the BOOKS of MAGIC

SUMMONINGS

JOHN NEY RIEBER
WRITER

PETER GROSS
PETER SNEJBJERG
GARY AMARO
DICK GIORDANO
ARTISTS

SHERILYN VAN VALKENBURGH
COLORS

STARKINGS & COMICRAFT
JOHN COSTANZA
JOHN WORKMAN
LETTERING

CHARLES VESS
COVERS

NEIL GAIMAN
CONSULTANT

TIMOTHY HUNTER AND THE BOOKS OF MAGIC
CREATED BY NEIL GAIMAN AND JOHN BOLTON

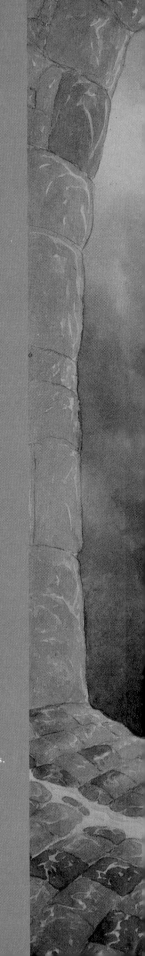

THE BOOKS OF MAGIC: SUMMONINGS
Published by DC Comics. Cover, introduction, and compilation copyright © 1996 DC Comics.
All Rights Reserved. Originally published in single magazine form in
THE BOOKS OF MAGIC 5-13 and VERTIGO RAVE 1. Copyright © 1994, 1995 DC Comics.
All Rights Reserved. VERTIGO and all characters, their distinctive likenesses and
related indicia featured in this publication are trademarks of DC Comics.
The stories, characters, and incidents featured in this publication are entirely fictional.

DC Comics, 1700 Broadway, New York, NY 10019
A division of Warner Bros. - A Time Warner Entertainment Company
Printed in Canada. Second Printing.
ISBN: 1-56389-265-0
Cover painting by Michael Kaluta.
Publication design by Eddie Ortiz.

CONTENTS

4
FOREWORD

*All stories written by John Ney Rieber and
colored by Sherilyn van Valkenburgh*

6
THE HIDDEN SCHOOL
(originally published in THE BOOKS OF MAGIC No. 5)
Artist-Peter Snejbjerg

SACRIFICES
(originally published in THE BOOKS OF MAGIC Nos. 6-8)
Artist-Peter Gross

31	56	82
PART I	PART II	PART III
INSTRUMENTS	VICTIMS	ALTARS

108
THE LOT
(originally published in VERTIGO RAVE No. 1)
Artists-Gary Amaro & Dick Giordano

THE ARTIFICIAL HEART
(originally published in THE BOOKS OF MAGIC Nos. 9-11)
Artists-Gary Amaro & Peter Gross

114	140	164
BOOK 1	BOOK 2	BOOK 3
HANDMEDOWNS OF	BLEAK HOUSES,	THE CLIMBING
THE RAGGED SCHOOL	HARD TIMES	BOY

SMALL GLASS WORLDS
(originally published in THE BOOKS OF MAGIC Nos. 12-13)
Artist-Peter Snejbjerg

189	214
BOOK ONE	BOOK TWO
MISSING COLORS	TRANSPARENT LIES

simple things

I've never been to London. I'm never entirely sure whether this is a good thing or a bad one, but I do know that it makes me feel like a long-tailed cat in a room full of rocking chairs several times a month. Ignorance complicates the simplest things.

Take ice cream, for instance.

It is no secret that Western civilization is based on cows, and the byproducts thereof. Or that when the cows of prehistory inspired our ancestors to invent real estate, chickens and eggs swiftly became crucial to the inner workings of Occidental society, especially in the mornings. Or that our culture has been running on sugar since the Industrial Revolution first brought heaping spoonfuls of the stuff within easy reach.

Which brings us back to London, and ice cream. The fundamental ingredients of ice cream are milk, eggs, sugar, and whipping cream. And Western civilization demonstrably has lots of them. We even have songs about ice cream[1]. So what could be simpler than sending two kids out on an ice-cream date, in the capital of that empire whose flag the sun used not to set on?

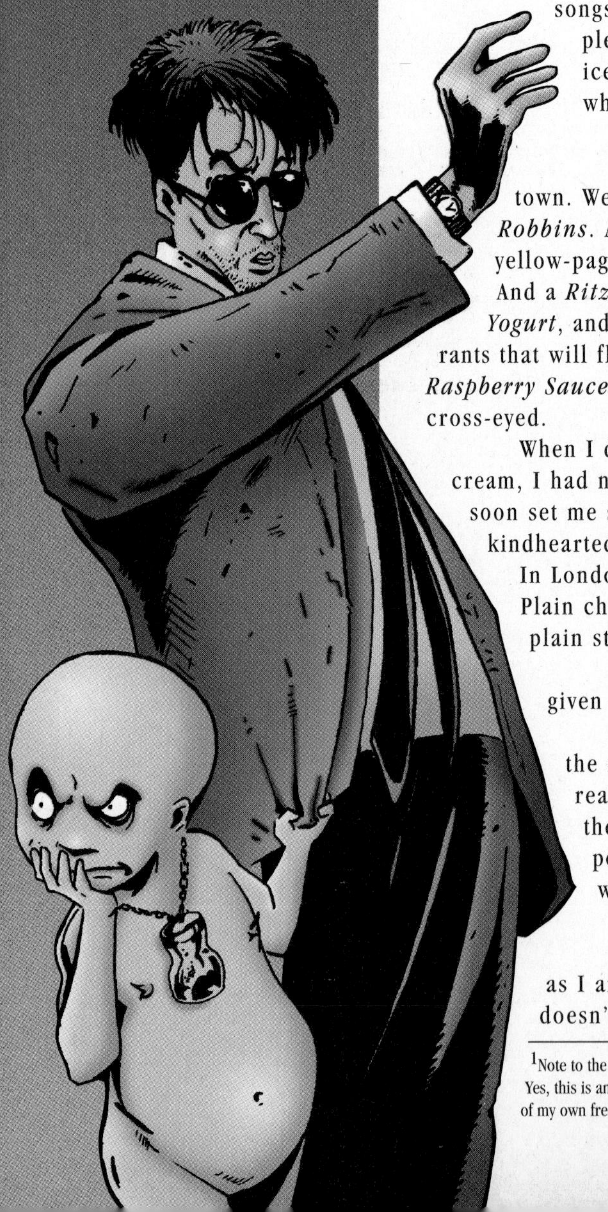

Just about anything, actually.

I live in a small Southern university-centric town. We have a *Ben & Jerry's* here, and a *Baskin-Robbins*. And a soda shop, which for some reason yellow-pages itself as *Swenson's Ice Cream Factory*. And a *Ritzie's Too Yogurt & Ice Cream*, and a *TCBY Yogurt*, and a *Yogurt Pump*. And several classy restaurants that will fling things like *Apricot Sorbet with Fresh Raspberry Sauce* at you if you so much as look at them cross-eyed.

When I decided to let Tim and Molly go out for ice cream, I had no idea what I was getting myself into. Neil soon set me straight — via Julie, since he was too kindhearted to burst my bubble himself.

In London, ice cream comes in three flavours. Plain chocolate. Plain vanilla. And, if you're lucky, plain strawberry.

As for *Baskin-Robbinses*? Gryphons, I was given to understand, were easier to find.

Now, I'm downright obsessive about keeping the real-world underpinnings of my stories realistic. My gunfire doesn't fill the room with the stench of cordite, if the room is contemporary. My blood doesn't taste coppery. My water runs downhill.

Neil, bless his heart, is just as obsessive as I am, or more so. Which is great, because he doesn't mind when I phone him at breakfast time

[1]Note to the readers of rec.arts.comics.vertigo, and subscribers to really-deep thoughts: Yes, this is an allusion to a Tori Amos song. No one *made* me do it, though. I'm alluding of my own free will.

to ask if British grocery stores use paper or plastic bags.[2] Or if old men are allowed to fish off the Palace Pier at Brighton. He takes great pains to ensure that Tim's Great Britain remains British.

Usually I think that's wonderful. In the context of this ice cream scenario, though?

I couldn't bring myself to accept the fact that in all the Greater London Metropolitan Area, there was not a scoop of pistachio ice cream to be found. Surely, I told myself, when Dr. Johnson said, "When a man is tired of London, he is tired of Life," he *couldn't* have meant "When a man craves Pistachio, he can bloody well ring his travel agent."

Seventeen or eighteen very long distance phone calls later, I succeeded in locating someone who *thought* he remembered seeing a *Baskin-Robbins* in a galleria near Mayfair, once. He was a little hazy about the timing of the incident, but what the heck.

I rang Julie, upon whom the sun rises. Julie rang Neil.

And Tim had his pistachio ice cream.

Molly, more sensibly, had chocolate.

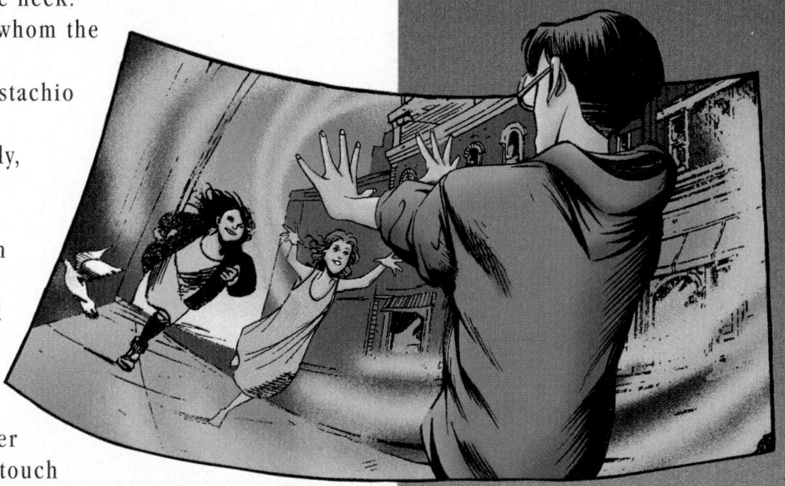

* * *

Fortunately, London is only peripherally the setting for The Books. Tim and Molly actually *live* in a realm that has never been mapped by the Royal Geographic Society and never will be. People who've lost touch with the place call it "Adolescence." Those of us who still spend time there never can seem to find the time to tack names onto it.

It's a place where anything can happen and probably will — the moment you blink, count on it. A place where nothing is real but the stuff you bang your head on, the stuff that dazzles you, and the stuff that makes your stomach feel all fluttery. A place where the only thing more mystifying than what's going on around you is what's going on inside you —

(With the possible exception of the fascinating girl or boy who sits next to you in Geometry class, solving quadratic equations In Beauty Like the Night. Who you really would ask out for ice cream or a movie, if only your tongue would stop tying itself in Gordian knots.)

In other words, a place of magic.

Have a nice time while you're here, kids. But don't stay out too late.

John Ney Rieber
Chapel Hill, North Carolina
December 15, 1995

---

[2] I'm sort of streching the truth a bit, here. Lorraine (Neil's assistant) and Mary (Neil's wife) actually settled the grocery-bag question for me. (Plastic.) Neil had been abducted by the BBC that morning.

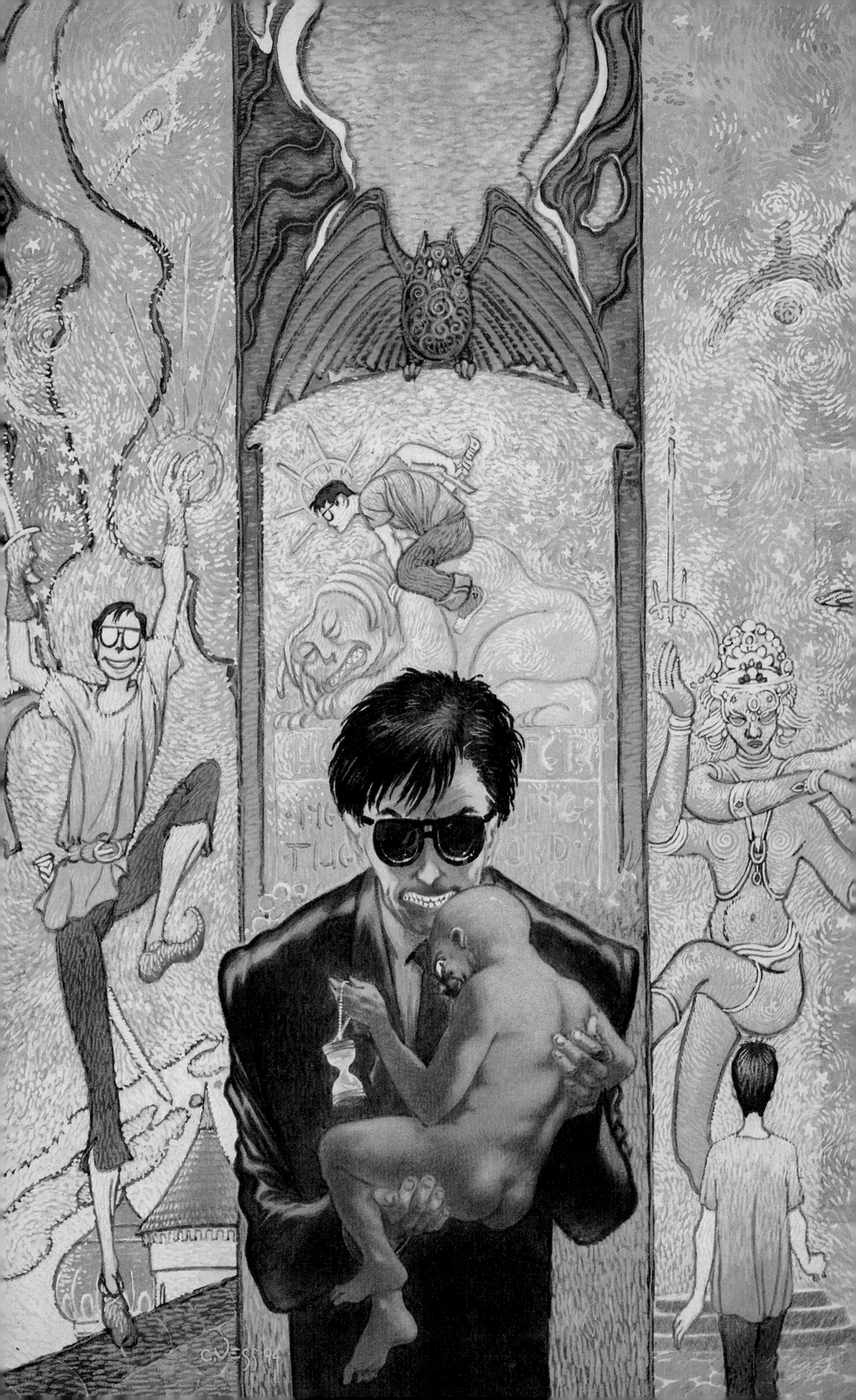

THE HIDDEN SCHOOL

John Ney Rieber, writer
Peter Snejbjerg, guest artist
Sherilyn Van Valkenburgh, colors
John Workman, letters
Julie Rottenberg, asst. editor
Stuart Moore, editor
Neil Gaiman, consultant

Timothy Hunter and The Books of Magic created by Neil Gaiman and John Bolton

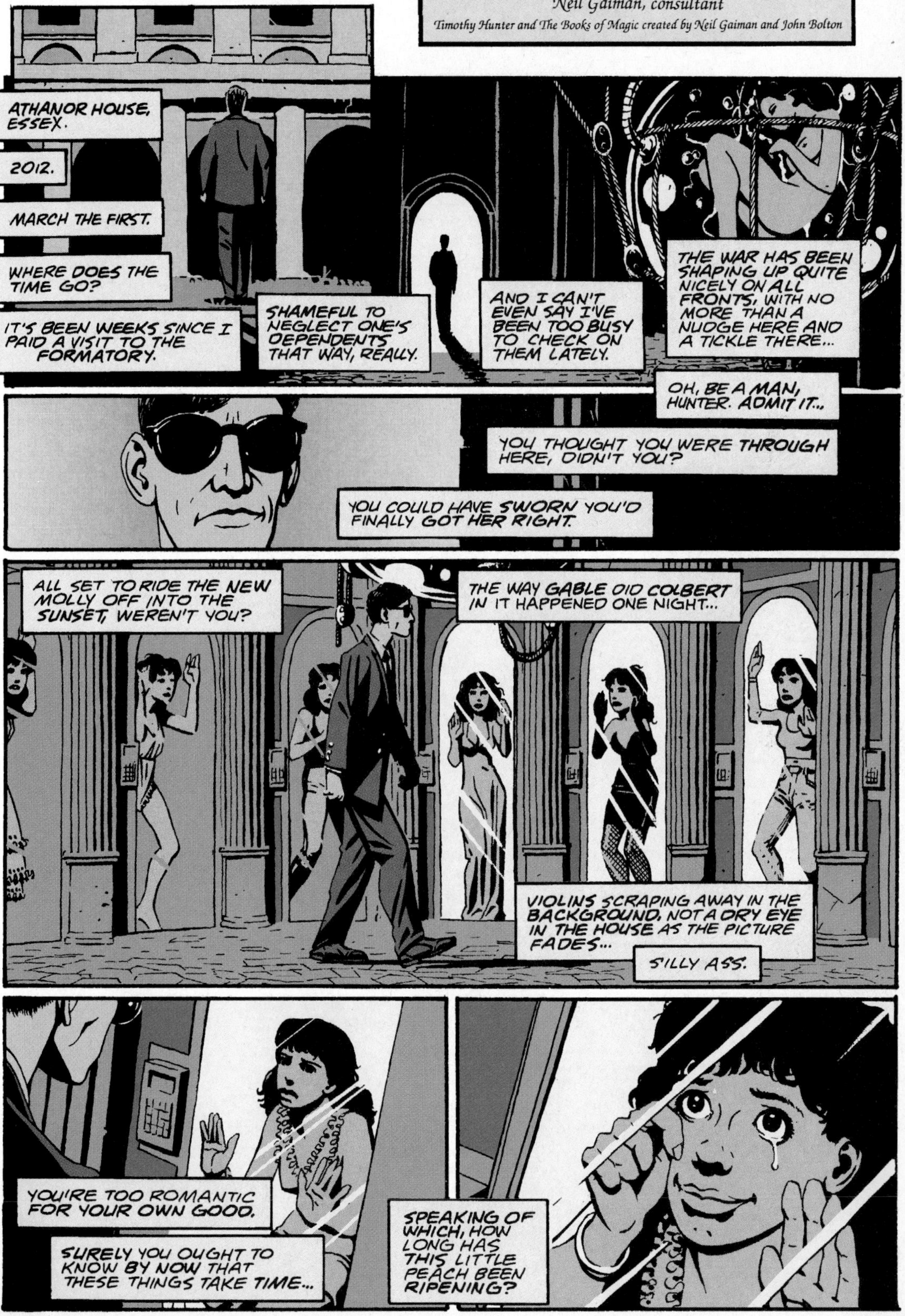

ATHANOR HOUSE, ESSEX.
2012.
MARCH THE FIRST.
WHERE DOES THE TIME GO?
IT'S BEEN WEEKS SINCE I PAID A VISIT TO THE FORMATORY.
SHAMEFUL TO NEGLECT ONE'S DEPENDENTS THAT WAY, REALLY.
AND I CAN'T EVEN SAY I'VE BEEN TOO BUSY TO CHECK ON THEM LATELY.
THE WAR HAS BEEN SHAPING UP QUITE NICELY ON ALL FRONTS, WITH NO MORE THAN A NUDGE HERE AND A TICKLE THERE...
OH, BE A MAN, HUNTER. ADMIT IT...
YOU THOUGHT YOU WERE THROUGH HERE, DIDN'T YOU?
YOU COULD HAVE SWORN YOU'D FINALLY GOT HER RIGHT.
ALL SET TO RIDE THE NEW MOLLY OFF INTO THE SUNSET, WEREN'T YOU?
THE WAY GABLE DID COLBERT IN IT HAPPENED ONE NIGHT...
VIOLINS SCRAPING AWAY IN THE BACKGROUND, NOT A DRY EYE IN THE HOUSE AS THE PICTURE FADES...
SILLY ASS.
YOU'RE TOO ROMANTIC FOR YOUR OWN GOOD.
SURELY YOU OUGHT TO KNOW BY NOW THAT THESE THINGS TAKE TIME...
SPEAKING OF WHICH, HOW LONG HAS THIS LITTLE PEACH BEEN RIPENING?

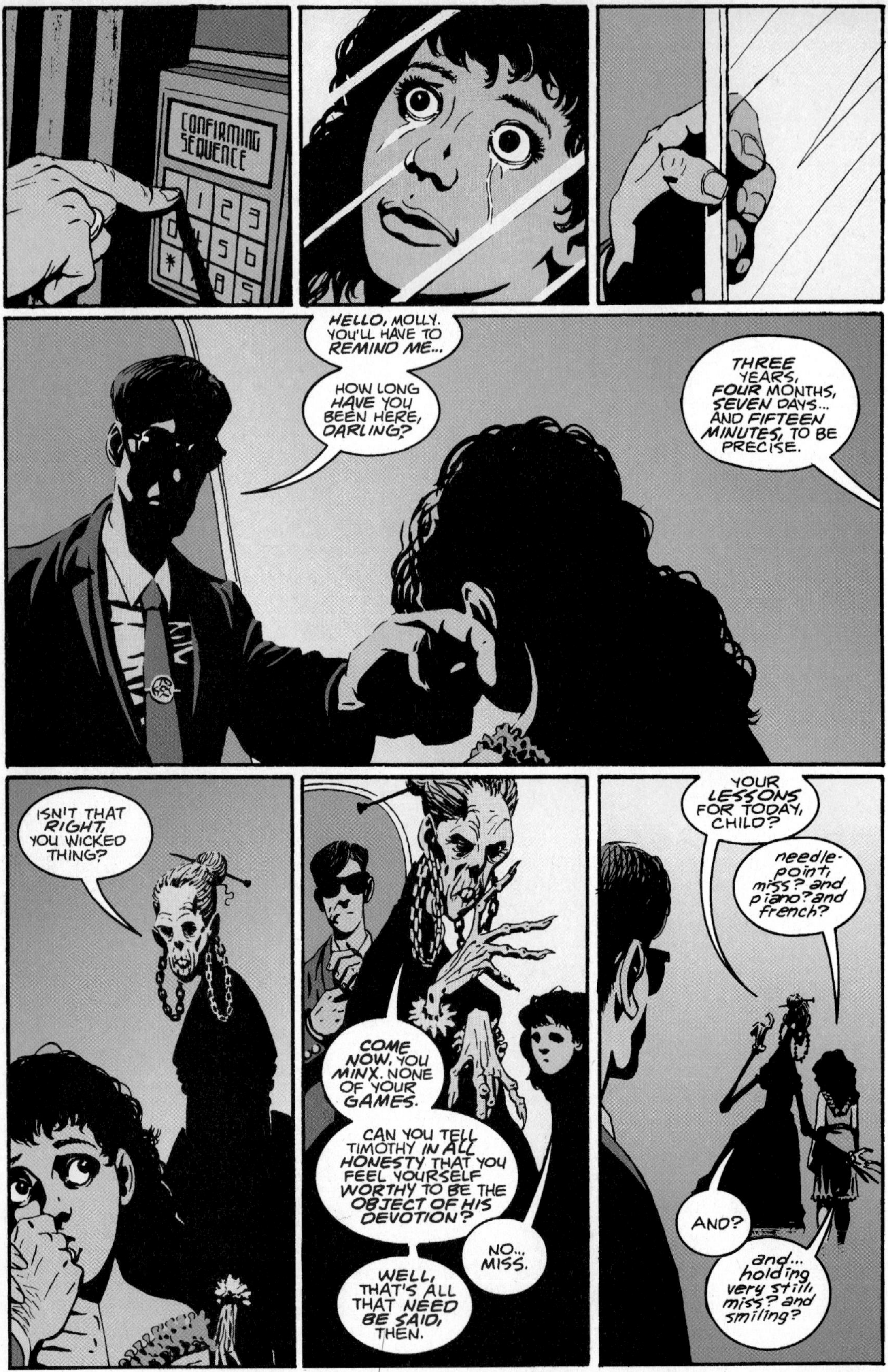
CONFIRMING SEQUENCE
HELLO, MOLLY. YOU'LL HAVE TO REMIND ME...
HOW LONG HAVE YOU BEEN HERE, DARLING?
THREE YEARS, FOUR MONTHS, SEVEN DAYS... AND FIFTEEN MINUTES, TO BE PRECISE.
ISN'T THAT RIGHT, YOU WICKED THING?
COME NOW, YOU MINX. NONE OF YOUR GAMES.
CAN YOU TELL TIMOTHY IN ALL HONESTY THAT YOU FEEL YOURSELF WORTHY TO BE THE OBJECT OF HIS DEVOTION?
NO... MISS.
WELL, THAT'S ALL THAT NEED BE SAID, THEN.
YOUR LESSONS FOR TODAY, CHILD?
needle-point, miss? and piano? and french?
AND?
and... holding very still, miss? and smiling?

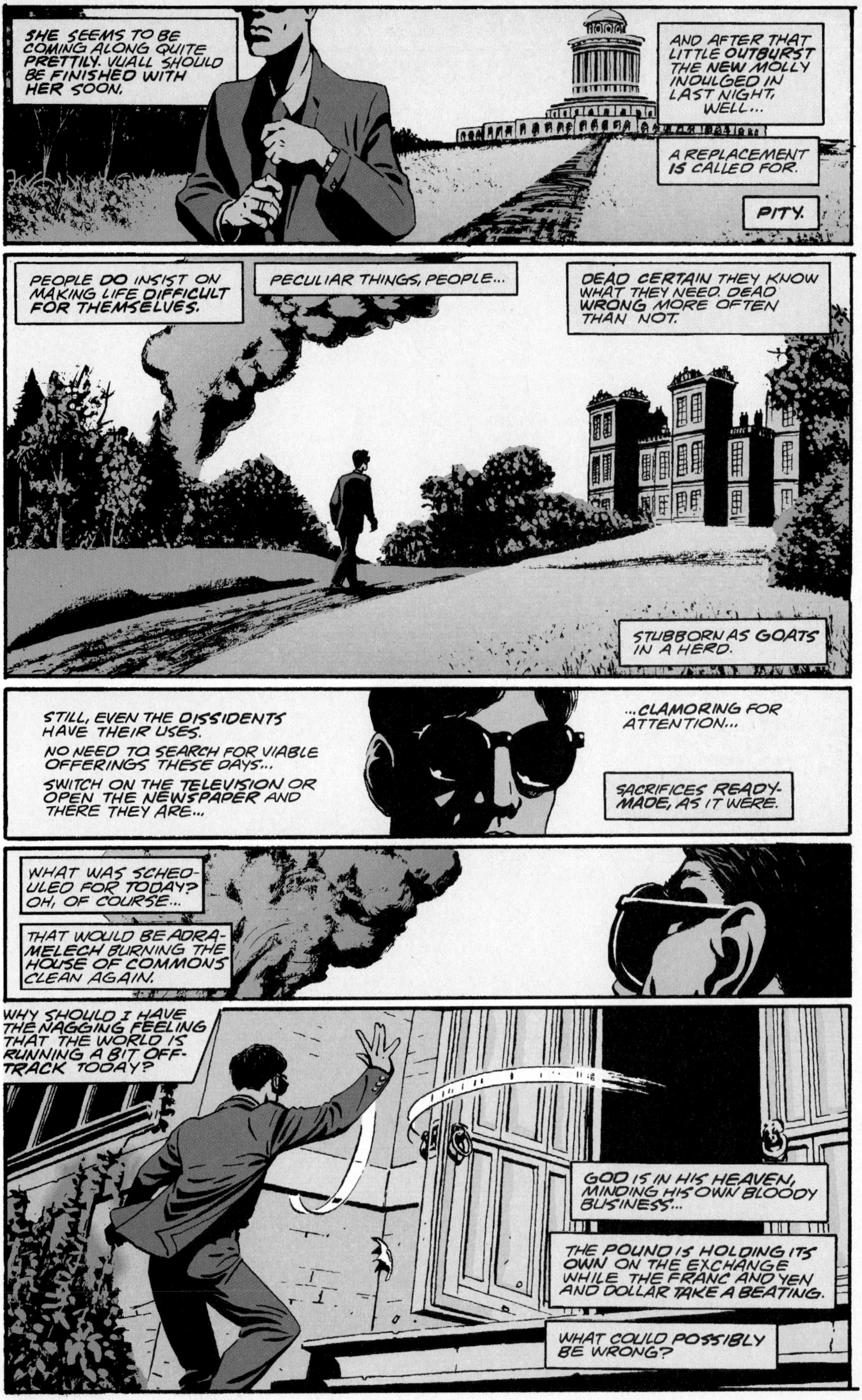
SHE SEEMS TO BE COMING ALONG QUITE PRETTILY. VUALL SHOULD BE FINISHED WITH HER SOON.
AND AFTER THAT LITTLE OUTBURST THE NEW MOLLY INDULGED IN LAST NIGHT, WELL...
A REPLACEMENT IS CALLED FOR.
PITY.
PEOPLE DO INSIST ON MAKING LIFE DIFFICULT FOR THEMSELVES.
PECULIAR THINGS, PEOPLE...
DEAD CERTAIN THEY KNOW WHAT THEY NEED. DEAD WRONG MORE OFTEN THAN NOT.
STUBBORN AS GOATS IN A HERD.
STILL, EVEN THE DISSIDENTS HAVE THEIR USES.
NO NEED TO SEARCH FOR VIABLE OFFERINGS THESE DAYS...
SWITCH ON THE TELEVISION OR OPEN THE NEWSPAPER AND THERE THEY ARE...
...CLAMORING FOR ATTENTION...
SACRIFICES READY-MADE, AS IT WERE.
WHAT WAS SCHEDULED FOR TODAY? OH, OF COURSE...
THAT WOULD BE ADRAMELECH BURNING THE HOUSE OF COMMONS CLEAN AGAIN.
WHY SHOULD I HAVE THE NAGGING FEELING THAT THE WORLD IS RUNNING A BIT OFF-TRACK TODAY?
GOD IS IN HIS HEAVEN, MINDING HIS OWN BLOODY BUSINESS...
THE POUND IS HOLDING ITS OWN ON THE EXCHANGE WHILE THE FRANC AND YEN AND DOLLAR TAKE A BEATING.
WHAT COULD POSSIBLY BE WRONG?

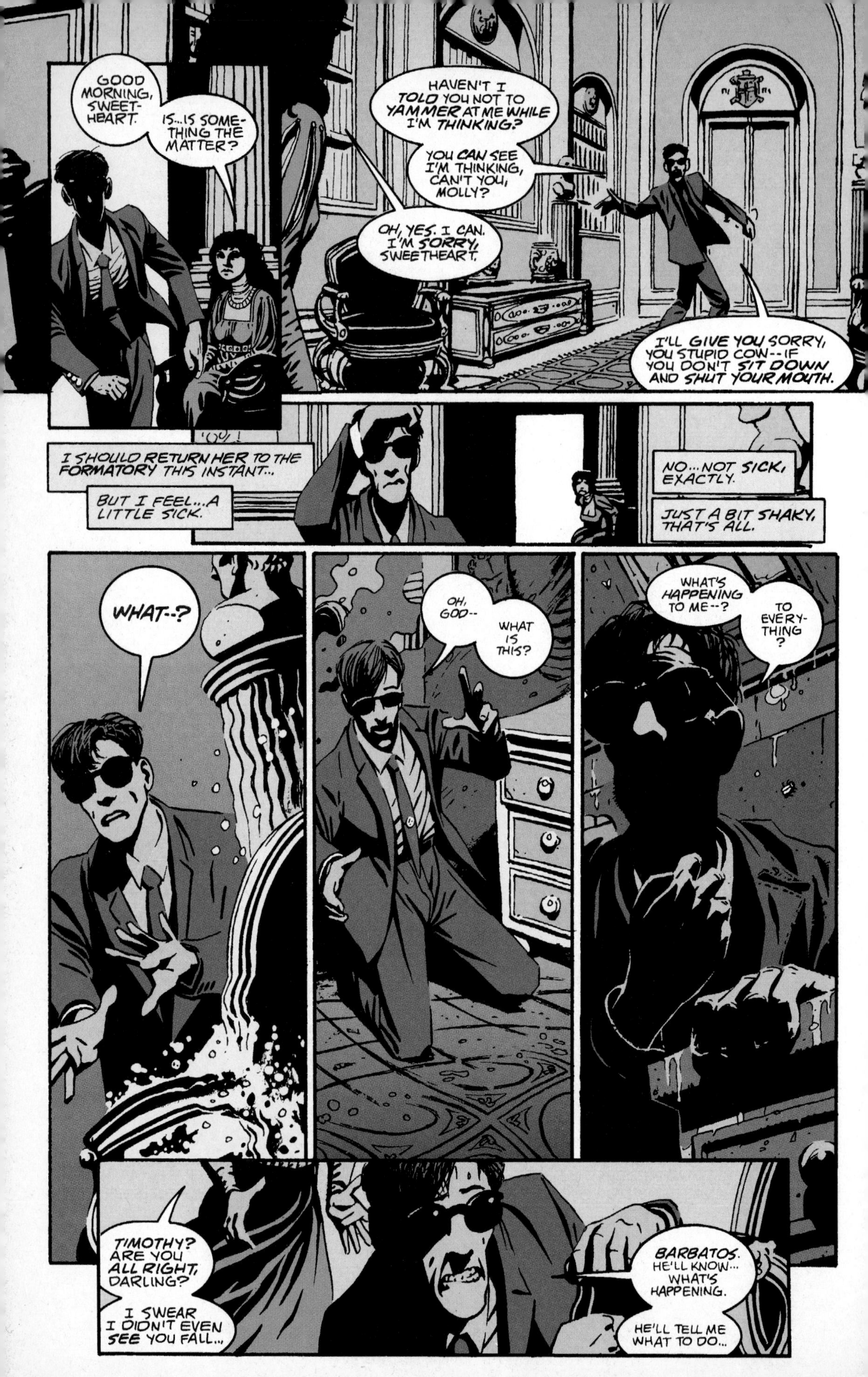

GOOD MORNING, SWEET-HEART.
IS...IS SOME-THING THE MATTER?
HAVEN'T I TOLD YOU NOT TO YAMMER AT ME WHILE I'M THINKING?
YOU CAN SEE I'M THINKING, CAN'T YOU, MOLLY?
OH, YES. I CAN. I'M SORRY, SWEETHEART.
I'LL GIVE YOU SORRY, YOU STUPID COW--IF YOU DON'T SIT DOWN AND SHUT YOUR MOUTH.
I SHOULD RETURN HER TO THE FORMATORY THIS INSTANT...
BUT I FEEL...A LITTLE SICK.
NO...NOT SICK, EXACTLY.
JUST A BIT SHAKY, THAT'S ALL.
WHAT--?
OH, GOD--
WHAT IS THIS?
WHAT'S HAPPENING TO ME--?
TO EVERY-THING?
TIMOTHY? ARE YOU ALL RIGHT, DARLING?
I SWEAR I DIDN'T EVEN SEE YOU FALL...
BARBATOS. HE'LL KNOW... WHAT'S HAPPENING.
HE'LL TELL ME WHAT TO DO...

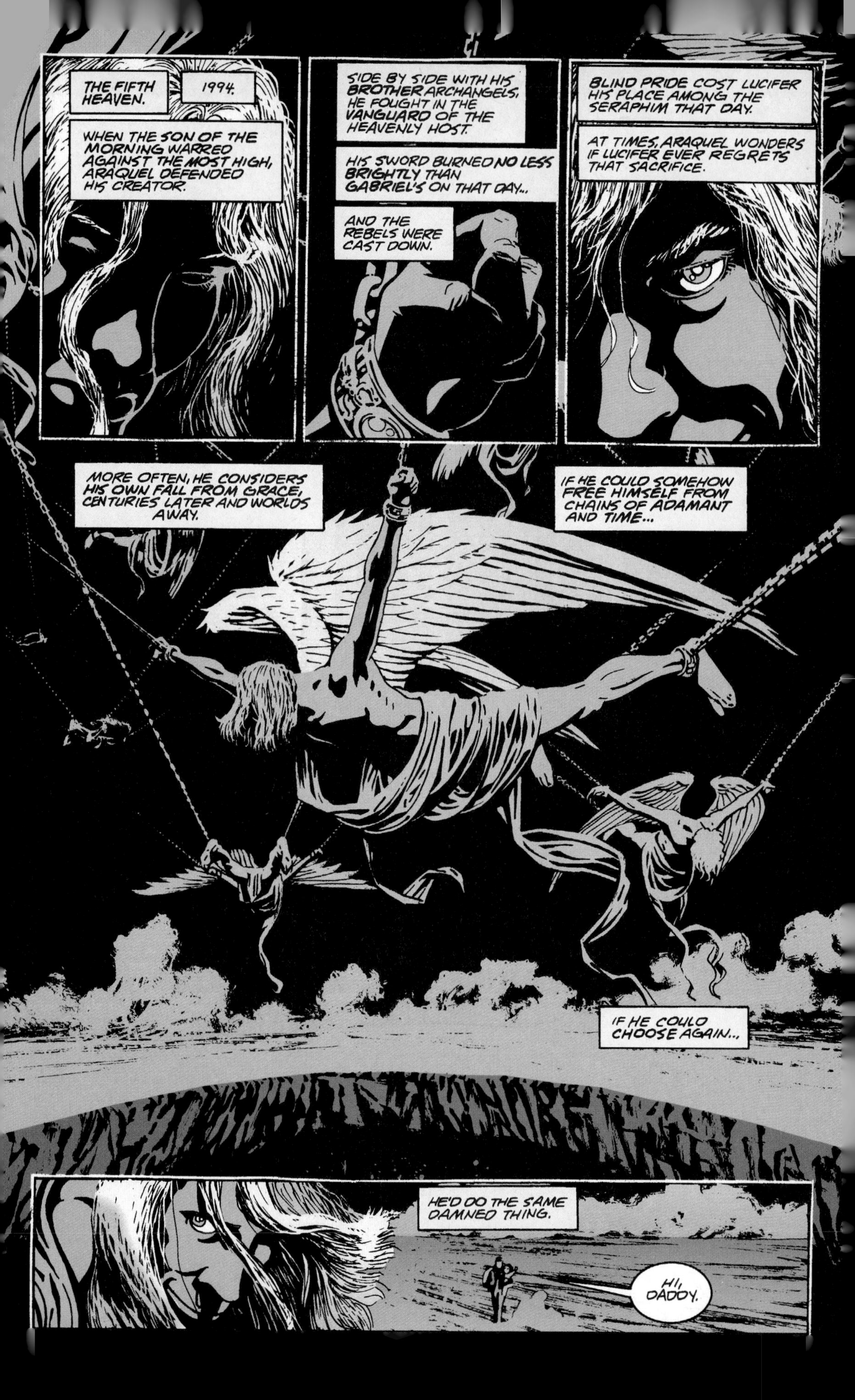
THE FIFTH HEAVEN.
1994.
WHEN THE SON OF THE MORNING WARRED AGAINST THE MOST HIGH, ARAQUEL DEFENDED HIS CREATOR.
SIDE BY SIDE WITH HIS BROTHER ARCHANGELS, HE FOUGHT IN THE VANGUARD OF THE HEAVENLY HOST.
HIS SWORD BURNED NO LESS BRIGHTLY THAN GABRIEL'S ON THAT DAY...
AND THE REBELS WERE CAST DOWN.
BLIND PRIDE COST LUCIFER HIS PLACE AMONG THE SERAPHIM THAT DAY.
AT TIMES, ARAQUEL WONDERS IF LUCIFER EVER REGRETS THAT SACRIFICE.
MORE OFTEN, HE CONSIDERS HIS OWN FALL FROM GRACE, CENTURIES LATER AND WORLDS AWAY.
IF HE COULD SOMEHOW FREE HIMSELF FROM CHAINS OF ADAMANT AND TIME...
IF HE COULD CHOOSE AGAIN...
HE'D DO THE SAME DAMNED THING.
HI, DADDY.

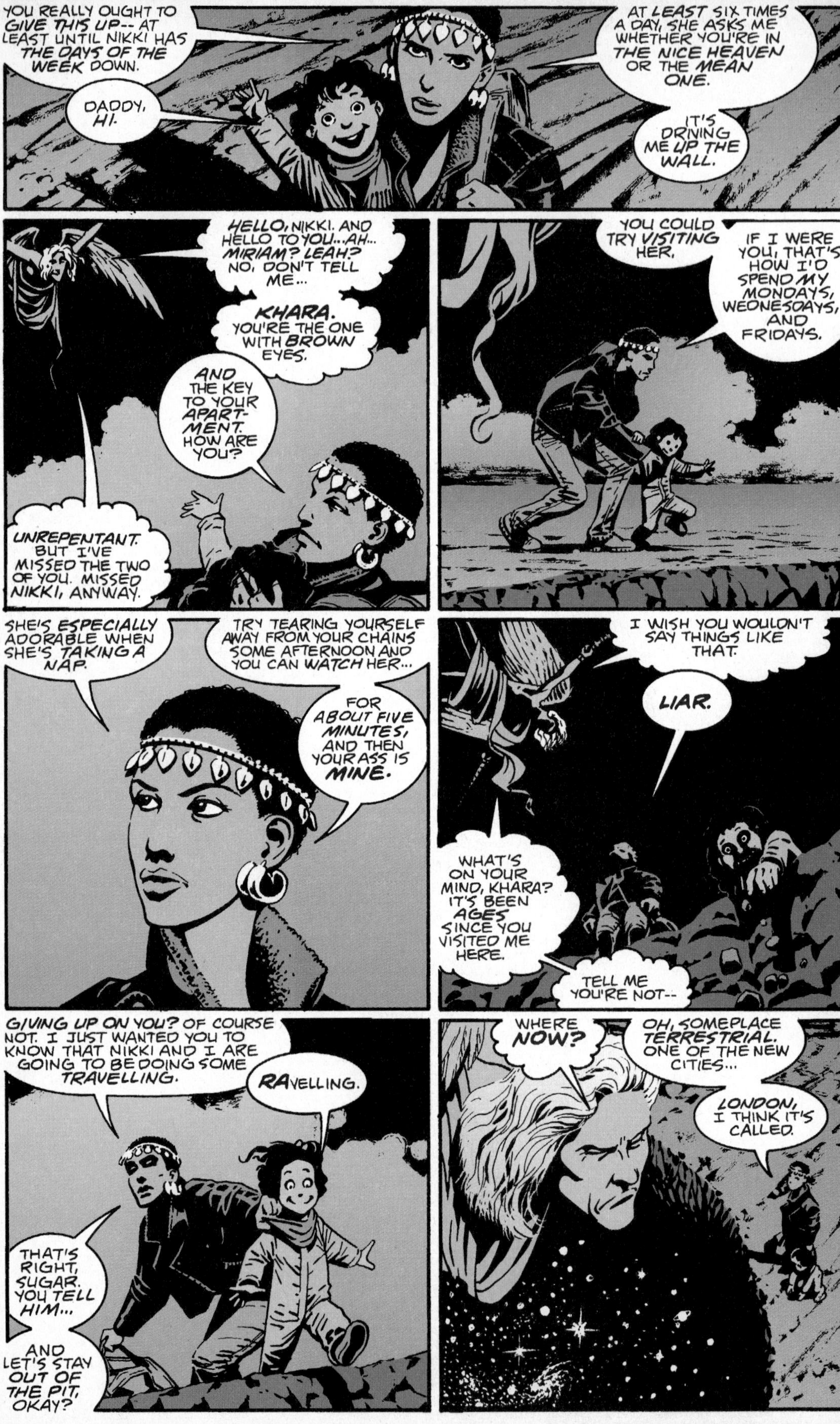
YOU REALLY OUGHT TO GIVE THIS UP-- AT LEAST UNTIL NIKKI HAS THE DAYS OF THE WEEK DOWN.
DADDY, HI.
AT LEAST SIX TIMES A DAY, SHE ASKS ME WHETHER YOU'RE IN THE NICE HEAVEN OR THE MEAN ONE.
IT'S DRIVING ME UP THE WALL.
HELLO, NIKKI. AND HELLO TO YOU... AH... MIRIAM? LEAH? NO, DON'T TELL ME...
KHARA. YOU'RE THE ONE WITH BROWN EYES.
AND THE KEY TO YOUR APARTMENT. HOW ARE YOU?
UNREPENTANT. BUT I'VE MISSED THE TWO OF YOU. MISSED NIKKI, ANYWAY.
YOU COULD TRY VISITING HER.
IF I WERE YOU, THAT'S HOW I'D SPEND MY MONDAYS, WEDNESDAYS, AND FRIDAYS.
SHE'S ESPECIALLY ADORABLE WHEN SHE'S TAKING A NAP.
TRY TEARING YOURSELF AWAY FROM YOUR CHAINS SOME AFTERNOON AND YOU CAN WATCH HER...
FOR ABOUT FIVE MINUTES, AND THEN YOUR ASS IS MINE.
I WISH YOU WOULDN'T SAY THINGS LIKE THAT.
LIAR.
WHAT'S ON YOUR MIND, KHARA? IT'S BEEN AGES SINCE YOU VISITED ME HERE.
TELL ME YOU'RE NOT--
GIVING UP ON YOU? OF COURSE NOT. I JUST WANTED YOU TO KNOW THAT NIKKI AND I ARE GOING TO BE DOING SOME TRAVELLING.
RAVELLING.
THAT'S RIGHT, SUGAR. YOU TELL HIM...
AND LET'S STAY OUT OF THE PIT, OKAY?
WHERE NOW?
OH, SOMEPLACE TERRESTRIAL. ONE OF THE NEW CITIES...
LONDON, I THINK IT'S CALLED.

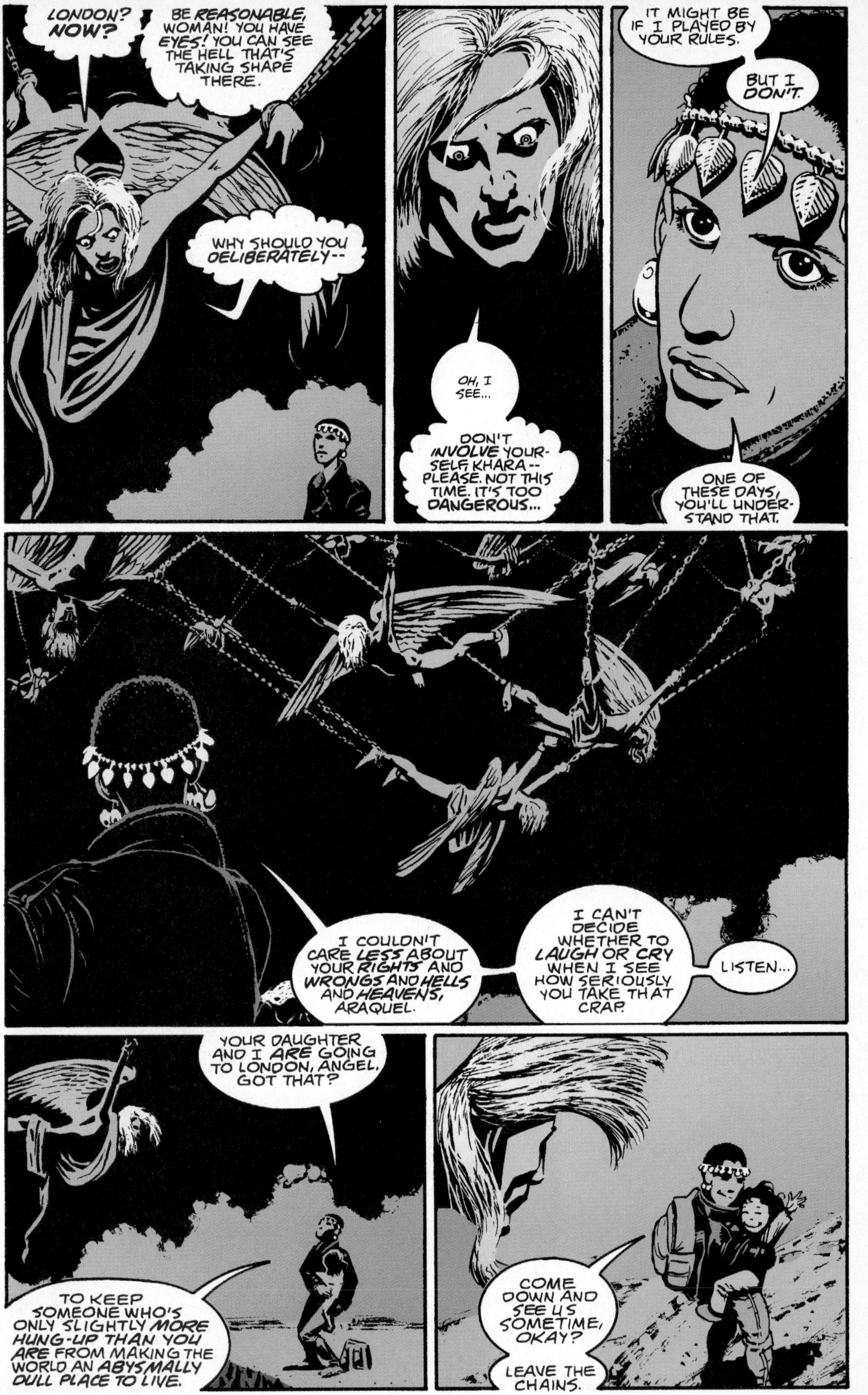

LONDON? NOW?
BE REASONABLE, WOMAN! YOU HAVE EYES! YOU CAN SEE THE HELL THAT'S TAKING SHAPE THERE.
WHY SHOULD YOU DELIBERATELY--
OH, I SEE...
DON'T INVOLVE YOURSELF, KHARA-- PLEASE. NOT THIS TIME. IT'S TOO DANGEROUS...
IT MIGHT BE IF I PLAYED BY YOUR RULES.
BUT I DON'T.
ONE OF THESE DAYS, YOU'LL UNDERSTAND THAT.
I COULDN'T CARE LESS ABOUT YOUR RIGHTS AND WRONGS AND HELLS AND HEAVENS, ARAQUEL.
I CAN'T DECIDE WHETHER TO LAUGH OR CRY WHEN I SEE HOW SERIOUSLY YOU TAKE THAT CRAP.
LISTEN...
YOUR DAUGHTER AND I ARE GOING TO LONDON, ANGEL, GOT THAT?
TO KEEP SOMEONE WHO'S ONLY SLIGHTLY MORE HUNG-UP THAN YOU ARE FROM MAKING THE WORLD AN ABYSMALLY DULL PLACE TO LIVE.
COME DOWN AND SEE US SOMETIME, OKAY?
LEAVE THE CHAINS.

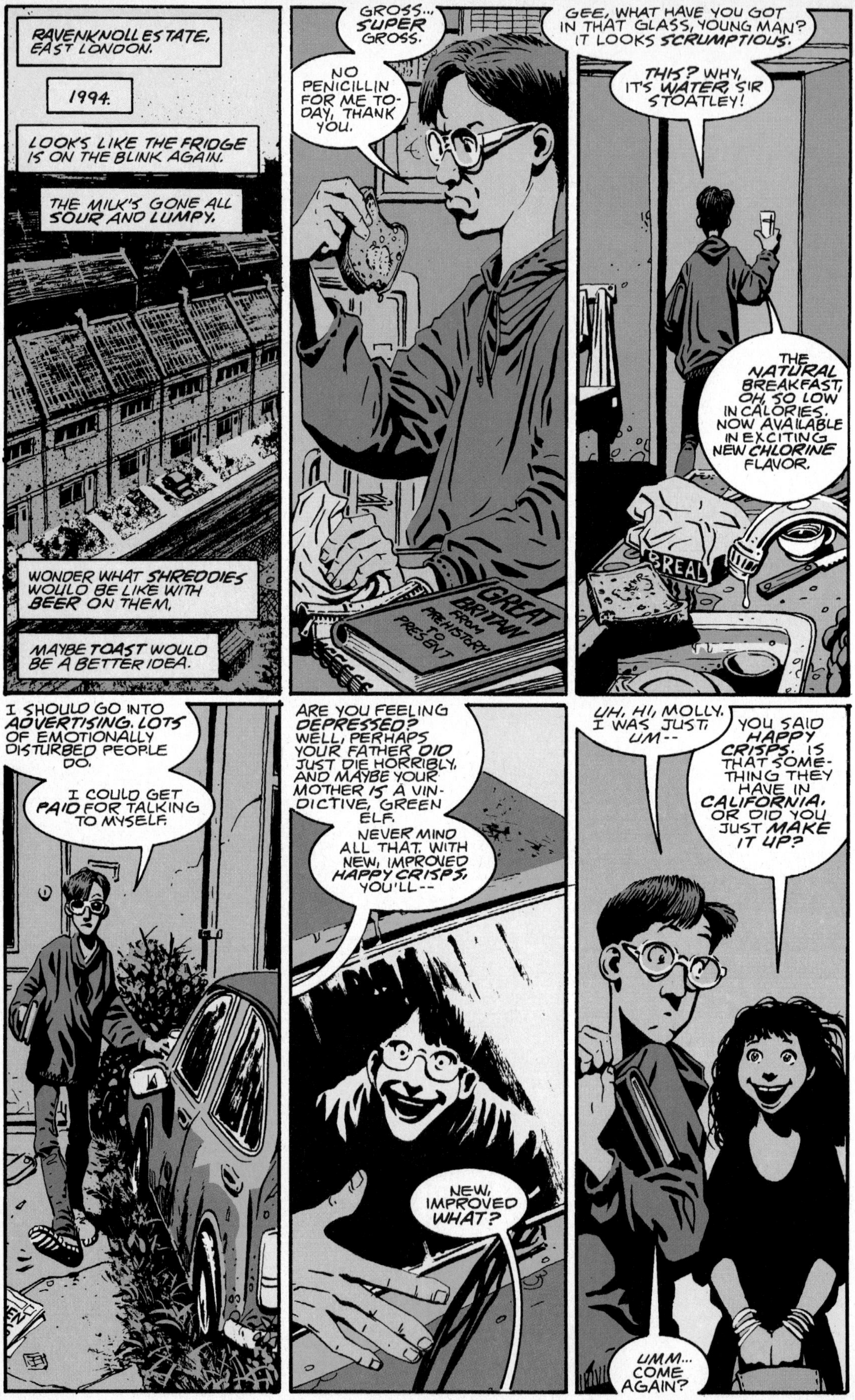
RAVENKNOLL ESTATE, EAST LONDON.
1994.
LOOKS LIKE THE FRIDGE IS ON THE BLINK AGAIN.
THE MILK'S GONE ALL SOUR AND LUMPY.
WONDER WHAT SHREDDIES WOULD BE LIKE WITH BEER ON THEM.
MAYBE TOAST WOULD BE A BETTER IDEA.
GROSS... SUPER GROSS.
NO PENICILLIN FOR ME TO-DAY, THANK YOU.
GREAT BRITAIN FROM PREHISTORY TO PRESENT
GEE, WHAT HAVE YOU GOT IN THAT GLASS, YOUNG MAN? IT LOOKS SCRUMPTIOUS.
THIS? WHY, IT'S WATER, SIR STOATLEY!
THE NATURAL BREAKFAST, OH, SO LOW IN CALORIES. NOW AVAILABLE IN EXCITING NEW CHLORINE FLAVOR.
I SHOULD GO INTO ADVERTISING. LOTS OF EMOTIONALLY DISTURBED PEOPLE DO.
I COULD GET PAID FOR TALKING TO MYSELF.
ARE YOU FEELING DEPRESSED? WELL, PERHAPS YOUR FATHER DID JUST DIE HORRIBLY, AND MAYBE YOUR MOTHER IS A VINDICTIVE, GREEN ELF.
NEVER MIND ALL THAT. WITH NEW, IMPROVED HAPPY CRISPS, YOU'LL--
NEW, IMPROVED WHAT?
UH, HI, MOLLY. I WAS JUST, UM--
YOU SAID HAPPY CRISPS. IS THAT SOMETHING THEY HAVE IN CALIFORNIA, OR DID YOU JUST MAKE IT UP?
UMM... COME AGAIN?

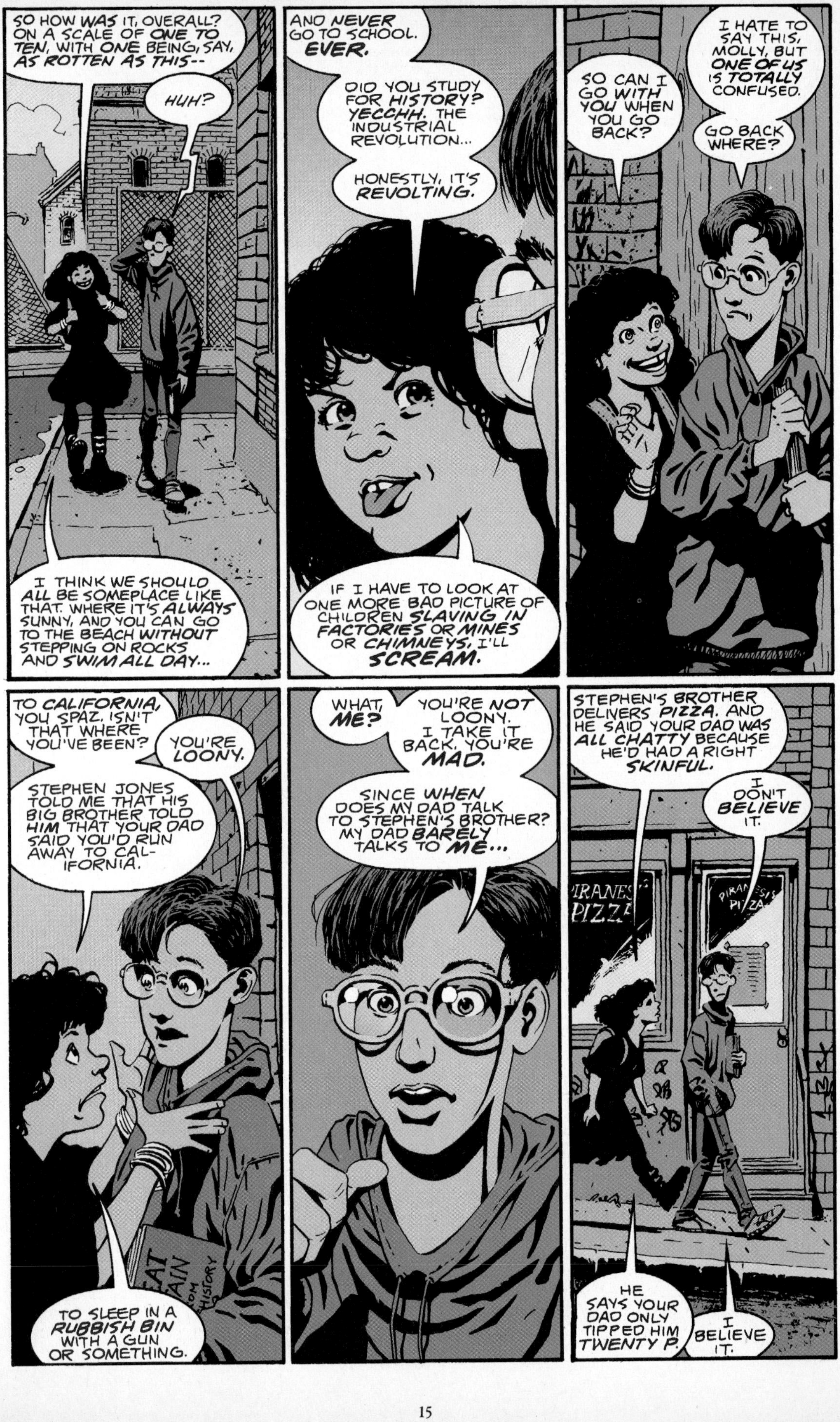
SO HOW WAS IT, OVERALL? ON A SCALE OF ONE TO TEN, WITH ONE BEING, SAY, AS ROTTEN AS THIS--
HUH?
I THINK WE SHOULD ALL BE SOMEPLACE LIKE THAT. WHERE IT'S ALWAYS SUNNY, AND YOU CAN GO TO THE BEACH WITHOUT STEPPING ON ROCKS AND SWIM ALL DAY...
AND NEVER GO TO SCHOOL. EVER.
DID YOU STUDY FOR HISTORY? YECCHH. THE INDUSTRIAL REVOLUTION...
HONESTLY, IT'S REVOLTING.
IF I HAVE TO LOOK AT ONE MORE BAD PICTURE OF CHILDREN SLAVING IN FACTORIES OR MINES OR CHIMNEYS, I'LL SCREAM.
SO CAN I GO WITH YOU WHEN YOU GO BACK?
I HATE TO SAY THIS, MOLLY, BUT ONE OF US IS TOTALLY CONFUSED.
GO BACK WHERE?
TO CALIFORNIA, YOU SPAZ. ISN'T THAT WHERE YOU'VE BEEN?
YOU'RE LOONY.
STEPHEN JONES TOLD ME THAT HIS BIG BROTHER TOLD HIM THAT YOUR DAD SAID YOU'D RUN AWAY TO CAL-IFORNIA.
TO SLEEP IN A RUBBISH BIN WITH A GUN OR SOMETHING.
WHAT, ME?
YOU'RE NOT LOONY. I TAKE IT BACK. YOU'RE MAD.
SINCE WHEN DOES MY DAD TALK TO STEPHEN'S BROTHER? MY DAD BARELY TALKS TO ME...
STEPHEN'S BROTHER DELIVERS PIZZA. AND HE SAID YOUR DAD WAS ALL CHATTY BECAUSE HE'D HAD A RIGHT SKINFUL.
I DON'T BELIEVE IT.
PIRANESI PIZZA
HE SAYS YOUR DAD ONLY TIPPED HIM TWENTY P.
I BELIEVE IT.

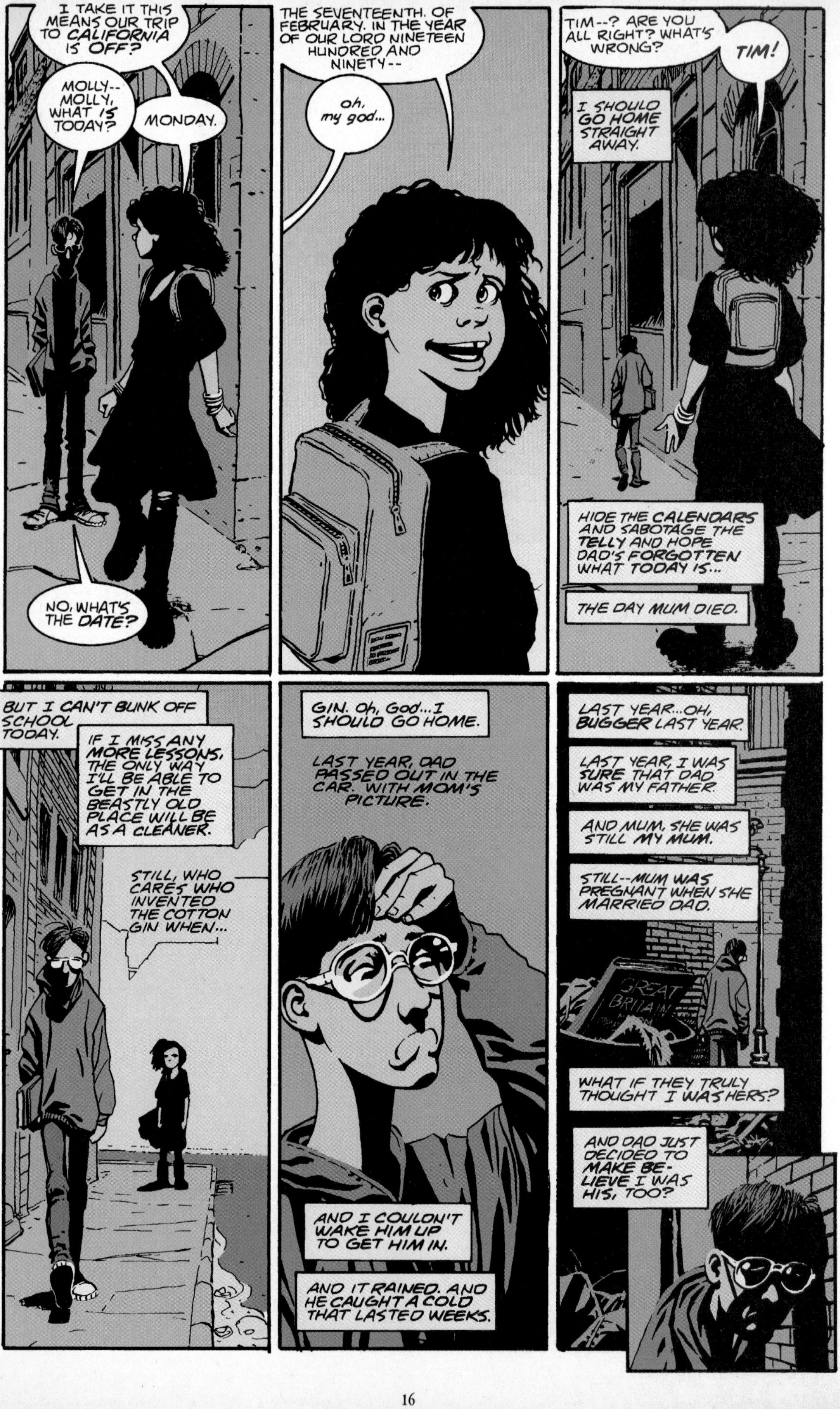
I TAKE IT THIS MEANS OUR TRIP TO CALIFORNIA IS OFF?
MOLLY--MOLLY, WHAT IS TODAY?
MONDAY.
NO, WHAT'S THE DATE?
THE SEVENTEENTH. OF FEBRUARY. IN THE YEAR OF OUR LORD NINETEEN HUNDRED AND NINETY--
oh, my god...
TIM--? ARE YOU ALL RIGHT? WHAT'S WRONG?
TIM!
I SHOULD GO HOME STRAIGHT AWAY.
HIDE THE CALENDARS AND SABOTAGE THE TELLY AND HOPE DAD'S FORGOTTEN WHAT TODAY IS...
THE DAY MUM DIED.
BUT I CAN'T BUNK OFF SCHOOL TODAY.
IF I MISS ANY MORE LESSONS, THE ONLY WAY I'LL BE ABLE TO GET IN THE BEASTLY OLD PLACE WILL BE AS A CLEANER.
STILL, WHO CARES WHO INVENTED THE COTTON GIN WHEN...
GIN. Oh, God... I SHOULD GO HOME.
LAST YEAR, DAD PASSED OUT IN THE CAR. WITH MOM'S PICTURE.
AND I COULDN'T WAKE HIM UP TO GET HIM IN.
AND IT RAINED. AND HE CAUGHT A COLD THAT LASTED WEEKS.
LAST YEAR...OH, BUGGER LAST YEAR.
LAST YEAR, I WAS SURE THAT DAD WAS MY FATHER.
AND MUM, SHE WAS STILL MY MUM.
STILL--MUM WAS PREGNANT WHEN SHE MARRIED DAD.
GREAT BRITAIN
WHAT IF THEY TRULY THOUGHT I WAS HERS?
AND DAD JUST DECIDED TO MAKE BE-LIEVE I WAS HIS, TOO?

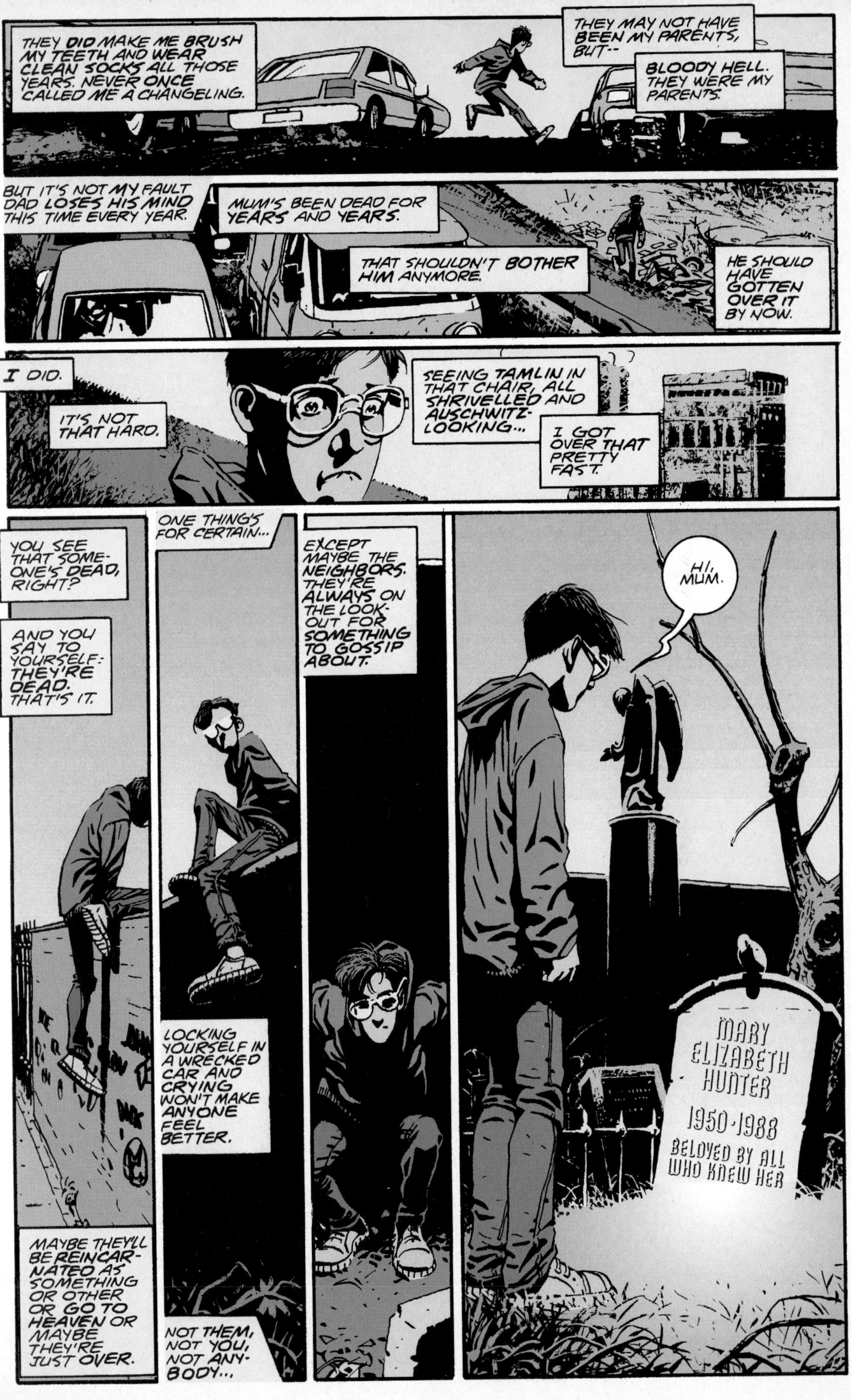
THEY DID MAKE ME BRUSH MY TEETH AND WEAR CLEAN SOCKS ALL THOSE YEARS. NEVER ONCE CALLED ME A CHANGELING.
THEY MAY NOT HAVE BEEN MY PARENTS, BUT--
BLOODY HELL. THEY WERE MY PARENTS.
BUT IT'S NOT MY FAULT DAD LOSES HIS MIND THIS TIME EVERY YEAR.
MUM'S BEEN DEAD FOR YEARS AND YEARS.
THAT SHOULDN'T BOTHER HIM ANYMORE.
HE SHOULD HAVE GOTTEN OVER IT BY NOW.
I DID.
IT'S NOT THAT HARD.
SEEING TAMLIN IN THAT CHAIR, ALL SHRIVELLED AND AUSCHWITZ-LOOKING...
I GOT OVER THAT PRETTY FAST.
YOU SEE THAT SOMEONE'S DEAD, RIGHT?
AND YOU SAY TO YOURSELF: THEY'RE DEAD. THAT'S IT.
MAYBE THEY'LL BE REINCARNATED AS SOMETHING OR OTHER OR GO TO HEAVEN OR MAYBE THEY'RE JUST OVER.
ONE THING'S FOR CERTAIN...
LOCKING YOURSELF IN A WRECKED CAR AND CRYING WON'T MAKE ANYONE FEEL BETTER.
NOT THEM, NOT YOU, NOT ANYBODY...
EXCEPT MAYBE THE NEIGHBORS. THEY'RE ALWAYS ON THE LOOK-OUT FOR SOMETHING TO GOSSIP ABOUT.
HI, MUM.
MARY ELIZABETH HUNTER
1950-1988
BELOVED BY ALL WHO KNEW HER

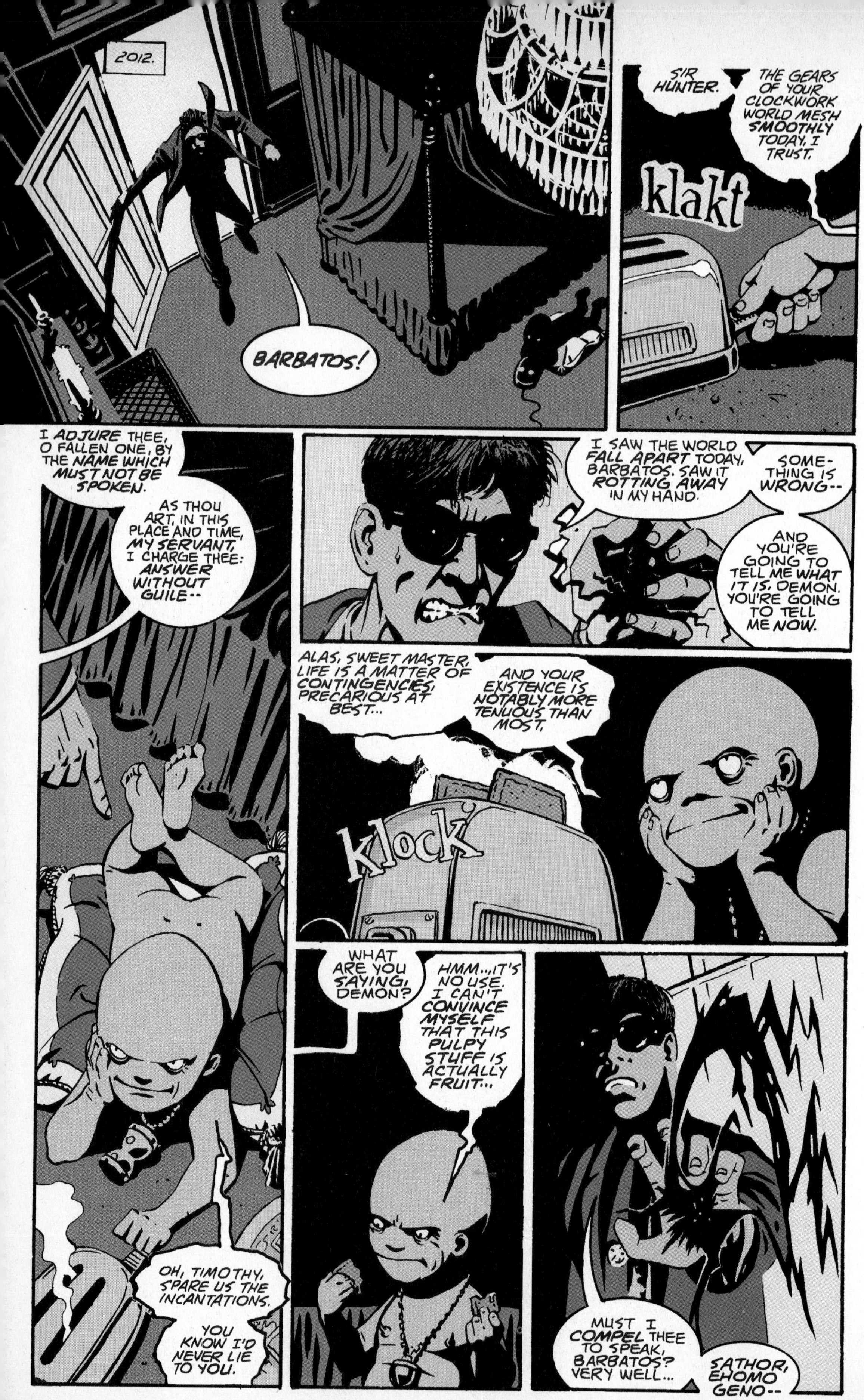

2012.
BARBATOS!
SIR HUNTER.
THE GEARS OF YOUR CLOCKWORK WORLD MESH SMOOTHLY TODAY, I TRUST.
klakt
I ADJURE THEE, O FALLEN ONE, BY THE NAME WHICH MUST NOT BE SPOKEN.
AS THOU ART, IN THIS PLACE AND TIME, MY SERVANT, I CHARGE THEE: ANSWER WITHOUT GUILE--
I SAW THE WORLD FALL APART TODAY, BARBATOS. SAW IT ROTTING AWAY IN MY HAND.
SOMETHING IS WRONG--
AND YOU'RE GOING TO TELL ME WHAT IT IS, DEMON. YOU'RE GOING TO TELL ME NOW.
ALAS, SWEET MASTER, LIFE IS A MATTER OF CONTINGENCIES, PRECARIOUS AT BEST...
AND YOUR EXISTENCE IS NOTABLY MORE TENUOUS THAN MOST.
klock
OH, TIMOTHY, SPARE US THE INCANTATIONS.
YOU KNOW I'D NEVER LIE TO YOU.
WHAT ARE YOU SAYING, DEMON?
HMM...IT'S NO USE. I CAN'T CONVINCE MYSELF THAT THIS PULPY STUFF IS ACTUALLY FRUIT...
MUST I COMPEL THEE TO SPEAK, BARBATOS? VERY WELL...
SATHOR, EHOMO GENO--

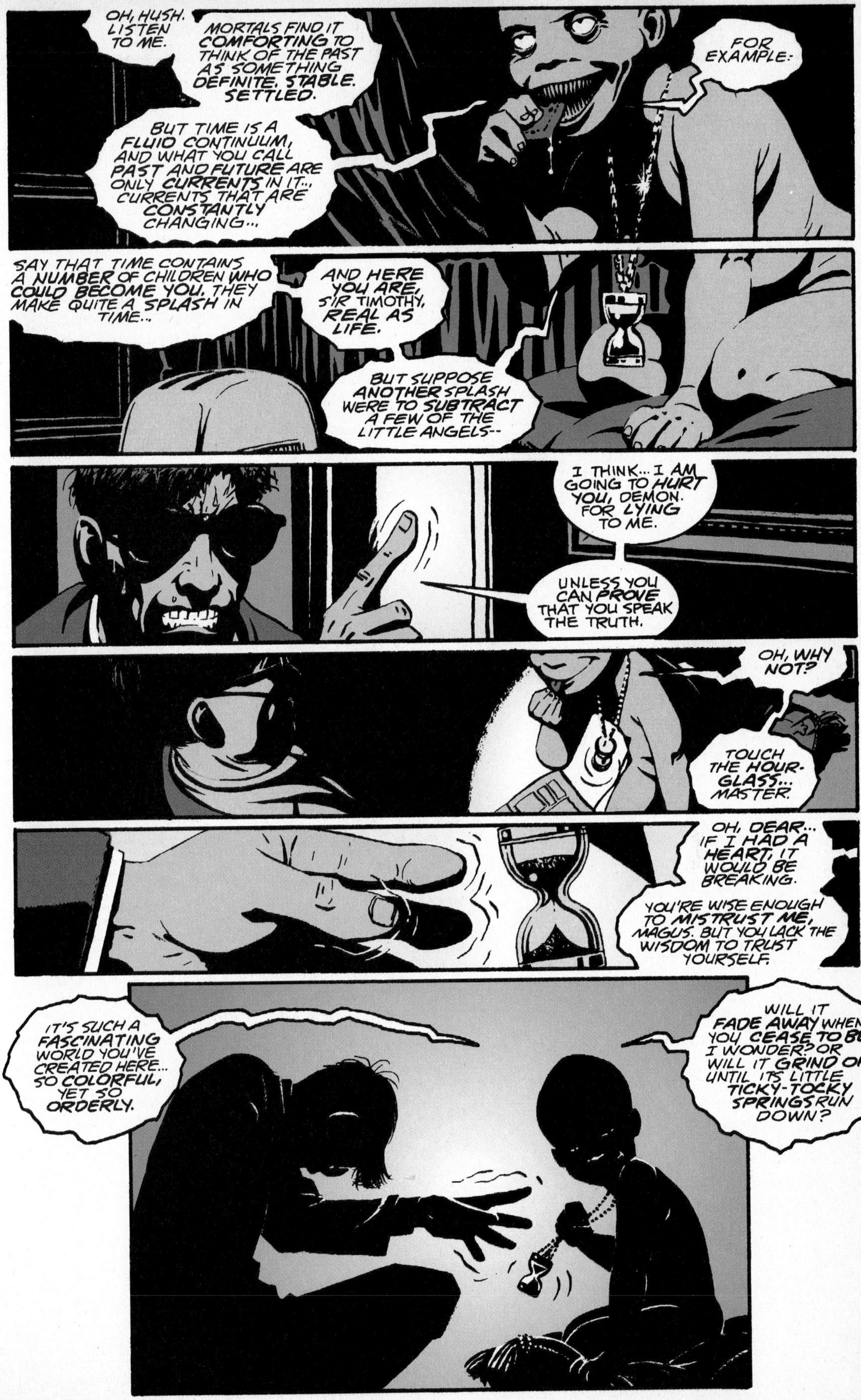

OH, HUSH. LISTEN TO ME.
MORTALS FIND IT COMFORTING TO THINK OF THE PAST AS SOMETHING DEFINITE. STABLE. SETTLED.
BUT TIME IS A FLUID CONTINUUM, AND WHAT YOU CALL PAST AND FUTURE ARE ONLY CURRENTS IN IT... CURRENTS THAT ARE CONSTANTLY CHANGING...
FOR EXAMPLE:
SAY THAT TIME CONTAINS A NUMBER OF CHILDREN WHO COULD BECOME YOU. THEY MAKE QUITE A SPLASH IN TIME...
AND HERE YOU ARE, SIR TIMOTHY, REAL AS LIFE.
BUT SUPPOSE ANOTHER SPLASH WERE TO SUBTRACT A FEW OF THE LITTLE ANGELS--
I THINK... I AM GOING TO HURT YOU, DEMON. FOR LYING TO ME.
UNLESS YOU CAN PROVE THAT YOU SPEAK THE TRUTH.
OH, WHY NOT?
TOUCH THE HOUR-GLASS... MASTER.
OH, DEAR... IF I HAD A HEART, IT WOULD BE BREAKING.
YOU'RE WISE ENOUGH TO MISTRUST ME, MAGUS. BUT YOU LACK THE WISDOM TO TRUST YOURSELF.
IT'S SUCH A FASCINATING WORLD YOU'VE CREATED HERE... SO COLORFUL, YET SO ORDERLY.
WILL IT FADE AWAY WHEN YOU CEASE TO BE, I WONDER? OR WILL IT GRIND ON UNTIL ITS LITTLE TICKY-TOCKY SPRINGS RUN DOWN?

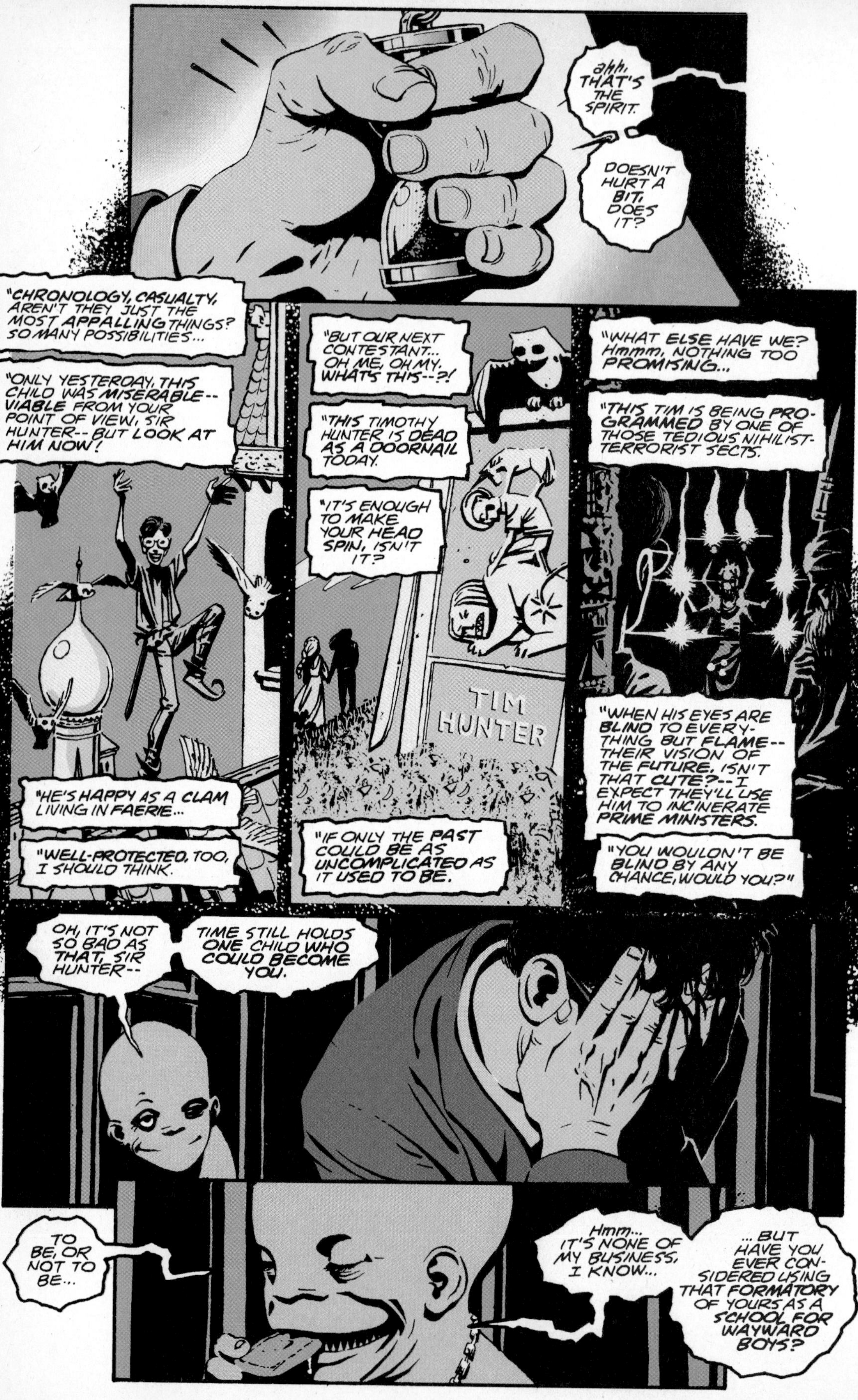
ahh, THAT'S THE SPIRIT.
DOESN'T HURT A BIT, DOES IT?
"CHRONOLOGY, CASUALTY. AREN'T THEY JUST THE MOST APPALLING THINGS? SO MANY POSSIBILITIES...
"ONLY YESTERDAY THIS CHILD WAS MISERABLE--VIABLE FROM YOUR POINT OF VIEW, SIR HUNTER-- BUT LOOK AT HIM NOW!
"HE'S HAPPY AS A CLAM LIVING IN FAERIE...
"WELL-PROTECTED, TOO, I SHOULD THINK.
"BUT OUR NEXT CONTESTANT... OH ME, OH MY. WHAT'S THIS--?!
"THIS TIMOTHY HUNTER IS DEAD AS A DOORNAIL TODAY.
"IT'S ENOUGH TO MAKE YOUR HEAD SPIN, ISN'T IT?
TIM HUNTER
"IF ONLY THE PAST COULD BE AS UNCOMPLICATED AS IT USED TO BE.
"WHAT ELSE HAVE WE? Hmmm, NOTHING TOO PROMISING...
"THIS TIM IS BEING PROGRAMMED BY ONE OF THOSE TEDIOUS NIHILIST-TERRORIST SECTS.
"WHEN HIS EYES ARE BLIND TO EVERYTHING BUT FLAME--THEIR VISION OF THE FUTURE. ISN'T THAT CUTE?-- I EXPECT THEY'LL USE HIM TO INCINERATE PRIME MINISTERS.
"YOU WOULDN'T BE BLIND BY ANY CHANCE, WOULD YOU?"
OH, IT'S NOT SO BAD AS THAT, SIR HUNTER--
TIME STILL HOLDS ONE CHILD WHO COULD BECOME YOU.
TO BE, OR NOT TO BE...
Hmm... IT'S NONE OF MY BUSINESS, I KNOW...
...BUT HAVE YOU EVER CONSIDERED USING THAT FORMATORY OF YOURS AS A SCHOOL FOR WAYWARD BOYS?

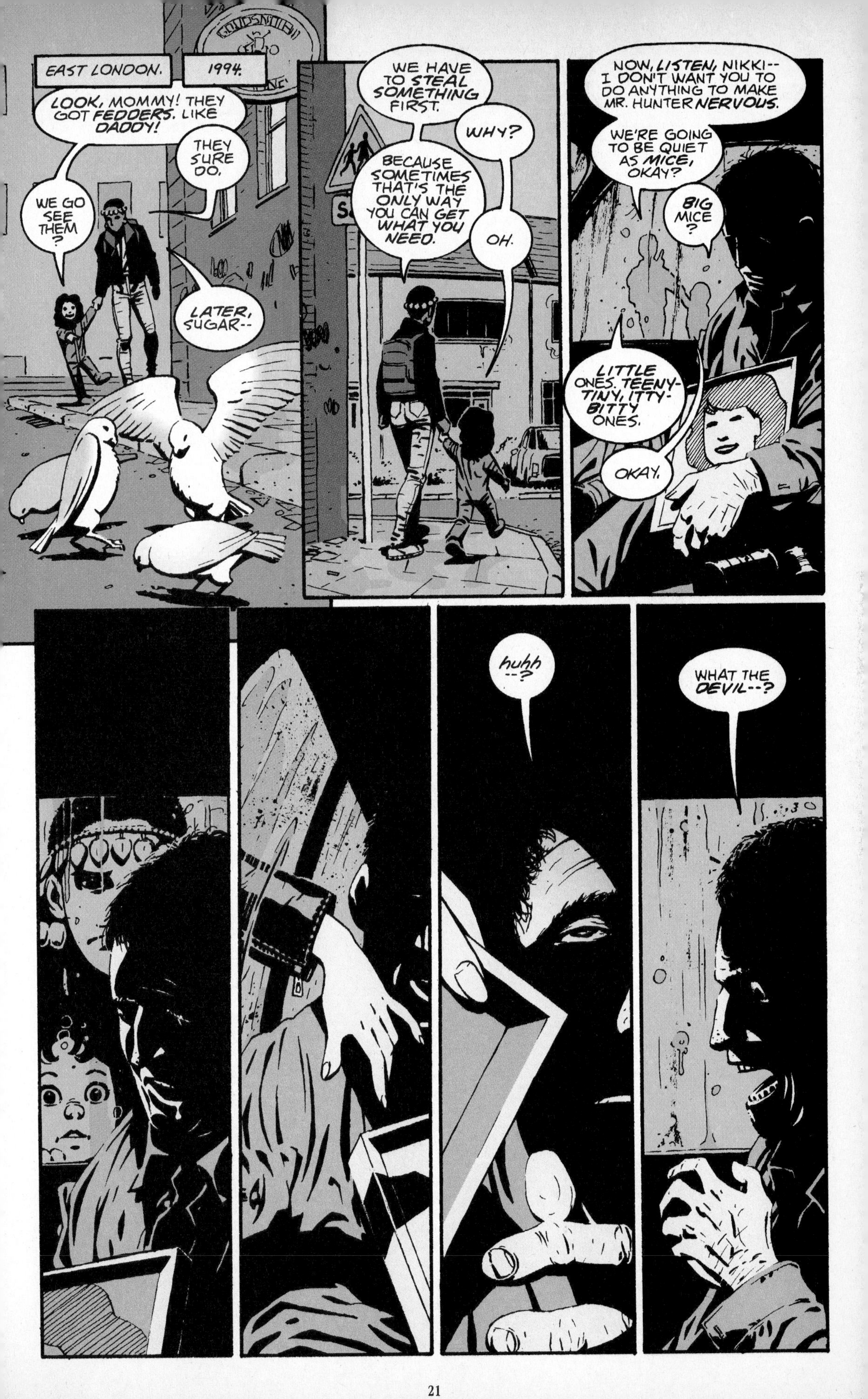
EAST LONDON.
1994.
LOOK, MOMMY! THEY GOT FEDDERS. LIKE DADDY!
THEY SURE DO.
WE GO SEE THEM?
LATER, SUGAR--
WE HAVE TO STEAL SOMETHING FIRST.
WHY?
BECAUSE SOMETIMES THAT'S THE ONLY WAY YOU CAN GET WHAT YOU NEED.
OH.
NOW, LISTEN, NIKKI-- I DON'T WANT YOU TO DO ANYTHING TO MAKE MR. HUNTER NERVOUS.
WE'RE GOING TO BE QUIET AS MICE, OKAY?
BIG MICE?
LITTLE ONES. TEENY-TINY, ITTY-BITTY ONES.
OKAY.
huhh --?
WHAT THE DEVIL--?

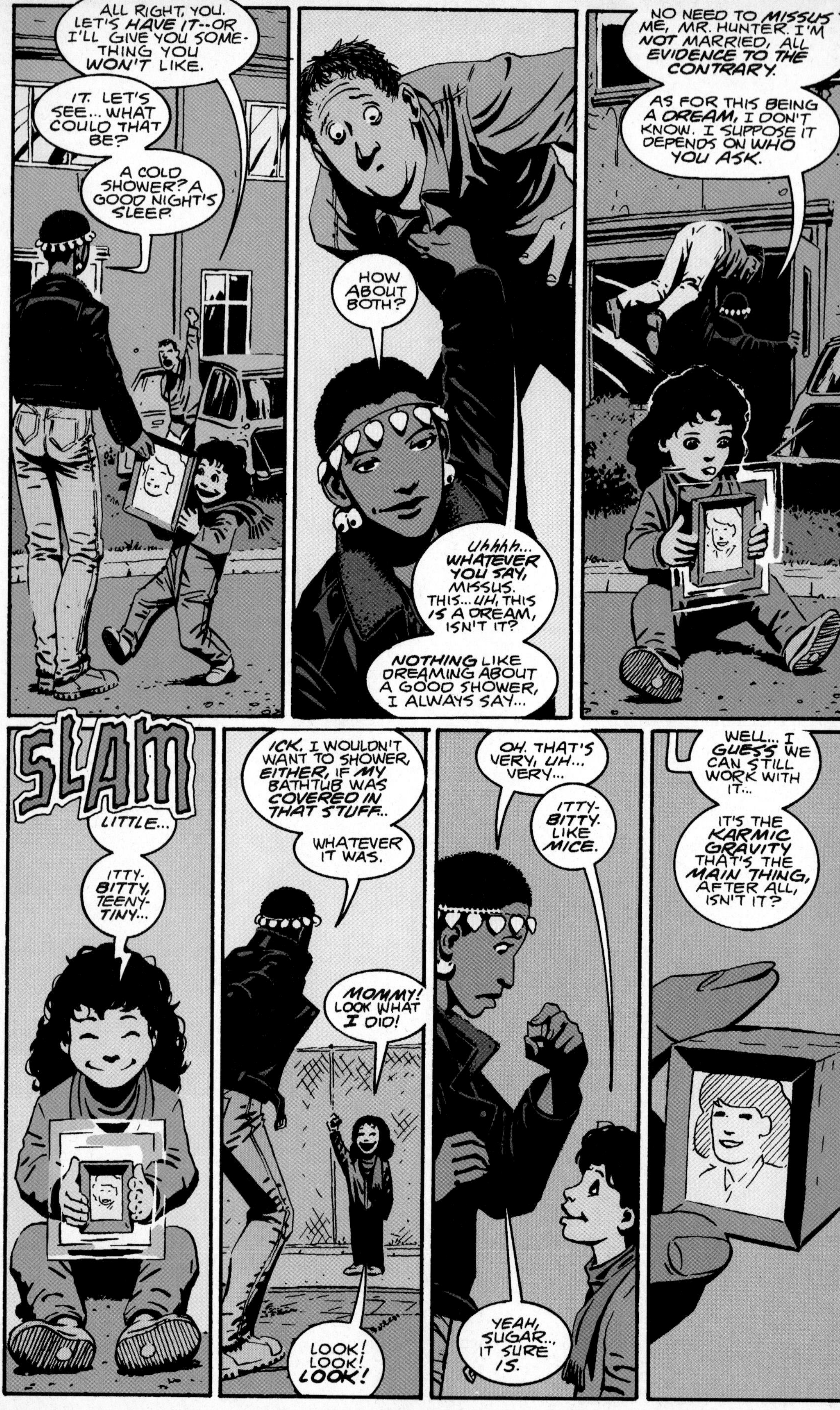

ALL RIGHT, YOU. LET'S HAVE IT--OR I'LL GIVE YOU SOMETHING YOU WON'T LIKE.
IT. LET'S SEE... WHAT COULD THAT BE?
A COLD SHOWER? A GOOD NIGHT'S SLEEP.
HOW ABOUT BOTH?
Uhhhh... WHATEVER YOU SAY, MISSUS. THIS... UH, THIS IS A DREAM, ISN'T IT?
NOTHING LIKE DREAMING ABOUT A GOOD SHOWER, I ALWAYS SAY...
NO NEED TO MISSUS ME, MR. HUNTER. I'M NOT MARRIED, ALL EVIDENCE TO THE CONTRARY.
AS FOR THIS BEING A DREAM, I DON'T KNOW. I SUPPOSE IT DEPENDS ON WHO YOU ASK.
SLAM
LITTLE...
ITTY-BITTY, TEENY-TINY...
ICK. I WOULDN'T WANT TO SHOWER, EITHER, IF MY BATHTUB WAS COVERED IN THAT STUFF..
WHATEVER IT WAS.
MOMMY! LOOK WHAT I DID!
LOOK! LOOK! LOOK!
OH. THAT'S VERY, UH... VERY...
ITTY-BITTY. LIKE MICE.
YEAH, SUGAR... IT SURE IS.
WELL... I GUESS WE CAN STILL WORK WITH IT...
IT'S THE KARMIC GRAVITY THAT'S THE MAIN THING, AFTER ALL, ISN'T IT?

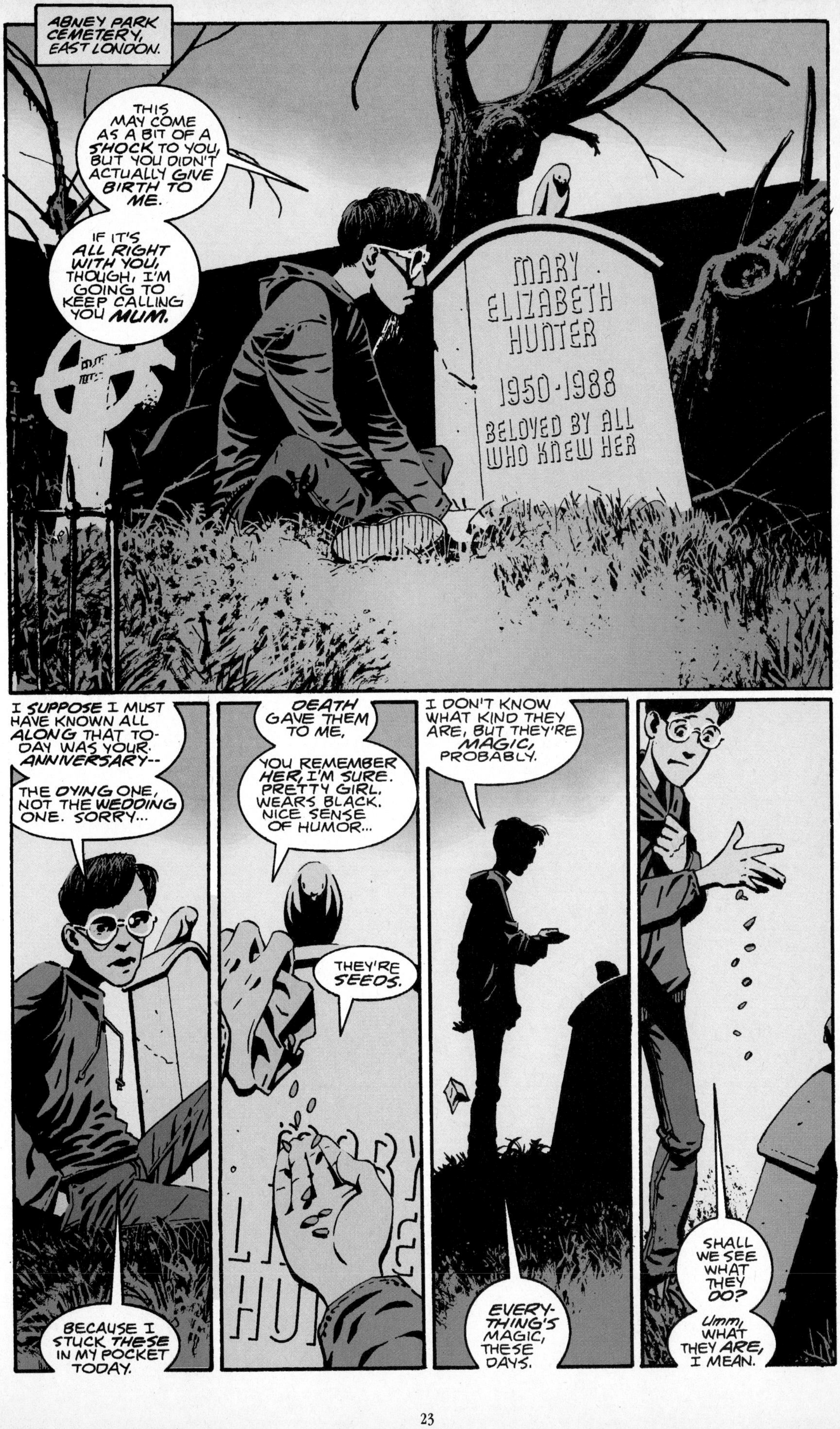
ABNEY PARK CEMETERY, EAST LONDON.
THIS MAY COME AS A BIT OF A SHOCK TO YOU, BUT YOU DIDN'T ACTUALLY GIVE BIRTH TO ME.
IF IT'S ALL RIGHT WITH YOU, THOUGH, I'M GOING TO KEEP CALLING YOU MUM.
MARY ELIZABETH HUNTER
1950-1988
BELOVED BY ALL WHO KNEW HER
I SUPPOSE I MUST HAVE KNOWN ALL ALONG THAT TO-DAY WAS YOUR ANNIVERSARY--
THE DYING ONE, NOT THE WEDDING ONE. SORRY...
BECAUSE I STUCK THESE IN MY POCKET TODAY.
DEATH GAVE THEM TO ME.
YOU REMEMBER HER, I'M SURE. PRETTY GIRL. WEARS BLACK. NICE SENSE OF HUMOR...
THEY'RE SEEDS.
I DON'T KNOW WHAT KIND THEY ARE, BUT THEY'RE MAGIC, PROBABLY.
EVERY-THING'S MAGIC, THESE DAYS.
SHALL WE SEE WHAT THEY DO?
Umm, WHAT THEY ARE, I MEAN.

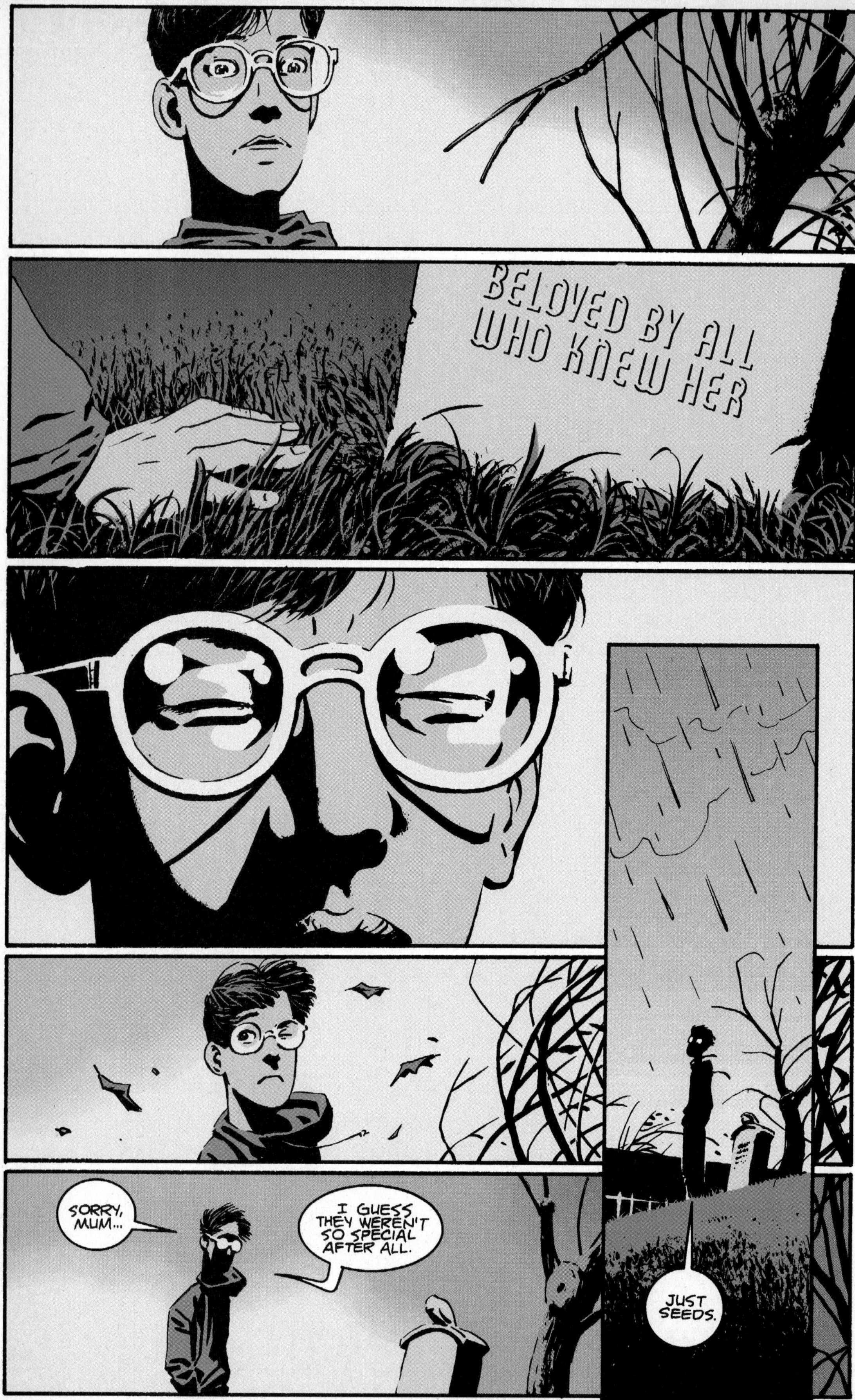
BELOVED BY ALL WHO KNEW HER
SORRY, MUM...
I GUESS THEY WEREN'T SO SPECIAL AFTER ALL.
JUST SEEDS.

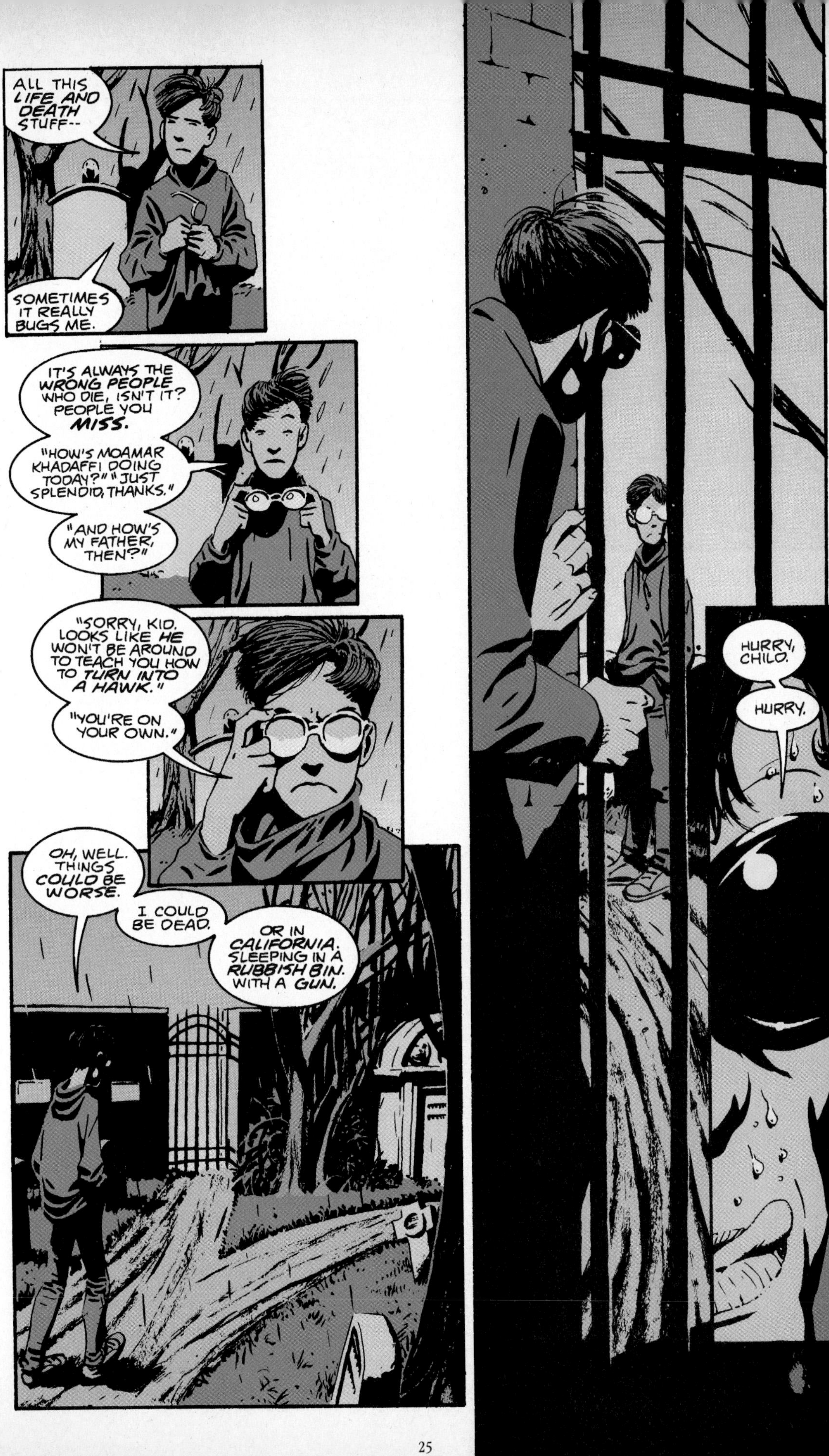
ALL THIS LIFE AND DEATH STUFF--
SOMETIMES IT REALLY BUGS ME.
IT'S ALWAYS THE WRONG PEOPLE WHO DIE, ISN'T IT? PEOPLE YOU MISS.
"HOW'S MOAMAR KHADAFFI DOING TODAY?" "JUST SPLENDID, THANKS."
"AND HOW'S MY FATHER, THEN?"
"SORRY, KID. LOOKS LIKE HE WON'T BE AROUND TO TEACH YOU HOW TO TURN INTO A HAWK."
"YOU'RE ON YOUR OWN."
OH, WELL. THINGS COULD BE WORSE.
I COULD BE DEAD.
OR IN CALIFORNIA. SLEEPING IN A RUBBISH BIN. WITH A GUN.
HURRY, CHILD.
HURRY.

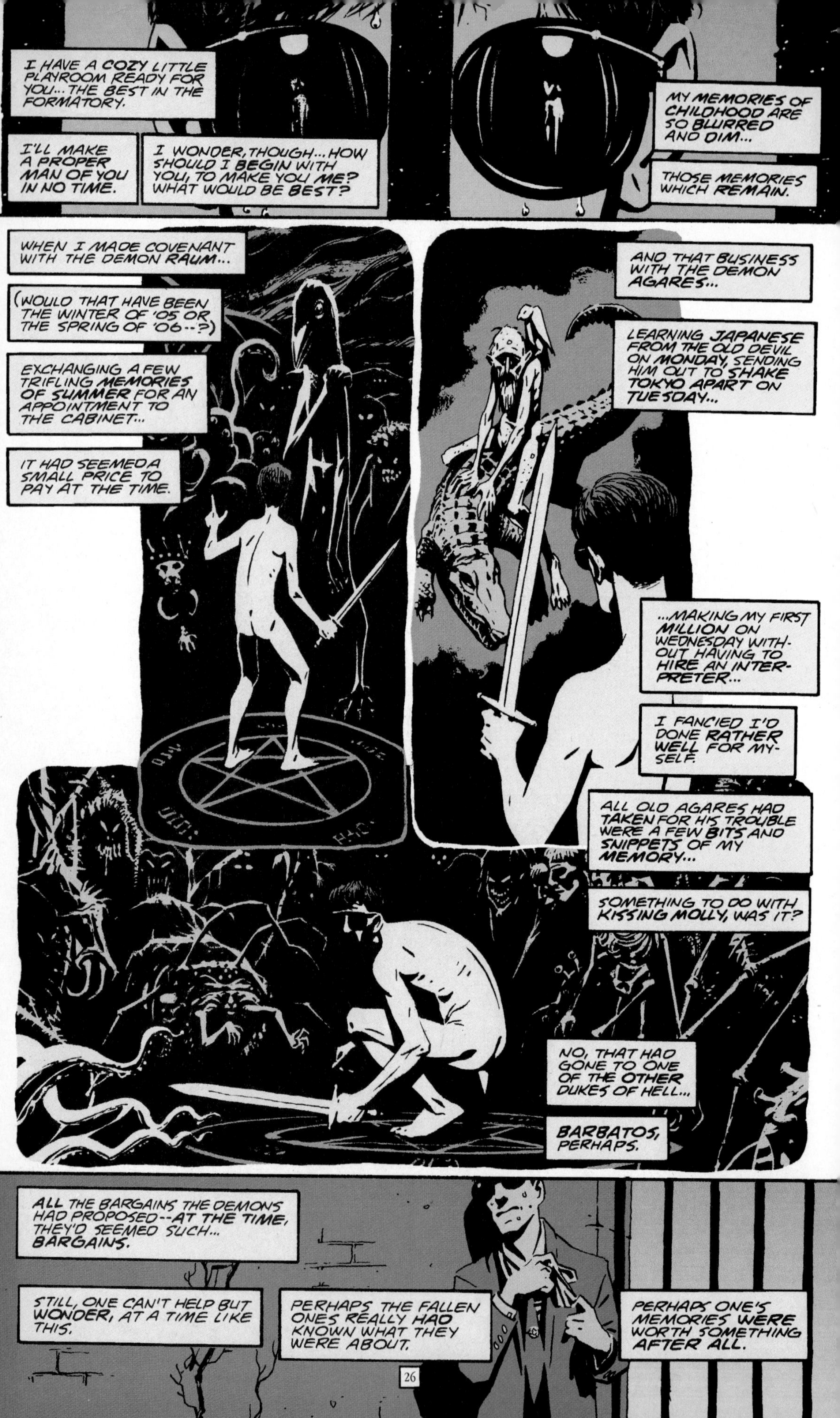
I HAVE A COZY LITTLE PLAYROOM READY FOR YOU... THE BEST IN THE FORMATORY.
I'LL MAKE A PROPER MAN OF YOU IN NO TIME.
I WONDER, THOUGH... HOW SHOULD I BEGIN WITH YOU, TO MAKE YOU ME? WHAT WOULD BE BEST?
MY MEMORIES OF CHILDHOOD ARE SO BLURRED AND DIM...
THOSE MEMORIES WHICH REMAIN.
WHEN I MADE COVENANT WITH THE DEMON RAUM...
(WOULD THAT HAVE BEEN THE WINTER OF '05 OR THE SPRING OF '06--?)
EXCHANGING A FEW TRIFLING MEMORIES OF SUMMER FOR AN APPOINTMENT TO THE CABINET...
IT HAD SEEMED A SMALL PRICE TO PAY AT THE TIME.
AND THAT BUSINESS WITH THE DEMON AGARES...
LEARNING JAPANESE FROM THE OLD DEVIL ON MONDAY, SENDING HIM OUT TO SHAKE TOKYO APART ON TUESDAY...
...MAKING MY FIRST MILLION ON WEDNESDAY WITH-OUT HAVING TO HIRE AN INTER-PRETER...
I FANCIED I'D DONE RATHER WELL FOR MY-SELF.
ALL OLD AGARES HAD TAKEN FOR HIS TROUBLE WERE A FEW BITS AND SNIPPETS OF MY MEMORY...
SOMETHING TO DO WITH KISSING MOLLY, WAS IT?
NO, THAT HAD GONE TO ONE OF THE OTHER DUKES OF HELL...
BARBATOS, PERHAPS.
ALL THE BARGAINS THE DEMONS HAD PROPOSED--AT THE TIME, THEY'D SEEMED SUCH... BARGAINS.
STILL, ONE CAN'T HELP BUT WONDER, AT A TIME LIKE THIS.
PERHAPS THE FALLEN ONES REALLY HAD KNOWN WHAT THEY WERE ABOUT.
PERHAPS ONE'S MEMORIES WERE WORTH SOMETHING AFTER ALL.

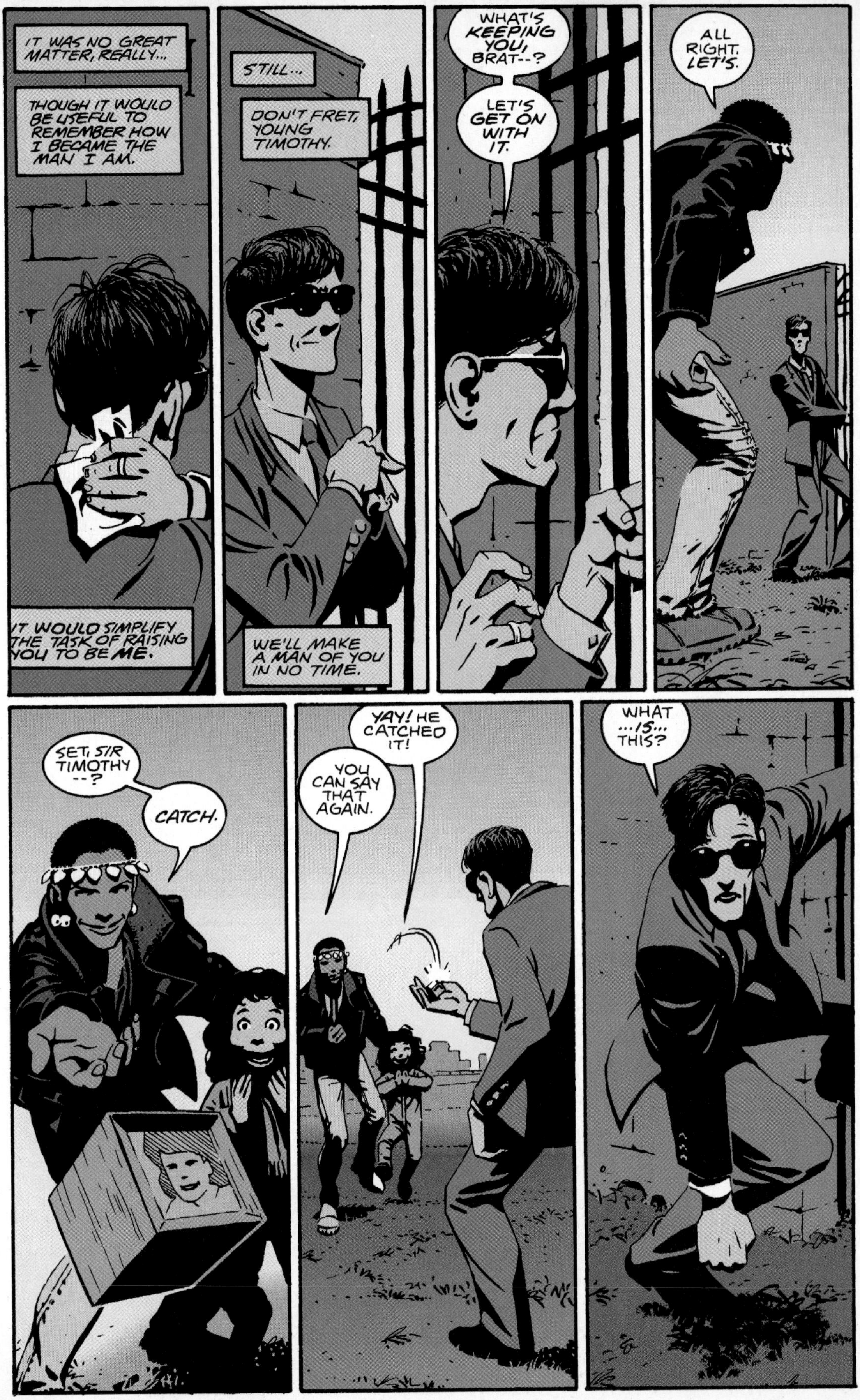
IT WAS NO GREAT MATTER, REALLY...
THOUGH IT WOULD BE USEFUL TO REMEMBER HOW I BECAME THE MAN I AM.
IT WOULD SIMPLIFY THE TASK OF RAISING YOU TO BE ME.
STILL...
DON'T FRET, YOUNG TIMOTHY.
WE'LL MAKE A MAN OF YOU IN NO TIME.
WHAT'S KEEPING YOU, BRAT--?
LET'S GET ON WITH IT.
ALL RIGHT. LET'S.
SET, SIR TIMOTHY--?
CATCH.
YAY! HE CATCHED IT!
YOU CAN SAY THAT AGAIN.
WHAT ...IS... THIS?

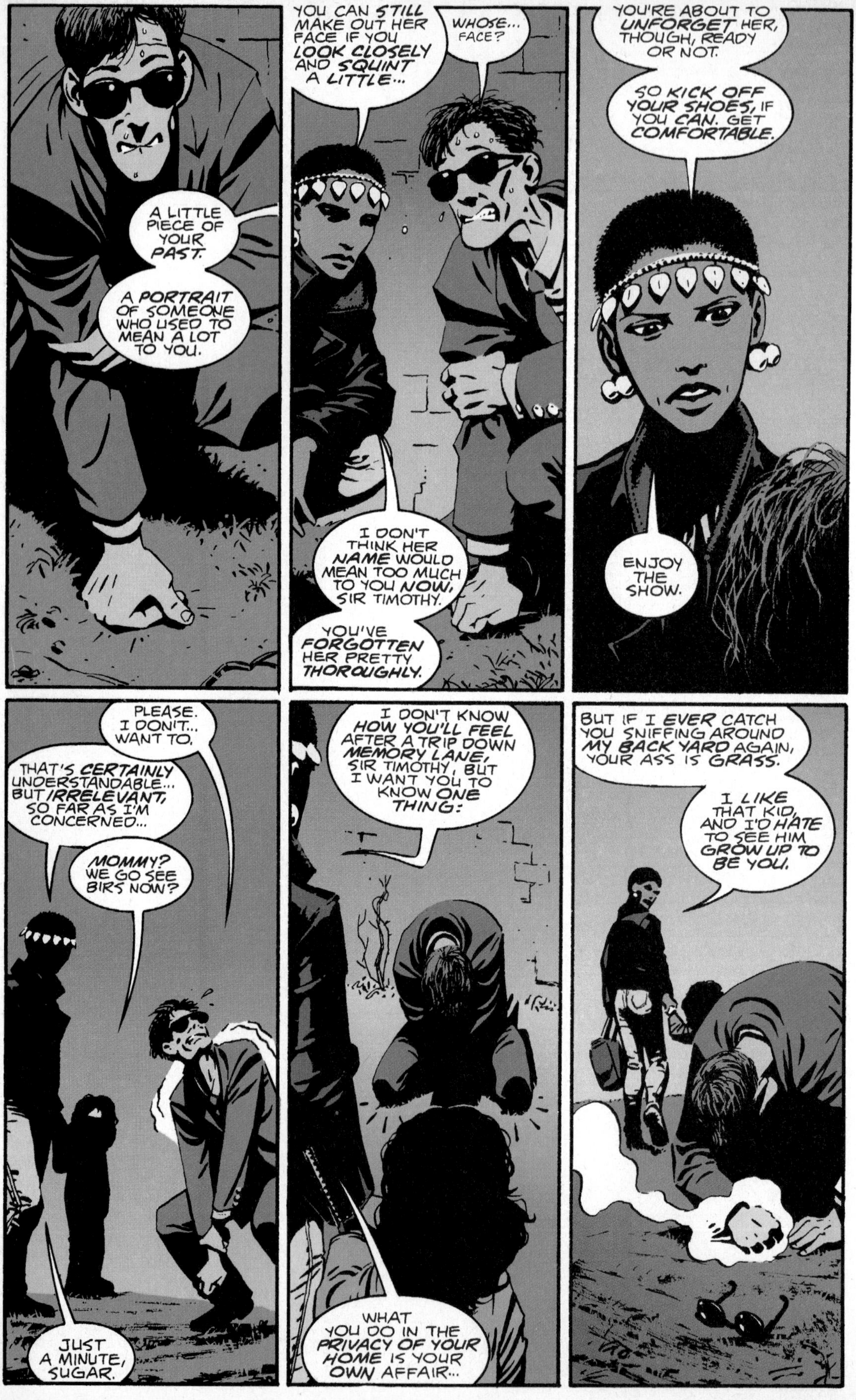
A LITTLE PIECE OF YOUR PAST.
A PORTRAIT OF SOMEONE WHO USED TO MEAN A LOT TO YOU.
YOU CAN STILL MAKE OUT HER FACE IF YOU LOOK CLOSELY AND SQUINT A LITTLE...
WHOSE... FACE?
I DON'T THINK HER NAME WOULD MEAN TOO MUCH TO YOU NOW, SIR TIMOTHY.
YOU'VE FORGOTTEN HER PRETTY THOROUGHLY.
YOU'RE ABOUT TO UNFORGET HER, THOUGH, READY OR NOT.
SO KICK OFF YOUR SHOES, IF YOU CAN. GET COMFORTABLE.
ENJOY THE SHOW.
PLEASE. I DON'T... WANT TO.
THAT'S CERTAINLY UNDERSTANDABLE... BUT IRRELEVANT, SO FAR AS I'M CONCERNED...
MOMMY? WE GO SEE BIRS NOW?
JUST A MINUTE, SUGAR.
I DON'T KNOW HOW YOU'LL FEEL AFTER A TRIP DOWN MEMORY LANE, SIR TIMOTHY, BUT I WANT YOU TO KNOW ONE THING:
WHAT YOU DO IN THE PRIVACY OF YOUR HOME IS YOUR OWN AFFAIR...
BUT IF I EVER CATCH YOU SNIFFING AROUND MY BACK YARD AGAIN, YOUR ASS IS GRASS.
I LIKE THAT KID, AND I'D HATE TO SEE HIM GROW UP TO BE YOU.

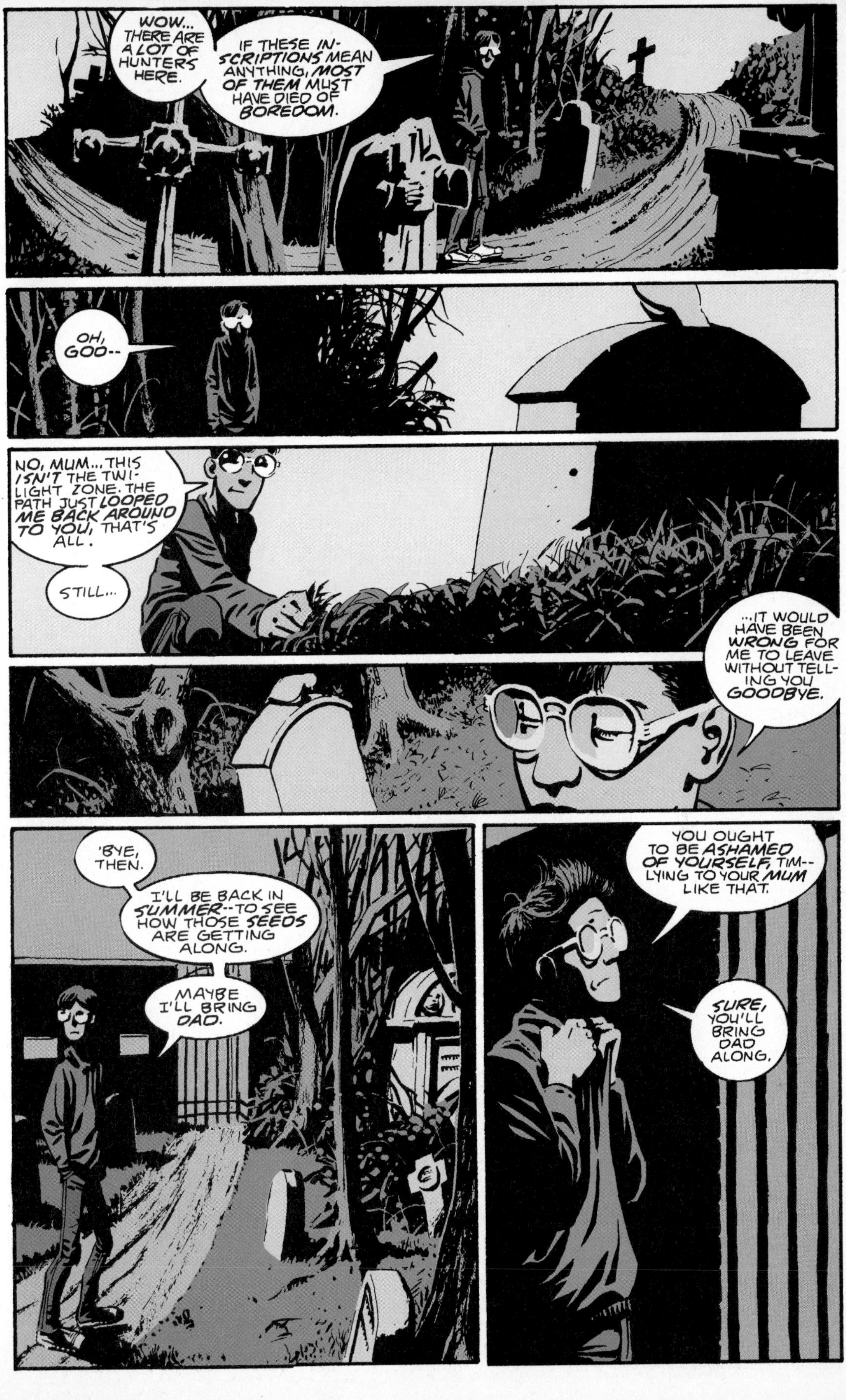
WOW... THERE ARE A LOT OF HUNTERS HERE.
IF THESE IN-SCRIPTIONS MEAN ANYTHING, MOST OF THEM MUST HAVE DIED OF BOREDOM.
OH, GOO--
NO, MUM... THIS ISN'T THE TWI-LIGHT ZONE. THE PATH JUST LOOPED ME BACK AROUND TO YOU, THAT'S ALL.
STILL...
...IT WOULD HAVE BEEN WRONG FOR ME TO LEAVE WITHOUT TELL-ING YOU GOODBYE.
'BYE, THEN.
I'LL BE BACK IN SUMMER--TO SEE HOW THOSE SEEDS ARE GETTING ALONG.
MAYBE I'LL BRING DAD.
YOU OUGHT TO BE ASHAMED OF YOURSELF, TIM-- LYING TO YOUR MUM LIKE THAT.
SURE, YOU'LL BRING DAD ALONG.

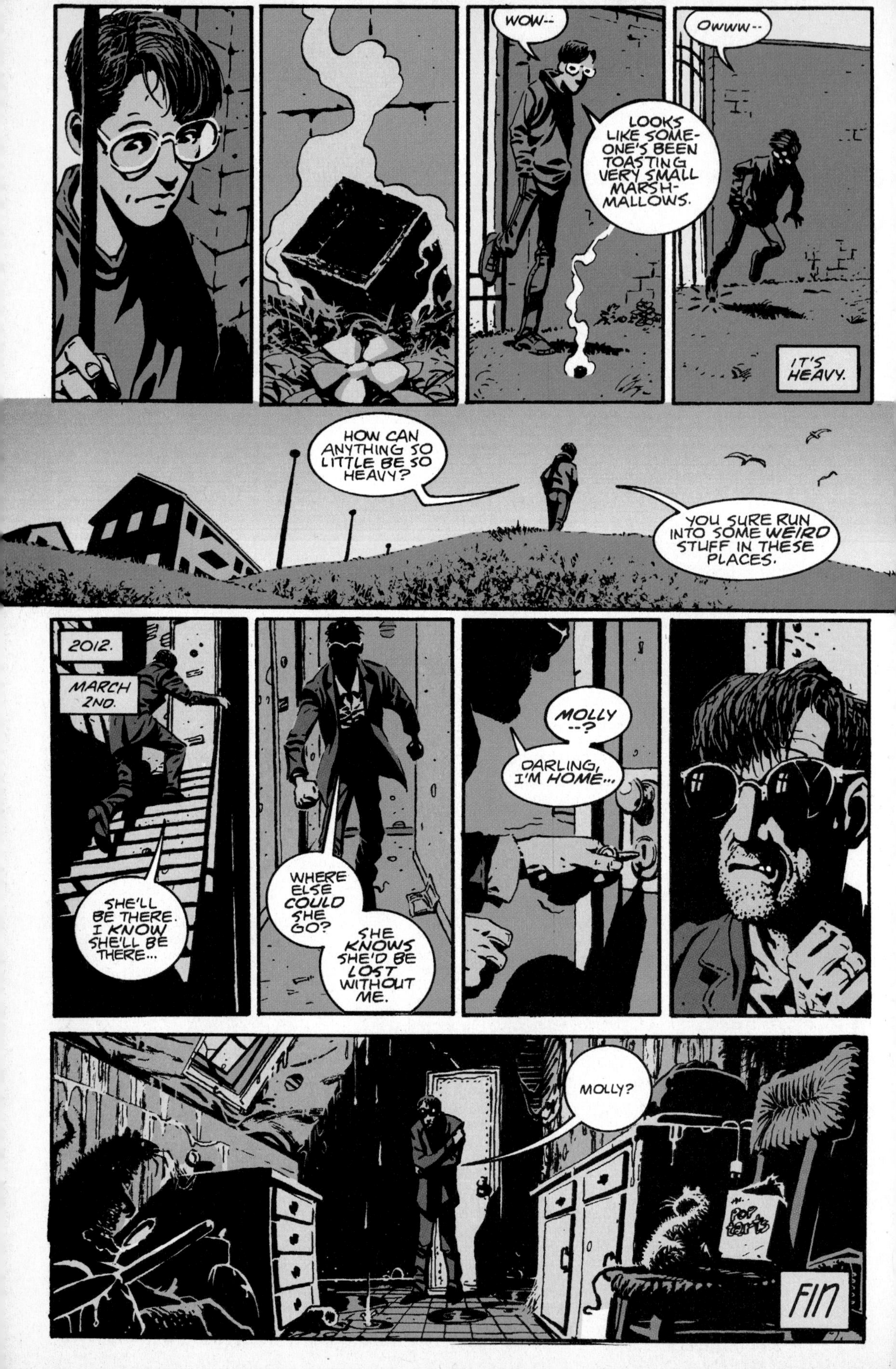
WOW--
LOOKS LIKE SOMEONE'S BEEN TOASTING VERY SMALL MARSH-MALLOWS.
OWWW--
IT'S HEAVY.
HOW CAN ANYTHING SO LITTLE BE SO HEAVY?
YOU SURE RUN INTO SOME WEIRD STUFF IN THESE PLACES.
2012.
MARCH 2ND.
SHE'LL BE THERE. I KNOW SHE'LL BE THERE...
WHERE ELSE COULD SHE GO?
SHE KNOWS SHE'D BE LOST WITHOUT ME.
MOLLY --?
DARLING, I'M HOME...
MOLLY?
FIN

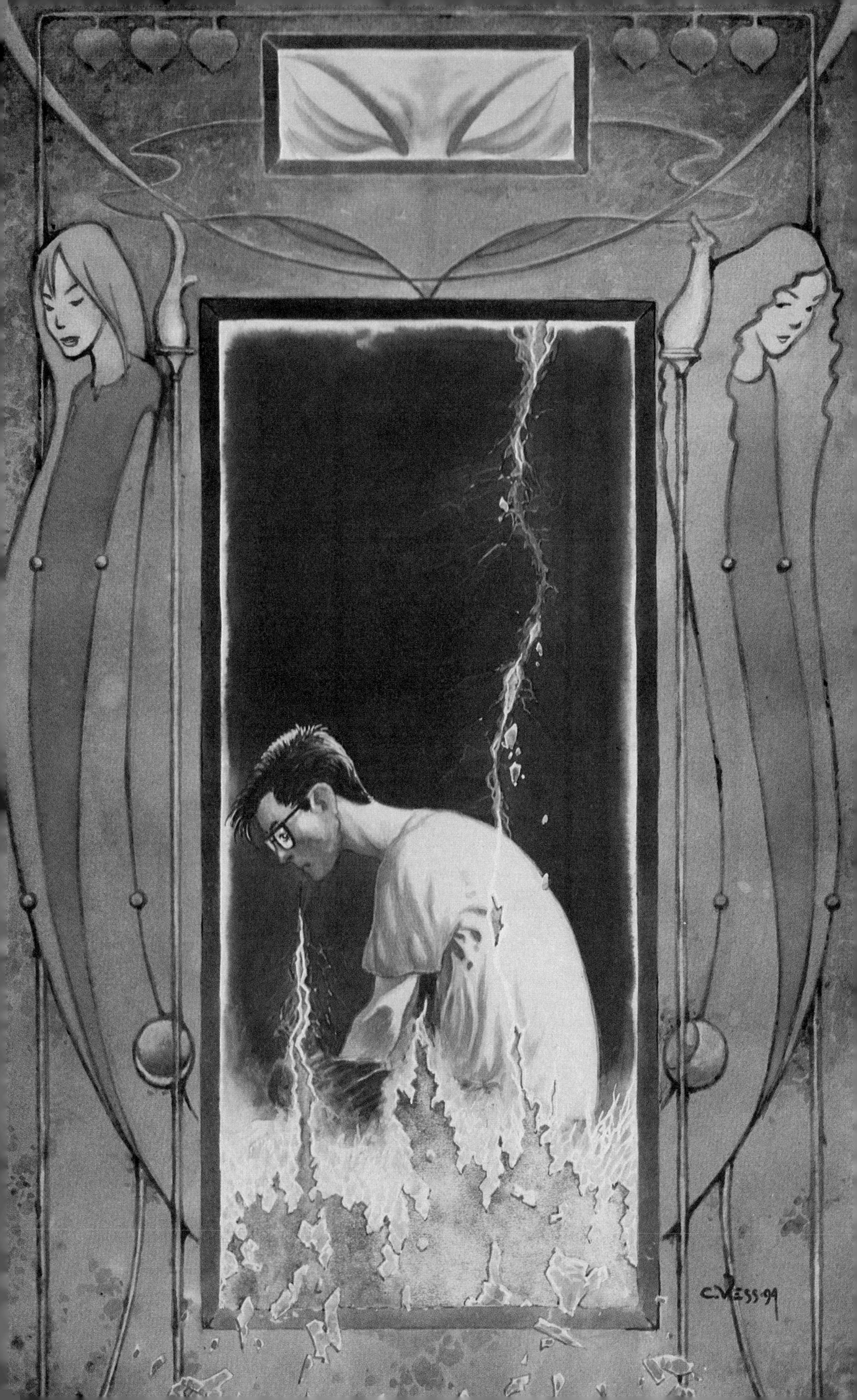
C. VESS·94

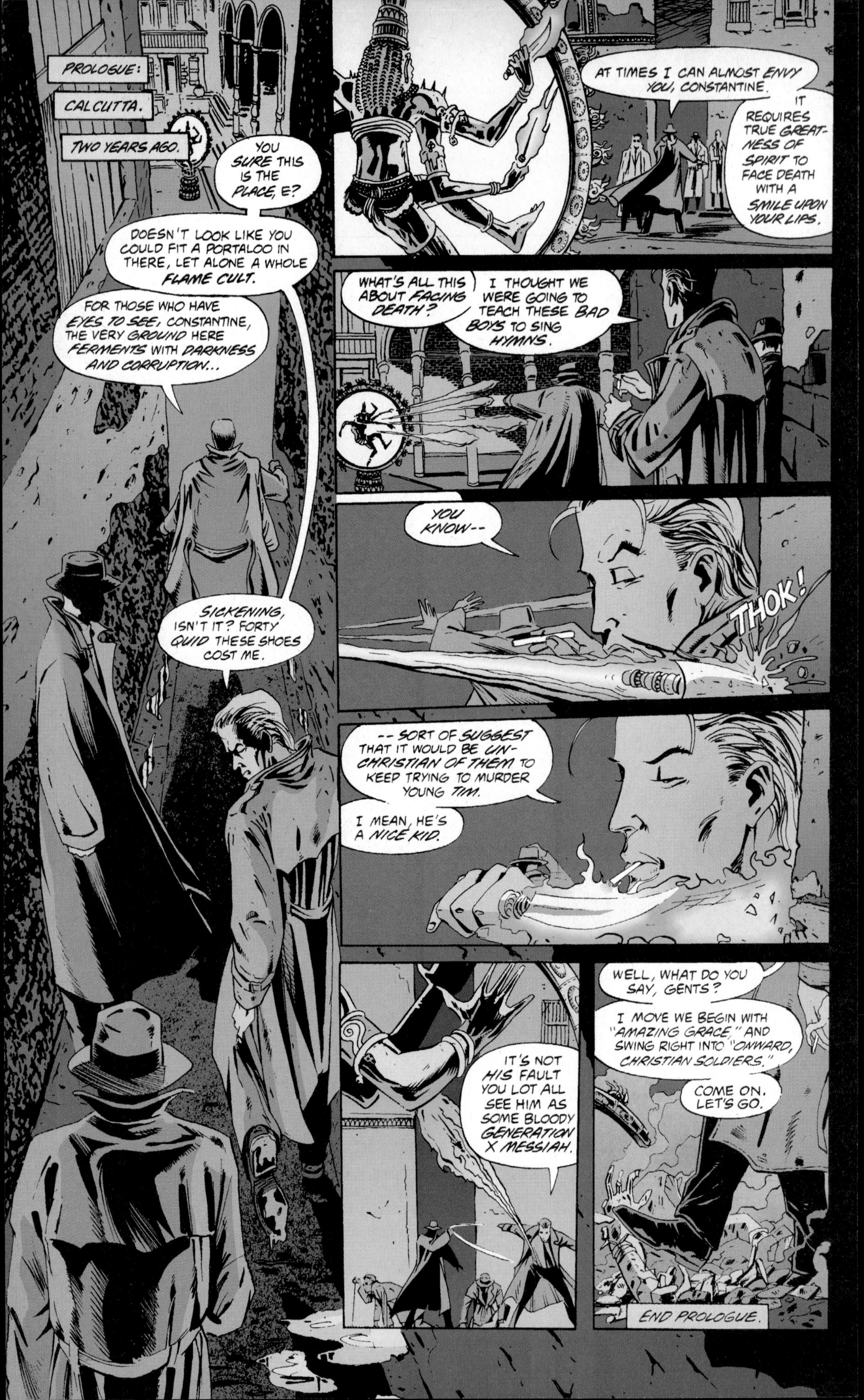
PROLOGUE:
CALCUTTA.
TWO YEARS AGO.
YOU SURE THIS IS THE PLACE, E?
DOESN'T LOOK LIKE YOU COULD FIT A PORTALOO IN THERE, LET ALONE A WHOLE FLAME CULT.
FOR THOSE WHO HAVE EYES TO SEE, CONSTANTINE, THE VERY GROUND HERE FERMENTS WITH DARKNESS AND CORRUPTION...
SICKENING, ISN'T IT? FORTY QUID THESE SHOES COST ME.
AT TIMES I CAN ALMOST ENVY YOU, CONSTANTINE.
IT REQUIRES TRUE GREATNESS OF SPIRIT TO FACE DEATH WITH A SMILE UPON YOUR LIPS.
WHAT'S ALL THIS ABOUT FACING DEATH?
I THOUGHT WE WERE GOING TO TEACH THESE BAD BOYS TO SING HYMNS.
YOU KNOW--
THOK!
-- SORT OF SUGGEST THAT IT WOULD BE UN-CHRISTIAN OF THEM TO KEEP TRYING TO MURDER YOUNG TIM.
I MEAN, HE'S A NICE KID.
IT'S NOT HIS FAULT YOU LOT ALL SEE HIM AS SOME BLOODY GENERATION X MESSIAH.
WELL, WHAT DO YOU SAY, GENTS?
I MOVE WE BEGIN WITH "AMAZING GRACE," AND SWING RIGHT INTO "ONWARD, CHRISTIAN SOLDIERS."
COME ON. LET'S GO.
END PROLOGUE.

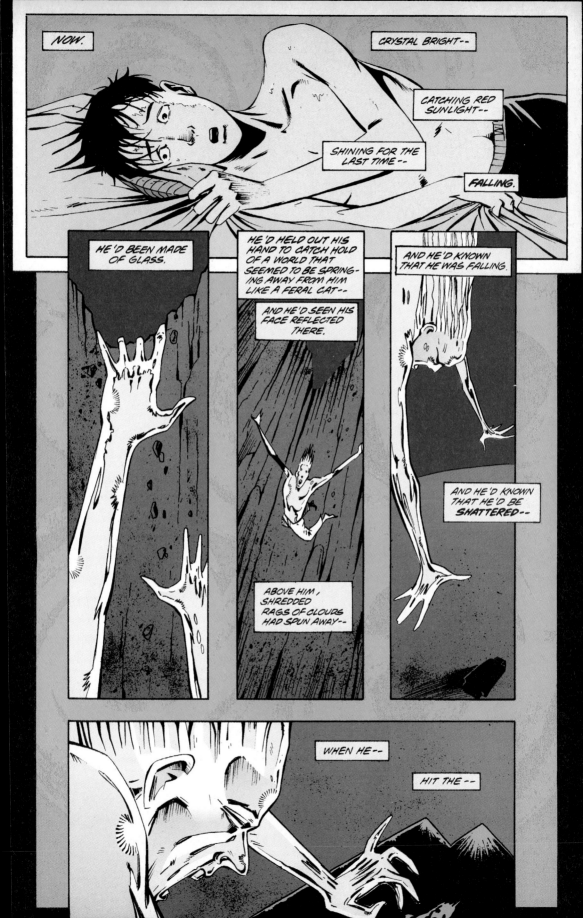

NOW.

CRYSTAL BRIGHT--

CATCHING RED SUNLIGHT--

SHINING FOR THE LAST TIME--

FALLING.

HE'D BEEN MADE OF GLASS.

HE'D HELD OUT HIS HAND TO CATCH HOLD OF A WORLD THAT SEEMED TO BE SPRINGING AWAY FROM HIM LIKE A FERAL CAT--

AND HE'D SEEN HIS FACE REFLECTED THERE.

AND HE'D KNOWN THAT HE WAS FALLING.

AND HE'D KNOWN THAT HE'D BE SHATTERED--

ABOVE HIM, SHREDDED RAGS OF CLOUDS HAD SPUN AWAY--

WHEN HE--

HIT THE--

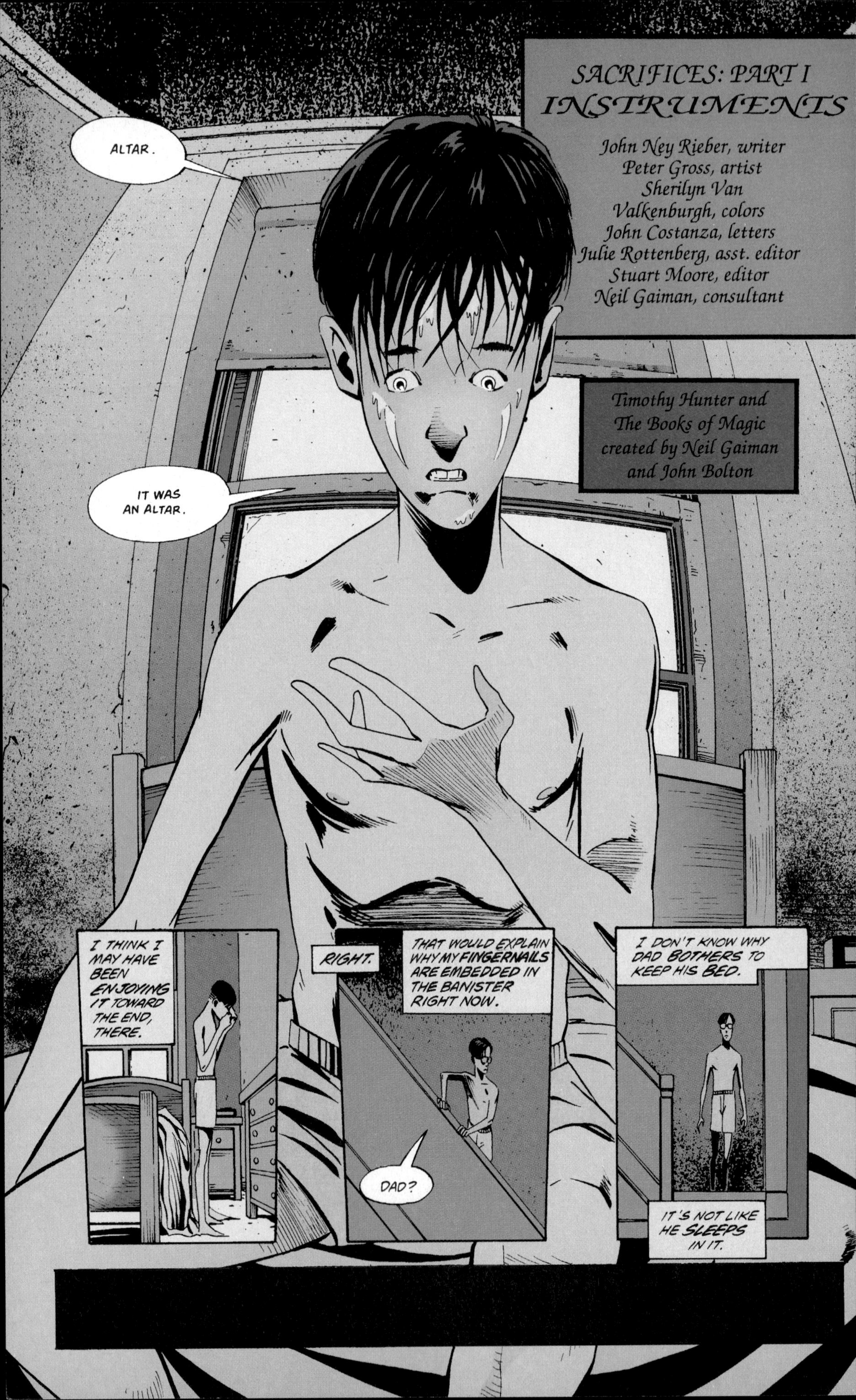
SACRIFICES: PART I
INSTRUMENTS
John Ney Rieber, writer
Peter Gross, artist
Sherilyn Van Valkenburgh, colors
John Costanza, letters
Julie Rottenberg, asst. editor
Stuart Moore, editor
Neil Gaiman, consultant
ALTAR.
IT WAS AN ALTAR.
Timothy Hunter and The Books of Magic created by Neil Gaiman and John Bolton
I THINK I MAY HAVE BEEN ENJOYING IT TOWARD THE END, THERE.
RIGHT.
THAT WOULD EXPLAIN WHY MY FINGERNAILS ARE EMBEDDED IN THE BANISTER RIGHT NOW.
DAD?
I DON'T KNOW WHY DAD BOTHERS TO KEEP HIS BED.
IT'S NOT LIKE HE SLEEPS IN IT.

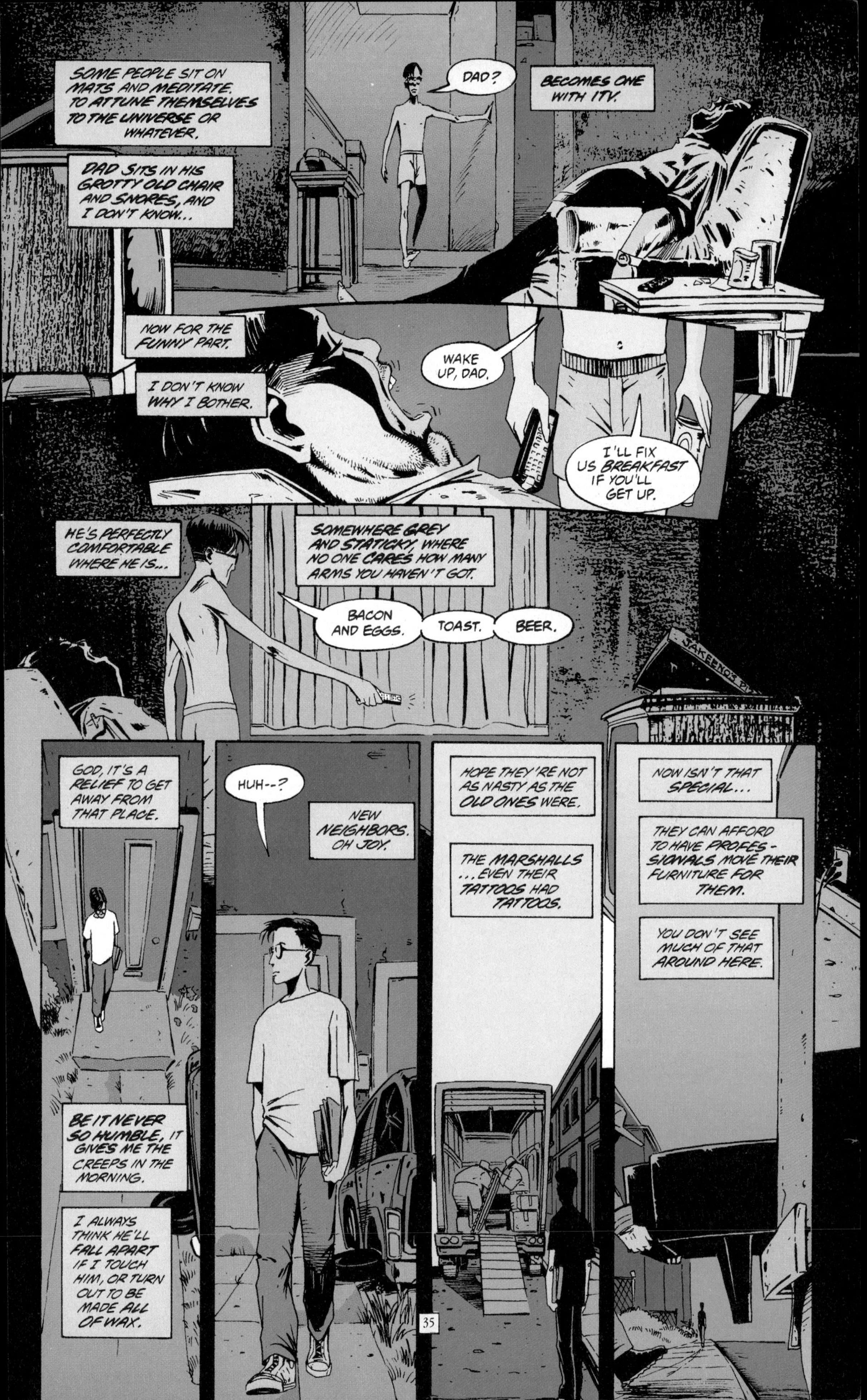

SOME PEOPLE SIT ON MATS AND MEDITATE. TO ATTUNE THEMSELVES TO THE UNIVERSE OR WHATEVER.
DAD?
BECOMES ONE WITH ITV.
DAD SITS IN HIS GROTTY OLD CHAIR AND SNORES, AND I DON'T KNOW...
NOW FOR THE FUNNY PART.
I DON'T KNOW WHY I BOTHER.
WAKE UP, DAD.
I'LL FIX US BREAKFAST IF YOU'LL GET UP.
HE'S PERFECTLY COMFORTABLE WHERE HE IS...
SOMEWHERE GREY AND STATICKY, WHERE NO ONE CARES HOW MANY ARMS YOU HAVEN'T GOT.
BACON AND EGGS.
TOAST.
BEER.
GOD, IT'S A RELIEF TO GET AWAY FROM THAT PLACE.
BE IT NEVER SO HUMBLE, IT GIVES ME THE CREEPS IN THE MORNING.
I ALWAYS THINK HE'LL FALL APART IF I TOUCH HIM, OR TURN OUT TO BE MADE ALL OF WAX.
HUH--?
NEW NEIGHBORS. OH JOY.
HOPE THEY'RE NOT AS NASTY AS THE OLD ONES WERE.
THE MARSHALLS ...EVEN THEIR TATTOOS HAD TATTOOS.
NOW ISN'T THAT SPECIAL...
THEY CAN AFFORD TO HAVE PROFES-SIONALS MOVE THEIR FURNITURE FOR THEM.
YOU DON'T SEE MUCH OF THAT AROUND HERE.

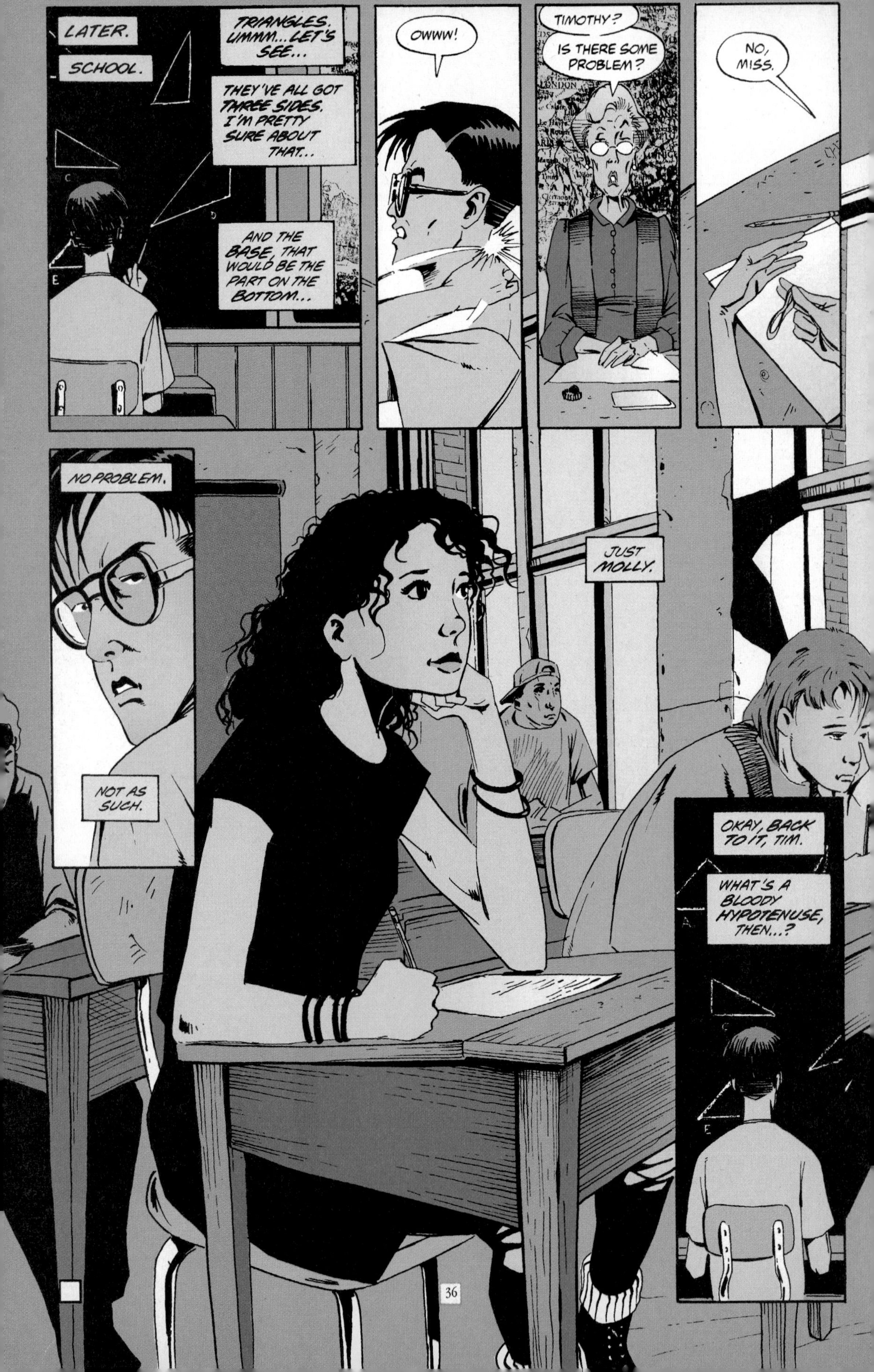

LATER.
SCHOOL.
TRIANGLES. UMMM... LET'S SEE...
THEY'VE ALL GOT THREE SIDES. I'M PRETTY SURE ABOUT THAT...
AND THE BASE, THAT WOULD BE THE PART ON THE BOTTOM...
OWWW!
TIMOTHY?
IS THERE SOME PROBLEM?
NO, MISS.
NO PROBLEM.
NOT AS SUCH.
JUST MOLLY.
OKAY, BACK TO IT, TIM.
WHAT'S A BLOODY HYPOTENUSE, THEN...?

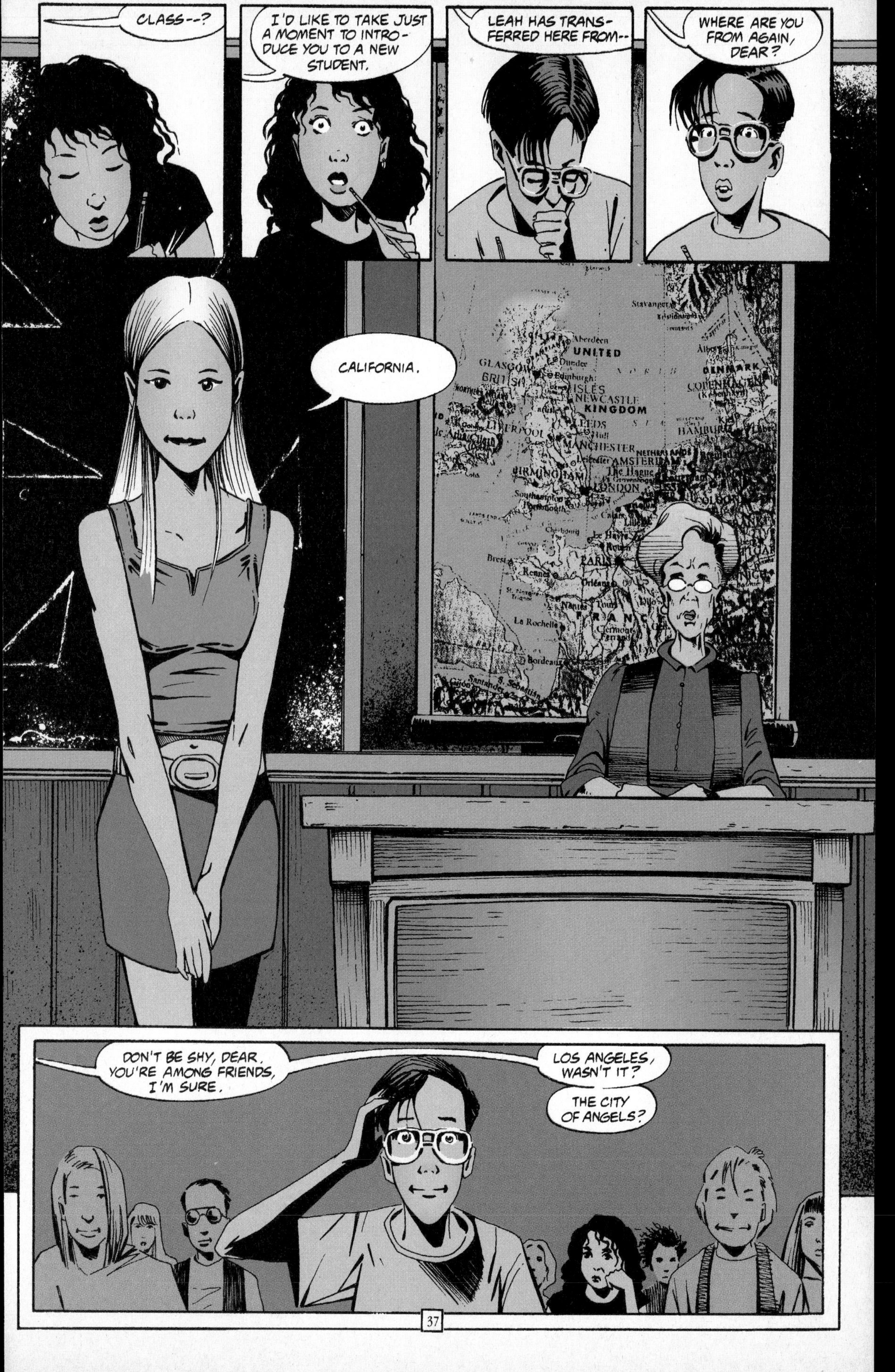
CLASS--?
I'D LIKE TO TAKE JUST A MOMENT TO INTRODUCE YOU TO A NEW STUDENT.
LEAH HAS TRANSFERRED HERE FROM--
WHERE ARE YOU FROM AGAIN, DEAR?
CALIFORNIA.
Stavanger
Aberdeen
UNITED
GLASGOW
Dundee
Edinburgh
BRITISH
ISLES
NEWCASTLE
KINGDOM
LEEDS
LIVERPOOL
MANCHESTER
AMSTERDAM
The Hague
LONDON
DENMARK
HAMBURG
Brest
Rennes
PARIS
Orléans
Nantes
La Rochelle
Bordeaux
DON'T BE SHY, DEAR. YOU'RE AMONG FRIENDS, I'M SURE.
LOS ANGELES, WASN'T IT?
THE CITY OF ANGELS?

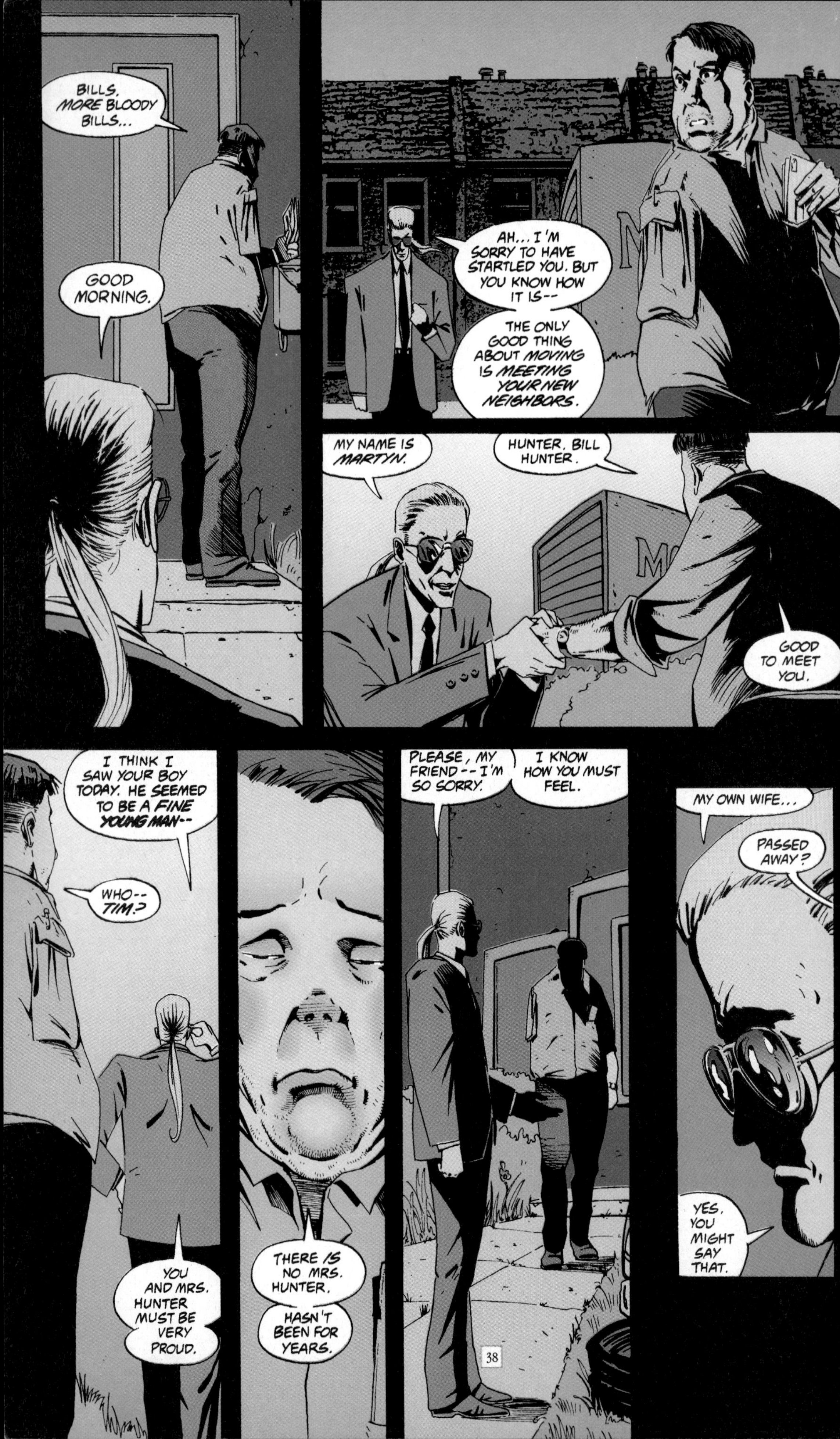

BILLS, MORE BLOODY BILLS...
GOOD MORNING.
AH... I'M SORRY TO HAVE STARTLED YOU. BUT YOU KNOW HOW IT IS--
THE ONLY GOOD THING ABOUT MOVING IS MEETING YOUR NEW NEIGHBORS.
MY NAME IS MARTYN.
HUNTER, BILL HUNTER.
GOOD TO MEET YOU.
I THINK I SAW YOUR BOY TODAY. HE SEEMED TO BE A FINE YOUNG MAN--
WHO-- TIM?
YOU AND MRS. HUNTER MUST BE VERY PROUD.
THERE IS NO MRS. HUNTER.
HASN'T BEEN FOR YEARS.
PLEASE, MY FRIEND -- I'M SO SORRY.
I KNOW HOW YOU MUST FEEL.
MY OWN WIFE...
PASSED AWAY?
YES, YOU MIGHT SAY THAT.

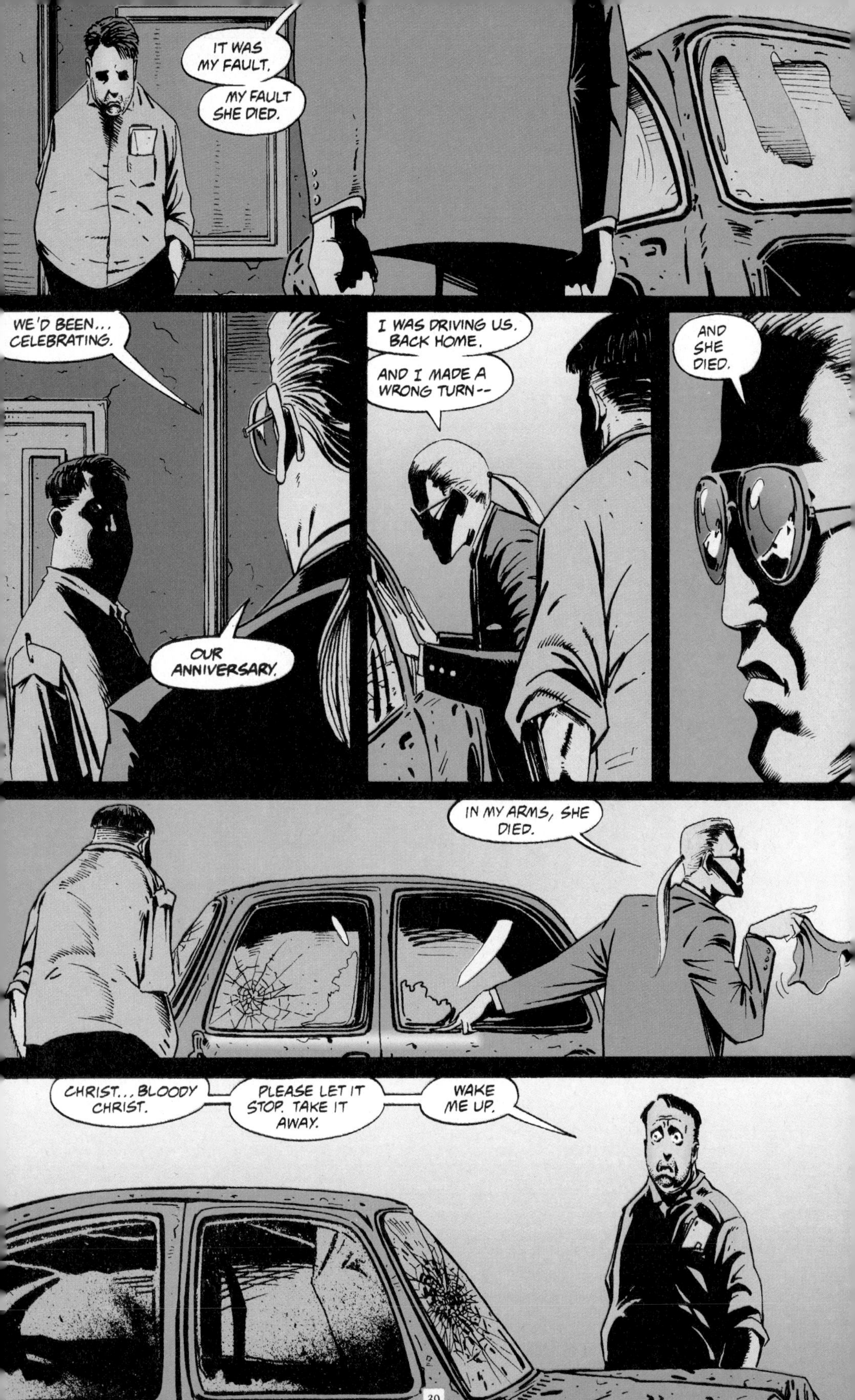
IT WAS MY FAULT.
MY FAULT SHE DIED.
WE'D BEEN... CELEBRATING.
OUR ANNIVERSARY.
I WAS DRIVING US. BACK HOME.
AND I MADE A WRONG TURN--
AND SHE DIED.
IN MY ARMS, SHE DIED.
CHRIST... BLOODY CHRIST.
PLEASE LET IT STOP. TAKE IT AWAY.
WAKE ME UP.

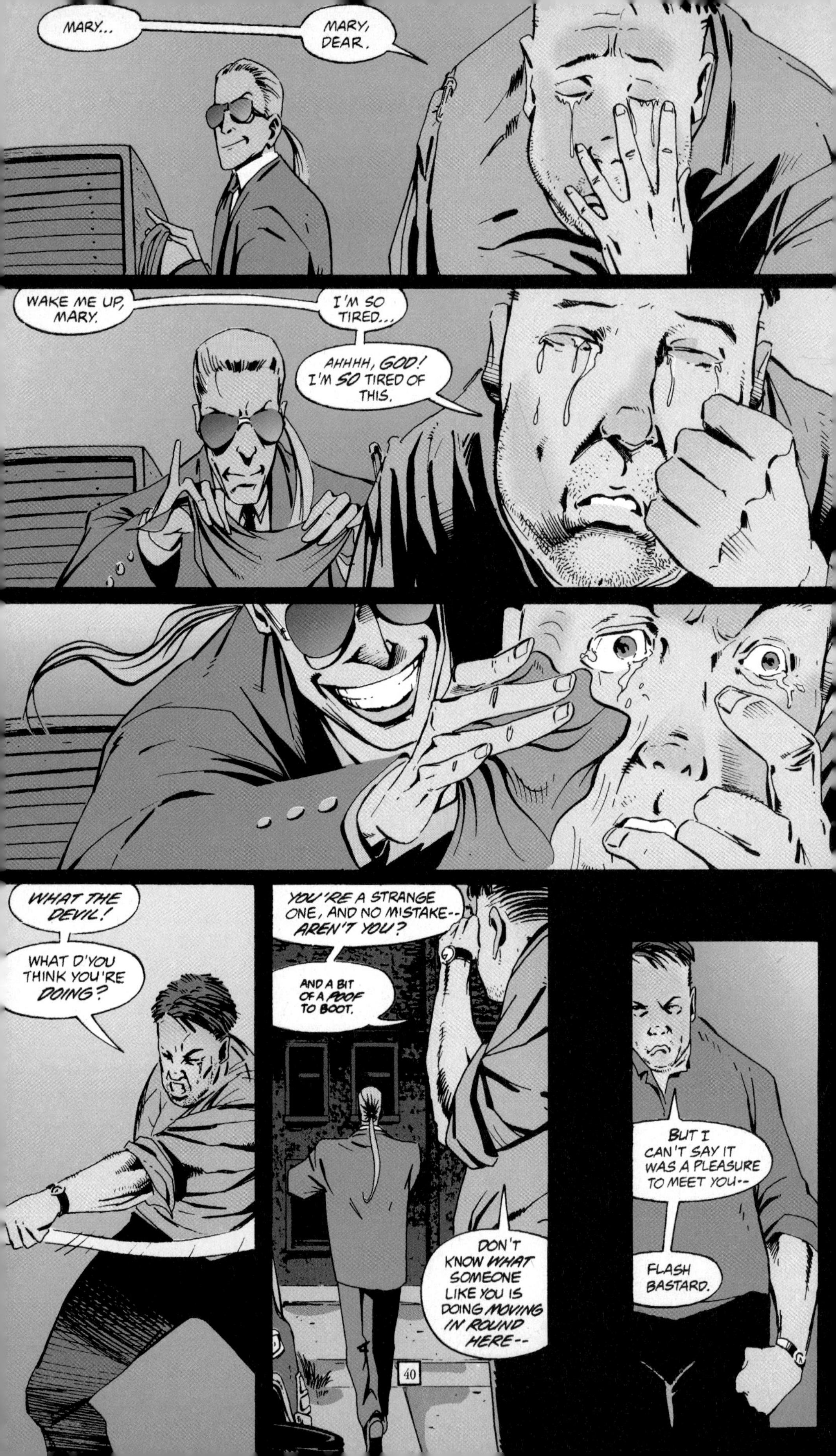

MARY...
MARY, DEAR.
WAKE ME UP, MARY.
I'M SO TIRED...
AHHHH, GOD! I'M SO TIRED OF THIS.
WHAT THE DEVIL!
WHAT D'YOU THINK YOU'RE DOING?
YOU'RE A STRANGE ONE, AND NO MISTAKE-- AREN'T YOU?
AND A BIT OF A POOF TO BOOT.
DON'T KNOW WHAT SOMEONE LIKE YOU IS DOING MOVING IN ROUND HERE--
BUT I CAN'T SAY IT WAS A PLEASURE TO MEET YOU--
FLASH BASTARD.

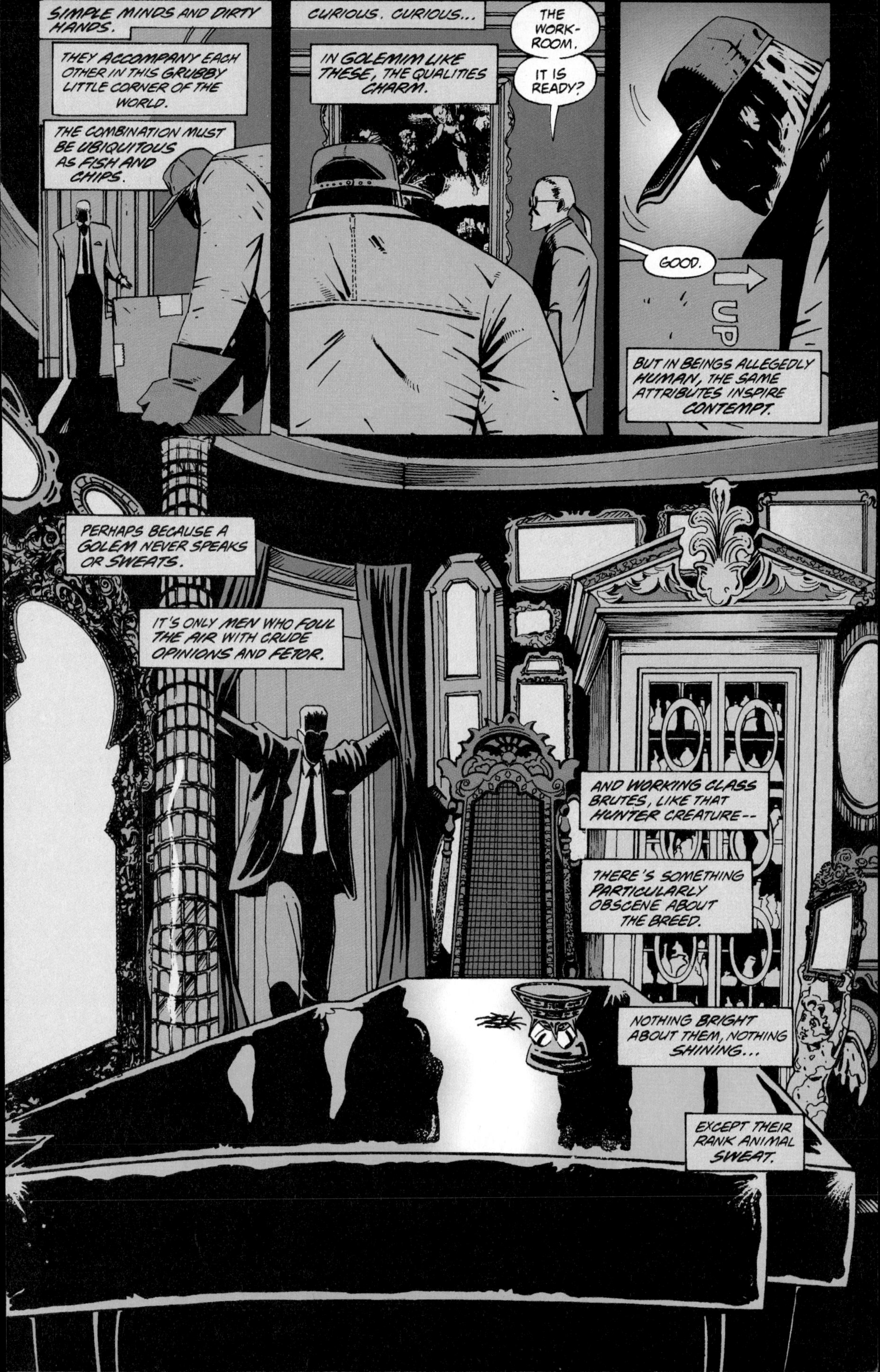
SIMPLE MINDS AND DIRTY HANDS.
THEY ACCOMPANY EACH OTHER IN THIS GRUBBY LITTLE CORNER OF THE WORLD.
THE COMBINATION MUST BE UBIQUITOUS AS FISH AND CHIPS.
CURIOUS. CURIOUS...
IN GOLEMIM LIKE THESE, THE QUALITIES CHARM.
THE WORK-ROOM.
IT IS READY?
GOOD.
UP
BUT IN BEINGS ALLEGEDLY HUMAN, THE SAME ATTRIBUTES INSPIRE CONTEMPT.
PERHAPS BECAUSE A GOLEM NEVER SPEAKS OR SWEATS.
IT'S ONLY MEN WHO FOUL THE AIR WITH CRUDE OPINIONS AND FETOR.
AND WORKING CLASS BRUTES, LIKE THAT HUNTER CREATURE--
THERE'S SOMETHING PARTICULARLY OBSCENE ABOUT THE BREED.
NOTHING BRIGHT ABOUT THEM, NOTHING SHINING...
EXCEPT THEIR RANK ANIMAL SWEAT.

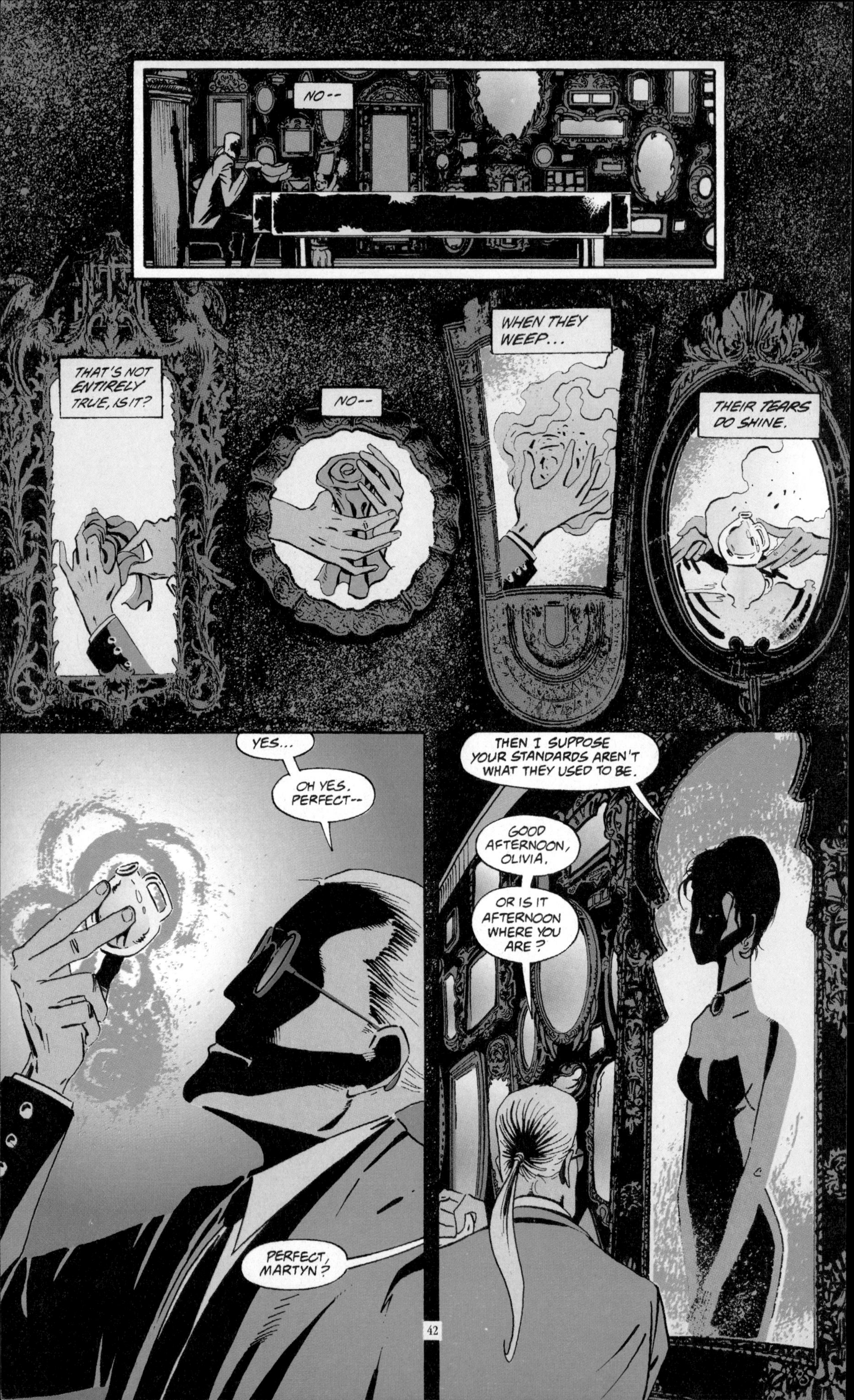
NO--
THAT'S NOT ENTIRELY TRUE, IS IT?
NO--
WHEN THEY WEEP...
THEIR TEARS DO SHINE.
YES...
OH YES. PERFECT--
PERFECT, MARTYN?
THEN I SUPPOSE YOUR STANDARDS AREN'T WHAT THEY USED TO BE.
GOOD AFTERNOON, OLIVIA.
OR IS IT AFTERNOON WHERE YOU ARE?

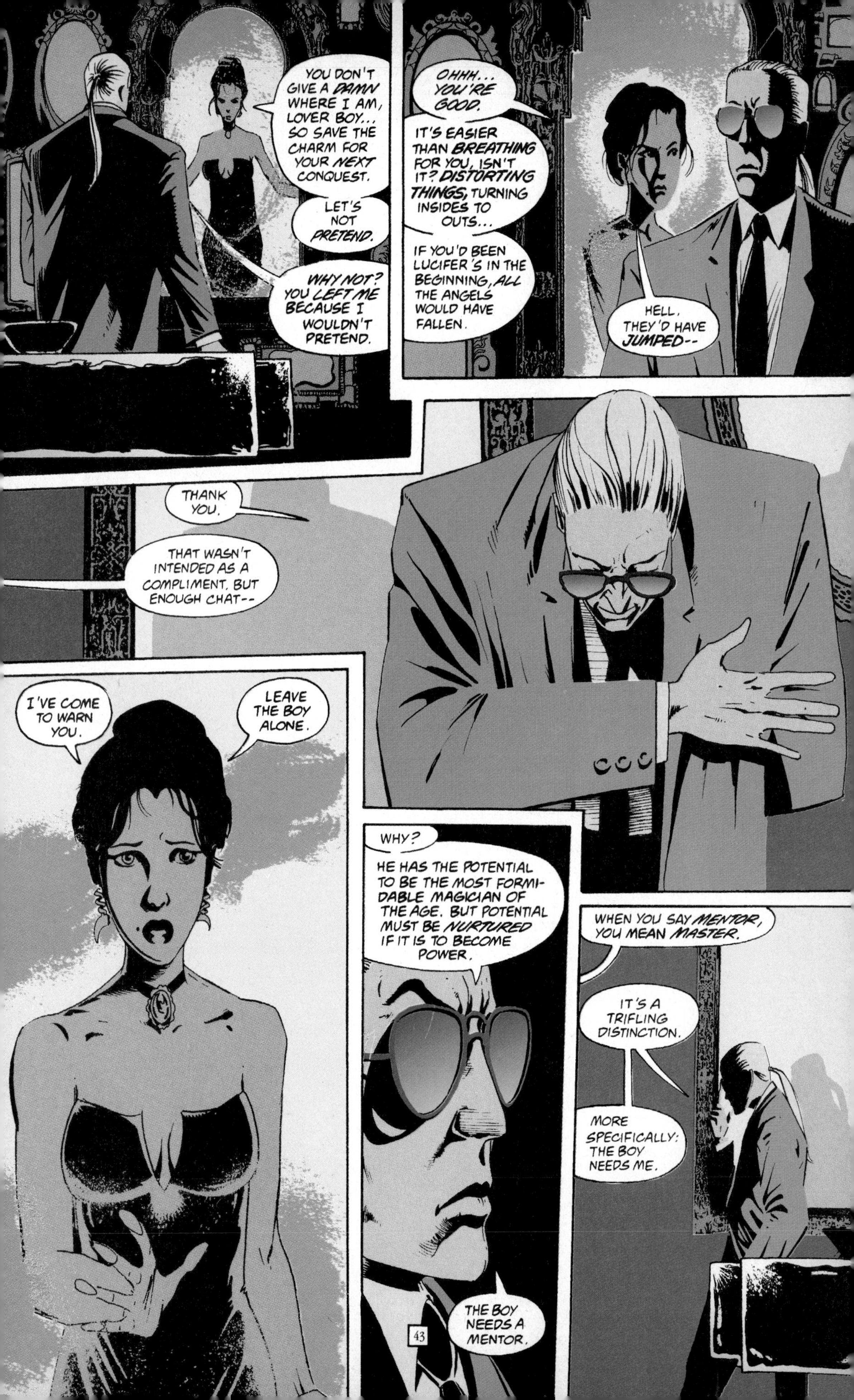
YOU DON'T GIVE A DAMN WHERE I AM, LOVER BOY... SO SAVE THE CHARM FOR YOUR NEXT CONQUEST.
LET'S NOT PRETEND.
WHY NOT? YOU LEFT ME BECAUSE I WOULDN'T PRETEND.
OHHH... YOU'RE GOOD.
IT'S EASIER THAN BREATHING FOR YOU, ISN'T IT? DISTORTING THINGS, TURNING INSIDES TO OUTS...
IF YOU'D BEEN LUCIFER'S IN THE BEGINNING, ALL THE ANGELS WOULD HAVE FALLEN.
HELL. THEY'D HAVE JUMPED--
THANK YOU.
THAT WASN'T INTENDED AS A COMPLIMENT. BUT ENOUGH CHAT--
I'VE COME TO WARN YOU.
LEAVE THE BOY ALONE.
WHY?
HE HAS THE POTENTIAL TO BE THE MOST FORMIDABLE MAGICIAN OF THE AGE. BUT POTENTIAL MUST BE NURTURED IF IT IS TO BECOME POWER.
THE BOY NEEDS A MENTOR.
WHEN YOU SAY MENTOR, YOU MEAN MASTER.
IT'S A TRIFLING DISTINCTION.
MORE SPECIFICALLY: THE BOY NEEDS ME.

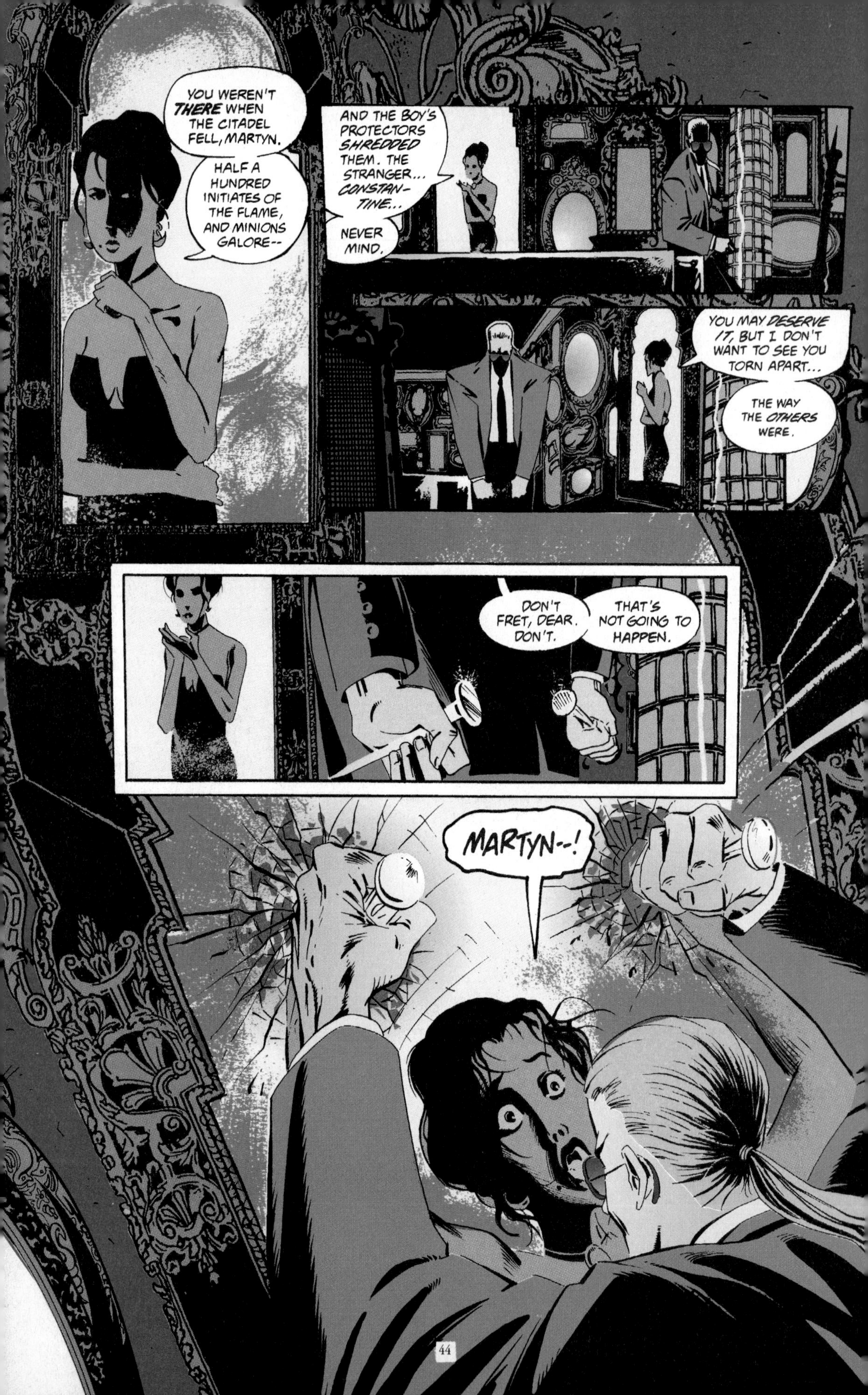

YOU WEREN'T THERE WHEN THE CITADEL FELL, MARTYN.
HALF A HUNDRED INITIATES OF THE FLAME, AND MINIONS GALORE--
AND THE BOY'S PROTECTORS SHREDDED THEM. THE STRANGER... CONSTAN-TINE...
NEVER MIND.
YOU MAY DESERVE IT, BUT I DON'T WANT TO SEE YOU TORN APART...
THE WAY THE OTHERS WERE.
DON'T FRET, DEAR. DON'T.
THAT'S NOT GOING TO HAPPEN.
MARTYN--!

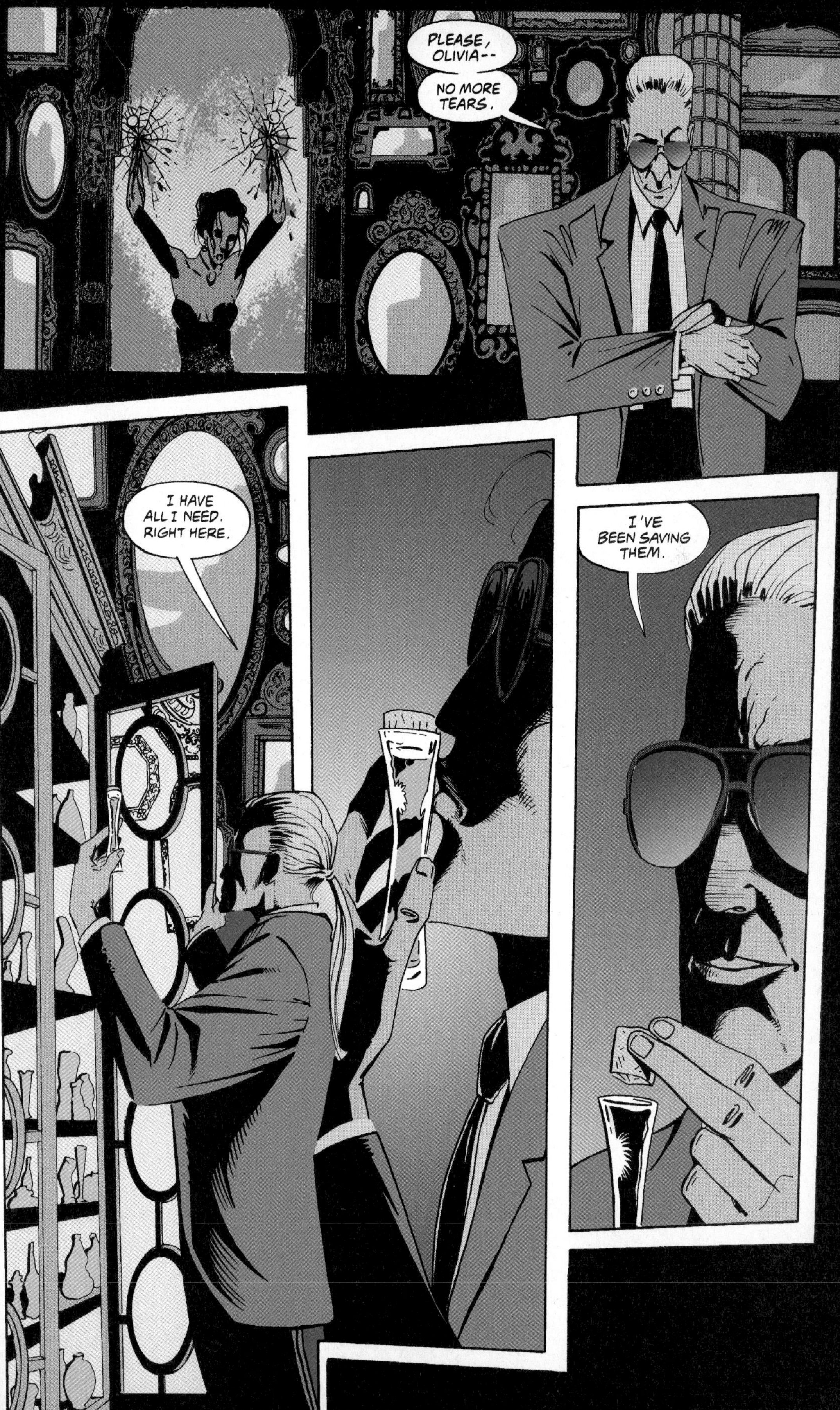
PLEASE, OLIVIA--
NO MORE TEARS.
I HAVE ALL I NEED. RIGHT HERE.
I'VE BEEN SAVING THEM.

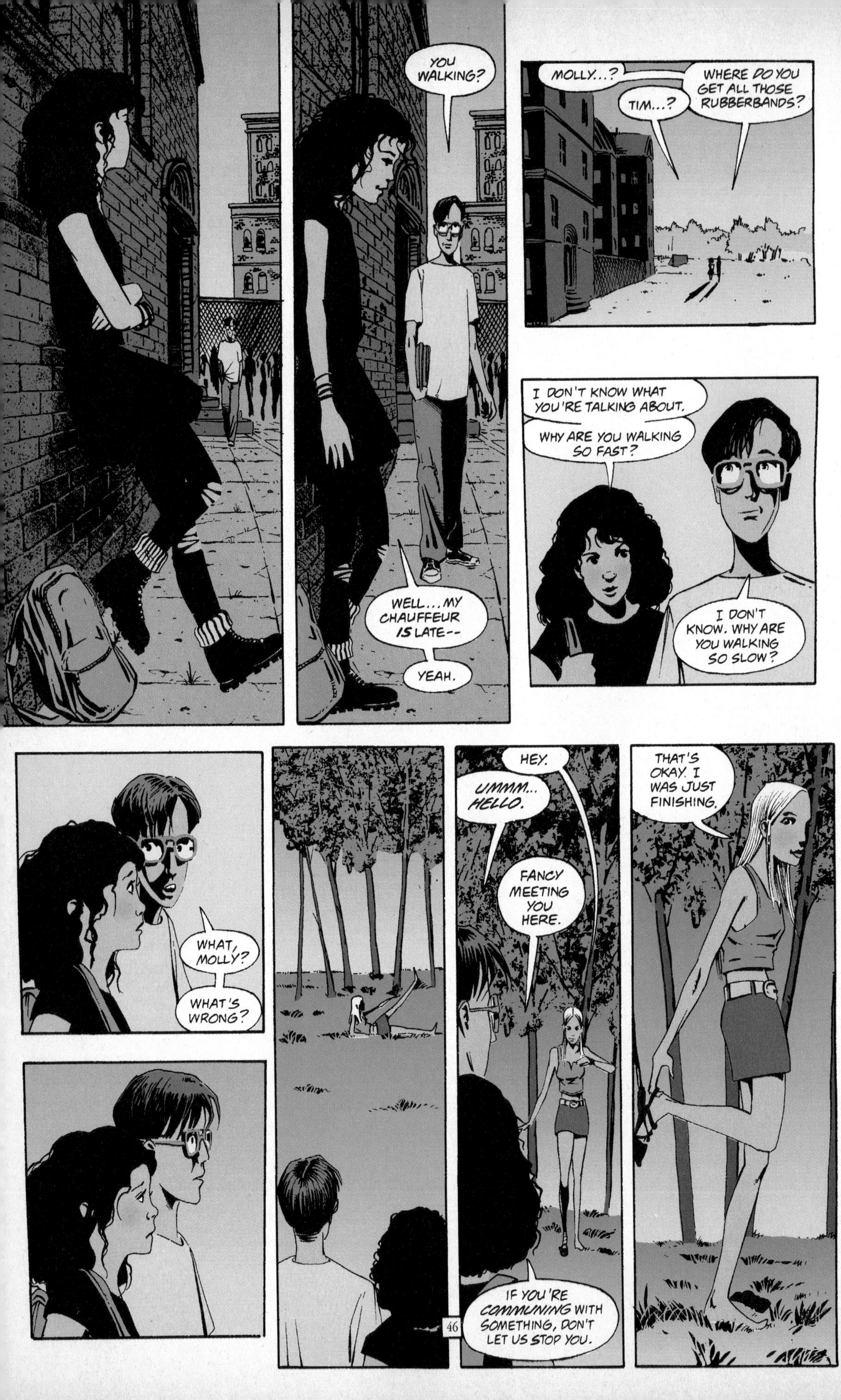
YOU WALKING?
WELL... MY CHAUFFEUR IS LATE--
YEAH.
MOLLY...?
TIM...?
WHERE DO YOU GET ALL THOSE RUBBERBANDS?
I DON'T KNOW WHAT YOU'RE TALKING ABOUT.
WHY ARE YOU WALKING SO FAST?
I DON'T KNOW. WHY ARE YOU WALKING SO SLOW?
WHAT, MOLLY?
WHAT'S WRONG?
HEY.
UMMM... HELLO.
FANCY MEETING YOU HERE.
IF YOU'RE COMMUNING WITH SOMETHING, DON'T LET US STOP YOU.
THAT'S OKAY. I WAS JUST FINISHING.

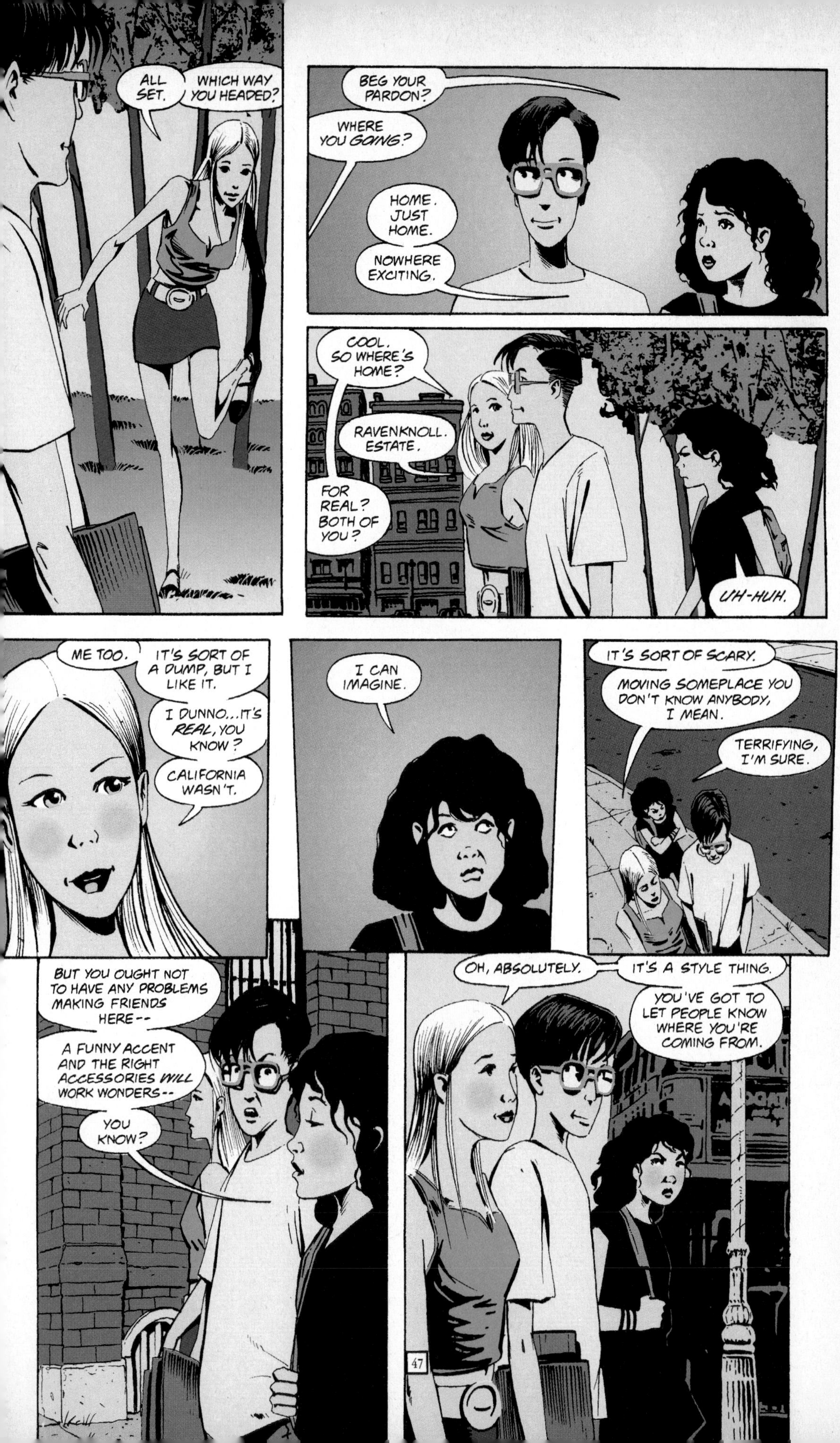
ALL SET.
WHICH WAY YOU HEADED?
BEG YOUR PARDON?
WHERE YOU GOING?
HOME. JUST HOME.
NOWHERE EXCITING.
COOL. SO WHERE'S HOME?
RAVENKNOLL. ESTATE.
FOR REAL? BOTH OF YOU?
UH-HUH.
ME TOO.
IT'S SORT OF A DUMP, BUT I LIKE IT.
I DUNNO... IT'S REAL, YOU KNOW?
CALIFORNIA WASN'T.
I CAN IMAGINE.
IT'S SORT OF SCARY.
MOVING SOMEPLACE YOU DON'T KNOW ANYBODY, I MEAN.
TERRIFYING, I'M SURE.
BUT YOU OUGHT NOT TO HAVE ANY PROBLEMS MAKING FRIENDS HERE--
A FUNNY ACCENT AND THE RIGHT ACCESSORIES WILL WORK WONDERS--
YOU KNOW?
OH, ABSOLUTELY.
IT'S A STYLE THING.
YOU'VE GOT TO LET PEOPLE KNOW WHERE YOU'RE COMING FROM.

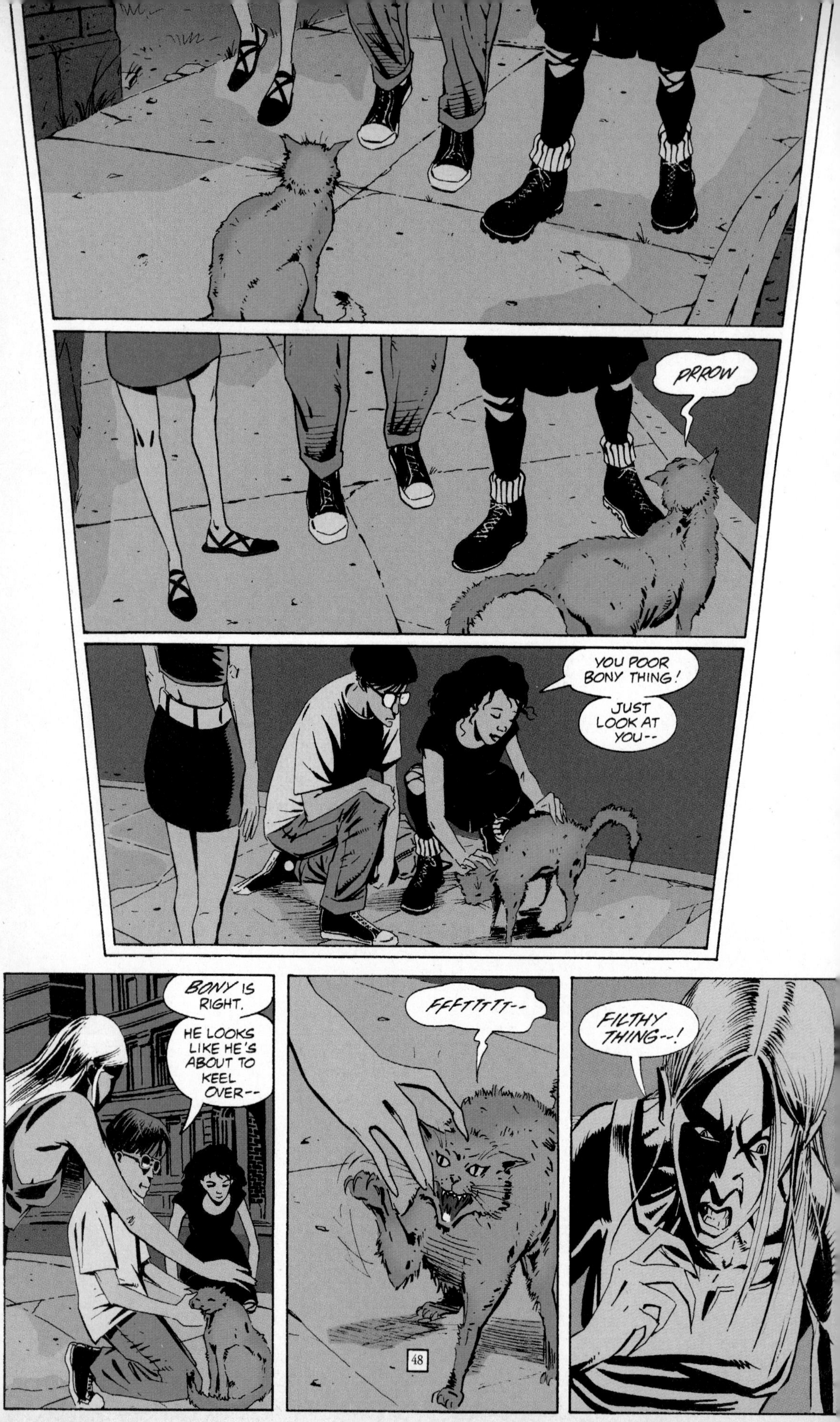
PRROW
YOU POOR BONY THING!
JUST LOOK AT YOU--
BONY IS RIGHT.
HE LOOKS LIKE HE'S ABOUT TO KEEL OVER--
FFFTTTTTT--
FILTHY THING--!

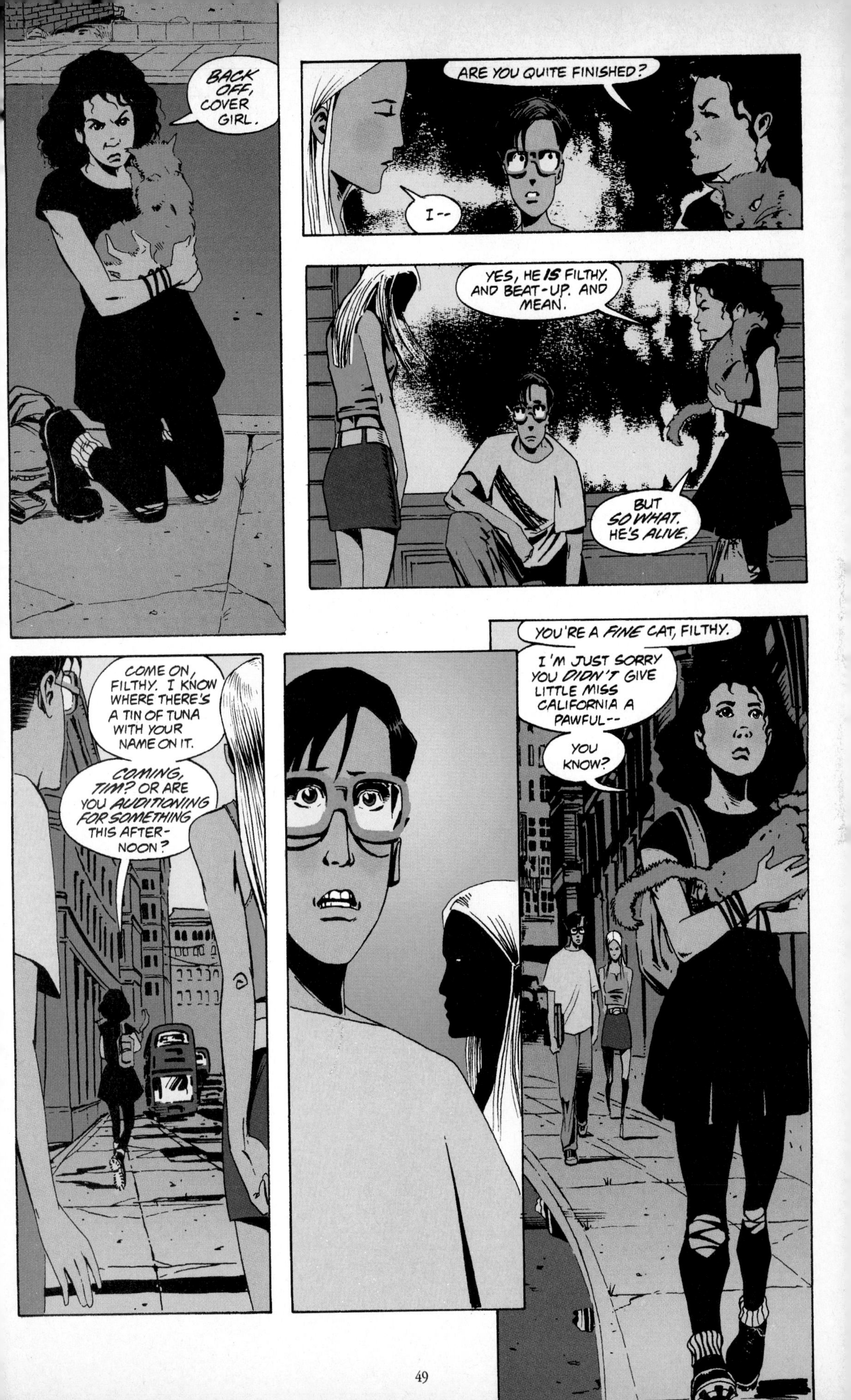
BACK OFF, COVER GIRL.
ARE YOU QUITE FINISHED?
I--
YES, HE IS FILTHY. AND BEAT-UP. AND MEAN.
BUT SO WHAT. HE'S ALIVE.
COME ON, FILTHY. I KNOW WHERE THERE'S A TIN OF TUNA WITH YOUR NAME ON IT.
COMING, TIM? OR ARE YOU AUDITIONING FOR SOMETHING THIS AFTER-NOON?
YOU'RE A FINE CAT, FILTHY.
I'M JUST SORRY YOU DIDN'T GIVE LITTLE MISS CALIFORNIA A PAWFUL--
YOU KNOW?

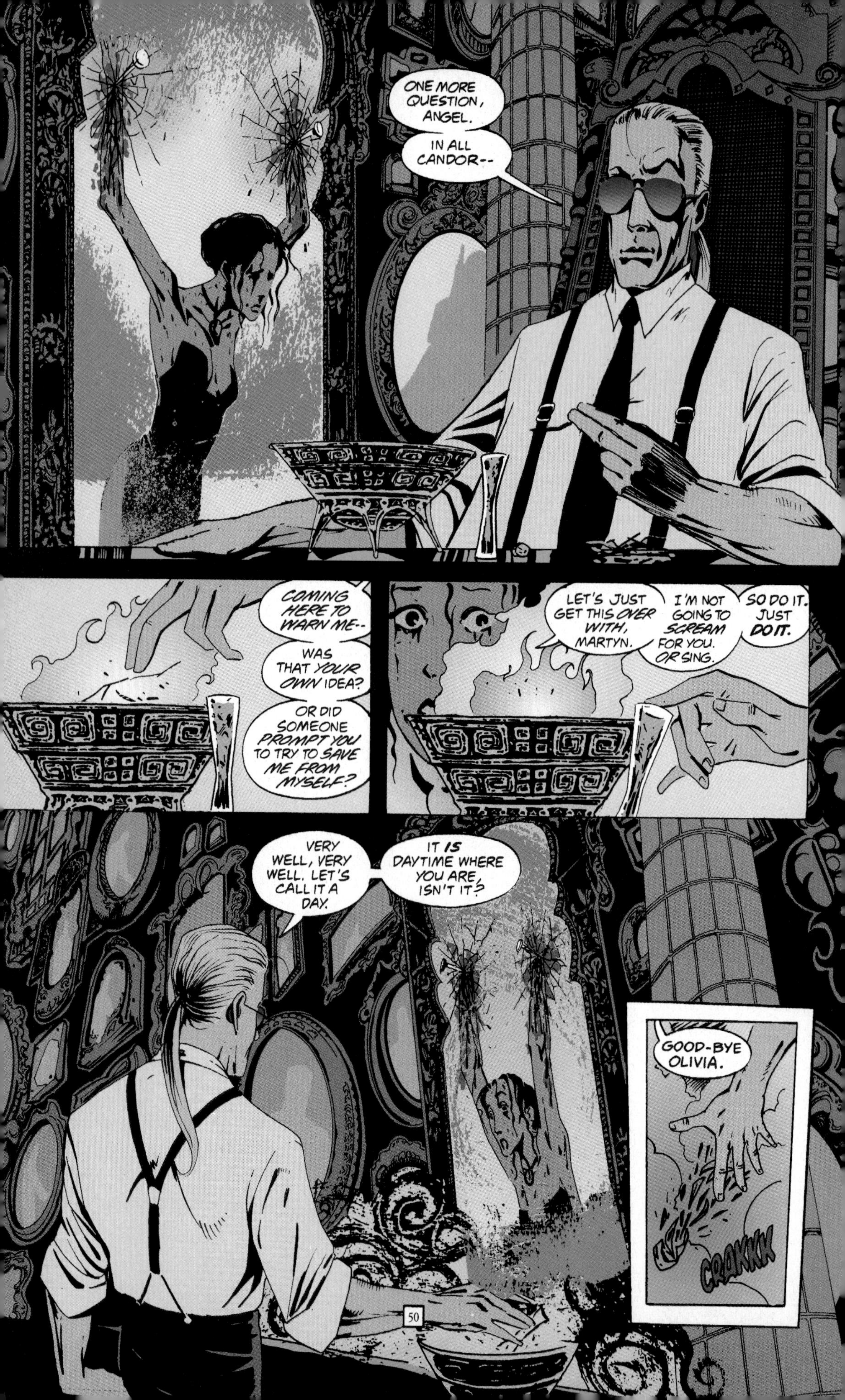
ONE MORE QUESTION, ANGEL.
IN ALL CANDOR--
COMING HERE TO WARN ME--
WAS THAT YOUR OWN IDEA?
OR DID SOMEONE PROMPT YOU TO TRY TO SAVE ME FROM MYSELF?
LET'S JUST GET THIS OVER WITH, MARTYN.
I'M NOT GOING TO SCREAM FOR YOU. OR SING.
SO DO IT. JUST DO IT.
VERY WELL, VERY WELL. LET'S CALL IT A DAY.
IT IS DAYTIME WHERE YOU ARE, ISN'T IT?
GOOD-BYE OLIVIA.
CRAKKK

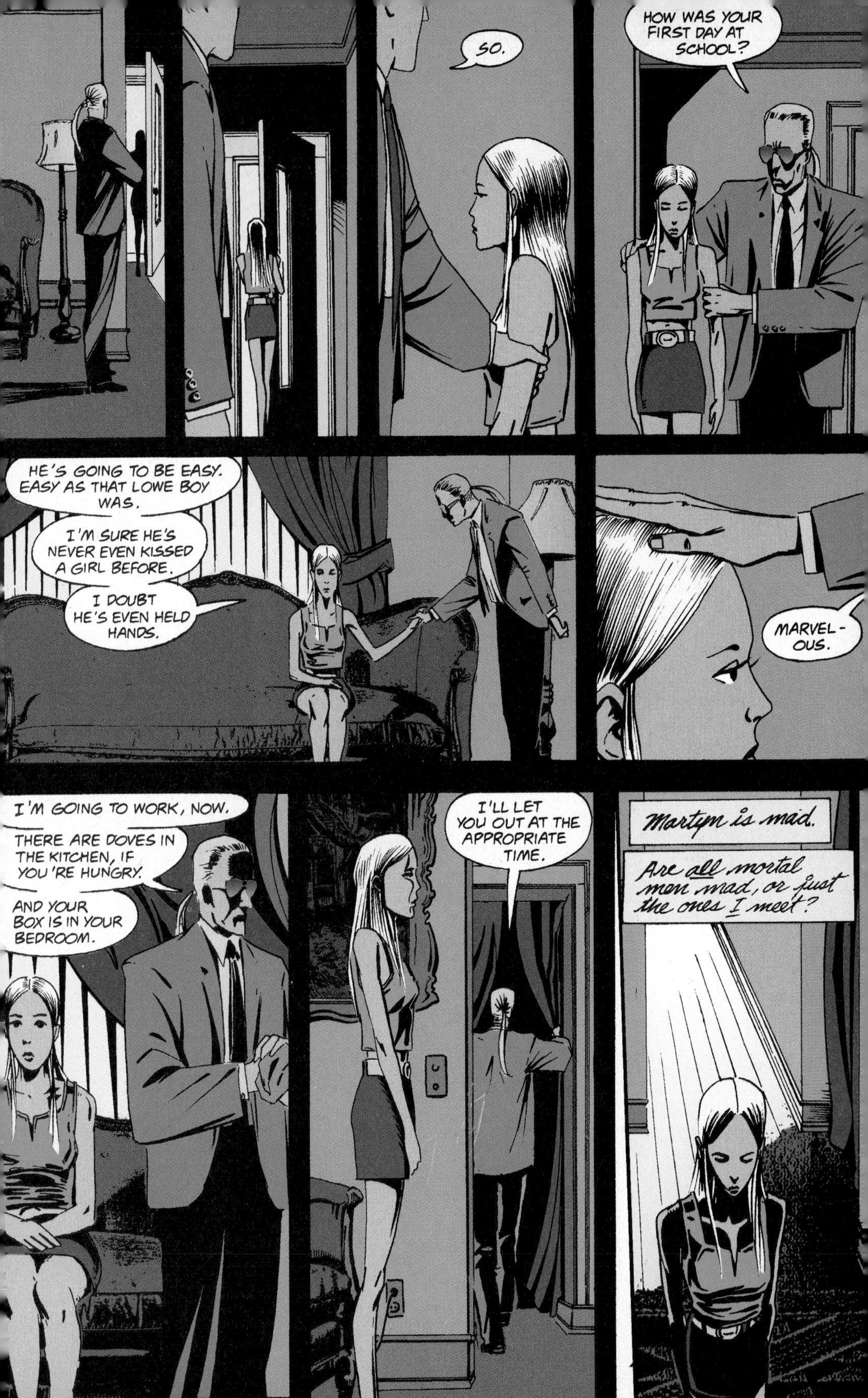
SO.
HOW WAS YOUR FIRST DAY AT SCHOOL?
HE'S GOING TO BE EASY. EASY AS THAT LOWE BOY WAS.
I'M SURE HE'S NEVER EVEN KISSED A GIRL BEFORE.
I DOUBT HE'S EVEN HELD HANDS.
MARVEL-OUS.
I'M GOING TO WORK, NOW.
THERE ARE DOVES IN THE KITCHEN, IF YOU'RE HUNGRY.
AND YOUR BOX IS IN YOUR BEDROOM.
I'LL LET YOU OUT AT THE APPROPRIATE TIME.
Martyn is mad.
Are all mortal men mad, or just the ones I meet?

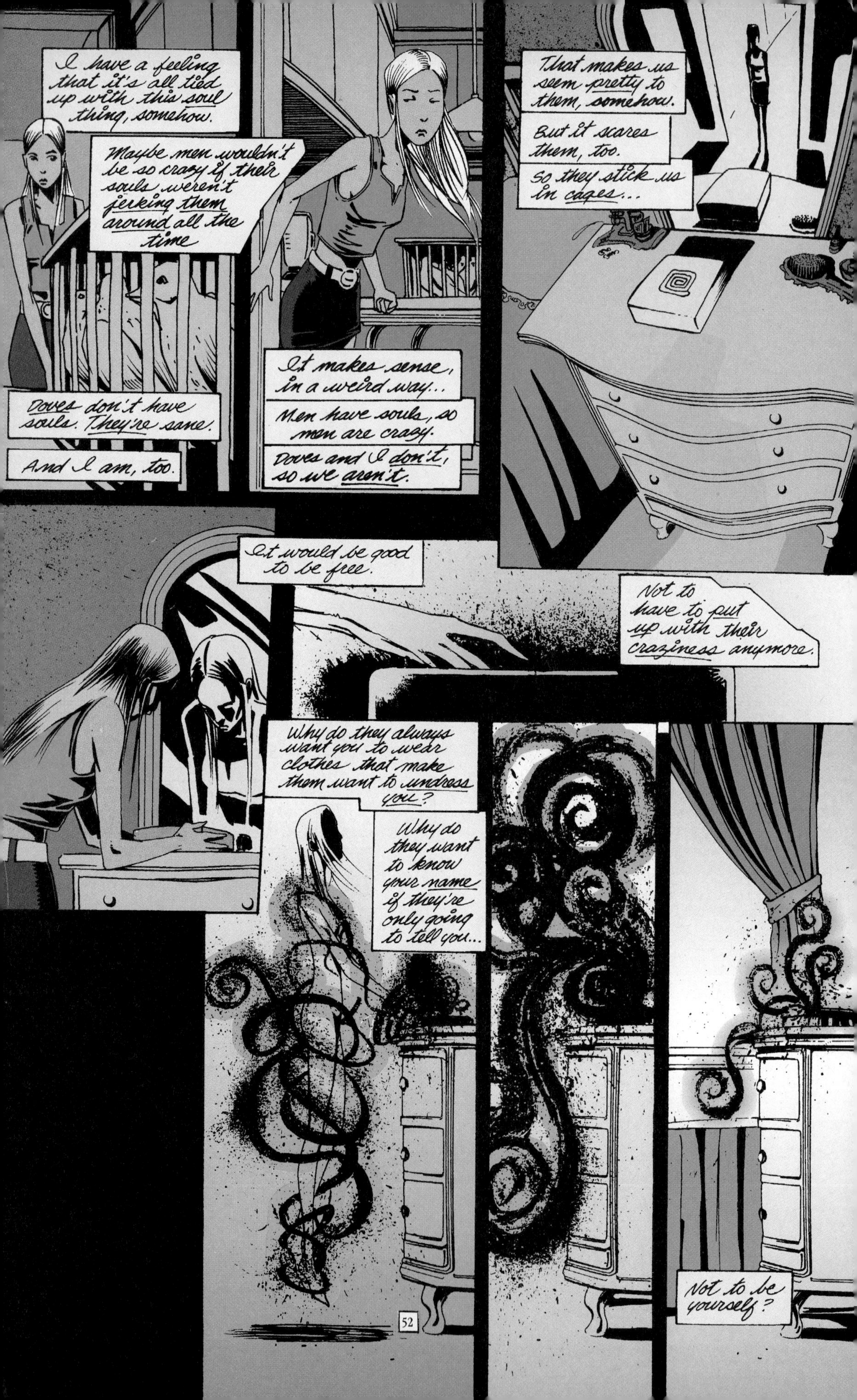

I have a feeling that it's all tied up with this soul thing, somehow.
Maybe men wouldn't be so crazy if their souls weren't jerking them around all the time
Doves don't have souls. They're sane.
And I am, too.
It makes sense, in a weird way...
Men have souls, so men are crazy.
Doves and I don't, so we aren't.
That makes us seem pretty to them, somehow.
But it scares them, too.
So they stick us in cages...
It would be good to be free.
Not to have to put up with their craziness anymore.
Why do they always want you to wear clothes that make them want to undress you?
Why do they want to know your name if they're only going to tell you...
Not to be yourself?

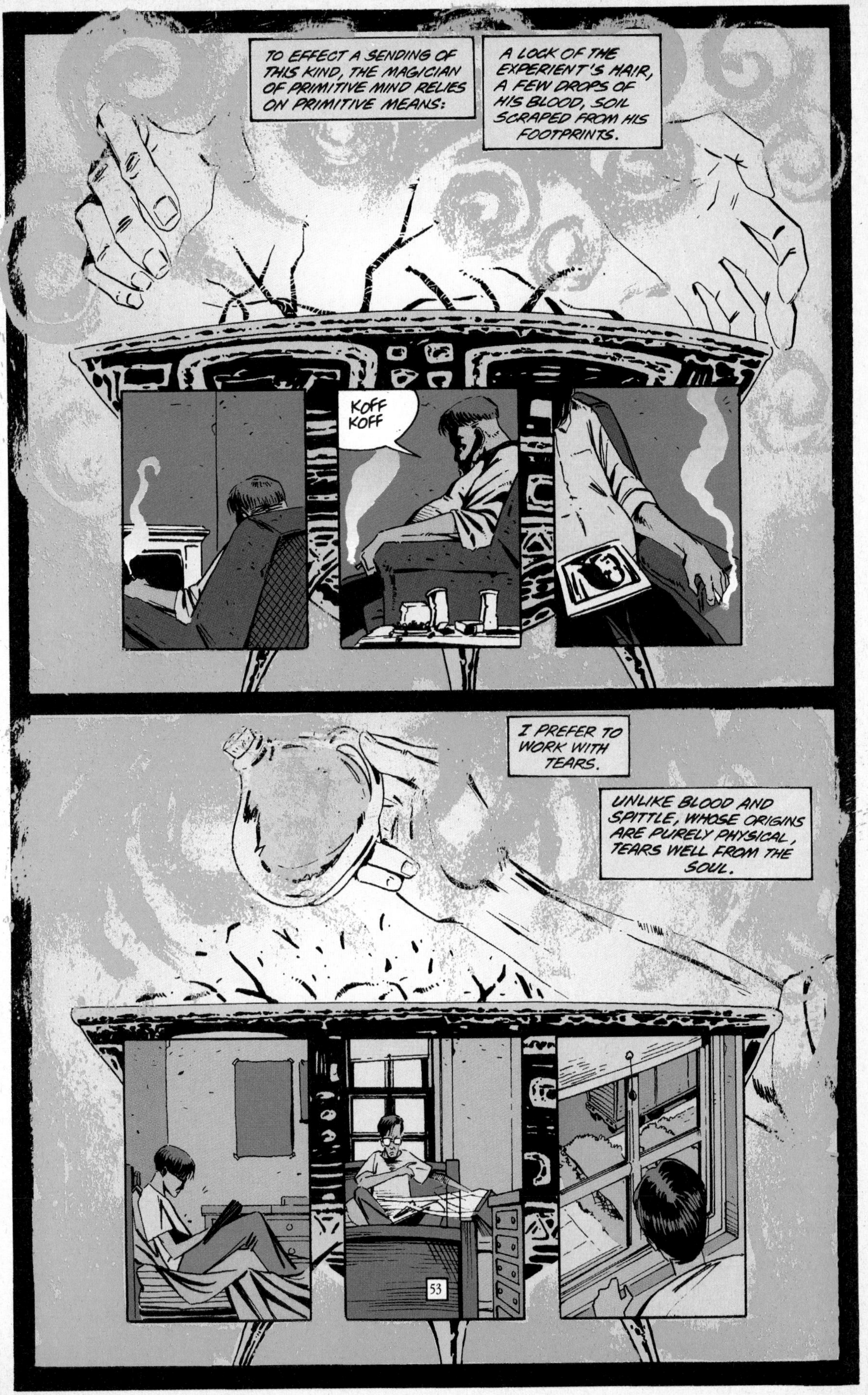
TO EFFECT A SENDING OF THIS KIND, THE MAGICIAN OF PRIMITIVE MIND RELIES ON PRIMITIVE MEANS:
A LOCK OF THE EXPERIENT'S HAIR, A FEW DROPS OF HIS BLOOD, SOIL SCRAPED FROM HIS FOOTPRINTS.
KOFF KOFF
I PREFER TO WORK WITH TEARS.
UNLIKE BLOOD AND SPITTLE, WHOSE ORIGINS ARE PURELY PHYSICAL, TEARS WELL FROM THE SOUL.

ADMITTEDLY, IT CAN BE SOMETHING OF A CHALLENGE TO OBTAIN THEM...
BUT I HAVE ALWAYS ENJOYED A CHALLENGE.
AIIIYAAAHHH!

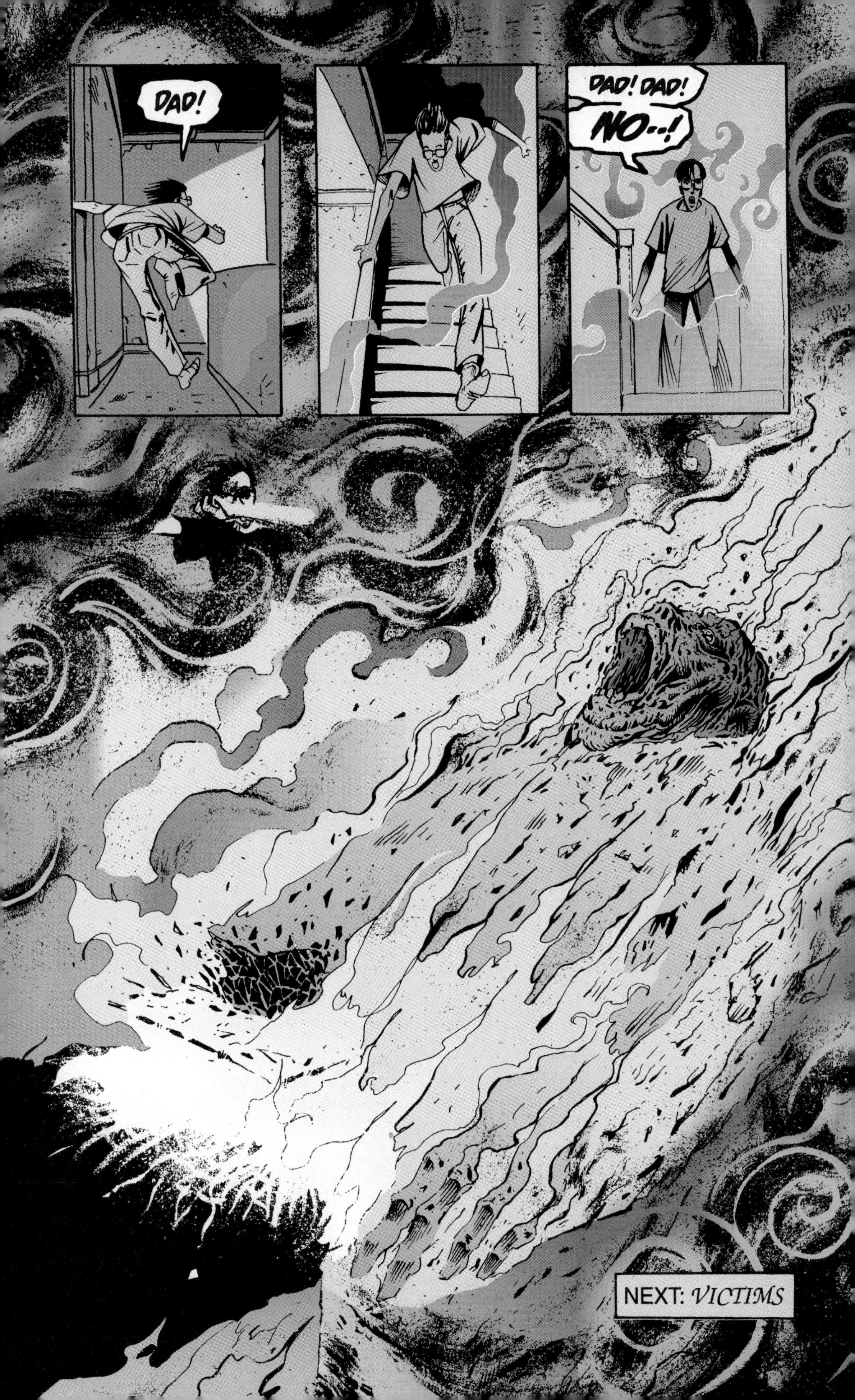
DAD!
DAD! DAD!
NO--!
NEXT: VICTIMS

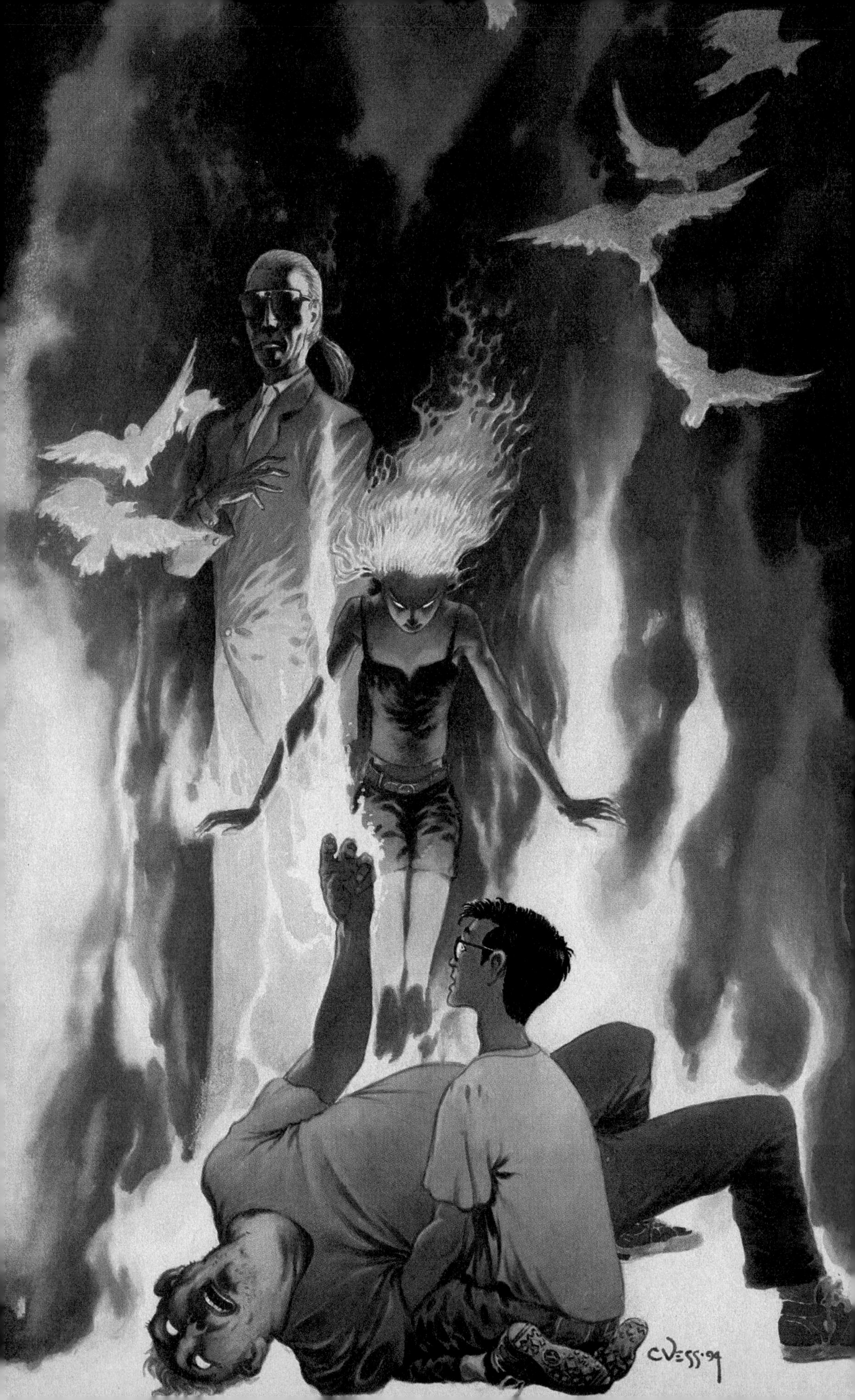
CVESS·94

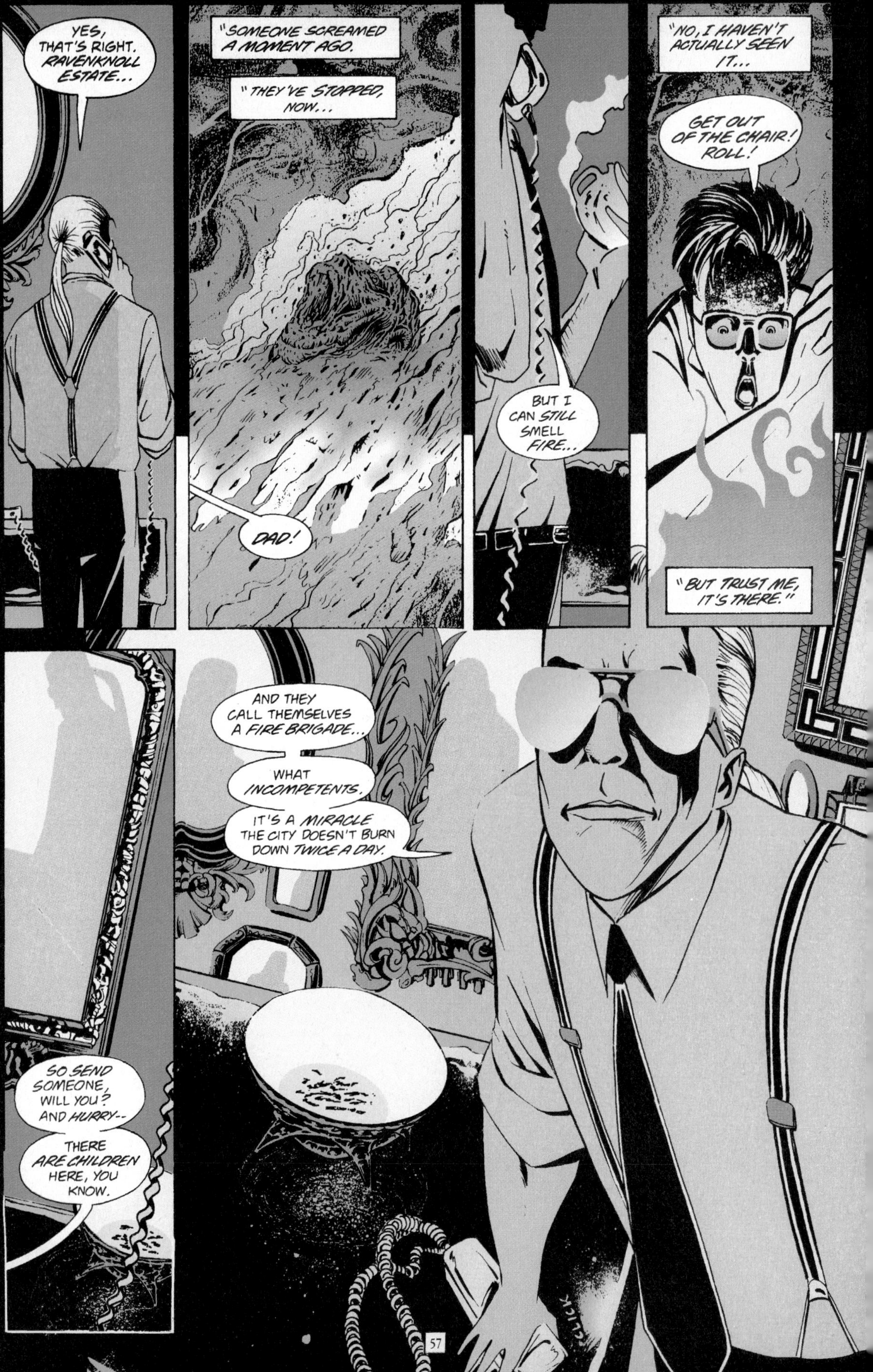
YES, THAT'S RIGHT. RAVENKNOLL ESTATE...
"SOMEONE SCREAMED A MOMENT AGO.
"THEY'VE STOPPED, NOW...
DAD!
BUT I CAN STILL SMELL FIRE...
"NO, I HAVEN'T ACTUALLY SEEN IT...
GET OUT OF THE CHAIR! ROLL!
"BUT TRUST ME, IT'S THERE."
AND THEY CALL THEMSELVES A FIRE BRIGADE...
WHAT INCOMPETENTS.
IT'S A MIRACLE THE CITY DOESN'T BURN DOWN TWICE A DAY.
SO SEND SOMEONE, WILL YOU? AND HURRY--
THERE ARE CHILDREN HERE, YOU KNOW.
CLICK

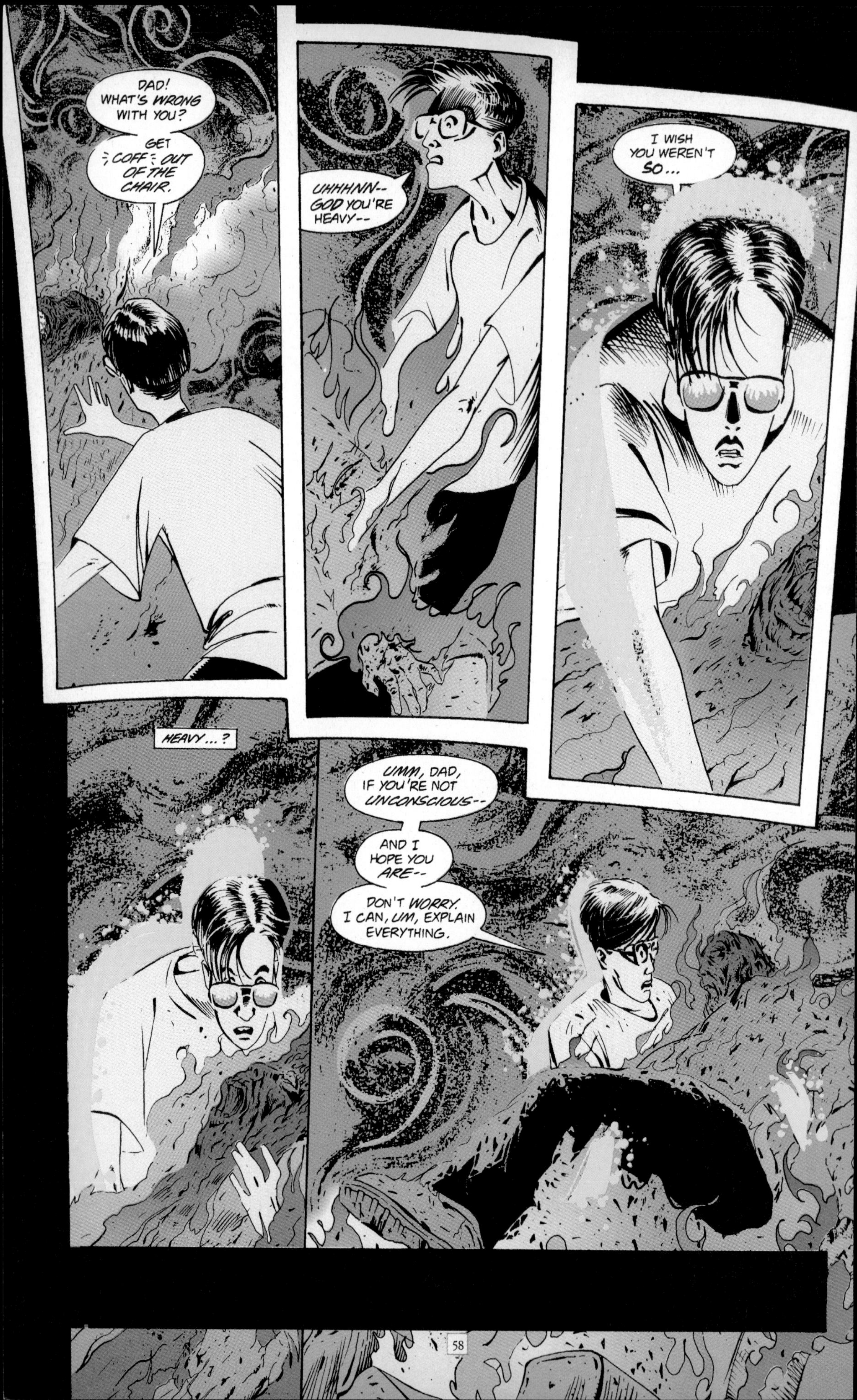
DAD! WHAT'S *WRONG* WITH YOU?
GET *COFF* OUT OF THE CHAIR.
UHHHNN-- GOD YOU'RE HEAVY--
I WISH YOU WEREN'T SO...
HEAVY...?
UMM, DAD, IF YOU'RE NOT UNCONSCIOUS--
AND I HOPE YOU *ARE*--
DON'T *WORRY*. I CAN, *UM*, EXPLAIN EVERYTHING.

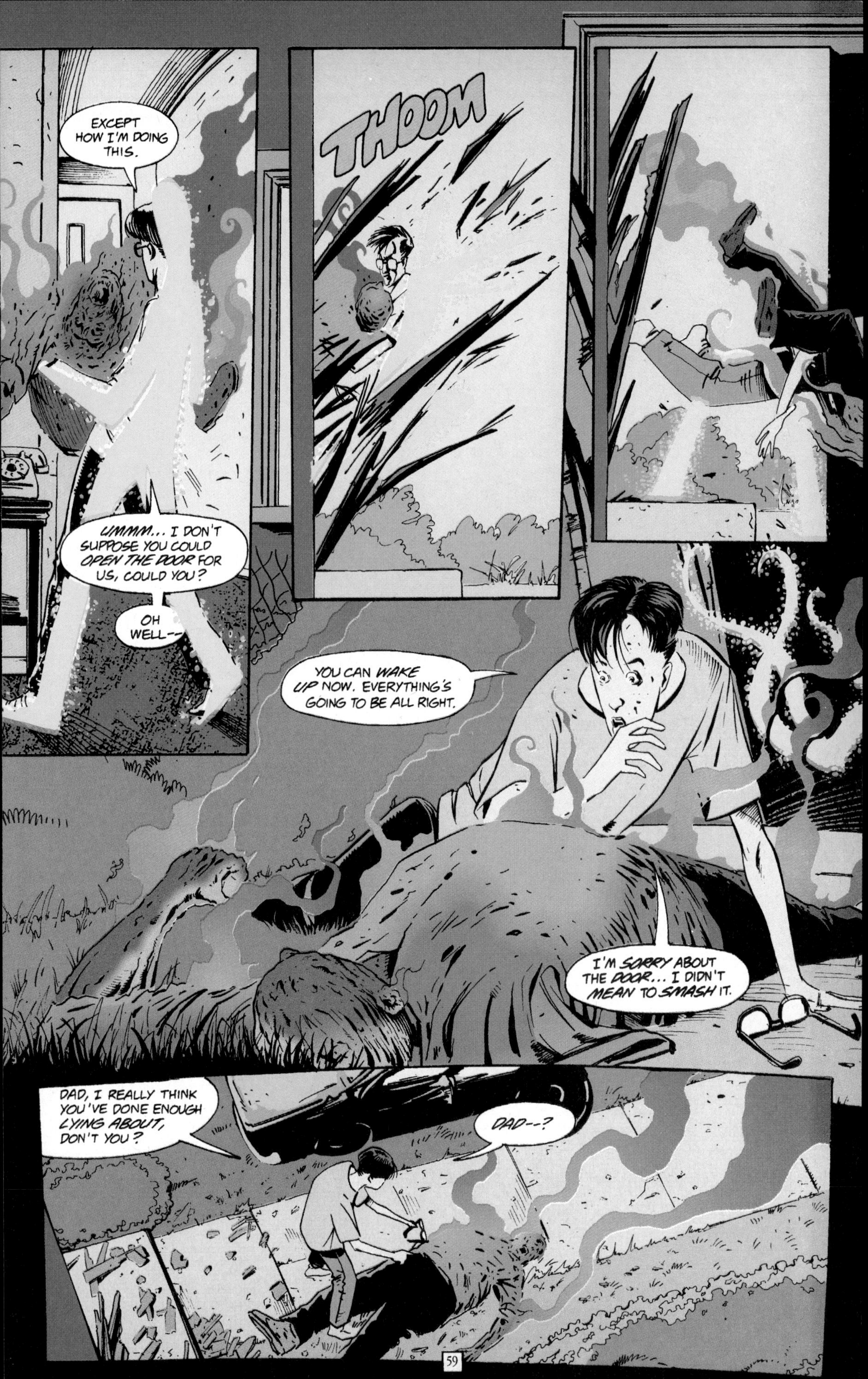
EXCEPT HOW I'M DOING THIS.
UMMM... I DON'T SUPPOSE YOU COULD OPEN THE DOOR FOR US, COULD YOU?
OH WELL--
THOOM
YOU CAN WAKE UP NOW. EVERYTHING'S GOING TO BE ALL RIGHT.
I'M SORRY ABOUT THE DOOR... I DIDN'T MEAN TO SMASH IT.
DAD, I REALLY THINK YOU'VE DONE ENOUGH LYING ABOUT, DON'T YOU?
DAD--?

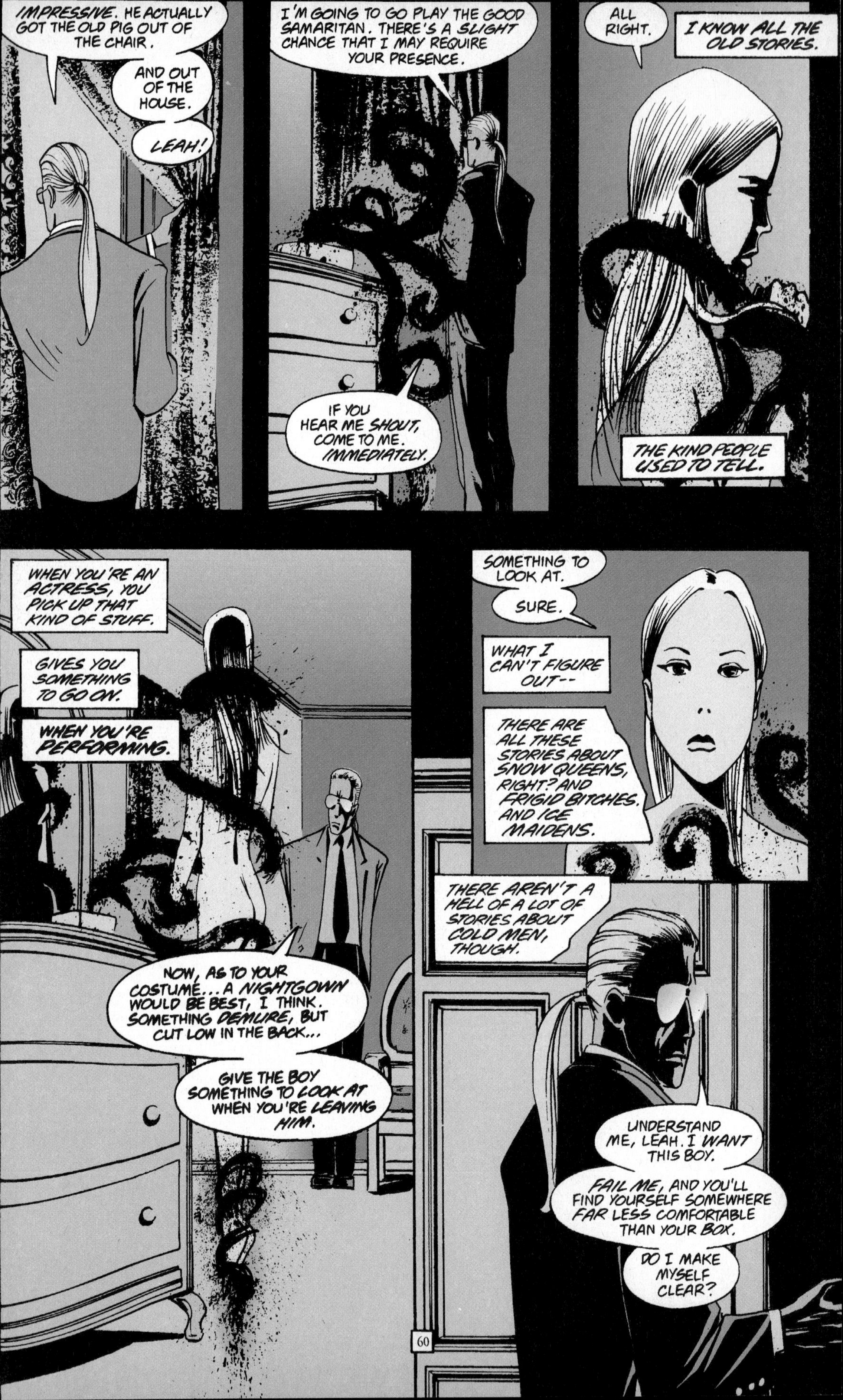
IMPRESSIVE. HE ACTUALLY GOT THE OLD PIG OUT OF THE CHAIR.
AND OUT OF THE HOUSE.
LEAH!
I'M GOING TO GO PLAY THE GOOD SAMARITAN. THERE'S A SLIGHT CHANCE THAT I MAY REQUIRE YOUR PRESENCE.
IF YOU HEAR ME SHOUT, COME TO ME. IMMEDIATELY.
ALL RIGHT.
I KNOW ALL THE OLD STORIES.
THE KIND PEOPLE USED TO TELL.
WHEN YOU'RE AN ACTRESS, YOU PICK UP THAT KIND OF STUFF.
GIVES YOU SOMETHING TO GO ON.
WHEN YOU'RE PERFORMING.
NOW, AS TO YOUR COSTUME... A NIGHTGOWN WOULD BE BEST, I THINK. SOMETHING DEMURE, BUT CUT LOW IN THE BACK...
GIVE THE BOY SOMETHING TO LOOK AT WHEN YOU'RE LEAVING HIM.
SOMETHING TO LOOK AT.
SURE.
WHAT I CAN'T FIGURE OUT--
THERE ARE ALL THESE STORIES ABOUT SNOW QUEENS, RIGHT? AND FRIGID BITCHES. AND ICE MAIDENS.
THERE AREN'T A HELL OF A LOT OF STORIES ABOUT COLD MEN, THOUGH.
UNDERSTAND ME, LEAH. I WANT THIS BOY.
FAIL ME, AND YOU'LL FIND YOURSELF SOMEWHERE FAR LESS COMFORTABLE THAN YOUR BOX.
DO I MAKE MYSELF CLEAR?

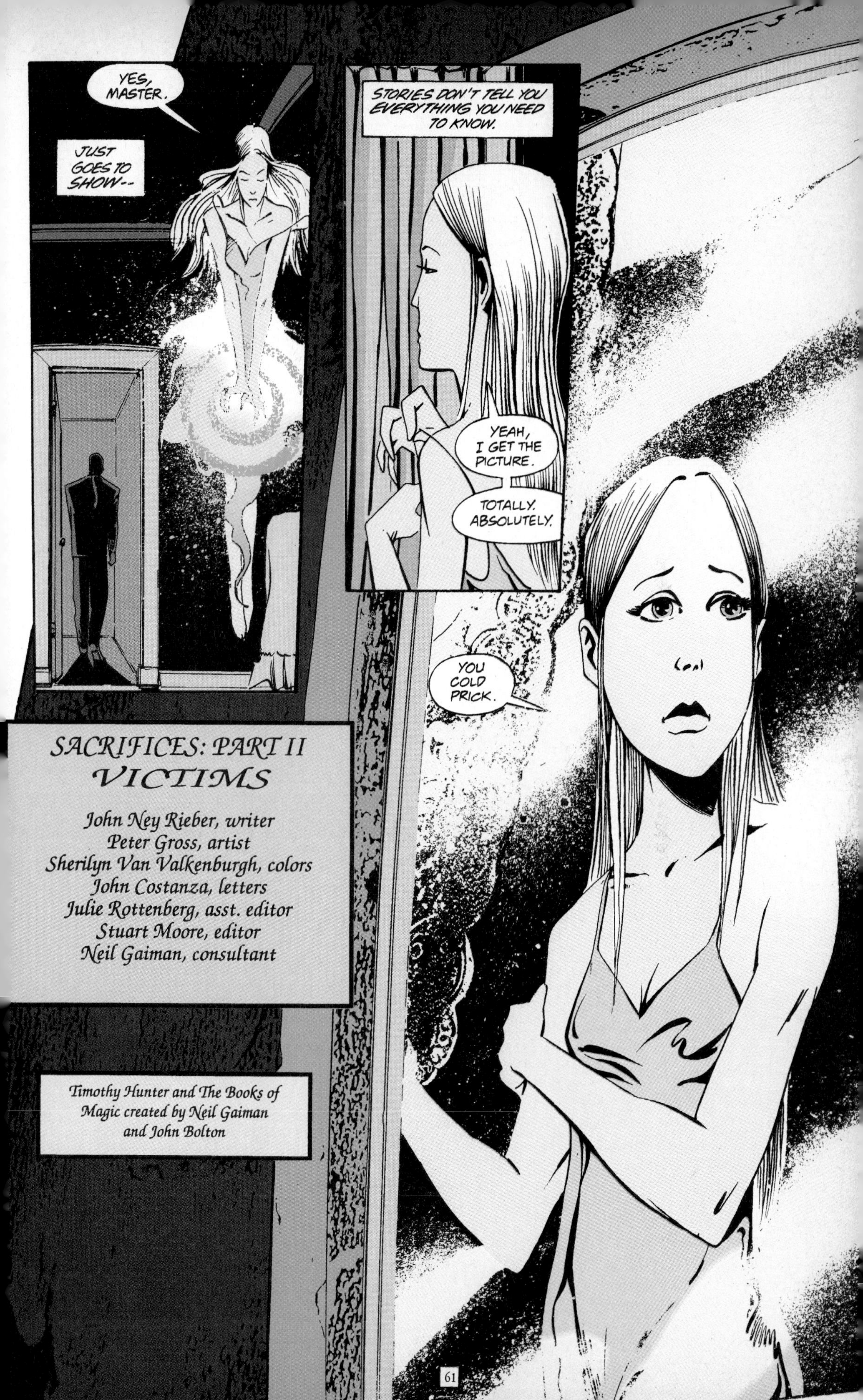
YES, MASTER.
JUST GOES TO SHOW--
STORIES DON'T TELL YOU EVERYTHING YOU NEED TO KNOW.
YEAH, I GET THE PICTURE.
TOTALLY. ABSOLUTELY.
YOU COLD PRICK.
SACRIFICES: PART II
VICTIMS
John Ney Rieber, writer
Peter Gross, artist
Sherilyn Van Valkenburgh, colors
John Costanza, letters
Julie Rottenberg, asst. editor
Stuart Moore, editor
Neil Gaiman, consultant
Timothy Hunter and The Books of Magic created by Neil Gaiman and John Bolton

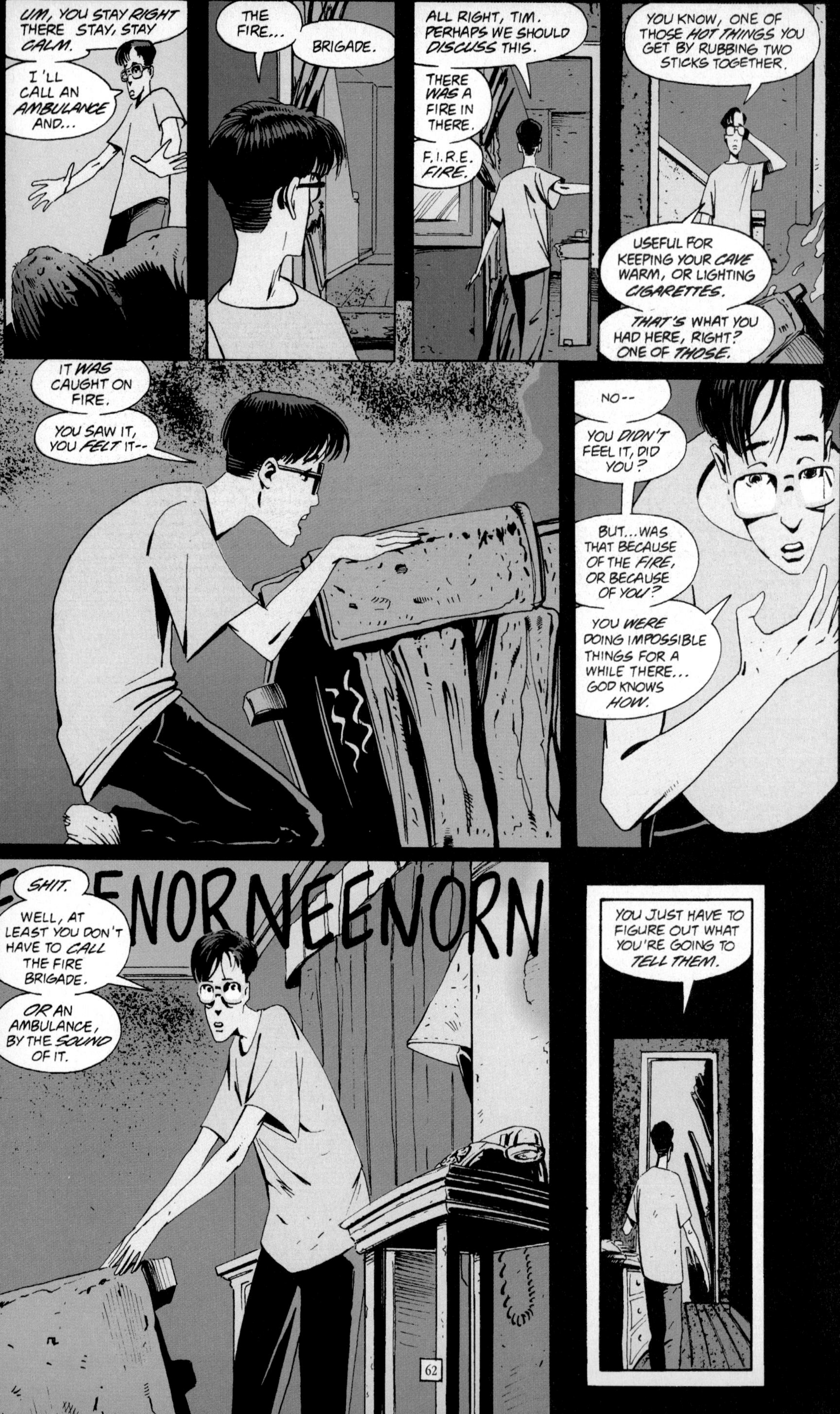
UM, YOU STAY RIGHT THERE STAY, STAY CALM.
I'LL CALL AN AMBULANCE AND...
THE FIRE...
BRIGADE.
ALL RIGHT, TIM. PERHAPS WE SHOULD DISCUSS THIS.
THERE WAS A FIRE IN THERE.
F.I.R.E. FIRE.
YOU KNOW, ONE OF THOSE HOT THINGS YOU GET BY RUBBING TWO STICKS TOGETHER.
USEFUL FOR KEEPING YOUR CAVE WARM, OR LIGHTING CIGARETTES.
THAT'S WHAT YOU HAD HERE, RIGHT? ONE OF THOSE.
IT WAS CAUGHT ON FIRE.
YOU SAW IT, YOU FELT IT--
NO--
YOU DIDN'T FEEL IT, DID YOU?
BUT...WAS THAT BECAUSE OF THE FIRE, OR BECAUSE OF YOU?
YOU WERE DOING IMPOSSIBLE THINGS FOR A WHILE THERE... GOD KNOWS HOW.
NEENORNEENORN
SHIT.
WELL, AT LEAST YOU DON'T HAVE TO CALL THE FIRE BRIGADE.
OR AN AMBULANCE, BY THE SOUND OF IT.
YOU JUST HAVE TO FIGURE OUT WHAT YOU'RE GOING TO TELL THEM.

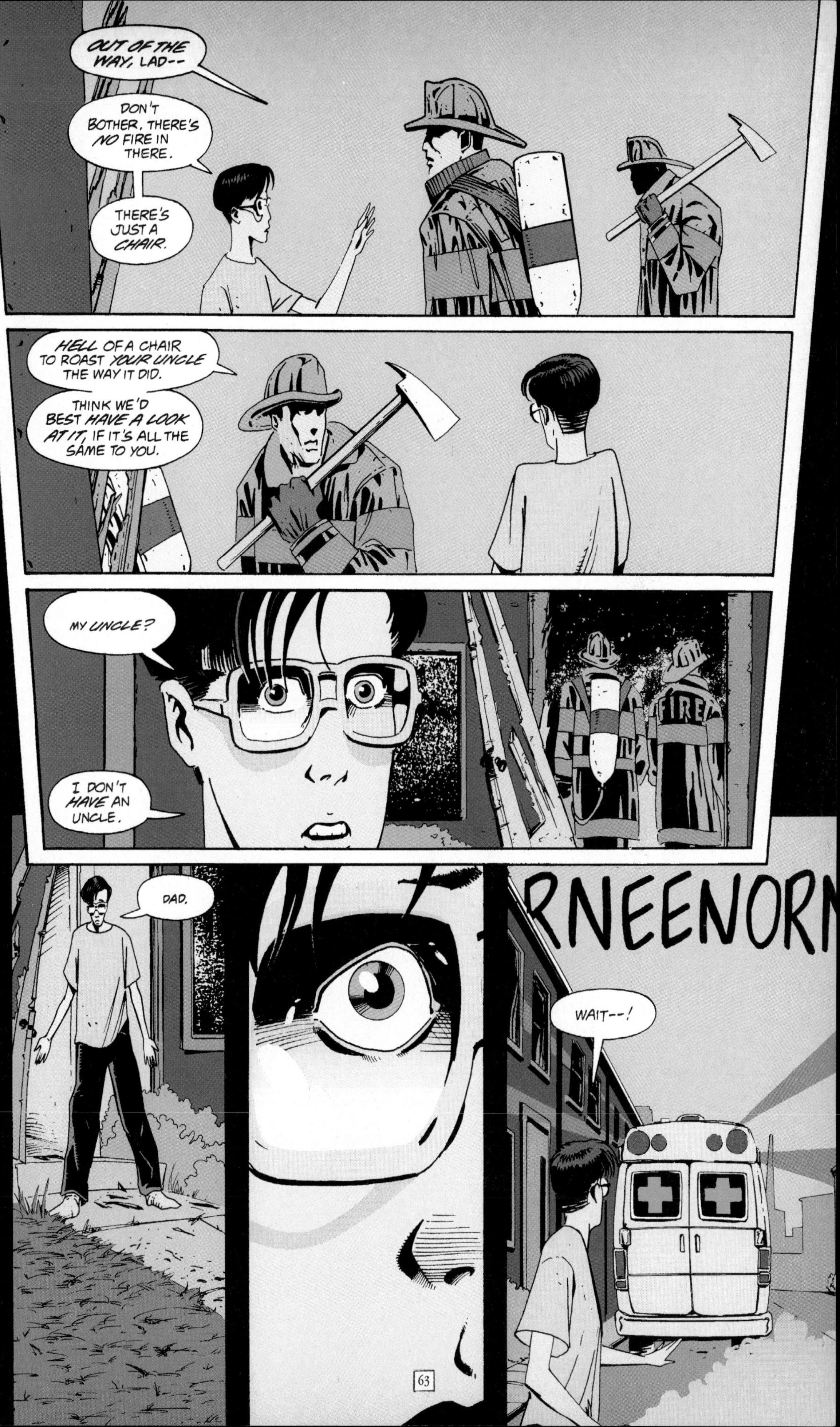
OUT OF THE WAY, LAD--
DON'T BOTHER. THERE'S NO FIRE IN THERE.
THERE'S JUST A CHAIR.
HELL OF A CHAIR TO ROAST YOUR UNCLE THE WAY IT DID.
THINK WE'D BEST HAVE A LOOK AT IT, IF IT'S ALL THE SAME TO YOU.
MY UNCLE?
FIRE
I DON'T HAVE AN UNCLE.
DAD.
RNEENORN
WAIT--!

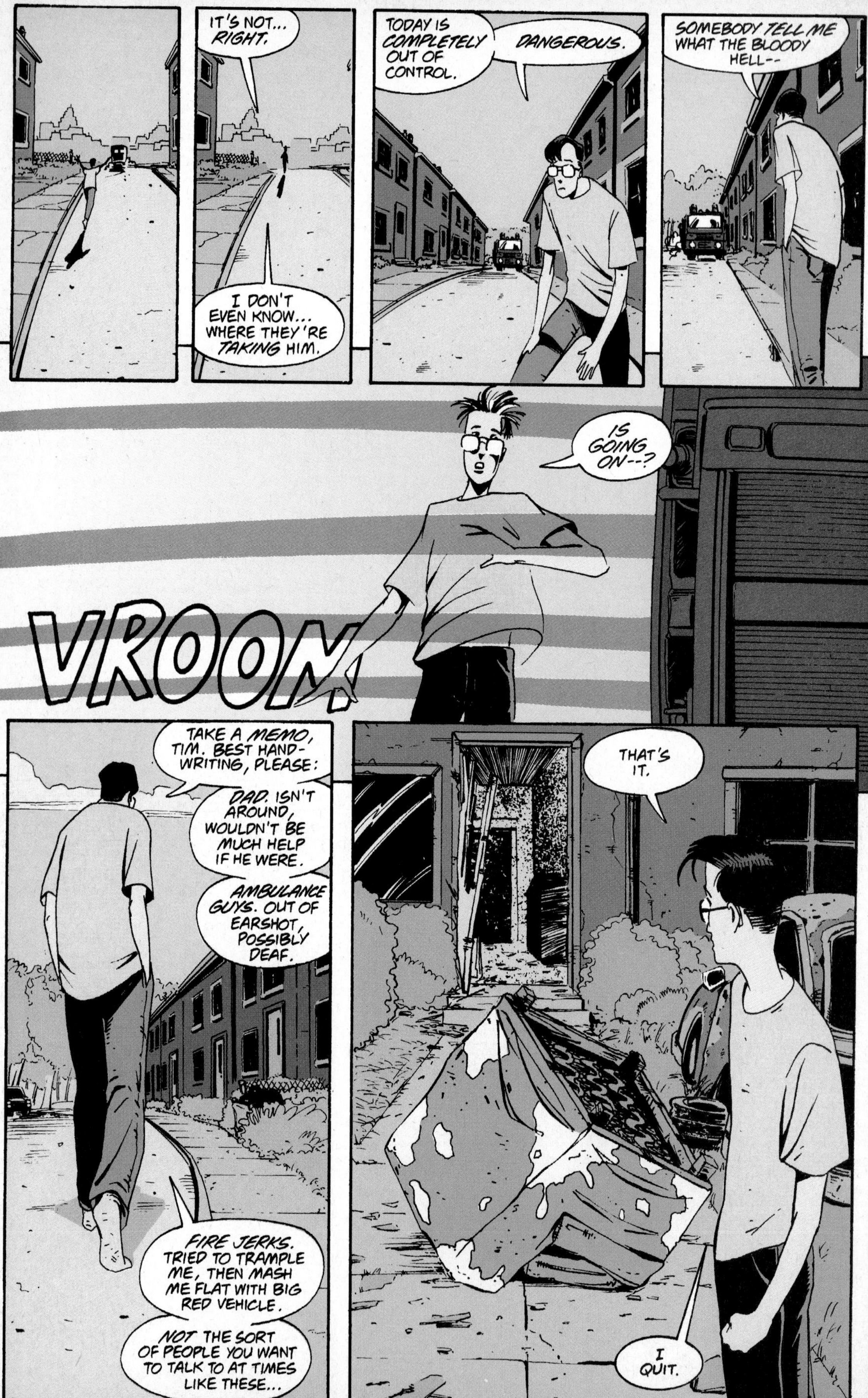
IT'S NOT... RIGHT.
I DON'T EVEN KNOW... WHERE THEY'RE TAKING HIM.
TODAY IS COMPLETELY OUT OF CONTROL.
DANGEROUS.
SOMEBODY TELL ME WHAT THE BLOODY HELL--
IS GOING ON--?
VROOM
TAKE A MEMO, TIM. BEST HAND-WRITING, PLEASE:
DAD. ISN'T AROUND, WOULDN'T BE MUCH HELP IF HE WERE.
AMBULANCE GUYS. OUT OF EARSHOT, POSSIBLY DEAF.
FIRE JERKS. TRIED TO TRAMPLE ME, THEN MASH ME FLAT WITH BIG RED VEHICLE.
NOT THE SORT OF PEOPLE YOU WANT TO TALK TO AT TIMES LIKE THESE...
THAT'S IT.
I QUIT.

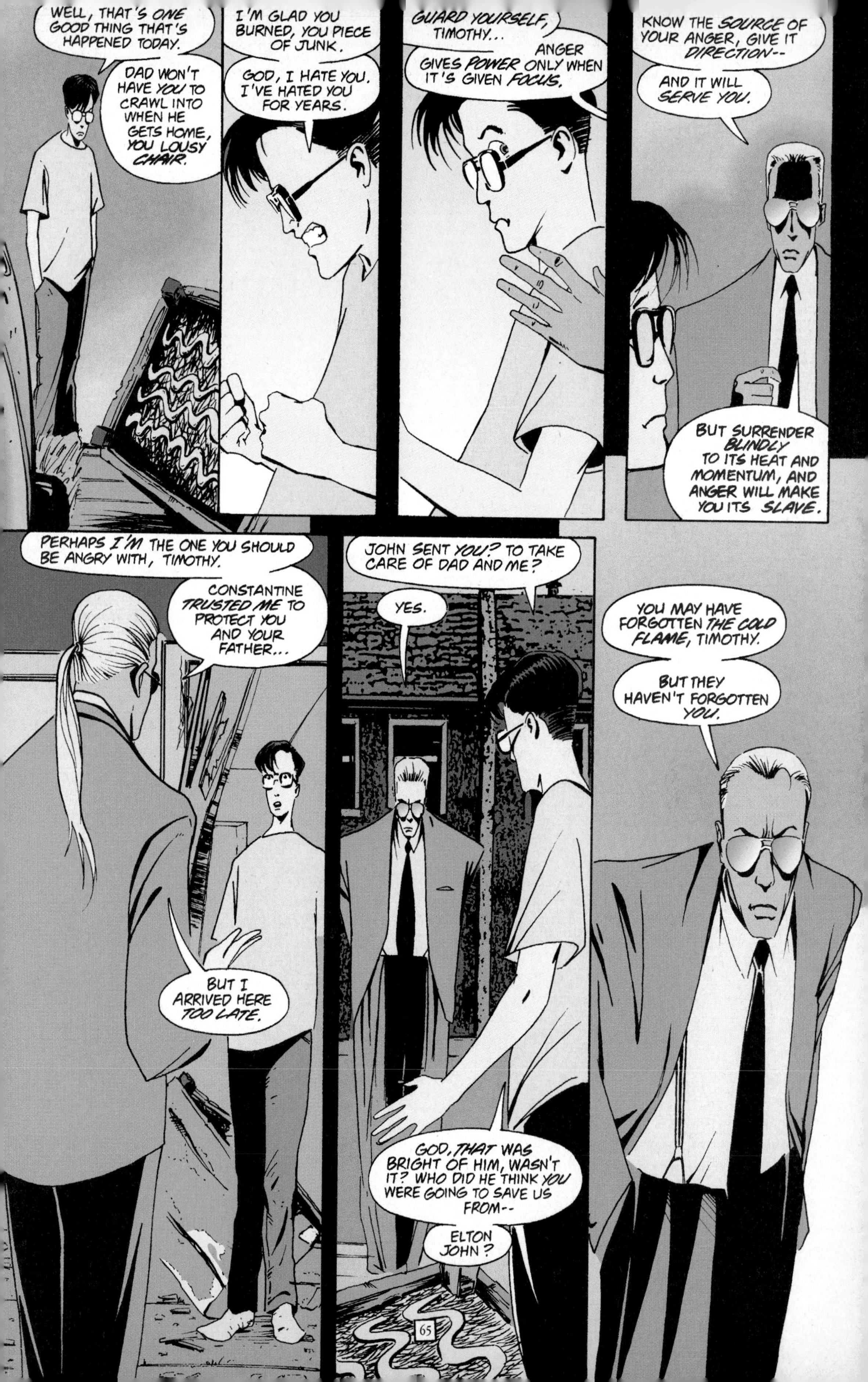
WELL, THAT'S ONE GOOD THING THAT'S HAPPENED TODAY.
DAD WON'T HAVE YOU TO CRAWL INTO WHEN HE GETS HOME, YOU LOUSY CHAIR.
I'M GLAD YOU BURNED, YOU PIECE OF JUNK.
GOD, I HATE YOU. I'VE HATED YOU FOR YEARS.
GUARD YOURSELF, TIMOTHY...
ANGER GIVES POWER ONLY WHEN IT'S GIVEN FOCUS.
KNOW THE SOURCE OF YOUR ANGER, GIVE IT DIRECTION--
AND IT WILL SERVE YOU.
BUT SURRENDER BLINDLY TO ITS HEAT AND MOMENTUM, AND ANGER WILL MAKE YOU ITS SLAVE.
PERHAPS I'M THE ONE YOU SHOULD BE ANGRY WITH, TIMOTHY.
CONSTANTINE TRUSTED ME TO PROTECT YOU AND YOUR FATHER...
BUT I ARRIVED HERE TOO LATE.
JOHN SENT YOU? TO TAKE CARE OF DAD AND ME?
YES.
GOD, THAT WAS BRIGHT OF HIM, WASN'T IT? WHO DID HE THINK YOU WERE GOING TO SAVE US FROM--
ELTON JOHN?
YOU MAY HAVE FORGOTTEN THE COLD FLAME, TIMOTHY.
BUT THEY HAVEN'T FORGOTTEN YOU.

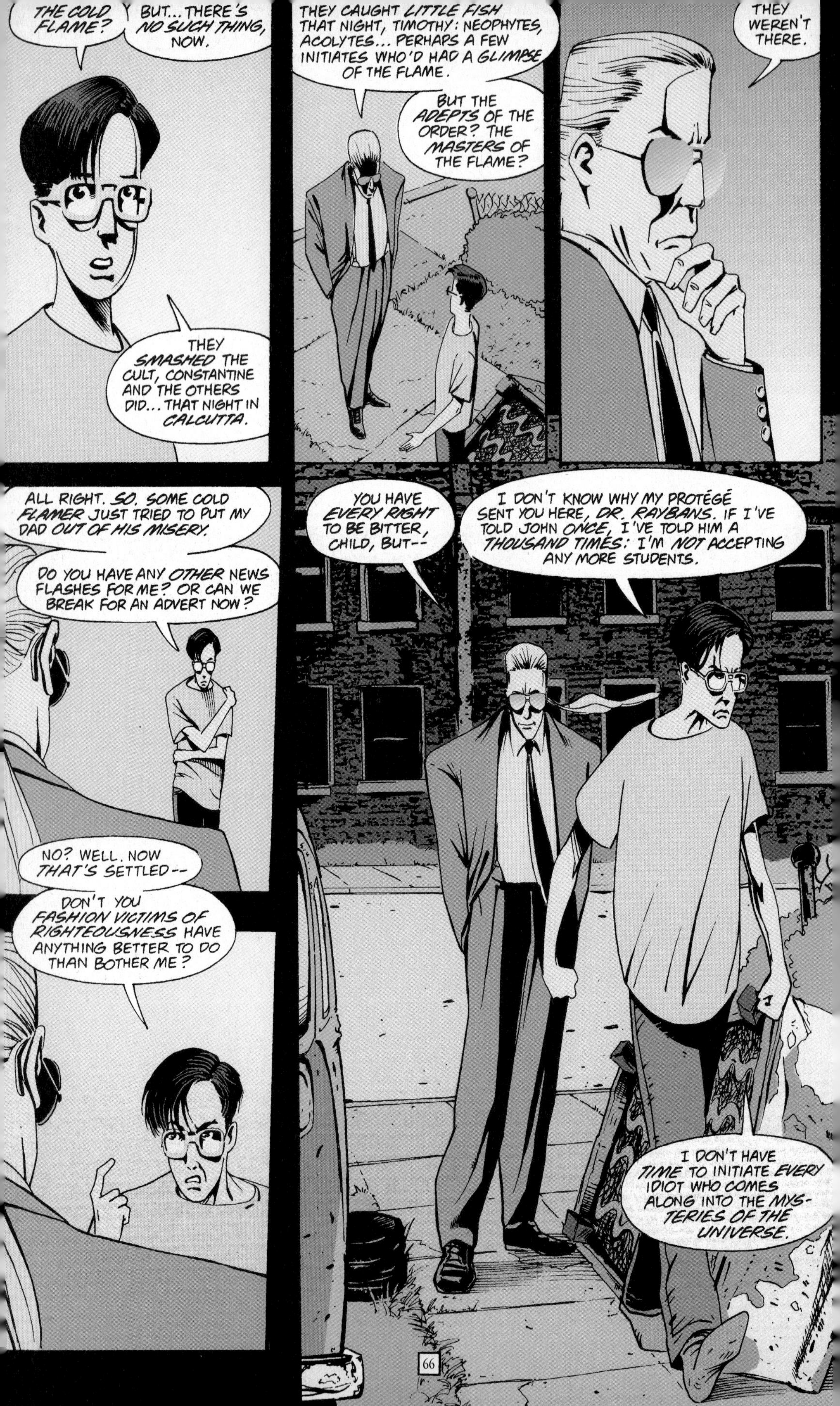
THE COLD FLAME?
BUT... THERE'S NO SUCH THING, NOW.
THEY SMASHED THE CULT, CONSTANTINE AND THE OTHERS DID... THAT NIGHT IN CALCUTTA.
THEY CAUGHT LITTLE FISH THAT NIGHT, TIMOTHY: NEOPHYTES, ACOLYTES... PERHAPS A FEW INITIATES WHO'D HAD A GLIMPSE OF THE FLAME.
BUT THE ADEPTS OF THE ORDER? THE MASTERS OF THE FLAME?
THEY WEREN'T THERE.
ALL RIGHT. SO. SOME COLD FLAMER JUST TRIED TO PUT MY DAD OUT OF HIS MISERY.
DO YOU HAVE ANY OTHER NEWS FLASHES FOR ME? OR CAN WE BREAK FOR AN ADVERT NOW?
NO? WELL. NOW THAT'S SETTLED--
DON'T YOU FASHION VICTIMS OF RIGHTEOUSNESS HAVE ANYTHING BETTER TO DO THAN BOTHER ME?
YOU HAVE EVERY RIGHT TO BE BITTER, CHILD, BUT--
I DON'T KNOW WHY MY PROTÉGÉ SENT YOU HERE, DR. RAYBANS. IF I'VE TOLD JOHN ONCE, I'VE TOLD HIM A THOUSAND TIMES: I'M NOT ACCEPTING ANY MORE STUDENTS.
I DON'T HAVE TIME TO INITIATE EVERY IDIOT WHO COMES ALONG INTO THE MYSTERIES OF THE UNIVERSE.

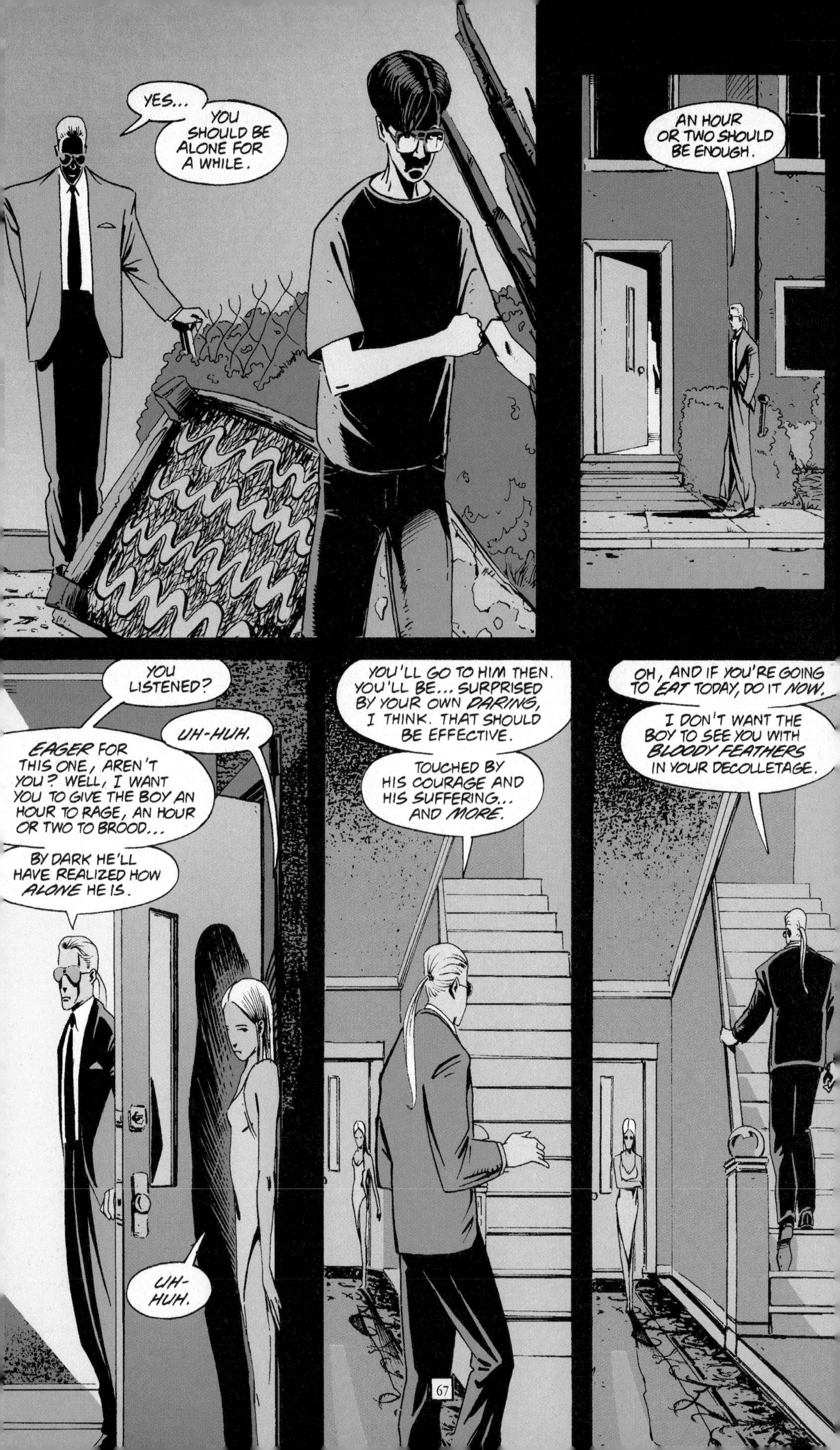
YES...
YOU SHOULD BE ALONE FOR A WHILE.
AN HOUR OR TWO SHOULD BE ENOUGH.
YOU LISTENED?
UH-HUH.
EAGER FOR THIS ONE, AREN'T YOU? WELL, I WANT YOU TO GIVE THE BOY AN HOUR TO RAGE, AN HOUR OR TWO TO BROOD...
BY DARK HE'LL HAVE REALIZED HOW ALONE HE IS.
UH-HUH.
YOU'LL GO TO HIM THEN. YOU'LL BE... SURPRISED BY YOUR OWN DARING, I THINK. THAT SHOULD BE EFFECTIVE.
TOUCHED BY HIS COURAGE AND HIS SUFFERING... AND MORE.
OH, AND IF YOU'RE GOING TO EAT TODAY, DO IT NOW.
I DON'T WANT THE BOY TO SEE YOU WITH BLOODY FEATHERS IN YOUR DECOLLETAGE.

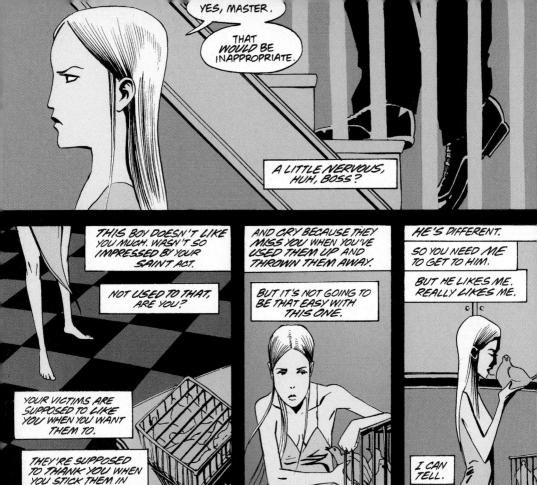

YES, MASTER.

THAT *WOULD BE* INAPPROPRIATE.

A LITTLE NERVOUS, HUH, BOSS?

THIS BOY DOESN'T LIKE YOU MUCH. WASN'T SO IMPRESSED BY YOUR *SAINT* ACT.

NOT USED TO THAT, ARE YOU?

YOUR VICTIMS ARE SUPPOSED TO LIKE YOU WHEN YOU WANT THEM TO.

THEY'RE SUPPOSED TO *THANK* YOU WHEN YOU STICK THEM IN THEIR CAGES.

AND CRY BECAUSE THEY *MISS* YOU WHEN YOU'VE USED THEM UP AND THROWN THEM AWAY.

BUT IT'S NOT GOING TO BE THAT EASY WITH THIS ONE.

HE'S DIFFERENT.

SO YOU NEED *ME* TO GET TO HIM.

BUT HE LIKES ME. *REALLY LIKES ME.*

I CAN TELL.

SO LET'S SEE IF I'VE GOT THIS *RIGHT.*

YOU WANT ME TO ACT SURPRISED, HUH? BY MY OWN DARING.

YOU WANT ME TO ACT TOUCHED.

WELL. I CAN DO BETTER THAN THAT.

TOUCHED...

OKAY, BOSS.

I CAN HANDLE THAT.

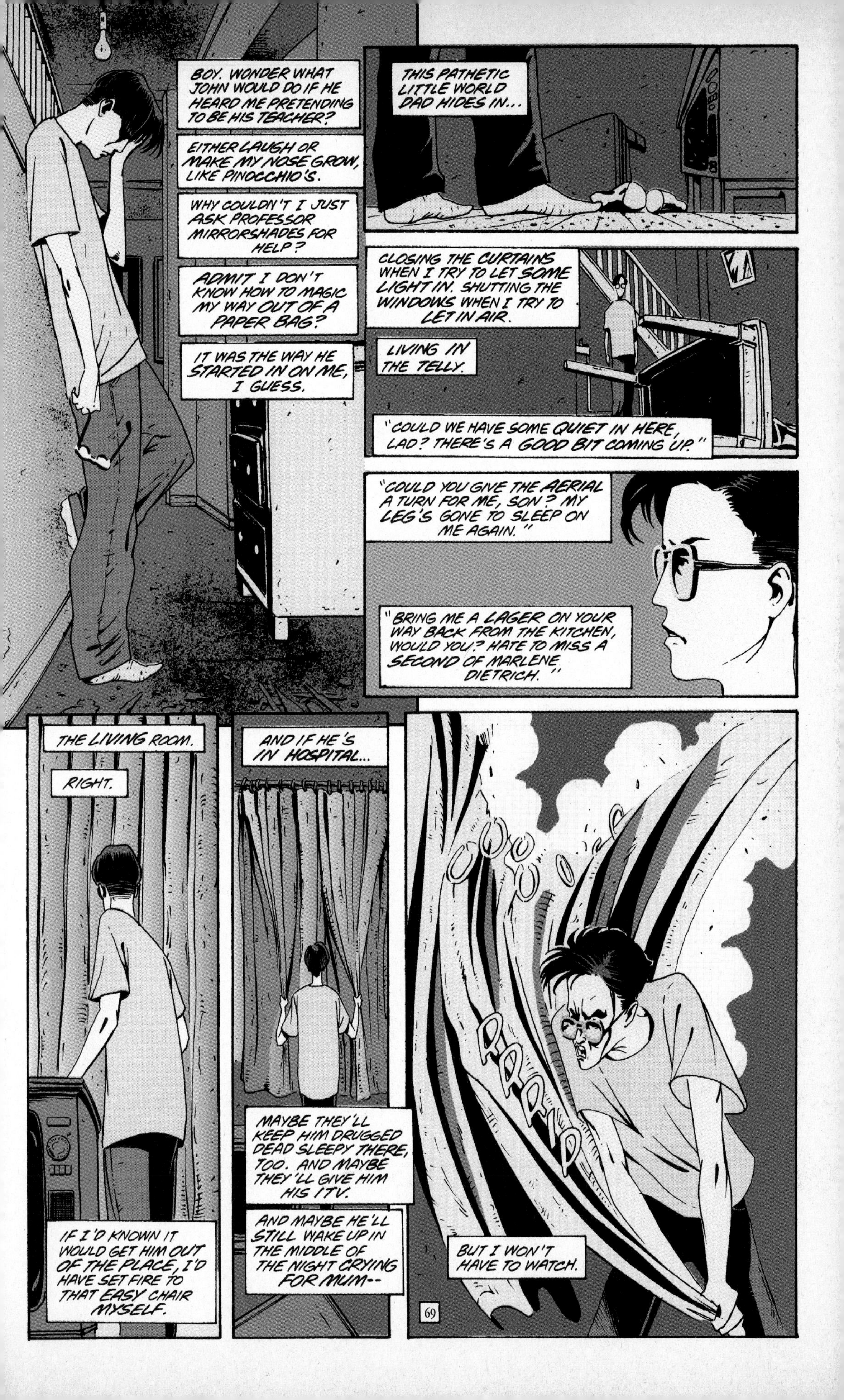
BOY. WONDER WHAT JOHN WOULD DO IF HE HEARD ME PRETENDING TO BE HIS TEACHER?
EITHER LAUGH OR MAKE MY NOSE GROW, LIKE PINOCCHIO'S.
WHY COULDN'T I JUST ASK PROFESSOR MIRRORSHADES FOR HELP?
ADMIT I DON'T KNOW HOW TO MAGIC MY WAY OUT OF A PAPER BAG?
IT WAS THE WAY HE STARTED IN ON ME, I GUESS.
THIS PATHETIC LITTLE WORLD DAD HIDES IN...
CLOSING THE CURTAINS WHEN I TRY TO LET SOME LIGHT IN. SHUTTING THE WINDOWS WHEN I TRY TO LET IN AIR.
LIVING IN THE TELLY.
"COULD WE HAVE SOME QUIET IN HERE, LAD? THERE'S A GOOD BIT COMING UP."
"COULD YOU GIVE THE AERIAL A TURN FOR ME, SON? MY LEG'S GONE TO SLEEP ON ME AGAIN."
"BRING ME A LAGER ON YOUR WAY BACK FROM THE KITCHEN, WOULD YOU? HATE TO MISS A SECOND OF MARLENE DIETRICH."
THE LIVING ROOM.
RIGHT.
IF I'D KNOWN IT WOULD GET HIM OUT OF THE PLACE, I'D HAVE SET FIRE TO THAT EASY CHAIR MYSELF.
AND IF HE'S IN HOSPITAL...
MAYBE THEY'LL KEEP HIM DRUGGED DEAD SLEEPY THERE, TOO. AND MAYBE THEY'LL GIVE HIM HIS ITV.
AND MAYBE HE'LL STILL WAKE UP IN THE MIDDLE OF THE NIGHT CRYING FOR MUM--
RRRRIP
BUT I WON'T HAVE TO WATCH.

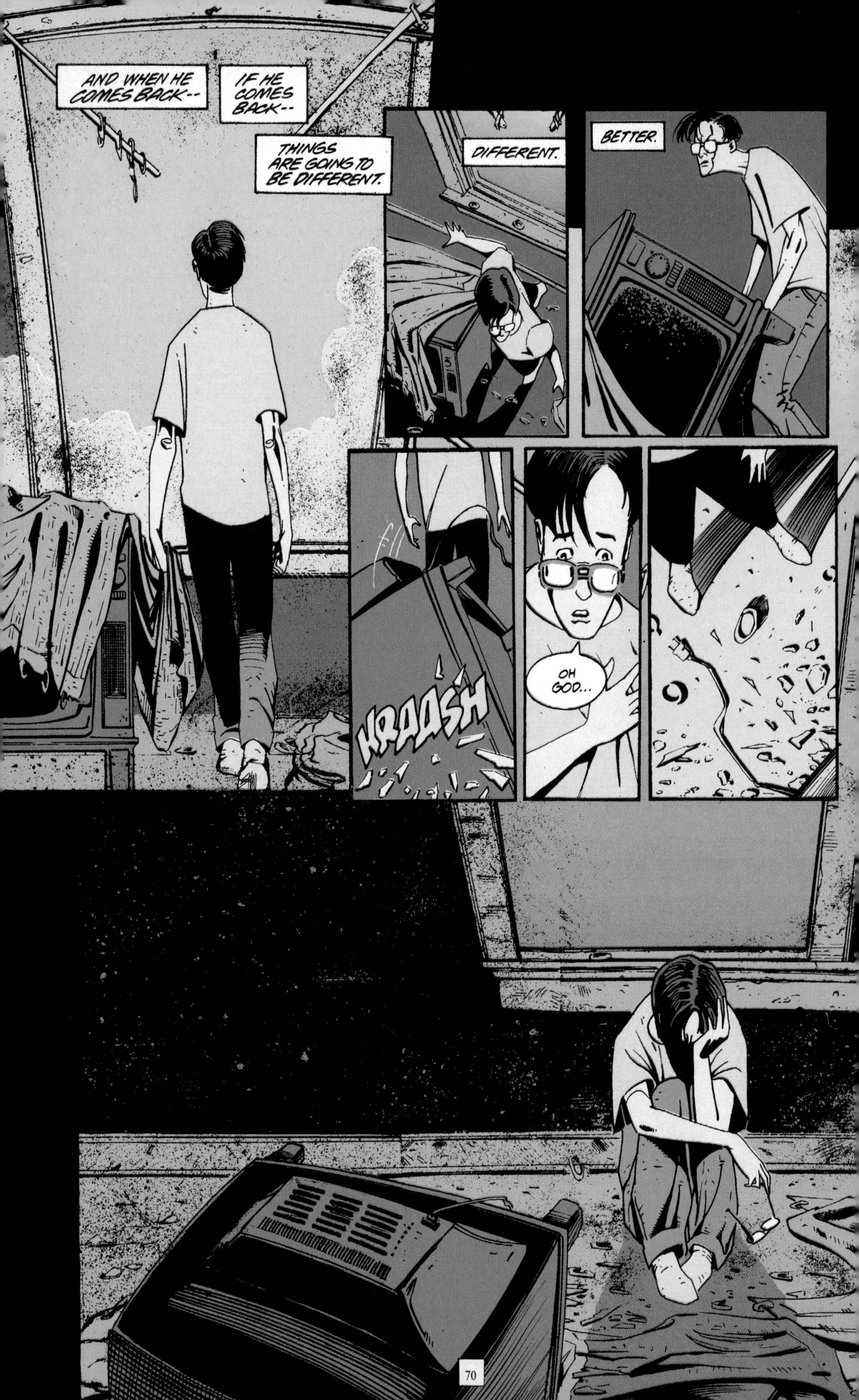
AND WHEN HE COMES BACK--
IF HE COMES BACK--
THINGS ARE GOING TO BE DIFFERENT.
DIFFERENT.
BETTER.
HRAASH
OH GOD...

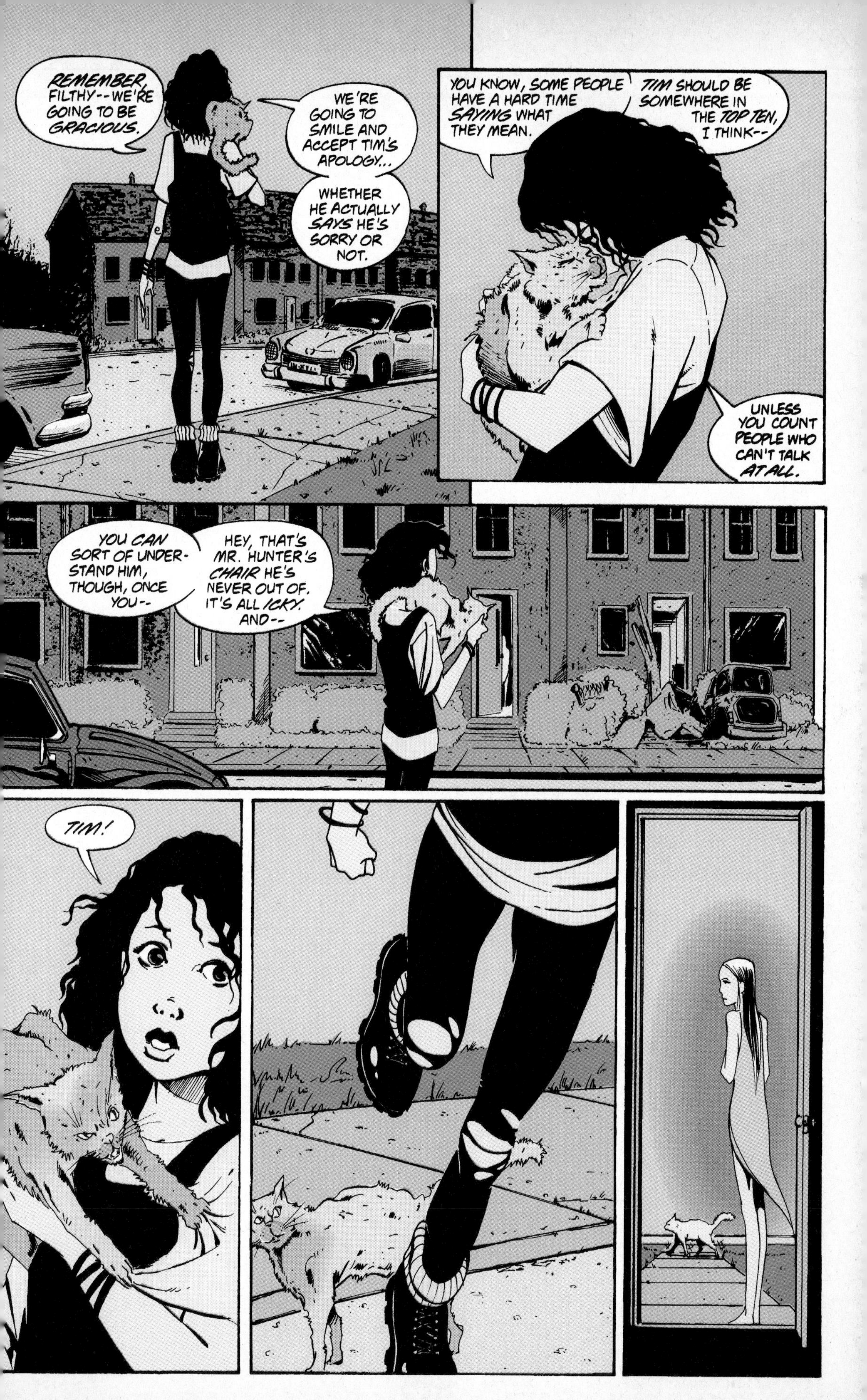
REMEMBER, FILTHY--WE'RE GOING TO BE GRACIOUS.
WE'RE GOING TO SMILE AND ACCEPT TIM'S APOLOGY...
WHETHER HE ACTUALLY SAYS HE'S SORRY OR NOT.
YOU KNOW, SOME PEOPLE HAVE A HARD TIME SAYING WHAT THEY MEAN.
TIM SHOULD BE SOMEWHERE IN THE TOP TEN, I THINK--
UNLESS YOU COUNT PEOPLE WHO CAN'T TALK AT ALL.
YOU CAN SORT OF UNDER-STAND HIM, THOUGH, ONCE YOU--
HEY, THAT'S MR. HUNTER'S CHAIR HE'S NEVER OUT OF. IT'S ALL ICKY. AND--
TIM!

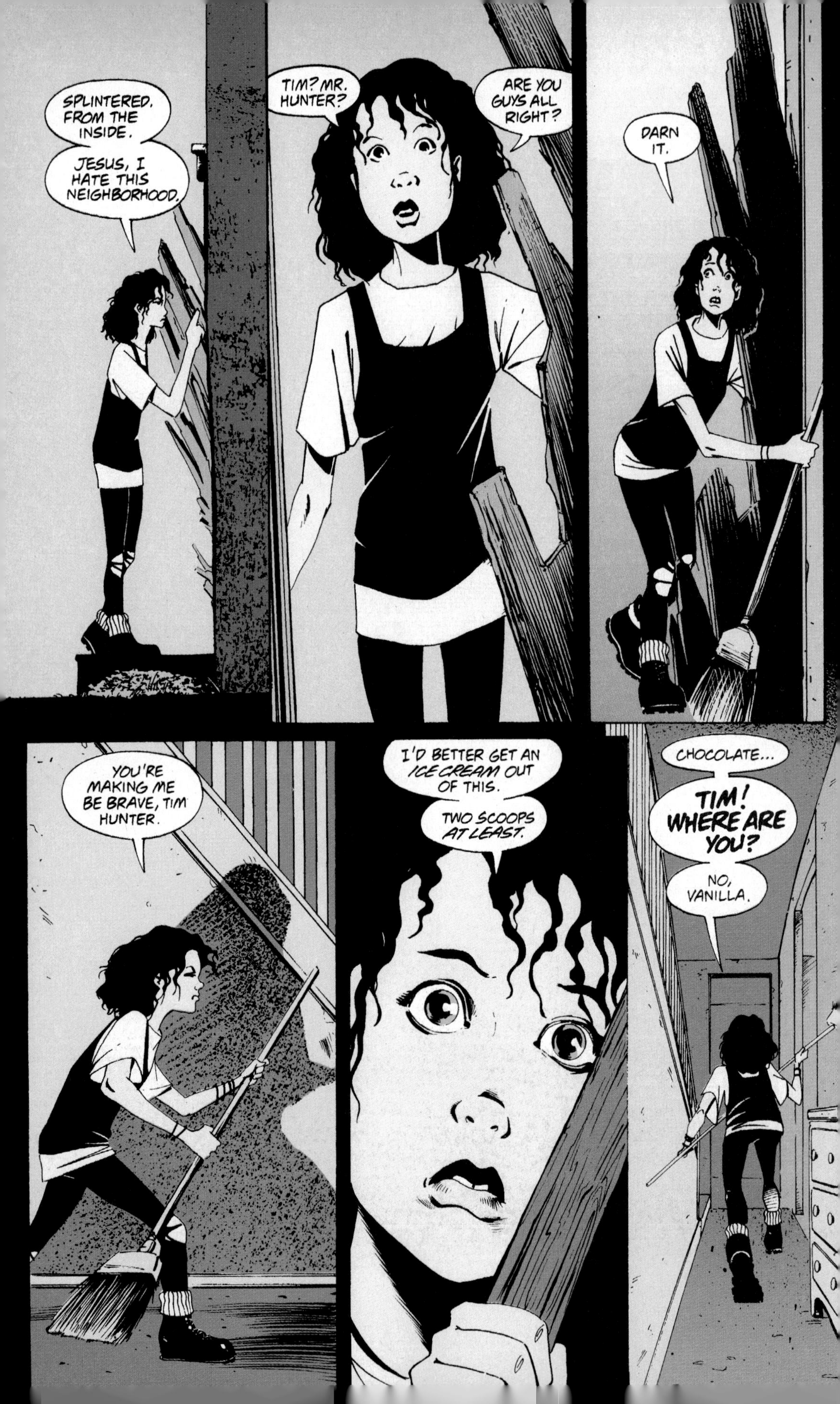
SPLINTERED. FROM THE INSIDE.
JESUS, I HATE THIS NEIGHBORHOOD.
TIM? MR. HUNTER?
ARE YOU GUYS ALL RIGHT?
DARN IT.
YOU'RE MAKING ME BE BRAVE, TIM HUNTER.
I'D BETTER GET AN ICE CREAM OUT OF THIS.
TWO SCOOPS AT LEAST.
CHOCOLATE...
TIM! WHERE ARE YOU?
NO, VANILLA.

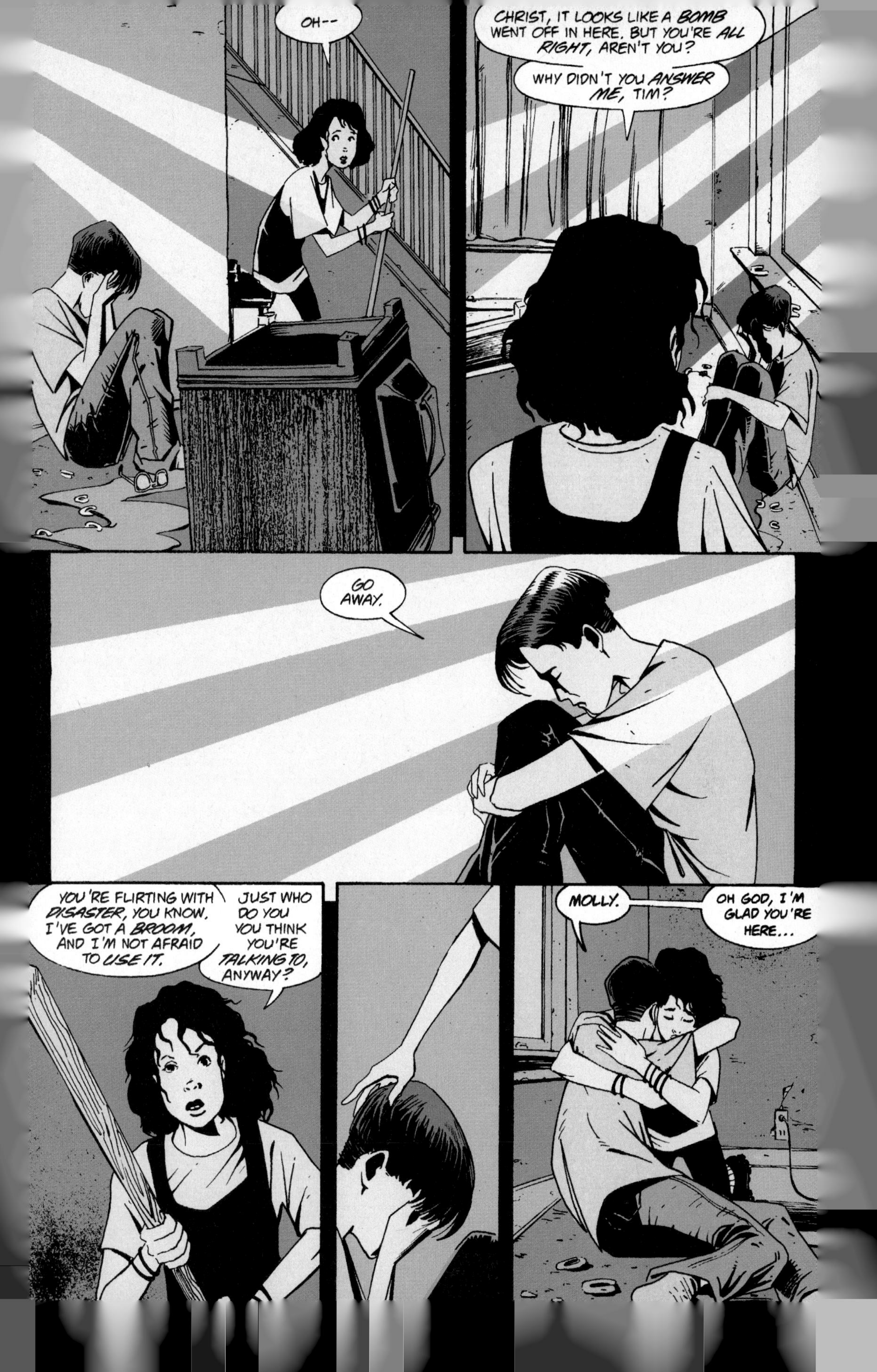
OH--
CHRIST, IT LOOKS LIKE A BOMB WENT OFF IN HERE. BUT YOU'RE ALL RIGHT, AREN'T YOU?
WHY DIDN'T YOU ANSWER ME, TIM?
GO AWAY.
YOU'RE FLIRTING WITH DISASTER, YOU KNOW. I'VE GOT A BROOM, AND I'M NOT AFRAID TO USE IT.
JUST WHO DO YOU YOU THINK YOU'RE TALKING TO, ANYWAY?
MOLLY.
OH GOD, I'M GLAD YOU'RE HERE...

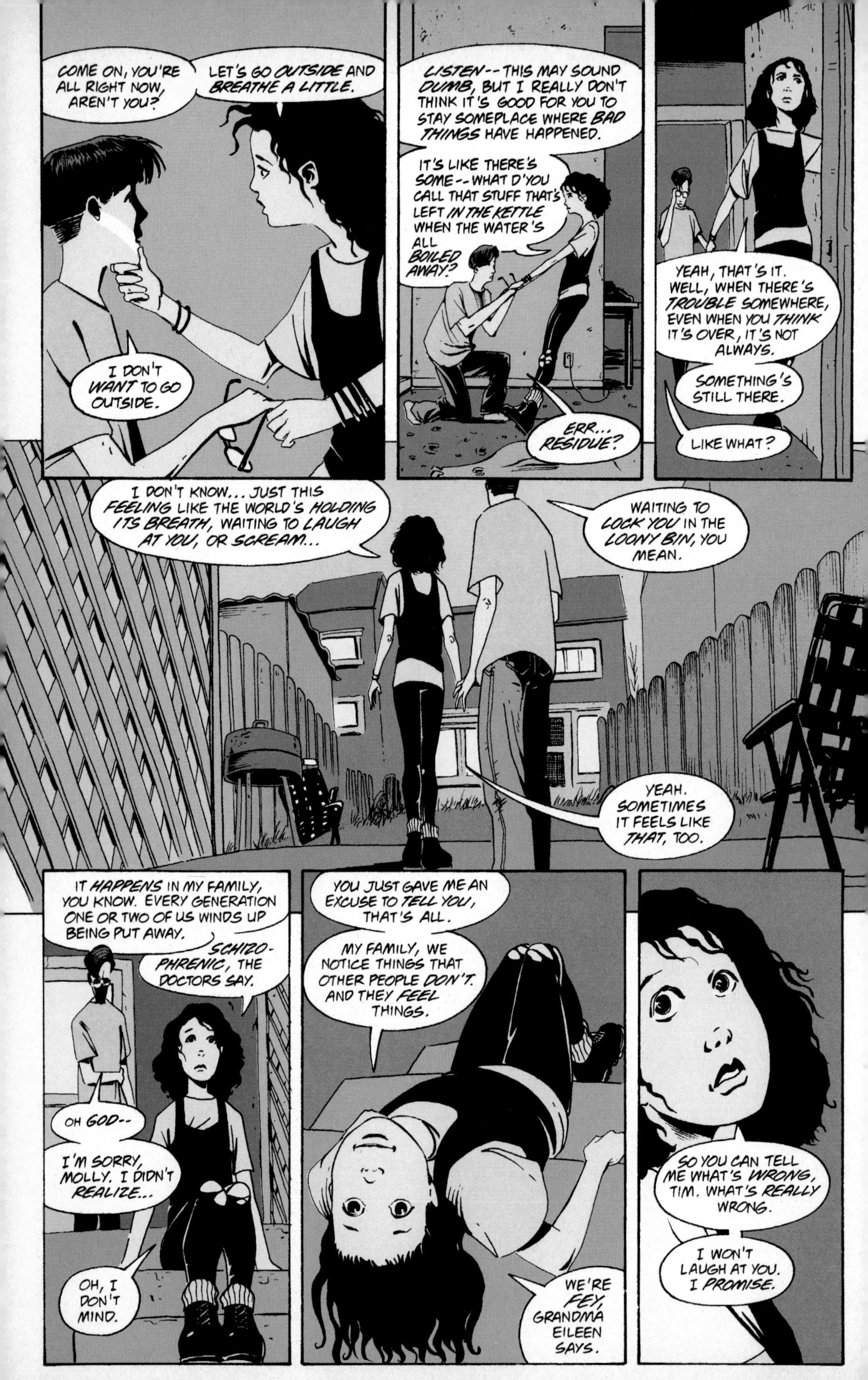
COME ON, YOU'RE ALL RIGHT NOW, AREN'T YOU?
LET'S GO OUTSIDE AND BREATHE A LITTLE.
I DON'T WANT TO GO OUTSIDE.
LISTEN-- THIS MAY SOUND DUMB, BUT I REALLY DON'T THINK IT'S GOOD FOR YOU TO STAY SOMEPLACE WHERE BAD THINGS HAVE HAPPENED.
IT'S LIKE THERE'S SOME-- WHAT D'YOU CALL THAT STUFF THAT'S LEFT IN THE KETTLE WHEN THE WATER'S ALL BOILED AWAY?
ERR... RESIDUE?
YEAH, THAT'S IT. WELL, WHEN THERE'S TROUBLE SOMEWHERE, EVEN WHEN YOU THINK IT'S OVER, IT'S NOT ALWAYS.
SOMETHING'S STILL THERE.
LIKE WHAT?
I DON'T KNOW... JUST THIS FEELING LIKE THE WORLD'S HOLDING ITS BREATH, WAITING TO LAUGH AT YOU, OR SCREAM...
WAITING TO LOCK YOU IN THE LOONY BIN, YOU MEAN.
YEAH. SOMETIMES IT FEELS LIKE THAT, TOO.
IT HAPPENS IN MY FAMILY, YOU KNOW. EVERY GENERATION ONE OR TWO OF US WINDS UP BEING PUT AWAY.
SCHIZO-PHRENIC, THE DOCTORS SAY.
OH GOD--
I'M SORRY, MOLLY. I DIDN'T REALIZE...
OH, I DON'T MIND.
YOU JUST GAVE ME AN EXCUSE TO TELL YOU, THAT'S ALL.
MY FAMILY, WE NOTICE THINGS THAT OTHER PEOPLE DON'T. AND THEY FEEL THINGS.
WE'RE FEY, GRANDMA EILEEN SAYS.
SO YOU CAN TELL ME WHAT'S WRONG, TIM. WHAT'S REALLY WRONG.
I WON'T LAUGH AT YOU. I PROMISE.

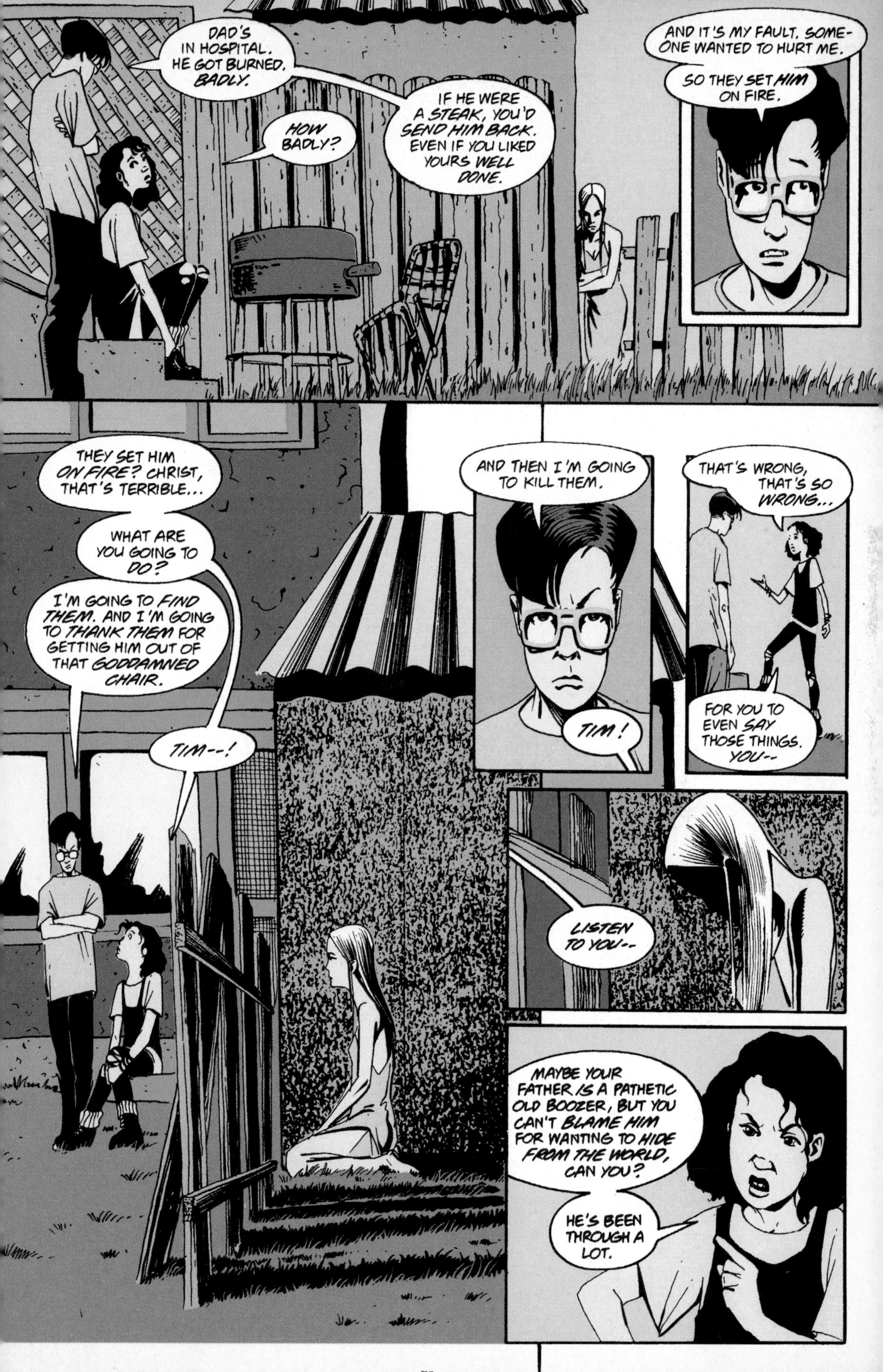
DAD'S IN HOSPITAL. HE GOT BURNED. BADLY.
HOW BADLY?
IF HE WERE A STEAK, YOU'D SEND HIM BACK. EVEN IF YOU LIKED YOURS WELL DONE.
AND IT'S MY FAULT. SOME-ONE WANTED TO HURT ME.
SO THEY SET HIM ON FIRE.
THEY SET HIM ON FIRE? CHRIST, THAT'S TERRIBLE...
WHAT ARE YOU GOING TO DO?
I'M GOING TO FIND THEM. AND I'M GOING TO THANK THEM FOR GETTING HIM OUT OF THAT GODDAMNED CHAIR.
TIM--!
AND THEN I'M GOING TO KILL THEM.
TIM!
THAT'S WRONG, THAT'S SO WRONG...
FOR YOU TO EVEN SAY THOSE THINGS. YOU--
LISTEN TO YOU--
MAYBE YOUR FATHER IS A PATHETIC OLD BOOZER, BUT YOU CAN'T BLAME HIM FOR WANTING TO HIDE FROM THE WORLD, CAN YOU?
HE'S BEEN THROUGH A LOT.

SHE'S SO WISE. SO GOOD.

LISTEN TO HER, TIM.

AND PROTECTING YOURSELF, I CAN UNDERSTAND THAT-- BUT TO HEAR YOU TALK ABOUT KILLING SOMEONE LIKE IT WOULD MAKE YOUR DAY--

IT MAKES ME SICK.

CHRIST, FOR A MINUTE I THOUGHT I WAS BACK IN CROSSMAGLEN, LISTENING TO THE BOYS IN THE STREET...

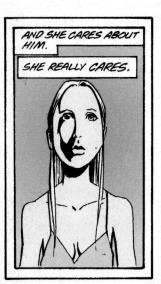

AND SHE CARES ABOUT HIM.

SHE REALLY CARES.

OH, THEY ALL HAD FATHERS TO AVENGE-- OR GREAT-GREAT-GRANDFATHERS, OR SISTERS--

AND SOME OF THEM TALKED ABOUT BLOWING HOLES IN THE BLOODY PARAS, AND SOME OF THEM DID IT.

SO I KNOW HOW IT GOES. AND HERE'S MY ADVICE TO YOU, BIG MAN--

SHOOT YOUR BAD GUYS IN THE BACK, ALL RIGHT? DON'T LET THEM SEE YOU COMING.

THAT'S THE WAY THE PROFESSIONALS DO IT.

AND WHEN YOU'RE DONE, DON'T SIT WITH YOUR BACK TO THE DOOR, KEEP AWAY FROM WINDOWS.

AND KEEP AWAY FROM ME.

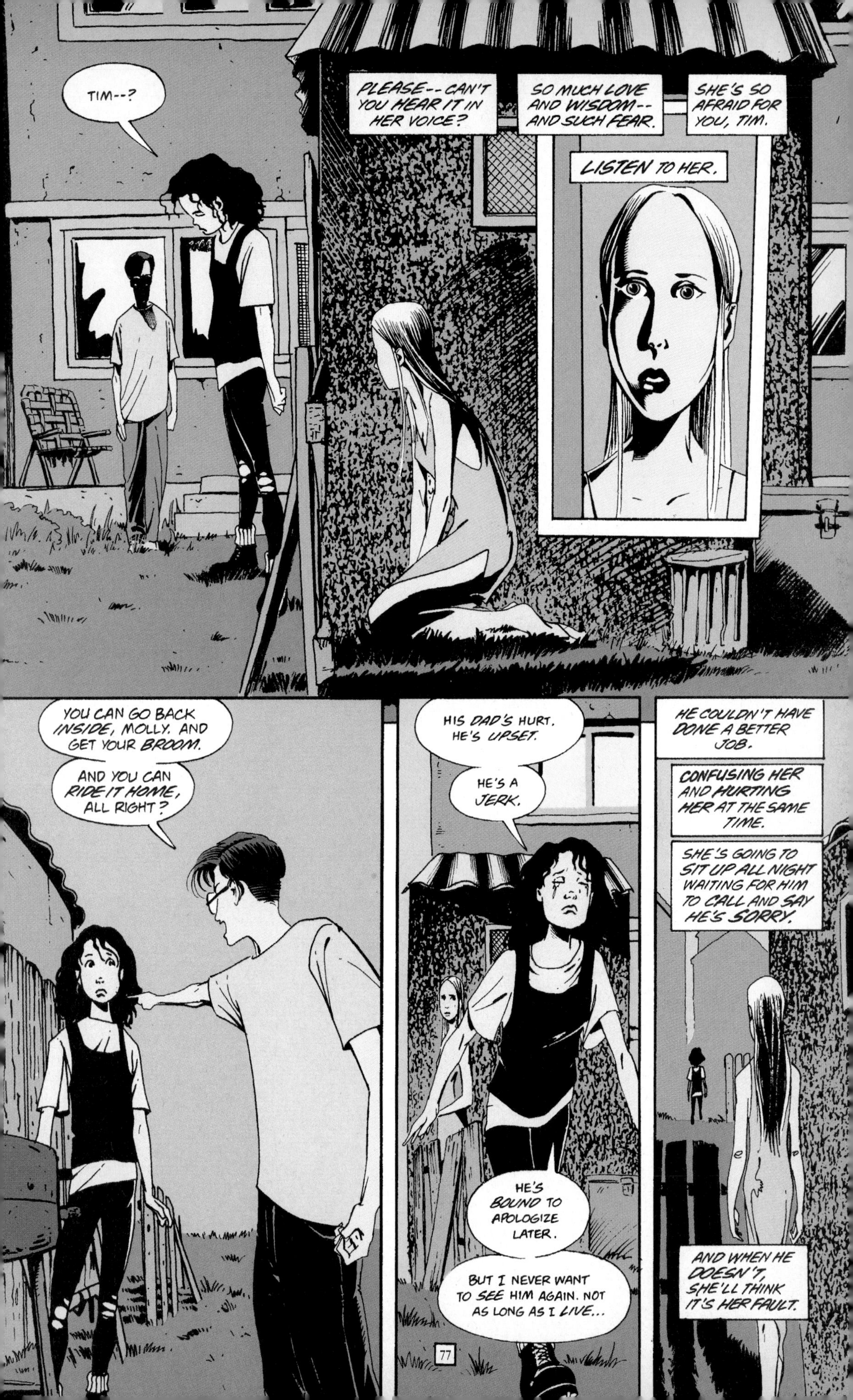
TIM--?
PLEASE--CAN'T YOU HEAR IT IN HER VOICE?
SO MUCH LOVE AND WISDOM--AND SUCH FEAR.
SHE'S SO AFRAID FOR YOU, TIM.
LISTEN TO HER.
YOU CAN GO BACK INSIDE, MOLLY. AND GET YOUR BROOM.
AND YOU CAN RIDE IT HOME, ALL RIGHT?
HIS DAD'S HURT. HE'S UPSET.
HE'S A JERK.
HE'S BOUND TO APOLOGIZE LATER.
BUT I NEVER WANT TO SEE HIM AGAIN. NOT AS LONG AS I LIVE...
HE COULDN'T HAVE DONE A BETTER JOB.
CONFUSING HER AND HURTING HER AT THE SAME TIME.
SHE'S GOING TO SIT UP ALL NIGHT WAITING FOR HIM TO CALL AND SAY HE'S SORRY.
AND WHEN HE DOESN'T, SHE'LL THINK IT'S HER FAULT.

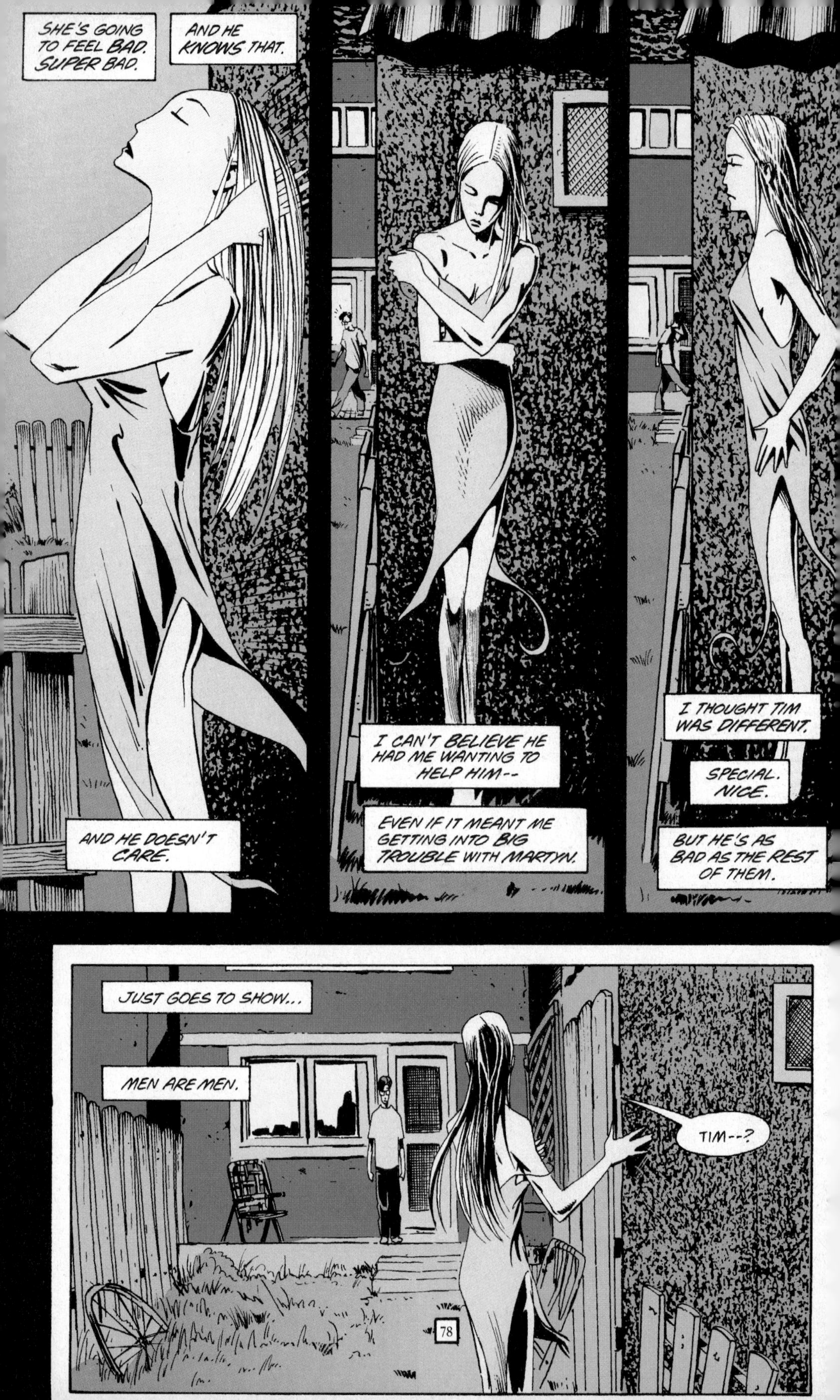
SHE'S GOING TO FEEL BAD. SUPER BAD.
AND HE KNOWS THAT.
AND HE DOESN'T CARE.
I CAN'T BELIEVE HE HAD ME WANTING TO HELP HIM--
EVEN IF IT MEANT ME GETTING INTO BIG TROUBLE WITH MARTYN.
I THOUGHT TIM WAS DIFFERENT.
SPECIAL. NICE.
BUT HE'S AS BAD AS THE REST OF THEM.
JUST GOES TO SHOW...
MEN ARE MEN.
TIM--?

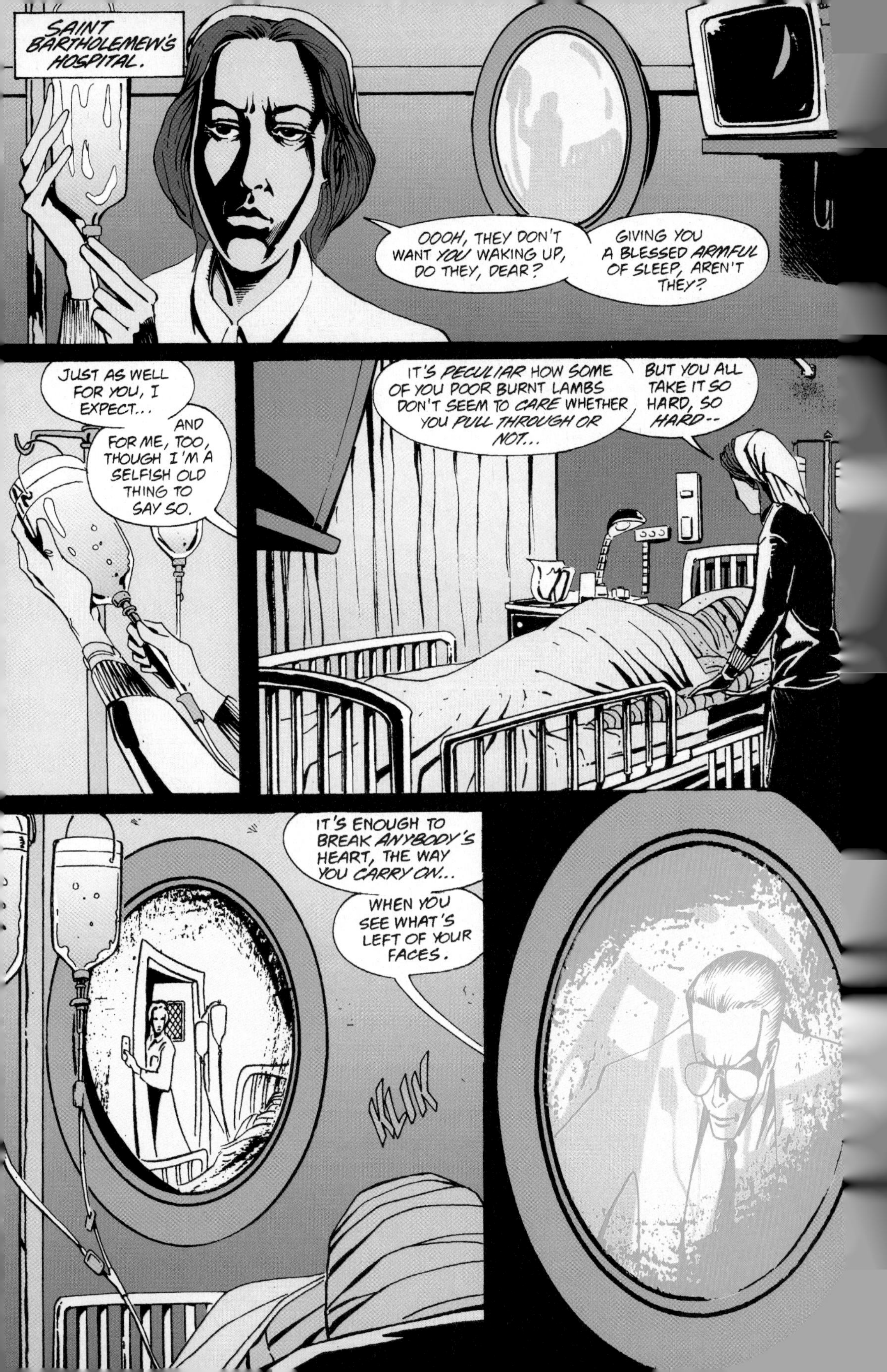
SAINT BARTHOLEMEW'S HOSPITAL.
OOOH, THEY DON'T WANT YOU WAKING UP, DO THEY, DEAR?
GIVING YOU A BLESSED ARMFUL OF SLEEP, AREN'T THEY?
JUST AS WELL FOR YOU, I EXPECT...
AND FOR ME, TOO, THOUGH I'M A SELFISH OLD THING TO SAY SO.
IT'S PECULIAR HOW SOME OF YOU POOR BURNT LAMBS DON'T SEEM TO CARE WHETHER YOU PULL THROUGH OR NOT...
BUT YOU ALL TAKE IT SO HARD, SO HARD--
IT'S ENOUGH TO BREAK ANYBODY'S HEART, THE WAY YOU CARRY ON...
WHEN YOU SEE WHAT'S LEFT OF YOUR FACES.
KLIK

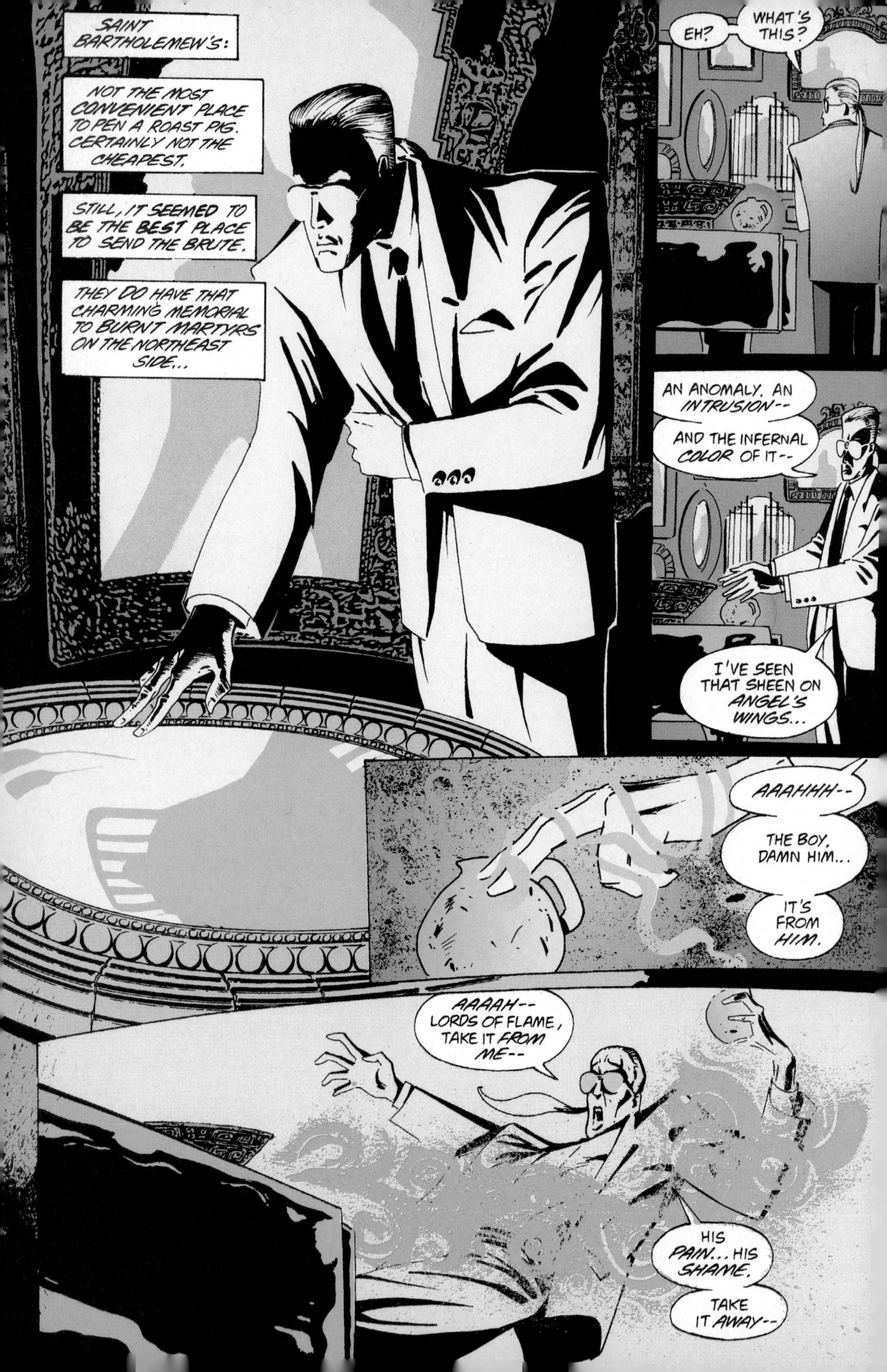
SAINT BARTHOLEMEW'S:
NOT THE MOST CONVENIENT PLACE TO PEN A ROAST PIG. CERTAINLY NOT THE CHEAPEST.
STILL, IT SEEMED TO BE THE BEST PLACE TO SEND THE BRUTE.
THEY DO HAVE THAT CHARMING MEMORIAL TO BURNT MARTYRS ON THE NORTHEAST SIDE...
EH?
WHAT'S THIS?
AN ANOMALY. AN INTRUSION--
AND THE INFERNAL COLOR OF IT--
I'VE SEEN THAT SHEEN ON ANGEL'S WINGS...
AAAHHH--
THE BOY, DAMN HIM...
IT'S FROM HIM.
AAAAH-- LORDS OF FLAME, TAKE IT FROM ME--
HIS PAIN... HIS SHAME.
TAKE IT AWAY--

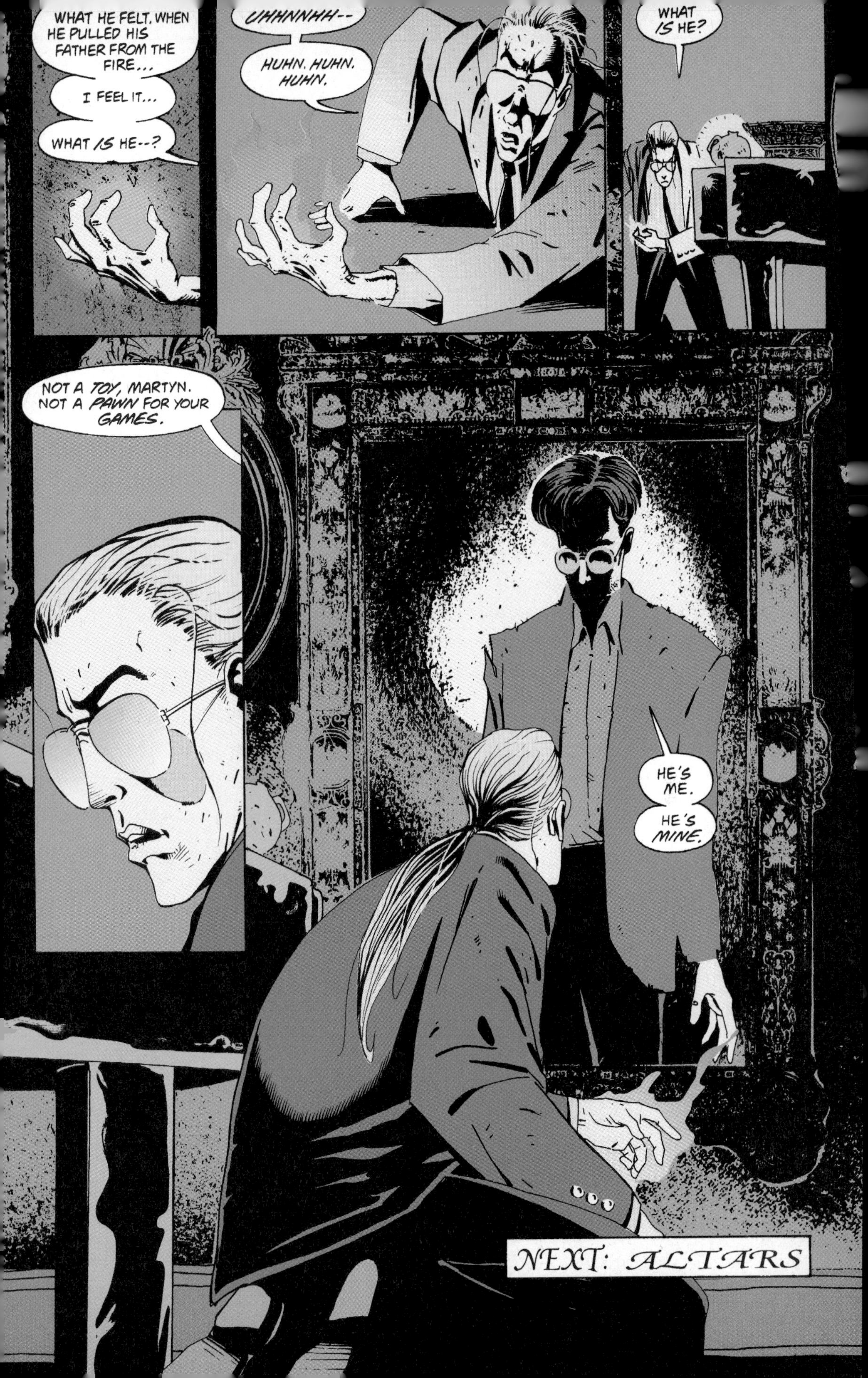
WHAT HE FELT, WHEN HE PULLED HIS FATHER FROM THE FIRE...
I FEEL IT...
WHAT IS HE--?
UHHNNHH--
HUHN. HUHN. HUHN.
WHAT IS HE?
NOT A TOY, MARTYN. NOT A PAWN FOR YOUR GAMES.
HE'S ME.
HE'S MINE.
NEXT: ALTARS

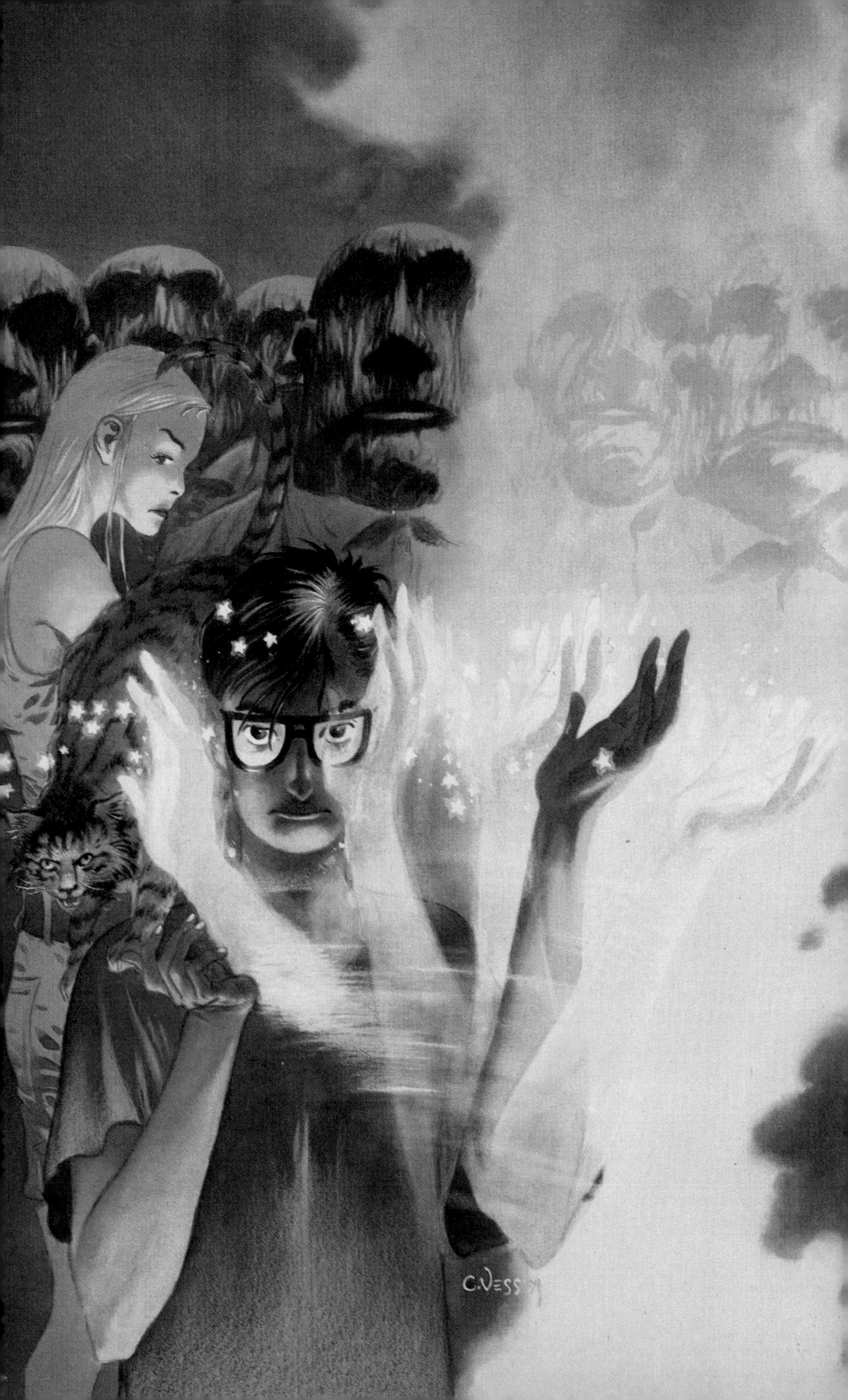
C.VESS

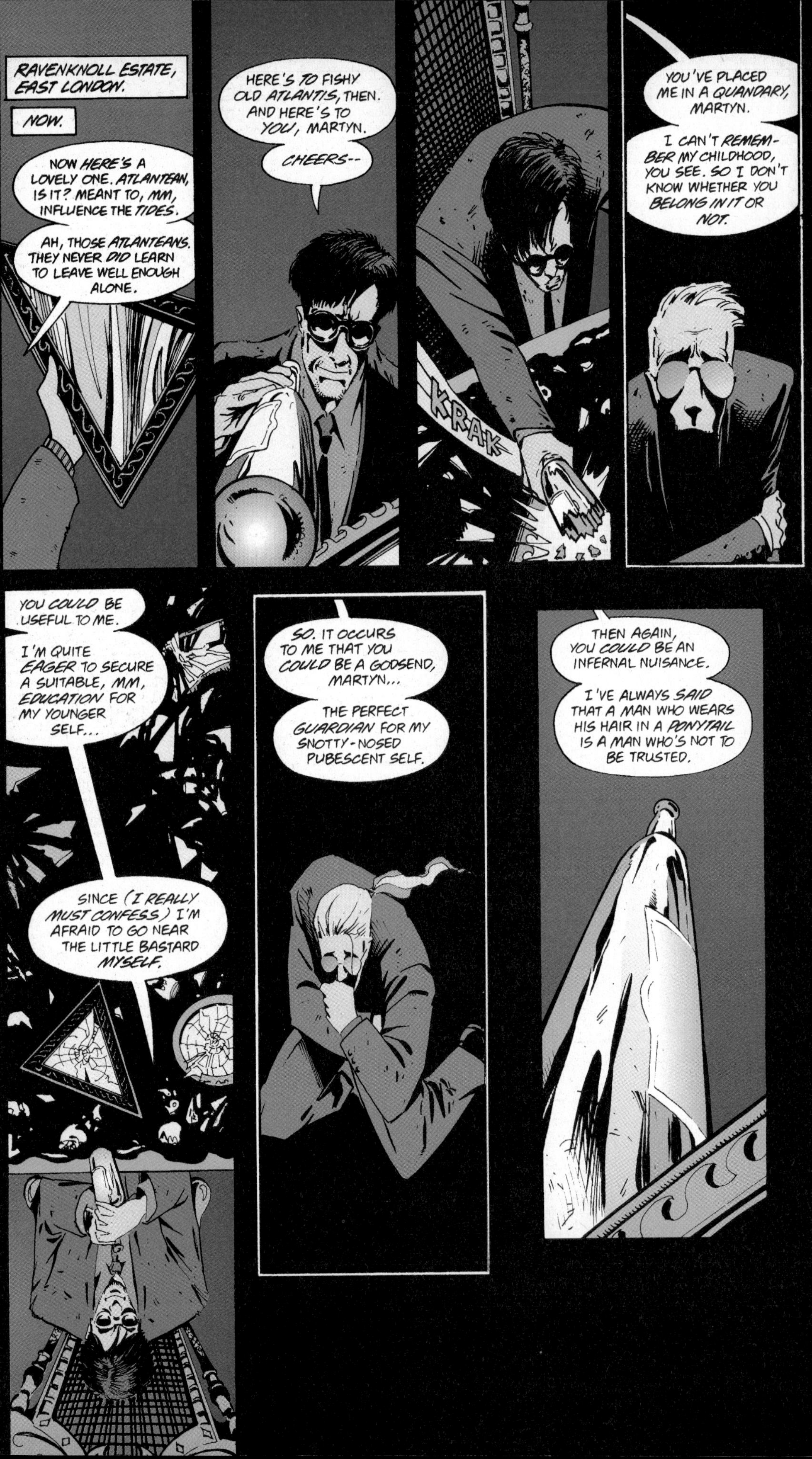
RAVENKNOLL ESTATE, EAST LONDON.
NOW.
NOW HERE'S A LOVELY ONE. ATLANTEAN, IS IT? MEANT TO, MM, INFLUENCE THE TIDES.
AH, THOSE ATLANTEANS. THEY NEVER DID LEARN TO LEAVE WELL ENOUGH ALONE.
HERE'S TO FISHY OLD ATLANTIS, THEN. AND HERE'S TO YOU, MARTYN.
CHEERS--
KRAK
YOU'VE PLACED ME IN A QUANDARY, MARTYN.
I CAN'T REMEMBER MY CHILDHOOD, YOU SEE. SO I DON'T KNOW WHETHER YOU BELONG IN IT OR NOT.
YOU COULD BE USEFUL TO ME.
I'M QUITE EAGER TO SECURE A SUITABLE, MM, EDUCATION FOR MY YOUNGER SELF...
SINCE (I REALLY MUST CONFESS) I'M AFRAID TO GO NEAR THE LITTLE BASTARD MYSELF.
SO. IT OCCURS TO ME THAT YOU COULD BE A GODSEND, MARTYN...
THE PERFECT GUARDIAN FOR MY SNOTTY-NOSED PUBESCENT SELF.
THEN AGAIN, YOU COULD BE AN INFERNAL NUISANCE.
I'VE ALWAYS SAID THAT A MAN WHO WEARS HIS HAIR IN A PONYTAIL IS A MAN WHO'S NOT TO BE TRUSTED.

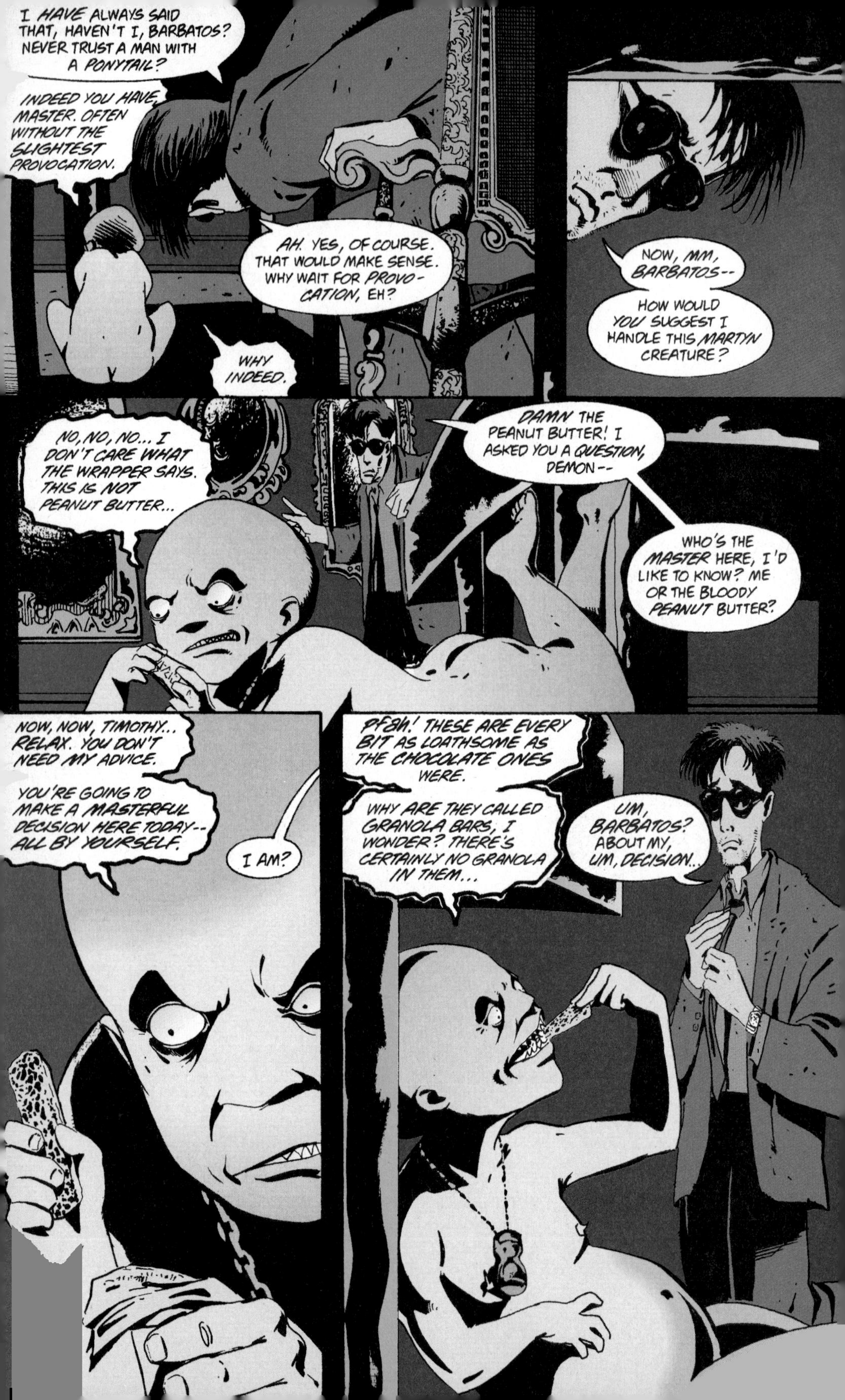
I HAVE ALWAYS SAID THAT, HAVEN'T I, BARBATOS? NEVER TRUST A MAN WITH A PONYTAIL?
INDEED YOU HAVE, MASTER. OFTEN WITHOUT THE SLIGHTEST PROVOCATION.
AH. YES, OF COURSE. THAT WOULD MAKE SENSE. WHY WAIT FOR PROVOCATION, EH?
WHY INDEED.
NOW, MM, BARBATOS--
HOW WOULD YOU SUGGEST I HANDLE THIS MARTYN CREATURE?
NO, NO, NO... I DON'T CARE WHAT THE WRAPPER SAYS. THIS IS NOT PEANUT BUTTER...
DAMN THE PEANUT BUTTER! I ASKED YOU A QUESTION, DEMON--
WHO'S THE MASTER HERE, I'D LIKE TO KNOW? ME OR THE BLOODY PEANUT BUTTER?
NOW, NOW, TIMOTHY... RELAX. YOU DON'T NEED MY ADVICE.
YOU'RE GOING TO MAKE A MASTERFUL DECISION HERE TODAY-- ALL BY YOURSELF.
I AM?
PFAH! THESE ARE EVERY BIT AS LOATHSOME AS THE CHOCOLATE ONES WERE.
WHY ARE THEY CALLED GRANOLA BARS, I WONDER? THERE'S CERTAINLY NO GRANOLA IN THEM...
UM, BARBATOS? ABOUT MY, UM, DECISION...

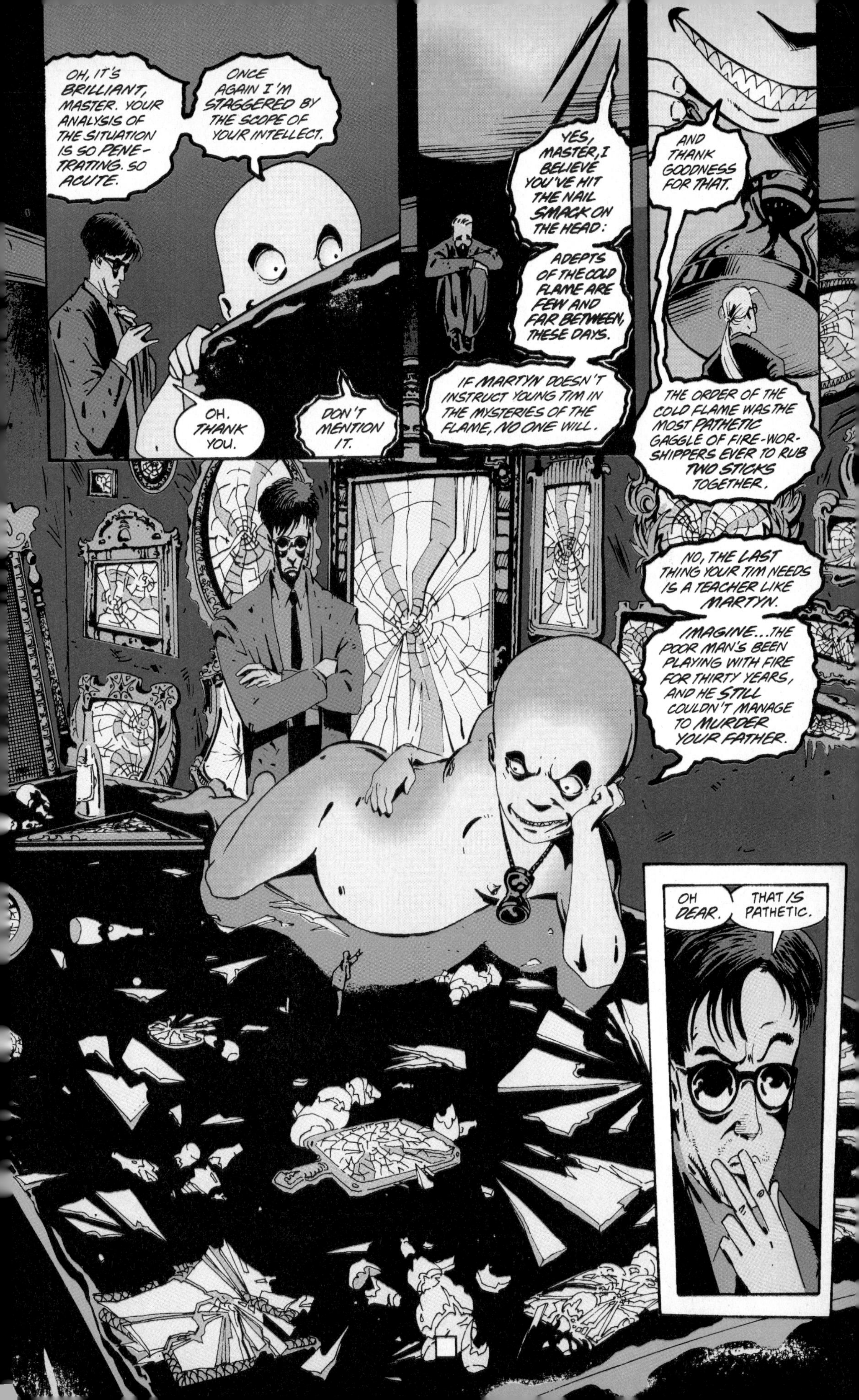
OH, IT'S BRILLIANT, MASTER. YOUR ANALYSIS OF THE SITUATION IS SO PENE-TRATING. SO ACUTE.
ONCE AGAIN I'M STAGGERED BY THE SCOPE OF YOUR INTELLECT.
OH. THANK YOU.
DON'T MENTION IT.
YES, MASTER, I BELIEVE YOU'VE HIT THE NAIL SMACK ON THE HEAD:
ADEPTS OF THE COLD FLAME ARE FEW AND FAR BETWEEN, THESE DAYS.
IF MARTYN DOESN'T INSTRUCT YOUNG TIM IN THE MYSTERIES OF THE FLAME, NO ONE WILL.
AND THANK GOODNESS FOR THAT.
THE ORDER OF THE COLD FLAME WAS THE MOST PATHETIC GAGGLE OF FIRE-WOR-SHIPPERS EVER TO RUB TWO STICKS TOGETHER.
NO, THE LAST THING YOUR TIM NEEDS IS A TEACHER LIKE MARTYN.
IMAGINE... THE POOR MAN'S BEEN PLAYING WITH FIRE FOR THIRTY YEARS, AND HE STILL COULDN'T MANAGE TO MURDER YOUR FATHER.
OH DEAR.
THAT IS PATHETIC.

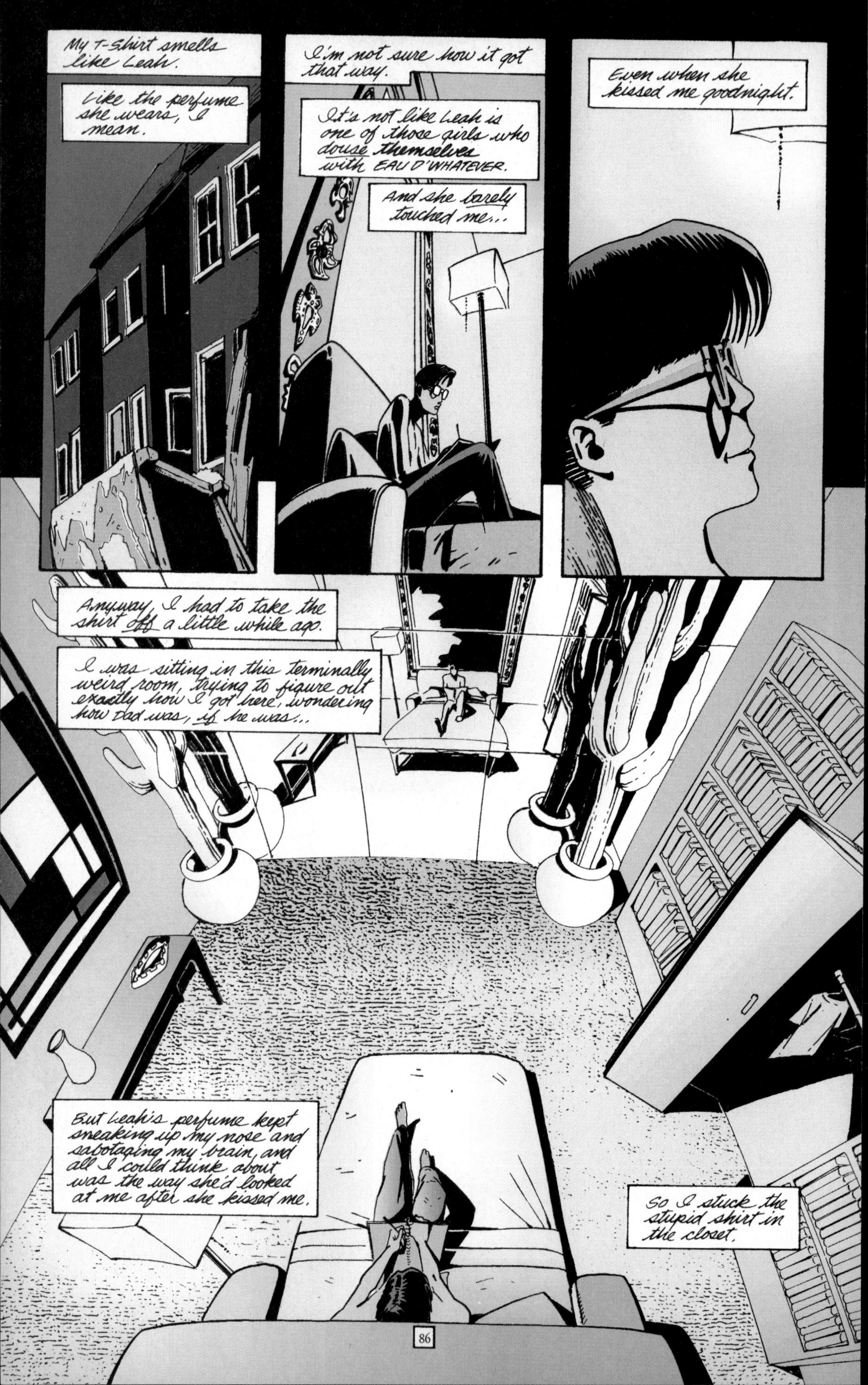

My T-shirt smells like Leah.
Like the perfume she wears, I mean.
I'm not sure how it got that way.
It's not like Leah is one of those girls who douse themselves with EAU D'WHATEVER.
And she barely touched me...
Even when she kissed me goodnight.
Anyway, I had to take the shirt off a little while ago.
I was sitting in this terminally weird room, trying to figure out exactly how I got here, wondering how Dad was, if he was...
But Leah's perfume kept sneaking up my nose and sabotaging my brain, and all I could think about was the way she'd looked at me after she kissed me.
So I stuck the stupid shirt in the closet.

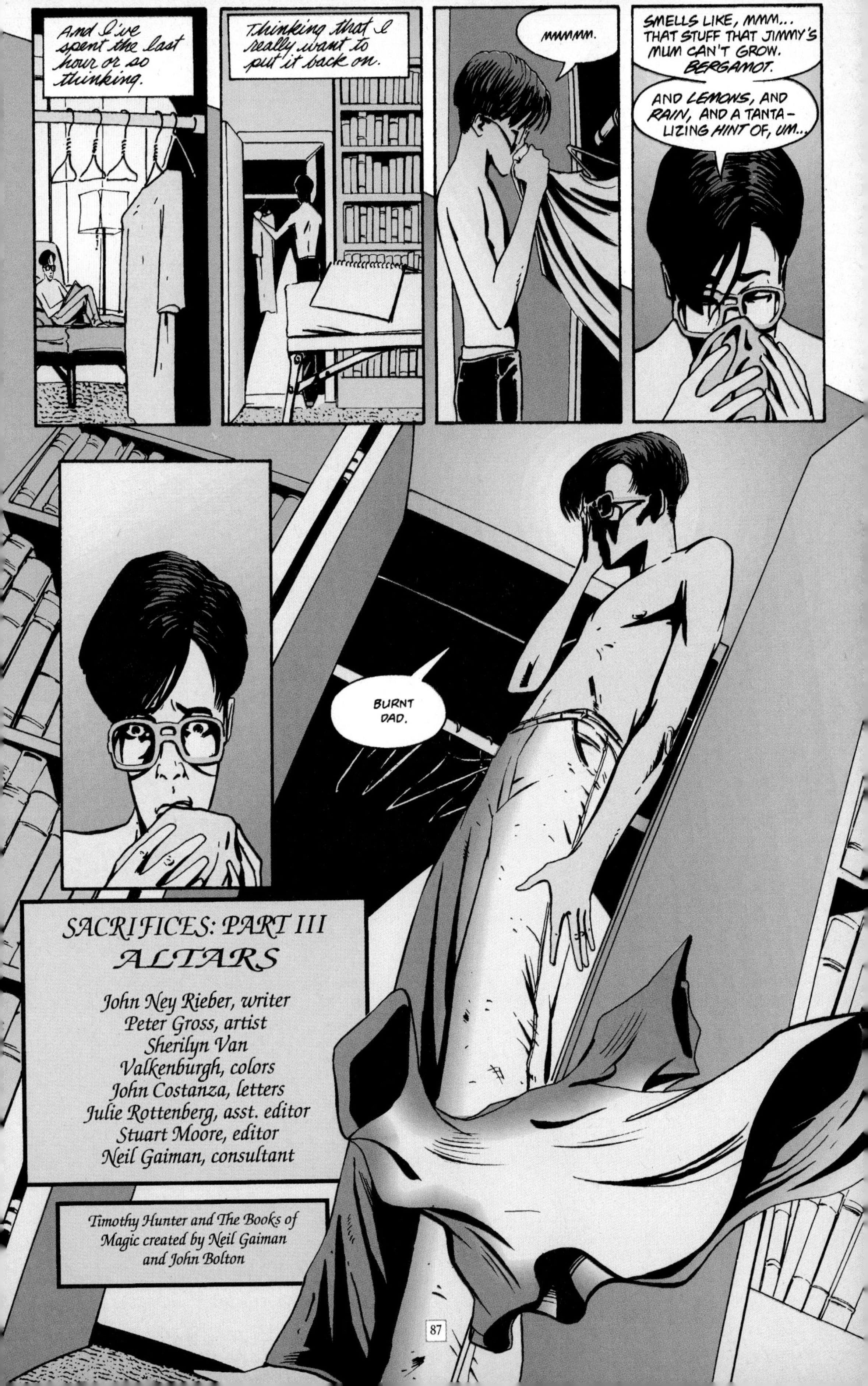
And I've spent the last hour or so thinking.
Thinking that I really want to put it back on.
MMMMMM.
SMELLS LIKE, MMM... THAT STUFF THAT JIMMY'S MUM CAN'T GROW. BERGAMOT.
AND LEMONS, AND RAIN, AND A TANTA-LIZING HINT OF, UM...
BURNT DAD.
SACRIFICES: PART III
ALTARS
John Ney Rieber, writer
Peter Gross, artist
Sherilyn Van Valkenburgh, colors
John Costanza, letters
Julie Rottenberg, asst. editor
Stuart Moore, editor
Neil Gaiman, consultant
Timothy Hunter and The Books of Magic created by Neil Gaiman and John Bolton

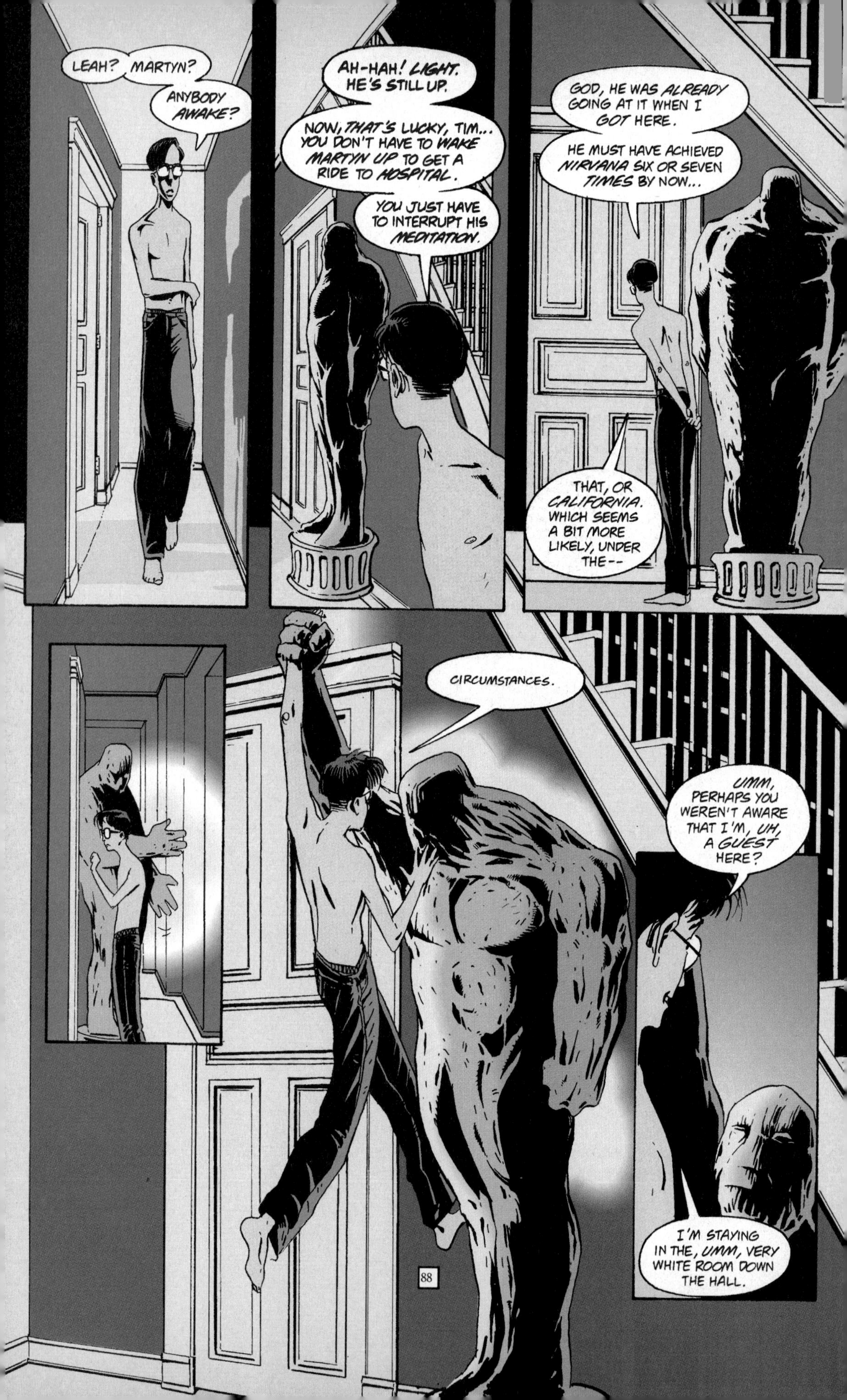
LEAH? MARTYN?
ANYBODY AWAKE?
AH-HAH! LIGHT. HE'S STILL UP.
NOW, THAT'S LUCKY, TIM... YOU DON'T HAVE TO WAKE MARTYN UP TO GET A RIDE TO HOSPITAL.
YOU JUST HAVE TO INTERRUPT HIS MEDITATION.
GOD, HE WAS ALREADY GOING AT IT WHEN I GOT HERE.
HE MUST HAVE ACHIEVED NIRVANA SIX OR SEVEN TIMES BY NOW...
THAT, OR CALIFORNIA. WHICH SEEMS A BIT MORE LIKELY, UNDER THE--
CIRCUMSTANCES.
UMM, PERHAPS YOU WEREN'T AWARE THAT I'M, UH, A GUEST HERE?
I'M STAYING IN THE, UMM, VERY WHITE ROOM DOWN THE HALL.

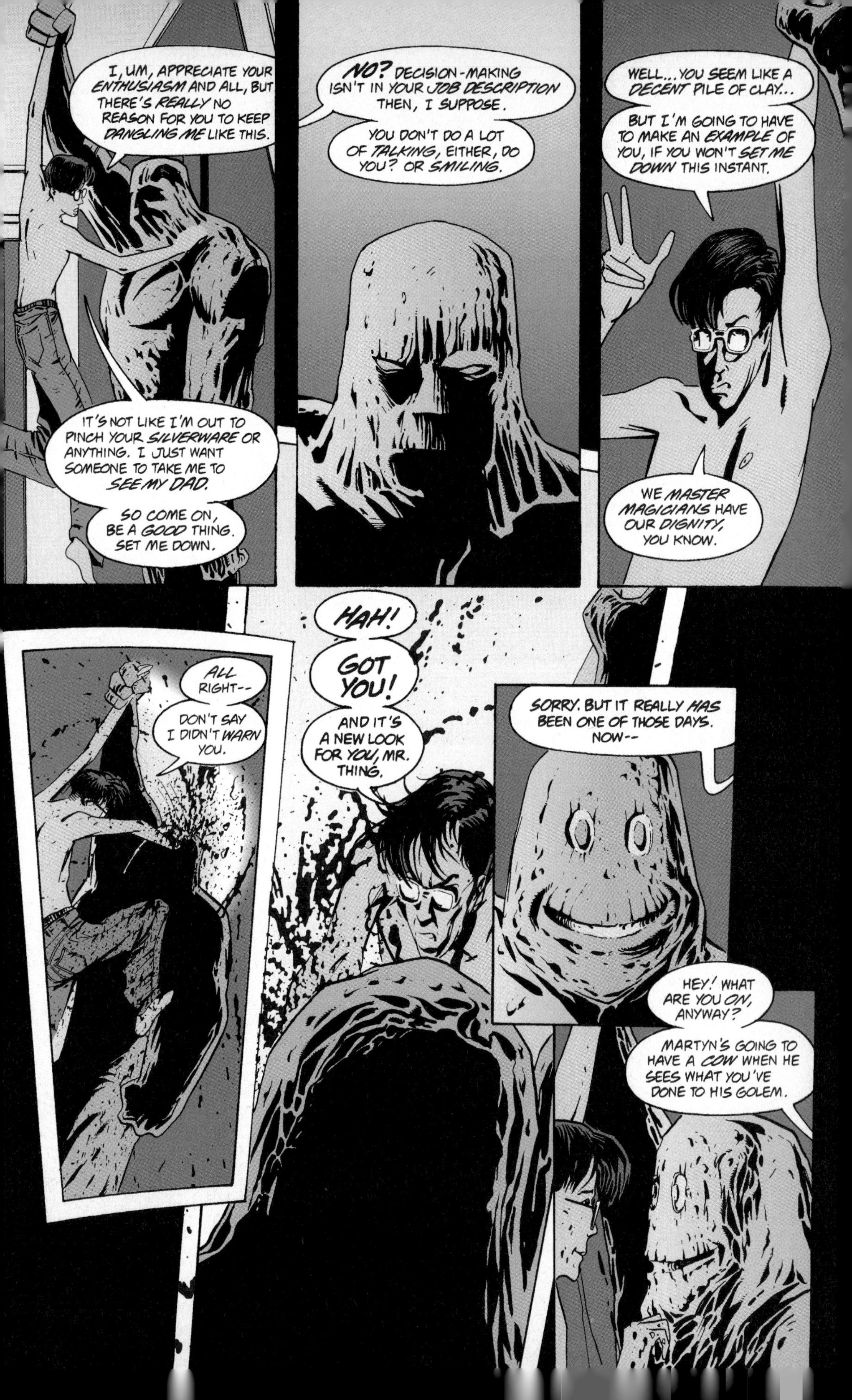
I, UM, APPRECIATE YOUR ENTHUSIASM AND ALL, BUT THERE'S REALLY NO REASON FOR YOU TO KEEP DANGLING ME LIKE THIS.
IT'S NOT LIKE I'M OUT TO PINCH YOUR SILVERWARE OR ANYTHING. I JUST WANT SOMEONE TO TAKE ME TO SEE MY DAD.
SO COME ON, BE A GOOD THING. SET ME DOWN.
NO? DECISION-MAKING ISN'T IN YOUR JOB DESCRIPTION THEN, I SUPPOSE.
YOU DON'T DO A LOT OF TALKING, EITHER, DO YOU? OR SMILING.
WELL... YOU SEEM LIKE A DECENT PILE OF CLAY...
BUT I'M GOING TO HAVE TO MAKE AN EXAMPLE OF YOU, IF YOU WON'T SET ME DOWN THIS INSTANT.
WE MASTER MAGICIANS HAVE OUR DIGNITY, YOU KNOW.
ALL RIGHT--
DON'T SAY I DIDN'T WARN YOU.
HAH!
GOT YOU!
AND IT'S A NEW LOOK FOR YOU, MR. THING.
SORRY. BUT IT REALLY HAS BEEN ONE OF THOSE DAYS. NOW--
HEY! WHAT ARE YOU ON, ANYWAY?
MARTYN'S GOING TO HAVE A COW WHEN HE SEES WHAT YOU'VE DONE TO HIS GOLEM.

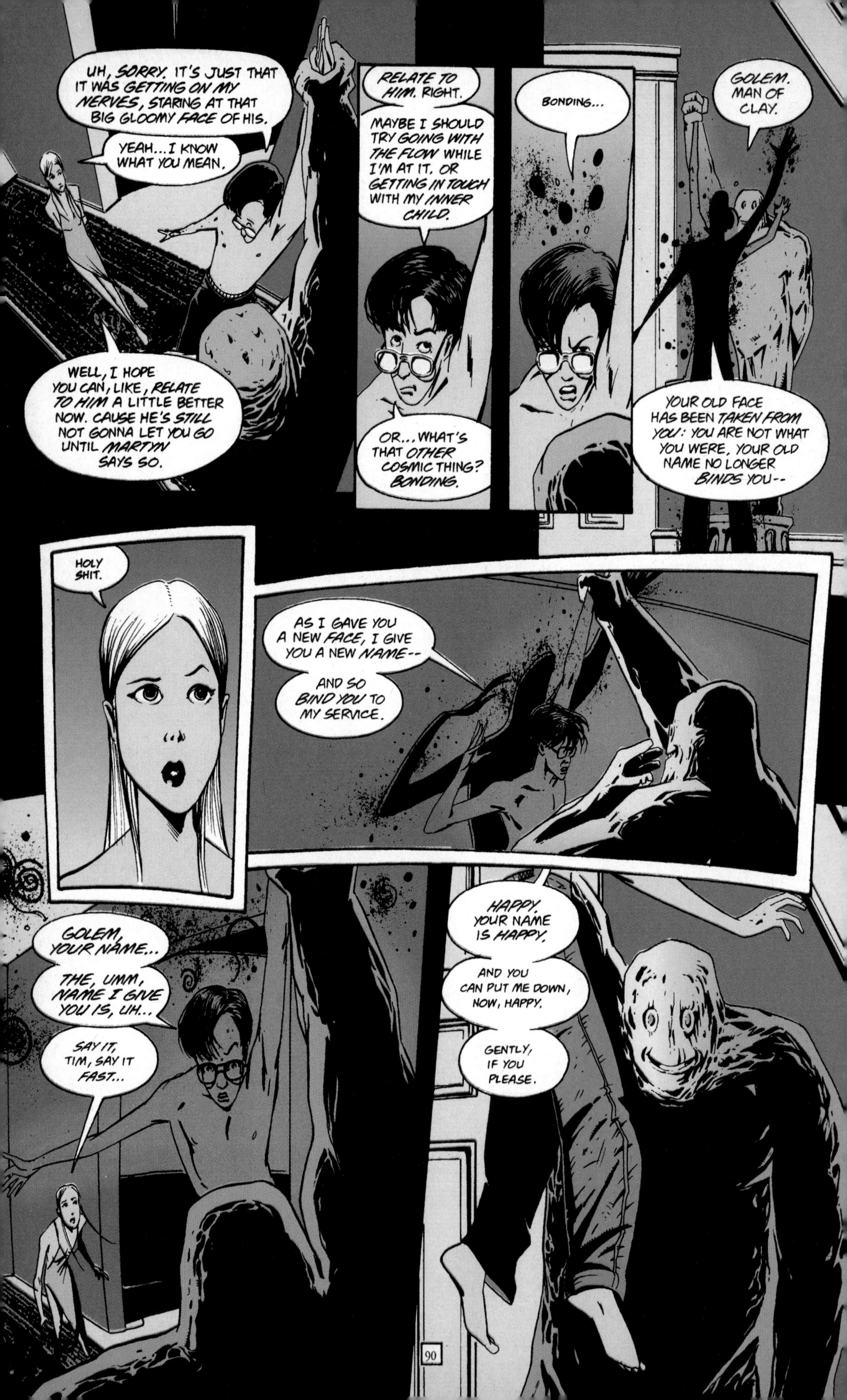
UH, SORRY. IT'S JUST THAT IT WAS GETTING ON MY NERVES, STARING AT THAT BIG GLOOMY FACE OF HIS.
YEAH... I KNOW WHAT YOU MEAN.
WELL, I HOPE YOU CAN, LIKE, RELATE TO HIM A LITTLE BETTER NOW. CAUSE HE'S STILL NOT GONNA LET YOU GO UNTIL MARTYN SAYS SO.
RELATE TO HIM. RIGHT.
MAYBE I SHOULD TRY GOING WITH THE FLOW WHILE I'M AT IT, OR GETTING IN TOUCH WITH MY INNER CHILD.
OR... WHAT'S THAT OTHER COSMIC THING? BONDING.
BONDING...
GOLEM. MAN OF CLAY.
YOUR OLD FACE HAS BEEN TAKEN FROM YOU: YOU ARE NOT WHAT YOU WERE, YOUR OLD NAME NO LONGER BINDS YOU--
HOLY SHIT.
AS I GAVE YOU A NEW FACE, I GIVE YOU A NEW NAME--
AND SO BIND YOU TO MY SERVICE.
GOLEM, YOUR NAME...
THE, UMM, NAME I GIVE YOU IS, UH...
SAY IT, TIM, SAY IT FAST...
HAPPY. YOUR NAME IS HAPPY.
AND YOU CAN PUT ME DOWN, NOW, HAPPY.
GENTLY, IF YOU PLEASE.

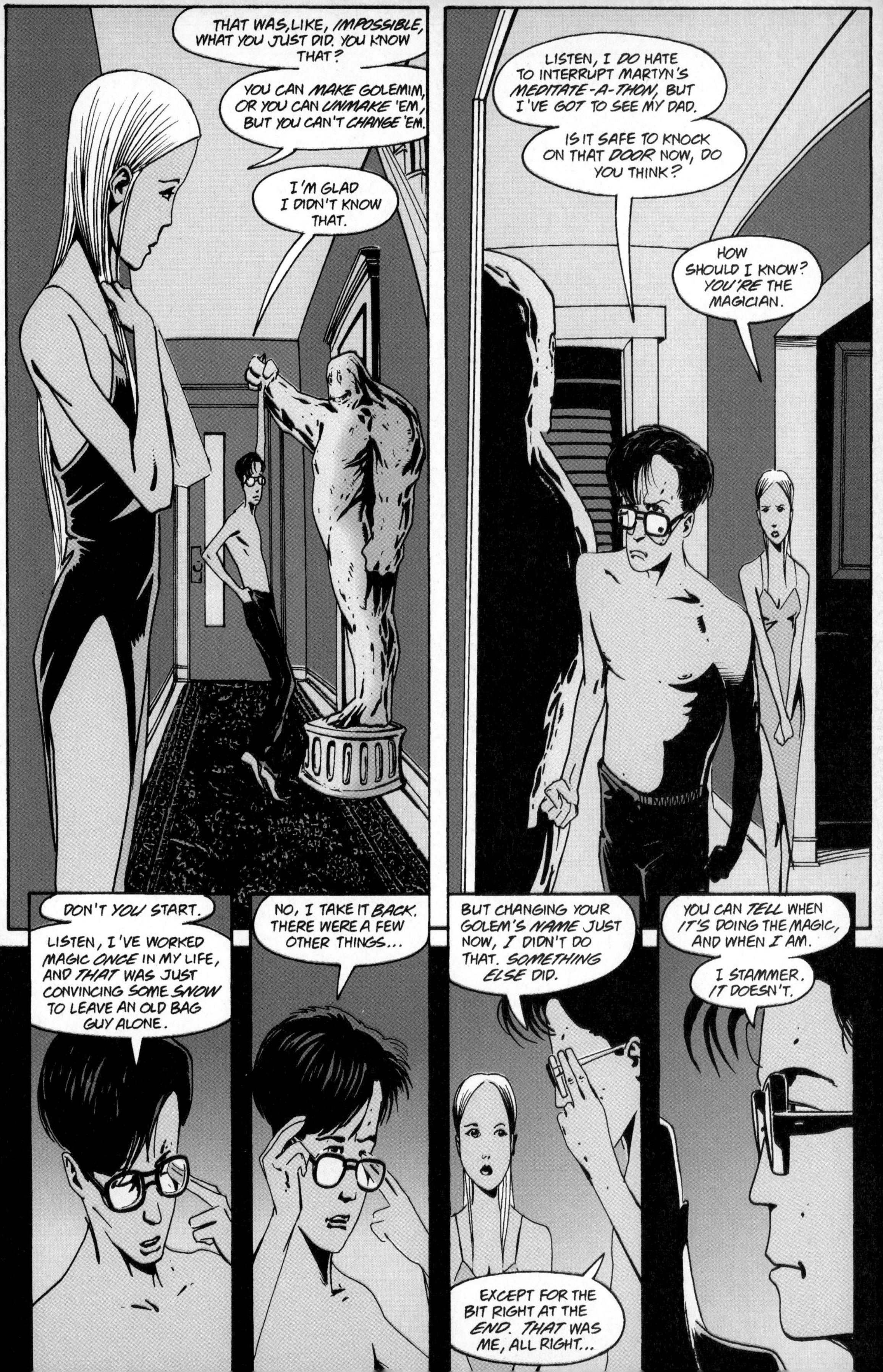

THAT WAS, LIKE, IMPOSSIBLE, WHAT YOU JUST DID. YOU KNOW THAT?
YOU CAN MAKE GOLEMIM, OR YOU CAN UNMAKE 'EM, BUT YOU CAN'T CHANGE 'EM.
I'M GLAD I DIDN'T KNOW THAT.
LISTEN, I DO HATE TO INTERRUPT MARTYN'S MEDITATE-A-THON, BUT I'VE GOT TO SEE MY DAD.
IS IT SAFE TO KNOCK ON THAT DOOR NOW, DO YOU THINK?
HOW SHOULD I KNOW? YOU'RE THE MAGICIAN.
DON'T YOU START.
LISTEN, I'VE WORKED MAGIC ONCE IN MY LIFE, AND THAT WAS JUST CONVINCING SOME SNOW TO LEAVE AN OLD BAG GUY ALONE.
NO, I TAKE IT BACK. THERE WERE A FEW OTHER THINGS...
BUT CHANGING YOUR GOLEM'S NAME JUST NOW, I DIDN'T DO THAT. SOMETHING ELSE DID.
EXCEPT FOR THE BIT RIGHT AT THE END. THAT WAS ME, ALL RIGHT...
YOU CAN TELL WHEN IT'S DOING THE MAGIC, AND WHEN I AM.
I STAMMER. IT DOESN'T.

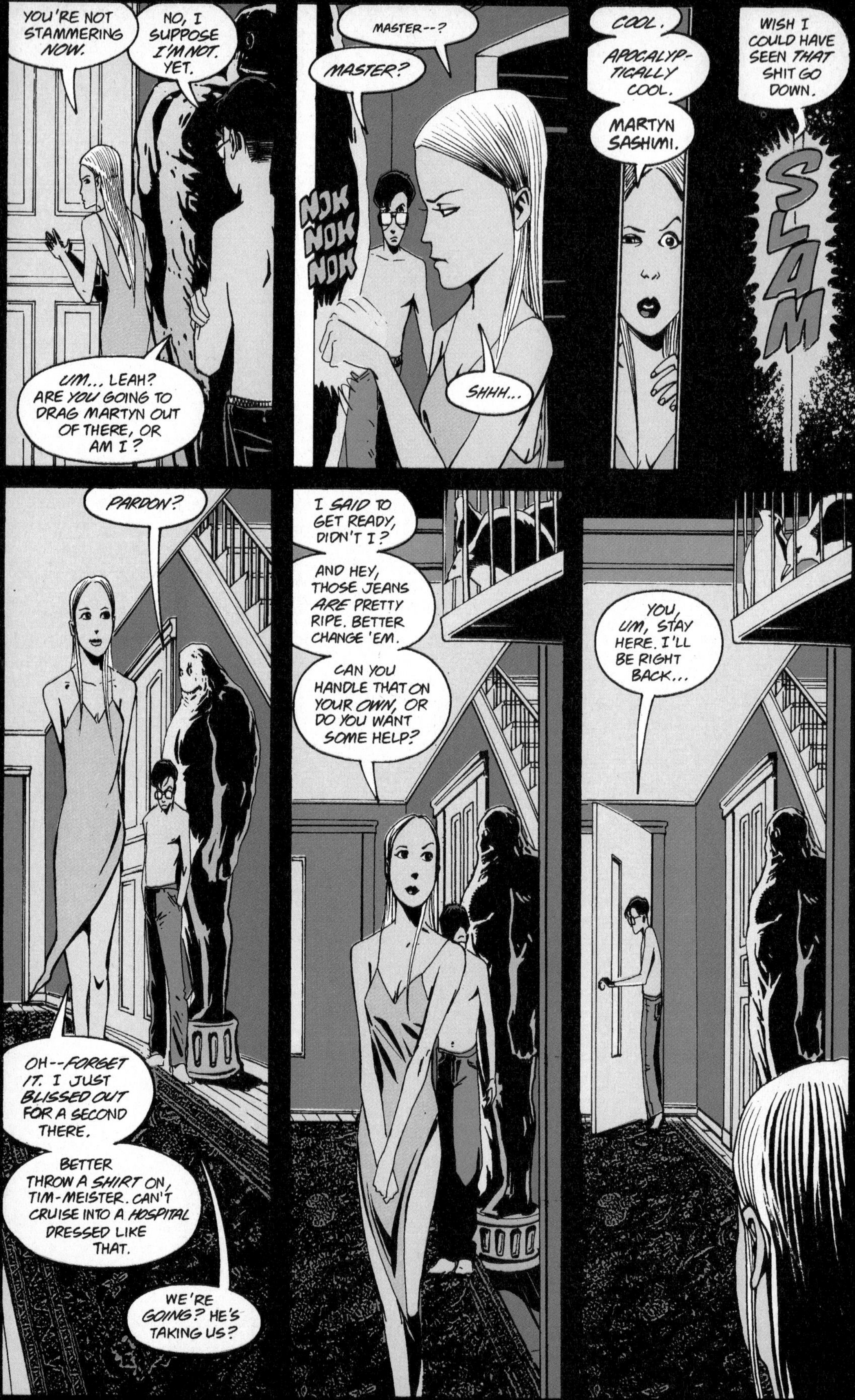
YOU'RE NOT STAMMERING NOW.
NO, I SUPPOSE I'M NOT. YET.
UM... LEAH? ARE YOU GOING TO DRAG MARTYN OUT OF THERE, OR AM I?
MASTER--?
MASTER?
NOK NOK NOK
SHHH...
COOL.
APOCALYPTICALLY COOL.
MARTYN SASHIMI.
WISH I COULD HAVE SEEN THAT SHIT GO DOWN.
SLAM
PARDON?
OH--FORGET IT. I JUST BLISSED OUT FOR A SECOND THERE.
BETTER THROW A SHIRT ON, TIM-MEISTER. CAN'T CRUISE INTO A HOSPITAL DRESSED LIKE THAT.
WE'RE GOING? HE'S TAKING US?
I SAID TO GET READY, DIDN'T I?
AND HEY, THOSE JEANS ARE PRETTY RIPE. BETTER CHANGE 'EM.
CAN YOU HANDLE THAT ON YOUR OWN, OR DO YOU WANT SOME HELP?
YOU, UM, STAY HERE. I'LL BE RIGHT BACK...

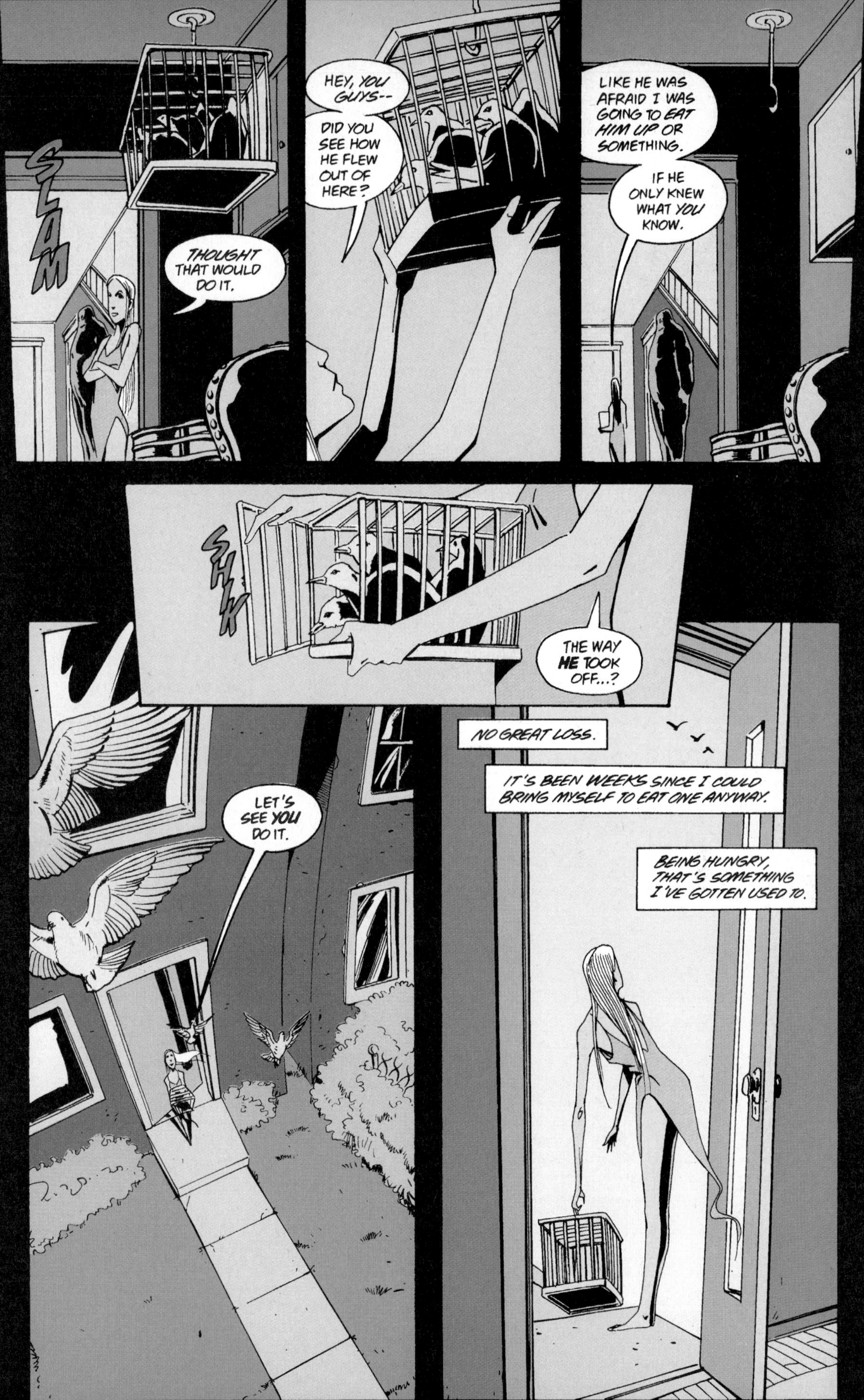
SLAM
THOUGHT THAT WOULD DO IT.
HEY, YOU GUYS--
DID YOU SEE HOW HE FLEW OUT OF HERE?
LIKE HE WAS AFRAID I WAS GOING TO EAT HIM UP OR SOMETHING.
IF HE ONLY KNEW WHAT YOU KNOW.
SHKK
THE WAY HE TOOK OFF...?
LET'S SEE YOU DO IT.
NO GREAT LOSS.
IT'S BEEN WEEKS SINCE I COULD BRING MYSELF TO EAT ONE ANYWAY.
BEING HUNGRY, THAT'S SOMETHING I'VE GOTTEN USED TO.

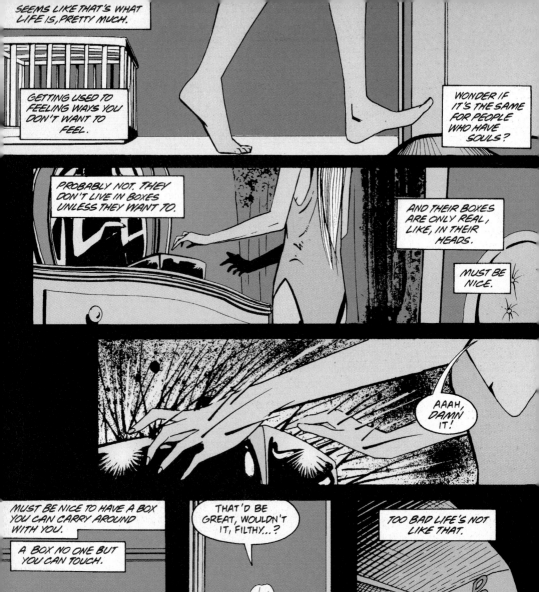

SEEMS LIKE THAT'S WHAT LIFE IS, PRETTY MUCH.

GETTING USED TO FEELING WAYS YOU DON'T WANT TO FEEL.

WONDER IF IT'S THE SAME FOR PEOPLE WHO HAVE SOULS?

PROBABLY NOT. THEY DON'T LIVE IN BOXES UNLESS THEY WANT TO.

AND THEIR BOXES ARE ONLY REAL, LIKE, IN THEIR HEADS.

MUST BE NICE.

AAAH, DAMN IT!

MUST BE NICE TO HAVE A BOX YOU CAN CARRY AROUND WITH YOU.

A BOX NO ONE BUT YOU CAN TOUCH.

THAT'D BE GREAT, WOULDN'T IT, FILTHY...?

TOO BAD LIFE'S NOT LIKE THAT.

A BOX YOU CAN GET OUT OF ANYTIME YOU WANT TO.

PRROW?

PRRT?

NOT FOR US.

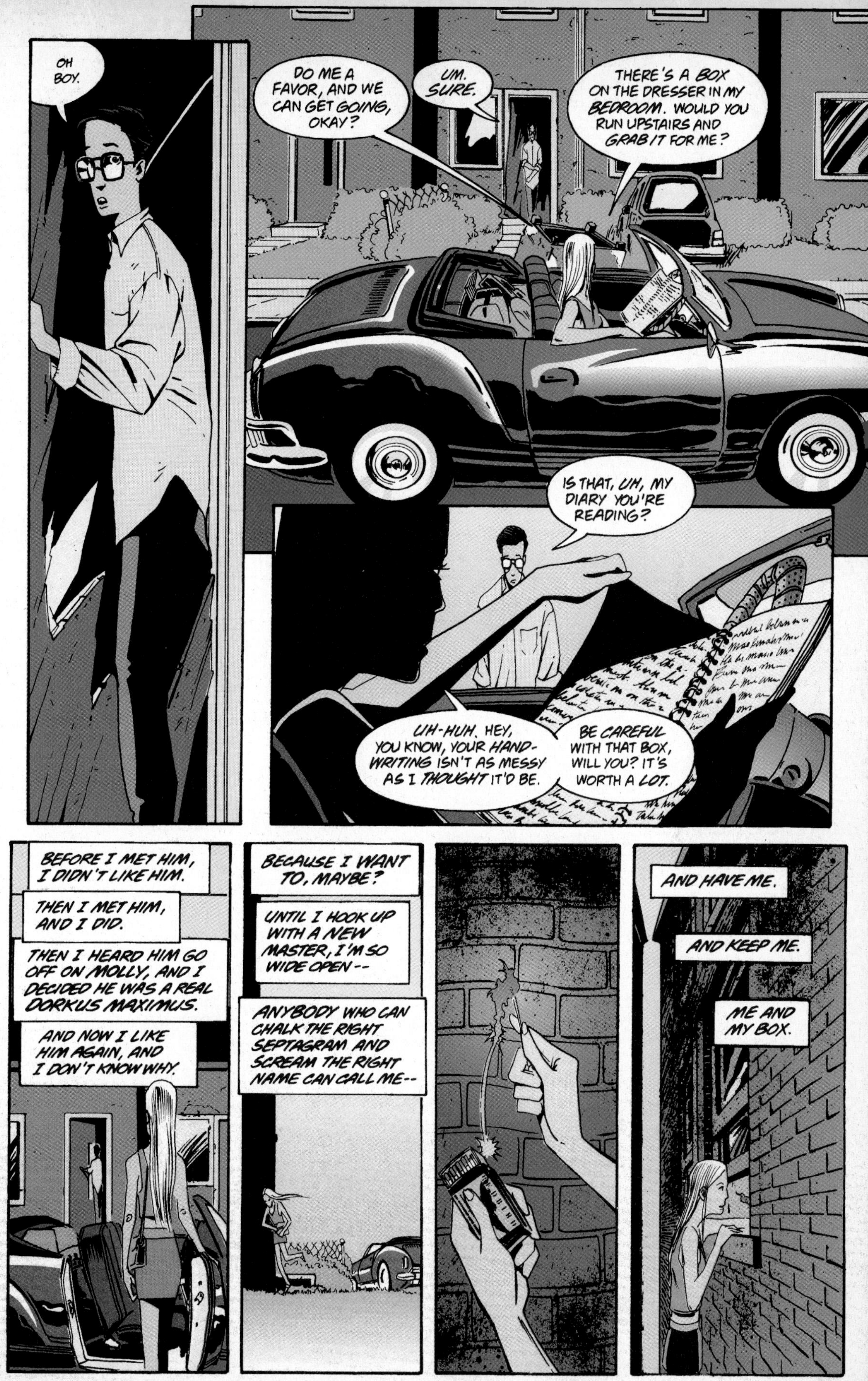

OH BOY.
DO ME A FAVOR, AND WE CAN GET GOING, OKAY?
UM. SURE.
THERE'S A BOX ON THE DRESSER IN MY BEDROOM. WOULD YOU RUN UPSTAIRS AND GRAB IT FOR ME?
IS THAT, UH, MY DIARY YOU'RE READING?
UH-HUH. HEY, YOU KNOW, YOUR HAND-WRITING ISN'T AS MESSY AS I THOUGHT IT'D BE.
BE CAREFUL WITH THAT BOX, WILL YOU? IT'S WORTH A LOT.
BEFORE I MET HIM, I DIDN'T LIKE HIM.
THEN I MET HIM, AND I DID.
THEN I HEARD HIM GO OFF ON MOLLY, AND I DECIDED HE WAS A REAL DORKUS MAXIMUS.
AND NOW I LIKE HIM AGAIN, AND I DON'T KNOW WHY.
BECAUSE I WANT TO, MAYBE?
UNTIL I HOOK UP WITH A NEW MASTER, I'M SO WIDE OPEN --
ANYBODY WHO CAN CHALK THE RIGHT SEPTAGRAM AND SCREAM THE RIGHT NAME CAN CALL ME--
AND HAVE ME.
AND KEEP ME.
ME AND MY BOX.

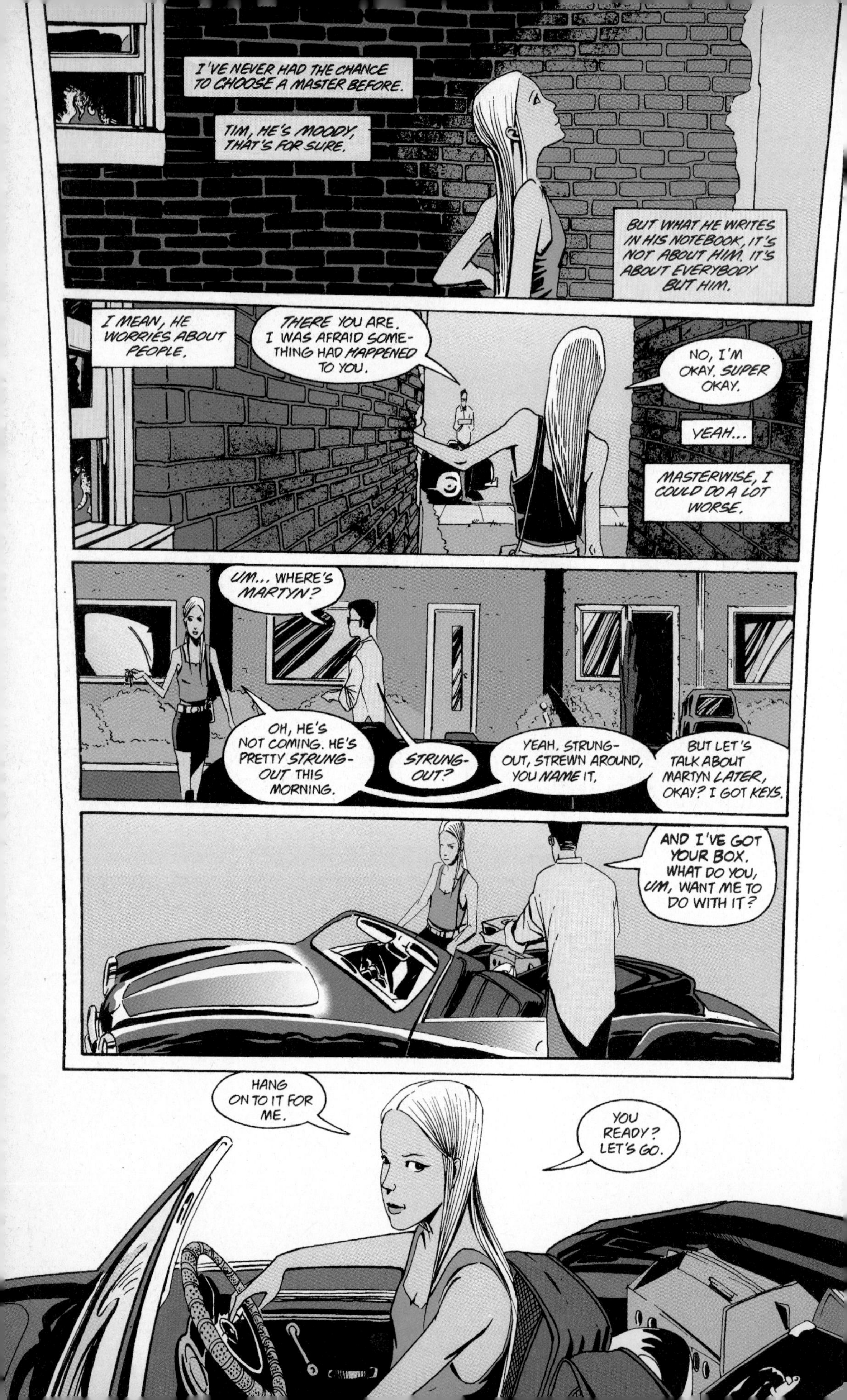
I'VE NEVER HAD THE CHANCE TO CHOOSE A MASTER BEFORE.
TIM, HE'S MOODY, THAT'S FOR SURE.
BUT WHAT HE WRITES IN HIS NOTEBOOK, IT'S NOT ABOUT HIM. IT'S ABOUT EVERYBODY BUT HIM.
I MEAN, HE WORRIES ABOUT PEOPLE.
THERE YOU ARE. I WAS AFRAID SOMETHING HAD HAPPENED TO YOU.
NO, I'M OKAY. SUPER OKAY.
YEAH...
MASTERWISE, I COULD DO A LOT WORSE.
UM... WHERE'S MARTYN?
OH, HE'S NOT COMING. HE'S PRETTY STRUNG-OUT THIS MORNING.
STRUNG-OUT?
YEAH. STRUNG-OUT, STREWN AROUND, YOU NAME IT.
BUT LET'S TALK ABOUT MARTYN LATER, OKAY? I GOT KEYS.
AND I'VE GOT YOUR BOX. WHAT DO YOU, UM, WANT ME TO DO WITH IT?
HANG ON TO IT FOR ME.
YOU READY? LET'S GO.

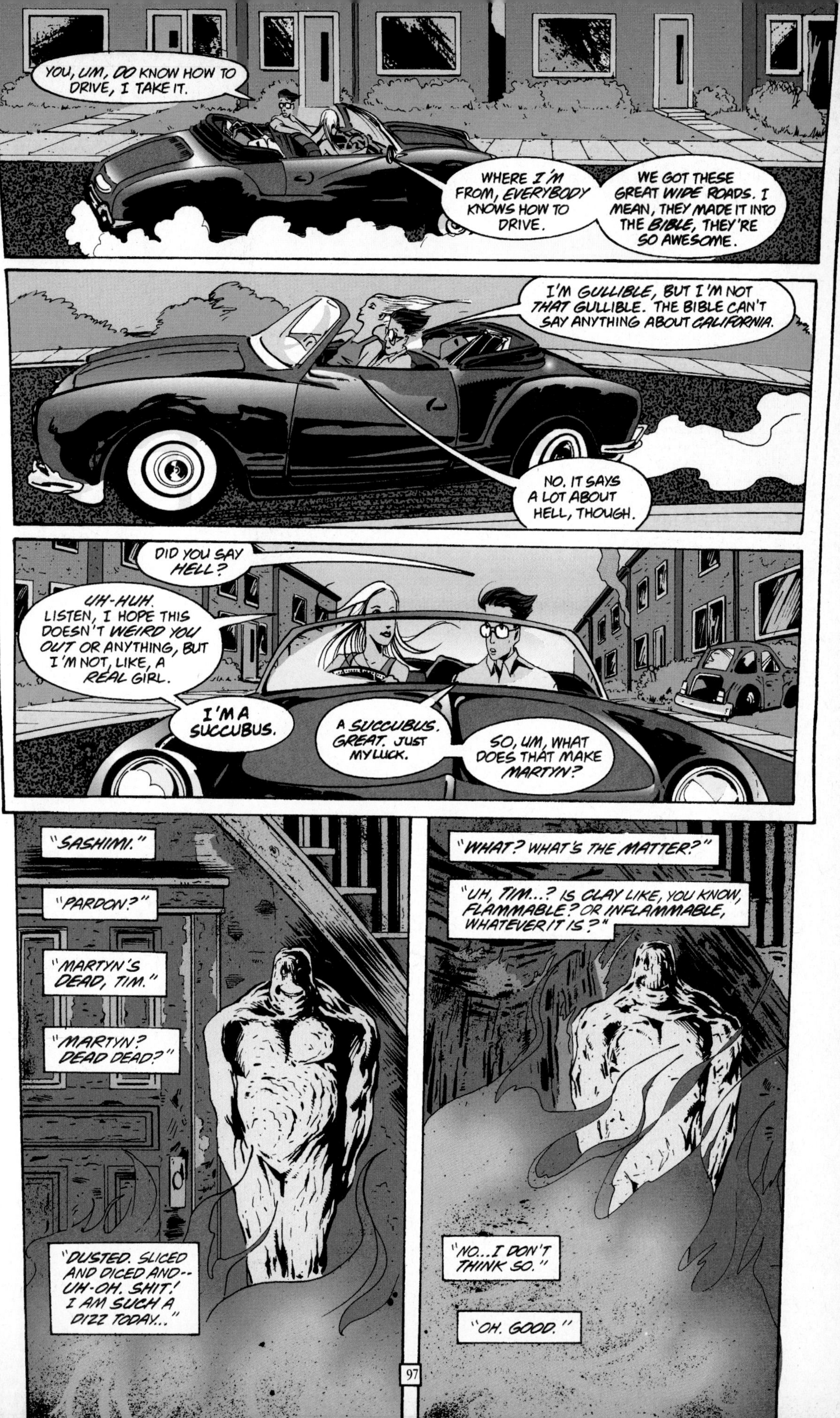

YOU, UM, DO KNOW HOW TO DRIVE, I TAKE IT.
WHERE I'M FROM, EVERYBODY KNOWS HOW TO DRIVE.
WE GOT THESE GREAT WIDE ROADS. I MEAN, THEY MADE IT INTO THE BIBLE, THEY'RE SO AWESOME.
I'M GULLIBLE, BUT I'M NOT THAT GULLIBLE. THE BIBLE CAN'T SAY ANYTHING ABOUT CALIFORNIA.
NO. IT SAYS A LOT ABOUT HELL, THOUGH.
DID YOU SAY HELL?
UH-HUH. LISTEN, I HOPE THIS DOESN'T WEIRD YOU OUT OR ANYTHING, BUT I'M NOT, LIKE, A REAL GIRL.
I'M A SUCCUBUS.
A SUCCUBUS. GREAT. JUST MY LUCK.
SO, UM, WHAT DOES THAT MAKE MARTYN?
"SASHIMI."
"PARDON?"
"MARTYN'S DEAD, TIM."
"MARTYN? DEAD DEAD?"
"DUSTED. SLICED AND DICED AND-- UH-OH. SHIT! I AM SUCH A DIZZ TODAY..."
"WHAT? WHAT'S THE MATTER?"
"UH, TIM...? IS CLAY LIKE, YOU KNOW, FLAMMABLE? OR INFLAMMABLE, WHATEVER IT IS?"
"NO...I DON'T THINK SO."
"OH. GOOD."

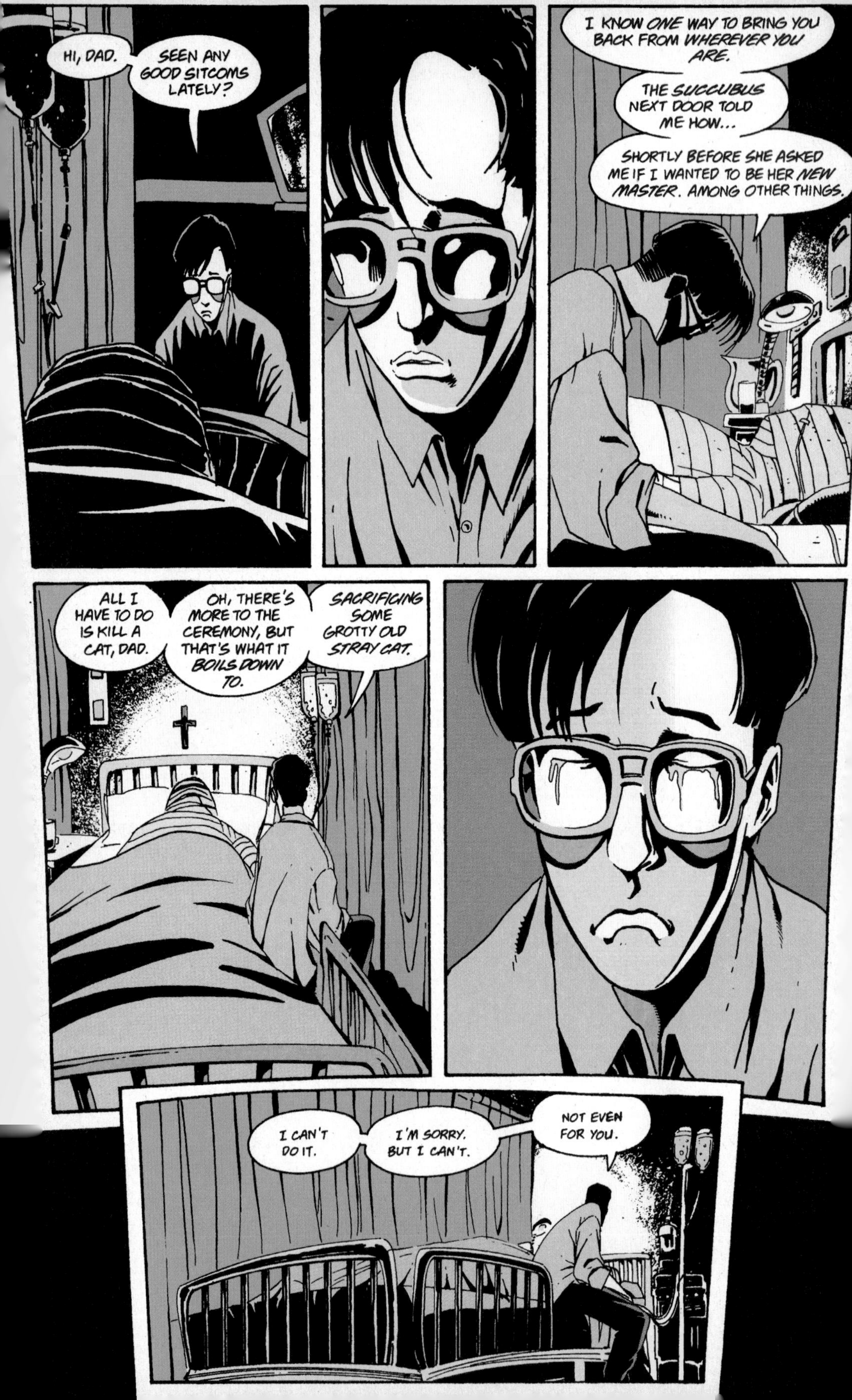
HI, DAD.
SEEN ANY GOOD SITCOMS LATELY?
I KNOW ONE WAY TO BRING YOU BACK FROM WHEREVER YOU ARE.
THE SUCCUBUS NEXT DOOR TOLD ME HOW...
SHORTLY BEFORE SHE ASKED ME IF I WANTED TO BE HER NEW MASTER. AMONG OTHER THINGS.
ALL I HAVE TO DO IS KILL A CAT, DAD.
OH, THERE'S MORE TO THE CEREMONY, BUT THAT'S WHAT IT BOILS DOWN TO.
SACRIFICING SOME GROTTY OLD STRAY CAT.
I CAN'T DO IT.
I'M SORRY. BUT I CAN'T.
NOT EVEN FOR YOU.

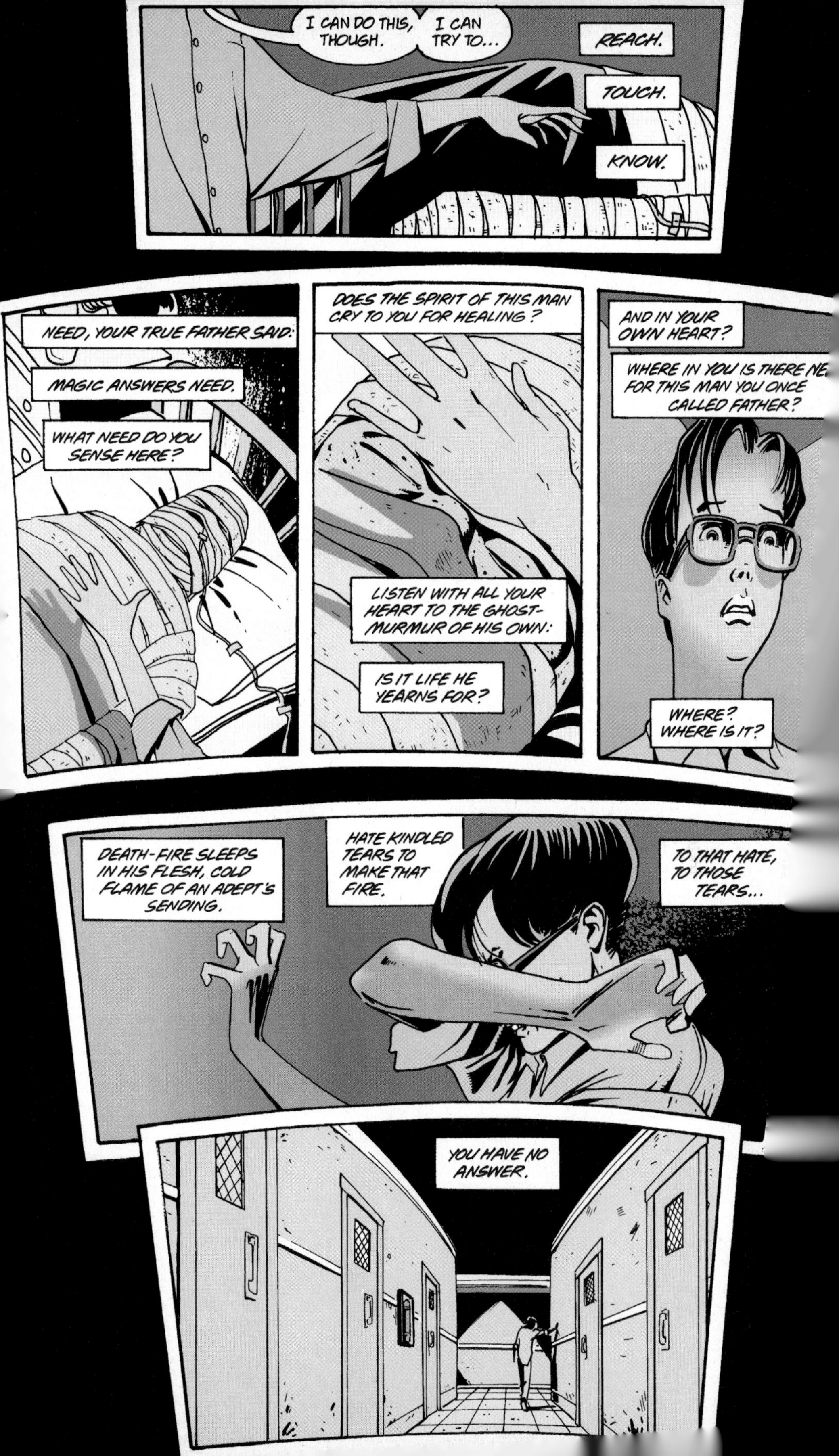
I CAN DO THIS, THOUGH.
I CAN TRY TO...
REACH.
TOUCH.
KNOW.
NEED, YOUR TRUE FATHER SAID:
MAGIC ANSWERS NEED.
WHAT NEED DO YOU SENSE HERE?
DOES THE SPIRIT OF THIS MAN CRY TO YOU FOR HEALING?
LISTEN WITH ALL YOUR HEART TO THE GHOST-MURMUR OF HIS OWN:
IS IT LIFE HE YEARNS FOR?
AND IN YOUR OWN HEART?
WHERE IN YOU IS THERE NE
FOR THIS MAN YOU ONCE CALLED FATHER?
WHERE? WHERE IS IT?
DEATH-FIRE SLEEPS IN HIS FLESH, COLD FLAME OF AN ADEPT'S SENDING.
HATE KINDLED TEARS TO MAKE THAT FIRE.
TO THAT HATE, TO THOSE TEARS...
YOU HAVE NO ANSWER.

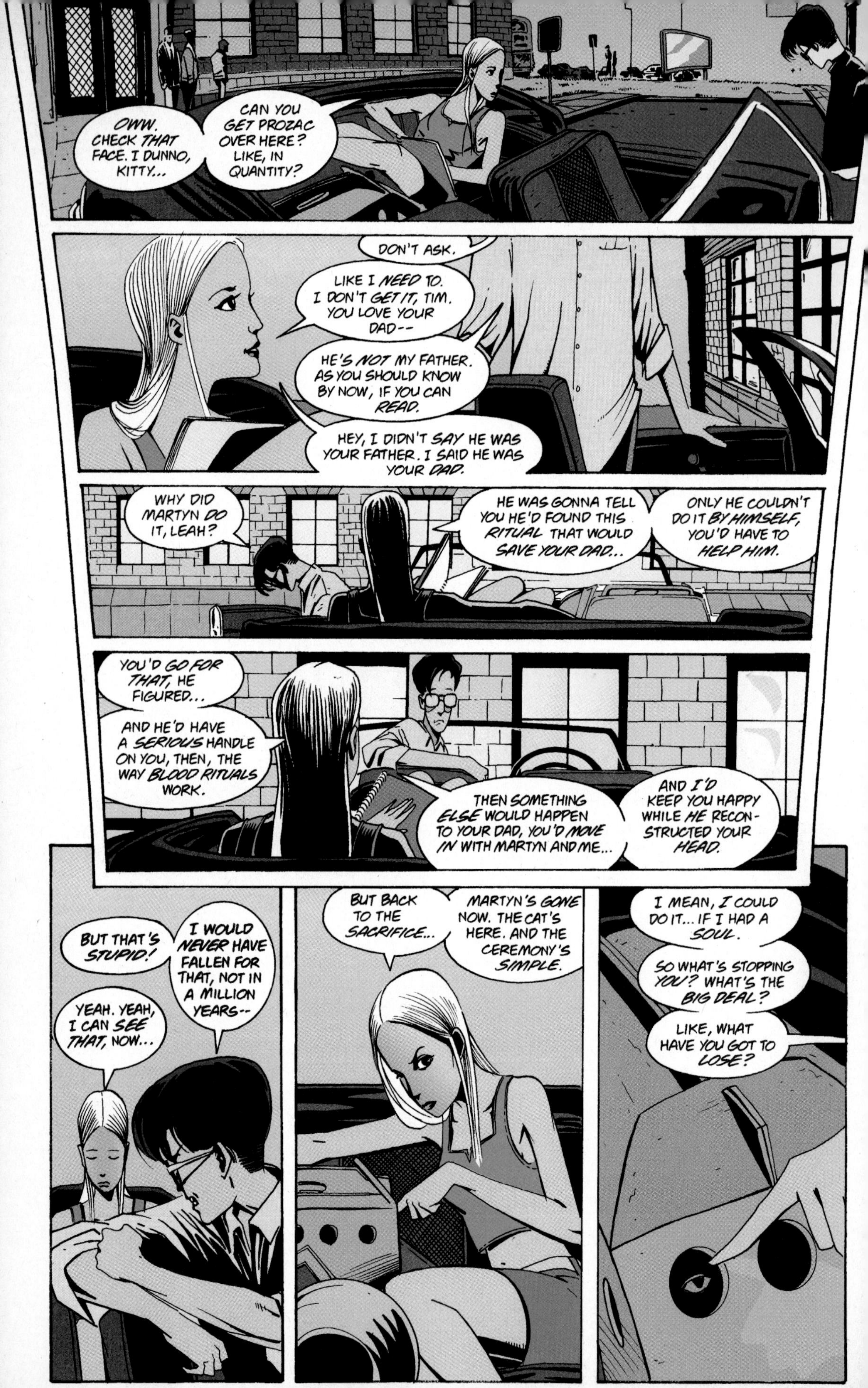
OWW. CHECK THAT FACE. I DUNNO, KITTY...
CAN YOU GET PROZAC OVER HERE? LIKE, IN QUANTITY?
DON'T ASK.
LIKE I NEED TO. I DON'T GET IT, TIM. YOU LOVE YOUR DAD--
HE'S NOT MY FATHER. AS YOU SHOULD KNOW BY NOW, IF YOU CAN READ.
HEY, I DIDN'T SAY HE WAS YOUR FATHER. I SAID HE WAS YOUR DAD.
WHY DID MARTYN DO IT, LEAH?
HE WAS GONNA TELL YOU HE'D FOUND THIS RITUAL THAT WOULD SAVE YOUR DAD...
ONLY HE COULDN'T DO IT BY HIMSELF, YOU'D HAVE TO HELP HIM.
YOU'D GO FOR THAT, HE FIGURED...
AND HE'D HAVE A SERIOUS HANDLE ON YOU, THEN, THE WAY BLOOD RITUALS WORK.
THEN SOMETHING ELSE WOULD HAPPEN TO YOUR DAD, YOU'D MOVE IN WITH MARTYN AND ME...
AND I'D KEEP YOU HAPPY WHILE HE RECON-STRUCTED YOUR HEAD.
BUT THAT'S STUPID!
I WOULD NEVER HAVE FALLEN FOR THAT, NOT IN A MILLION YEARS--
YEAH. YEAH, I CAN SEE THAT, NOW...
BUT BACK TO THE SACRIFICE...
MARTYN'S GONE NOW. THE CAT'S HERE. AND THE CEREMONY'S SIMPLE.
I MEAN, I COULD DO IT... IF I HAD A SOUL.
SO WHAT'S STOPPING YOU? WHAT'S THE BIG DEAL?
LIKE, WHAT HAVE YOU GOT TO LOSE?

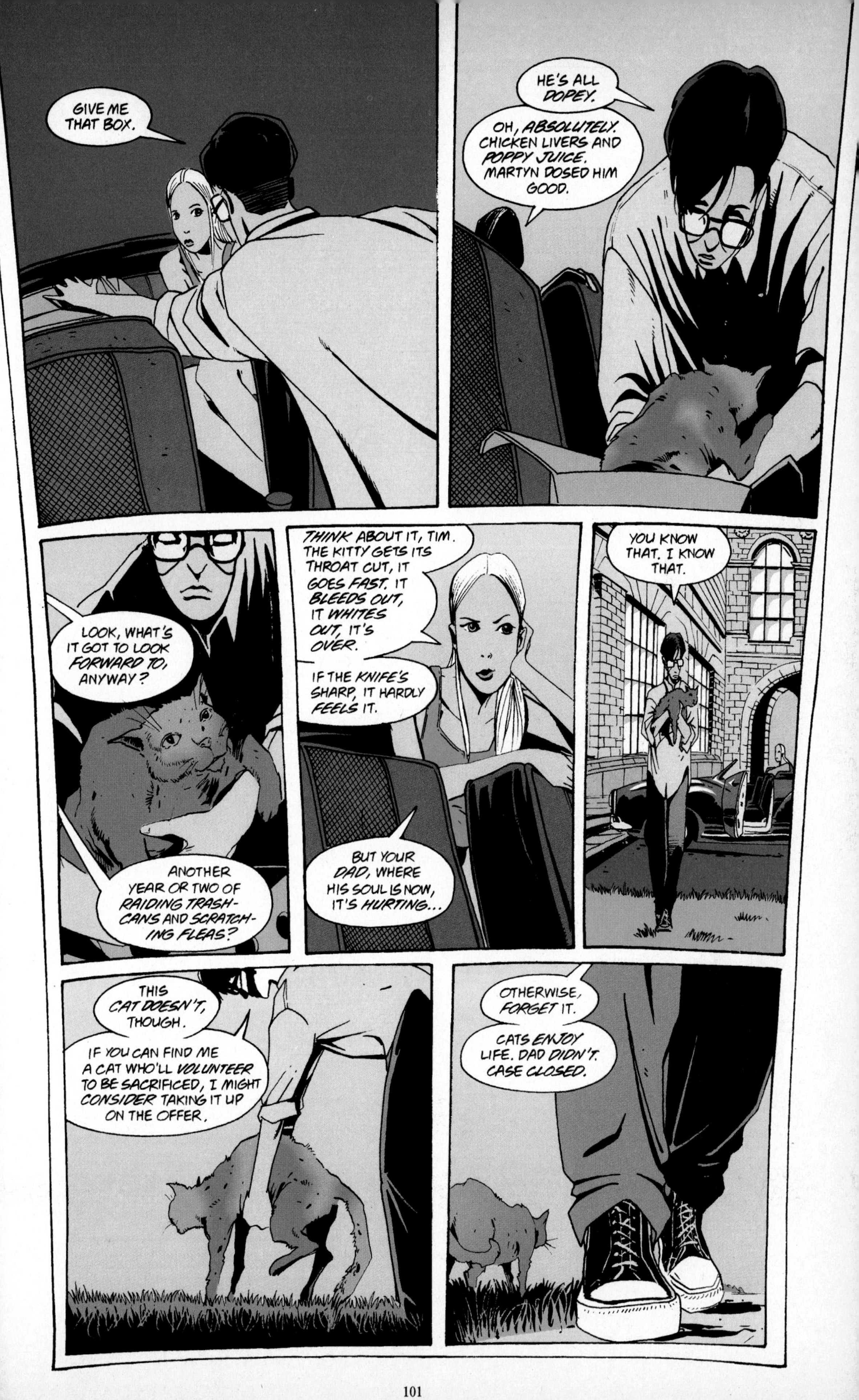
GIVE ME THAT BOX.
HE'S ALL DOPEY.
OH, ABSOLUTELY. CHICKEN LIVERS AND POPPY JUICE. MARTYN DOSED HIM GOOD.
LOOK, WHAT'S IT GOT TO LOOK FORWARD TO, ANYWAY?
ANOTHER YEAR OR TWO OF RAIDING TRASH-CANS AND SCRATCHING FLEAS?
THINK ABOUT IT, TIM. THE KITTY GETS ITS THROAT CUT, IT GOES FAST. IT BLEEDS OUT, IT WHITES OUT, IT'S OVER.
IF THE KNIFE'S SHARP, IT HARDLY FEELS IT.
BUT YOUR DAD, WHERE HIS SOUL IS NOW, IT'S HURTING...
YOU KNOW THAT. I KNOW THAT.
THIS CAT DOESN'T, THOUGH.
IF YOU CAN FIND ME A CAT WHO'LL VOLUNTEER TO BE SACRIFICED, I MIGHT CONSIDER TAKING IT UP ON THE OFFER.
OTHERWISE, FORGET IT.
CATS ENJOY LIFE. DAD DIDN'T. CASE CLOSED.

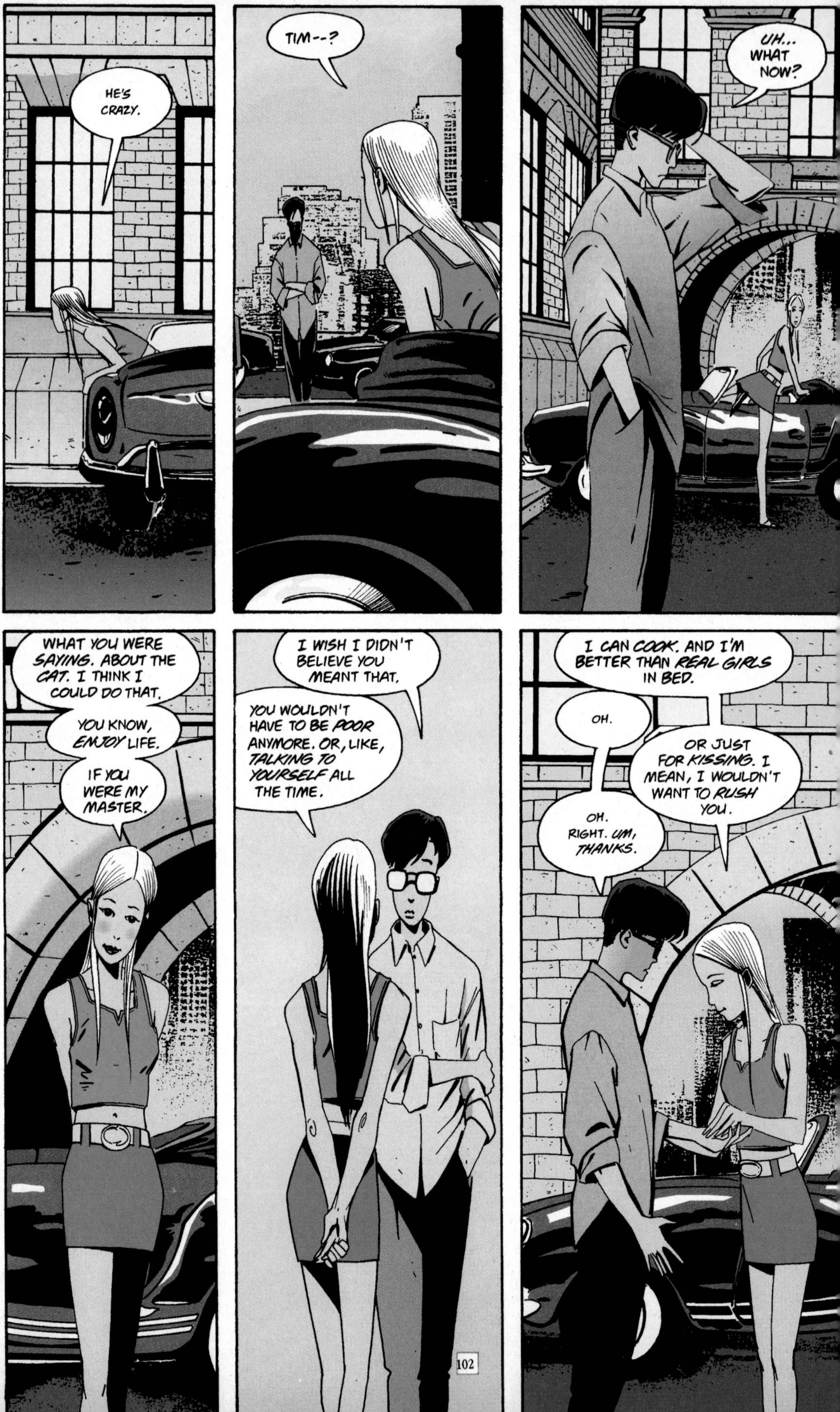
HE'S CRAZY.
TIM--?
UH... WHAT NOW?
WHAT YOU WERE SAYING. ABOUT THE CAT. I THINK I COULD DO THAT.
YOU KNOW, ENJOY LIFE.
IF YOU WERE MY MASTER.
I WISH I DIDN'T BELIEVE YOU MEANT THAT.
YOU WOULDN'T HAVE TO BE POOR ANYMORE. OR, LIKE, TALKING TO YOURSELF ALL THE TIME.
I CAN COOK. AND I'M BETTER THAN REAL GIRLS IN BED.
OH.
OR JUST FOR KISSING. I MEAN, I WOULDN'T WANT TO RUSH YOU.
OH. RIGHT. UM, THANKS.

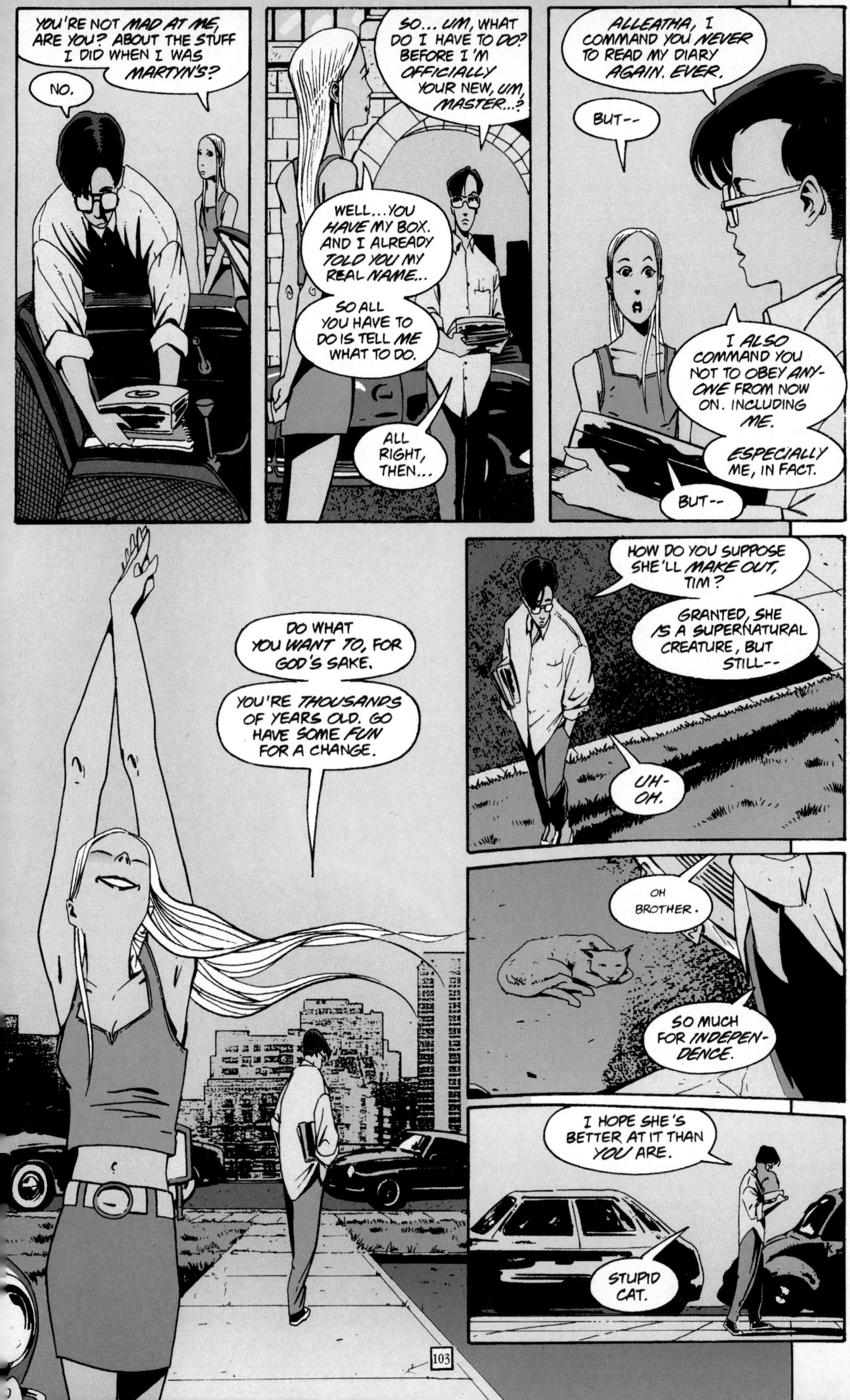
YOU'RE NOT MAD AT ME, ARE YOU? ABOUT THE STUFF I DID WHEN I WAS MARTYN'S?
NO.
SO... UM, WHAT DO I HAVE TO DO? BEFORE I'M OFFICIALLY YOUR NEW, UM, MASTER...?
WELL... YOU HAVE MY BOX. AND I ALREADY TOLD YOU MY REAL NAME...
SO ALL YOU HAVE TO DO IS TELL ME WHAT TO DO.
ALL RIGHT, THEN...
ALLEATHA, I COMMAND YOU NEVER TO READ MY DIARY AGAIN. EVER.
BUT--
I ALSO COMMAND YOU NOT TO OBEY ANY-ONE FROM NOW ON. INCLUDING ME.
ESPECIALLY ME, IN FACT.
BUT--
DO WHAT YOU WANT TO, FOR GOD'S SAKE.
YOU'RE THOUSANDS OF YEARS OLD. GO HAVE SOME FUN FOR A CHANGE.
HOW DO YOU SUPPOSE SHE'LL MAKE OUT, TIM?
GRANTED, SHE IS A SUPERNATURAL CREATURE, BUT STILL--
UH-OH.
OH BROTHER.
SO MUCH FOR INDEPEN-DENCE.
I HOPE SHE'S BETTER AT IT THAN YOU ARE.
STUPID CAT.

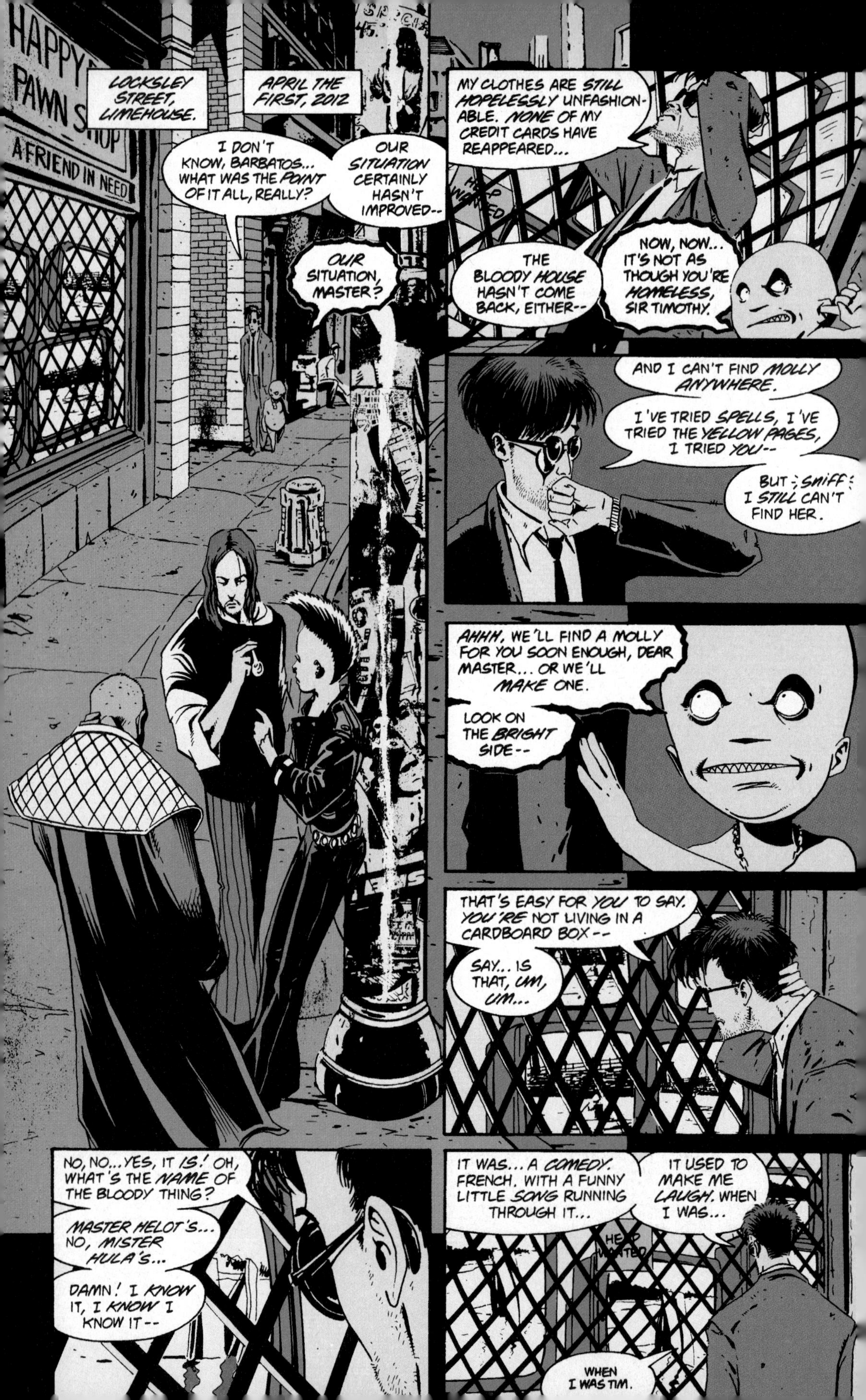
HAPPY PAWN SHOP
A FRIEND IN NEED
LOCKSLEY STREET, LIMEHOUSE.
APRIL THE FIRST, 2012
I DON'T KNOW, BARBATOS... WHAT WAS THE POINT OF IT ALL, REALLY?
OUR SITUATION CERTAINLY HASN'T IMPROVED--
OUR SITUATION, MASTER?
MY CLOTHES ARE STILL HOPELESSLY UNFASHIONABLE. NONE OF MY CREDIT CARDS HAVE REAPPEARED...
THE BLOODY HOUSE HASN'T COME BACK, EITHER--
NOW, NOW... IT'S NOT AS THOUGH YOU'RE HOMELESS, SIR TIMOTHY.
AND I CAN'T FIND MOLLY ANYWHERE.
I'VE TRIED SPELLS, I'VE TRIED THE YELLOW PAGES, I TRIED YOU--
BUT -SNIFF- I STILL CAN'T FIND HER.
AHHH. WE'LL FIND A MOLLY FOR YOU SOON ENOUGH, DEAR MASTER... OR WE'LL MAKE ONE.
LOOK ON THE BRIGHT SIDE--
THAT'S EASY FOR YOU TO SAY. YOU'RE NOT LIVING IN A CARDBOARD BOX--
SAY... IS THAT, UM, UM...
NO, NO... YES, IT IS! OH, WHAT'S THE NAME OF THE BLOODY THING?
MASTER HELOT'S... NO, MISTER HULA'S...
DAMN! I KNOW IT, I KNOW I KNOW IT--
IT WAS... A COMEDY. FRENCH. WITH A FUNNY LITTLE SONG RUNNING THROUGH IT...
IT USED TO MAKE ME LAUGH. WHEN I WAS...
HELP WANTED
WHEN I WAS TIM.

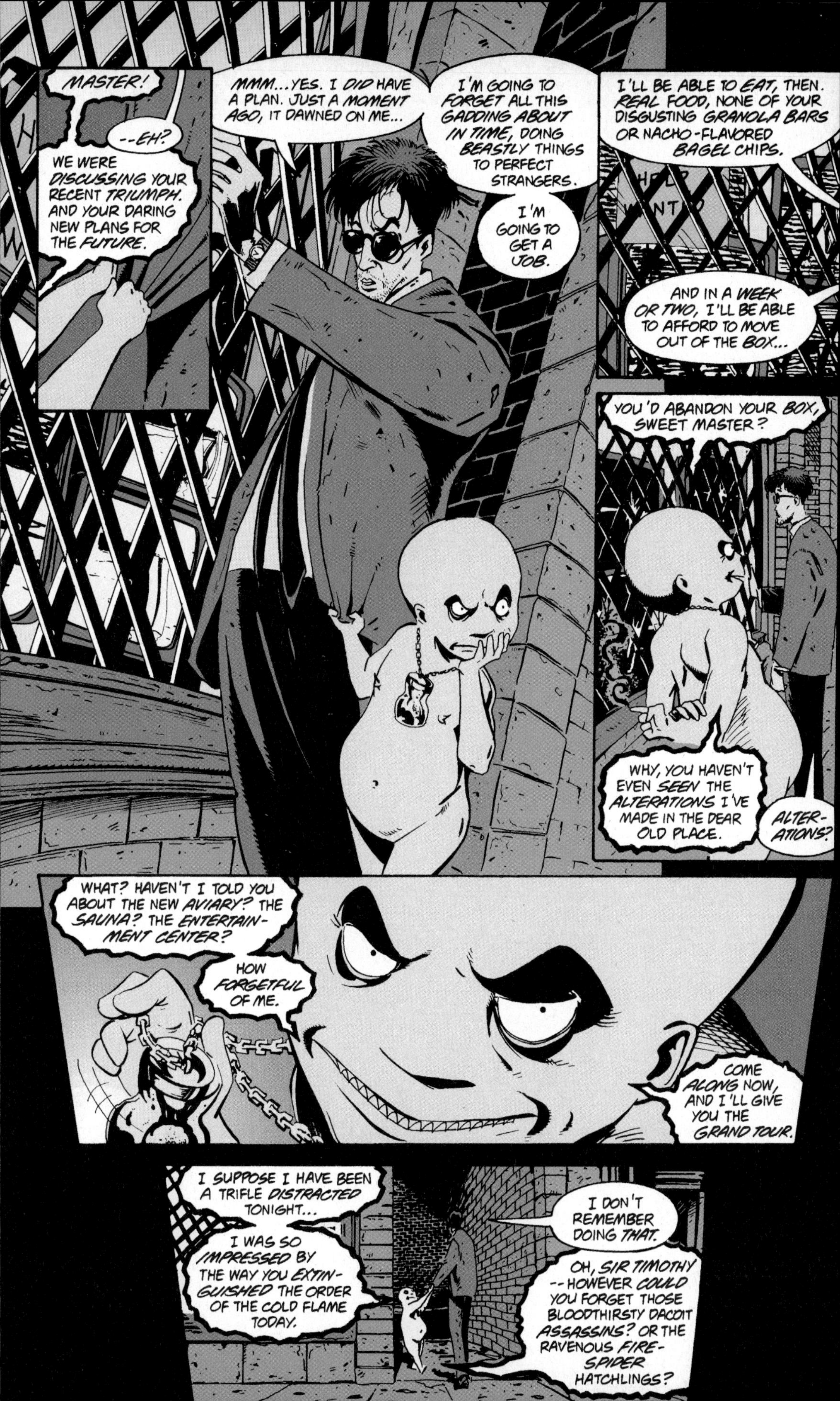

MASTER!
--EH?
WE WERE DISCUSSING YOUR RECENT TRIUMPH. AND YOUR DARING NEW PLANS FOR THE FUTURE.
MMM...YES. I DID HAVE A PLAN. JUST A MOMENT AGO, IT DAWNED ON ME...
I'M GOING TO FORGET ALL THIS GADDING ABOUT IN TIME, DOING BEASTLY THINGS TO PERFECT STRANGERS.
I'M GOING TO GET A JOB.
I'LL BE ABLE TO EAT, THEN. REAL FOOD, NONE OF YOUR DISGUSTING GRANOLA BARS OR NACHO-FLAVORED BAGEL CHIPS.
AND IN A WEEK OR TWO, I'LL BE ABLE TO AFFORD TO MOVE OUT OF THE BOX...
YOU'D ABANDON YOUR BOX, SWEET MASTER?
WHY, YOU HAVEN'T EVEN SEEN THE ALTERATIONS I'VE MADE IN THE DEAR OLD PLACE.
ALTER-ATIONS?
WHAT? HAVEN'T I TOLD YOU ABOUT THE NEW AVIARY? THE SAUNA? THE ENTERTAIN-MENT CENTER?
HOW FORGETFUL OF ME.
COME ALONG NOW, AND I'LL GIVE YOU THE GRAND TOUR.
I SUPPOSE I HAVE BEEN A TRIFLE DISTRACTED TONIGHT...
I WAS SO IMPRESSED BY THE WAY YOU EXTIN-GUISHED THE ORDER OF THE COLD FLAME TODAY.
I DON'T REMEMBER DOING THAT.
OH, SIR TIMOTHY --HOWEVER COULD YOU FORGET THOSE BLOODTHIRSTY DACOIT ASSASSINS? OR THE RAVENOUS FIRE-SPIDER HATCHLINGS?

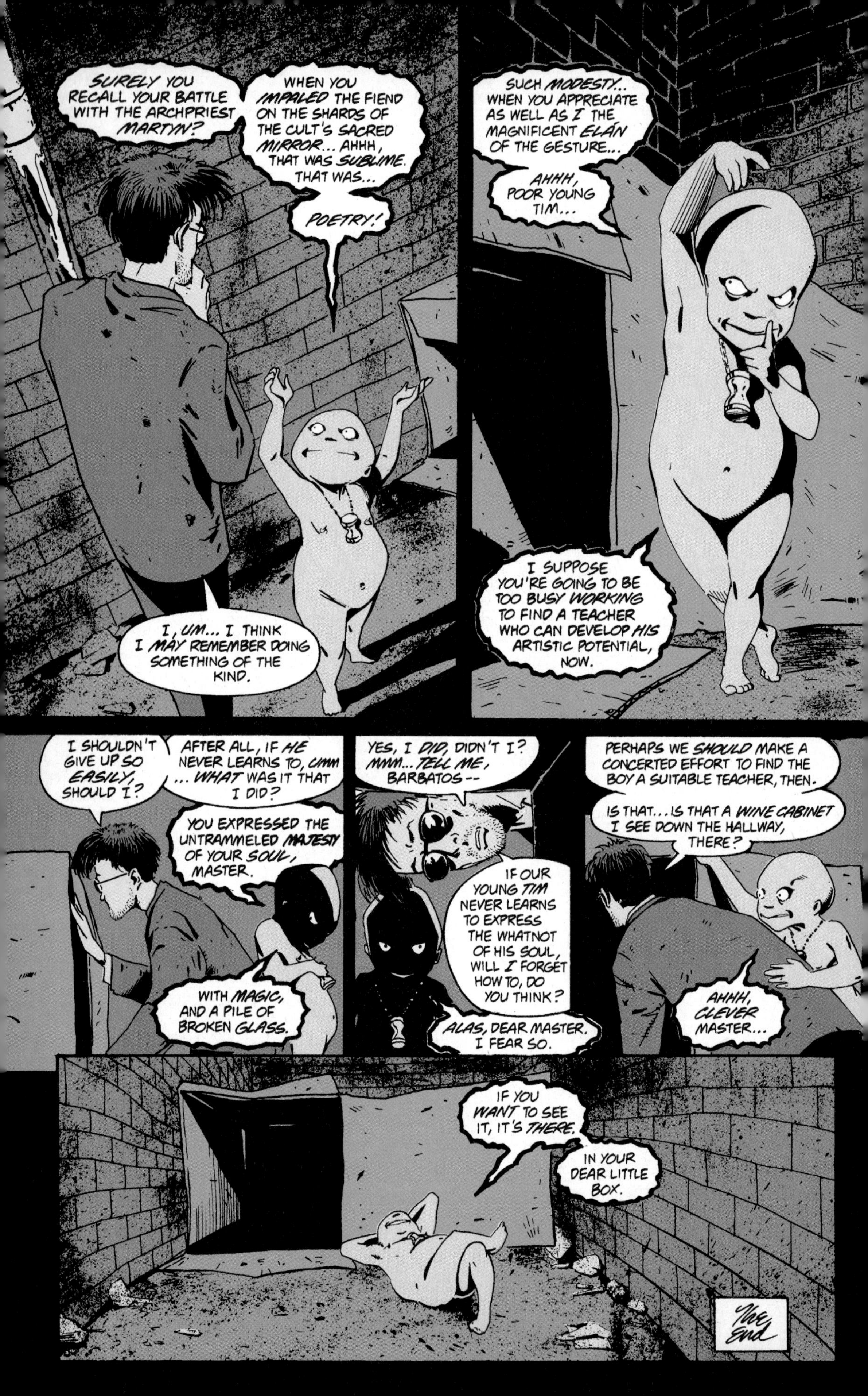

SURELY YOU RECALL YOUR BATTLE WITH THE ARCHPRIEST MARTYN?
WHEN YOU IMPALED THE FIEND ON THE SHARDS OF THE CULT'S SACRED MIRROR... AHHH, THAT WAS SUBLIME. THAT WAS...
POETRY!
I, UM... I THINK I MAY REMEMBER DOING SOMETHING OF THE KIND.
SUCH MODESTY... WHEN YOU APPRECIATE AS WELL AS I THE MAGNIFICENT ELÁN OF THE GESTURE...
AHHH, POOR YOUNG TIM...
I SUPPOSE YOU'RE GOING TO BE TOO BUSY WORKING TO FIND A TEACHER WHO CAN DEVELOP HIS ARTISTIC POTENTIAL, NOW.
I SHOULDN'T GIVE UP SO EASILY, SHOULD I?
AFTER ALL, IF HE NEVER LEARNS TO, UMM ... WHAT WAS IT THAT I DID?
YOU EXPRESSED THE UNTRAMMELED MAJESTY OF YOUR SOUL, MASTER.
WITH MAGIC, AND A PILE OF BROKEN GLASS.
YES, I DID, DIDN'T I? MMM... TELL ME, BARBATOS --
IF OUR YOUNG TIM NEVER LEARNS TO EXPRESS THE WHATNOT OF HIS SOUL, WILL I FORGET HOW TO, DO YOU THINK?
ALAS, DEAR MASTER. I FEAR SO.
PERHAPS WE SHOULD MAKE A CONCERTED EFFORT TO FIND THE BOY A SUITABLE TEACHER, THEN.
IS THAT... IS THAT A WINE CABINET I SEE DOWN THE HALLWAY, THERE?
AHHH, CLEVER MASTER...
IF YOU WANT TO SEE IT, IT'S THERE.
IN YOUR DEAR LITTLE BOX.
The End

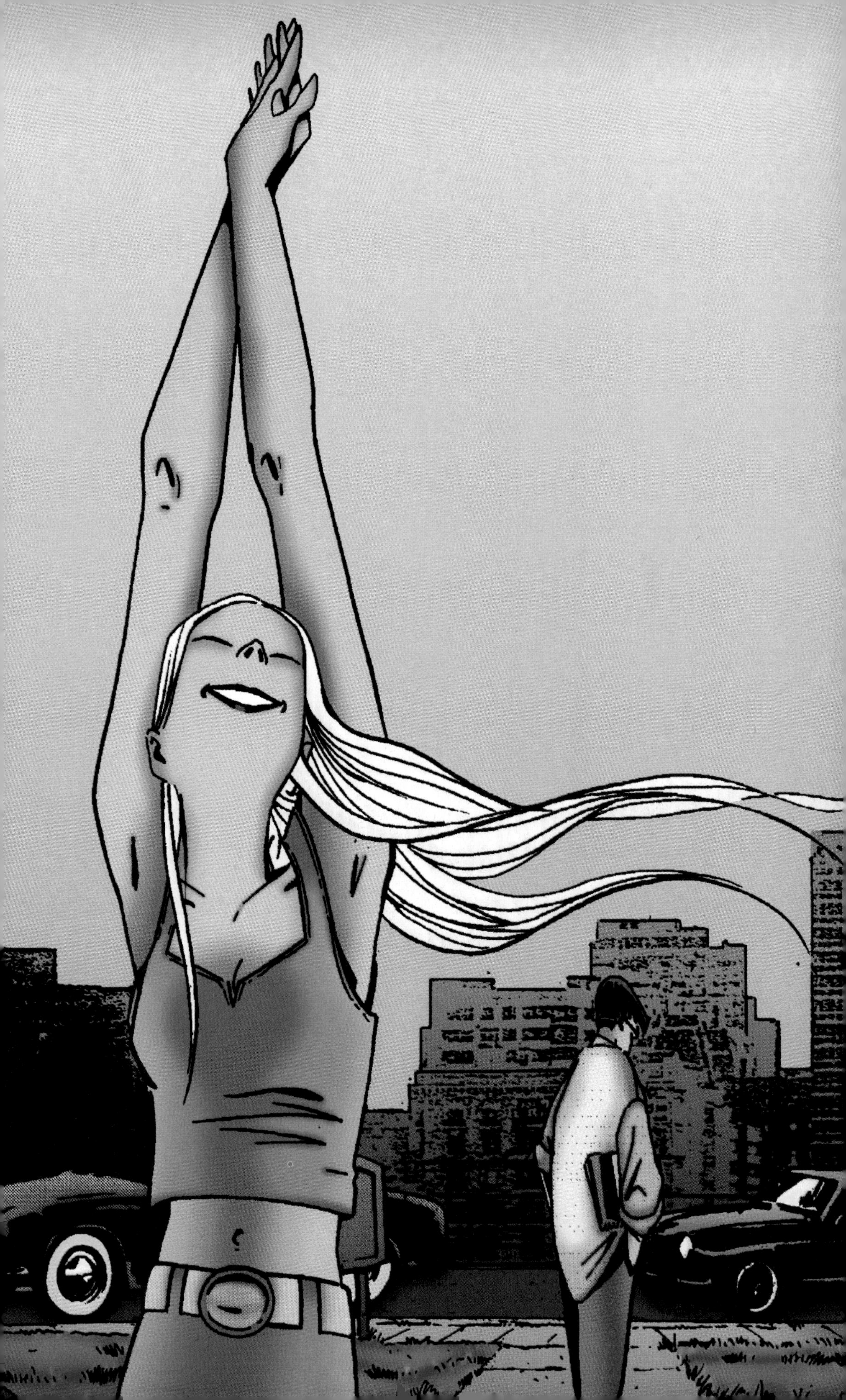

SO YOU MAKE THE CHOICE.

TO BELIEVE IN MAGIC, BE MAGIC. LIVE IN A MAGIC WORLD.

BUT THINGS DON'T TURN OUT QUITE THE WAY THE TRAVEL BROCHURE SAID THEY WOULD.

YOU'RE SUPPOSED TO HAVE ALL THIS POWER, RIGHT? OR SO ANY NUMBER OF GUYS IN TRENCHCOATS TELL YOU.

BUT YOU'RE ALWAYS IN SO MUCH TROUBLE THAT YOU NEVER GET A CHANCE TO FIGURE OUT HOW TO USE IT.

OAK PROSPECT HOTEL PLEASANT LODGING

SO I WAS THINKING. MAYBE...

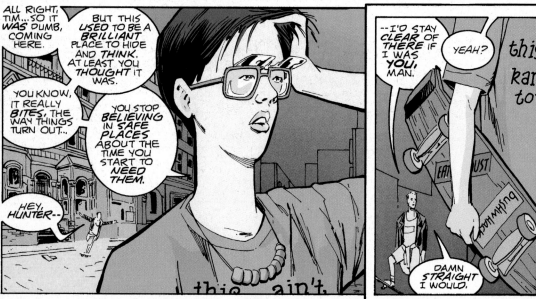

ALL RIGHT, TIM...SO IT WAS DUMB, COMING HERE.

BUT THIS USED TO BE A BRILLIANT PLACE TO HIDE AND THINK. AT LEAST YOU THOUGHT IT WAS.

YOU KNOW, IT REALLY BITES, THE WAY THINGS TURN OUT...

YOU STOP BELIEVING IN SAFE PLACES ABOUT THE TIME YOU START TO NEED THEM.

HEY, HUNTER--

this ain't

--I'D STAY CLEAR OF THERE IF I WAS YOU, MAN.

YEAH?

DAMN STRAIGHT I WOULD.

HAD DARLENE OUT HERE THE OTHER NIGHT. MOONLIGHT...IT SETS HER OFF, Y'KNOW--?

AWW, WHERE'S THE BLOODY THING GOT TO? CHUCKED IT SOMEWHERE HERE, FOR SURE.

ANYWAYS, SOON'S WE'RE IN, I'M HEARING STUFF OUT IN THE GRASS...RUSTLING. LIKE SOMEBODY'S DOGGING US AROUND.

ONLY DARLENE, SHE SAYS IT AIN'T JUST GRASS SHE'S HEARING.

IT'S SOMETHING TALKING. WHISPERING AT US.

THEN SHE STEPS ON THIS.

AND SOMEBODY LAUGHS. NASTY. RIGHT BEHIND US...

AND WE RUN.

108

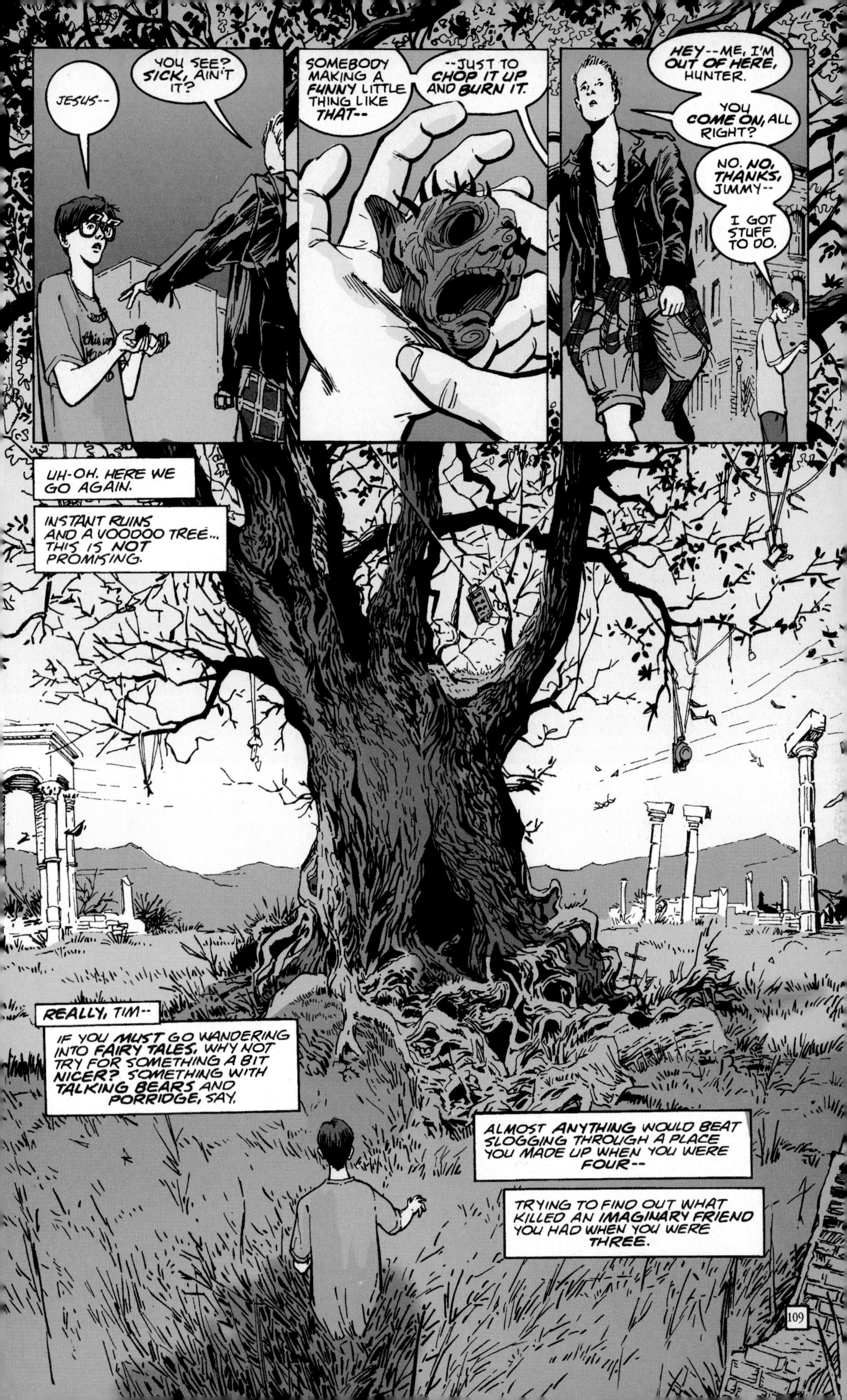
JESUS--
YOU SEE? SICK, AIN'T IT?
SOMEBODY MAKING A FUNNY LITTLE THING LIKE THAT--
--JUST TO CHOP IT UP AND BURN IT.
HEY--ME, I'M OUT OF HERE, HUNTER.
YOU COME ON, ALL RIGHT?
NO. NO, THANKS, JIMMY--
I GOT STUFF TO DO.
UH-OH. HERE WE GO AGAIN.
INSTANT RUINS AND A VOODOO TREE... THIS IS NOT PROMISING.
REALLY, TIM--
IF YOU MUST GO WANDERING INTO FAIRY TALES, WHY NOT TRY FOR SOMETHING A BIT NICER? SOMETHING WITH TALKING BEARS AND PORRIDGE, SAY.
ALMOST ANYTHING WOULD BEAT SLOGGING THROUGH A PLACE YOU MADE UP WHEN YOU WERE FOUR--
TRYING TO FIND OUT WHAT KILLED AN IMAGINARY FRIEND YOU HAD WHEN YOU WERE THREE.

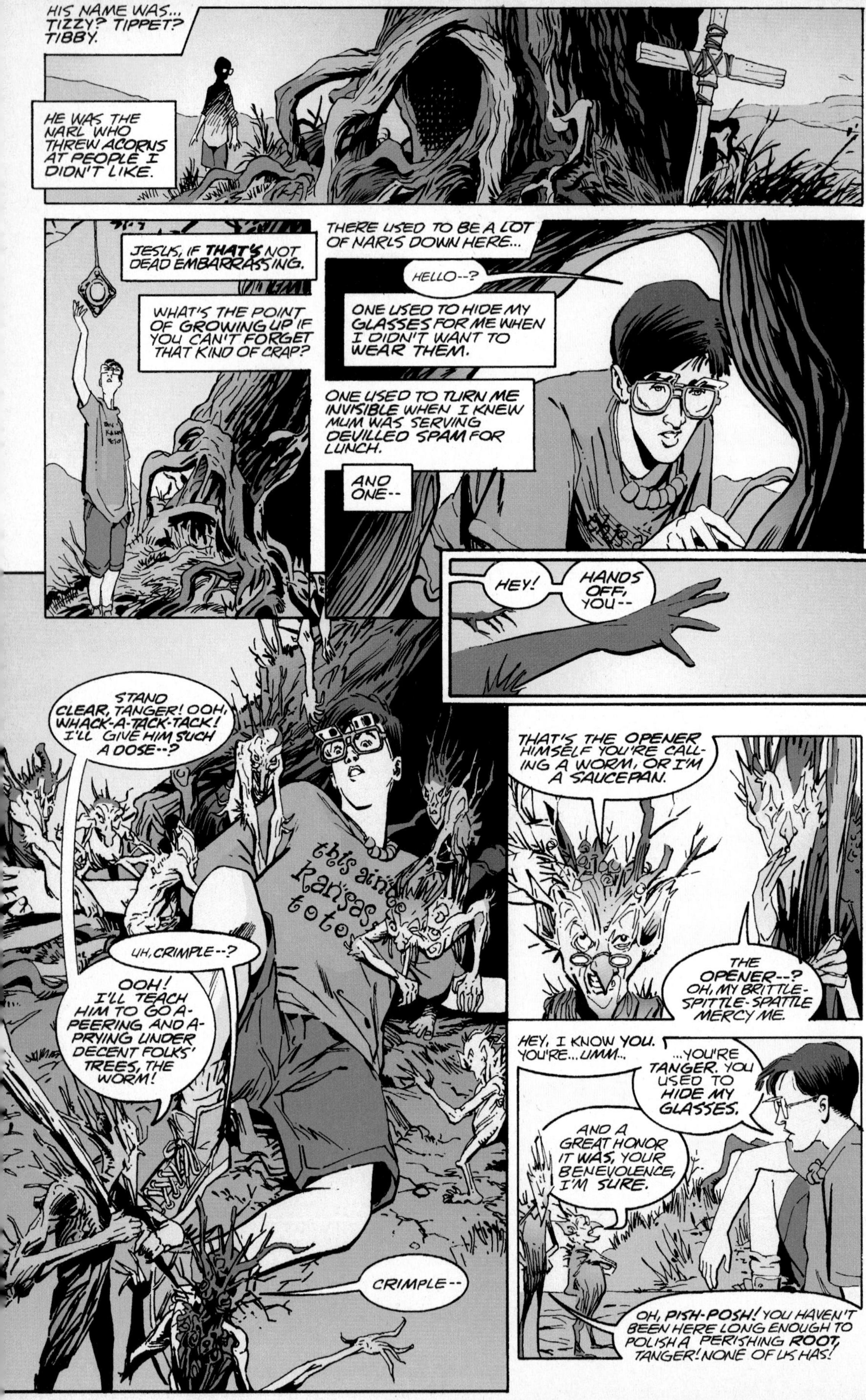
HIS NAME WAS... TIZZY? TIPPET? TIBBY.
HE WAS THE NARL WHO THREW ACORNS AT PEOPLE I DIDN'T LIKE.
JESUS, IF THAT'S NOT DEAD EMBARRASSING.
WHAT'S THE POINT OF GROWING UP IF YOU CAN'T FORGET THAT KIND OF CRAP?
THERE USED TO BE A LOT OF NARLS DOWN HERE...
HELLO--?
ONE USED TO HIDE MY GLASSES FOR ME WHEN I DIDN'T WANT TO WEAR THEM.
ONE USED TO TURN ME INVISIBLE WHEN I KNEW MUM WAS SERVING DEVILLED SPAM FOR LUNCH.
AND ONE--
HEY!
HANDS OFF, YOU--
STAND CLEAR, TANGER! OOH, WHACK-A-TACK-TACK! I'LL GIVE HIM SUCH A DOSE--?
this ain't kansas toto
UH, CRIMPLE--?
OOH! I'LL TEACH HIM TO GO A-PEERING AND A-PRYING UNDER DECENT FOLKS' TREES, THE WORM!
CRIMPLE--
THAT'S THE OPENER HIMSELF YOU'RE CALLING A WORM, OR I'M A SAUCEPAN.
THE OPENER--? OH, MY BRITTLE-SPITTLE-SPATTLE MERCY ME.
HEY, I KNOW YOU. YOU'RE... UMM...
...YOU'RE TANGER. YOU USED TO HIDE MY GLASSES.
AND A GREAT HONOR IT WAS, YOUR BENEVOLENCE, I'M SURE.
OH, PISH-POSH! YOU HAVEN'T BEEN HERE LONG ENOUGH TO POLISH A PERISHING ROOT, TANGER! NONE OF US HAS!

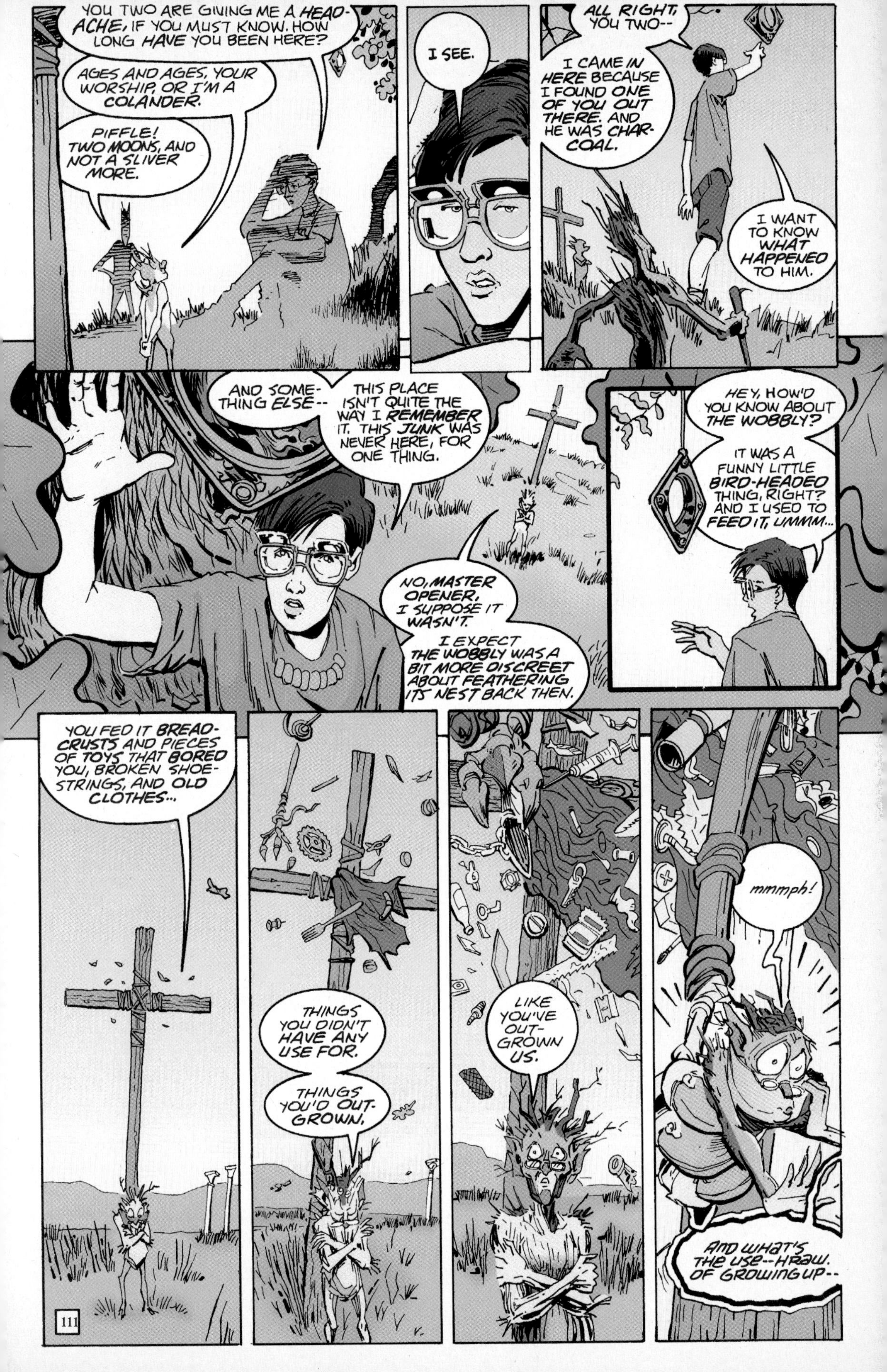
YOU TWO ARE GIVING ME A HEADACHE, IF YOU MUST KNOW. HOW LONG HAVE YOU BEEN HERE?
AGES AND AGES, YOUR WORSHIP, OR I'M A COLANDER.
PIFFLE! TWO MOONS, AND NOT A SLIVER MORE.
I SEE.
ALL RIGHT, YOU TWO--
I CAME IN HERE BECAUSE I FOUND ONE OF YOU OUT THERE. AND HE WAS CHARCOAL.
I WANT TO KNOW WHAT HAPPENED TO HIM.
AND SOMETHING ELSE--
THIS PLACE ISN'T QUITE THE WAY I REMEMBER IT. THIS JUNK WAS NEVER HERE, FOR ONE THING.
NO, MASTER OPENER, I SUPPOSE IT WASN'T.
I EXPECT THE WOBBLY WAS A BIT MORE DISCREET ABOUT FEATHERING ITS NEST BACK THEN.
HEY, HOW'D YOU KNOW ABOUT THE WOBBLY?
IT WAS A FUNNY LITTLE BIRD-HEADED THING, RIGHT? AND I USED TO FEED IT, UMMM...
YOU FED IT BREADCRUSTS AND PIECES OF TOYS THAT BORED YOU, BROKEN SHOESTRINGS, AND OLD CLOTHES...
THINGS YOU DIDN'T HAVE ANY USE FOR.
THINGS YOU'D OUTGROWN.
LIKE YOU'VE OUTGROWN US.
mmmph!
AND WHAT'S THE USE--HRAW. OF GROWING UP--

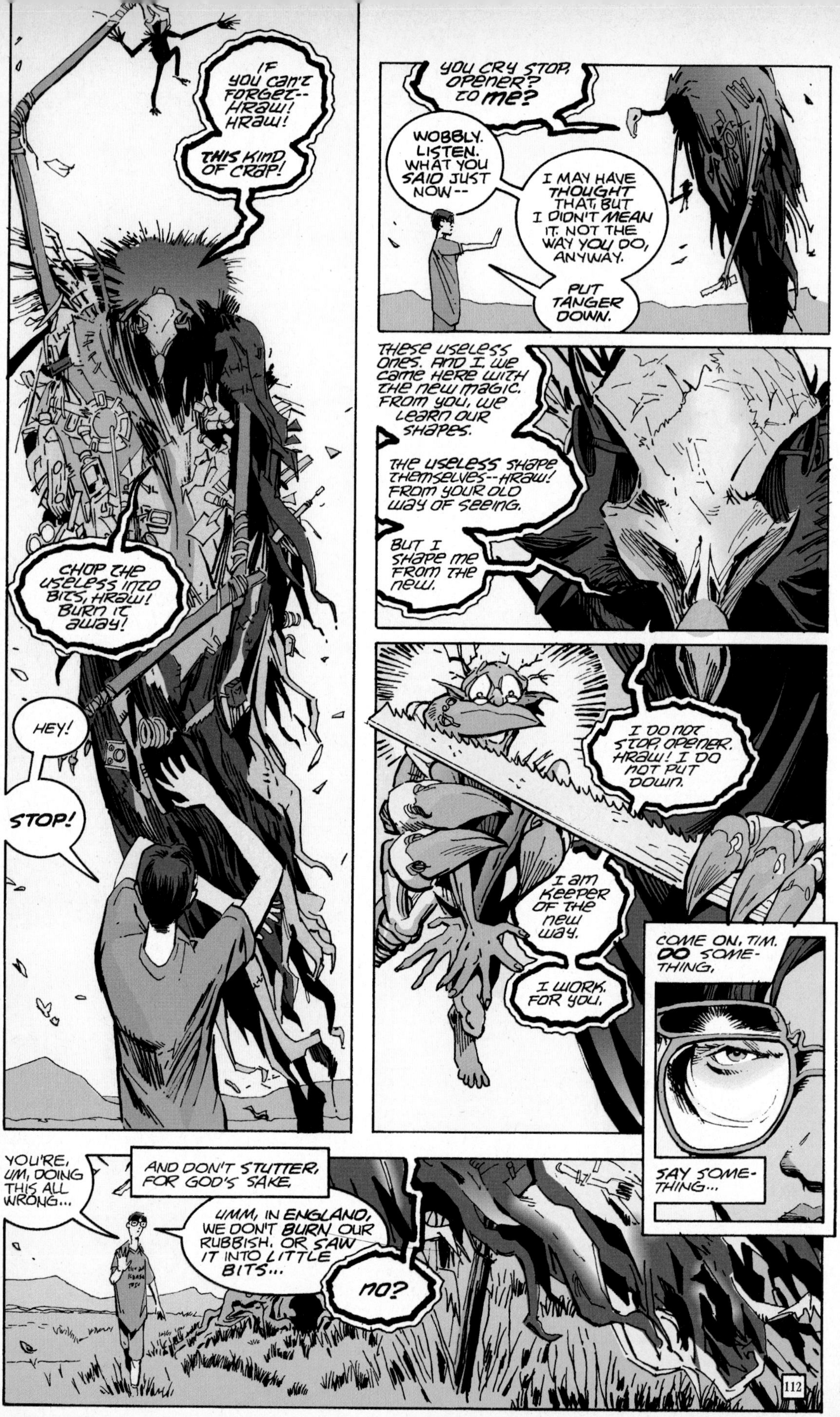
IF YOU CAN'T FORGET-- HRAW! HRAW!
THIS KIND OF CRAP!
CHOP THE USELESS INTO BITS, HRAW! BURN IT AWAY!
HEY!
STOP!
YOU CRY STOP, OPENER? TO ME?
WOBBLY. LISTEN. WHAT YOU SAID JUST NOW--
I MAY HAVE THOUGHT THAT, BUT I DIDN'T MEAN IT. NOT THE WAY YOU DO, ANYWAY.
PUT TANGER DOWN.
THESE USELESS ONES. AND I, WE CAME HERE WITH THE NEW MAGIC. FROM YOU, WE LEARN OUR SHAPES.
THE USELESS SHAPE THEMSELVES--HRAW! FROM YOUR OLD WAY OF SEEING.
BUT I SHAPE ME FROM THE NEW.
I DO NOT STOP, OPENER. HRAW! I DO NOT PUT DOWN.
I AM KEEPER OF THE NEW WAY.
I WORK. FOR YOU.
COME ON, TIM. DO SOMETHING.
SAY SOMETHING...
YOU'RE, UM, DOING THIS ALL WRONG...
AND DON'T STUTTER, FOR GOD'S SAKE.
UMM, IN ENGLAND, WE DON'T BURN OUR RUBBISH. OR SAW IT INTO LITTLE BITS...
NO?

KEEP IT UP, TIM... YOU CAN HANDLE THE OLD VULTURE...

YOU MADE IT OUT OF STICKS AND RAGS, REMEMBER? IT *CAN'T* BE VERY BRIGHT.

ERRR, NO.

SAWING UP THROWAYS, BURNING THEM... THAT'S CONSIDERED VERY, UMMM... OLD-FASHIONED.

UMMMM... RECYCLING IS THE *NEW* THING.

HRRAWW-W...

WHAT MEANS IT, OPENER? TO RE-CYCLE?

PITCHING THE, UM, USELESS INTO A BIN. OR, UM, UNDER A TREE.

THEN PRETENDING IT'S *NOT* THERE.

BEAUTIFUL CONCEPT, HEY? QUITE INGENIOUS, REALLY...

HRAW...

NOW, IF YOU'LL JUST PUT ME DOWN, I'LL PITCH MYSELF UNDER THE, AH, GOOD OLD RECYCLING TREE...

AND YOU CAN GET RIGHT TO WORK PRETENDING I'M NOT THERE.

HRAW--

GO, USELESS. AND I GO. TO WAIT FOR OTHER RUBBISH.

MUCH OBLIGED, YOUR WOBBLY-SHIP.

AND YOU, YOUNG MASTER-- IF YOU EVER NEED SOMEONE TO HIDE THOSE GLASSES FOR YOU, COUNT ON ME.

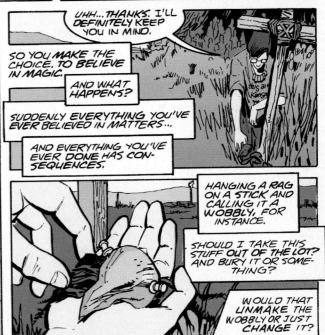

UHH...THANKS. I'LL DEFINITELY KEEP YOU IN MIND.

SO YOU MAKE THE CHOICE, TO BELIEVE IN MAGIC.

AND WHAT HAPPENS?

SUDDENLY EVERYTHING YOU'VE EVER BELIEVED IN MATTERS...

AND EVERYTHING YOU'VE EVER DONE HAS CON-SEQUENCES.

HANGING A RAG ON A STICK AND CALLING IT A WOBBLY, FOR INSTANCE.

SHOULD I TAKE THIS STUFF OUT OF THE LOT? AND BURY IT OR SOME-THING?

WOULD THAT UNMAKE THE WOBBLY OR JUST CHANGE IT?

MAYBE IT WOULD BE SAFEST JUST TO CHANGE ME.

YEAH. THAT WOULD BE THE SENSIBLE THING TO DO...

IF I COULD ONLY FIGURE OUT WHAT TO CHANGE ME INTO.

THE END

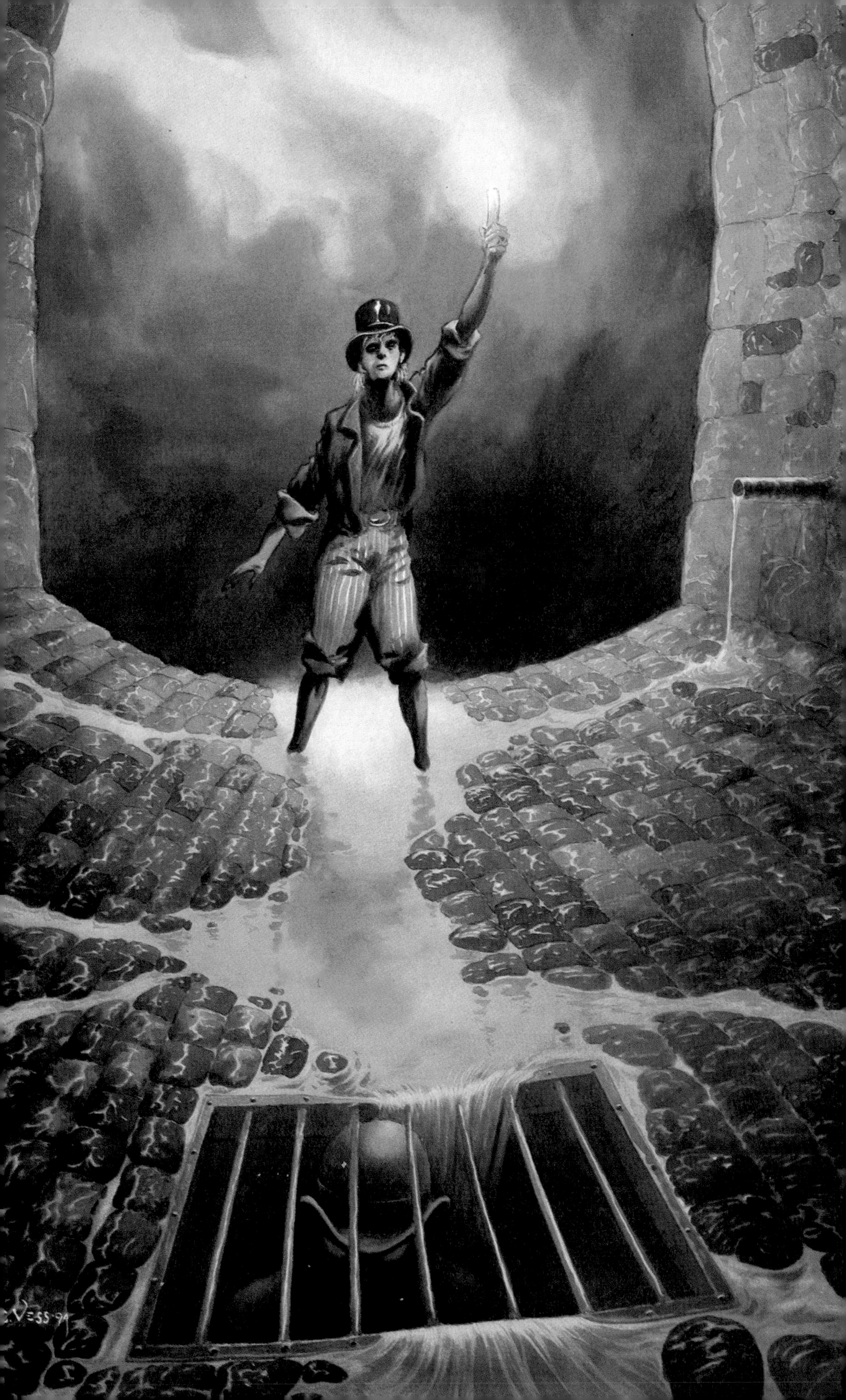

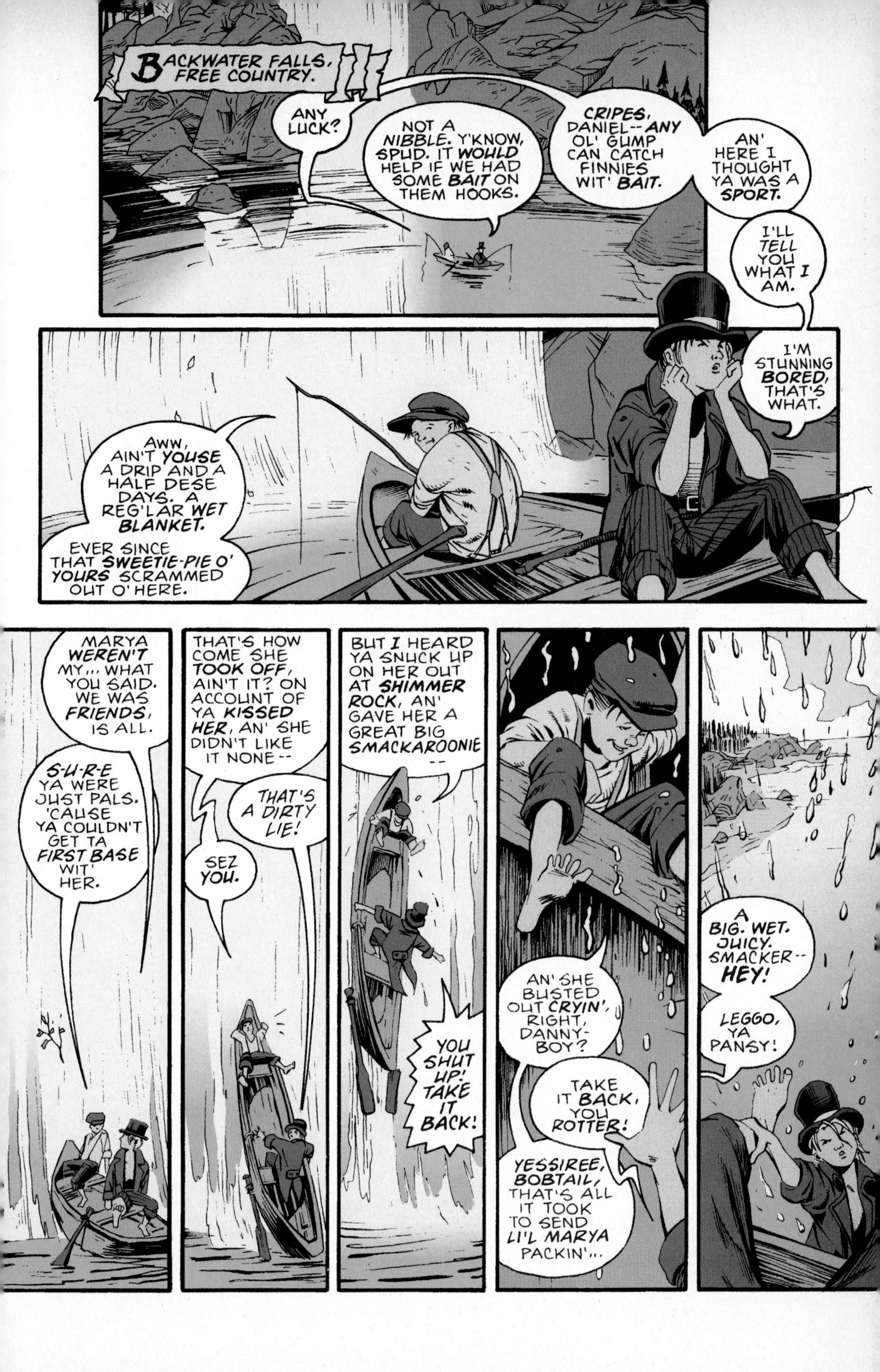
BACKWATER FALLS, FREE COUNTRY.
ANY LUCK?
NOT A NIBBLE. Y'KNOW, SPUD. IT WOULD HELP IF WE HAD SOME BAIT ON THEM HOOKS.
CRIPES, DANIEL-- ANY OL' GUMP CAN CATCH FINNIES WIT' BAIT.
AN' HERE I THOUGHT YA WAS A SPORT.
I'LL TELL YOU WHAT I AM.
I'M STUNNING BORED, THAT'S WHAT.
AWW, AIN'T YOUSE A DRIP AND A HALF DESE DAYS. A REG'LAR WET BLANKET.
EVER SINCE THAT SWEETIE-PIE O' YOURS SCRAMMED OUT O' HERE.
MARYA WEREN'T MY... WHAT YOU SAID. WE WAS FRIENDS, IS ALL.
S-U-R-E YA WERE JUST PALS. 'CAUSE YA COULDN'T GET TA FIRST BASE WIT' HER.
THAT'S HOW COME SHE TOOK OFF, AIN'T IT? ON ACCOUNT OF YA KISSED HER, AN' SHE DIDN'T LIKE IT NONE --
THAT'S A DIRTY LIE!
SEZ YOU.
BUT I HEARD YA SNUCK UP ON HER OUT AT SHIMMER ROCK, AN' GAVE HER A GREAT BIG SMACKAROONIE --
YOU SHUT UP! TAKE IT BACK!
AN' SHE BUSTED OUT CRYIN', RIGHT, DANNY-BOY?
TAKE IT BACK, YOU ROTTER!
YESSIREE, BOBTAIL, THAT'S ALL IT TOOK TO SEND LI'L MARYA PACKIN'...
A BIG. WET. JUICY. SMACKER-- HEY!
LEGGO, YA PANSY!

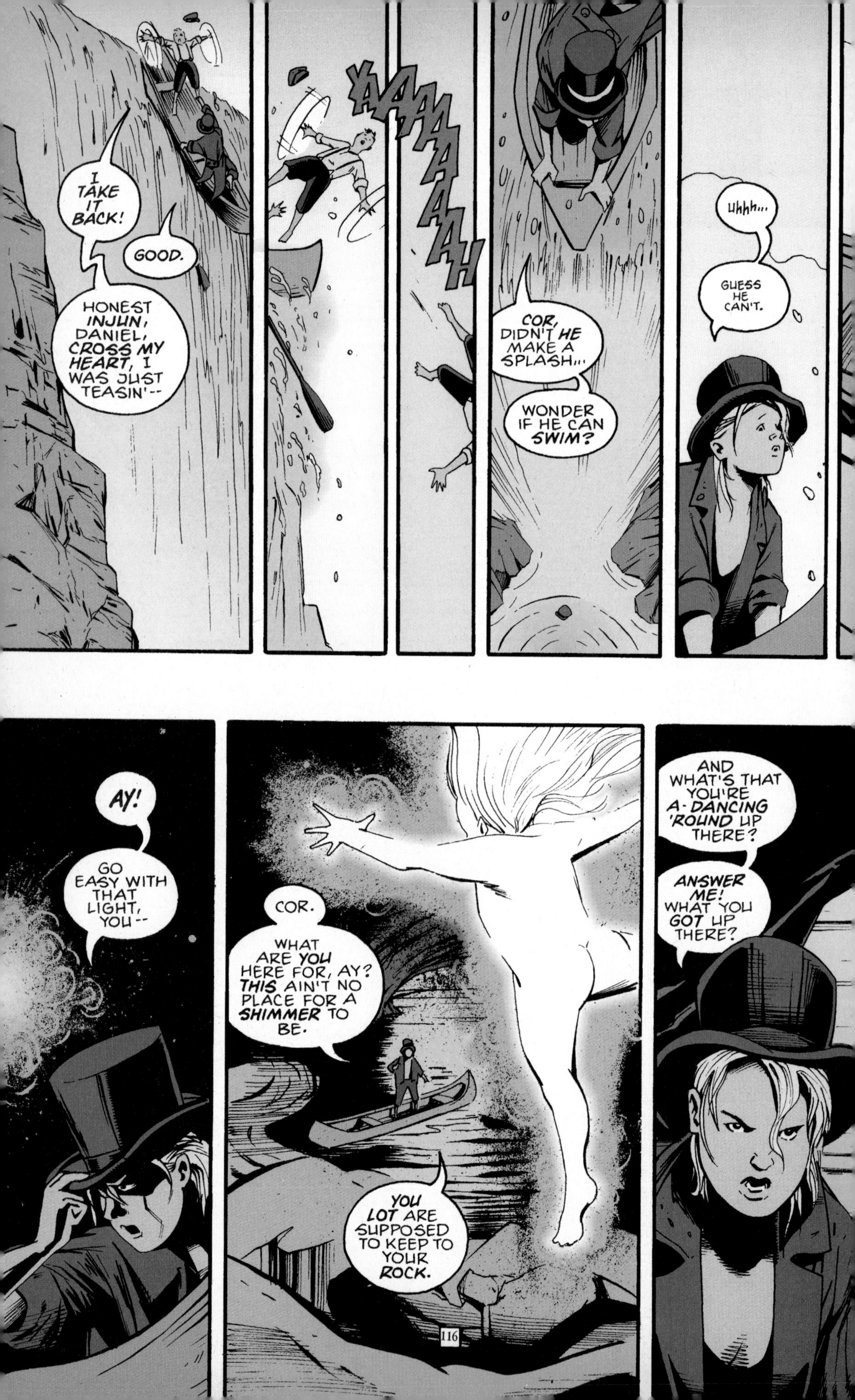
I TAKE IT BACK!
GOOD.
HONEST INJUN, DANIEL, CROSS MY HEART, I WAS JUST TEASIN'--
YAAAAAAAAH
COR, DIDN'T HE MAKE A SPLASH...
WONDER IF HE CAN SWIM?
Uhhh...
GUESS HE CAN'T.
AY!
GO EASY WITH THAT LIGHT, YOU--
COR.
WHAT ARE YOU HERE FOR, AY? THIS AIN'T NO PLACE FOR A SHIMMER TO BE.
YOU LOT ARE SUPPOSED TO KEEP TO YOUR ROCK.
AND WHAT'S THAT YOU'RE A-DANCING 'ROUND UP THERE?
ANSWER ME! WHAT YOU GOT UP THERE?

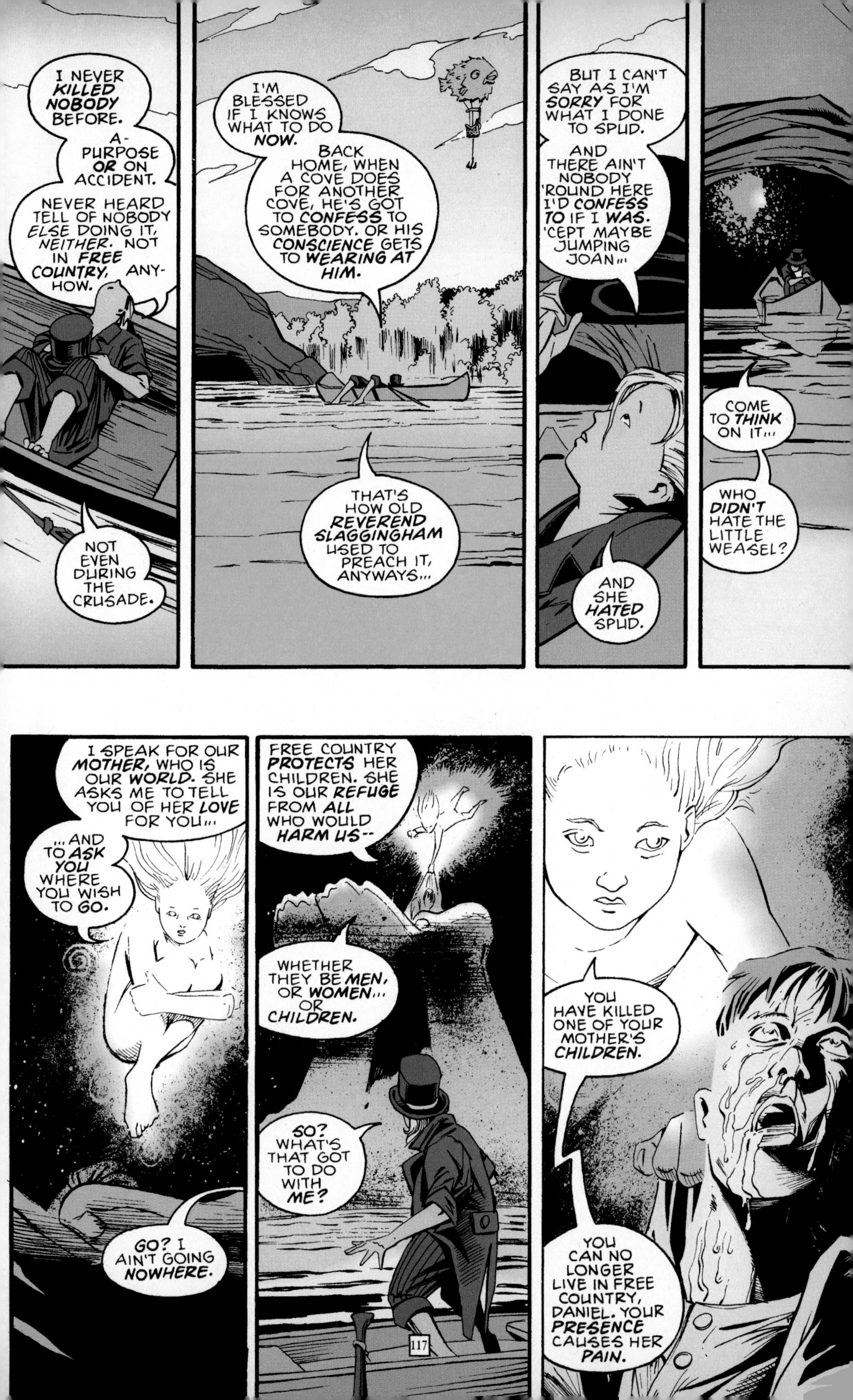
I NEVER KILLED NOBODY BEFORE.
A-PURPOSE OR ON ACCIDENT.
NEVER HEARD TELL OF NOBODY ELSE DOING IT, NEITHER. NOT IN FREE COUNTRY, ANY-HOW.
NOT EVEN DURING THE CRUSADE.
I'M BLESSED IF I KNOWS WHAT TO DO NOW.
BACK HOME, WHEN A COVE DOES FOR ANOTHER COVE, HE'S GOT TO CONFESS TO SOMEBODY. OR HIS CONSCIENCE GETS TO WEARING AT HIM.
THAT'S HOW OLD REVEREND SLAGGINGHAM USED TO PREACH IT, ANYWAYS...
BUT I CAN'T SAY AS I'M SORRY FOR WHAT I DONE TO SPUD.
AND THERE AIN'T NOBODY 'ROUND HERE I'D CONFESS TO IF I WAS. 'CEPT MAYBE JUMPING JOAN...
AND SHE HATED SPUD.
COME TO THINK ON IT...
WHO DIDN'T HATE THE LITTLE WEASEL?
I SPEAK FOR OUR MOTHER, WHO IS OUR WORLD. SHE ASKS ME TO TELL YOU OF HER LOVE FOR YOU...
...AND TO ASK YOU WHERE YOU WISH TO GO.
GO? I AIN'T GOING NOWHERE.
FREE COUNTRY PROTECTS HER CHILDREN. SHE IS OUR REFUGE FROM ALL WHO WOULD HARM US--
WHETHER THEY BE MEN, OR WOMEN... OR CHILDREN.
SO? WHAT'S THAT GOT TO DO WITH ME?
YOU HAVE KILLED ONE OF YOUR MOTHER'S CHILDREN.
YOU CAN NO LONGER LIVE IN FREE COUNTRY, DANIEL. YOUR PRESENCE CAUSES HER PAIN.

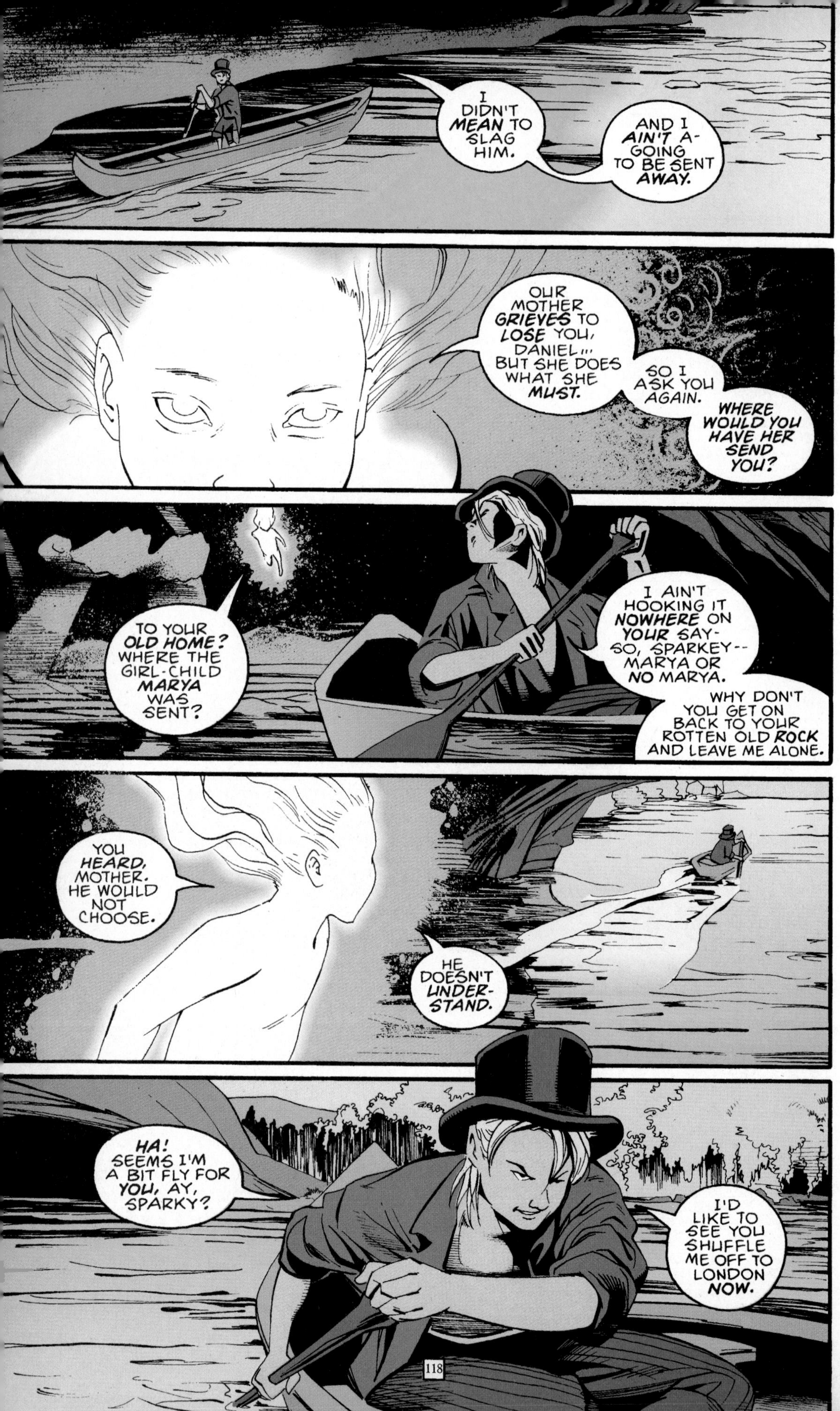
I DIDN'T MEAN TO SLAG HIM.
AND I AIN'T A-GOING TO BE SENT AWAY.
OUR MOTHER GRIEVES TO LOSE YOU, DANIEL... BUT SHE DOES WHAT SHE MUST.
SO I ASK YOU AGAIN.
WHERE WOULD YOU HAVE HER SEND YOU?
TO YOUR OLD HOME? WHERE THE GIRL-CHILD MARYA WAS SENT?
I AIN'T HOOKING IT NOWHERE ON YOUR SAY-SO, SPARKEY-- MARYA OR NO MARYA.
WHY DON'T YOU GET ON BACK TO YOUR ROTTEN OLD ROCK AND LEAVE ME ALONE.
YOU HEARD, MOTHER. HE WOULD NOT CHOOSE.
HE DOESN'T UNDER-STAND.
HA! SEEMS I'M A BIT FLY FOR YOU, AY, SPARKY?
I'D LIKE TO SEE YOU SHUFFLE ME OFF TO LONDON NOW.

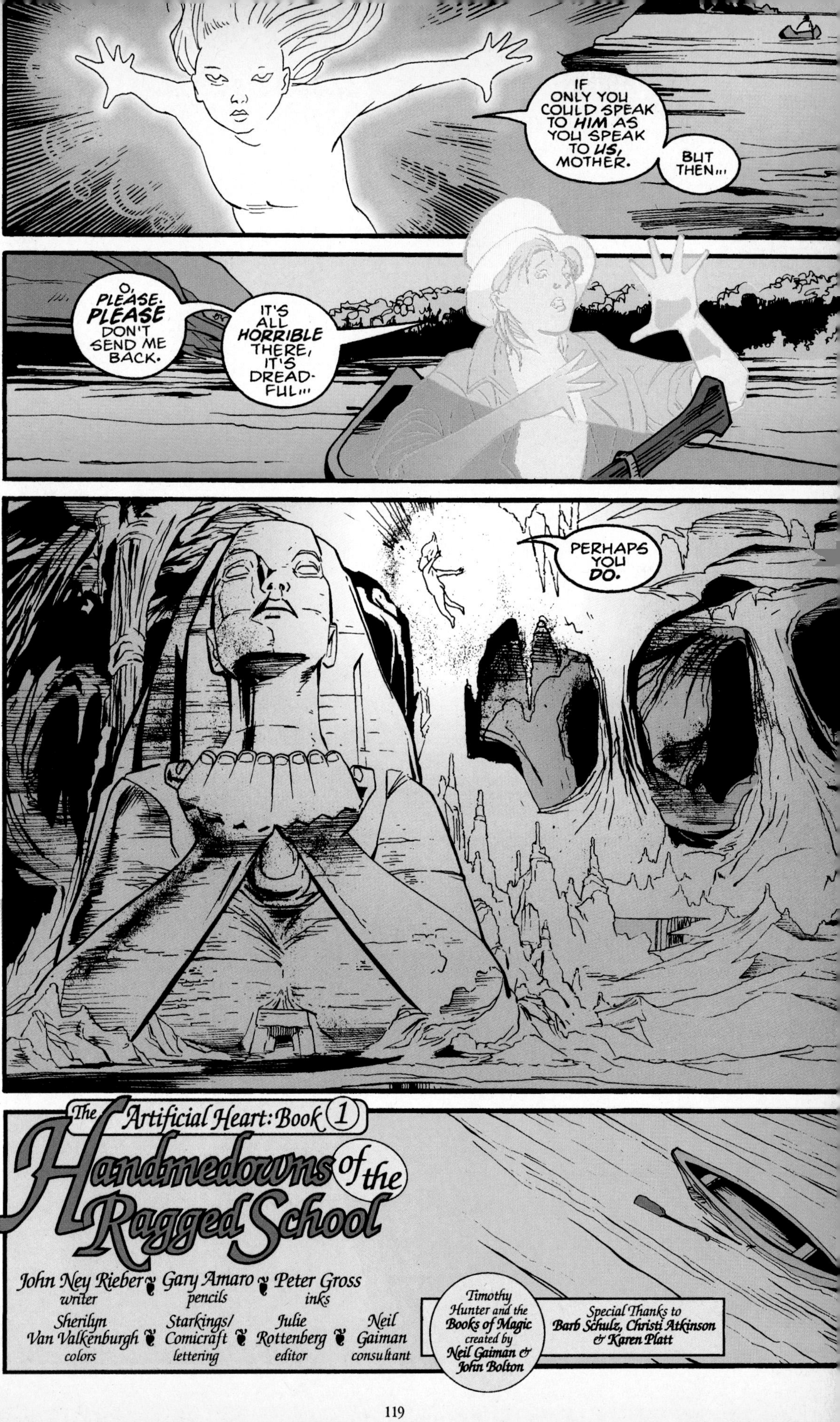
IF ONLY YOU COULD SPEAK TO HIM AS YOU SPEAK TO US, MOTHER.
BUT THEN...
O, PLEASE. PLEASE DON'T SEND ME BACK.
IT'S ALL HORRIBLE THERE, IT'S DREADFUL...
PERHAPS YOU DO.
The Artificial Heart: Book 1
Handmedowns of the Ragged School
John Ney Rieber writer
Gary Amaro pencils
Peter Gross inks
Sherilyn Van Valkenburgh colors
Starkings/ Comicraft lettering
Julie Rottenberg editor
Neil Gaiman consultant
Timothy Hunter and the Books of Magic created by Neil Gaiman & John Bolton
Special Thanks to Barb Schulz, Christi Atkinson & Karen Platt

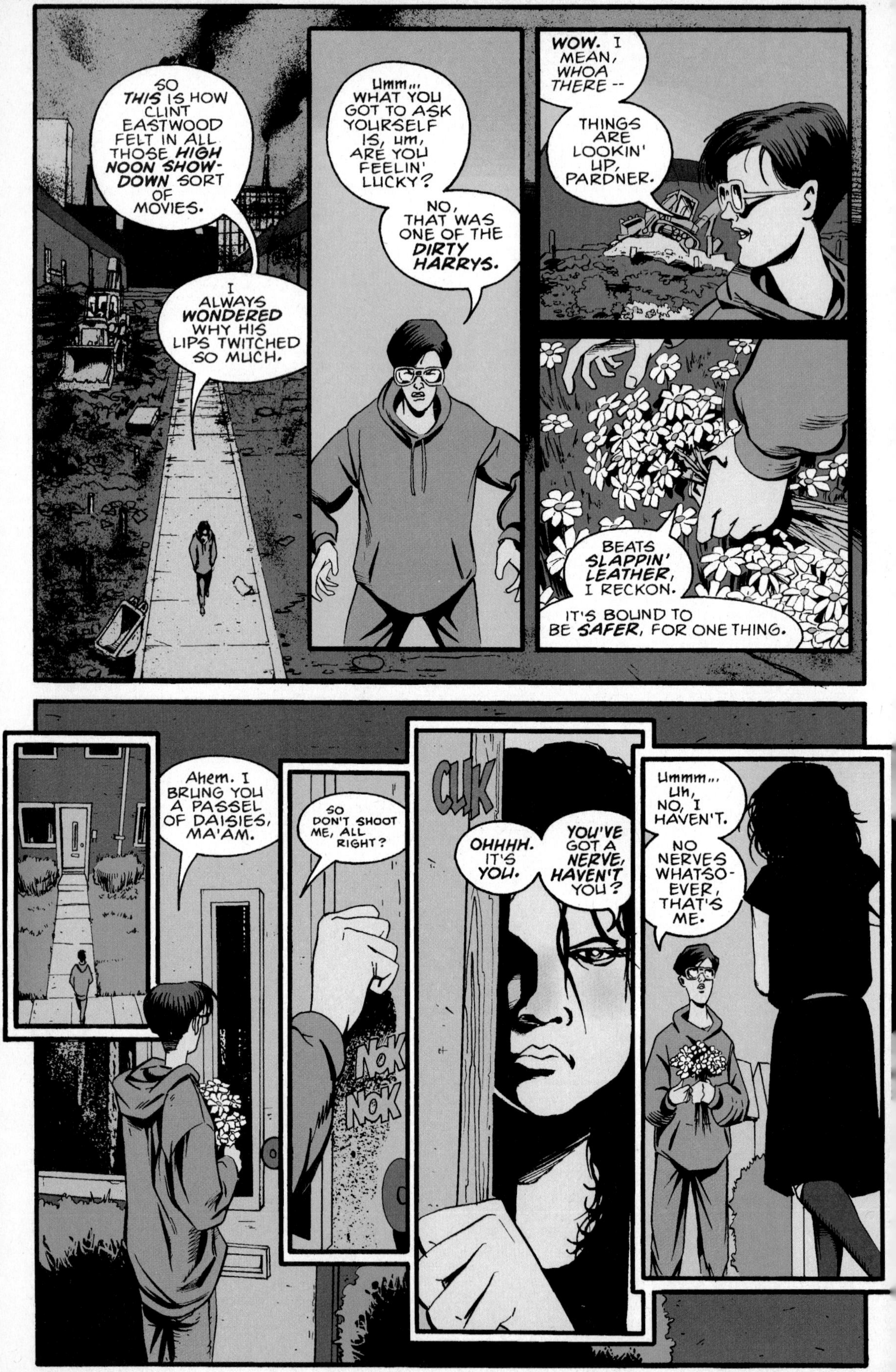
SO THIS IS HOW CLINT EASTWOOD FELT IN ALL THOSE HIGH NOON SHOW-DOWN SORT OF MOVIES.
I ALWAYS WONDERED WHY HIS LIPS TWITCHED SO MUCH.
Umm... WHAT YOU GOT TO ASK YOURSELF IS, um, ARE YOU FEELIN' LUCKY?
NO, THAT WAS ONE OF THE DIRTY HARRYS.
WOW. I MEAN, WHOA THERE --
THINGS ARE LOOKIN' UP, PARDNER.
BEATS SLAPPIN' LEATHER, I RECKON.
IT'S BOUND TO BE SAFER, FOR ONE THING.
Ahem. I BRUNG YOU A PASSEL OF DAISIES, MA'AM.
SO DON'T SHOOT ME, ALL RIGHT?
NOK NOK
CLIK
OHHHH. IT'S YOU.
YOU'VE GOT A NERVE, HAVEN'T YOU?
Ummm... Uh, NO, I HAVEN'T.
NO NERVES WHATSO-EVER, THAT'S ME.

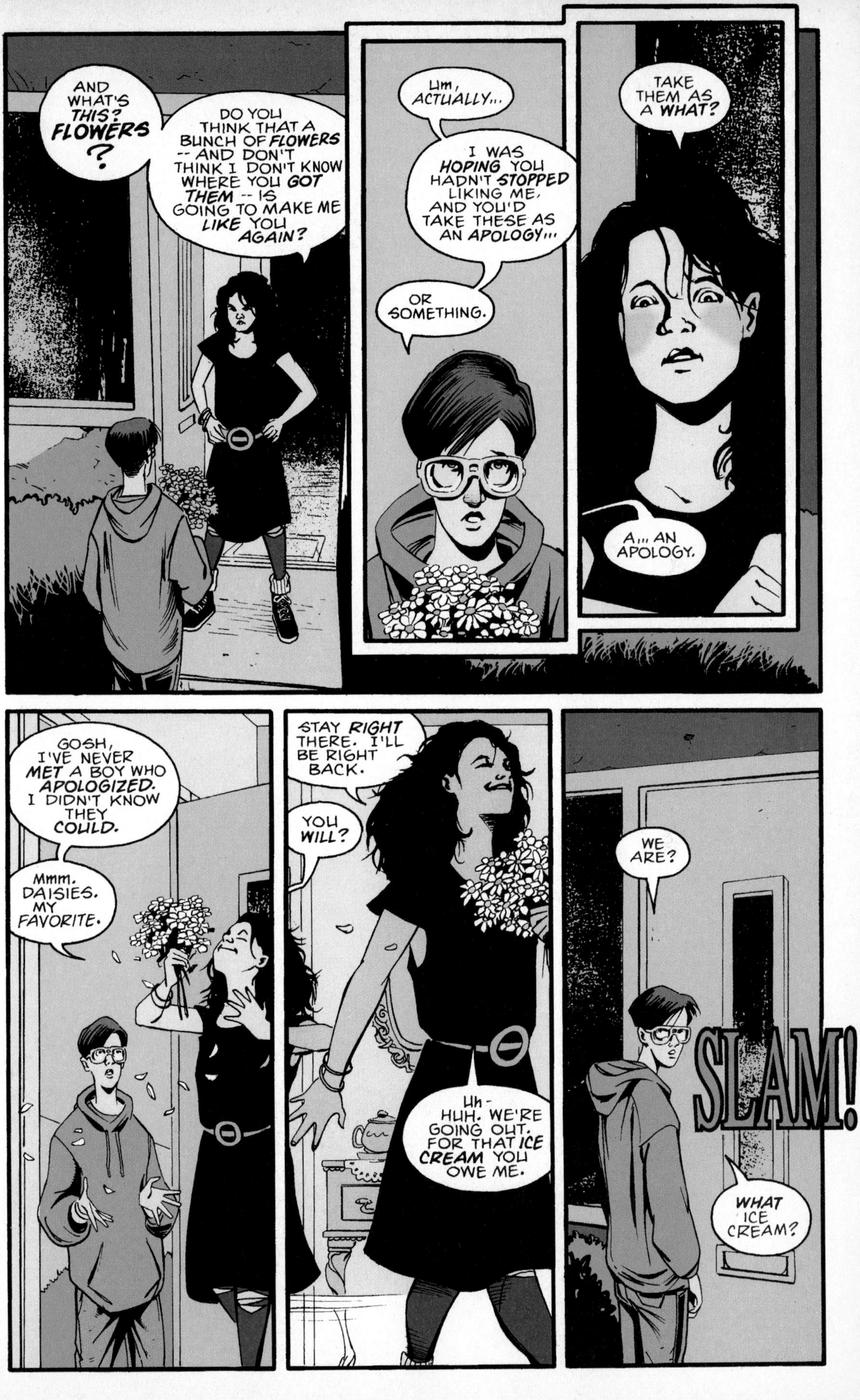
AND WHAT'S THIS? FLOWERS?
DO YOU THINK THAT A BUNCH OF FLOWERS -- AND DON'T THINK I DON'T KNOW WHERE YOU GOT THEM -- IS GOING TO MAKE ME LIKE YOU AGAIN?
UM, ACTUALLY...
I WAS HOPING YOU HADN'T STOPPED LIKING ME, AND YOU'D TAKE THESE AS AN APOLOGY...
OR SOMETHING.
TAKE THEM AS A WHAT?
A... AN APOLOGY.
GOSH, I'VE NEVER MET A BOY WHO APOLOGIZED. I DIDN'T KNOW THEY COULD.
MMM. DAISIES. MY FAVORITE.
STAY RIGHT THERE. I'LL BE RIGHT BACK.
YOU WILL?
UH-HUH. WE'RE GOING OUT. FOR THAT ICE CREAM YOU OWE ME.
WE ARE?
SLAM!
WHAT ICE CREAM?

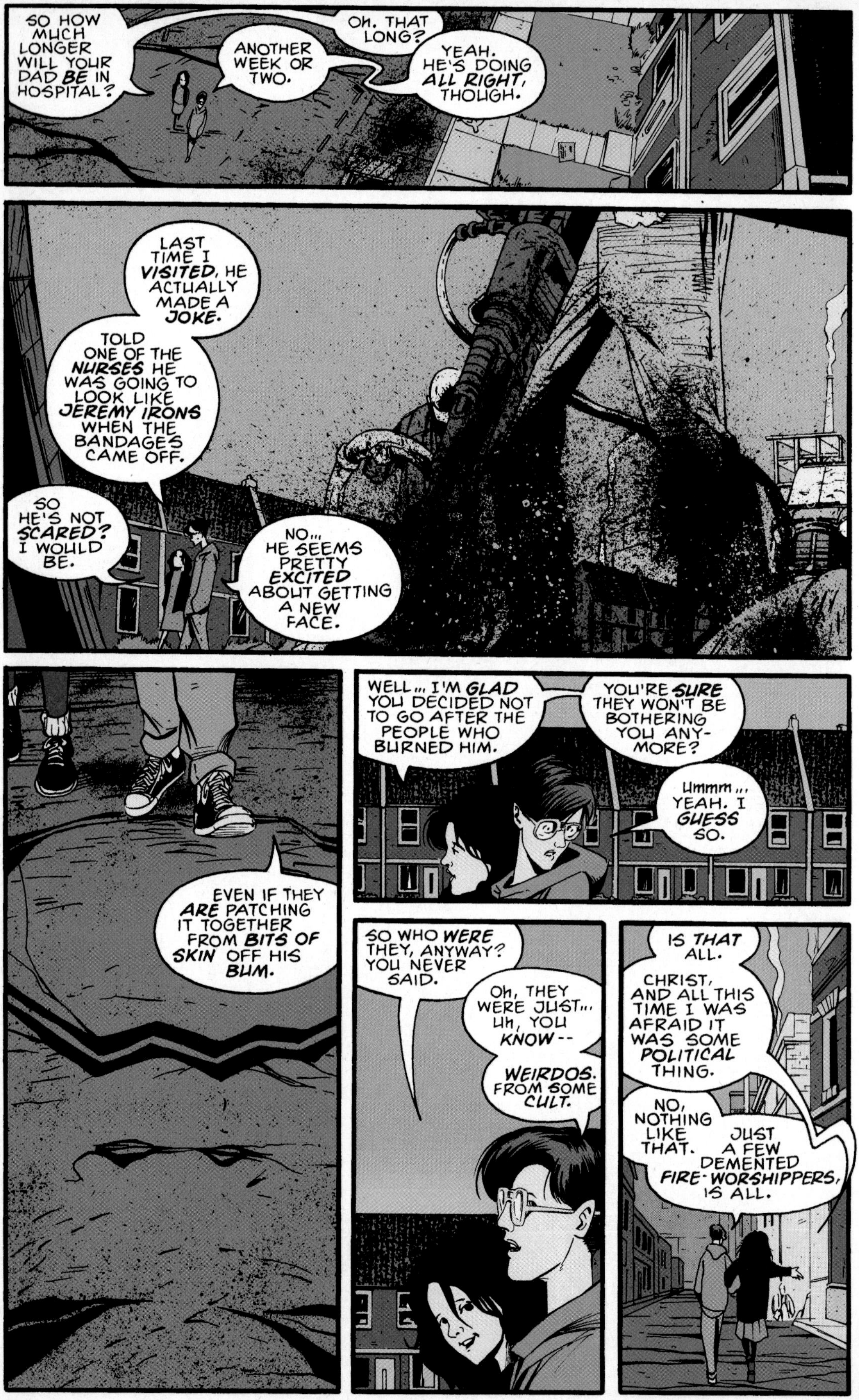
SO HOW MUCH LONGER WILL YOUR DAD BE IN HOSPITAL?
ANOTHER WEEK OR TWO.
OH. THAT LONG?
YEAH. HE'S DOING ALL RIGHT, THOUGH.
LAST TIME I VISITED, HE ACTUALLY MADE A JOKE.
TOLD ONE OF THE NURSES HE WAS GOING TO LOOK LIKE JEREMY IRONS WHEN THE BANDAGES CAME OFF.
SO HE'S NOT SCARED? I WOULD BE.
NO... HE SEEMS PRETTY EXCITED ABOUT GETTING A NEW FACE.
EVEN IF THEY ARE PATCHING IT TOGETHER FROM BITS OF SKIN OFF HIS BUM.
WELL... I'M GLAD YOU DECIDED NOT TO GO AFTER THE PEOPLE WHO BURNED HIM.
YOU'RE SURE THEY WON'T BE BOTHERING YOU ANY-MORE?
UMMM... YEAH. I GUESS SO.
SO WHO WERE THEY, ANYWAY? YOU NEVER SAID.
OH, THEY WERE JUST... UH, YOU KNOW --
WEIRDOS. FROM SOME CULT.
IS THAT ALL.
CHRIST, AND ALL THIS TIME I WAS AFRAID IT WAS SOME POLITICAL THING.
NO, NOTHING LIKE THAT.
JUST A FEW DEMENTED FIRE-WORSHIPPERS, IS ALL.

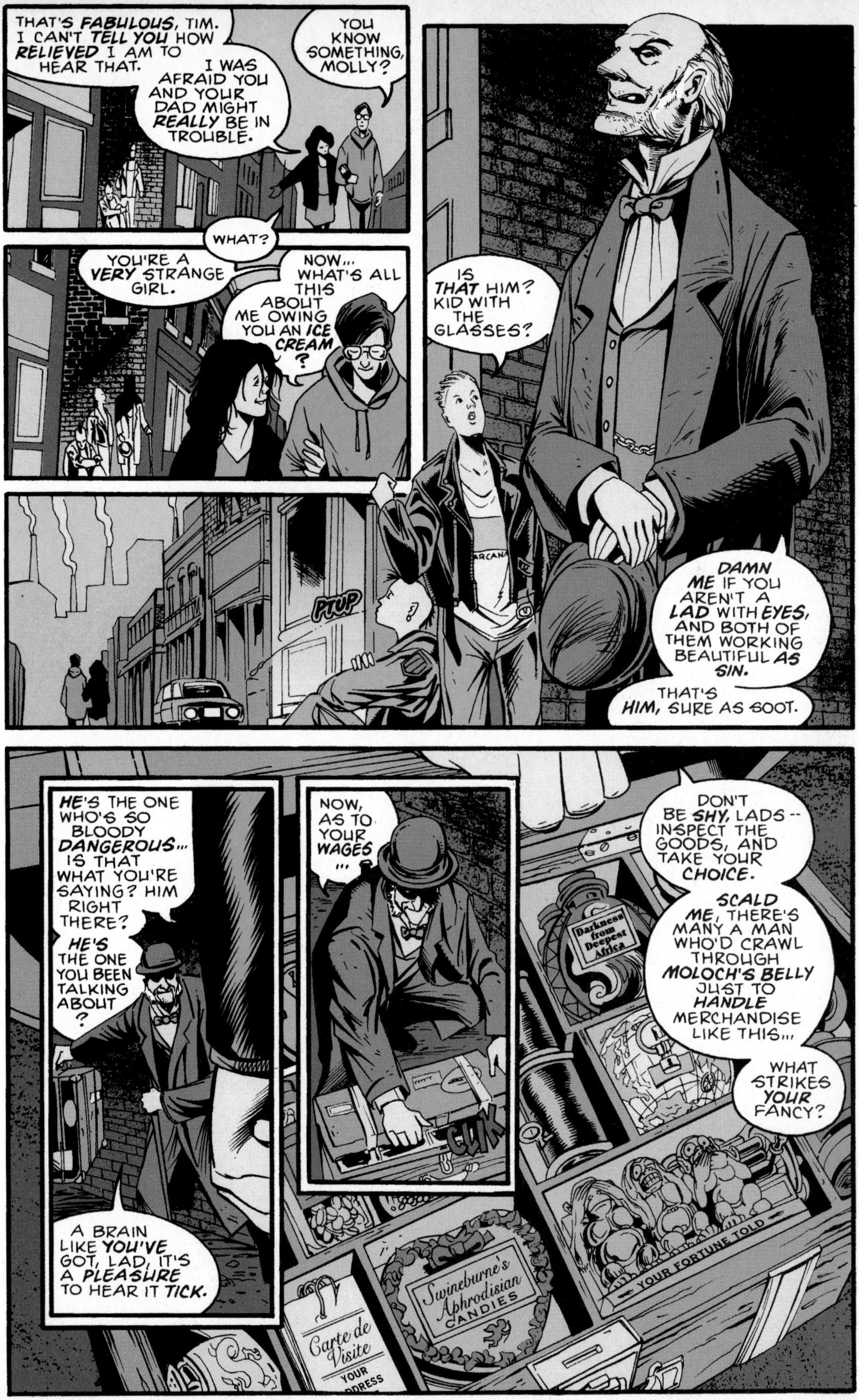
THAT'S FABULOUS, TIM. I CAN'T TELL YOU HOW RELIEVED I AM TO HEAR THAT.
I WAS AFRAID YOU AND YOUR DAD MIGHT REALLY BE IN TROUBLE.
YOU KNOW SOMETHING, MOLLY?
WHAT?
YOU'RE A VERY STRANGE GIRL.
NOW... WHAT'S ALL THIS ABOUT ME OWING YOU AN ICE CREAM?
IS THAT HIM? KID WITH THE GLASSES?
ARCANA
PTUP
DAMN ME IF YOU AREN'T A LAD WITH EYES, AND BOTH OF THEM WORKING BEAUTIFUL AS SIN.
THAT'S HIM, SURE AS SOOT.
HE'S THE ONE WHO'S SO BLOODY DANGEROUS... IS THAT WHAT YOU'RE SAYING? HIM RIGHT THERE?
HE'S THE ONE YOU BEEN TALKING ABOUT?
A BRAIN LIKE YOU'VE GOT, LAD, IT'S A PLEASURE TO HEAR IT TICK.
NOW, AS TO YOUR WAGES...
CLIK
DON'T BE SHY, LADS -- INSPECT THE GOODS, AND TAKE YOUR CHOICE.
SCALD ME, THERE'S MANY A MAN WHO'D CRAWL THROUGH MOLOCH'S BELLY JUST TO HANDLE MERCHANDISE LIKE THIS...
WHAT STRIKES YOUR FANCY?
Darkness from Deepest Africa
YOUR FORTUNE TOLD
Swineburne's Aphrodisian CANDIES
Carte de Visite
YOUR

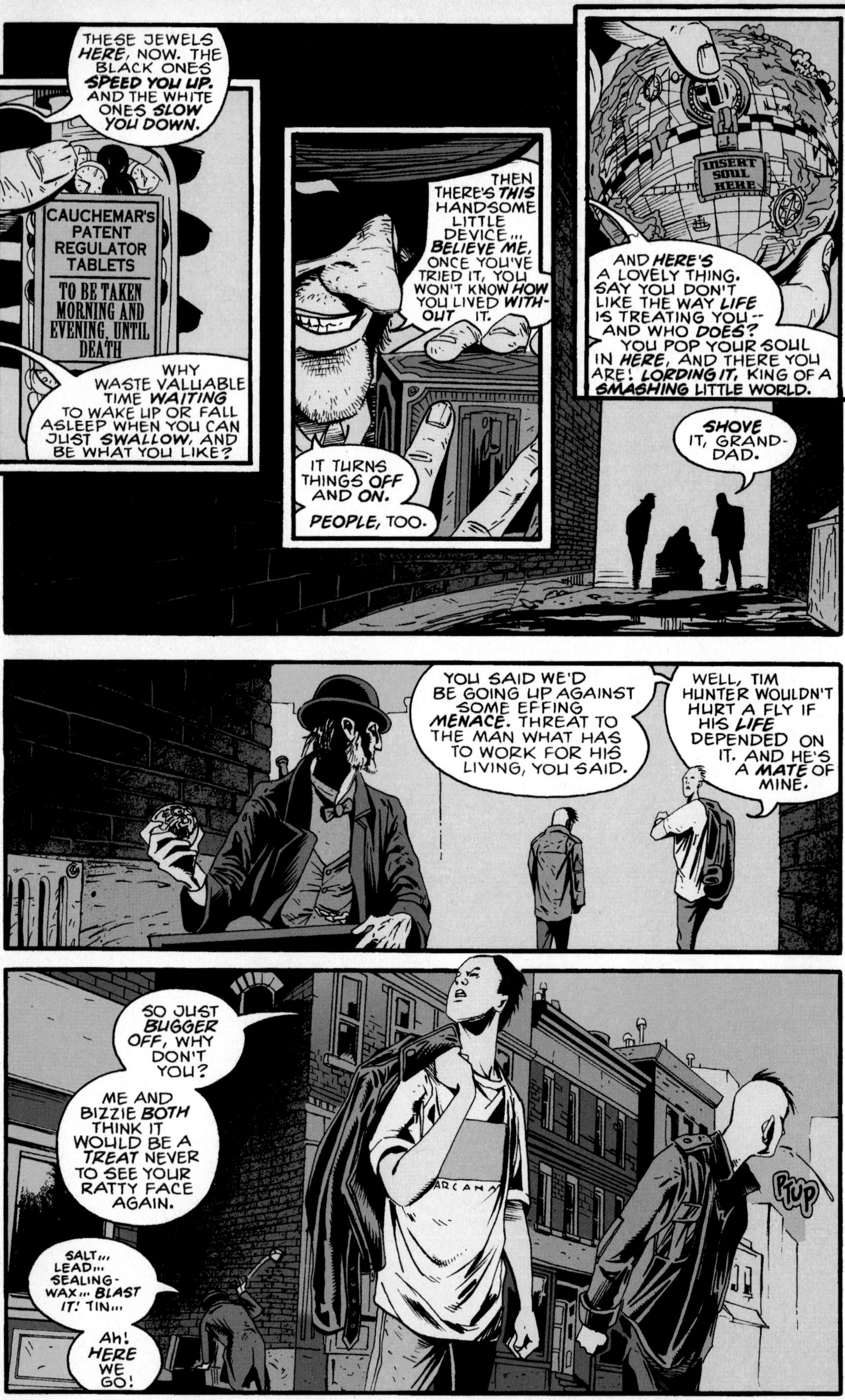
THESE JEWELS HERE, NOW. THE BLACK ONES SPEED YOU UP. AND THE WHITE ONES SLOW YOU DOWN.
CAUCHEMAR's PATENT REGULATOR TABLETS
TO BE TAKEN MORNING AND EVENING, UNTIL DEATH
WHY WASTE VALUABLE TIME WAITING TO WAKE UP OR FALL ASLEEP WHEN YOU CAN JUST SWALLOW, AND BE WHAT YOU LIKE?
THEN THERE'S THIS HANDSOME LITTLE DEVICE... BELIEVE ME, ONCE YOU'VE TRIED IT, YOU WON'T KNOW HOW YOU LIVED WITH-OUT IT.
IT TURNS THINGS OFF AND ON.
PEOPLE, TOO.
INSERT SOUL HERE
AND HERE'S A LOVELY THING. SAY YOU DON'T LIKE THE WAY LIFE IS TREATING YOU -- AND WHO DOES? YOU POP YOUR SOUL IN HERE, AND THERE YOU ARE! LORDING IT, KING OF A SMASHING LITTLE WORLD.
SHOVE IT, GRAND-DAD.
YOU SAID WE'D BE GOING UP AGAINST SOME EFFING MENACE. THREAT TO THE MAN WHAT HAS TO WORK FOR HIS LIVING, YOU SAID.
WELL, TIM HUNTER WOULDN'T HURT A FLY IF HIS LIFE DEPENDED ON IT. AND HE'S A MATE OF MINE.
SO JUST BUGGER OFF, WHY DON'T YOU?
ME AND BIZZIE BOTH THINK IT WOULD BE A TREAT NEVER TO SEE YOUR RATTY FACE AGAIN.
ARCANA
PTUP
SALT... LEAD... SEALING-WAX... BLAST IT! TIN...
Ah! HERE WE GO!

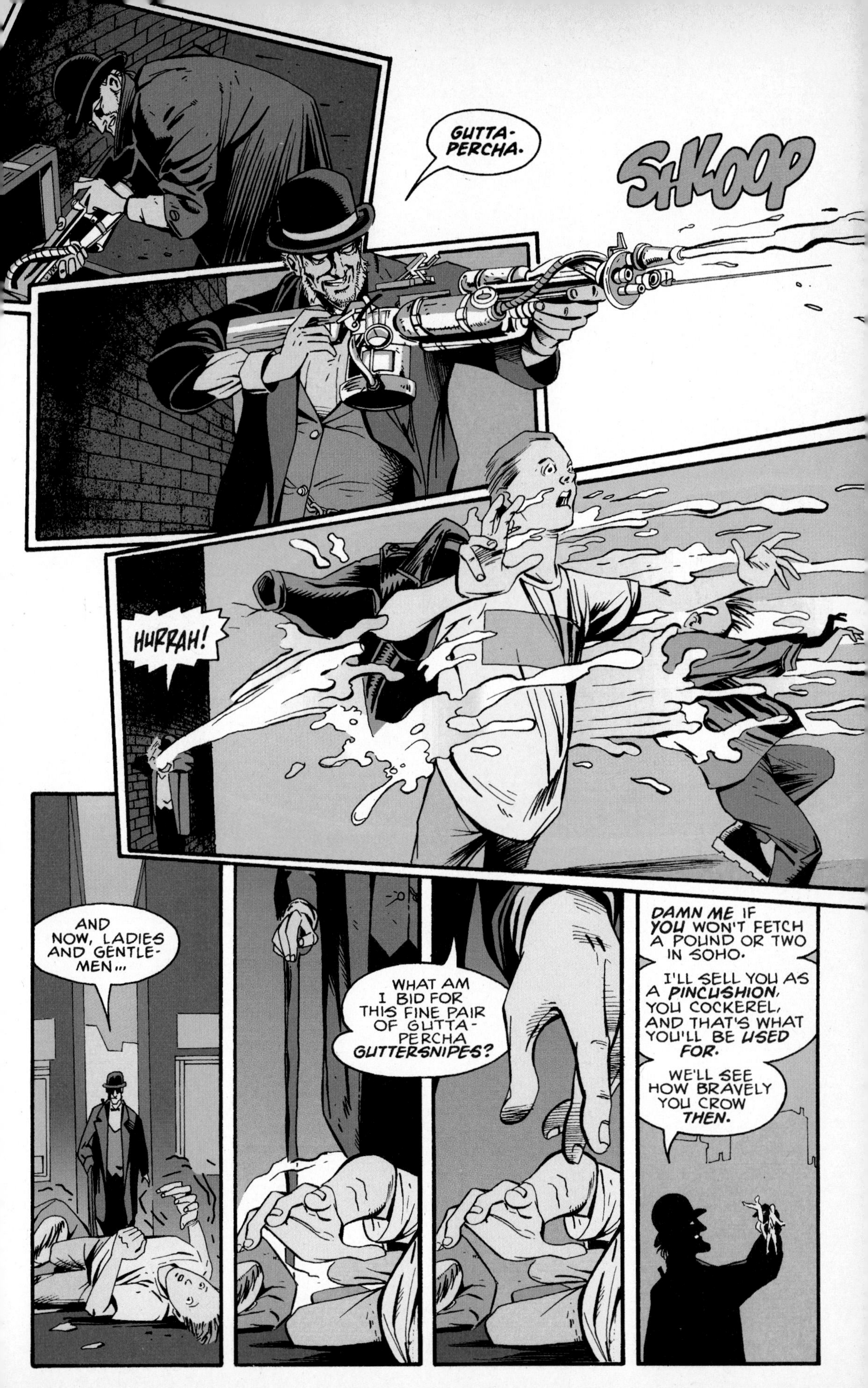

GUTTA-PERCHA.
SHLOOP
HURRAH!
AND NOW, LADIES AND GENTLE-MEN...
WHAT AM I BID FOR THIS FINE PAIR OF GUTTA-PERCHA GUTTERSNIPES?
DAMN ME IF YOU WON'T FETCH A POUND OR TWO IN SOHO.
I'LL SELL YOU AS A PINCUSHION, YOU COCKEREL, AND THAT'S WHAT YOU'LL BE USED FOR.
WE'LL SEE HOW BRAVELY YOU CROW THEN.

DAYS AND DAYS HE'S BEEN LOOKING FOR HER.

NIGHTS, TOO.

TALKING TO MARYA ALWAYS HAD HELPED HIM GET HIS THOUGHTS STRAIGHT.

ONLY HE HADN'T FOUND HER. AND HE WEREN'T GOING TO, NEITHER.

THIS LONDON, IT'S TOO BIG. TOO STRANGE.

HE DON'T KNOW HIS WAY AROUND NO MORE.

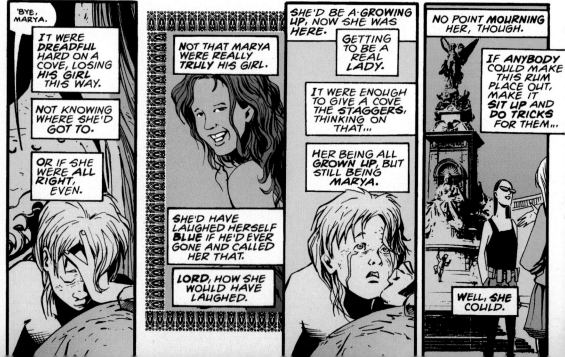

'BYE, MARYA.

IT WERE DREADFUL HARD ON A COVE, LOSING HIS GIRL THIS WAY.

NOT KNOWING WHERE SHE'D GOT TO.

OR IF SHE WERE ALL RIGHT, EVEN.

NOT THAT MARYA WERE REALLY TRULY HIS GIRL.

SHE'D HAVE LAUGHED HERSELF BLUE IF HE'D EVER GONE AND CALLED HER THAT.

LORD, HOW SHE WOULD HAVE LAUGHED.

SHE'D BE A-GROWING UP, NOW SHE WAS HERE.

GETTING TO BE A REAL LADY.

IT WERE ENOUGH TO GIVE A COVE THE STAGGERS, THINKING ON THAT...

HER BEING ALL GROWN UP, BUT STILL BEING MARYA.

NO POINT MOURNING HER, THOUGH.

IF ANYBODY COULD MAKE THIS RUM PLACE OUT, MAKE IT SIT UP AND DO TRICKS FOR THEM...

WELL, SHE COULD.

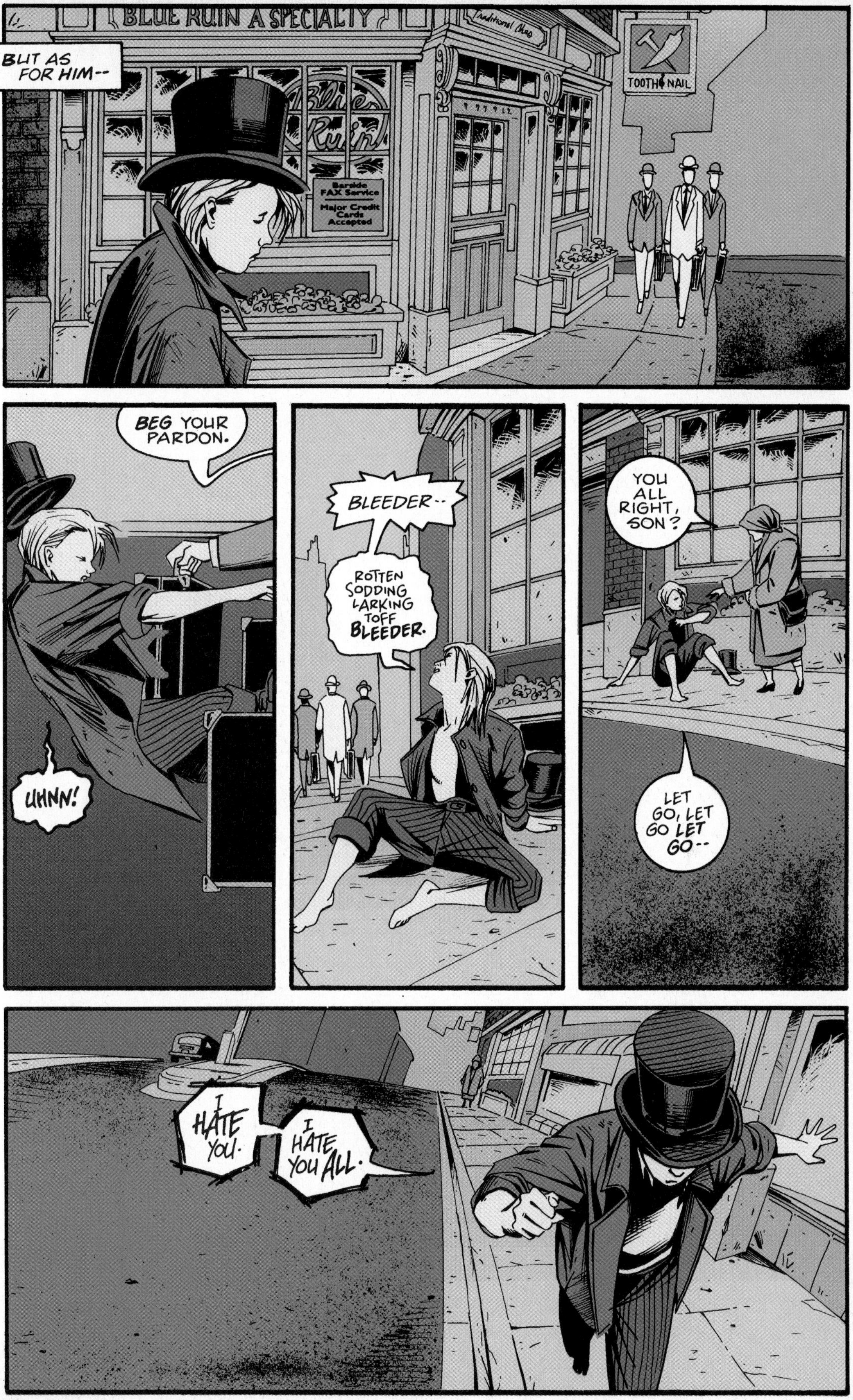
BLUE RUIN A SPECIALTY
BUT AS FOR HIM--
Blue Ruin
Barside FAX Service
Major Credit Cards Accepted
TOOTH & NAIL
BEG YOUR PARDON.
UHNN!
BLEEDER--
ROTTEN SODDING LARKING TOFF BLEEDER.
YOU ALL RIGHT, SON?
LET GO, LET GO LET GO--
I HATE YOU.
I HATE YOU ALL.

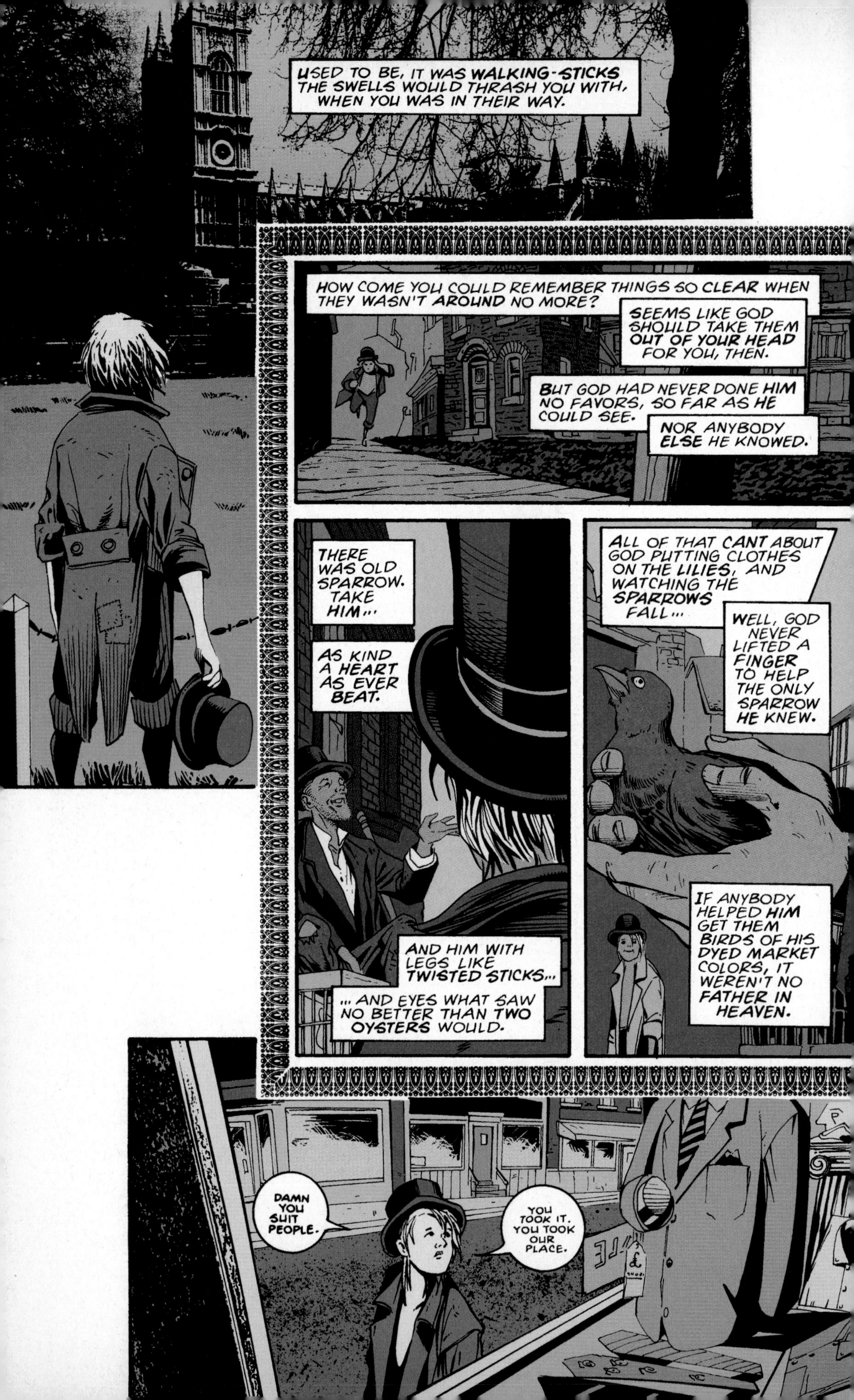

USED TO BE, IT WAS WALKING-STICKS THE SWELLS WOULD THRASH YOU WITH, WHEN YOU WAS IN THEIR WAY.
HOW COME YOU COULD REMEMBER THINGS SO CLEAR WHEN THEY WASN'T AROUND NO MORE?
SEEMS LIKE GOD SHOULD TAKE THEM OUT OF YOUR HEAD FOR YOU, THEN.
BUT GOD HAD NEVER DONE HIM NO FAVORS, SO FAR AS HE COULD SEE.
NOR ANYBODY ELSE HE KNOWED.
THERE WAS OLD SPARROW. TAKE HIM...
AS KIND A HEART AS EVER BEAT.
AND HIM WITH LEGS LIKE TWISTED STICKS...
...AND EYES WHAT SAW NO BETTER THAN TWO OYSTERS WOULD.
ALL OF THAT CANT ABOUT GOD PUTTING CLOTHES ON THE LILIES, AND WATCHING THE SPARROWS FALL...
WELL, GOD NEVER LIFTED A FINGER TO HELP THE ONLY SPARROW HE KNEW.
IF ANYBODY HELPED HIM GET THEM BIRDS OF HIS DYED MARKET COLORS, IT WEREN'T NO FATHER IN HEAVEN.
DAMN YOU SUIT PEOPLE.
YOU TOOK IT. YOU TOOK OUR PLACE.

OLD SPARROW'S PLACE. LAUGHING JENNY'S PLACE.
MY PLACE.
YOU AIN'T LEFT US NOTHING.
NOT A DROP OF ALE NOR CRUST OF BREAD. NOR A SPARK OF FIRE TO WARM OUR HANDS AT.
BUT YOU CAN'T... unhhhh...
CAN'T HAVE CHANGED... huhnn... EVERY-THING --
--UUHF!
THERE'S GOT TO BE SOMEPLACE THEM SUIT-CASE BLOKES AIN'T GOT 'ROUND TO SPOILING YET.
SOME-WHERE, SOME-THING'S GOT TO BE--
SPLOSHH
THE WAY IT USED TO BE.

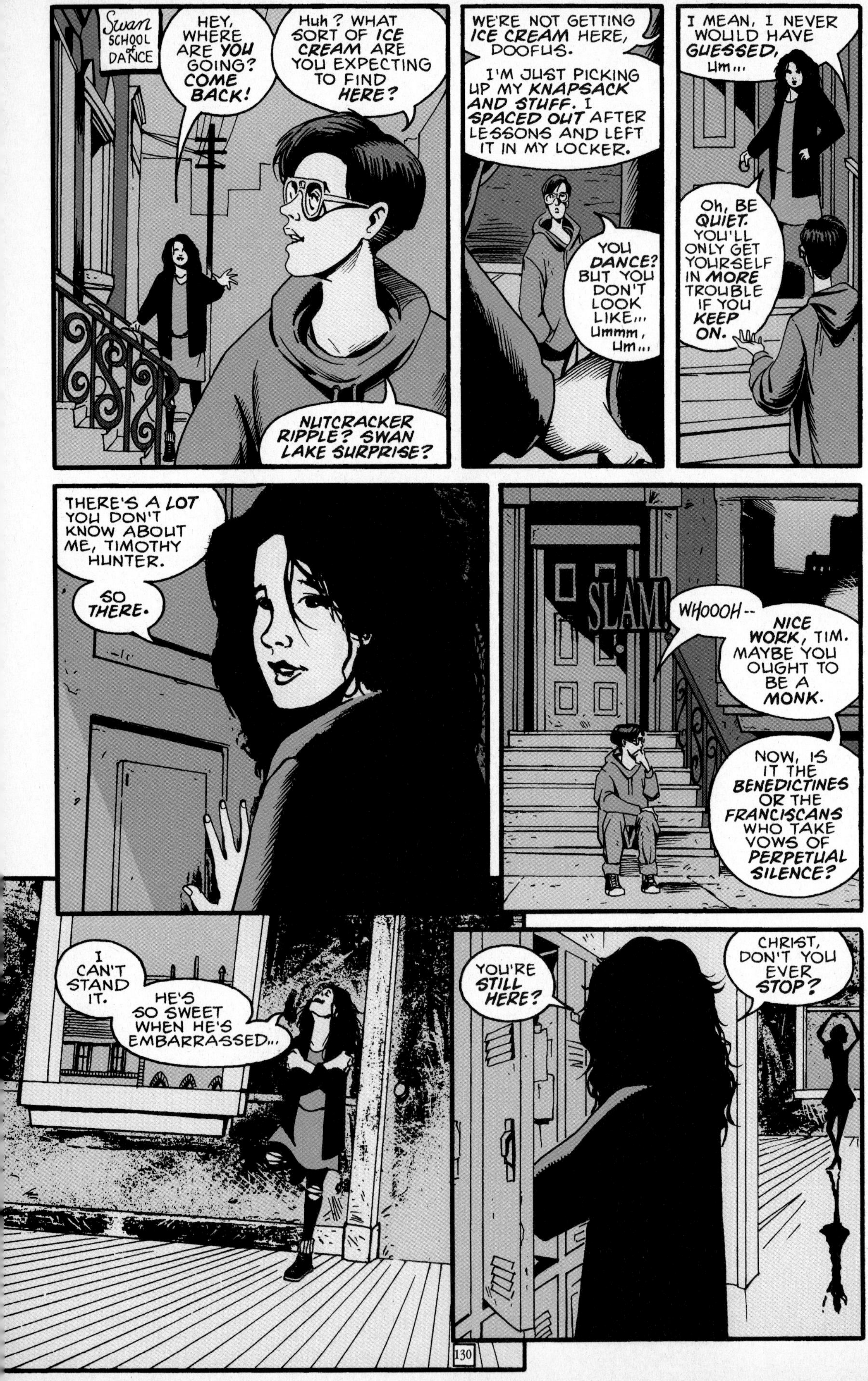
Swan SCHOOL of DANCE
HEY, WHERE ARE YOU GOING? COME BACK!
Huh? WHAT SORT OF ICE CREAM ARE YOU EXPECTING TO FIND HERE?
NUTCRACKER RIPPLE? SWAN LAKE SURPRISE?
WE'RE NOT GETTING ICE CREAM HERE, DOOFUS.
I'M JUST PICKING UP MY KNAPSACK AND STUFF. I SPACED OUT AFTER LESSONS AND LEFT IT IN MY LOCKER.
YOU DANCE? BUT YOU DON'T LOOK LIKE... UMMM, UM...
I MEAN, I NEVER WOULD HAVE GUESSED, UM...
Oh, BE QUIET. YOU'LL ONLY GET YOURSELF IN MORE TROUBLE IF YOU KEEP ON.
THERE'S A LOT YOU DON'T KNOW ABOUT ME, TIMOTHY HUNTER.
SO THERE.
SLAM!
WHOOOH-- NICE WORK, TIM. MAYBE YOU OUGHT TO BE A MONK.
NOW, IS IT THE BENEDICTINES OR THE FRANCISCANS WHO TAKE VOWS OF PERPETUAL SILENCE?
I CAN'T STAND IT.
HE'S SO SWEET WHEN HE'S EMBARRASSED...
YOU'RE STILL HERE?
CHRIST, DON'T YOU EVER STOP?

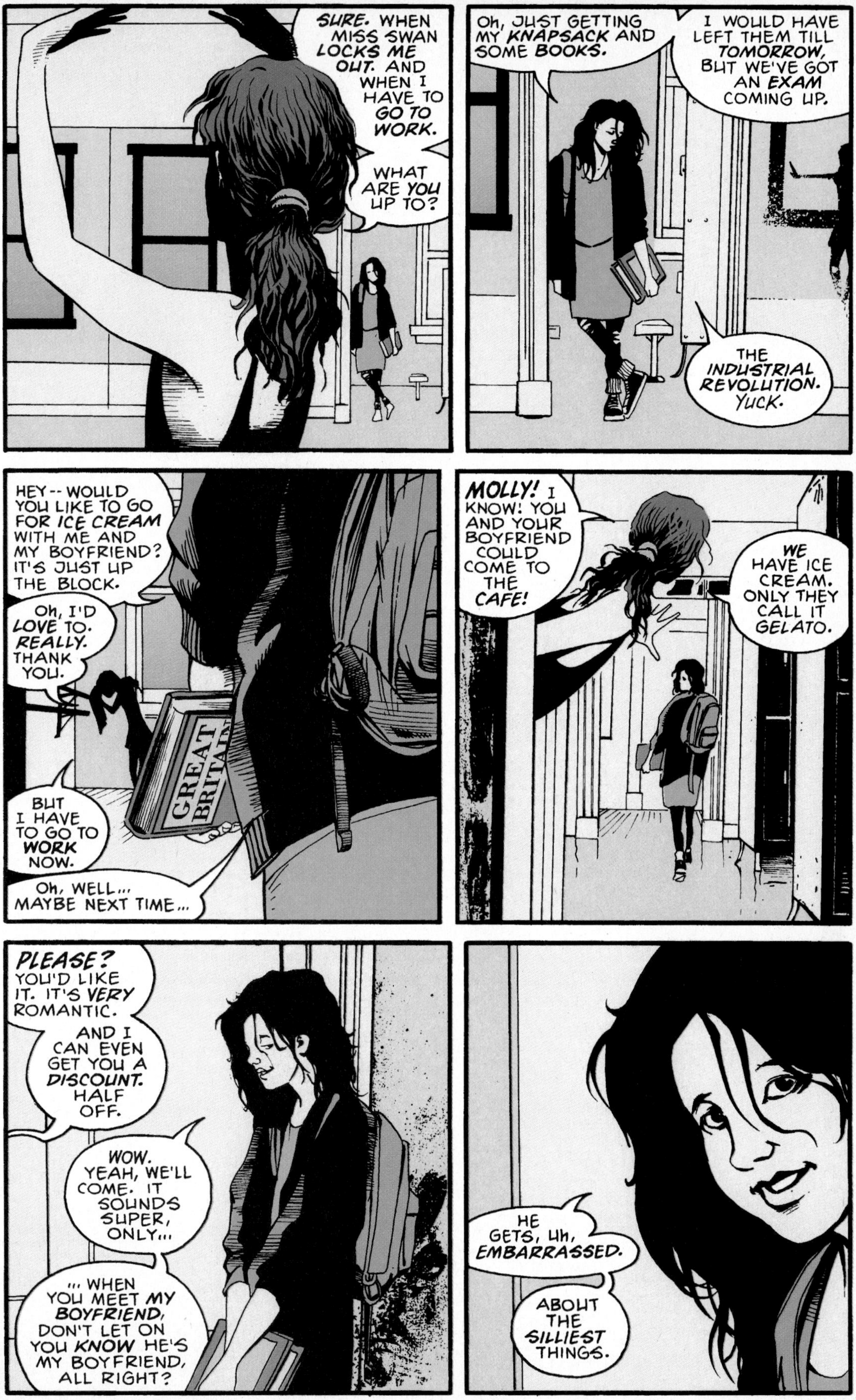
SURE. WHEN MISS SWAN LOCKS ME OUT. AND WHEN I HAVE TO GO TO WORK.
WHAT ARE YOU UP TO?
Oh, JUST GETTING MY KNAPSACK AND SOME BOOKS.
I WOULD HAVE LEFT THEM TILL TOMORROW, BUT WE'VE GOT AN EXAM COMING UP.
THE INDUSTRIAL REVOLUTION. Yuck.
HEY -- WOULD YOU LIKE TO GO FOR ICE CREAM WITH ME AND MY BOYFRIEND? IT'S JUST UP THE BLOCK.
Oh, I'D LOVE TO. REALLY. THANK YOU.
GREAT
BUT I HAVE TO GO TO WORK NOW.
Oh, WELL... MAYBE NEXT TIME...
MOLLY! I KNOW: YOU AND YOUR BOYFRIEND COULD COME TO THE CAFE!
WE HAVE ICE CREAM. ONLY THEY CALL IT GELATO.
PLEASE? YOU'D LIKE IT. IT'S VERY ROMANTIC.
AND I CAN EVEN GET YOU A DISCOUNT. HALF OFF.
WOW. YEAH, WE'LL COME. IT SOUNDS SUPER, ONLY...
... WHEN YOU MEET MY BOYFRIEND, DON'T LET ON YOU KNOW HE'S MY BOYFRIEND, ALL RIGHT?
HE GETS, Uh, EMBARRASSED.
ABOUT THE SILLIEST THINGS.

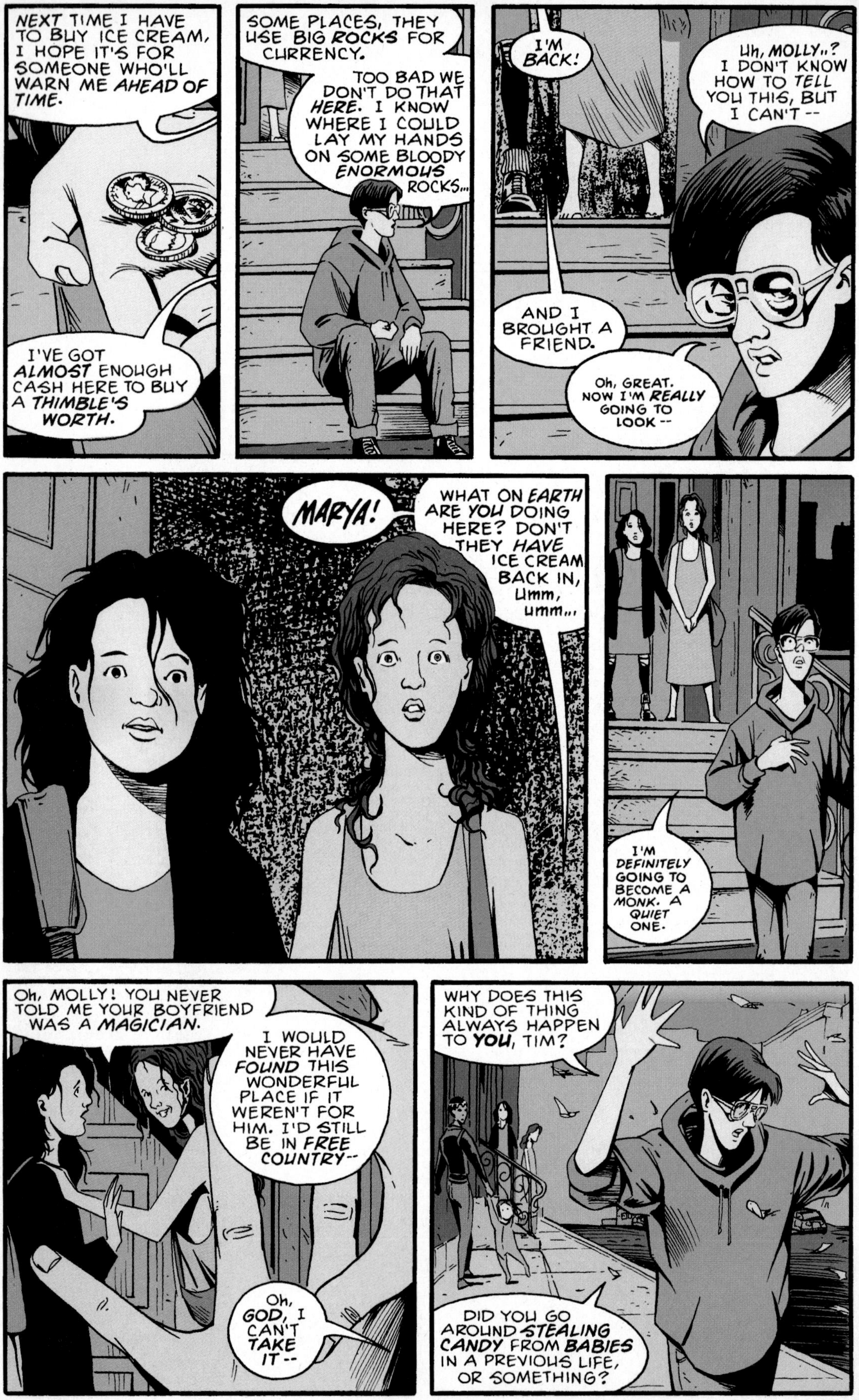

NEXT TIME I HAVE TO BUY ICE CREAM, I HOPE IT'S FOR SOMEONE WHO'LL WARN ME AHEAD OF TIME.
I'VE GOT ALMOST ENOUGH CASH HERE TO BUY A THIMBLE'S WORTH.
SOME PLACES, THEY USE BIG ROCKS FOR CURRENCY.
TOO BAD WE DON'T DO THAT HERE. I KNOW WHERE I COULD LAY MY HANDS ON SOME BLOODY ENORMOUS ROCKS...
I'M BACK!
AND I BROUGHT A FRIEND.
Uh, MOLLY..? I DON'T KNOW HOW TO TELL YOU THIS, BUT I CAN'T --
Oh, GREAT. NOW I'M REALLY GOING TO LOOK --
MARYA!
WHAT ON EARTH ARE YOU DOING HERE? DON'T THEY HAVE ICE CREAM BACK IN, umm, umm...
I'M DEFINITELY GOING TO BECOME A MONK. A QUIET ONE.
Oh, MOLLY! YOU NEVER TOLD ME YOUR BOYFRIEND WAS A MAGICIAN.
I WOULD NEVER HAVE FOUND THIS WONDERFUL PLACE IF IT WEREN'T FOR HIM. I'D STILL BE IN FREE COUNTRY--
Oh, GOD, I CAN'T TAKE IT --
WHY DOES THIS KIND OF THING ALWAYS HAPPEN TO YOU, TIM?
DID YOU GO AROUND STEALING CANDY FROM BABIES IN A PREVIOUS LIFE, OR SOMETHING?

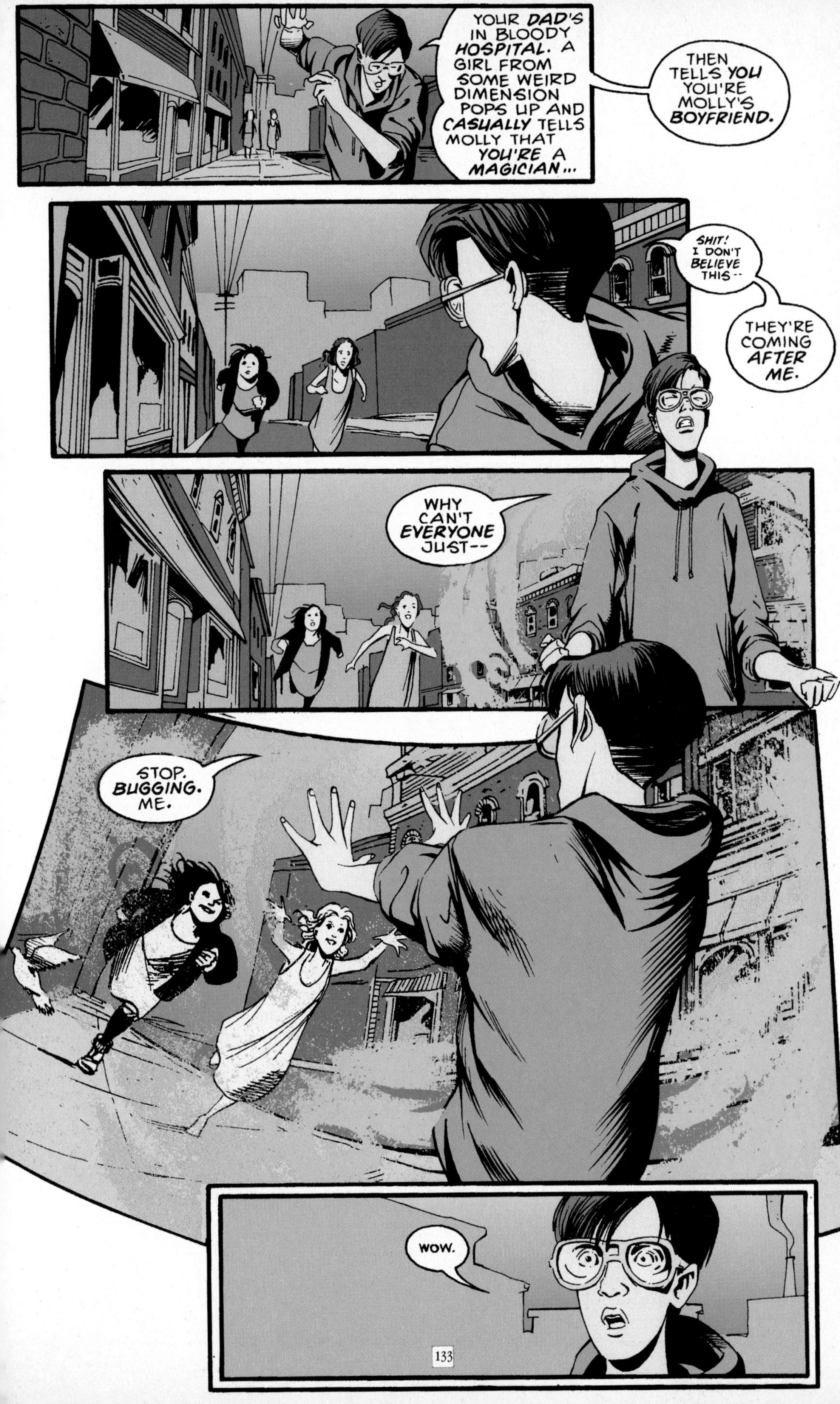
YOUR DAD'S IN BLOODY HOSPITAL. A GIRL FROM SOME WEIRD DIMENSION POPS UP AND CASUALLY TELLS MOLLY THAT YOU'RE A MAGICIAN...
THEN TELLS YOU YOU'RE MOLLY'S BOYFRIEND.
SHIT! I DON'T BELIEVE THIS--
THEY'RE COMING AFTER ME.
WHY CAN'T EVERYONE JUST--
STOP. BUGGING. ME.
WOW.

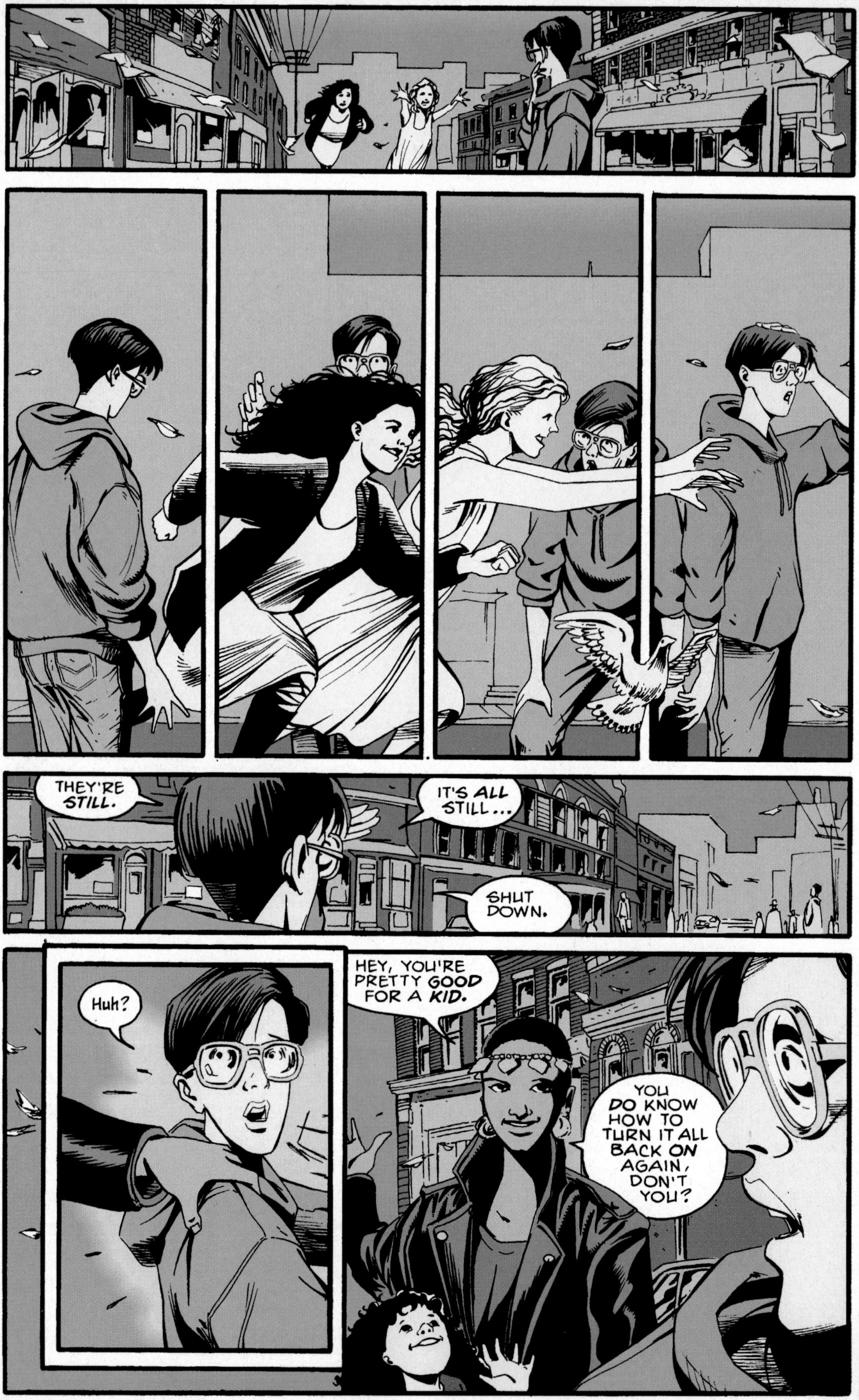
THEY'RE STILL.
IT'S ALL STILL...
SHUT DOWN.
Huh?
HEY, YOU'RE PRETTY GOOD FOR A KID.
YOU DO KNOW HOW TO TURN IT ALL BACK ON AGAIN, DON'T YOU?

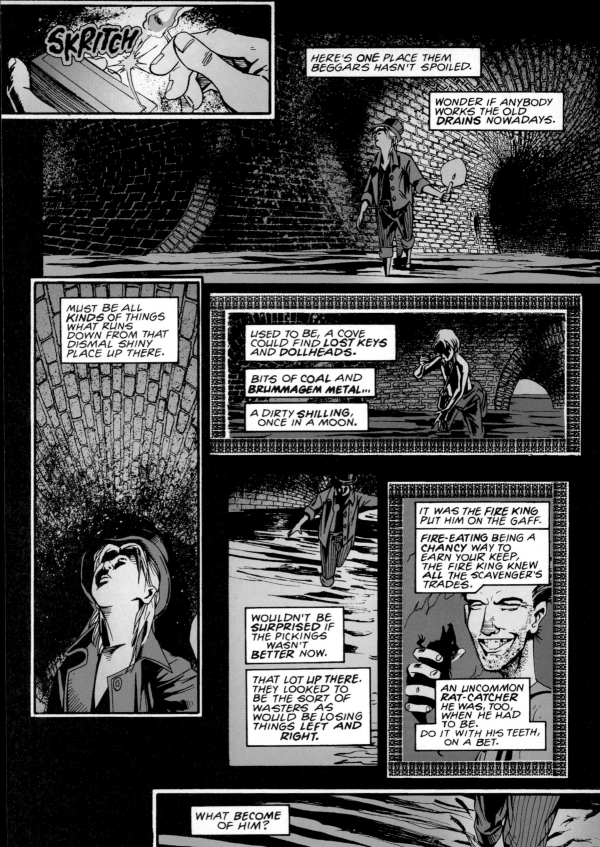

SKRITCH

HERE'S ONE PLACE THEM BEGGARS HASN'T SPOILED.

WONDER IF ANYBODY WORKS THE OLD DRAINS NOWADAYS.

MUST BE ALL KINDS OF THINGS WHAT RUNS DOWN FROM THAT DISMAL SHINY PLACE UP THERE.

USED TO BE, A COVE COULD FIND LOST KEYS AND DOLLHEADS.

BITS OF COAL AND BRUMMAGEM METAL...

A DIRTY SHILLING, ONCE IN A MOON.

WOULDN'T BE SURPRISED IF THE PICKINGS WASN'T BETTER NOW.

THAT LOT UP THERE. THEY LOOKED TO BE THE SORT OF WASTERS AS WOULD BE LOSING THINGS LEFT AND RIGHT.

IT WAS THE FIRE KING PUT HIM ON THE GAFF.

FIRE-EATING BEING A CHANCY WAY TO EARN YOUR KEEP, THE FIRE KING KNEW ALL THE SCAVENGER'S TRADES.

AN UNCOMMON RAT-CATCHER HE WAS, TOO, WHEN HE HAD TO BE. DO IT WITH HIS TEETH, ON A BET.

WHAT BECOME OF HIM?

LORD, IT'D BE WORTH A PENNY TO SEE HIM AGAIN.

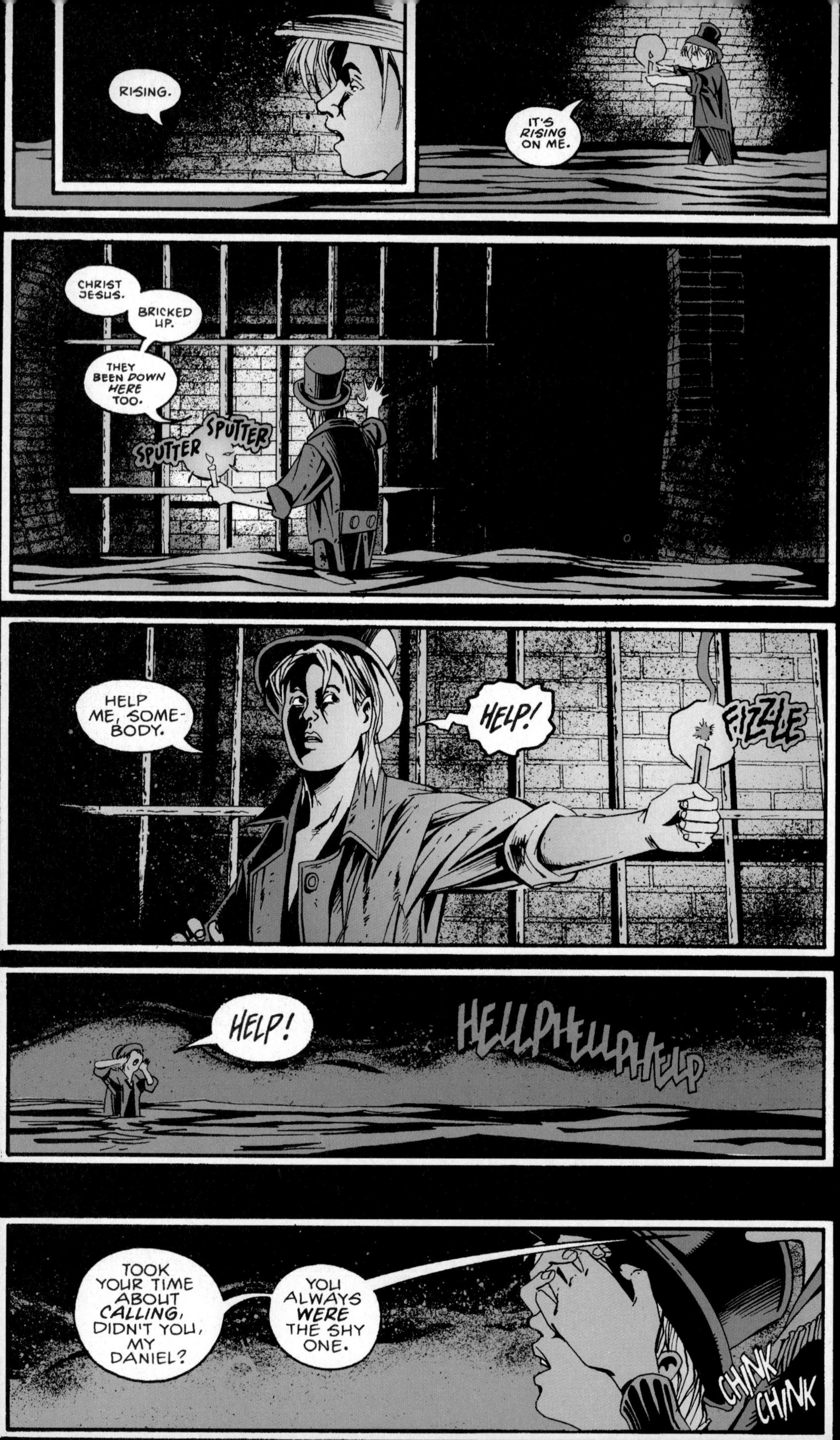
RISING.
IT'S RISING ON ME.
CHRIST JESUS.
BRICKED UP.
THEY BEEN DOWN HERE TOO.
SPUTTER SPUTTER
HELP ME, SOMEBODY.
HELP!
FIZZLE
HELP!
HELLPHELLPHELP
TOOK YOUR TIME ABOUT CALLING, DIDN'T YOU, MY DANIEL?
YOU ALWAYS WERE THE SHY ONE.
CHINK CHINK

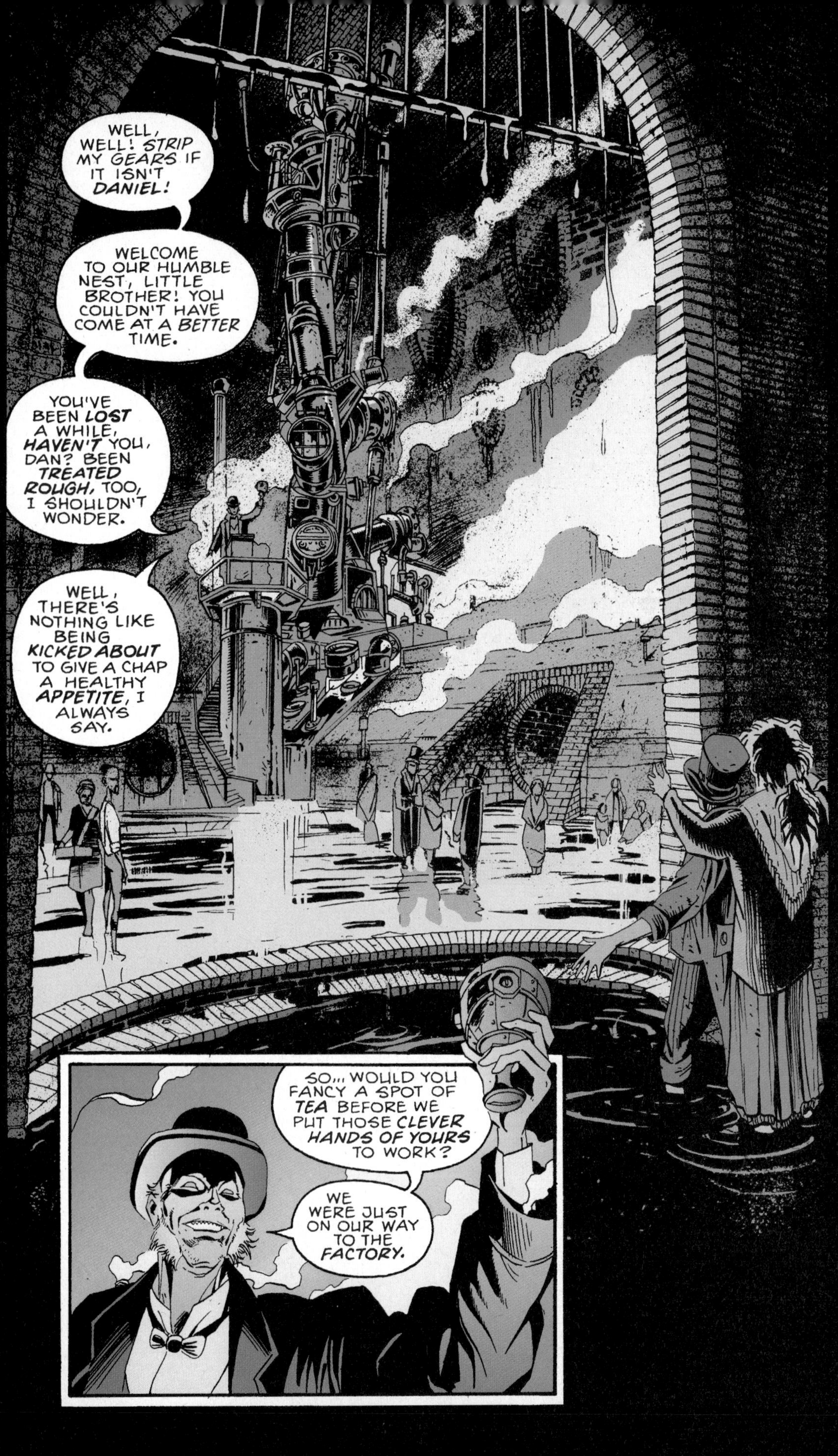
WELL, WELL! STRIP MY GEARS IF IT ISN'T DANIEL!
WELCOME TO OUR HUMBLE NEST, LITTLE BROTHER! YOU COULDN'T HAVE COME AT A BETTER TIME.
YOU'VE BEEN LOST A WHILE, HAVEN'T YOU, DAN? BEEN TREATED ROUGH, TOO, I SHOULDN'T WONDER.
WELL, THERE'S NOTHING LIKE BEING KICKED ABOUT TO GIVE A CHAP A HEALTHY APPETITE, I ALWAYS SAY.
SO... WOULD YOU FANCY A SPOT OF TEA BEFORE WE PUT THOSE CLEVER HANDS OF YOURS TO WORK?
WE WERE JUST ON OUR WAY TO THE FACTORY.

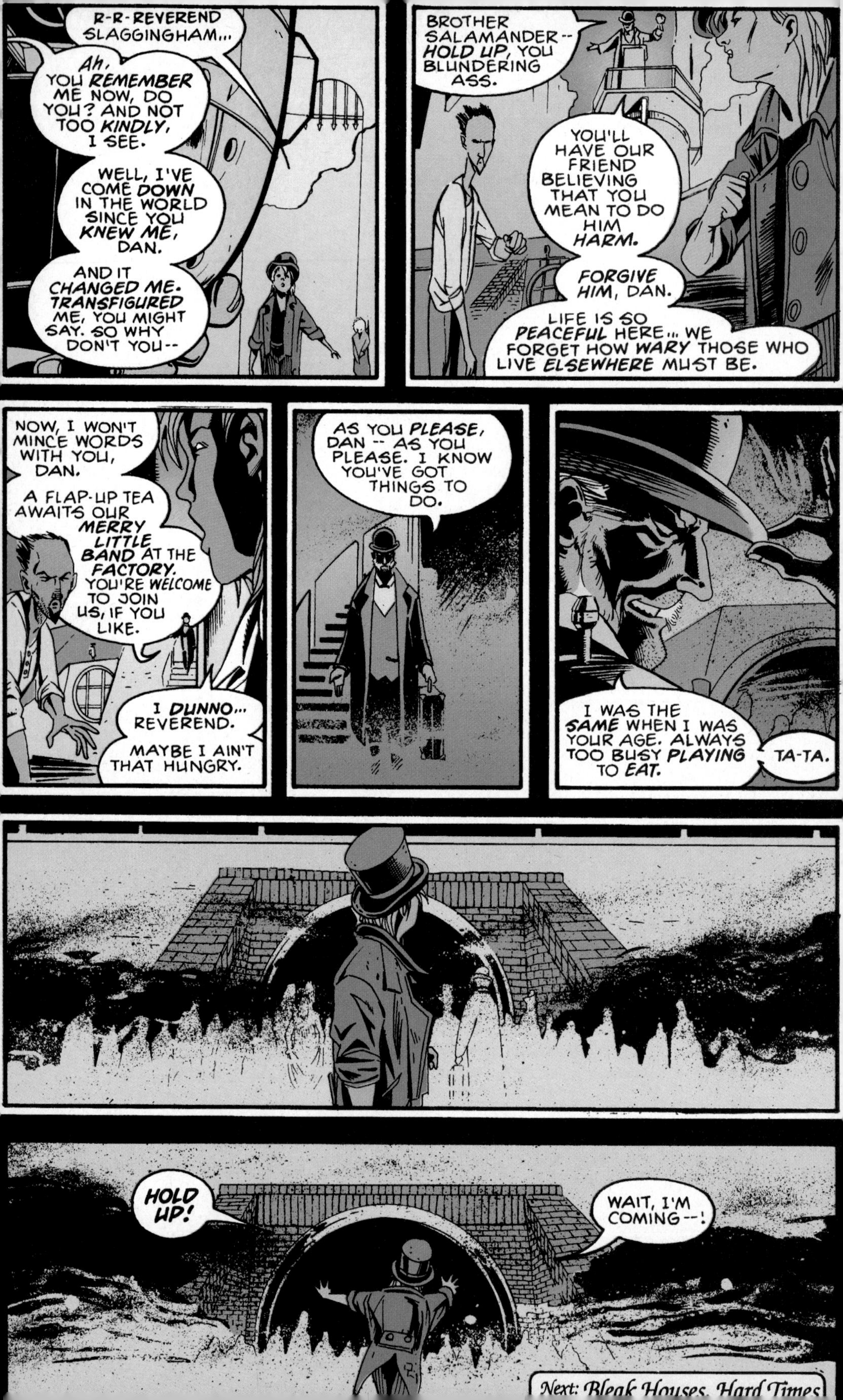
R-R-REVEREND SLAGGINGHAM...
Ah, YOU REMEMBER ME NOW, DO YOU? AND NOT TOO KINDLY, I SEE.
WELL, I'VE COME DOWN IN THE WORLD SINCE YOU KNEW ME, DAN.
AND IT CHANGED ME. TRANSFIGURED ME, YOU MIGHT SAY. SO WHY DON'T YOU--
BROTHER SALAMANDER-- HOLD UP, YOU BLUNDERING ASS.
YOU'LL HAVE OUR FRIEND BELIEVING THAT YOU MEAN TO DO HIM HARM.
FORGIVE HIM, DAN.
LIFE IS SO PEACEFUL HERE... WE FORGET HOW WARY THOSE WHO LIVE ELSEWHERE MUST BE.
NOW, I WON'T MINCE WORDS WITH YOU, DAN.
A FLAP-UP TEA AWAITS OUR MERRY LITTLE BAND AT THE FACTORY. YOU'RE WELCOME TO JOIN US, IF YOU LIKE.
I DUNNO... REVEREND.
MAYBE I AIN'T THAT HUNGRY.
AS YOU PLEASE, DAN -- AS YOU PLEASE. I KNOW YOU'VE GOT THINGS TO DO.
I WAS THE SAME WHEN I WAS YOUR AGE. ALWAYS TOO BUSY PLAYING TO EAT.
TA-TA.
HOLD UP!
WAIT, I'M COMING--!
Next: Bleak Houses, Hard Times

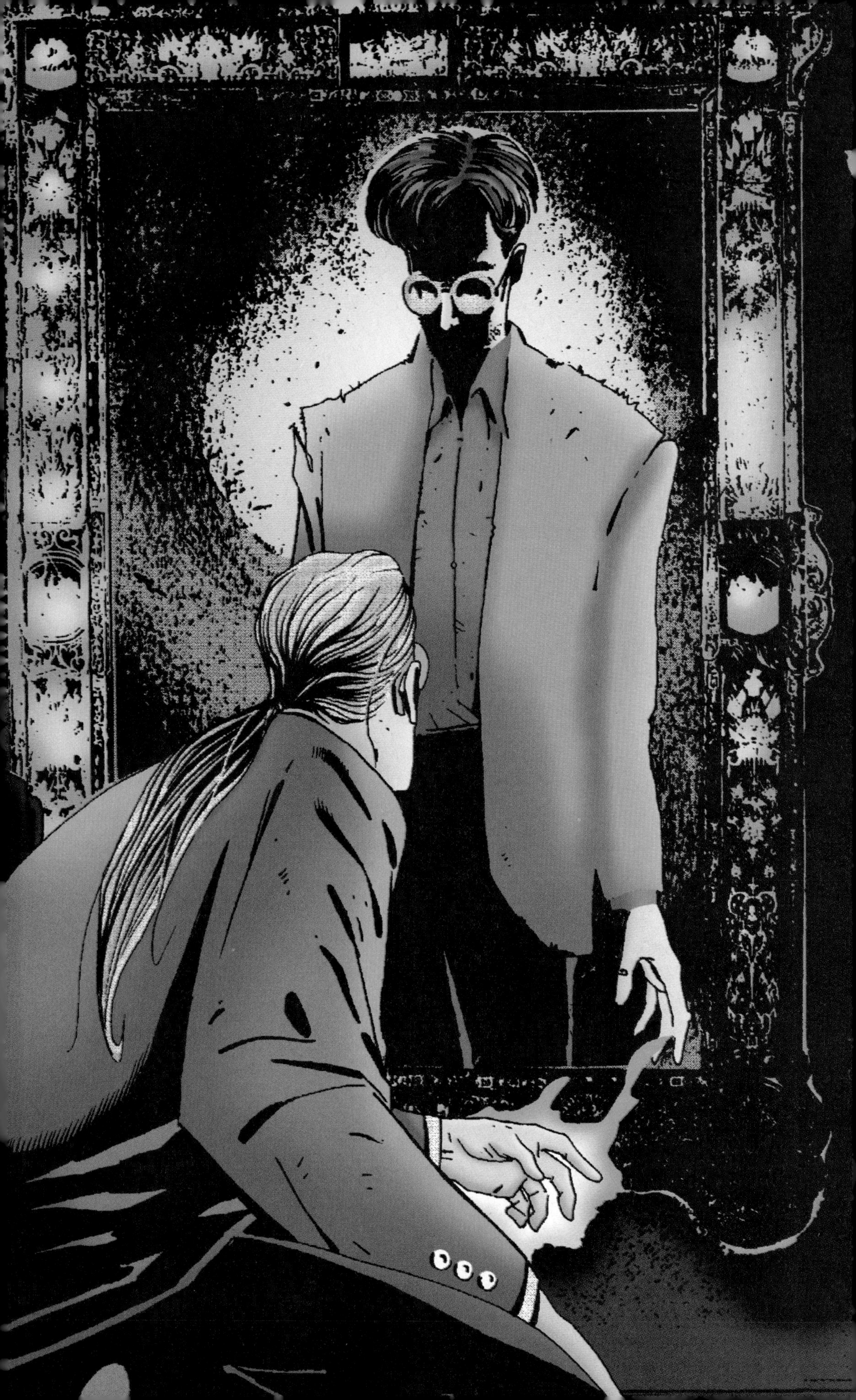

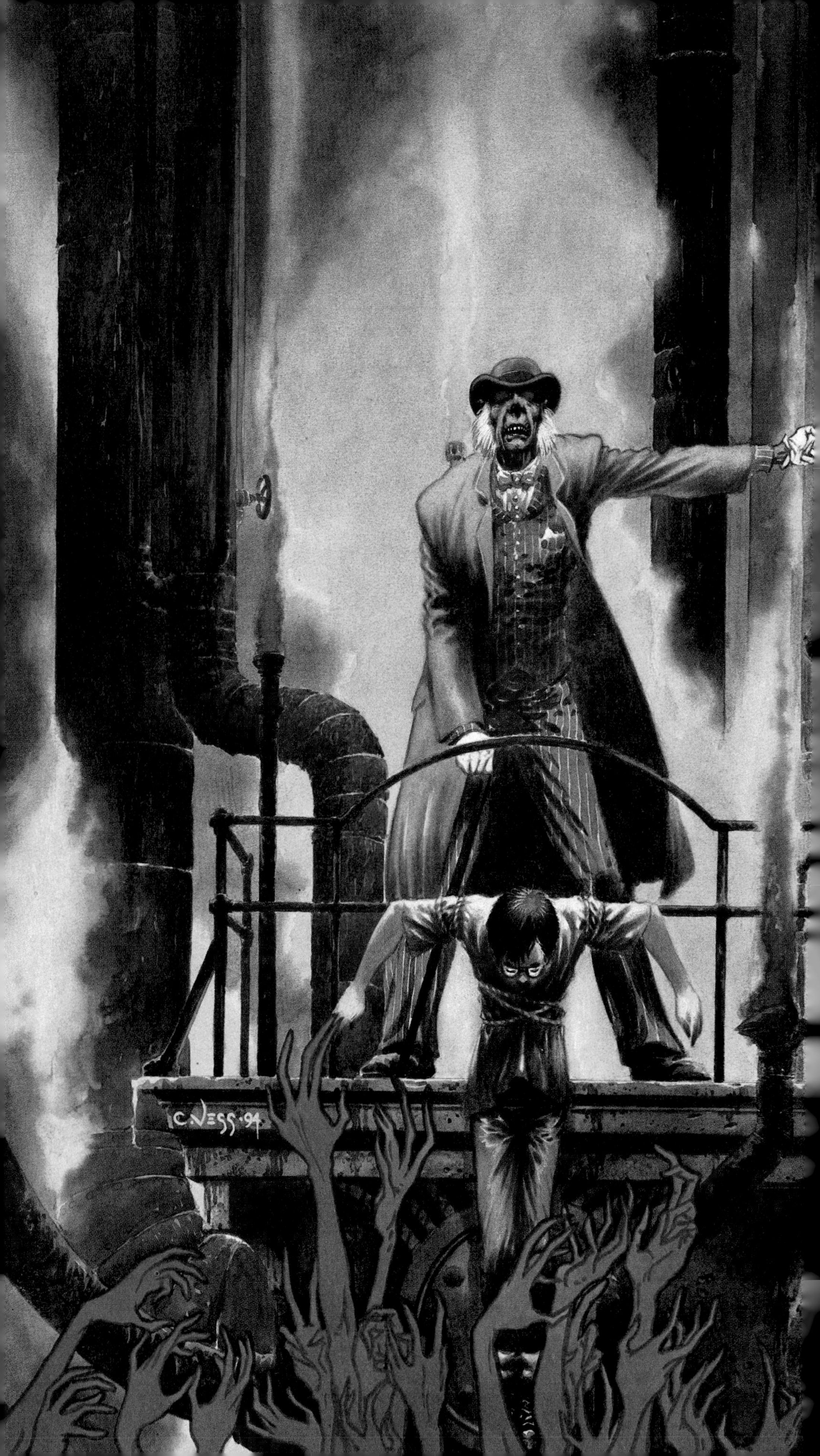
C.VESS·94

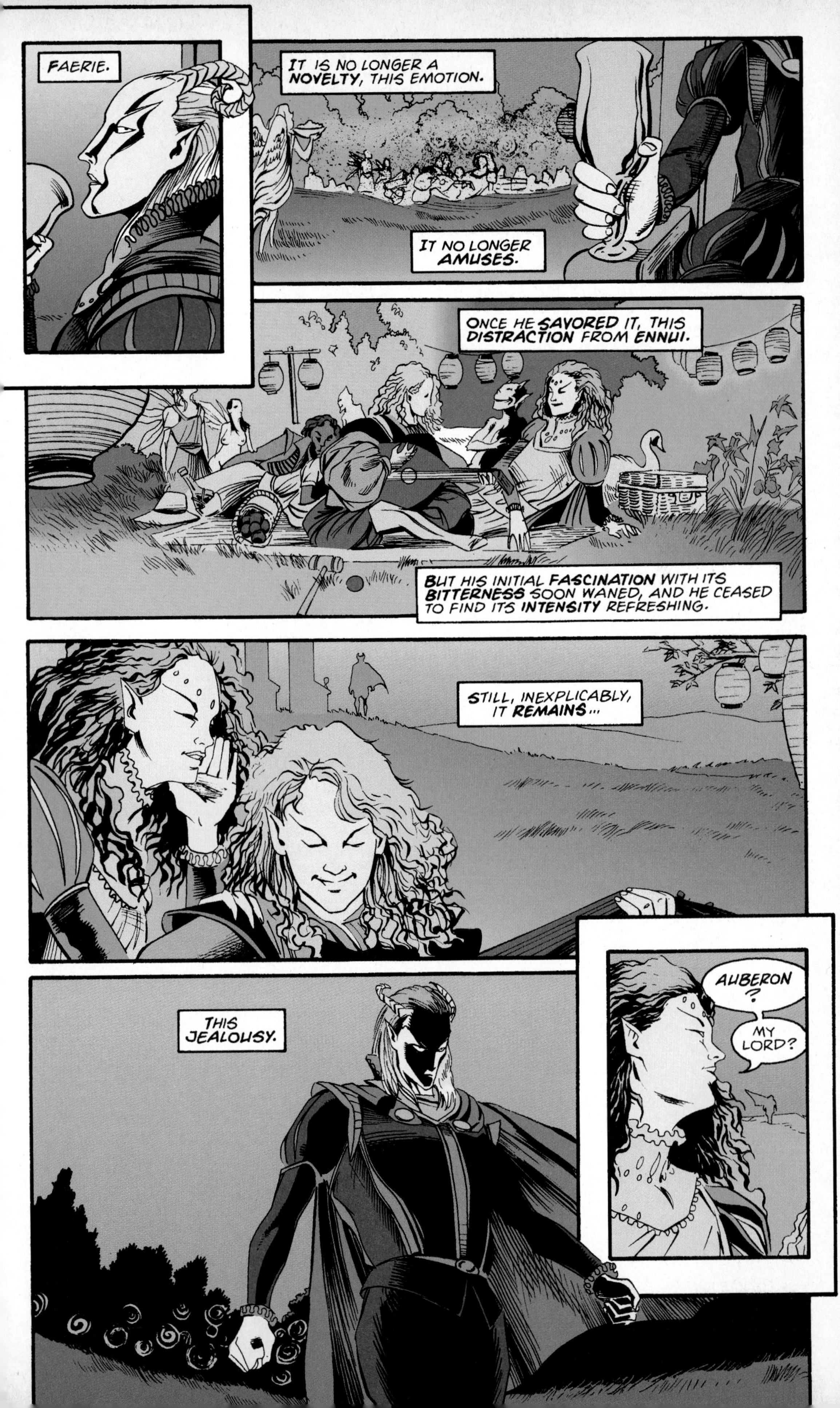
FAERIE.
IT IS NO LONGER A NOVELTY, THIS EMOTION.
IT NO LONGER AMUSES.
ONCE HE SAVORED IT, THIS DISTRACTION FROM ENNUI.
BUT HIS INITIAL FASCINATION WITH ITS BITTERNESS SOON WANED, AND HE CEASED TO FIND ITS INTENSITY REFRESHING.
STILL, INEXPLICABLY, IT REMAINS...
THIS JEALOUSY.
AUBERON?
MY LORD?

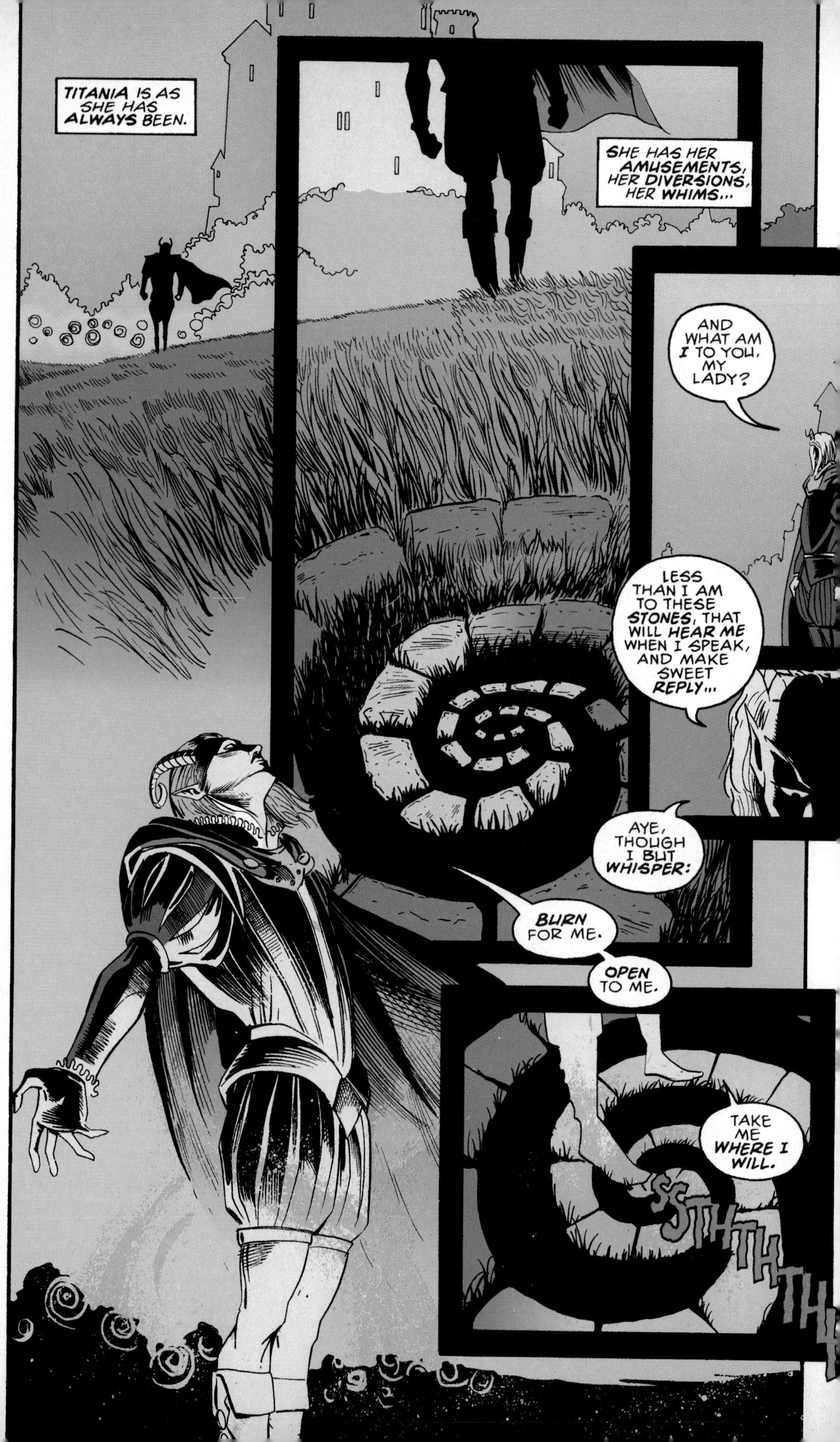
TITANIA IS AS SHE HAS ALWAYS BEEN.
SHE HAS HER AMUSEMENTS, HER DIVERSIONS, HER WHIMS...
AND WHAT AM I TO YOU, MY LADY?
LESS THAN I AM TO THESE STONES, THAT WILL HEAR ME WHEN I SPEAK, AND MAKE SWEET REPLY...
AYE, THOUGH I BUT WHISPER:
BURN FOR ME.
OPEN TO ME.
TAKE ME WHERE I WILL.
SSTHTHTHTH

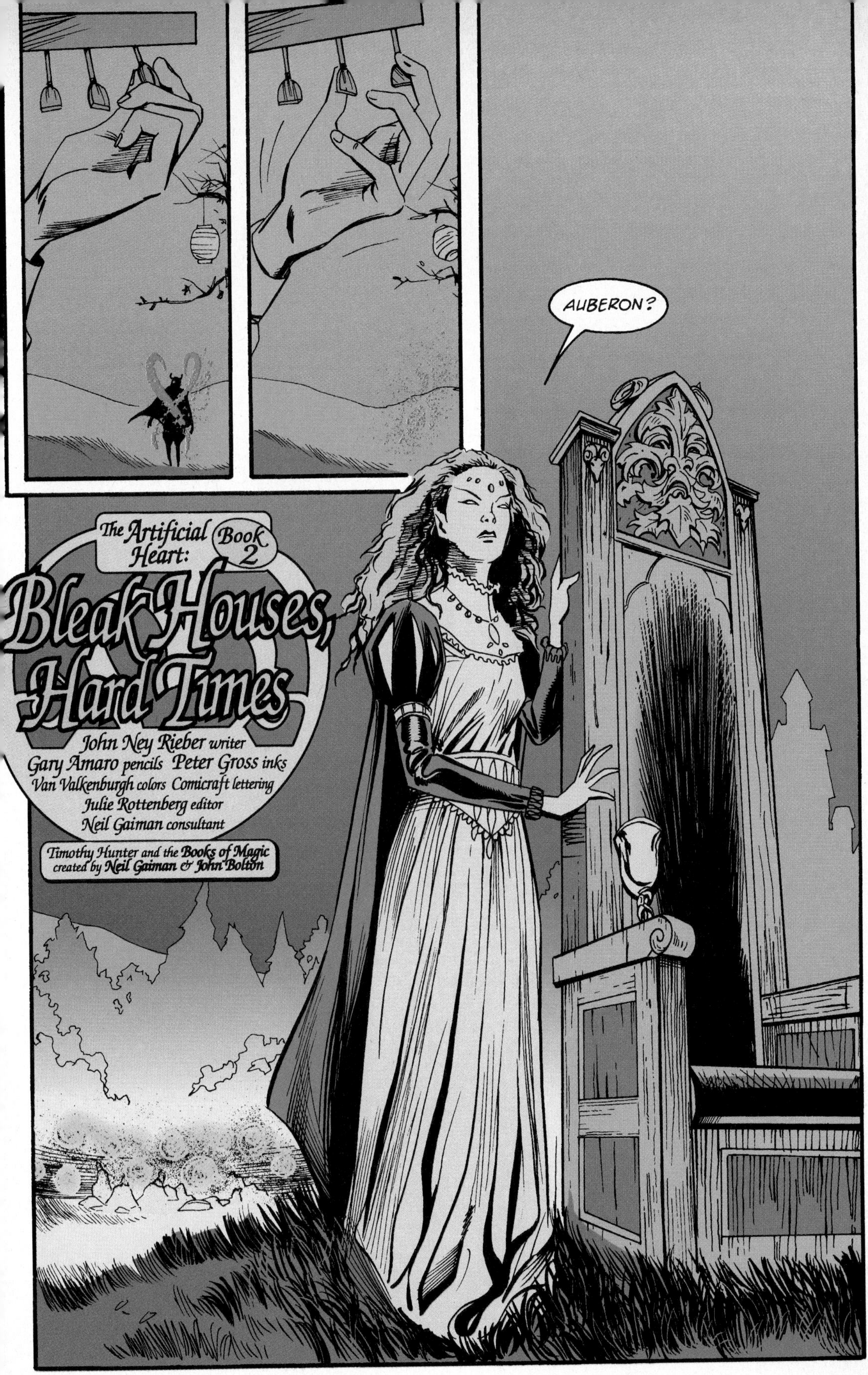
AUBERON?
The Artificial Heart: Book 2
Bleak Houses, Hard Times
John Ney Rieber writer
Gary Amaro pencils Peter Gross inks
Van Valkenburgh colors Comicraft lettering
Julie Rottenberg editor
Neil Gaiman consultant
Timothy Hunter and the Books of Magic created by Neil Gaiman & John Bolton

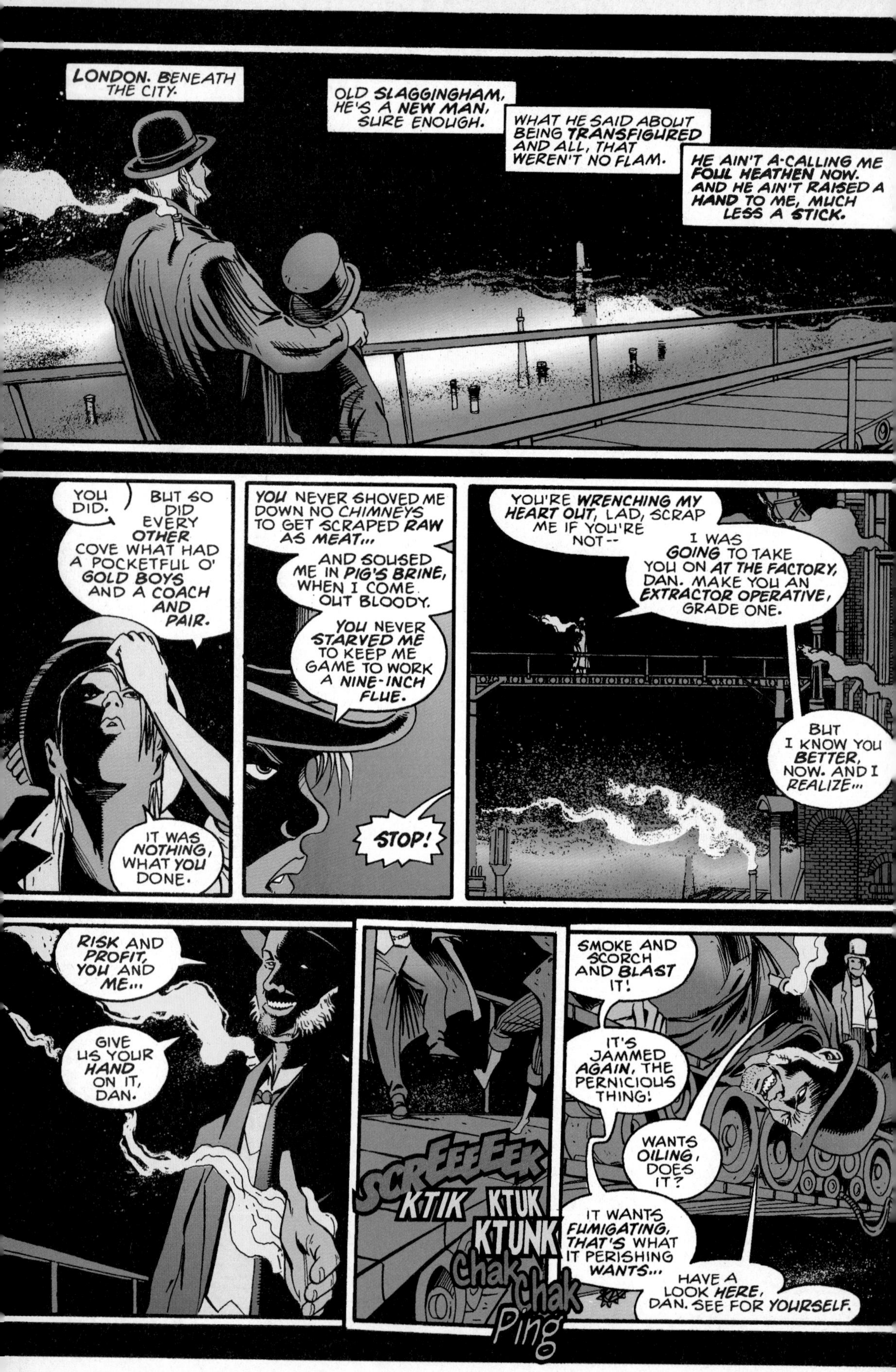
LONDON. BENEATH THE CITY.
OLD SLAGGINGHAM, HE'S A NEW MAN, SURE ENOUGH.
WHAT HE SAID ABOUT BEING TRANSFIGURED AND ALL, THAT WEREN'T NO FLAM.
HE AIN'T A-CALLING ME FOUL HEATHEN NOW. AND HE AIN'T RAISED A HAND TO ME, MUCH LESS A STICK.
YOU DID.
BUT SO DID EVERY OTHER COVE WHAT HAD A POCKETFUL O' GOLD BOYS AND A COACH AND PAIR.
IT WAS NOTHING, WHAT YOU DONE.
YOU NEVER SHOVED ME DOWN NO CHIMNEYS TO GET SCRAPED RAW AS MEAT...
AND SOUSED ME IN PIG'S BRINE, WHEN I COME OUT BLOODY.
YOU NEVER STARVED ME TO KEEP ME GAME TO WORK A NINE-INCH FLUE.
STOP!
YOU'RE WRENCHING MY HEART OUT, LAD, SCRAP ME IF YOU'RE NOT--
I WAS GOING TO TAKE YOU ON AT THE FACTORY, DAN. MAKE YOU AN EXTRACTOR OPERATIVE, GRADE ONE.
BUT I KNOW YOU BETTER, NOW. AND I REALIZE...
RISK AND PROFIT, YOU AND ME...
GIVE US YOUR HAND ON IT, DAN.
SCREEEEEK
KTIK KTUK
KTUNK
Chak Chak
Ping
SMOKE AND SCORCH AND BLAST IT!
IT'S JAMMED AGAIN, THE PERNICIOUS THING!
WANTS OILING, DOES IT?
IT WANTS FUMIGATING, THAT'S WHAT IT PERISHING WANTS...
HAVE A LOOK HERE, DAN. SEE FOR YOURSELF.

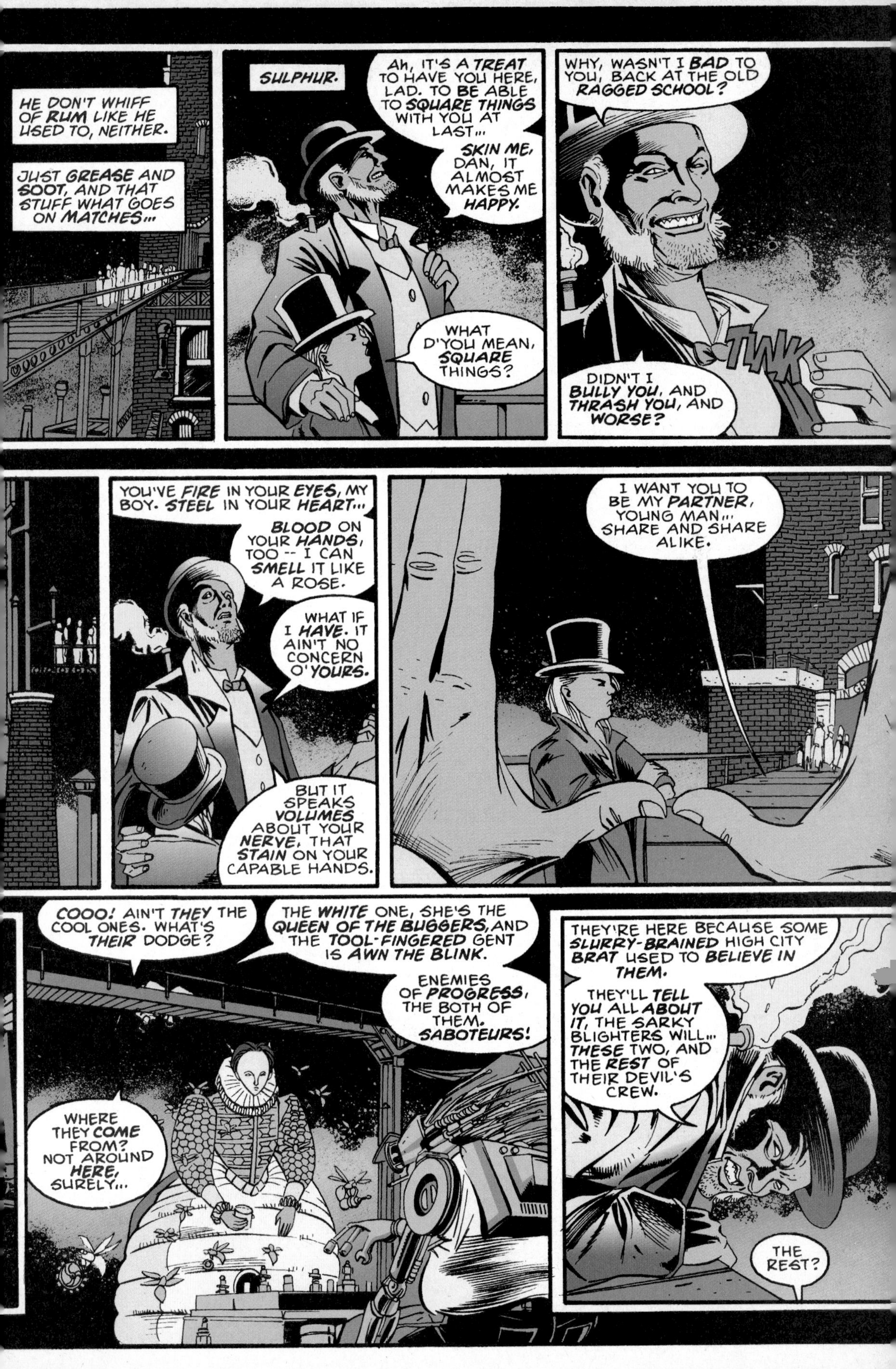
HE DON'T WHIFF OF RUM LIKE HE USED TO, NEITHER.
JUST GREASE AND SOOT, AND THAT STUFF WHAT GOES ON MATCHES...
SULPHUR.
AH, IT'S A TREAT TO HAVE YOU HERE, LAD. TO BE ABLE TO SQUARE THINGS WITH YOU AT LAST...
SKIN ME, DAN, IT ALMOST MAKES ME HAPPY.
WHAT D'YOU MEAN, SQUARE THINGS?
WHY, WASN'T I BAD TO YOU, BACK AT THE OLD RAGGED SCHOOL?
TINK
DIDN'T I BULLY YOU, AND THRASH YOU, AND WORSE?
YOU'VE FIRE IN YOUR EYES, MY BOY. STEEL IN YOUR HEART...
BLOOD ON YOUR HANDS, TOO -- I CAN SMELL IT LIKE A ROSE.
WHAT IF I HAVE. IT AIN'T NO CONCERN O'YOURS.
BUT IT SPEAKS VOLUMES ABOUT YOUR NERVE, THAT STAIN ON YOUR CAPABLE HANDS.
I WANT YOU TO BE MY PARTNER, YOUNG MAN... SHARE AND SHARE ALIKE.
COOO! AIN'T THEY THE COOL ONES. WHAT'S THEIR DODGE?
THE WHITE ONE, SHE'S THE QUEEN OF THE BUGGERS, AND THE TOOL-FINGERED GENT IS AWN THE BLINK.
ENEMIES OF PROGRESS, THE BOTH OF THEM. SABOTEURS!
WHERE THEY COME FROM? NOT AROUND HERE, SURELY...
THEY'RE HERE BECAUSE SOME SLURRY-BRAINED HIGH CITY BRAT USED TO BELIEVE IN THEM.
THEY'LL TELL YOU ALL ABOUT IT, THE SARKY BLIGHTERS WILL... THESE TWO, AND THE REST OF THEIR DEVIL'S CREW.
THE REST?

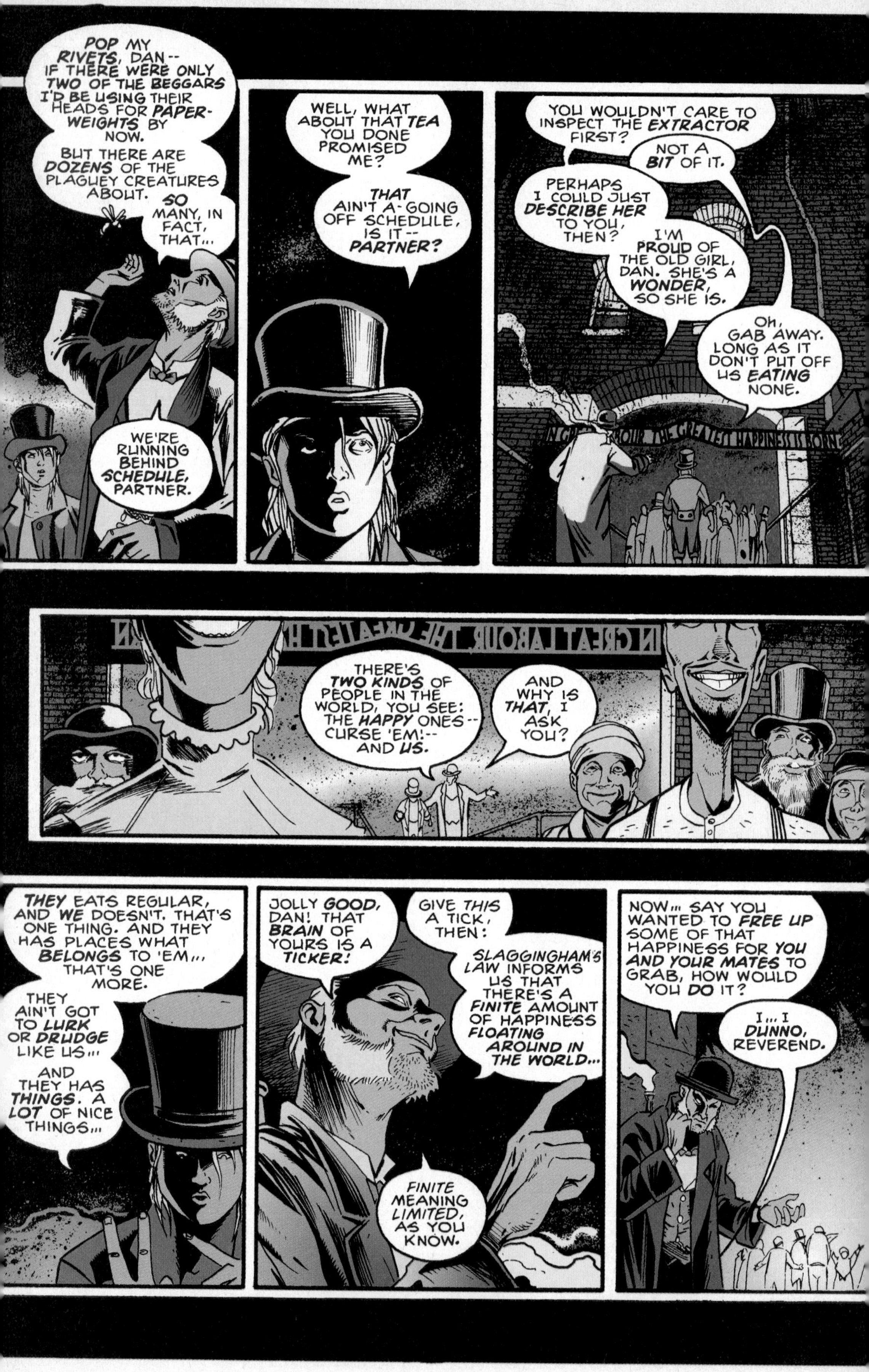

POP MY RIVETS, DAN -- IF THERE WERE ONLY TWO OF THE BEGGARS I'D BE USING THEIR HEADS FOR PAPER-WEIGHTS BY NOW.
BUT THERE ARE DOZENS OF THE PLAGUEY CREATURES ABOUT.
SO MANY, IN FACT, THAT...
WE'RE RUNNING BEHIND SCHEDULE, PARTNER.
WELL, WHAT ABOUT THAT TEA YOU DONE PROMISED ME?
THAT AIN'T A-GOING OFF SCHEDULE, IS IT -- PARTNER?
YOU WOULDN'T CARE TO INSPECT THE EXTRACTOR FIRST?
NOT A BIT OF IT.
PERHAPS I COULD JUST DESCRIBE HER TO YOU, THEN?
I'M PROUD OF THE OLD GIRL, DAN. SHE'S A WONDER, SO SHE IS.
OH, GAB AWAY. LONG AS IT DON'T PUT OFF US EATING NONE.
IN GREAT LABOUR THE GREATEST HAPPINESS IS BORN
THERE'S TWO KINDS OF PEOPLE IN THE WORLD, YOU SEE: THE HAPPY ONES -- CURSE 'EM! -- AND US.
AND WHY IS THAT, I ASK YOU?
THEY EATS REGULAR, AND WE DOESN'T. THAT'S ONE THING. AND THEY HAS PLACES WHAT BELONGS TO 'EM... THAT'S ONE MORE.
THEY AIN'T GOT TO LURK OR DRUDGE LIKE US...
AND THEY HAS THINGS. A LOT OF NICE THINGS...
JOLLY GOOD, DAN! THAT BRAIN OF YOURS IS A TICKER!
GIVE THIS A TICK, THEN:
SLAGGINGHAM'S LAW INFORMS US THAT THERE'S A FINITE AMOUNT OF HAPPINESS FLOATING AROUND IN THE WORLD...
FINITE MEANING LIMITED, AS YOU KNOW.
NOW... SAY YOU WANTED TO FREE UP SOME OF THAT HAPPINESS FOR YOU AND YOUR MATES TO GRAB, HOW WOULD YOU DO IT?
I... I DUNNO, REVEREND.

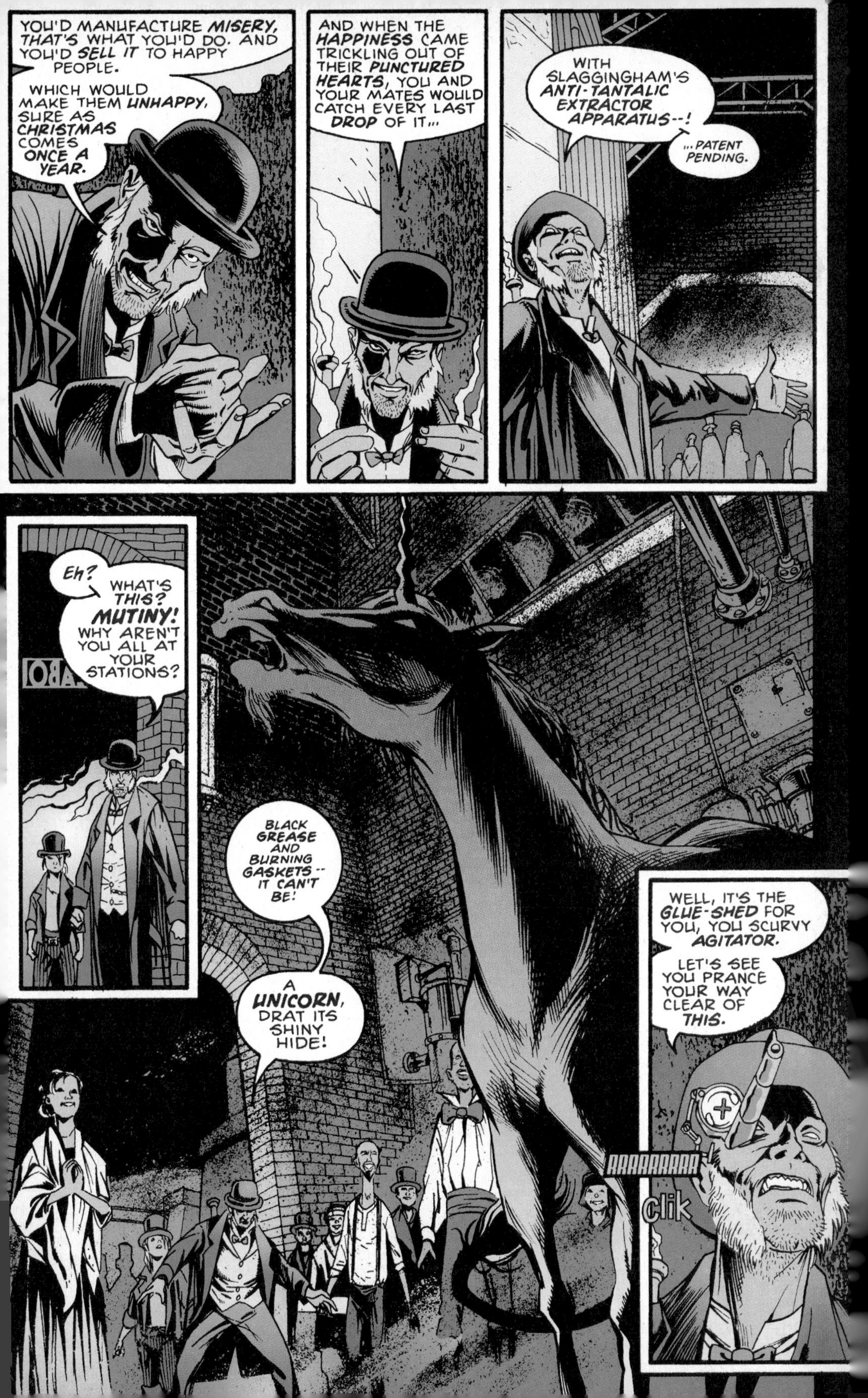
YOU'D MANUFACTURE MISERY, THAT'S WHAT YOU'D DO. AND YOU'D SELL IT TO HAPPY PEOPLE.
WHICH WOULD MAKE THEM UNHAPPY, SURE AS CHRISTMAS COMES ONCE A YEAR.
AND WHEN THE HAPPINESS CAME TRICKLING OUT OF THEIR PUNCTURED HEARTS, YOU AND YOUR MATES WOULD CATCH EVERY LAST DROP OF IT...
WITH SLAGGINGHAM'S ANTI-TANTALIC EXTRACTOR APPARATUS--!
...PATENT PENDING.
Eh?
WHAT'S THIS? MUTINY! WHY AREN'T YOU ALL AT YOUR STATIONS?
BLACK GREASE AND BURNING GASKETS-- IT CAN'T BE!
A UNICORN, DRAT ITS SHINY HIDE!
WELL, IT'S THE GLUE-SHED FOR YOU, YOU SCURVY AGITATOR.
LET'S SEE YOU PRANCE YOUR WAY CLEAR OF THIS.
AAAAAAAA
clik

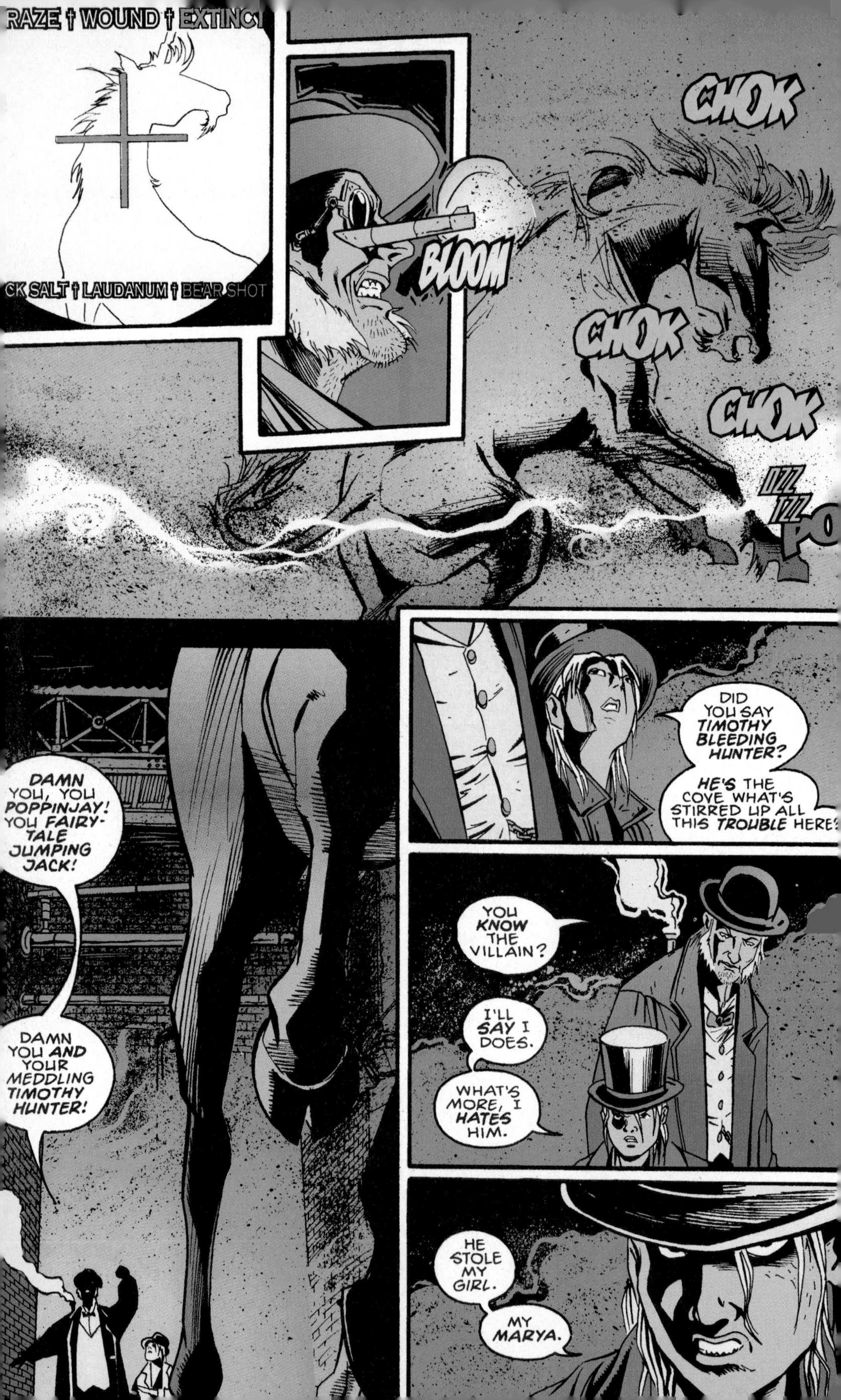

RAZE † WOUND † EXTINCT
CK SALT † LAUDANUM † BEAR SHOT
BLOOM
CHOK
CHOK
CHOK
DAMN YOU, YOU POPPINJAY! YOU FAIRY-TALE JUMPING JACK!
DAMN YOU AND YOUR MEDDLING TIMOTHY HUNTER!
DID YOU SAY TIMOTHY BLEEDING HUNTER?
HE'S THE COVE WHAT'S STIRRED UP ALL THIS TROUBLE HERE?
YOU KNOW THE VILLAIN?
I'LL SAY I DOES.
WHAT'S MORE, I HATES HIM.
HE STOLE MY GIRL.
MY MARYA.

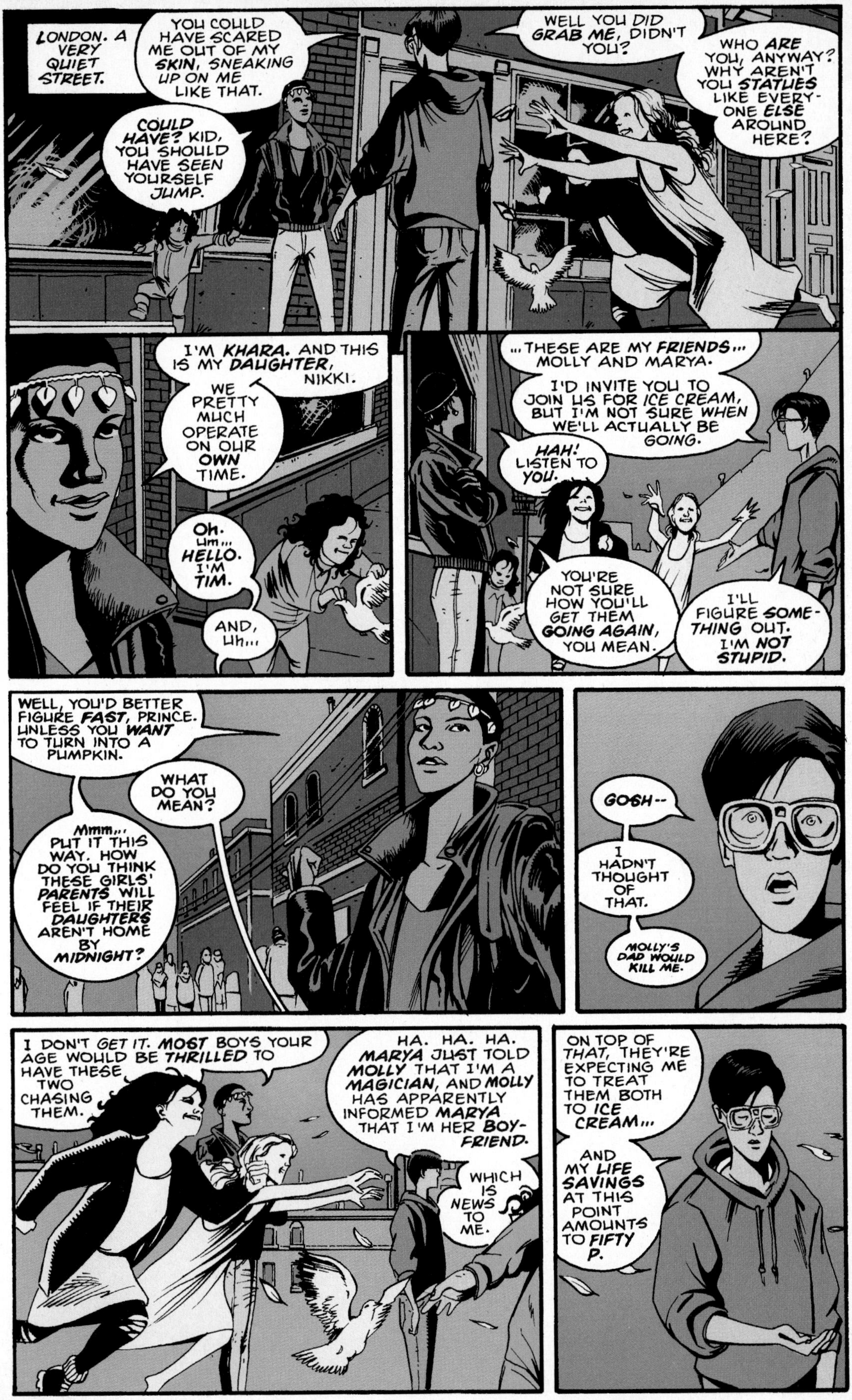

LONDON. A VERY QUIET STREET.
YOU COULD HAVE SCARED ME OUT OF MY SKIN, SNEAKING UP ON ME LIKE THAT.
COULD HAVE? KID, YOU SHOULD HAVE SEEN YOURSELF JUMP.
WELL YOU DID GRAB ME, DIDN'T YOU?
WHO ARE YOU, ANYWAY? WHY AREN'T YOU STATUES LIKE EVERY-ONE ELSE AROUND HERE?
I'M KHARA. AND THIS IS MY DAUGHTER, NIKKI.
WE PRETTY MUCH OPERATE ON OUR OWN TIME.
Oh. Um... HELLO. I'M TIM.
AND, Uh...
...THESE ARE MY FRIENDS... MOLLY AND MARYA.
I'D INVITE YOU TO JOIN US FOR ICE CREAM, BUT I'M NOT SURE WHEN WE'LL ACTUALLY BE GOING.
HAH! LISTEN TO YOU.
YOU'RE NOT SURE HOW YOU'LL GET THEM GOING AGAIN, YOU MEAN.
I'LL FIGURE SOME-THING OUT. I'M NOT STUPID.
WELL, YOU'D BETTER FIGURE FAST, PRINCE. UNLESS YOU WANT TO TURN INTO A PUMPKIN.
WHAT DO YOU MEAN?
Mmm... PUT IT THIS WAY. HOW DO YOU THINK THESE GIRLS' PARENTS WILL FEEL IF THEIR DAUGHTERS AREN'T HOME BY MIDNIGHT?
GOSH--
I HADN'T THOUGHT OF THAT.
MOLLY'S DAD WOULD KILL ME.
I DON'T GET IT. MOST BOYS YOUR AGE WOULD BE THRILLED TO HAVE THESE TWO CHASING THEM.
HA. HA. HA. MARYA JUST TOLD MOLLY THAT I'M A MAGICIAN, AND MOLLY HAS APPARENTLY INFORMED MARYA THAT I'M HER BOY-FRIEND.
WHICH IS NEWS TO ME.
ON TOP OF THAT, THEY'RE EXPECTING ME TO TREAT THEM BOTH TO ICE CREAM...
AND MY LIFE SAVINGS AT THIS POINT AMOUNTS TO FIFTY P.

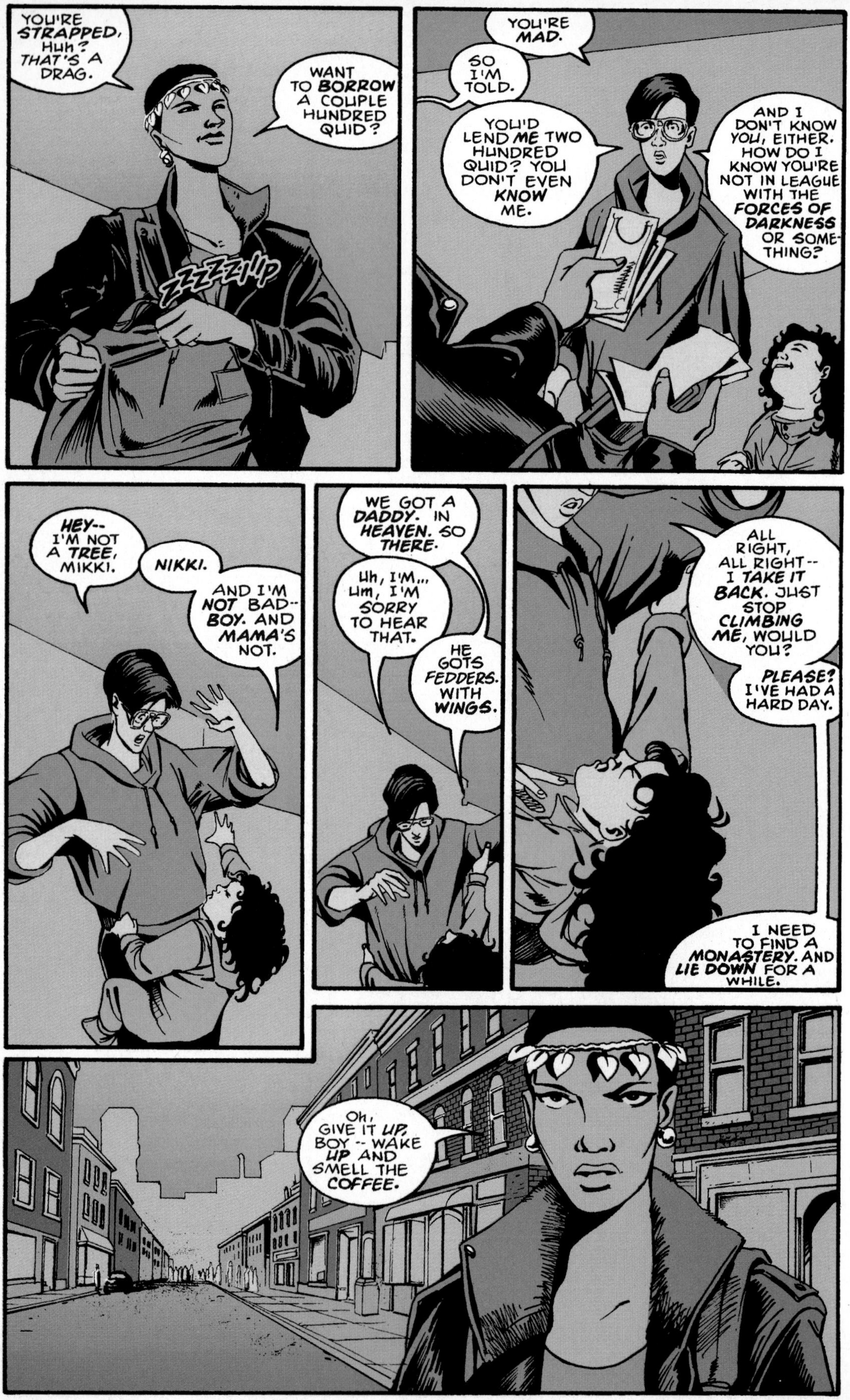
YOU'RE STRAPPED, Huh? THAT'S A DRAG.
WANT TO BORROW A COUPLE HUNDRED QUID?
ZZZZZIIIP
YOU'RE MAD.
SO I'M TOLD.
YOU'D LEND ME TWO HUNDRED QUID? YOU DON'T EVEN KNOW ME.
AND I DON'T KNOW YOU, EITHER. HOW DO I KNOW YOU'RE NOT IN LEAGUE WITH THE FORCES OF DARKNESS OR SOME-THING?
HEY-- I'M NOT A TREE, MIKKI.
NIKKI.
AND I'M NOT BAD-BOY. AND MAMA'S NOT.
WE GOT A DADDY. IN HEAVEN. SO THERE.
Uh, I'M... Um, I'M SORRY TO HEAR THAT.
HE GOTS FEDDERS. WITH WINGS.
ALL RIGHT, ALL RIGHT-- I TAKE IT BACK. JUST STOP CLIMBING ME, WOULD YOU?
PLEASE? I'VE HAD A HARD DAY.
I NEED TO FIND A MONASTERY. AND LIE DOWN FOR A WHILE.
Oh, GIVE IT UP, BOY -- WAKE UP AND SMELL THE COFFEE.

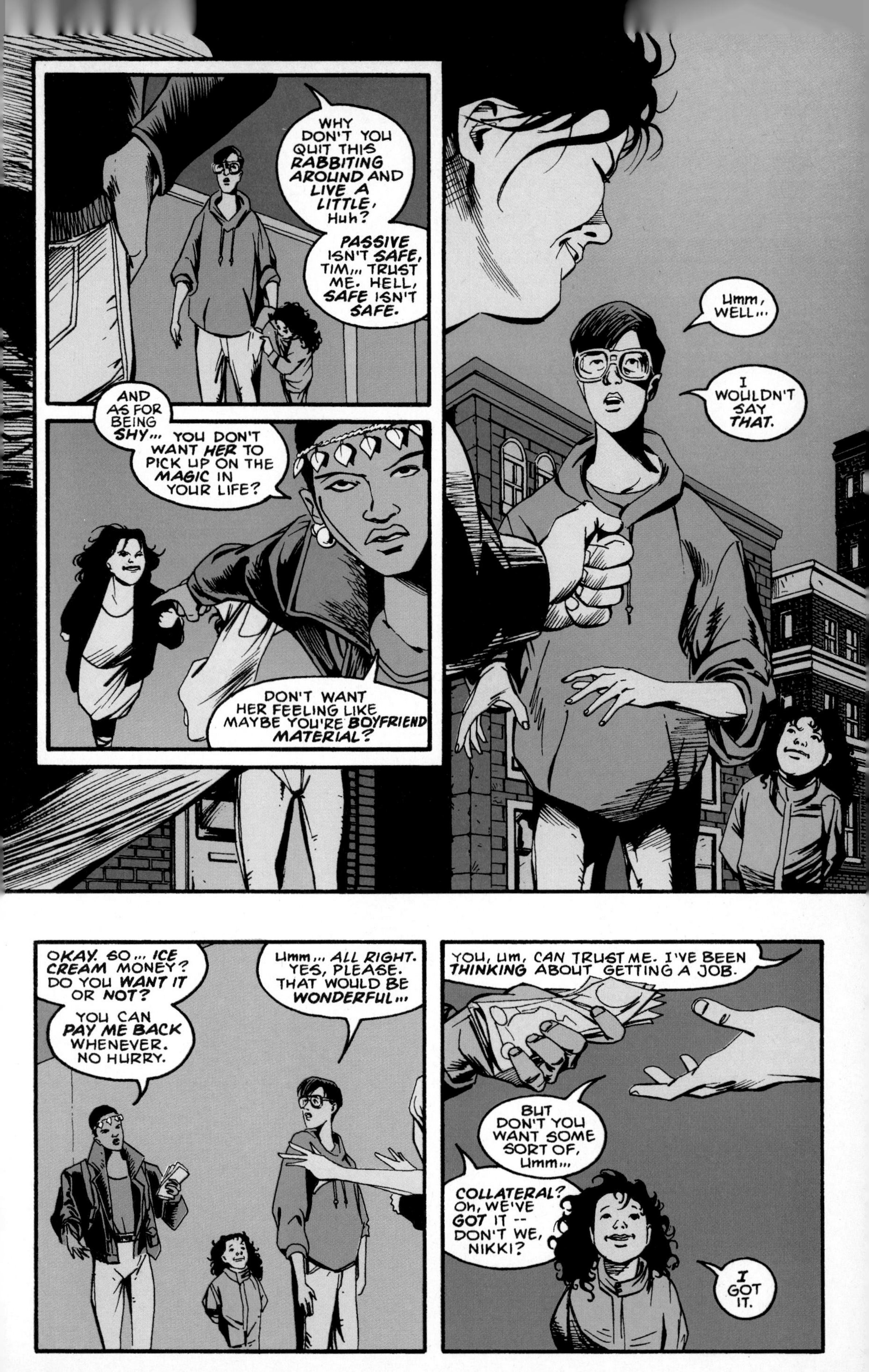
WHY DON'T YOU QUIT THIS RABBITING AROUND AND LIVE A LITTLE, Huh?
PASSIVE ISN'T SAFE, TIM... TRUST ME. HELL, SAFE ISN'T SAFE.
Umm, WELL...
I WOULDN'T SAY THAT.
AND AS FOR BEING SHY... YOU DON'T WANT HER TO PICK UP ON THE MAGIC IN YOUR LIFE?
DON'T WANT HER FEELING LIKE MAYBE YOU'RE BOYFRIEND MATERIAL?
OKAY. SO... ICE CREAM MONEY? DO YOU WANT IT OR NOT?
YOU CAN PAY ME BACK WHENEVER. NO HURRY.
Umm... ALL RIGHT. YES, PLEASE. THAT WOULD BE WONDERFUL...
YOU, UM, CAN TRUST ME. I'VE BEEN THINKING ABOUT GETTING A JOB.
BUT DON'T YOU WANT SOME SORT OF, Umm...
COLLATERAL? Oh, WE'VE GOT IT -- DON'T WE, NIKKI?
I GOT IT.

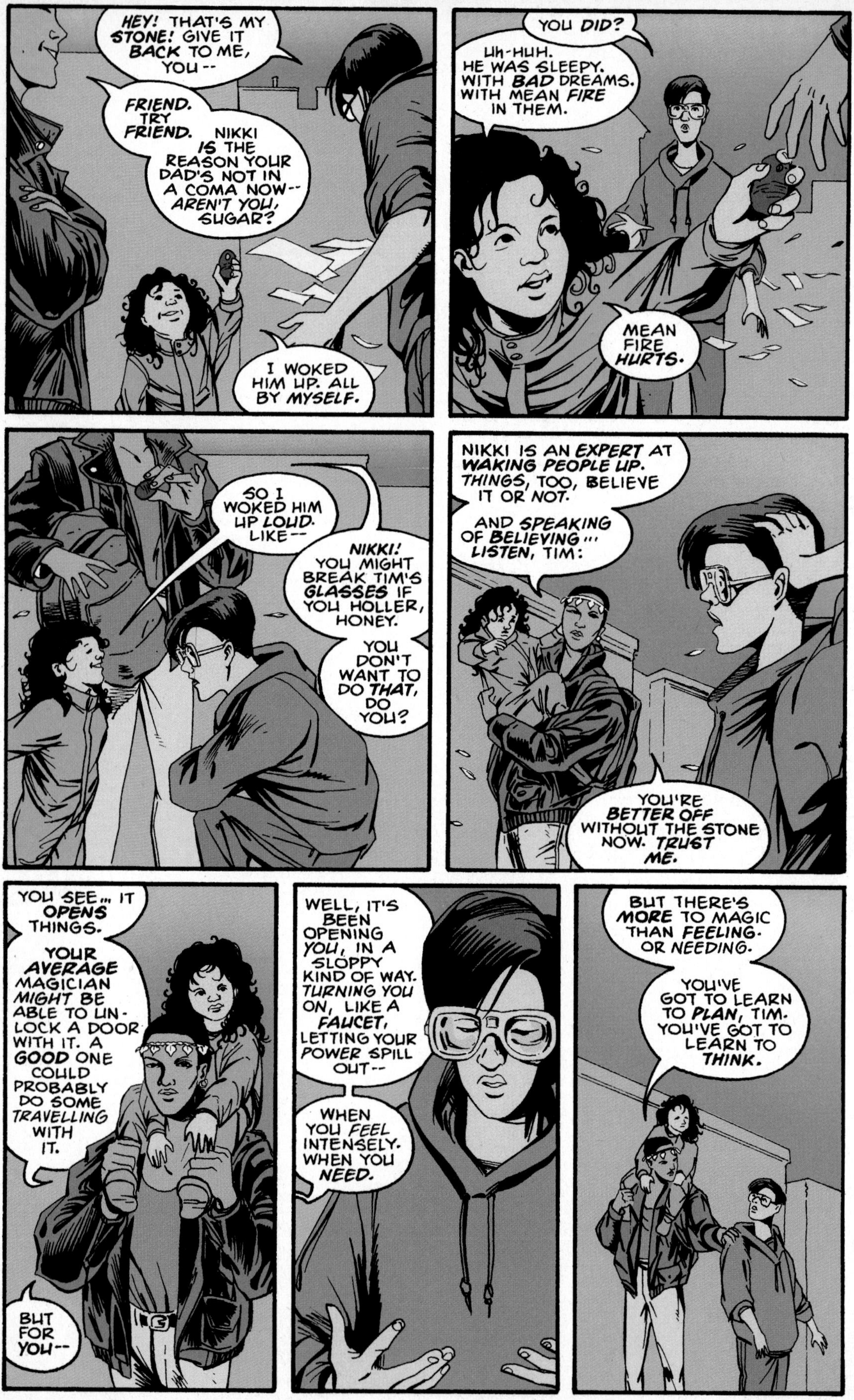
HEY! THAT'S MY STONE! GIVE IT BACK TO ME, YOU --
FRIEND. TRY FRIEND. NIKKI IS THE REASON YOUR DAD'S NOT IN A COMA NOW-- AREN'T YOU, SUGAR?
I WOKED HIM UP. ALL BY MYSELF.
YOU DID?
UH-HUH. HE WAS SLEEPY. WITH BAD DREAMS. WITH MEAN FIRE IN THEM.
MEAN FIRE HURTS.
SO I WOKED HIM UP LOUD. LIKE--
NIKKI! YOU MIGHT BREAK TIM'S GLASSES IF YOU HOLLER, HONEY.
YOU DON'T WANT TO DO THAT, DO YOU?
NIKKI IS AN EXPERT AT WAKING PEOPLE UP. THINGS, TOO, BELIEVE IT OR NOT.
AND SPEAKING OF BELIEVING... LISTEN, TIM:
YOU'RE BETTER OFF WITHOUT THE STONE NOW. TRUST ME.
YOU SEE... IT OPENS THINGS.
YOUR AVERAGE MAGICIAN MIGHT BE ABLE TO UNLOCK A DOOR WITH IT. A GOOD ONE COULD PROBABLY DO SOME TRAVELLING WITH IT.
BUT FOR YOU--
WELL, IT'S BEEN OPENING YOU, IN A SLOPPY KIND OF WAY. TURNING YOU ON, LIKE A FAUCET, LETTING YOUR POWER SPILL OUT--
WHEN YOU FEEL INTENSELY. WHEN YOU NEED.
BUT THERE'S MORE TO MAGIC THAN FEELING. OR NEEDING.
YOU'VE GOT TO LEARN TO PLAN, TIM. YOU'VE GOT TO LEARN TO THINK.

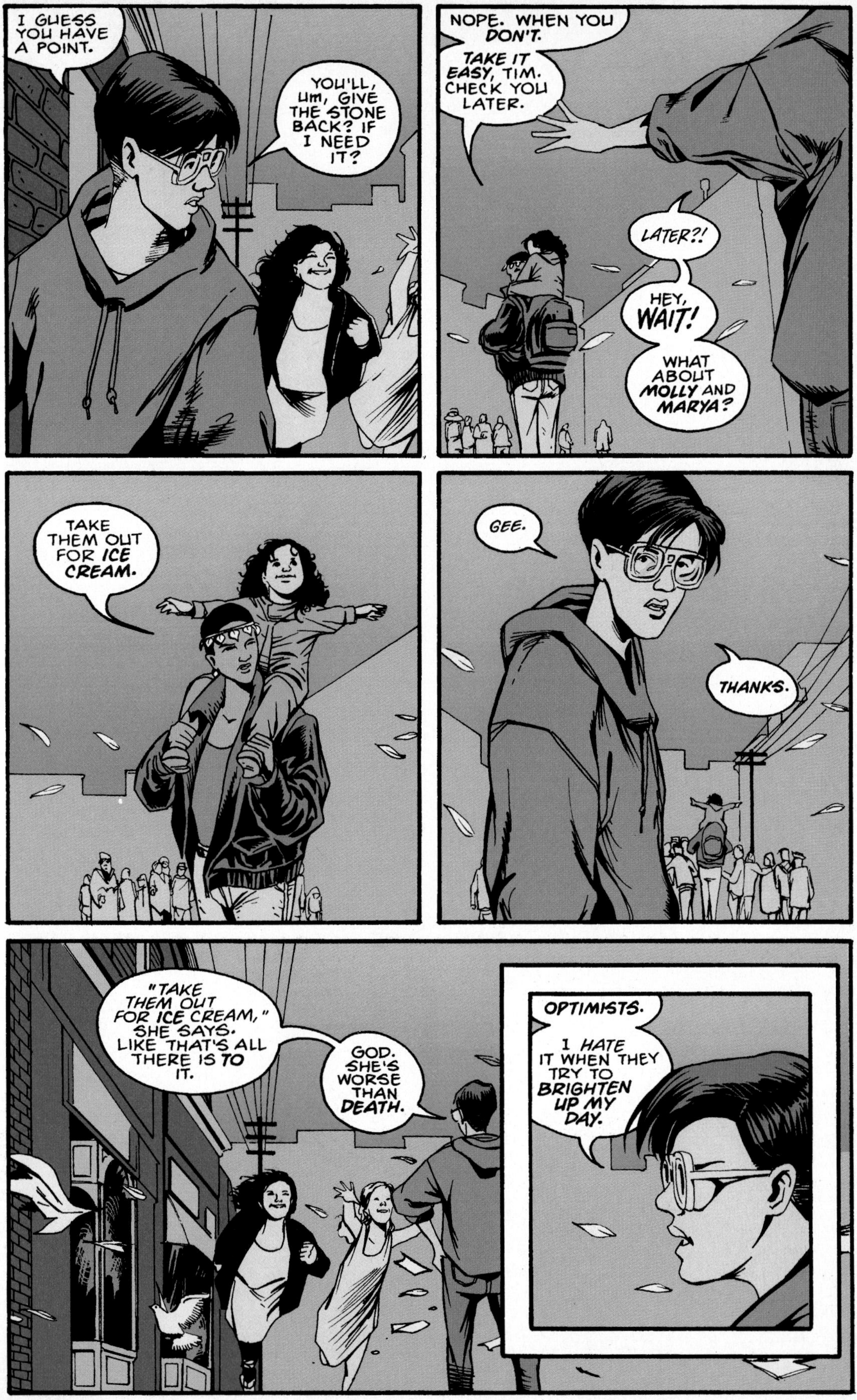
I GUESS YOU HAVE A POINT.
YOU'LL, UM, GIVE THE STONE BACK? IF I NEED IT?
NOPE. WHEN YOU DON'T.
TAKE IT EASY, TIM. CHECK YOU LATER.
LATER?!
HEY, WAIT!
WHAT ABOUT MOLLY AND MARYA?
TAKE THEM OUT FOR ICE CREAM.
GEE.
THANKS.
"TAKE THEM OUT FOR ICE CREAM," SHE SAYS. LIKE THAT'S ALL THERE IS TO IT.
GOD. SHE'S WORSE THAN DEATH.
OPTIMISTS.
I HATE IT WHEN THEY TRY TO BRIGHTEN UP MY DAY.

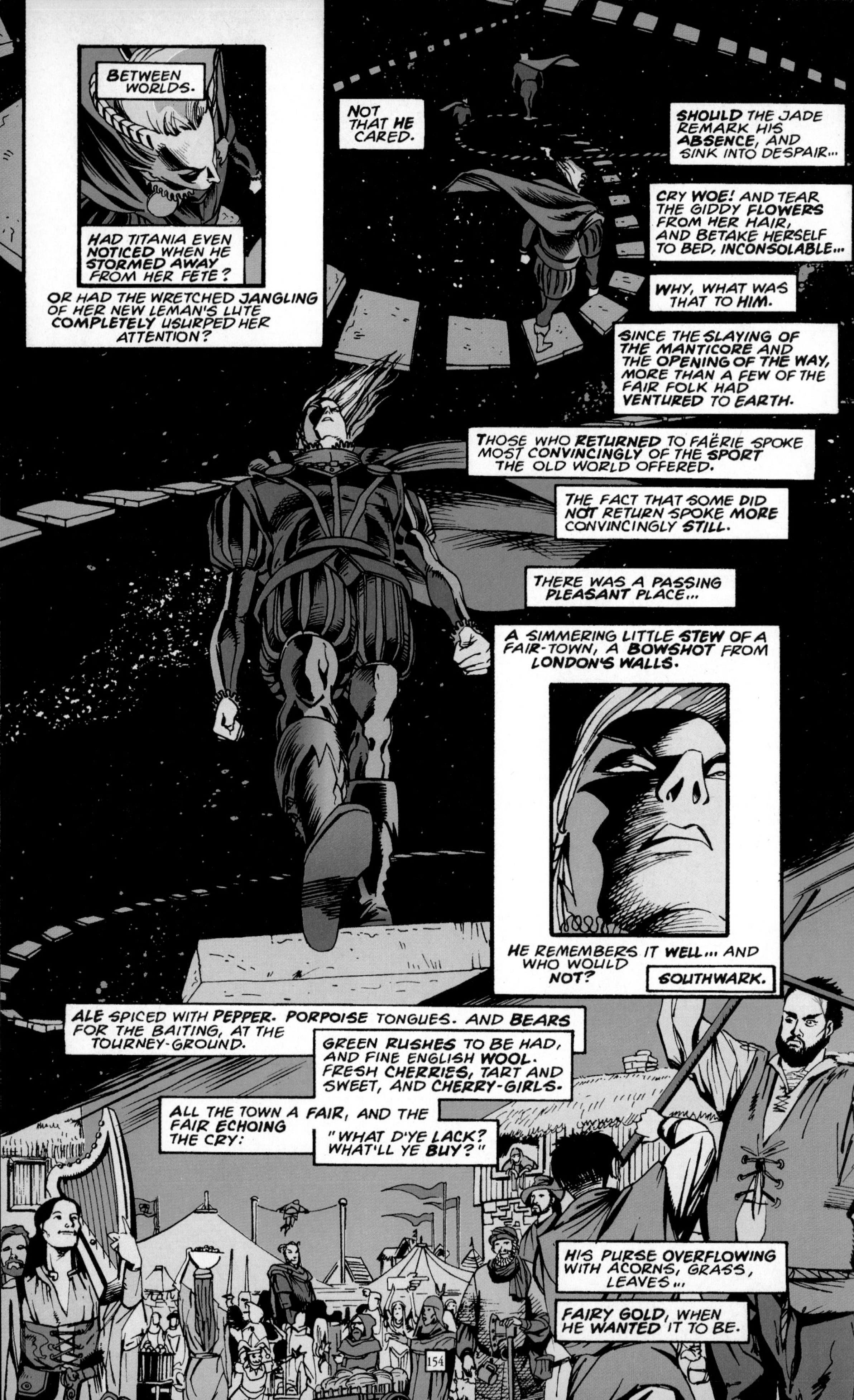
BETWEEN WORLDS.
HAD TITANIA EVEN NOTICED WHEN HE STORMED AWAY FROM HER FETE?
OR HAD THE WRETCHED JANGLING OF HER NEW LEMAN'S LUTE COMPLETELY USURPED HER ATTENTION?
NOT THAT HE CARED.
SHOULD THE JADE REMARK HIS ABSENCE, AND SINK INTO DESPAIR...
CRY WOE! AND TEAR THE GIDDY FLOWERS FROM HER HAIR, AND BETAKE HERSELF TO BED, INCONSOLABLE...
WHY, WHAT WAS THAT TO HIM.
SINCE THE SLAYING OF THE MANTICORE AND THE OPENING OF THE WAY, MORE THAN A FEW OF THE FAIR FOLK HAD VENTURED TO EARTH.
THOSE WHO RETURNED TO FAËRIE SPOKE MOST CONVINCINGLY OF THE SPORT THE OLD WORLD OFFERED.
THE FACT THAT SOME DID NOT RETURN SPOKE MORE CONVINCINGLY STILL.
THERE WAS A PASSING PLEASANT PLACE...
A SIMMERING LITTLE STEW OF A FAIR-TOWN, A BOWSHOT FROM LONDON'S WALLS.
HE REMEMBERS IT WELL... AND WHO WOULD NOT?
SOUTHWARK.
ALE SPICED WITH PEPPER. PORPOISE TONGUES. AND BEARS FOR THE BAITING, AT THE TOURNEY-GROUND.
GREEN RUSHES TO BE HAD, AND FINE ENGLISH WOOL. FRESH CHERRIES, TART AND SWEET, AND CHERRY-GIRLS.
ALL THE TOWN A FAIR, AND THE FAIR ECHOING THE CRY:
"WHAT D'YE LACK? WHAT'LL YE BUY?"
HIS PURSE OVERFLOWING WITH ACORNS, GRASS, LEAVES...
FAIRY GOLD, WHEN HE WANTED IT TO BE.

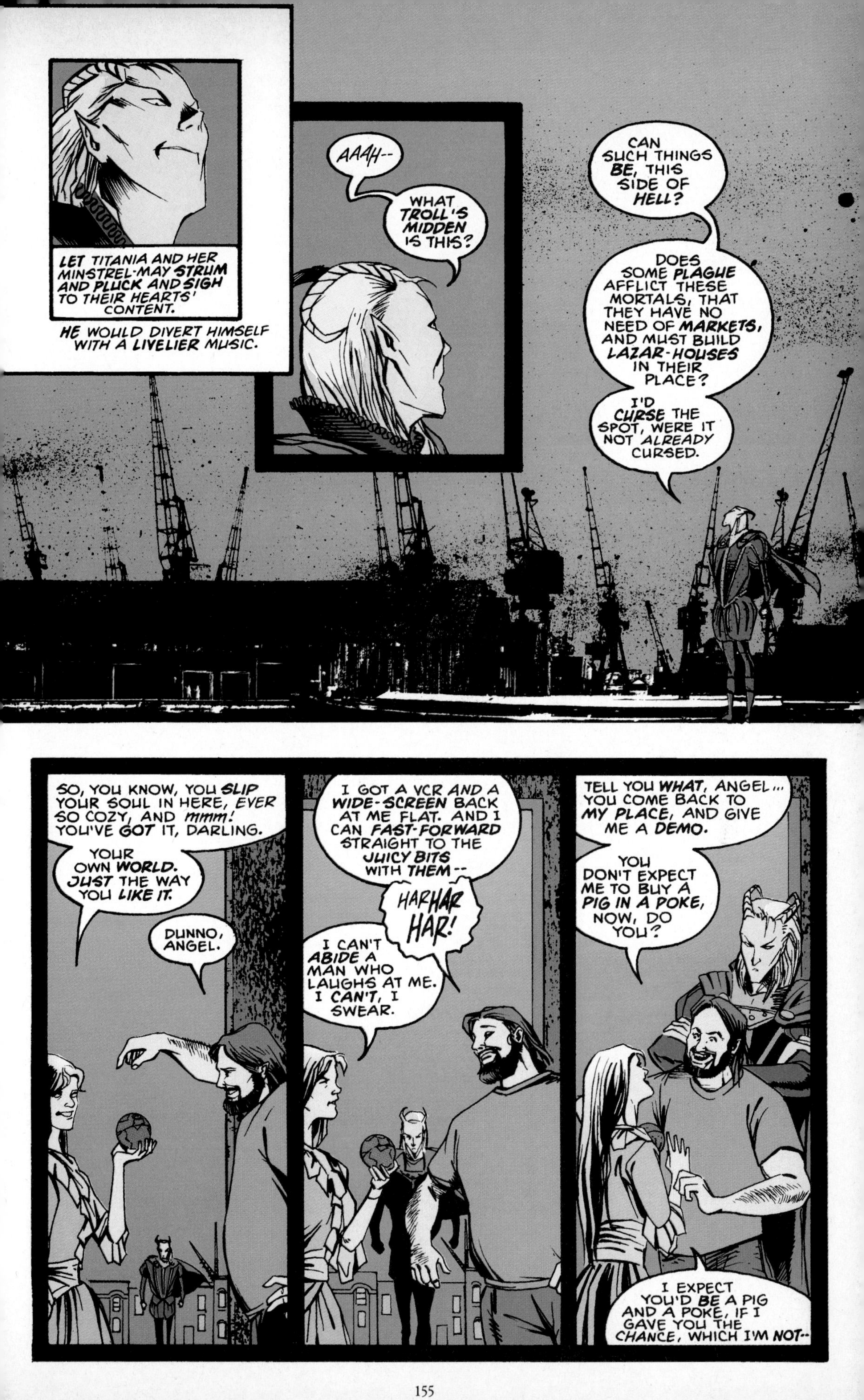
LET TITANIA AND HER MINSTREL-MAY STRUM AND PLUCK AND SIGH TO THEIR HEARTS' CONTENT.
HE WOULD DIVERT HIMSELF WITH A LIVELIER MUSIC.
AAAH--
WHAT TROLL'S MIDDEN IS THIS?
CAN SUCH THINGS BE, THIS SIDE OF HELL?
DOES SOME PLAGUE AFFLICT THESE MORTALS, THAT THEY HAVE NO NEED OF MARKETS, AND MUST BUILD LAZAR-HOUSES IN THEIR PLACE?
I'D CURSE THE SPOT, WERE IT NOT ALREADY CURSED.
SO, YOU KNOW, YOU SLIP YOUR SOUL IN HERE, EVER SO COZY, AND mmm! YOU'VE GOT IT, DARLING.
YOUR OWN WORLD. JUST THE WAY YOU LIKE IT.
DUNNO, ANGEL.
I GOT A VCR AND A WIDE-SCREEN BACK AT ME FLAT. AND I CAN FAST-FORWARD STRAIGHT TO THE JUICY BITS WITH THEM--
HAR HAR HAR!
I CAN'T ABIDE A MAN WHO LAUGHS AT ME. I CAN'T, I SWEAR.
TELL YOU WHAT, ANGEL... YOU COME BACK TO MY PLACE, AND GIVE ME A DEMO.
YOU DON'T EXPECT ME TO BUY A PIG IN A POKE, NOW, DO YOU?
I EXPECT YOU'D BE A PIG AND A POKE, IF I GAVE YOU THE CHANCE, WHICH I'M NOT--

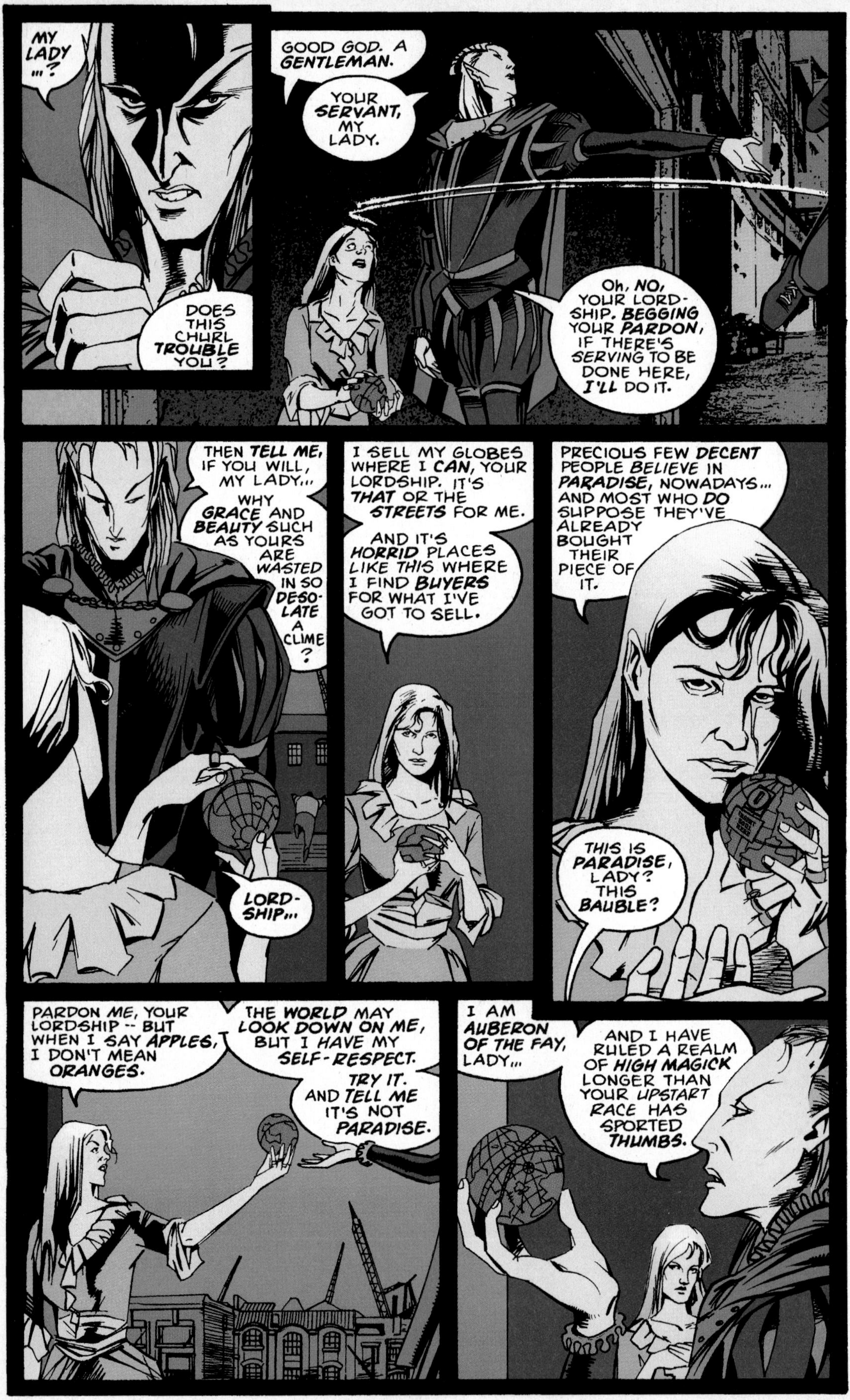
MY LADY ...?
DOES THIS CHURL TROUBLE YOU?
GOOD GOD. A GENTLEMAN.
YOUR SERVANT, MY LADY.
Oh, NO, YOUR LORDSHIP. BEGGING YOUR PARDON, IF THERE'S SERVING TO BE DONE HERE, I'LL DO IT.
THEN TELL ME, IF YOU WILL, MY LADY... WHY GRACE AND BEAUTY SUCH AS YOURS ARE WASTED IN SO DESOLATE A CLIME?
LORDSHIP...
I SELL MY GLOBES WHERE I CAN, YOUR LORDSHIP. IT'S THAT OR THE STREETS FOR ME.
AND IT'S HORRID PLACES LIKE THIS WHERE I FIND BUYERS FOR WHAT I'VE GOT TO SELL.
PRECIOUS FEW DECENT PEOPLE BELIEVE IN PARADISE, NOWADAYS... AND MOST WHO DO SUPPOSE THEY'VE ALREADY BOUGHT THEIR PIECE OF IT.
THIS IS PARADISE, LADY? THIS BAUBLE?
PARDON ME, YOUR LORDSHIP -- BUT WHEN I SAY APPLES, I DON'T MEAN ORANGES.
THE WORLD MAY LOOK DOWN ON ME, BUT I HAVE MY SELF-RESPECT.
TRY IT. AND TELL ME IT'S NOT PARADISE.
I AM AUBERON OF THE FAY, LADY...
AND I HAVE RULED A REALM OF HIGH MAGICK LONGER THAN YOUR UPSTART RACE HAS SPORTED THUMBS.

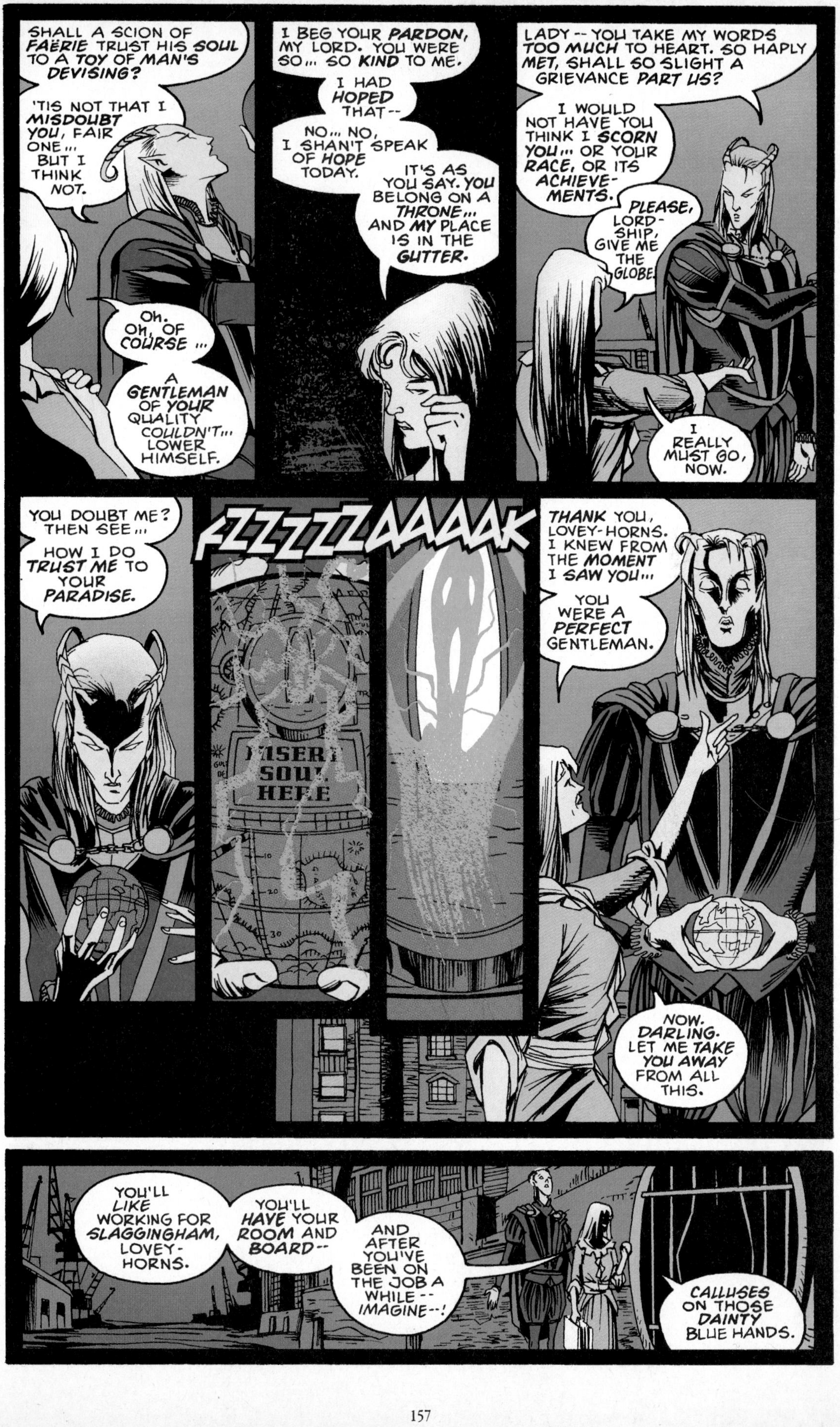
SHALL A SCION OF FAËRIE TRUST HIS SOUL TO A TOY OF MAN'S DEVISING?
'TIS NOT THAT I MISDOUBT YOU, FAIR ONE... BUT I THINK NOT.
Oh. Oh, OF COURSE ...
A GENTLEMAN OF YOUR QUALITY COULDN'T... LOWER HIMSELF.
I BEG YOUR PARDON, MY LORD. YOU WERE SO... SO KIND TO ME.
I HAD HOPED THAT--
NO... NO, I SHAN'T SPEAK OF HOPE TODAY.
IT'S AS YOU SAY. YOU BELONG ON A THRONE... AND MY PLACE IS IN THE GUTTER.
LADY -- YOU TAKE MY WORDS TOO MUCH TO HEART. SO HAPLY MET, SHALL SO SLIGHT A GRIEVANCE PART US?
I WOULD NOT HAVE YOU THINK I SCORN YOU... OR YOUR RACE, OR ITS ACHIEVEMENTS.
PLEASE, LORDSHIP, GIVE ME THE GLOBE!
I REALLY MUST GO, NOW.
YOU DOUBT ME? THEN SEE...
HOW I DO TRUST ME TO YOUR PARADISE.
FZZZZZAAAAK
THANK YOU, LOVEY-HORNS. I KNEW FROM THE MOMENT I SAW YOU...
YOU WERE A PERFECT GENTLEMAN.
NOW. DARLING. LET ME TAKE YOU AWAY FROM ALL THIS.
YOU'LL LIKE WORKING FOR SLAGGINGHAM, LOVEY-HORNS.
YOU'LL HAVE YOUR ROOM AND BOARD--
AND AFTER YOU'VE BEEN ON THE JOB A WHILE -- IMAGINE--!
CALLUSES ON THOSE DAINTY BLUE HANDS.

ALL RIGHT, COMRADES, THE SIDESHOW'S OVER.

BACK TO YOUR STATIONS, EVERY JACK AND JILL OF YOU.

KANK KANK

NOW, DANIEL. LET'S GET YOU THAT TEA, SHALL WE?

AFTER THAT BROUHAHA, I COULD DO WITH A SPOT OF REFRESHMENT MYSELF.

COMMISSARY

SO... THAT SLY DOG HUNTER STOLE YOUR GIRL, DID HE?

SHE RUN OFF TO LONDON TO FIND HIM. AND I AIN'T SEEN HER SINCE.

SOME MIGHT NOT CALL THAT STEALING HER. BUT I AIN'T SUCH A FOOL.

YOU DONE TOOK OFF YOUR SKIN.

GLOVES, DAN. MY GLOVES.

BLESS YOU, YOU CAN'T EXPECT A MAN TO EAT WHILE HE'S GOT HIS RUDDY GLOVES ON.

NOW. WE'VE BOTH GOT REASONS FOR WANTING THIS TIM HUNTER DEAD AS JUDAS.

I SAY WE GET RIGHT TO IT.

BZZZ ZZZ

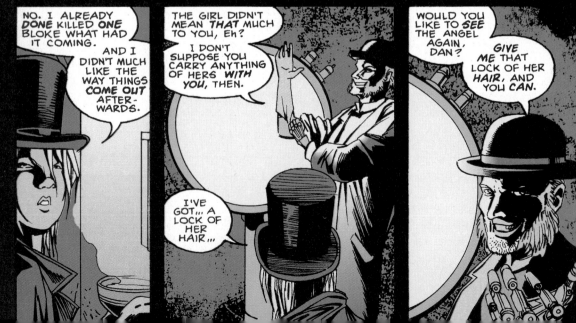

NO. I ALREADY DONE KILLED ONE BLOKE WHAT HAD IT COMING.

AND I DIDN'T MUCH LIKE THE WAY THINGS COME OUT AFTER-WARDS.

THE GIRL DIDN'T MEAN THAT MUCH TO YOU, EH?

I DON'T SUPPOSE YOU CARRY ANYTHING OF HERS WITH YOU, THEN.

I'VE GOT... A LOCK OF HER HAIR...

WOULD YOU LIKE TO SEE THE ANGEL AGAIN, DAN?

GIVE ME THAT LOCK OF HER HAIR, AND YOU CAN.

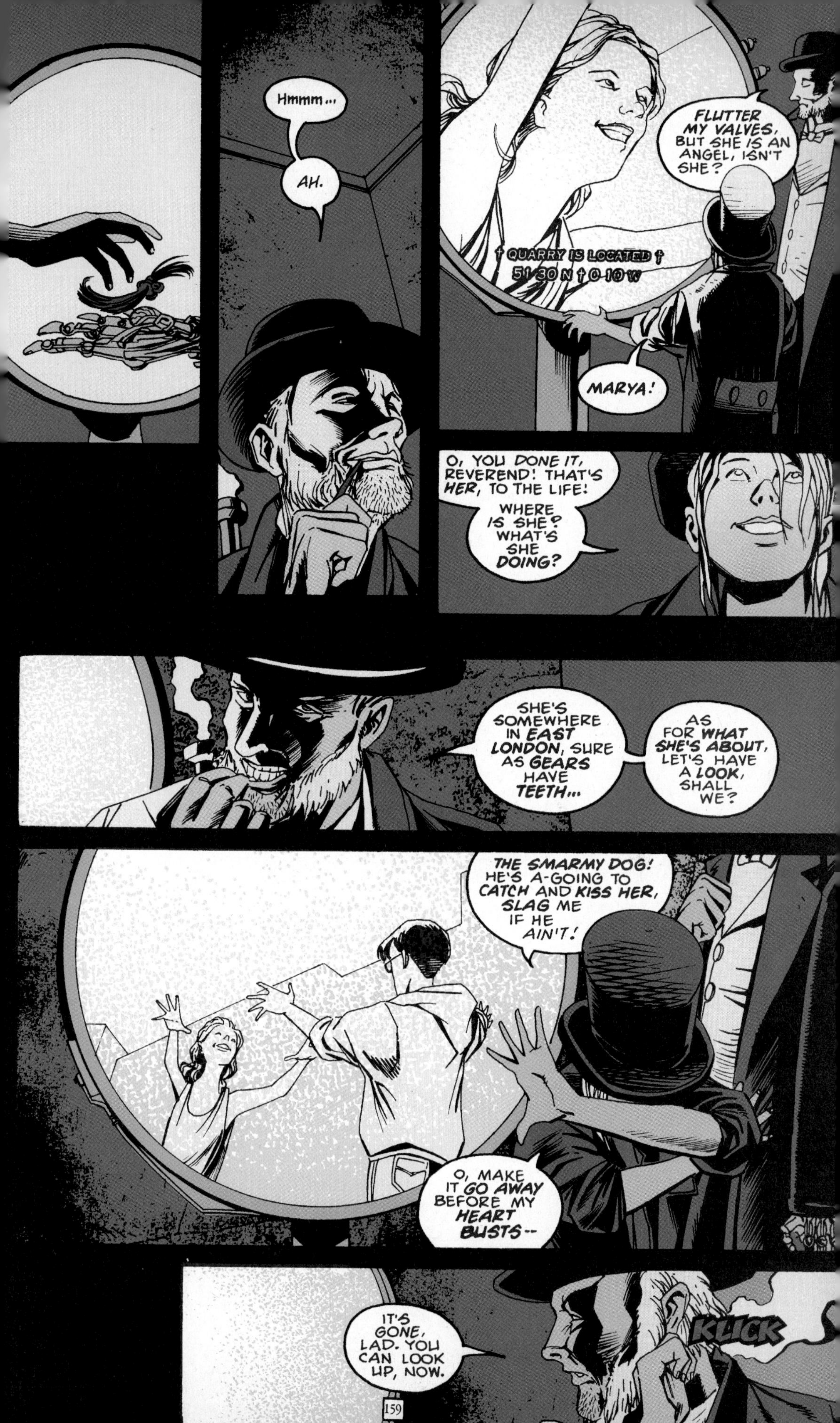
Hmmm...
AH.
FLUTTER MY VALVES, BUT SHE IS AN ANGEL, ISN'T SHE?
† QUARRY IS LOCATED †
51 30 N † 0 10 W
MARYA!
O, YOU DONE IT, REVEREND! THAT'S HER, TO THE LIFE!
WHERE IS SHE? WHAT'S SHE DOING?
SHE'S SOMEWHERE IN EAST LONDON, SURE AS GEARS HAVE TEETH...
AS FOR WHAT SHE'S ABOUT, LET'S HAVE A LOOK, SHALL WE?
THE SMARMY DOG! HE'S A-GOING TO CATCH AND KISS HER, SLAG ME IF HE AIN'T!
O, MAKE IT GO AWAY BEFORE MY HEART BUSTS--
IT'S GONE, LAD. YOU CAN LOOK UP, NOW.
KLICK

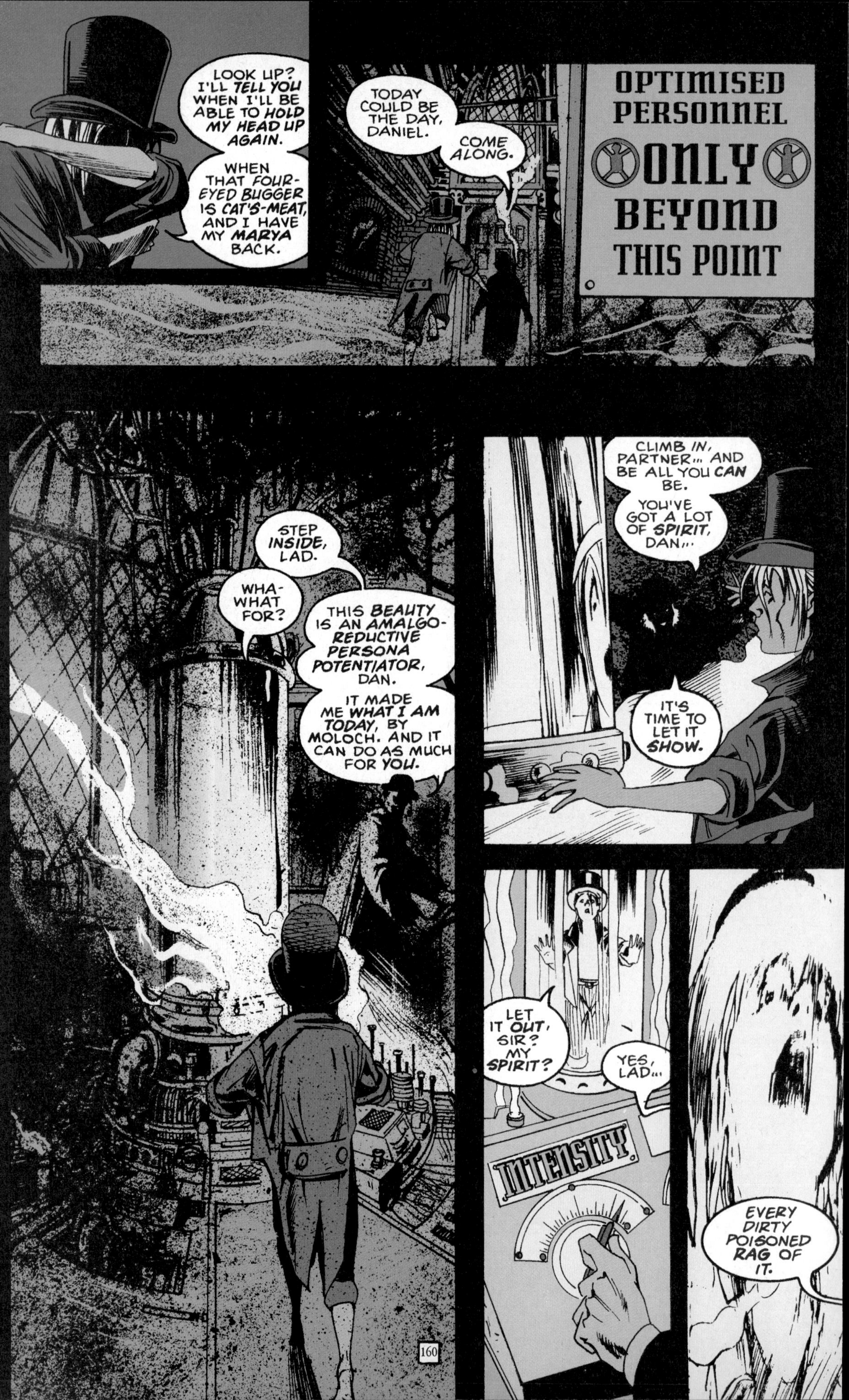

LOOK UP? I'LL TELL YOU WHEN I'LL BE ABLE TO HOLD MY HEAD UP AGAIN.
WHEN THAT FOUR-EYED BUGGER IS CAT'S-MEAT, AND I HAVE MY MARYA BACK.
TODAY COULD BE THE DAY, DANIEL.
COME ALONG.
OPTIMISED PERSONNEL ONLY BEYOND THIS POINT
STEP INSIDE, LAD.
WHA-WHAT FOR?
THIS BEAUTY IS AN AMALGO-REDUCTIVE PERSONA POTENTIATOR, DAN.
IT MADE ME WHAT I AM TODAY, BY MOLOCH. AND IT CAN DO AS MUCH FOR YOU.
CLIMB IN, PARTNER... AND BE ALL YOU CAN BE.
YOU'VE GOT A LOT OF SPIRIT, DAN...
IT'S TIME TO LET IT SHOW.
LET IT OUT, SIR? MY SPIRIT?
YES, LAD...
INTENSITY.
EVERY DIRTY POISONED RAG OF IT.

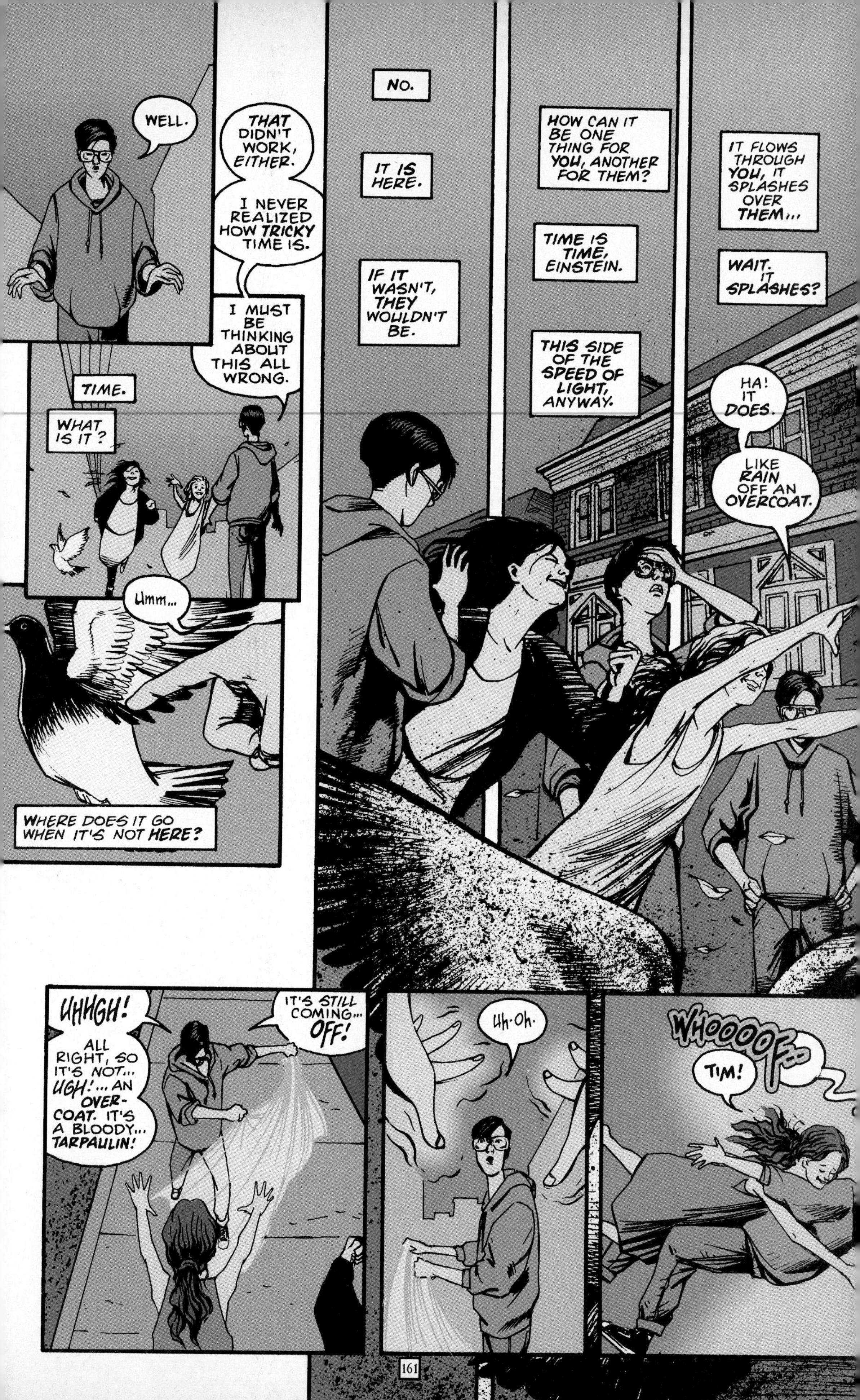

WELL.
THAT DIDN'T WORK, EITHER.
I NEVER REALIZED HOW TRICKY TIME IS.
I MUST BE THINKING ABOUT THIS ALL WRONG.
TIME.
WHAT IS IT?
Umm...
WHERE DOES IT GO WHEN IT'S NOT HERE?
NO.
IT IS HERE.
IF IT WASN'T, THEY WOULDN'T BE.
HOW CAN IT BE ONE THING FOR YOU, ANOTHER FOR THEM?
TIME IS TIME, EINSTEIN.
THIS SIDE OF THE SPEED OF LIGHT, ANYWAY.
IT FLOWS THROUGH YOU, IT SPLASHES OVER THEM...
WAIT. IT SPLASHES?
HA! IT DOES.
LIKE RAIN OFF AN OVERCOAT.
UHHGH!
ALL RIGHT, SO IT'S NOT... UGH!... AN OVERCOAT. IT'S A BLOODY... TARPAULIN!
IT'S STILL COMING... OFF!
Uh-Oh.
WHOOOOF
TIM!

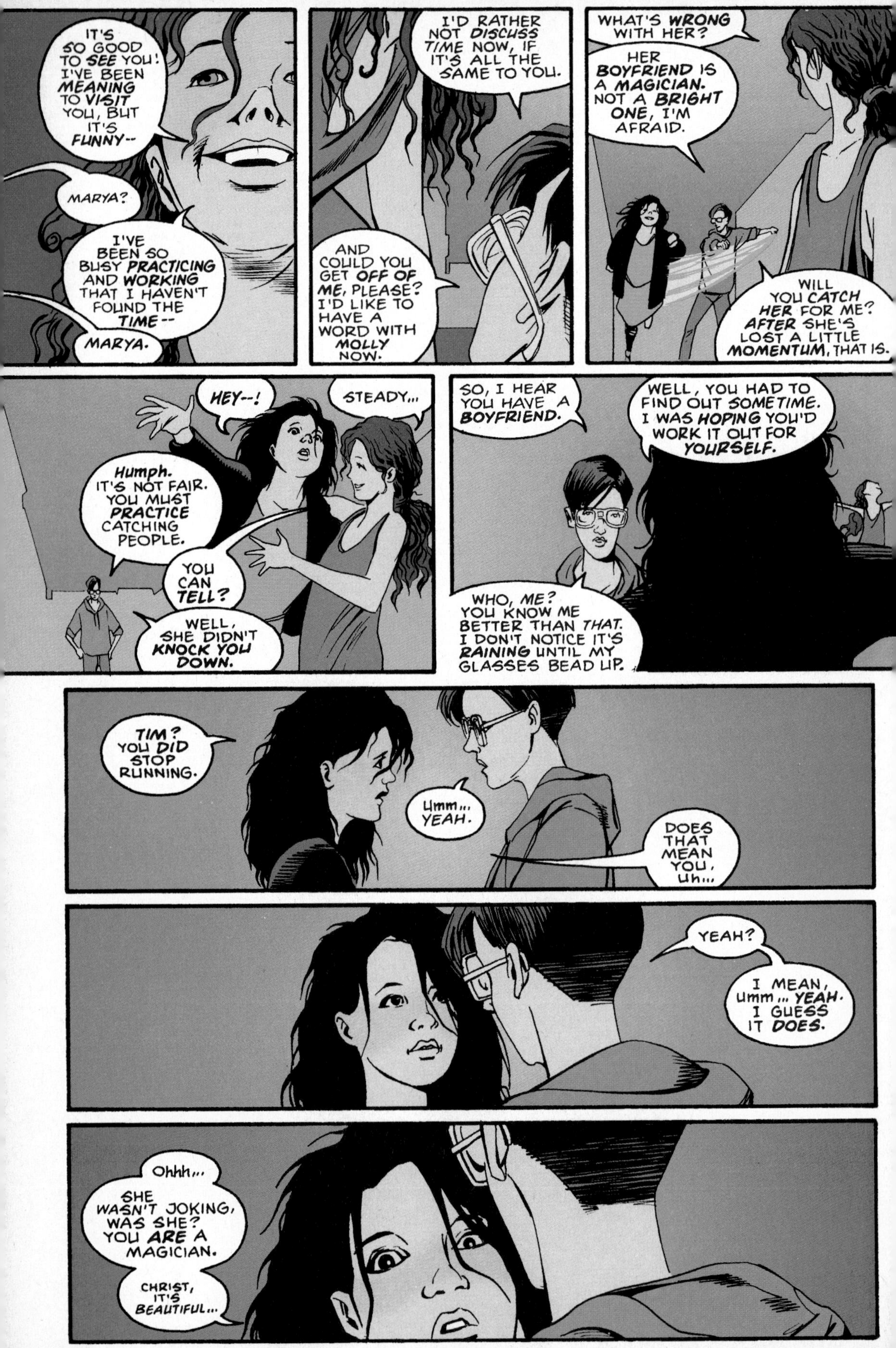
IT'S SO GOOD TO SEE YOU! I'VE BEEN MEANING TO VISIT YOU, BUT IT'S FUNNY--
MARYA?
I'VE BEEN SO BUSY PRACTICING AND WORKING THAT I HAVEN'T FOUND THE TIME--
MARYA.
I'D RATHER NOT DISCUSS TIME NOW, IF IT'S ALL THE SAME TO YOU.
AND COULD YOU GET OFF OF ME, PLEASE? I'D LIKE TO HAVE A WORD WITH MOLLY NOW.
WHAT'S WRONG WITH HER?
HER BOYFRIEND IS A MAGICIAN. NOT A BRIGHT ONE, I'M AFRAID.
WILL YOU CATCH HER FOR ME? AFTER SHE'S LOST A LITTLE MOMENTUM, THAT IS.
HEY--!
STEADY...
Humph. IT'S NOT FAIR. YOU MUST PRACTICE CATCHING PEOPLE.
YOU CAN TELL?
WELL, SHE DIDN'T KNOCK YOU DOWN.
SO, I HEAR YOU HAVE A BOYFRIEND.
WELL, YOU HAD TO FIND OUT SOMETIME. I WAS HOPING YOU'D WORK IT OUT FOR YOURSELF.
WHO, ME? YOU KNOW ME BETTER THAN THAT. I DON'T NOTICE IT'S RAINING UNTIL MY GLASSES BEAD UP.
TIM? YOU DID STOP RUNNING.
Umm... YEAH.
DOES THAT MEAN YOU, Uh...
YEAH?
I MEAN, Umm... YEAH. I GUESS IT DOES.
Ohhh...
SHE WASN'T JOKING, WAS SHE? YOU ARE A MAGICIAN.
CHRIST, IT'S BEAUTIFUL...

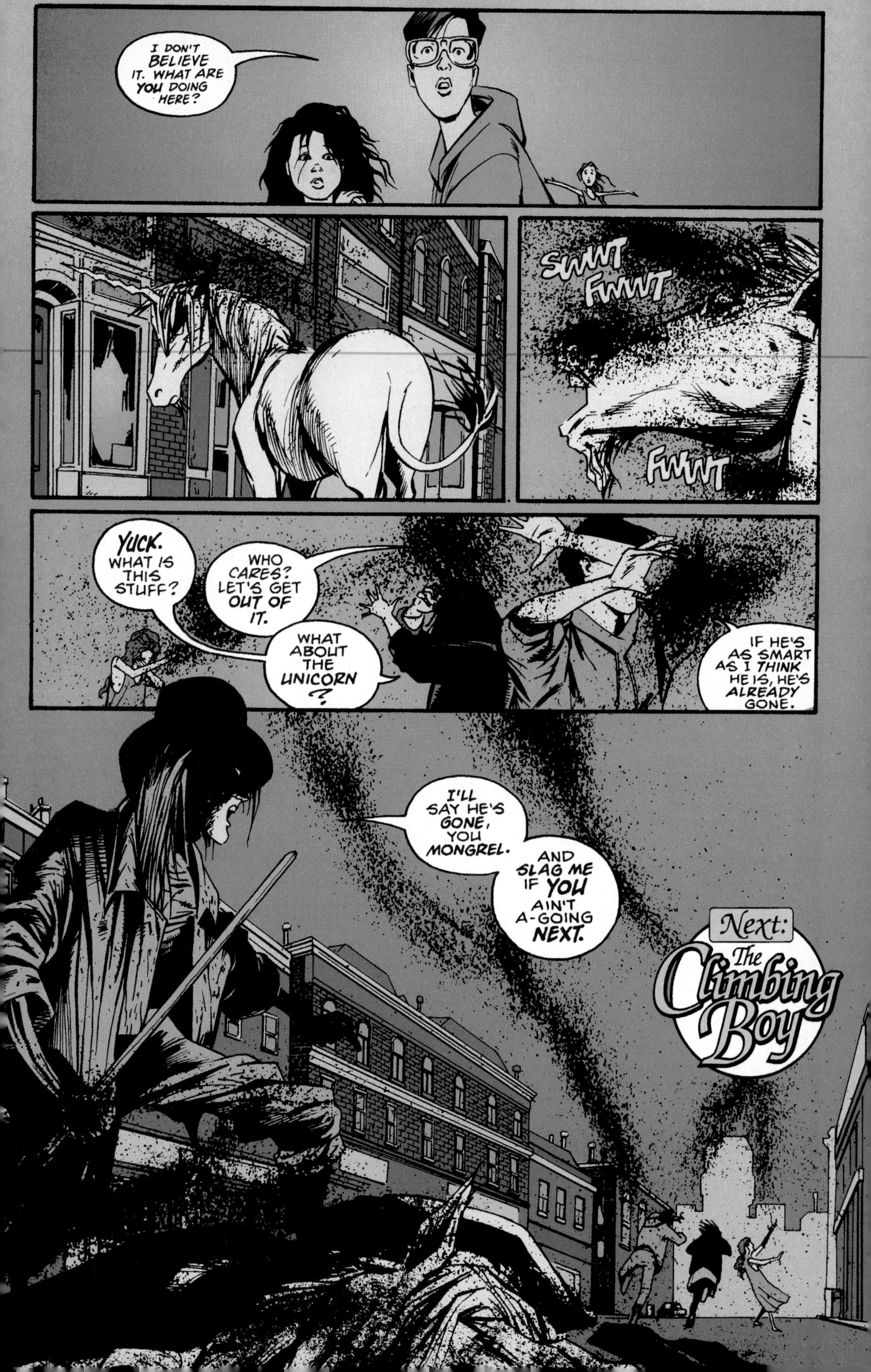
I DON'T BELIEVE IT. WHAT ARE YOU DOING HERE?
SWWT FWWT
FWWT
YUCK. WHAT IS THIS STUFF?
WHO CARES? LET'S GET OUT OF IT.
WHAT ABOUT THE UNICORN?
IF HE'S AS SMART AS I THINK HE IS, HE'S ALREADY GONE.
I'LL SAY HE'S GONE, YOU MONGREL.
AND SLAG ME IF YOU AIN'T A-GOING NEXT.
Next: The Climbing Boy

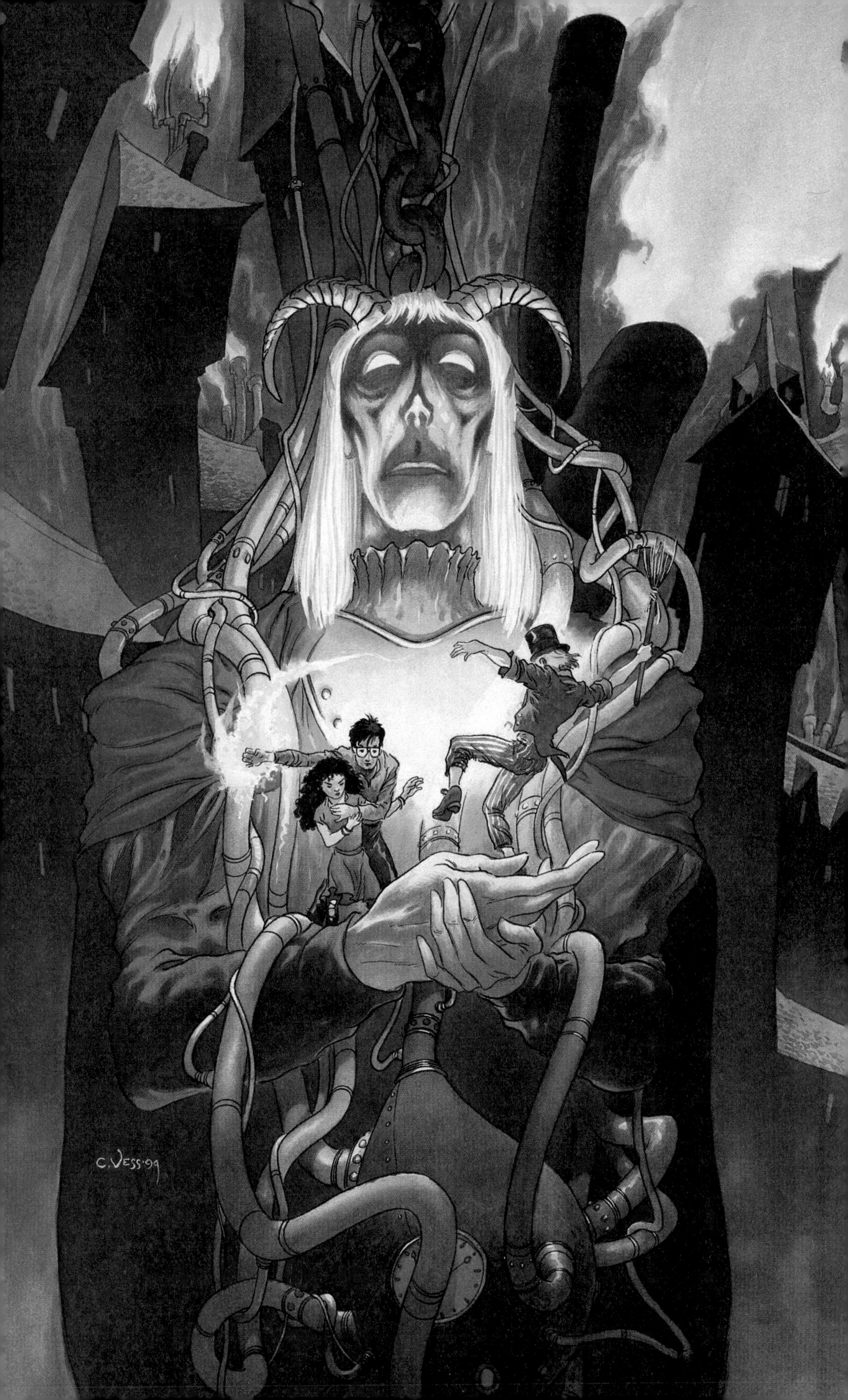
C. VESS·99

BENEATH LONDON.

GRACIOUS SAKES, LOVEY-HORNS.

WHAT'S BECOME OF YOUR DIGNITY?

IT'S NOT AS THOUGH YOU'RE THE *FIRST* KING TO BE *CAPTIVATED* BY THE LIKES OF ME.

ARE YOU KEEN ON *HISTORY*, DEAR? YOU *OUGHT* TO BE.

IT *REPEATS* ITSELF, YOU KNOW.

GO BACK AS *FAR AS YOU LIKE*. THERE'S ALWAYS *SOMETHING* TO BE LEARNED.

TAKE THE ANCIENT *ROMANS*, FOR INSTANCE. SOME OF *THOSE* GENTS COULD TELL YOU *WHAT WAS WHAT*.

A BIT OF THE OLD *CAVEAT EMPTOR* WOULD'VE DONE YOU A *WORLD* OF GOOD TODAY, LOVEY-HORNS.

JUST *IMAGINE!* YOU'D STILL BE IN CHARGE OF YOUR *BODY*...

...IF YOU HADN'T BEEN SO *ANXIOUS* TO MAKE FREE WITH *MINE*.

STILL... IT'S *LIVE* AND *LEARN* FOR *ALL* OF US, ISN'T IT? RICH AND POOR *ALIKE*.

I EXPECT YOU'VE LEARNED A *GREAT DEAL* TODAY, LORDSHIP...

I HOPE IT HASN'T LEFT YOU TOO *SHAKEN* FOR ONE *TINY* LESSON MORE.

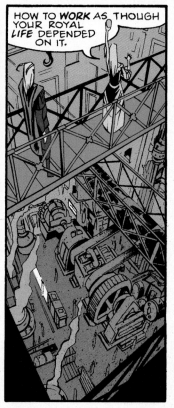

HOW TO *WORK* AS THOUGH YOUR ROYAL *LIFE* DEPENDED ON IT.

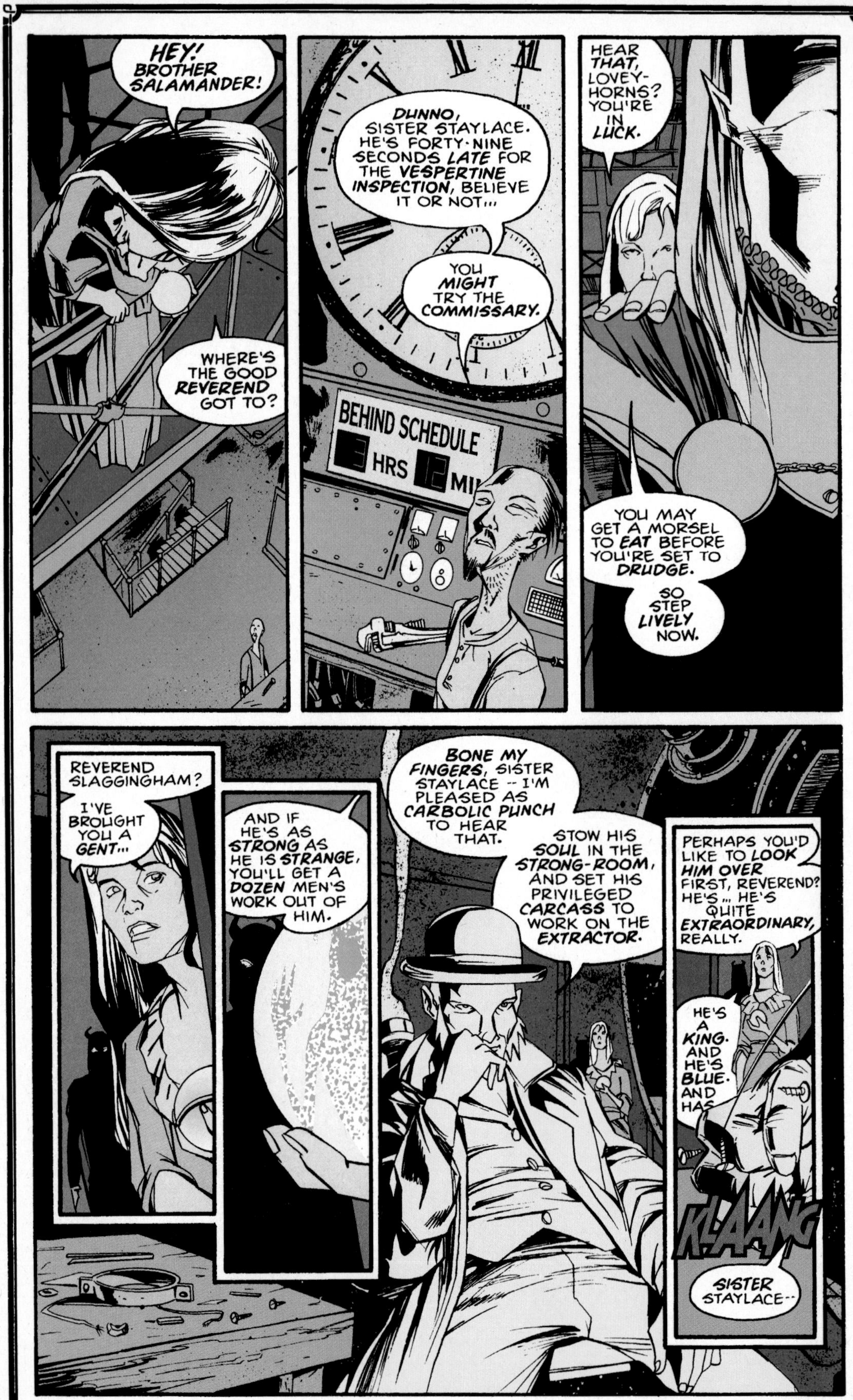
HEY! BROTHER SALAMANDER!
WHERE'S THE GOOD REVEREND GOT TO?
DUNNO, SISTER STAYLACE. HE'S FORTY-NINE SECONDS LATE FOR THE VESPERTINE INSPECTION, BELIEVE IT OR NOT...
YOU MIGHT TRY THE COMMISSARY.
BEHIND SCHEDULE
HRS
HEAR THAT, LOVEY-HORNS? YOU'RE IN LUCK.
YOU MAY GET A MORSEL TO EAT BEFORE YOU'RE SET TO DRUDGE.
SO STEP LIVELY NOW.
REVEREND SLAGGINGHAM?
I'VE BROUGHT YOU A GENT...
AND IF HE'S AS STRONG AS HE IS STRANGE, YOU'LL GET A DOZEN MEN'S WORK OUT OF HIM.
BONE MY FINGERS, SISTER STAYLACE -- I'M PLEASED AS CARBOLIC PUNCH TO HEAR THAT.
STOW HIS SOUL IN THE STRONG-ROOM, AND SET HIS PRIVILEGED CARCASS TO WORK ON THE EXTRACTOR.
PERHAPS YOU'D LIKE TO LOOK HIM OVER FIRST, REVEREND? HE'S... HE'S QUITE EXTRAORDINARY, REALLY.
HE'S A KING. AND HE'S BLUE. AND HAS
KLAANG
SISTER STAYLACE--

I DON'T CARE IF THE WASTER HAS A **BRASS MONKEY'S** TAIL. I'LL INSPECT HIM **LATER.**

I'M **BUSY,** D'YOU HEAR? **BUSY!**

YOU **HAVE** YOUR INSTRUCTIONS, DOLLY-MOP. FOLLOW THEM.

AS YOU PLEASE... **REVEREND.**

COME ALONG, LOVEY-HORNS.

SO I'M A **DOLLY-MOP** NOW, AM I? *Hmph!*

I MAY FLASH A **SMILE** AND AN **ANKLE** NOW AND THEN, LORDSHIP, BUT I DO IT FOR **THE CAUSE.**

I'M AS **RESPECTABLE** A SEAMSTRESS AS EVER **STARVED IN A GARRET,** I'LL HAVE YOU KNOW.

YOU KNOW WHAT I REMEMBER **CLEAREST** ABOUT MY OLD LIFE?

NOT THE **WORK** -- THOUGH GOD KNOWS I WAS **HARD AT IT** FROM THE DAY I WAS OLD ENOUGH TO **THREAD A NEEDLE.**

IT'S THE **FOOD** I REMEMBER.

WITH MY **MOTHER** AND MY **SISTER** AND ME ALL STITCHING AWAY, WE COULD EAT **TWICE A DAY,** MOST DAYS...

COLD BOILED POTATOES FOR **BREAKFAST. HOT** BOILED POTATOES FOR **SUPPER.**

NOT BECAUSE WE **FANCIED THEM.** BECAUSE THEY WERE **CHEAP.**

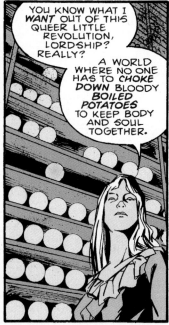

YOU KNOW WHAT I **WANT** OUT OF THIS QUEER LITTLE REVOLUTION, LORDSHIP? REALLY?

A WORLD WHERE NO ONE HAS TO **CHOKE DOWN** BLOODY **BOILED POTATOES** TO KEEP BODY AND SOUL TOGETHER.

THAT'S MY IDEA OF **PARADISE,** LOVEY-HORNS.

AMUSING, DON'T YOU THINK?

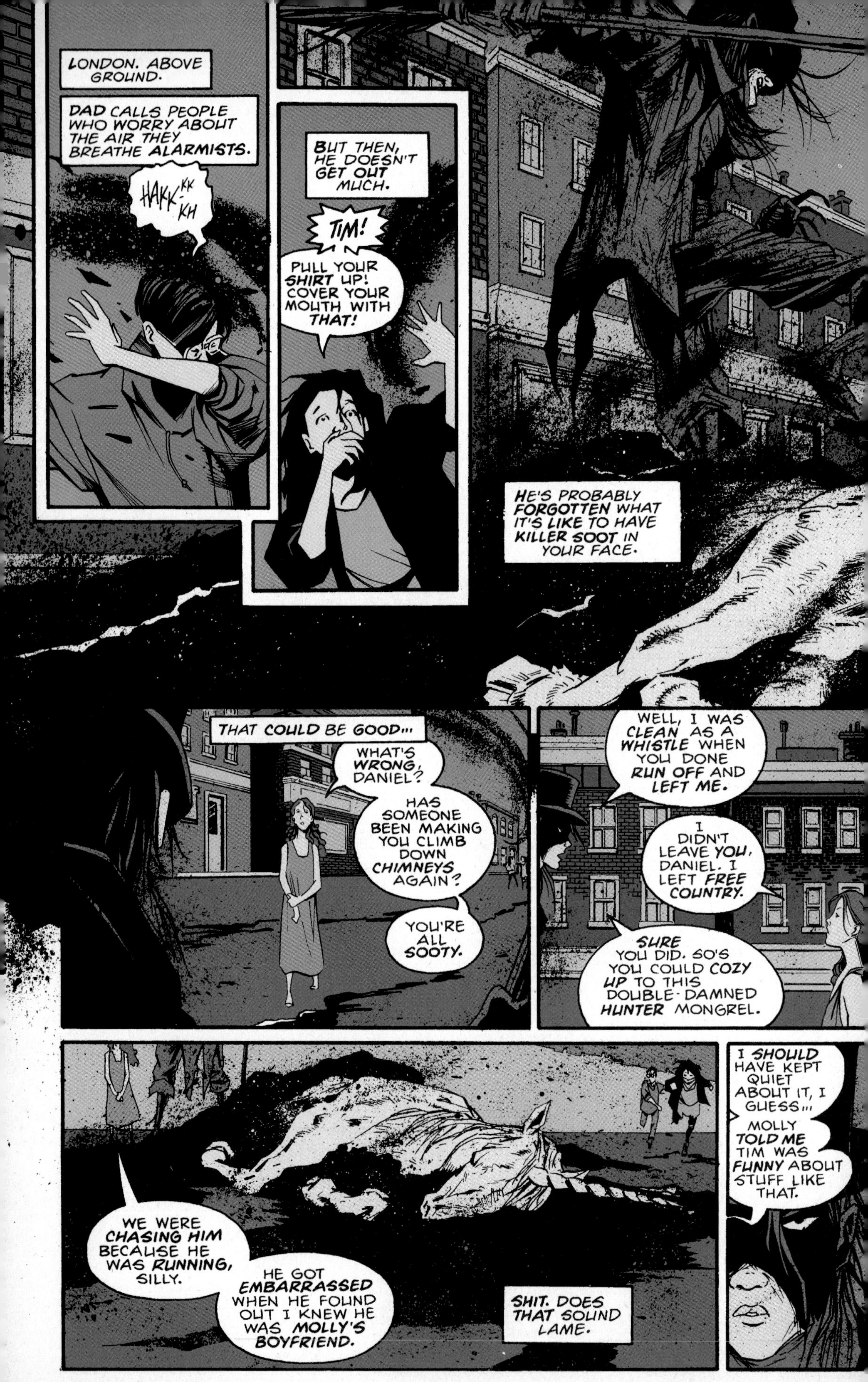
LONDON. ABOVE GROUND.
DAD CALLS PEOPLE WHO WORRY ABOUT THE AIR THEY BREATHE ALARMISTS.
HAKK-KK-KH
BUT THEN, HE DOESN'T GET OUT MUCH.
TIM!
PULL YOUR SHIRT UP! COVER YOUR MOUTH WITH THAT!
HE'S PROBABLY FORGOTTEN WHAT IT'S LIKE TO HAVE KILLER SOOT IN YOUR FACE.
THAT COULD BE GOOD...
WHAT'S WRONG, DANIEL?
HAS SOMEONE BEEN MAKING YOU CLIMB DOWN CHIMNEYS AGAIN?
YOU'RE ALL SOOTY.
WELL, I WAS CLEAN AS A WHISTLE WHEN YOU DONE RUN OFF AND LEFT ME.
I DIDN'T LEAVE YOU, DANIEL. I LEFT FREE COUNTRY.
SURE YOU DID. SO'S YOU COULD COZY UP TO THIS DOUBLE-DAMNED HUNTER MONGREL.
WE WERE CHASING HIM BECAUSE HE WAS RUNNING, SILLY.
HE GOT EMBARRASSED WHEN HE FOUND OUT I KNEW HE WAS MOLLY'S BOYFRIEND.
SHIT. DOES THAT SOUND LAME.
I SHOULD HAVE KEPT QUIET ABOUT IT, I GUESS...
MOLLY TOLD ME TIM WAS FUNNY ABOUT STUFF LIKE THAT.

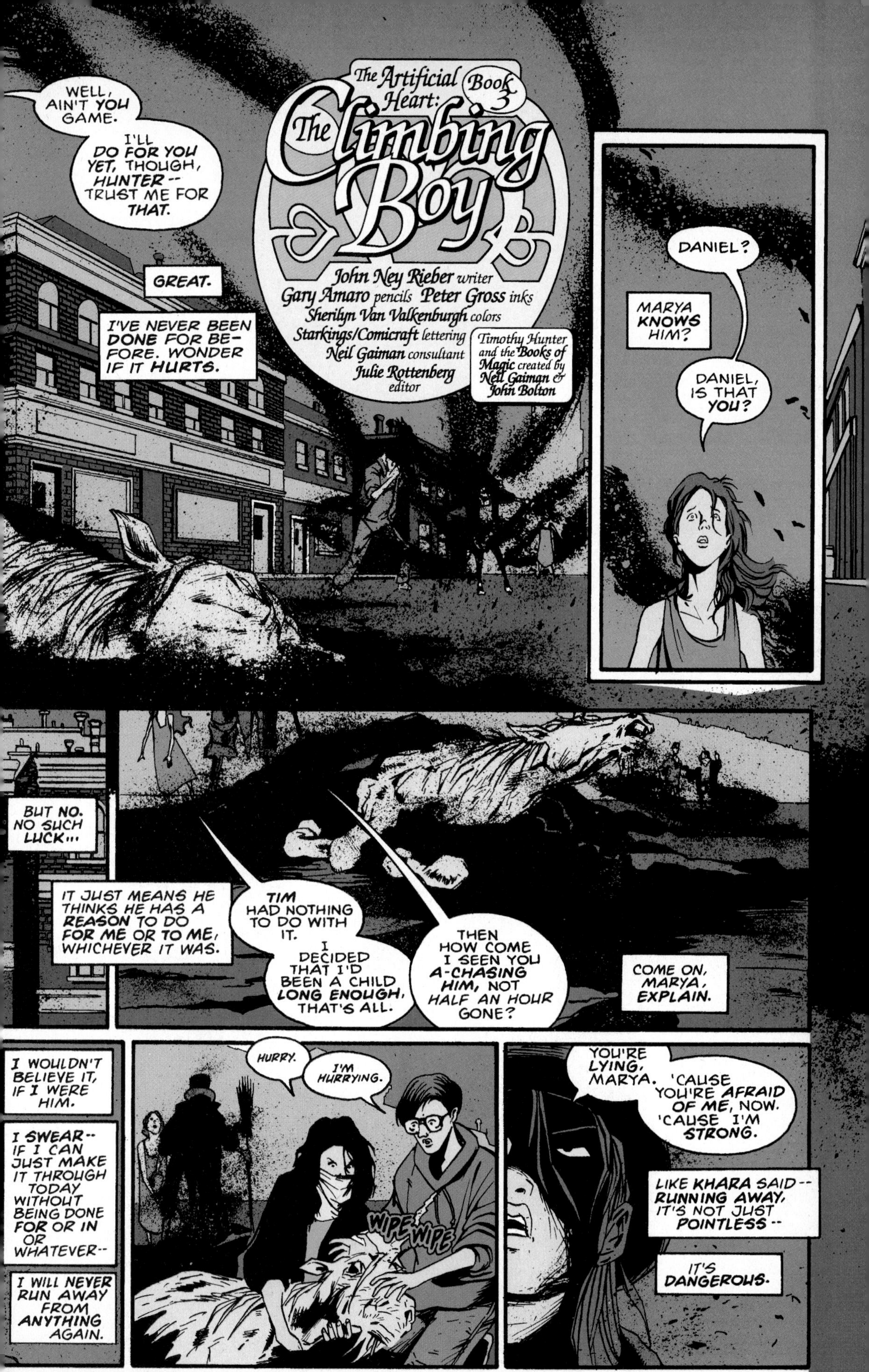
WELL, AIN'T YOU GAME.
I'LL DO FOR YOU YET, THOUGH, HUNTER -- TRUST ME FOR THAT.
The Artificial Heart: Book 3
The Climbing Boy
John Ney Rieber writer
Gary Amaro pencils Peter Gross inks
Sherilyn Van Valkenburgh colors
Starkings/Comicraft lettering
Neil Gaiman consultant
Julie Rottenberg editor
Timothy Hunter and the Books of Magic created by Neil Gaiman & John Bolton
GREAT.
I'VE NEVER BEEN DONE FOR BEFORE. WONDER IF IT HURTS.
DANIEL?
MARYA KNOWS HIM?
DANIEL, IS THAT YOU?
BUT NO. NO SUCH LUCK...
IT JUST MEANS HE THINKS HE HAS A REASON TO DO FOR ME OR TO ME, WHICHEVER IT WAS.
TIM HAD NOTHING TO DO WITH IT.
I DECIDED THAT I'D BEEN A CHILD LONG ENOUGH, THAT'S ALL.
THEN HOW COME I SEEN YOU A-CHASING HIM, NOT HALF AN HOUR GONE?
COME ON, MARYA, EXPLAIN.
I WOULDN'T BELIEVE IT, IF I WERE HIM.
I SWEAR -- IF I CAN JUST MAKE IT THROUGH TODAY WITHOUT BEING DONE FOR OR IN OR WHATEVER --
I WILL NEVER RUN AWAY FROM ANYTHING AGAIN.
HURRY.
I'M HURRYING.
WIPE WIPE
YOU'RE LYING, MARYA. 'CAUSE YOU'RE AFRAID OF ME, NOW. 'CAUSE I'M STRONG.
LIKE KHARA SAID -- RUNNING AWAY, IT'S NOT JUST POINTLESS --
IT'S DANGEROUS.

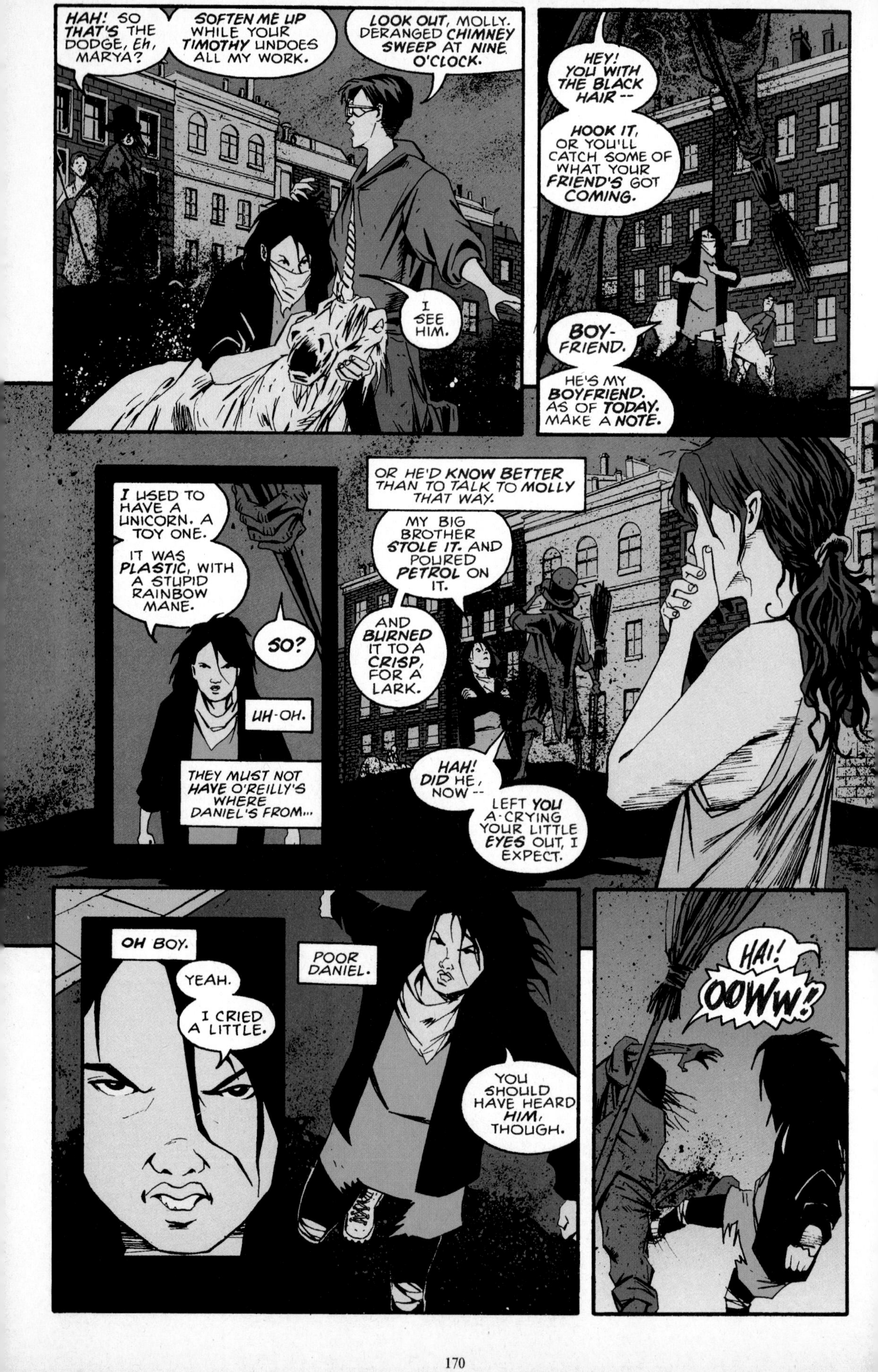
HAH! SO THAT'S THE DODGE, EH, MARYA?
SOFTEN ME UP WHILE YOUR TIMOTHY UNDOES ALL MY WORK.
LOOK OUT, MOLLY. DERANGED CHIMNEY SWEEP AT NINE O'CLOCK.
I SEE HIM.
HEY! YOU WITH THE BLACK HAIR --
HOOK IT, OR YOU'LL CATCH SOME OF WHAT YOUR FRIEND'S GOT COMING.
BOY-FRIEND.
HE'S MY BOYFRIEND. AS OF TODAY. MAKE A NOTE.
I USED TO HAVE A UNICORN. A TOY ONE.
IT WAS PLASTIC, WITH A STUPID RAINBOW MANE.
SO?
UH-OH.
THEY MUST NOT HAVE O'REILLY'S WHERE DANIEL'S FROM...
OR HE'D KNOW BETTER THAN TO TALK TO MOLLY THAT WAY.
MY BIG BROTHER STOLE IT. AND POURED PETROL ON IT.
AND BURNED IT TO A CRISP, FOR A LARK.
HAH! DID HE, NOW --
LEFT YOU A-CRYING YOUR LITTLE EYES OUT, I EXPECT.
OH BOY.
YEAH.
I CRIED A LITTLE.
POOR DANIEL.
YOU SHOULD HAVE HEARD HIM, THOUGH.
HAI!
OOWW!

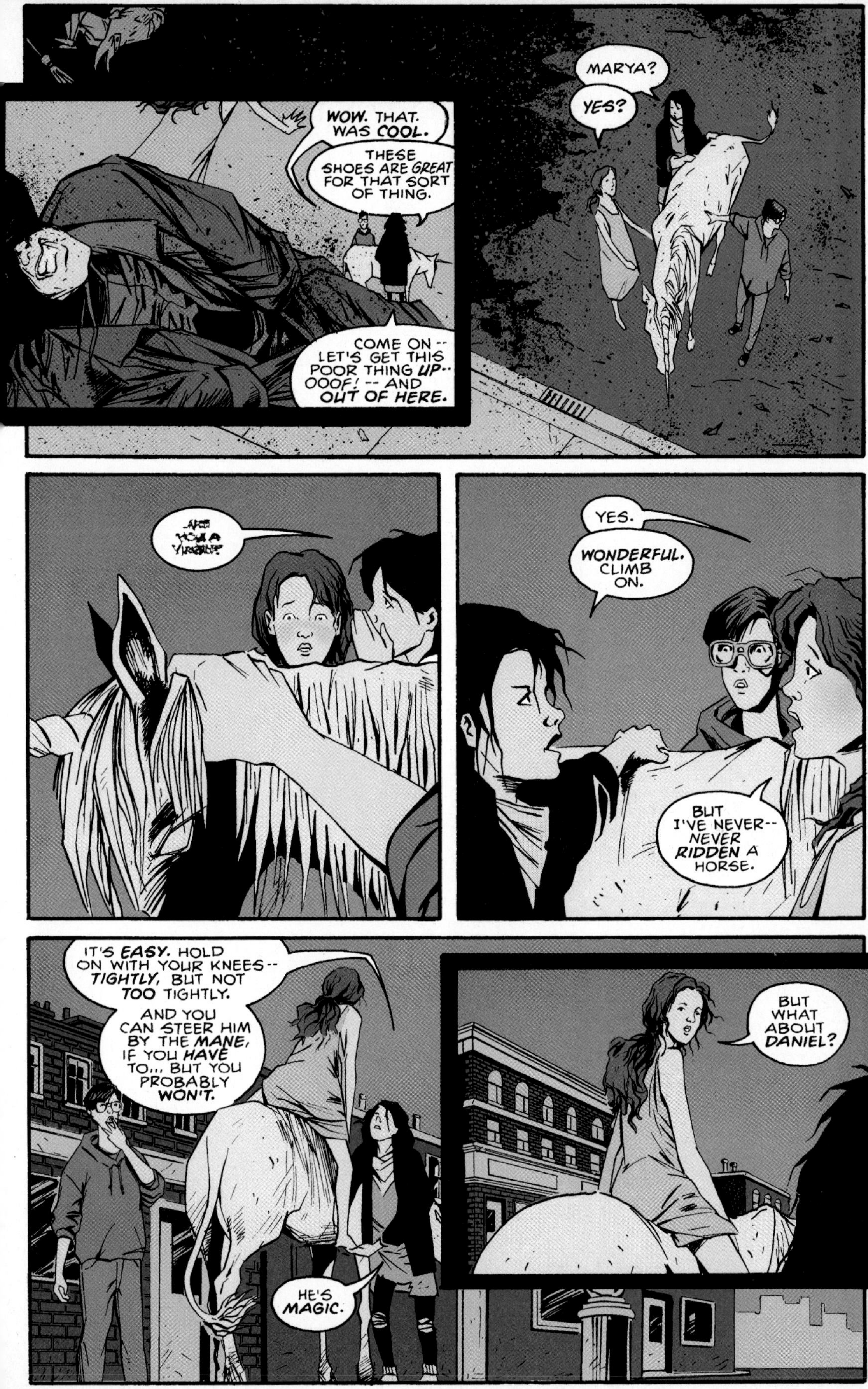
WOW. THAT. WAS COOL.
THESE SHOES ARE GREAT FOR THAT SORT OF THING.
COME ON -- LET'S GET THIS POOR THING UP-- OOOF! -- AND OUT OF HERE.
MARYA?
YES?
YES.
WONDERFUL. CLIMB ON.
BUT I'VE NEVER-- NEVER RIDDEN A HORSE.
IT'S EASY. HOLD ON WITH YOUR KNEES-- TIGHTLY, BUT NOT TOO TIGHTLY.
AND YOU CAN STEER HIM BY THE MANE, IF YOU HAVE TO... BUT YOU PROBABLY WON'T.
HE'S MAGIC.
BUT WHAT ABOUT DANIEL?

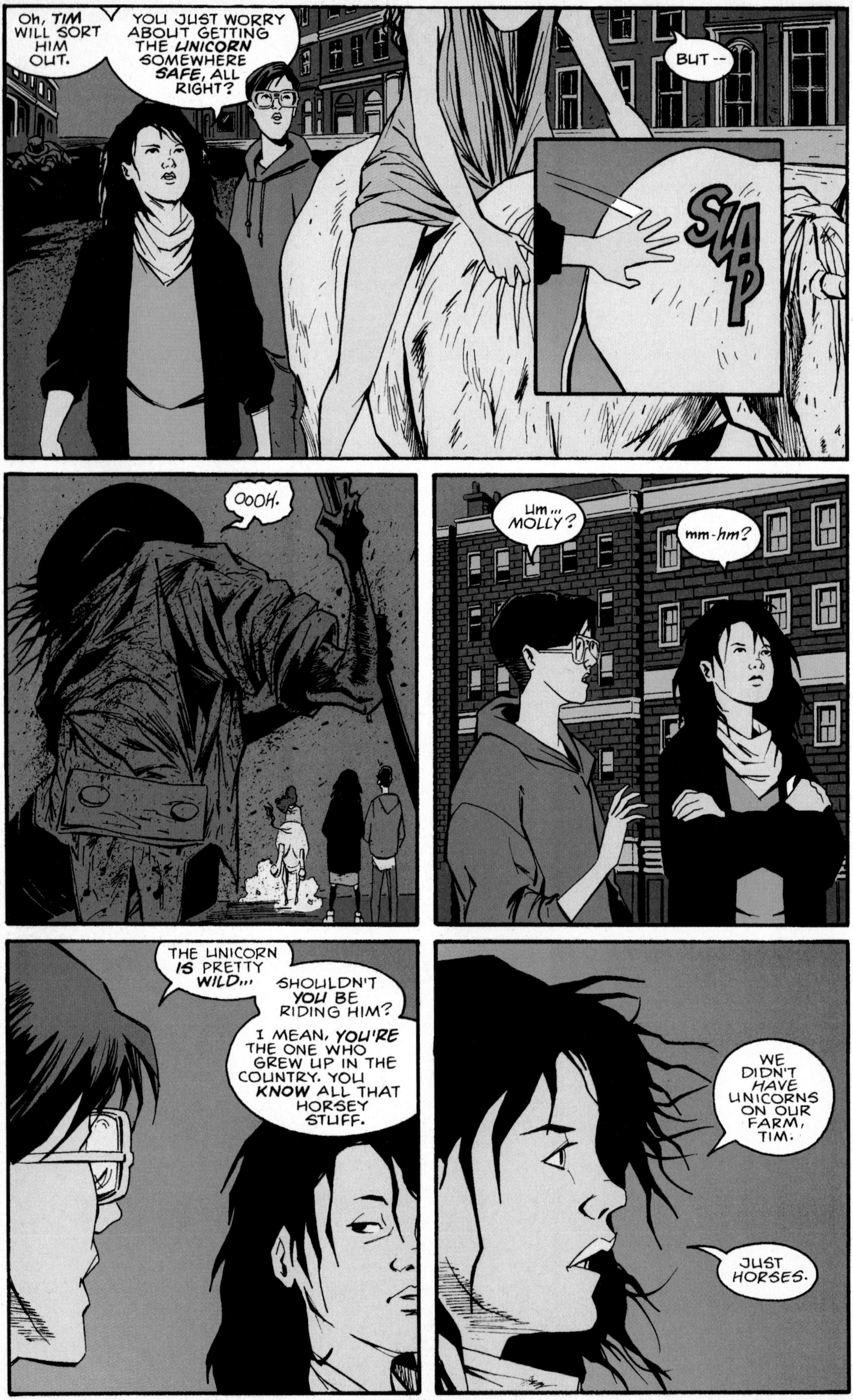

Oh, TIM WILL SORT HIM OUT.
YOU JUST WORRY ABOUT GETTING THE UNICORN SOMEWHERE SAFE, ALL RIGHT?
BUT --
SLAP
OOOH.
UM... MOLLY?
mm-hm?
THE UNICORN IS PRETTY WILD...
SHOULDN'T YOU BE RIDING HIM?
I MEAN, YOU'RE THE ONE WHO GREW UP IN THE COUNTRY. YOU KNOW ALL THAT HORSEY STUFF.
WE DIDN'T HAVE UNICORNS ON OUR FARM, TIM.
JUST HORSES.

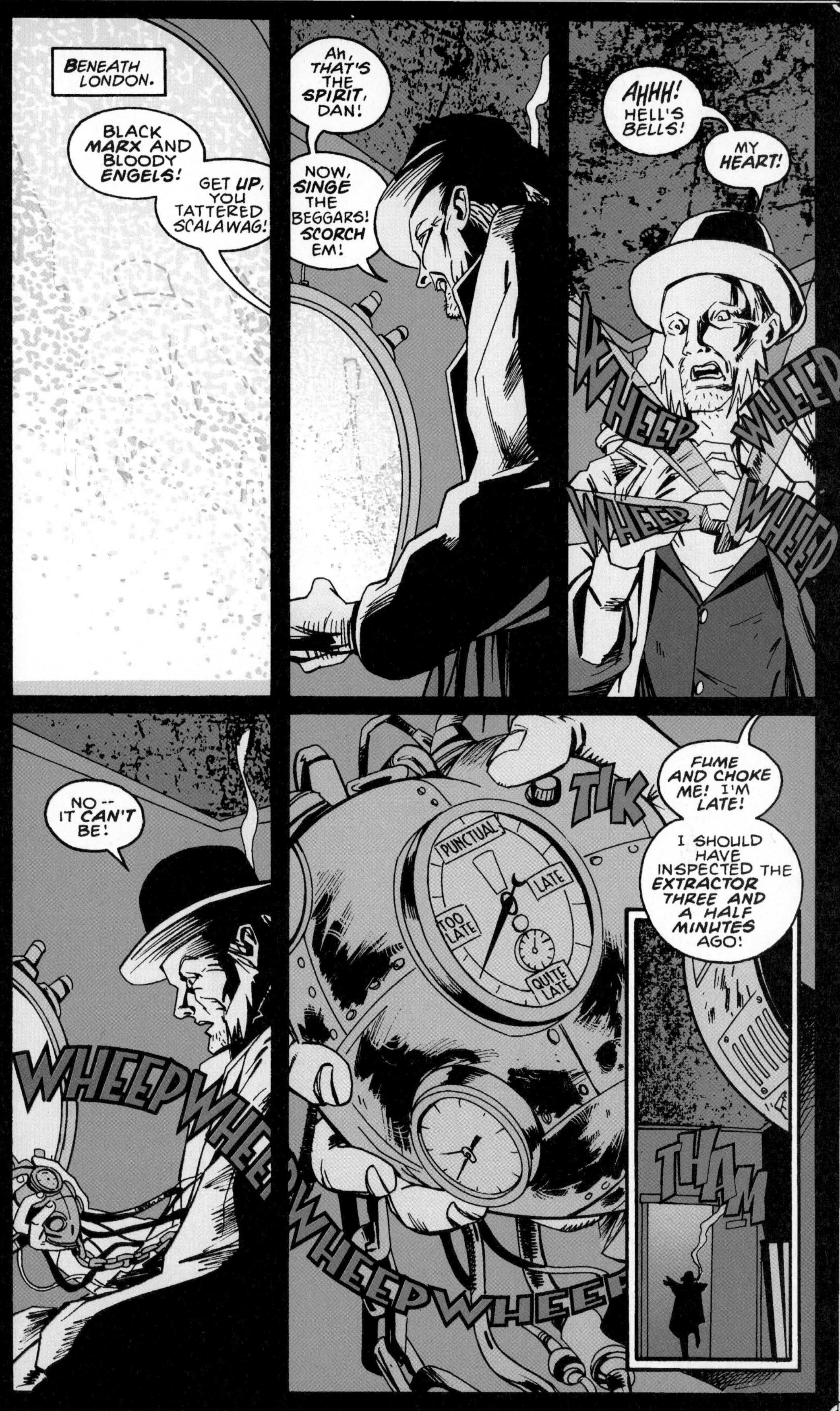
BENEATH LONDON.
BLACK MARX AND BLOODY ENGELS!
GET UP, YOU TATTERED SCALAWAG!
Ah, THAT'S THE SPIRIT, DAN!
NOW, SINGE THE BEGGARS! SCORCH EM!
AHHH! HELL'S BELLS!
MY HEART!
WHEEP WHEEP
WHEEP WHEEP
NO -- IT CAN'T BE!
WHEEP WHEEP WHEEP WHEEP
TIK
FUME AND CHOKE ME! I'M LATE!
I SHOULD HAVE INSPECTED THE EXTRACTOR THREE AND A HALF MINUTES AGO!
PUNCTUAL
LATE
TOO LATE
QUITE LATE
THAM

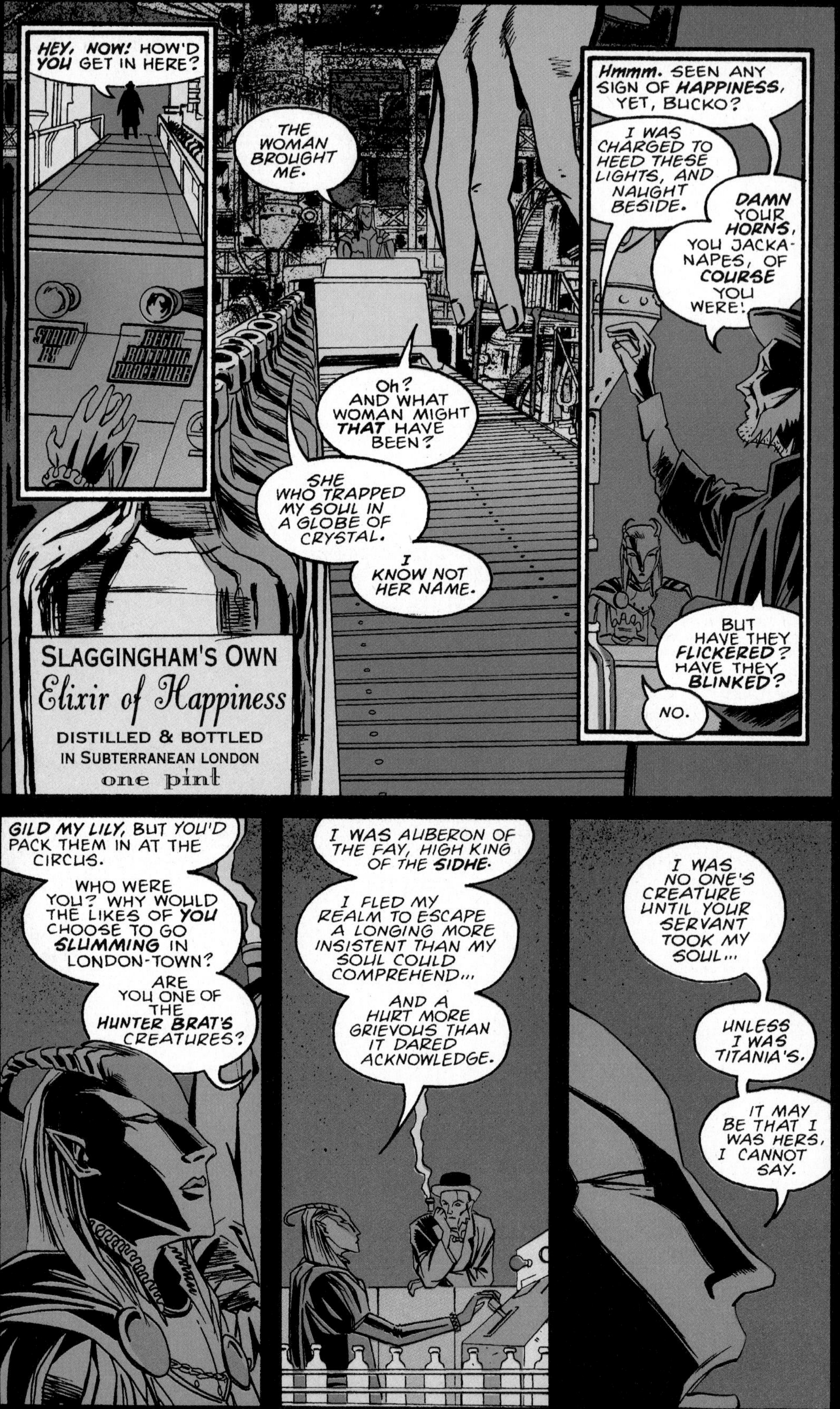
HEY, NOW! HOW'D YOU GET IN HERE?
STAND BY
BEGIN BOTTLING PROCEDURE
THE WOMAN BROUGHT ME.
Oh? AND WHAT WOMAN MIGHT THAT HAVE BEEN?
SHE WHO TRAPPED MY SOUL IN A GLOBE OF CRYSTAL.
I KNOW NOT HER NAME.
SLAGGINGHAM'S OWN
Elixir of Happiness
DISTILLED & BOTTLED
IN SUBTERRANEAN LONDON
one pint
Hmmm. SEEN ANY SIGN OF HAPPINESS, YET, BUCKO?
I WAS CHARGED TO HEED THESE LIGHTS, AND NAUGHT BESIDE.
DAMN YOUR HORNS, YOU JACKANAPES, OF COURSE YOU WERE!
BUT HAVE THEY FLICKERED? HAVE THEY BLINKED?
NO.
GILD MY LILY, BUT YOU'D PACK THEM IN AT THE CIRCUS.
WHO WERE YOU? WHY WOULD THE LIKES OF YOU CHOOSE TO GO SLUMMING IN LONDON-TOWN?
ARE YOU ONE OF THE HUNTER BRAT'S CREATURES?
I WAS AUBERON OF THE FAY, HIGH KING OF THE SIDHE.
I FLED MY REALM TO ESCAPE A LONGING MORE INSISTENT THAN MY SOUL COULD COMPREHEND...
AND A HURT MORE GRIEVOUS THAN IT DARED ACKNOWLEDGE.
I WAS NO ONE'S CREATURE UNTIL YOUR SERVANT TOOK MY SOUL...
UNLESS I WAS TITANIA'S.
IT MAY BE THAT I WAS HERS, I CANNOT SAY.

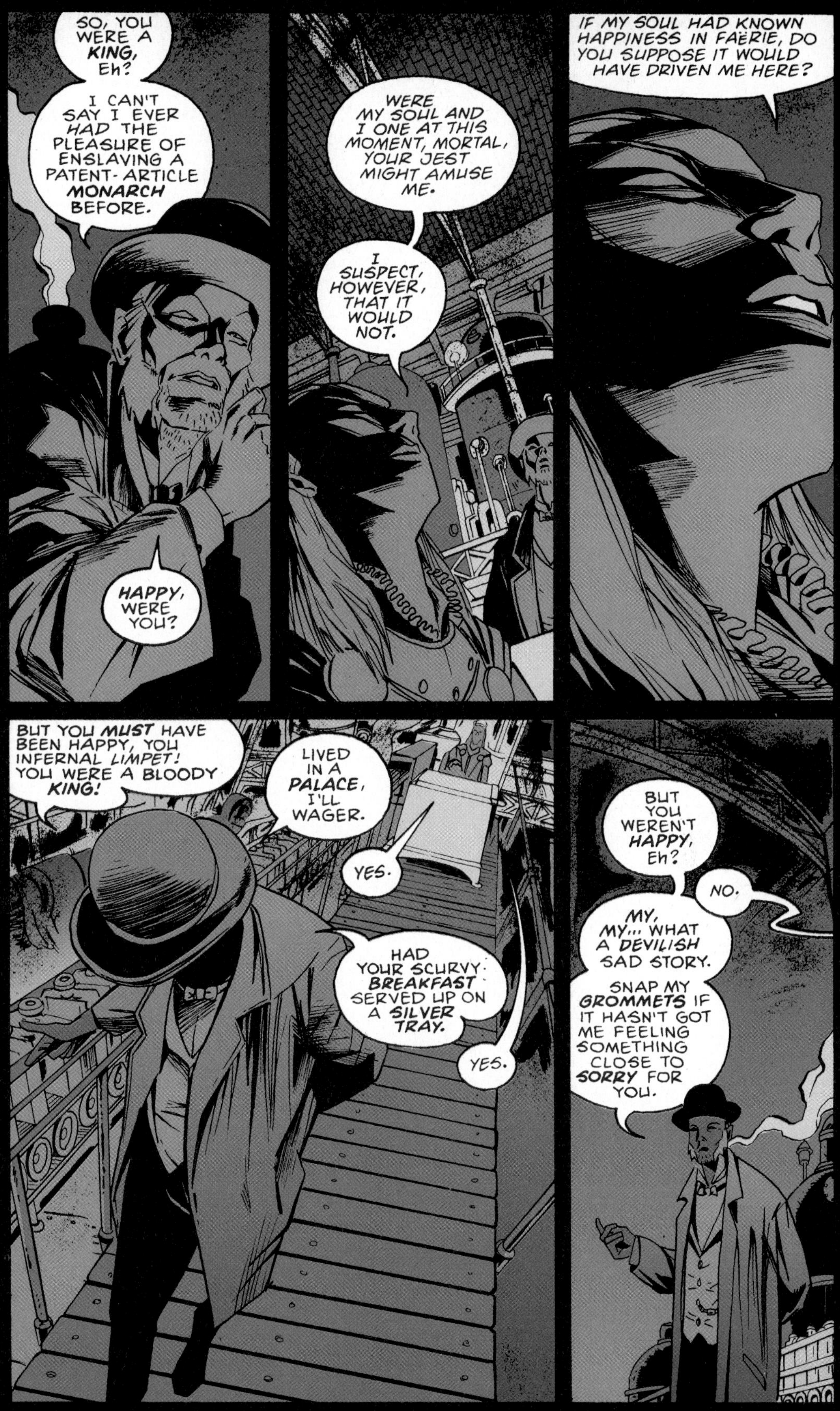
SO, YOU WERE A KING, Eh?
I CAN'T SAY I EVER HAD THE PLEASURE OF ENSLAVING A PATENT-ARTICLE MONARCH BEFORE.
HAPPY, WERE YOU?
WERE MY SOUL AND I ONE AT THIS MOMENT, MORTAL, YOUR JEST MIGHT AMUSE ME.
I SUSPECT, HOWEVER, THAT IT WOULD NOT.
IF MY SOUL HAD KNOWN HAPPINESS IN FAËRIE, DO YOU SUPPOSE IT WOULD HAVE DRIVEN ME HERE?
BUT YOU MUST HAVE BEEN HAPPY, YOU INFERNAL LIMPET! YOU WERE A BLOODY KING!
LIVED IN A PALACE, I'LL WAGER.
YES.
HAD YOUR SCURVY BREAKFAST SERVED UP ON A SILVER TRAY.
YES.
BUT YOU WEREN'T HAPPY, Eh?
NO.
MY, MY... WHAT A DEVILISH SAD STORY.
SNAP MY GROMMETS IF IT HASN'T GOT ME FEELING SOMETHING CLOSE TO SORRY FOR YOU.

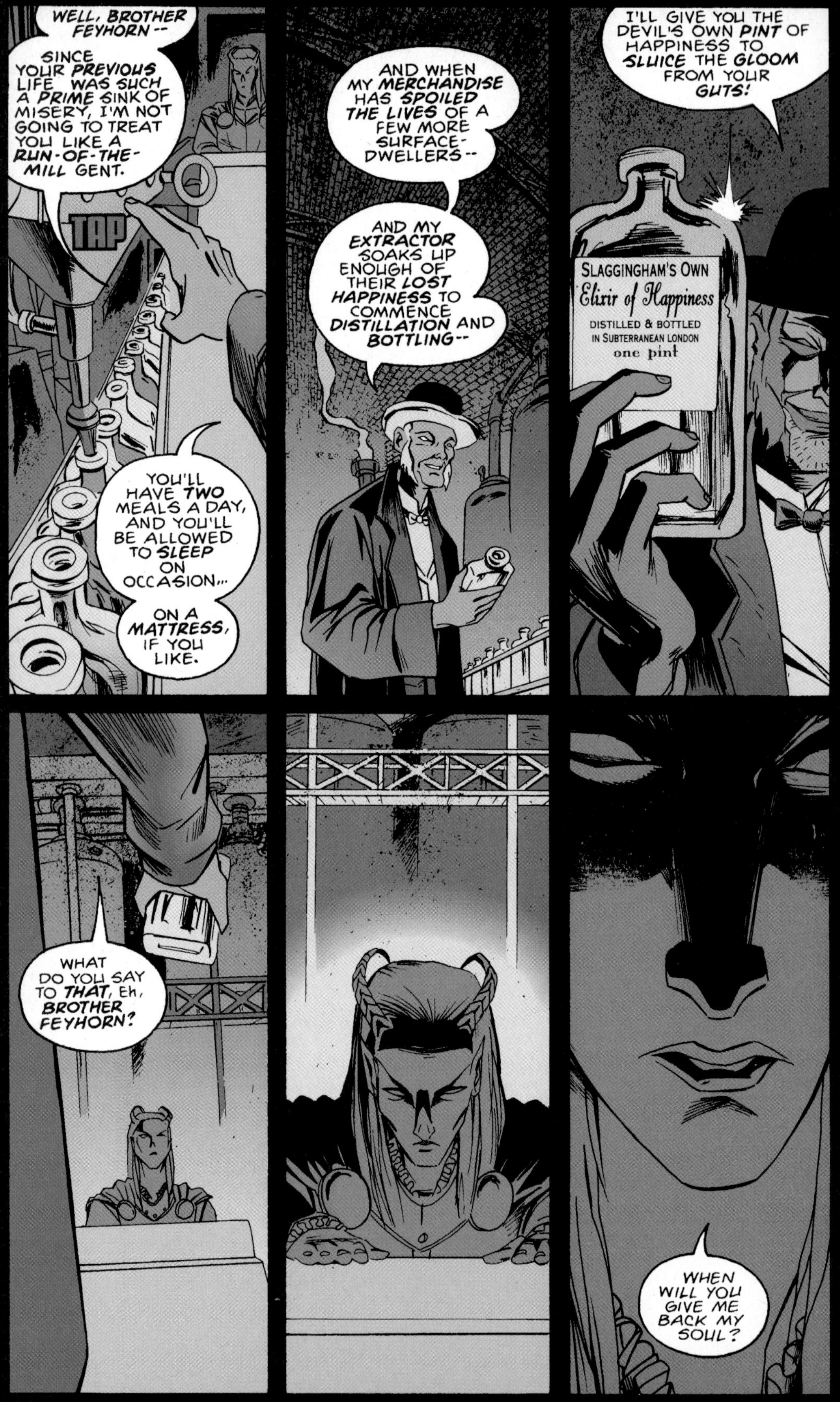
WELL, BROTHER FEYHORN --
SINCE YOUR PREVIOUS LIFE WAS SUCH A PRIME SINK OF MISERY, I'M NOT GOING TO TREAT YOU LIKE A RUN-OF-THE-MILL GENT.
TAP
YOU'LL HAVE TWO MEALS A DAY, AND YOU'LL BE ALLOWED TO SLEEP ON OCCASION...
ON A MATTRESS, IF YOU LIKE.
AND WHEN MY MERCHANDISE HAS SPOILED THE LIVES OF A FEW MORE SURFACE-DWELLERS --
AND MY EXTRACTOR SOAKS UP ENOUGH OF THEIR LOST HAPPINESS TO COMMENCE DISTILLATION AND BOTTLING --
I'LL GIVE YOU THE DEVIL'S OWN PINT OF HAPPINESS TO SLUICE THE GLOOM FROM YOUR GUTS!
SLAGGINGHAM'S OWN
Elixir of Happiness
DISTILLED & BOTTLED
IN SUBTERRANEAN LONDON
one pint
WHAT DO YOU SAY TO THAT, Eh, BROTHER FEYHORN?
WHEN WILL YOU GIVE ME BACK MY SOUL?

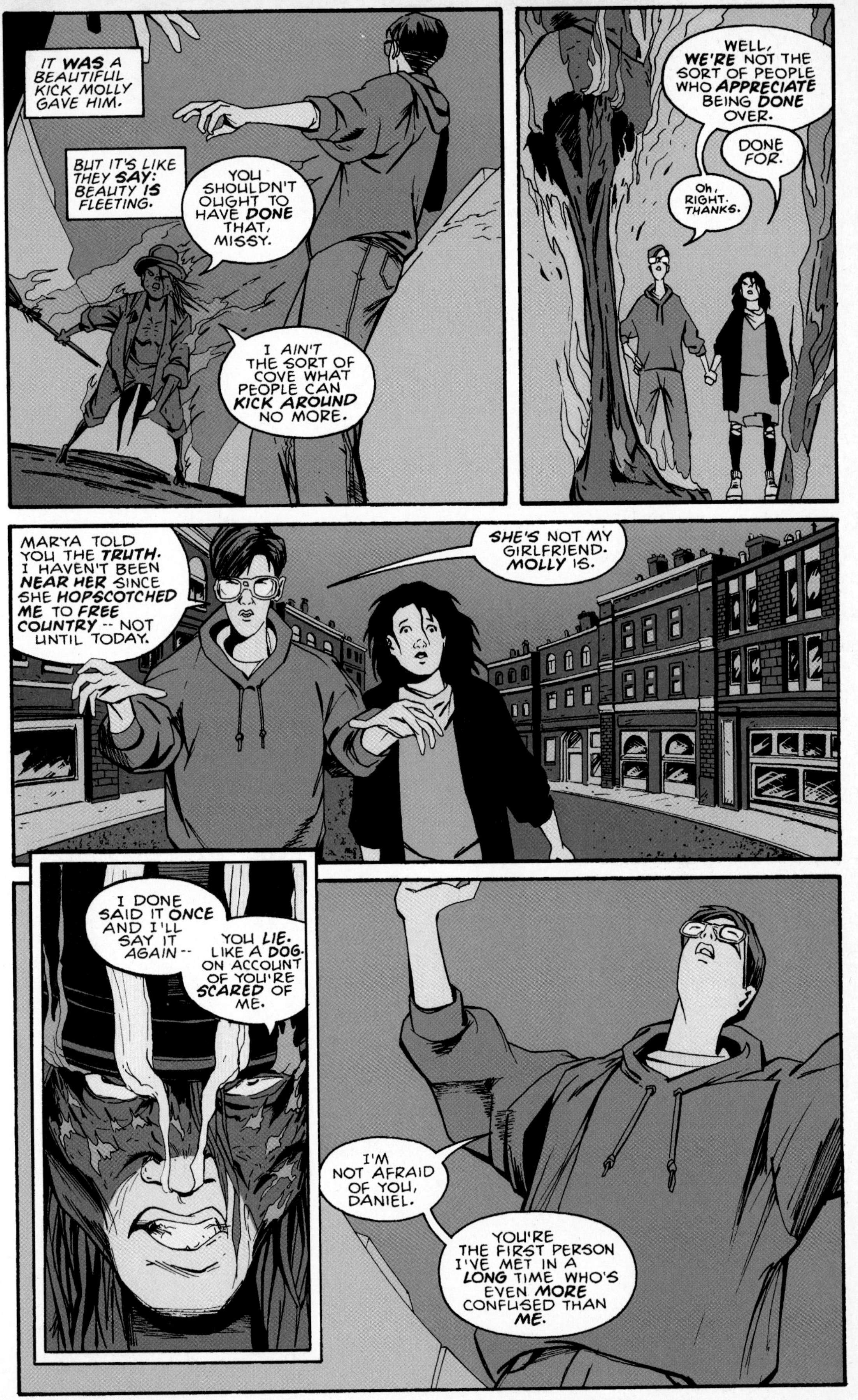
IT WAS A BEAUTIFUL KICK MOLLY GAVE HIM.
BUT IT'S LIKE THEY SAY: BEAUTY IS FLEETING.
YOU SHOULDN'T OUGHT TO HAVE DONE THAT, MISSY.
I AIN'T THE SORT OF COVE WHAT PEOPLE CAN KICK AROUND NO MORE.
WELL, WE'RE NOT THE SORT OF PEOPLE WHO APPRECIATE BEING DONE OVER.
DONE FOR.
Oh, RIGHT. THANKS.
MARYA TOLD YOU THE TRUTH. I HAVEN'T BEEN NEAR HER SINCE SHE HOPSCOTCHED ME TO FREE COUNTRY -- NOT UNTIL TODAY.
SHE'S NOT MY GIRLFRIEND. MOLLY IS.
I DONE SAID IT ONCE AND I'LL SAY IT AGAIN --
YOU LIE. LIKE A DOG. ON ACCOUNT OF YOU'RE SCARED OF ME.
I'M NOT AFRAID OF YOU, DANIEL.
YOU'RE THE FIRST PERSON I'VE MET IN A LONG TIME WHO'S EVEN MORE CONFUSED THAN ME.

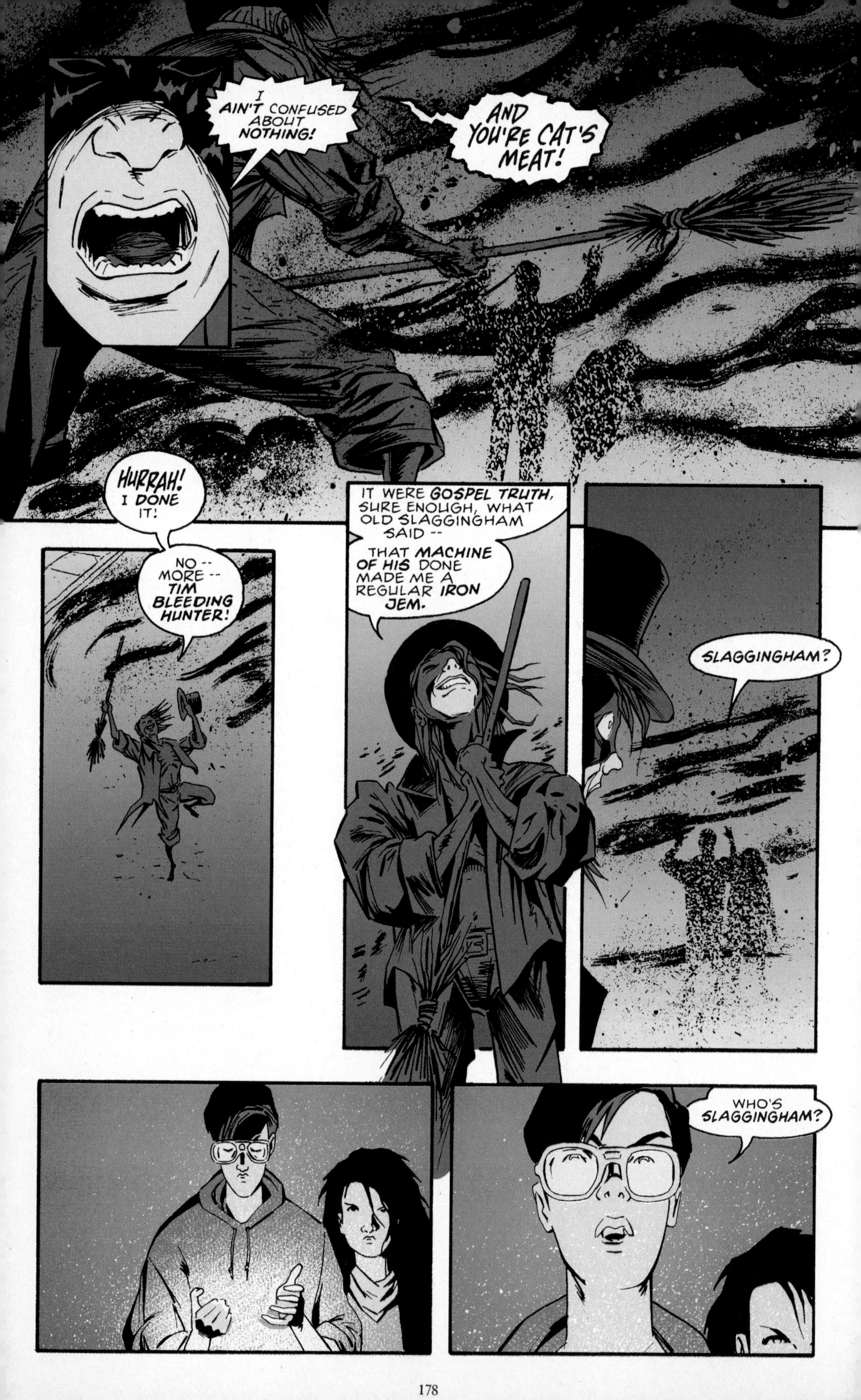
I AIN'T CONFUSED ABOUT NOTHING!
AND YOU'RE CAT'S MEAT!
HURRAH! I DONE IT!
NO -- MORE -- TIM BLEEDING HUNTER!
IT WERE GOSPEL TRUTH, SURE ENOUGH, WHAT OLD SLAGGINGHAM SAID --
THAT MACHINE OF HIS DONE MADE ME A REGULAR IRON JEM.
SLAGGINGHAM?
WHO'S SLAGGINGHAM?

DAMN YOU.

Y-YOU AIN'T EVEN SINGED. IT AIN'T FAIR!

I AIN'T NO GOOD.

EVEN THIS WAY I AIN'T NO GOOD AT NOTHING.

WELL, ALL RIGHT. BEAT ON ME. KICK ME AGAIN.

I DOESN'T CARE. I CAN TAKE IT.

UH, DANIEL... WE AREN'T GOING TO HURT YOU. WE JUST WANT YOU TO CALM DOWN.

YOU KNOW... JUST BE A BIT LESS HOMICIDAL.

SO ... YOU WEREN'T ALWAYS, UM, LIKE YOU ARE NOW, IS THAT RIGHT?

YOU KNOW, MARYA BARELY RECOGNIZED YOU.

I DON'T WONDER.

I HAS FELT SORT OF INSIDE-OUT-LIKE SINCE SLAGGINGHAM RUN ME THROUGH THAT PER-SONA MACHINE.

TIM, TAKE OFF YOUR GLASSES.

MY GLASSES?

YOUR GLASSES.

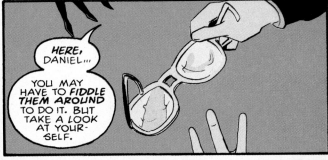

HERE, DANIEL...

YOU MAY HAVE TO FIDDLE THEM AROUND TO DO IT. BUT TAKE A LOOK AT YOUR-SELF.

--BUT-- THAT'S NOT--

IS THAT ME?

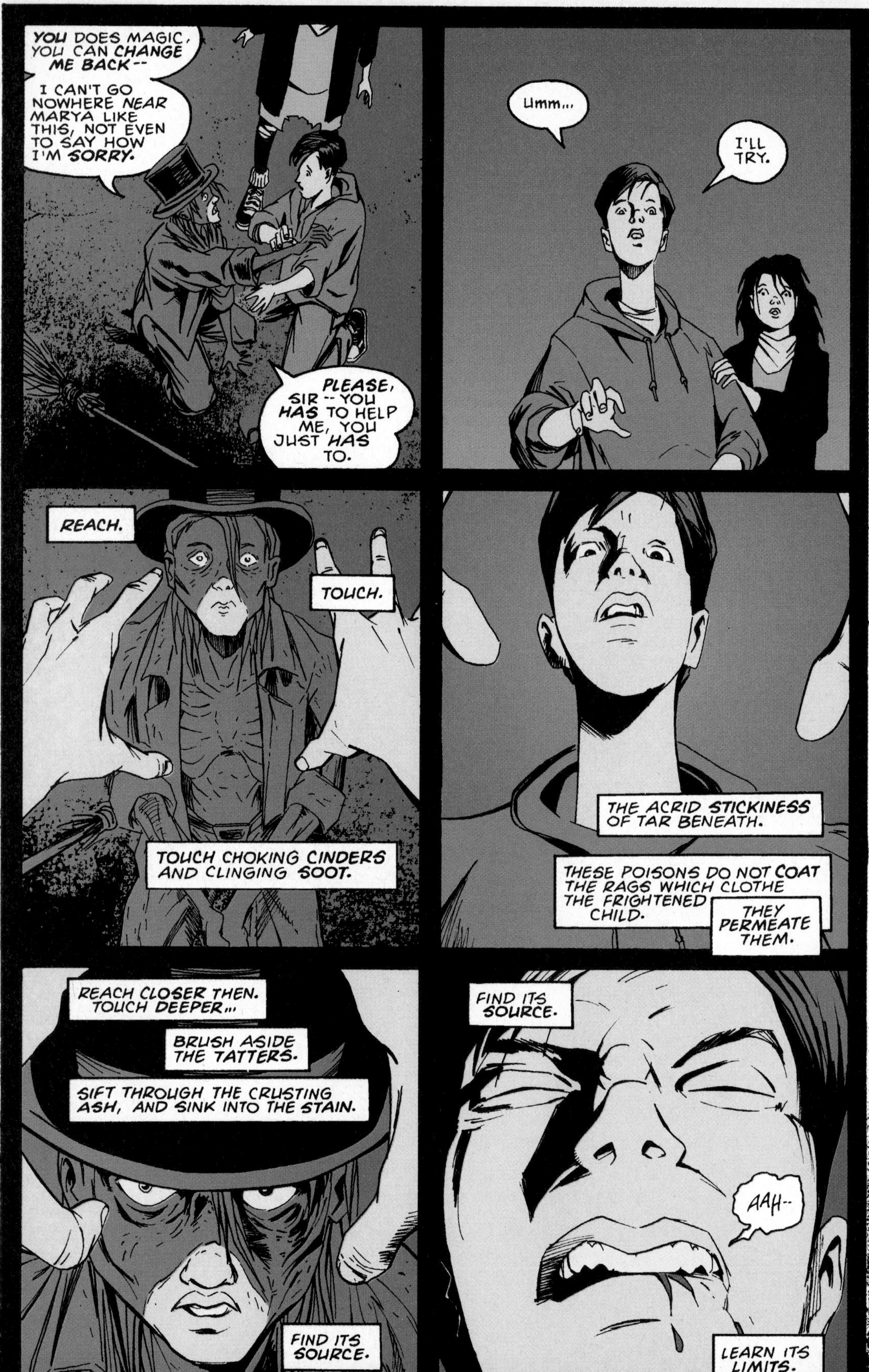
YOU DOES MAGIC, YOU CAN CHANGE ME BACK--
I CAN'T GO NOWHERE NEAR MARYA LIKE THIS, NOT EVEN TO SAY HOW I'M SORRY.
PLEASE, SIR -- YOU HAS TO HELP ME, YOU JUST HAS TO.
Umm...
I'LL TRY.
REACH.
TOUCH.
TOUCH CHOKING CINDERS AND CLINGING SOOT.
THE ACRID STICKINESS OF TAR BENEATH.
THESE POISONS DO NOT COAT THE RAGS WHICH CLOTHE THE FRIGHTENED CHILD.
THEY PERMEATE THEM.
REACH CLOSER THEN. TOUCH DEEPER...
BRUSH ASIDE THE TATTERS.
SIFT THROUGH THE CRUSTING ASH, AND SINK INTO THE STAIN.
FIND ITS SOURCE.
FIND ITS SOURCE.
AAH--
LEARN ITS LIMITS.

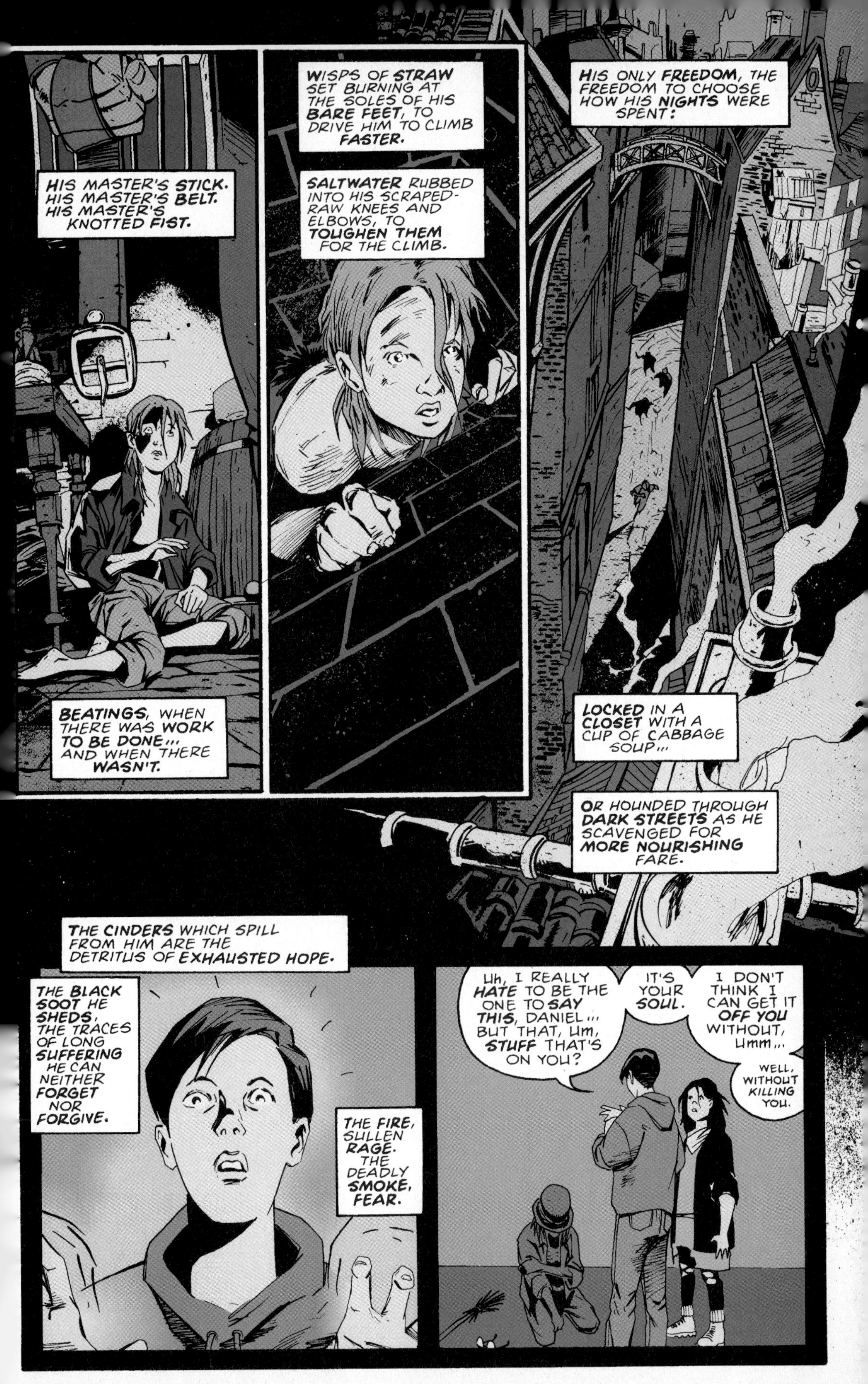
HIS MASTER'S STICK. HIS MASTER'S BELT. HIS MASTER'S KNOTTED FIST.
BEATINGS, WHEN THERE WAS WORK TO BE DONE... AND WHEN THERE WASN'T.
WISPS OF STRAW SET BURNING AT THE SOLES OF HIS BARE FEET, TO DRIVE HIM TO CLIMB FASTER.
SALTWATER RUBBED INTO HIS SCRAPED-RAW KNEES AND ELBOWS, TO TOUGHEN THEM FOR THE CLIMB.
HIS ONLY FREEDOM, THE FREEDOM TO CHOOSE HOW HIS NIGHTS WERE SPENT:
LOCKED IN A CLOSET WITH A CUP OF CABBAGE SOUP...
OR HOUNDED THROUGH DARK STREETS AS HE SCAVENGED FOR MORE NOURISHING FARE.
THE CINDERS WHICH SPILL FROM HIM ARE THE DETRITUS OF EXHAUSTED HOPE.
THE BLACK SOOT HE SHEDS, THE TRACES OF LONG SUFFERING HE CAN NEITHER FORGET NOR FORGIVE.
THE FIRE, SULLEN RAGE. THE DEADLY SMOKE, FEAR.
Uh, I REALLY HATE TO BE THE ONE TO SAY THIS, DANIEL... BUT THAT, Um, STUFF THAT'S ON YOU?
IT'S YOUR SOUL.
I DON'T THINK I CAN GET IT OFF YOU WITHOUT, Umm...
WELL, WITHOUT KILLING YOU.

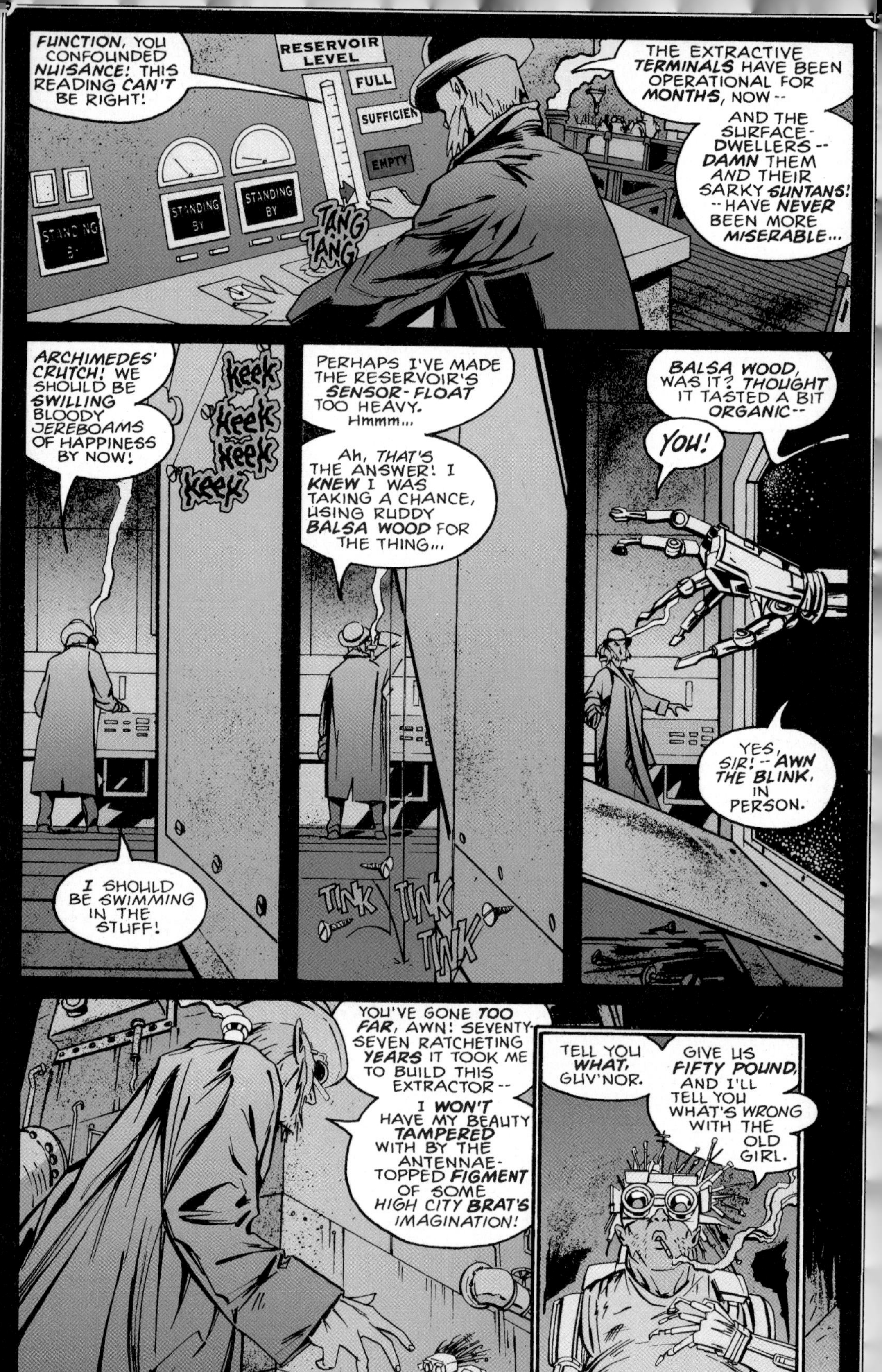
FUNCTION, YOU CONFOUNDED NUISANCE! THIS READING CAN'T BE RIGHT!
RESERVOIR LEVEL
FULL
SUFFICIEN
EMPTY
STANDING BY
STANDING BY
TANG TANG
THE EXTRACTIVE TERMINALS HAVE BEEN OPERATIONAL FOR MONTHS, NOW --
AND THE SURFACE-DWELLERS -- DAMN THEM AND THEIR SARKY SUNTANS! -- HAVE NEVER BEEN MORE MISERABLE...
ARCHIMEDES' CRUTCH! WE SHOULD BE SWILLING BLOODY JEREBOAMS OF HAPPINESS BY NOW!
KEEK KEEK KEEK KEEK
I SHOULD BE SWIMMING IN THE STUFF!
PERHAPS I'VE MADE THE RESERVOIR'S SENSOR-FLOAT TOO HEAVY. Hmmm...
Ah, THAT'S THE ANSWER! I KNEW I WAS TAKING A CHANCE, USING RUDDY BALSA WOOD FOR THE THING...
TINK TINK TINK
BALSA WOOD, WAS IT? THOUGHT IT TASTED A BIT ORGANIC--
YOU!
YES, SIR! -- AWN THE BLINK, IN PERSON.
YOU'VE GONE TOO FAR, AWN! SEVENTY-SEVEN RATCHETING YEARS IT TOOK ME TO BUILD THIS EXTRACTOR --
I WON'T HAVE MY BEAUTY TAMPERED WITH BY THE ANTENNAE-TOPPED FIGMENT OF SOME HIGH CITY BRAT'S IMAGINATION!
TELL YOU WHAT, GUV'NOR.
GIVE US FIFTY POUND, AND I'LL TELL YOU WHAT'S WRONG WITH THE OLD GIRL.

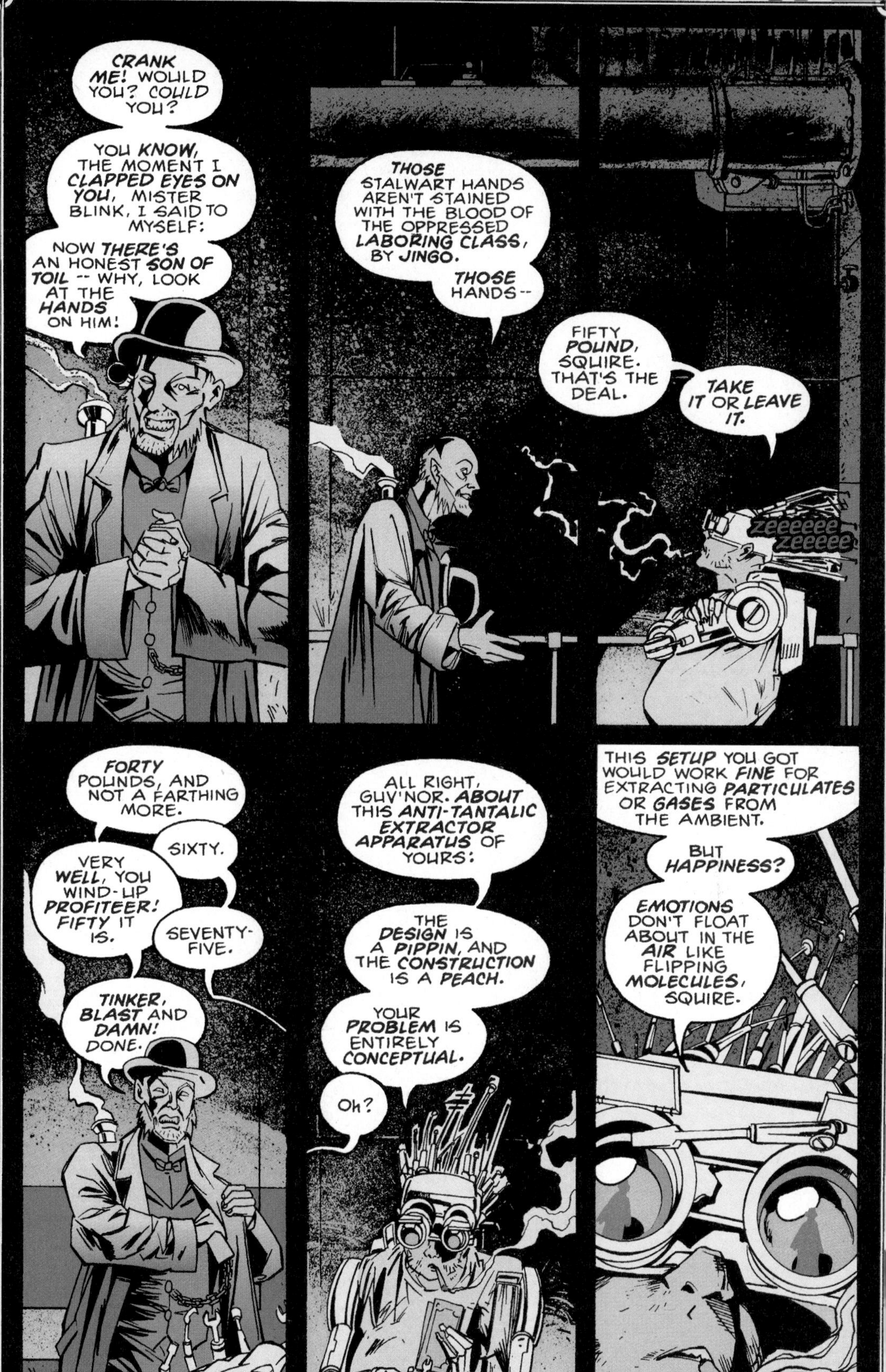
CRANK ME! WOULD YOU? COULD YOU?
YOU KNOW, THE MOMENT I CLAPPED EYES ON YOU, MISTER BLINK, I SAID TO MYSELF:
NOW THERE'S AN HONEST SON OF TOIL -- WHY, LOOK AT THE HANDS ON HIM!
THOSE STALWART HANDS AREN'T STAINED WITH THE BLOOD OF THE OPPRESSED LABORING CLASS, BY JINGO.
THOSE HANDS--
FIFTY POUND, SQUIRE. THAT'S THE DEAL.
TAKE IT OR LEAVE IT.
zeeeeee zeeeee
FORTY POUNDS, AND NOT A FARTHING MORE.
SIXTY.
VERY WELL, YOU WIND-UP PROFITEER! FIFTY IT IS.
SEVENTY-FIVE.
TINKER, BLAST AND DAMN! DONE.
ALL RIGHT, GUV'NOR. ABOUT THIS ANTI-TANTALIC EXTRACTOR APPARATUS OF YOURS:
THE DESIGN IS A PIPPIN, AND THE CONSTRUCTION IS A PEACH.
YOUR PROBLEM IS ENTIRELY CONCEPTUAL.
Oh?
THIS SETUP YOU GOT WOULD WORK FINE FOR EXTRACTING PARTICULATES OR GASES FROM THE AMBIENT.
BUT HAPPINESS?
EMOTIONS DON'T FLOAT ABOUT IN THE AIR LIKE FLIPPING MOLECULES, SQUIRE.

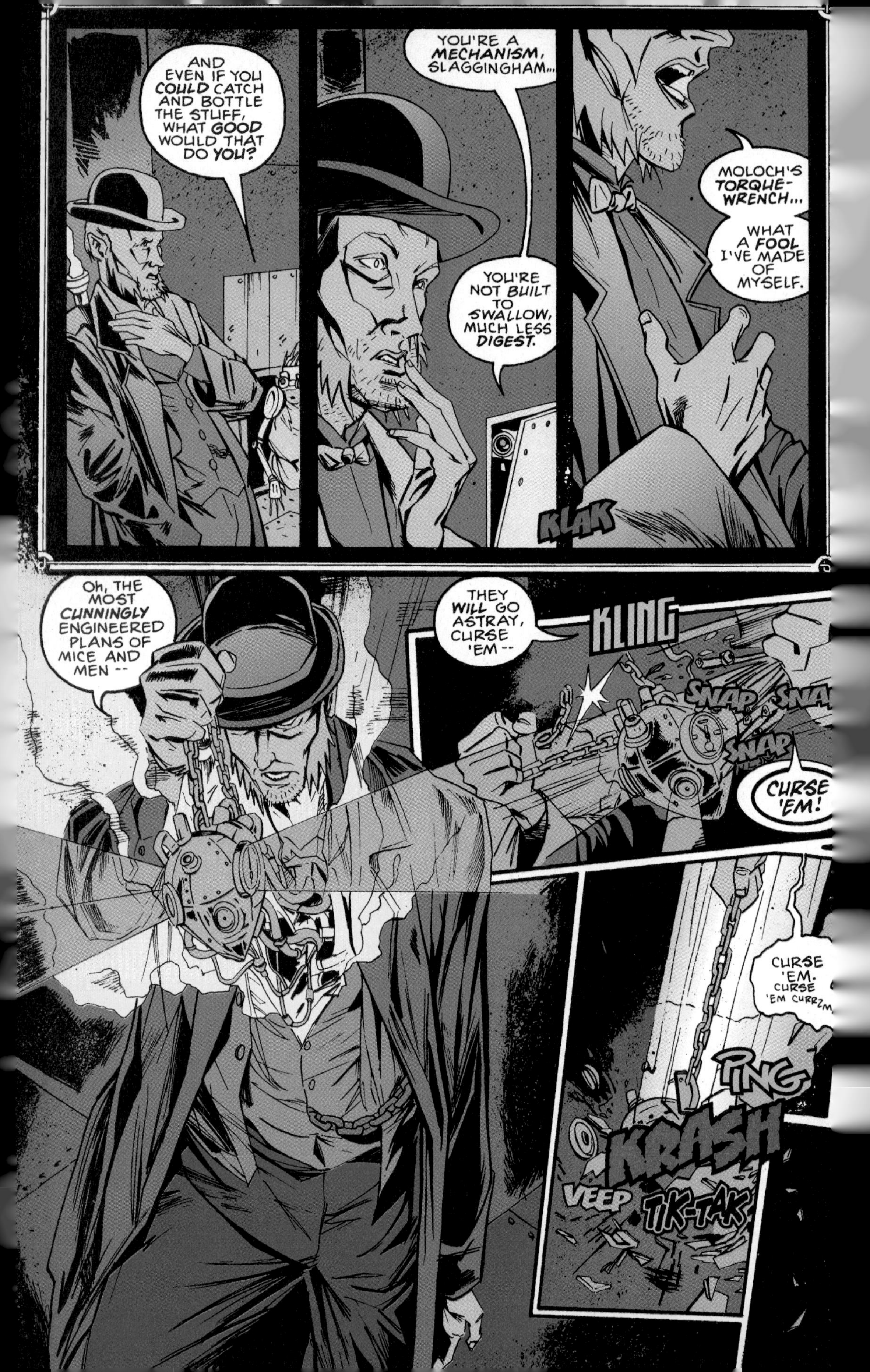
AND EVEN IF YOU COULD CATCH AND BOTTLE THE STUFF, WHAT GOOD WOULD THAT DO YOU?
YOU'RE A MECHANISM, SLAGGINGHAM...
YOU'RE NOT BUILT TO SWALLOW, MUCH LESS DIGEST.
MOLOCH'S TORQUE-WRENCH...
WHAT A FOOL I'VE MADE OF MYSELF.
KLAK
Oh, THE MOST CUNNINGLY ENGINEERED PLANS OF MICE AND MEN --
THEY WILL GO ASTRAY, CURSE 'EM --
KLING
SNAP
SNAP
CURSE 'EM!
CURSE 'EM. CURSE 'EM CURRZM
PING
KRASH
VEEP
TIK-TAK

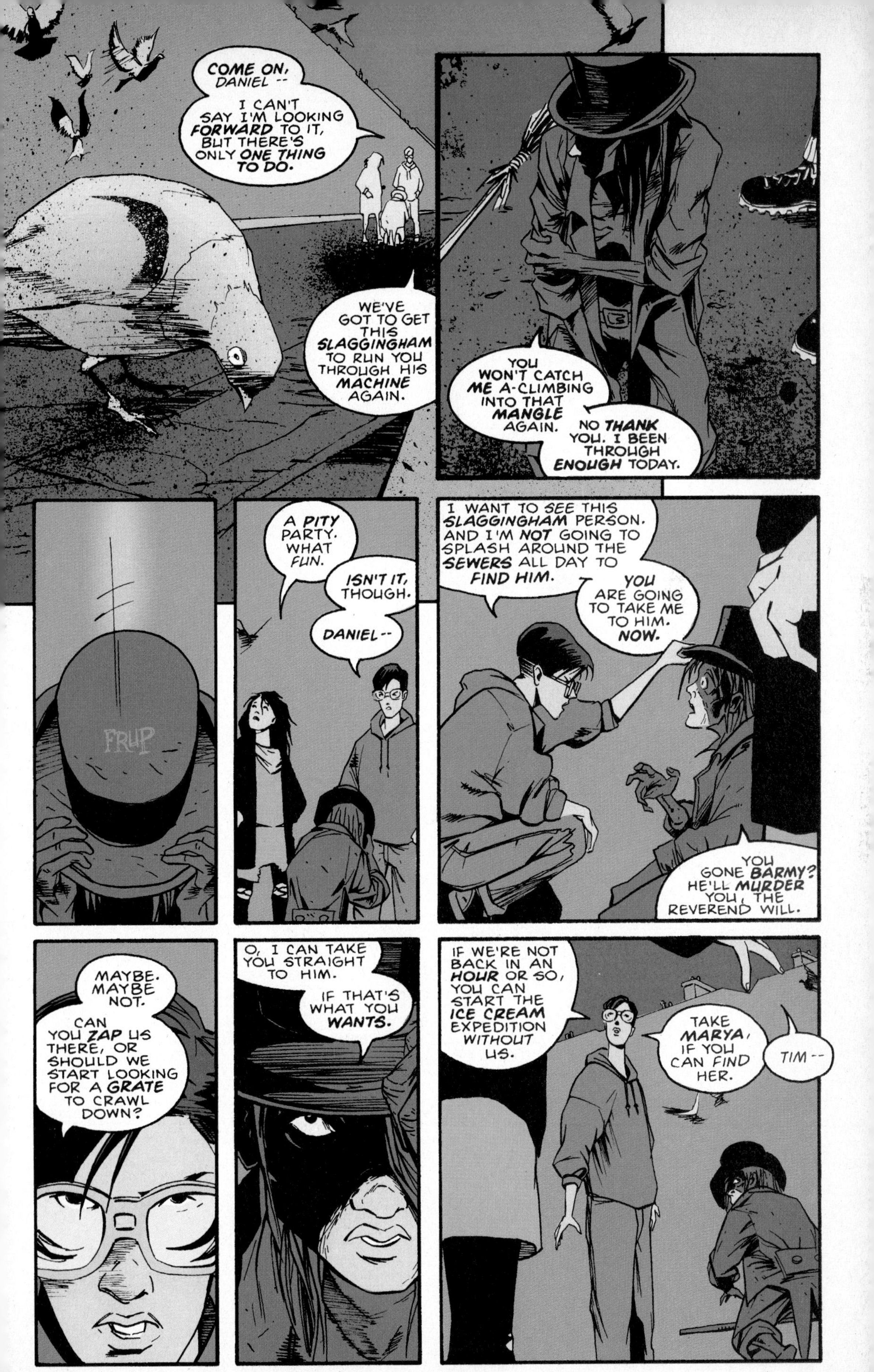
COME ON, DANIEL --
I CAN'T SAY I'M LOOKING FORWARD TO IT, BUT THERE'S ONLY ONE THING TO DO.
WE'VE GOT TO GET THIS SLAGGINGHAM TO RUN YOU THROUGH HIS MACHINE AGAIN.
YOU WON'T CATCH ME A-CLIMBING INTO THAT MANGLE AGAIN.
NO THANK YOU. I BEEN THROUGH ENOUGH TODAY.
FRUP
A PITY PARTY. WHAT FUN.
ISN'T IT, THOUGH.
DANIEL --
I WANT TO SEE THIS SLAGGINGHAM PERSON. AND I'M NOT GOING TO SPLASH AROUND THE SEWERS ALL DAY TO FIND HIM.
YOU ARE GOING TO TAKE ME TO HIM. NOW.
YOU GONE BARMY? HE'LL MURDER YOU, THE REVEREND WILL.
MAYBE. MAYBE NOT.
CAN YOU ZAP US THERE, OR SHOULD WE START LOOKING FOR A GRATE TO CRAWL DOWN?
O, I CAN TAKE YOU STRAIGHT TO HIM.
IF THAT'S WHAT YOU WANTS.
IF WE'RE NOT BACK IN AN HOUR OR SO, YOU CAN START THE ICE CREAM EXPEDITION WITHOUT US.
TAKE MARYA, IF YOU CAN FIND HER.
TIM --

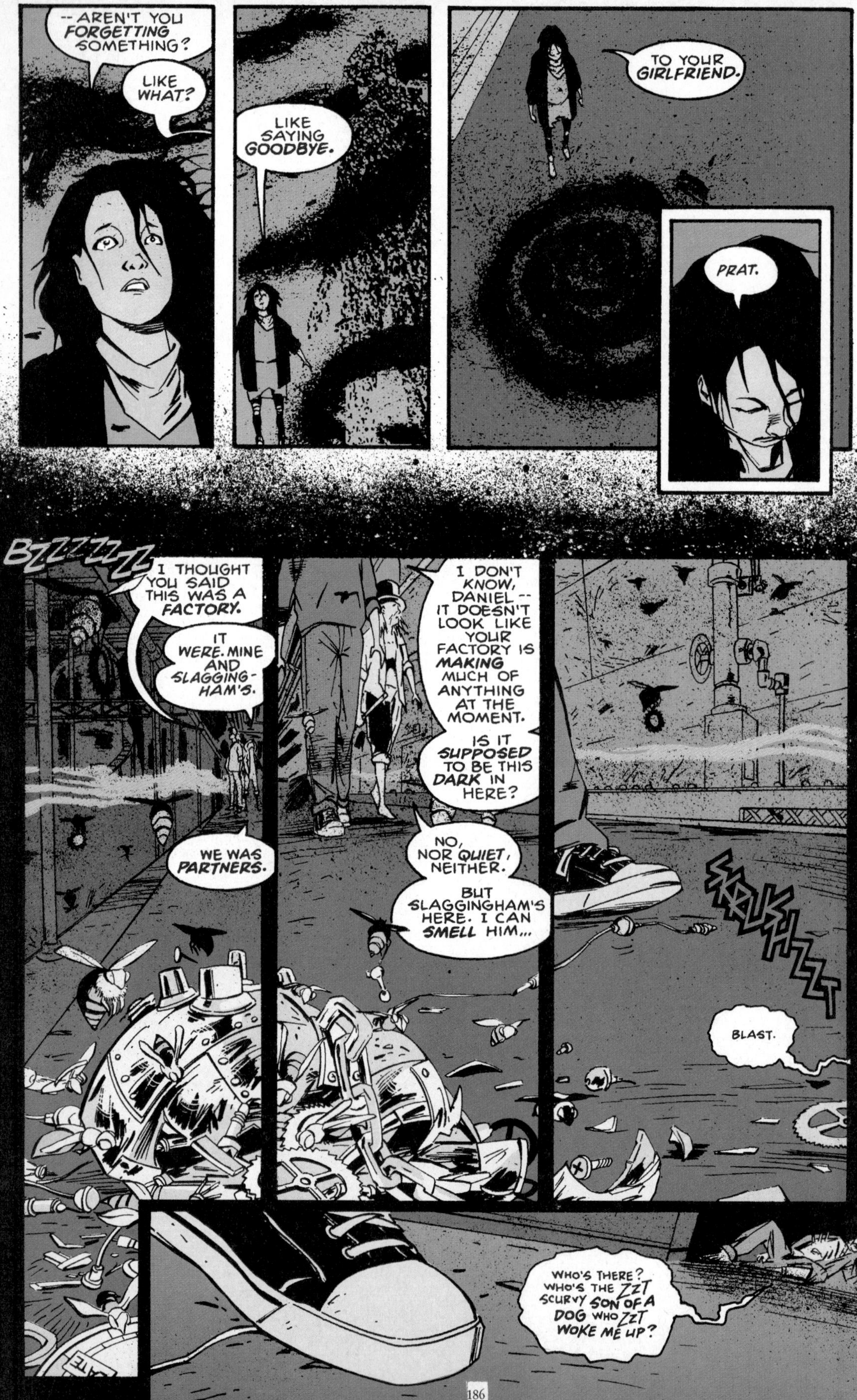

-- ARE'N'T YOU FORGETTING SOMETHING?
LIKE WHAT?
LIKE SAYING GOODBYE.
TO YOUR GIRLFRIEND.
PRAT.
BZZZZZZZ
I THOUGHT YOU SAID THIS WAS A FACTORY.
IT WERE. MINE AND SLAGGINGHAM'S.
WE WAS PARTNERS.
I DON'T KNOW, DANIEL -- IT DOESN'T LOOK LIKE YOUR FACTORY IS MAKING MUCH OF ANYTHING AT THE MOMENT.
IS IT SUPPOSED TO BE THIS DARK IN HERE?
NO, NOR QUIET, NEITHER.
BUT SLAGGINGHAM'S HERE. I CAN SMELL HIM...
SKRUSHZZZT
BLAST.
WHO'S THERE? WHO'S THE ZZT SCURVY SON OF A DOG WHO ZZT WOKE ME UP?

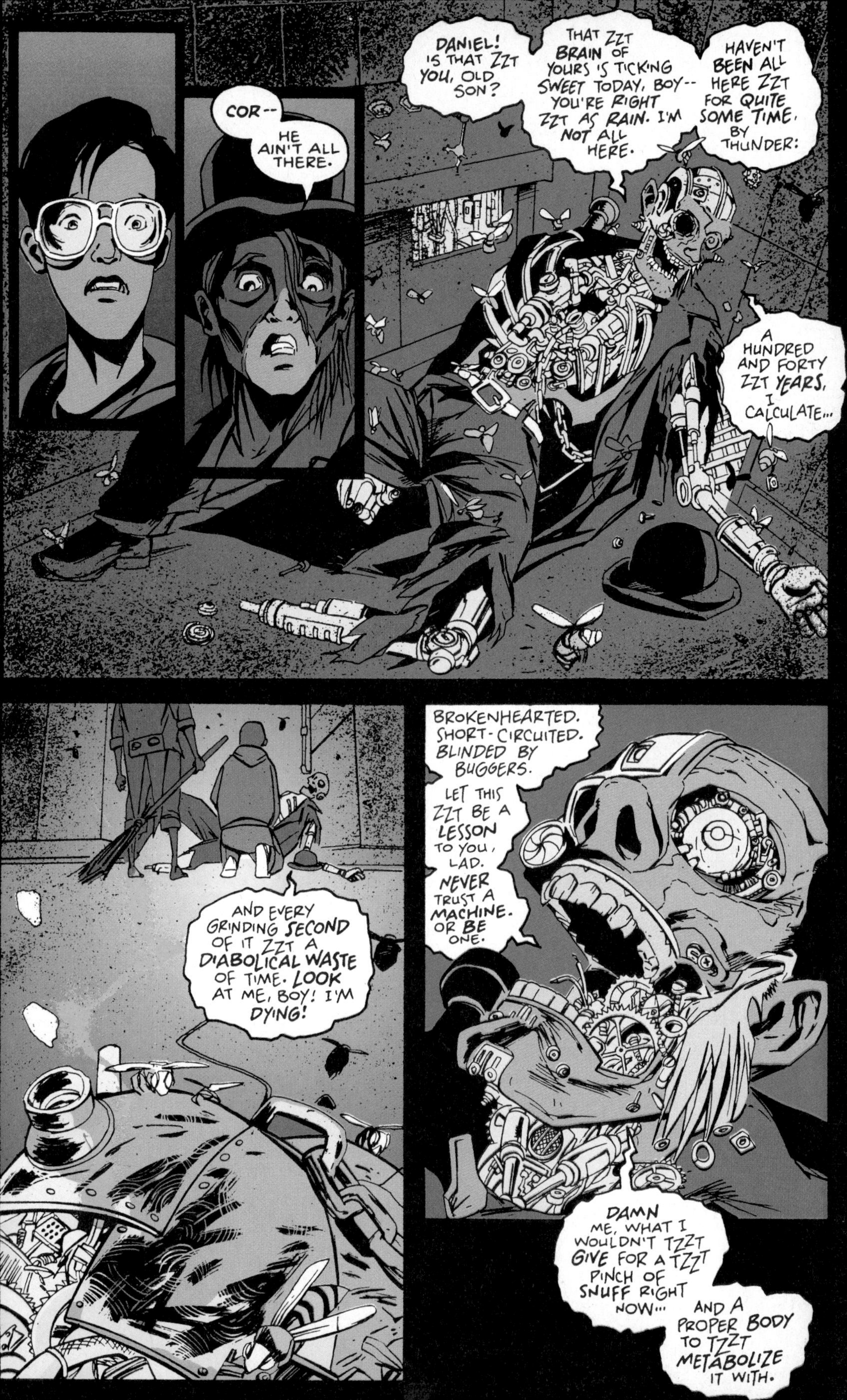
COR--
HE AIN'T ALL THERE.
DANIEL! IS THAT ZZT YOU, OLD SON?
THAT ZZT BRAIN OF YOURS IS TICKING SWEET TODAY, BOY-- YOU'RE RIGHT ZZT AS RAIN. I'M NOT ALL HERE.
HAVEN'T BEEN ALL HERE ZZT FOR QUITE SOME TIME, BY THUNDER:
A HUNDRED AND FORTY ZZT YEARS, I CALCULATE...
AND EVERY GRINDING SECOND OF IT ZZT A DIABOLICAL WASTE OF TIME. LOOK AT ME, BOY! I'M DYING!
BROKENHEARTED. SHORT-CIRCUITED. BLINDED BY BUGGERS.
LET THIS ZZT BE A LESSON TO YOU, LAD. NEVER TRUST A MACHINE. OR BE ONE.
DAMN ME, WHAT I WOULDN'T TZZT GIVE FOR A TZZT PINCH OF SNUFF RIGHT NOW...
AND A PROPER BODY TO TZZT METABOLIZE IT WITH.

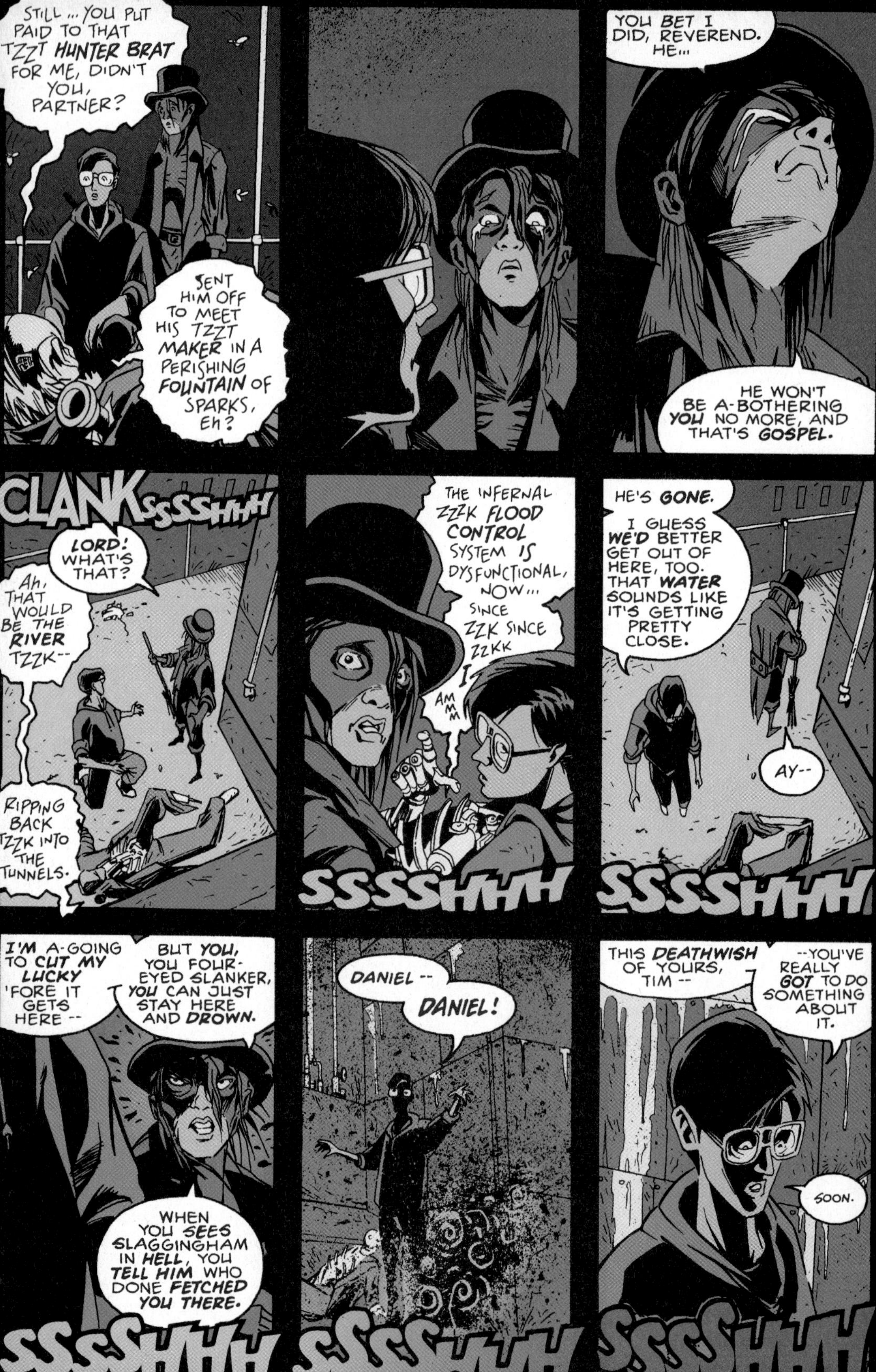
STILL ... YOU PUT PAID TO THAT TZZT HUNTER BRAT FOR ME, DIDN'T YOU, PARTNER?
SENT HIM OFF TO MEET HIS TZZT MAKER IN A PERISHING FOUNTAIN OF SPARKS, EH?
YOU BET I DID, REVEREND. HE...
HE WON'T BE A-BOTHERING YOU NO MORE, AND THAT'S GOSPEL.
CLANK SSSSHHH
LORD! WHAT'S THAT?
AH, THAT WOULD BE THE RIVER TZZK--
RIPPING BACK TZZK INTO THE TUNNELS.
THE INFERNAL ZZZK FLOOD CONTROL SYSTEM IS DYSFUNCTIONAL, NOW... SINCE ZZK SINCE ZZKK
I AMM
SSSSHHH
HE'S GONE.
I GUESS WE'D BETTER GET OUT OF HERE, TOO. THAT WATER SOUNDS LIKE IT'S GETTING PRETTY CLOSE.
AY--
SSSSHHH
I'M A-GOING TO CUT MY LUCKY 'FORE IT GETS HERE --
BUT YOU, YOU FOUR-EYED SLANKER, YOU CAN JUST STAY HERE AND DROWN.
WHEN YOU SEES SLAGGINGHAM IN HELL, YOU TELL HIM WHO DONE FETCHED YOU THERE.
SSSSHHH
DANIEL --
DANIEL!
SSSSHHH
THIS DEATHWISH OF YOURS, TIM --
--YOU'VE REALLY GOT TO DO SOMETHING ABOUT IT.
SOON.
SSSSHHH

NEXT: MISSING COLORS

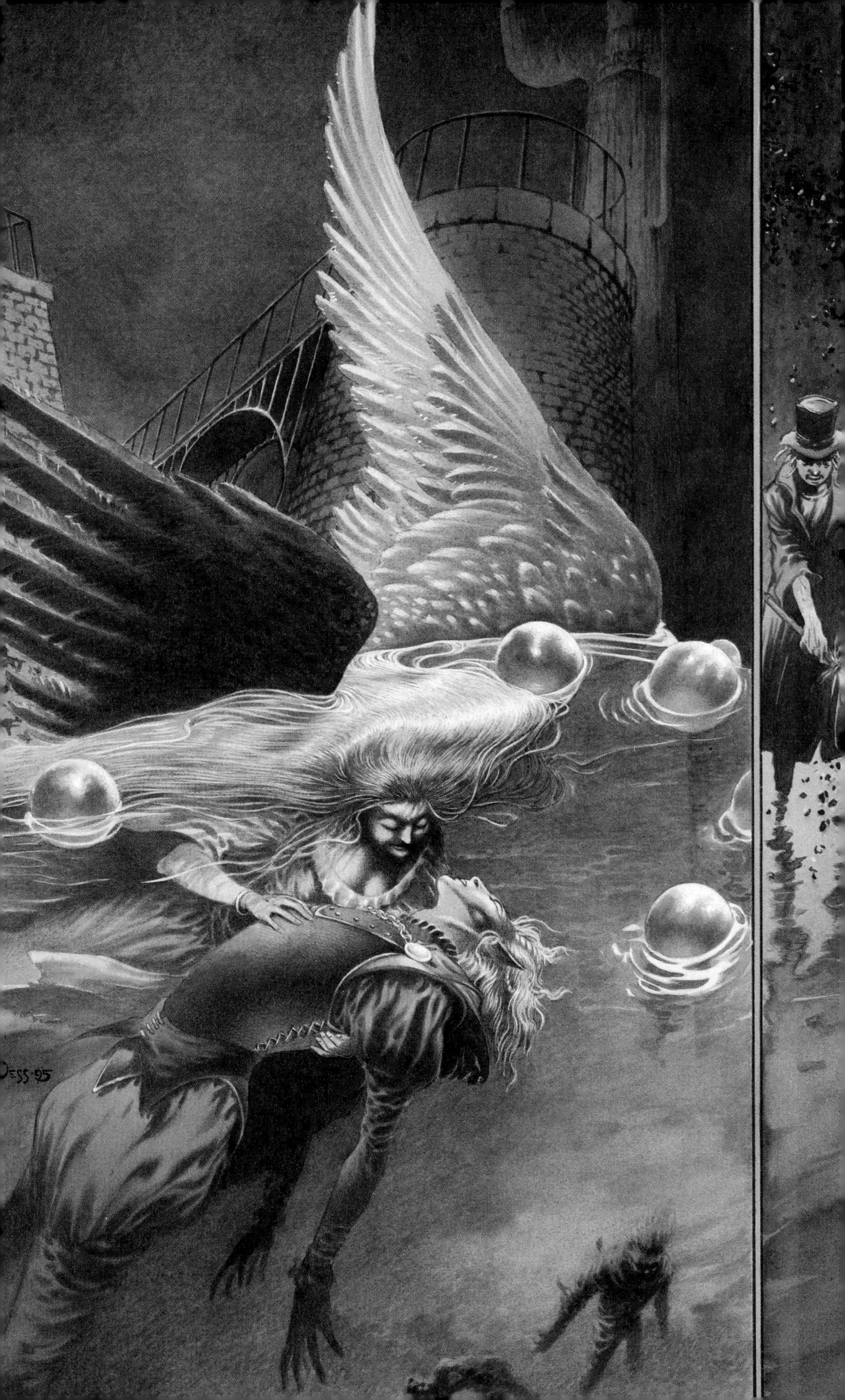

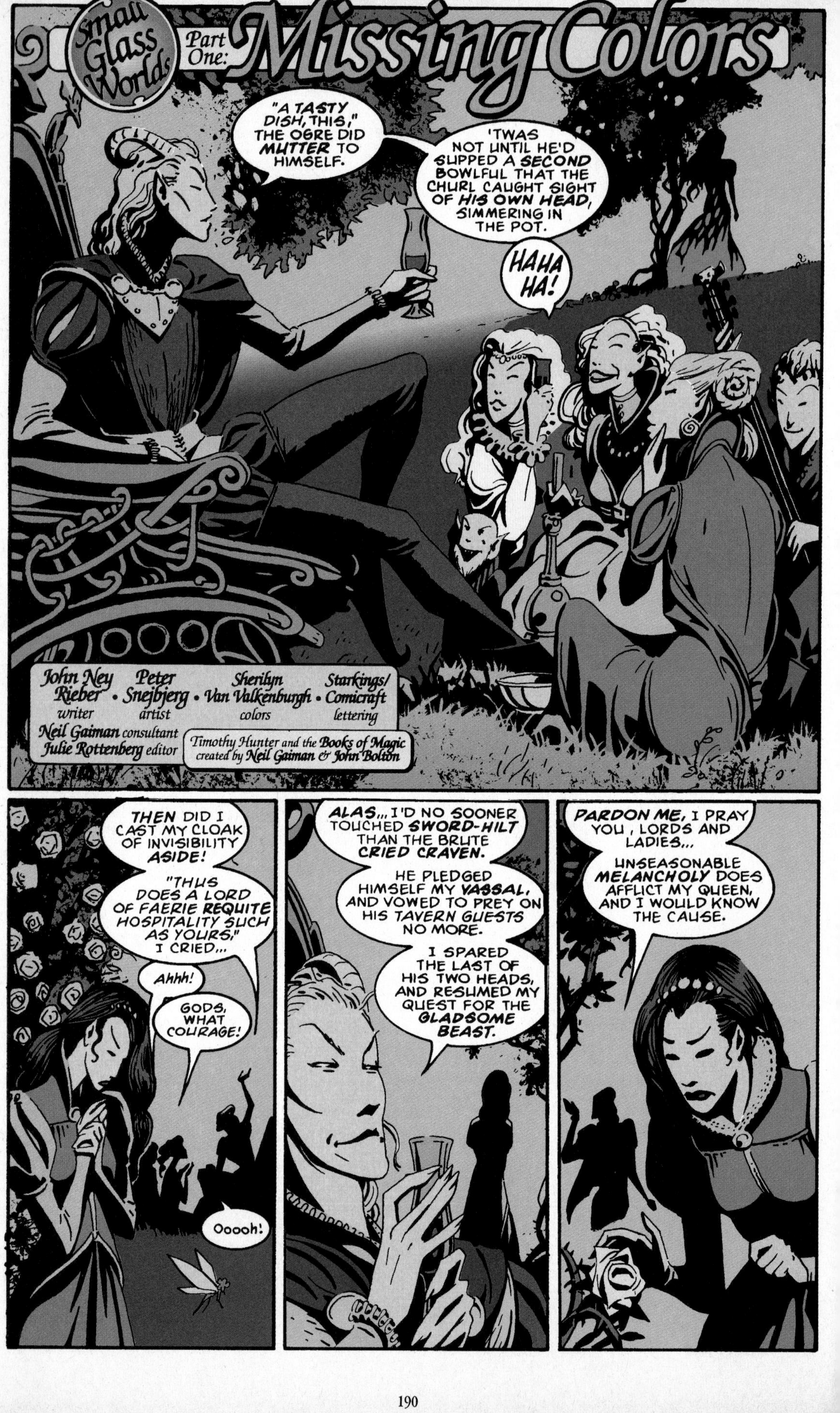
Small Glass Worlds
Part One: Missing Colors
"A TASTY DISH, THIS," THE OGRE DID MUTTER TO HIMSELF.
'TWAS NOT UNTIL HE'D SLIPPED A SECOND BOWLFUL THAT THE CHURL CAUGHT SIGHT OF HIS OWN HEAD, SIMMERING IN THE POT.
HAHA HA!
John Ney Rieber writer • Peter Snejbjerg artist • Sherilyn Van Valkenburgh colors • Starkings/ Comicraft lettering
Neil Gaiman consultant
Julie Rottenberg editor
Timothy Hunter and the Books of Magic created by Neil Gaiman & John Bolton
THEN DID I CAST MY CLOAK OF INVISIBILITY ASIDE!
"THUS DOES A LORD OF FAERIE REQUITE HOSPITALITY SUCH AS YOURS," I CRIED...
Ahhh!
GODS, WHAT COURAGE!
Ooooh!
ALAS... I'D NO SOONER TOUCHED SWORD-HILT THAN THE BRUTE CRIED CRAVEN.
HE PLEDGED HIMSELF MY VASSAL, AND VOWED TO PREY ON HIS TAVERN GUESTS NO MORE.
I SPARED THE LAST OF HIS TWO HEADS, AND RESUMED MY QUEST FOR THE GLADSOME BEAST.
PARDON ME, I PRAY YOU, LORDS AND LADIES...
UNSEASONABLE MELANCHOLY DOES AFFLICT MY QUEEN, AND I WOULD KNOW THE CAUSE.

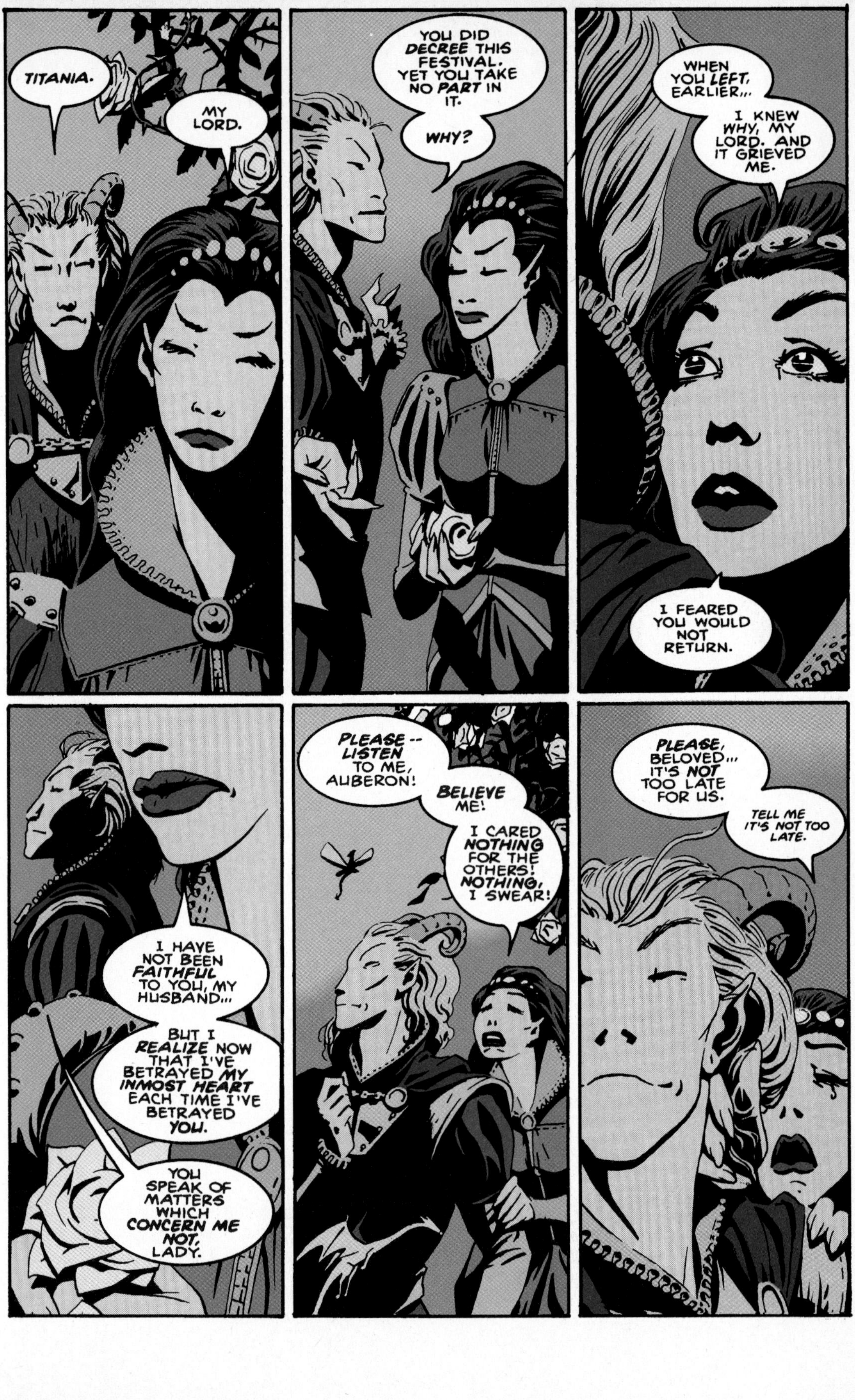
TITANIA.
MY LORD.
YOU DID DECREE THIS FESTIVAL. YET YOU TAKE NO PART IN IT.
WHY?
WHEN YOU LEFT, EARLIER...
I KNEW WHY, MY LORD. AND IT GRIEVED ME.
I FEARED YOU WOULD NOT RETURN.
I HAVE NOT BEEN FAITHFUL TO YOU, MY HUSBAND...
BUT I REALIZE NOW THAT I'VE BETRAYED MY INMOST HEART EACH TIME I'VE BETRAYED YOU.
YOU SPEAK OF MATTERS WHICH CONCERN ME NOT, LADY.
PLEASE -- LISTEN TO ME, AUBERON!
BELIEVE ME!
I CARED NOTHING FOR THE OTHERS! NOTHING, I SWEAR!
PLEASE, BELOVED... IT'S NOT TOO LATE FOR US.
TELL ME IT'S NOT TOO LATE.

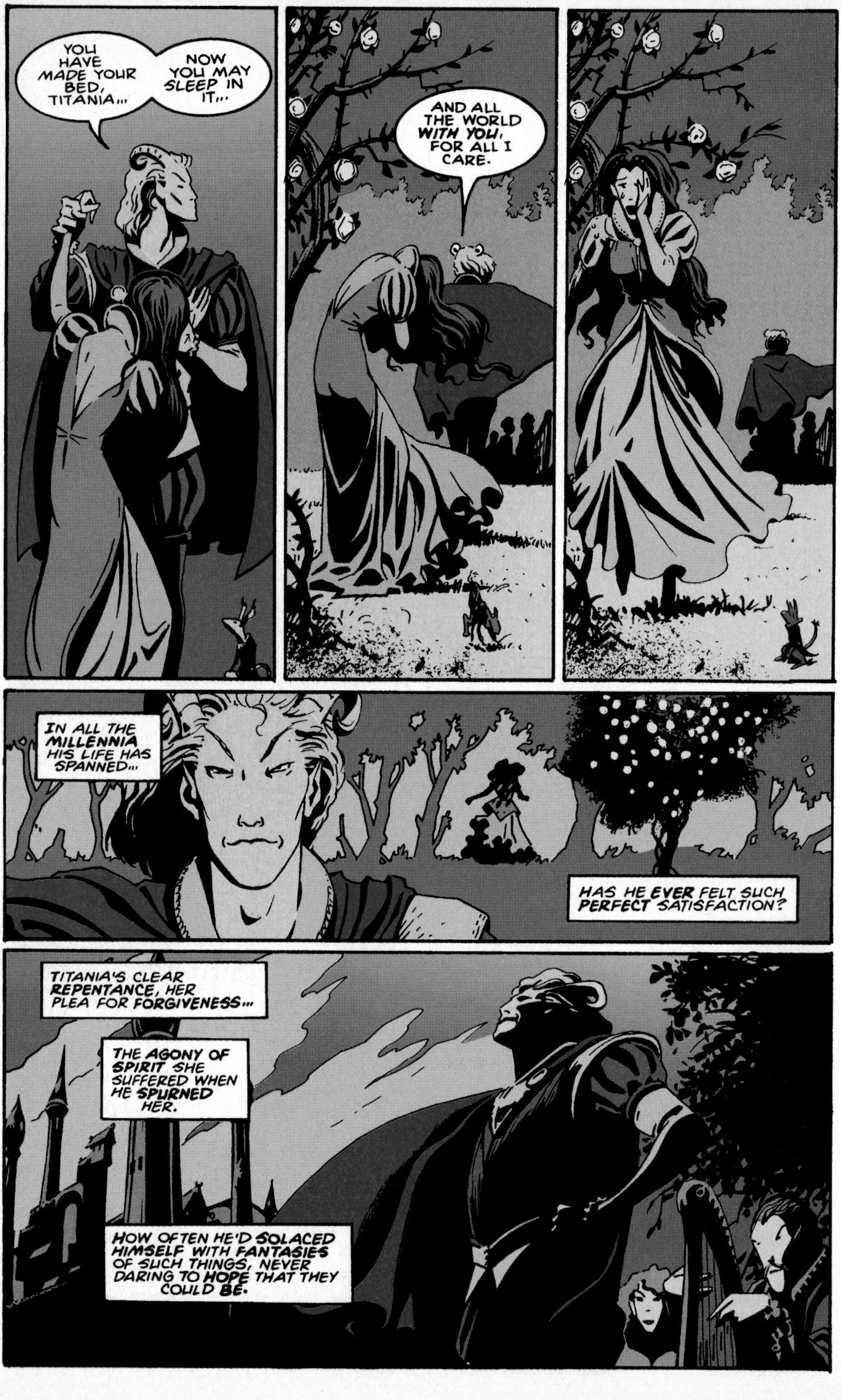
YOU HAVE MADE YOUR BED, TITANIA...
NOW YOU MAY SLEEP IN IT...
AND ALL THE WORLD WITH YOU, FOR ALL I CARE.
IN ALL THE MILLENNIA HIS LIFE HAS SPANNED...
HAS HE EVER FELT SUCH PERFECT SATISFACTION?
TITANIA'S CLEAR REPENTANCE, HER PLEA FOR FORGIVENESS...
THE AGONY OF SPIRIT SHE SUFFERED WHEN HE SPURNED HER.
HOW OFTEN HE'D SOLACED HIMSELF WITH FANTASIES OF SUCH THINGS, NEVER DARING TO HOPE THAT THEY COULD BE.

A WARM SHIVER RUNS DOWN HIS SPINE, AS THOUGH LIGHTNING HAS KISSED HIM.

THE WORLD IS PARADISE, HE REALIZES...

AND HE THE LORD AND MASTER OF IT.

THE TRUTH DAWNS ON HIM, THEN.

ONCE HE SPOKE TO A MORTAL MAID OF PARADISE AND REVOLUTION.

AS HE RECALLS, HE WAS SURPRISED TO LEARN THAT A COMMON SEAMSTRESS COULD ASPIRE TO EITHER STATE.

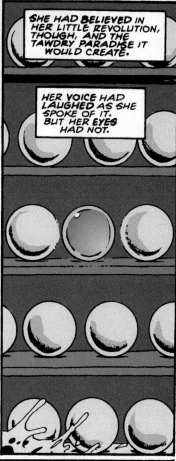

SHE HAD BELIEVED IN HER LITTLE REVOLUTION, THOUGH, AND THE TAWDRY PARADISE IT WOULD CREATE.

HER VOICE HAD LAUGHED AS SHE SPOKE OF IT. BUT HER EYES HAD NOT.

IF ONLY HE COULD SPEAK TO HER AGAIN.

TO ANSWER HER, AS HE COULD NOT AT THE TIME:

THE GATES OF PARADISE ARE NOT OPENED BY IDEALS AND REVOLUTIONS.

PATIENCE IS THE KEY.

PATIENCE.

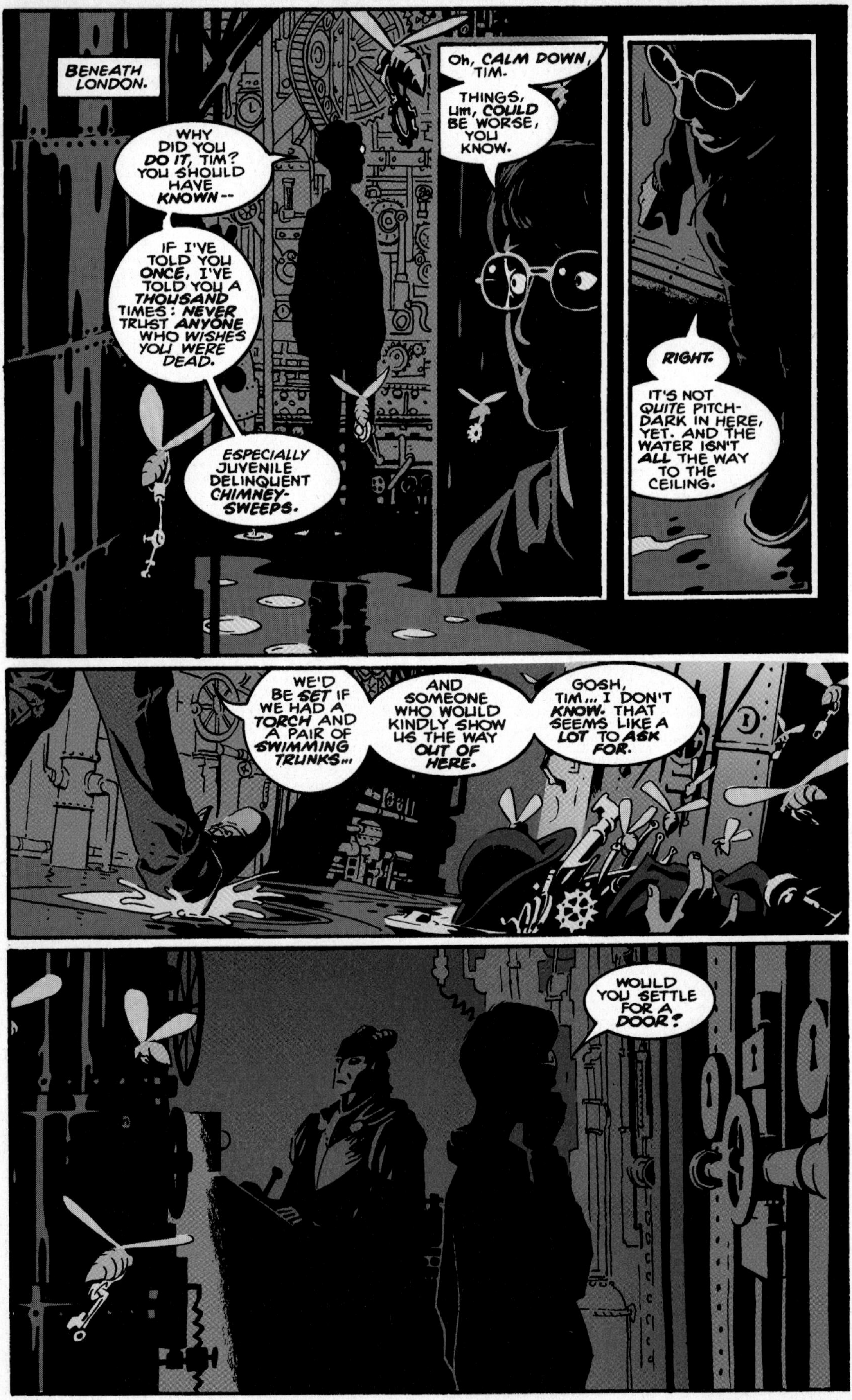
BENEATH LONDON.
WHY DID YOU DO IT, TIM? YOU SHOULD HAVE KNOWN--
IF I'VE TOLD YOU ONCE, I'VE TOLD YOU A THOUSAND TIMES: NEVER TRUST ANYONE WHO WISHES YOU WERE DEAD.
ESPECIALLY JUVENILE DELINQUENT CHIMNEY-SWEEPS.
Oh, CALM DOWN, TIM.
THINGS, UM, COULD BE WORSE, YOU KNOW.
RIGHT.
IT'S NOT QUITE PITCH-DARK IN HERE, YET. AND THE WATER ISN'T ALL THE WAY TO THE CEILING.
WE'D BE SET IF WE HAD A TORCH AND A PAIR OF SWIMMING TRUNKS...
AND SOMEONE WHO WOULD KINDLY SHOW US THE WAY OUT OF HERE.
GOSH, TIM... I DON'T KNOW. THAT SEEMS LIKE A LOT TO ASK FOR.
WOULD YOU SETTLE FOR A DOOR?

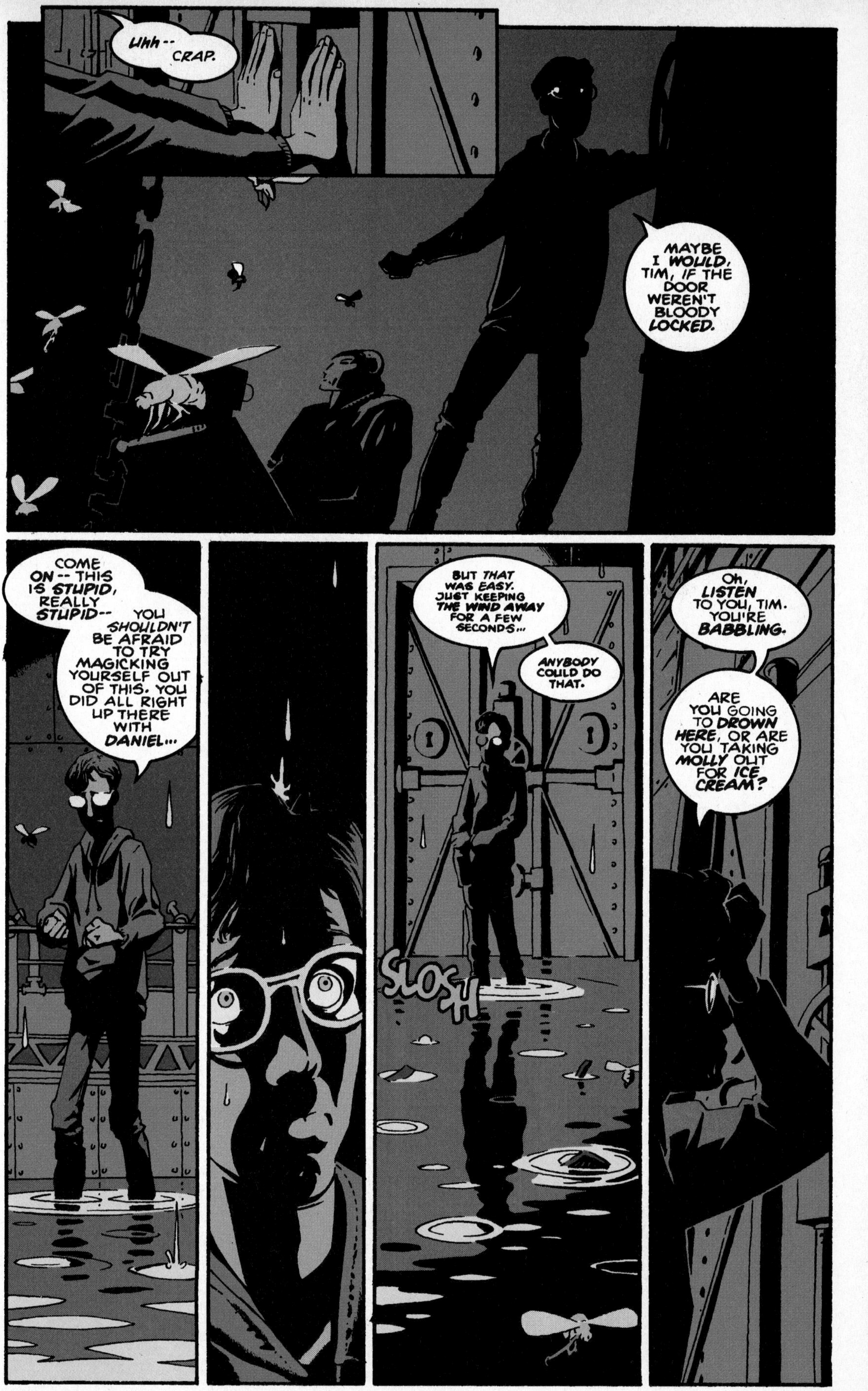
Uhh -- CRAP.
MAYBE I WOULD, TIM, IF THE DOOR WEREN'T BLOODY LOCKED.
COME ON -- THIS IS STUPID, REALLY STUPID--
YOU SHOULDN'T BE AFRAID TO TRY MAGICKING YOURSELF OUT OF THIS. YOU DID ALL RIGHT UP THERE WITH DANIEL...
BUT THAT WAS EASY. JUST KEEPING THE WIND AWAY FOR A FEW SECONDS...
ANYBODY COULD DO THAT.
SLOSH
Oh, LISTEN TO YOU, TIM. YOU'RE BABBLING.
ARE YOU GOING TO DROWN HERE, OR ARE YOU TAKING MOLLY OUT FOR ICE CREAM?

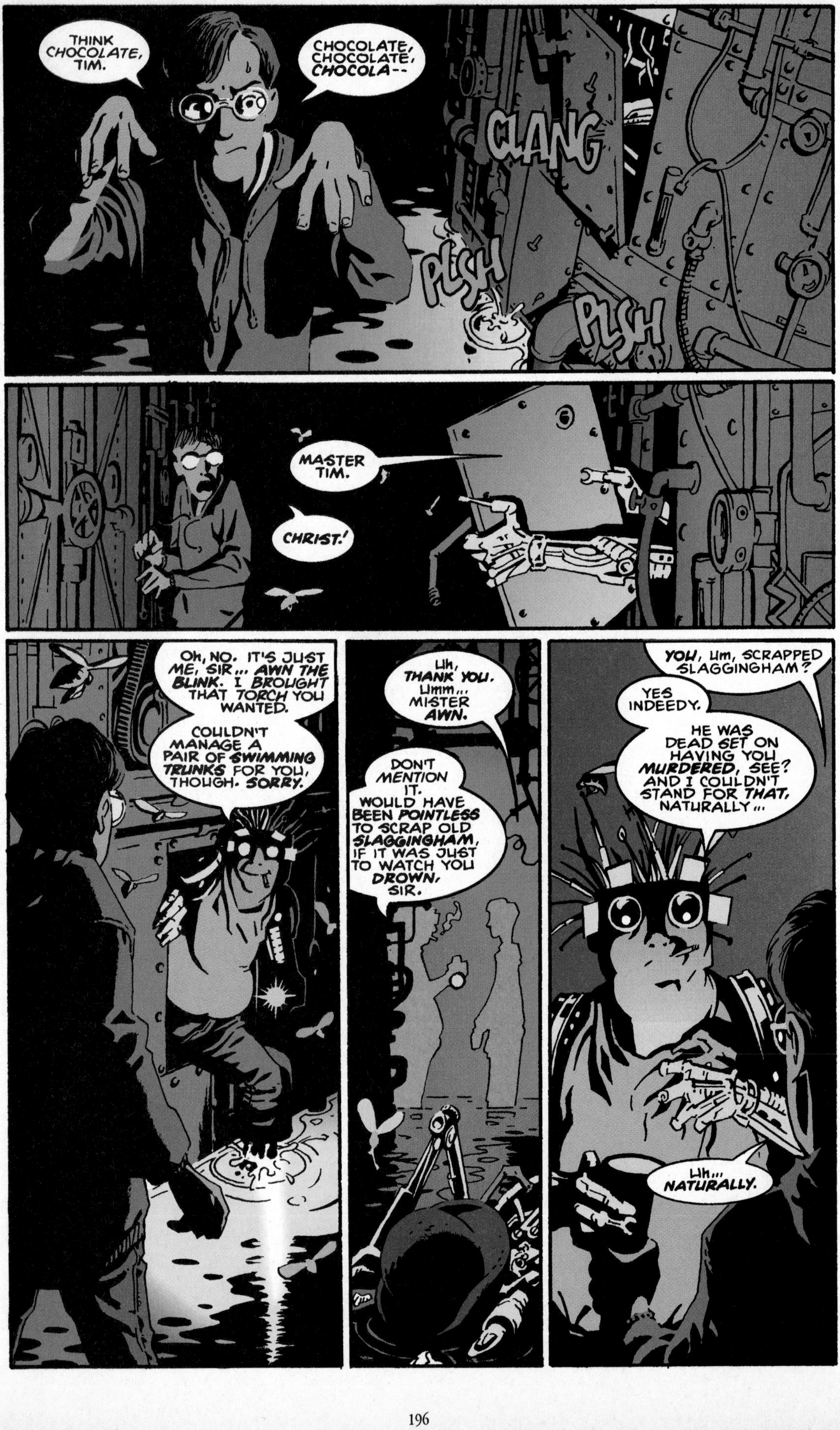
THINK CHOCOLATE, TIM.
CHOCOLATE, CHOCOLATE, CHOCOLA--
CLANG
PLSH
PLSH
MASTER TIM.
CHRIST!
Oh, NO. IT'S JUST ME, SIR... AWN THE BLINK. I BROUGHT THAT TORCH YOU WANTED.
COULDN'T MANAGE A PAIR OF SWIMMING TRUNKS FOR YOU, THOUGH. SORRY.
Uh, THANK YOU. Umm... MISTER AWN.
DON'T MENTION IT. WOULD HAVE BEEN POINTLESS TO SCRAP OLD SLAGGINGHAM, IF IT WAS JUST TO WATCH YOU DROWN, SIR.
YOU, Um, SCRAPPED SLAGGINGHAM?
YES INDEEDY.
HE WAS DEAD SET ON HAVING YOU MURDERED, SEE? AND I COULDN'T STAND FOR THAT, NATURALLY...
Uh... NATURALLY.

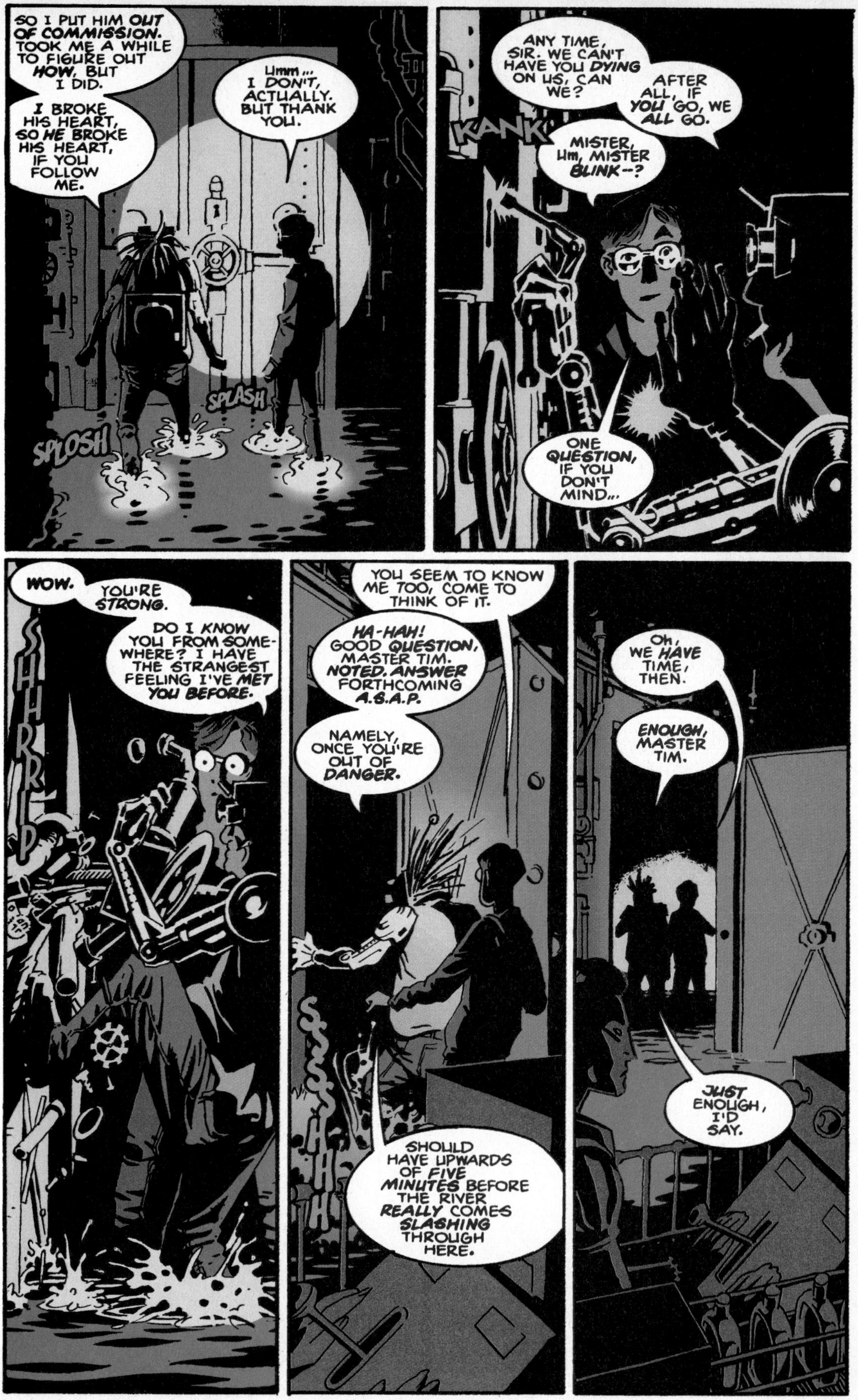
SO I PUT HIM OUT OF COMMISSION. TOOK ME A WHILE TO FIGURE OUT HOW, BUT I DID.
I BROKE HIS HEART, SO HE BROKE HIS HEART, IF YOU FOLLOW ME.
Umm... I DON'T, ACTUALLY. BUT THANK YOU.
SPLASH
SPLOSH
ANY TIME, SIR. WE CAN'T HAVE YOU DYING ON US, CAN WE?
AFTER ALL, IF YOU GO, WE ALL GO.
KANK
MISTER, Um, MISTER BLINK--?
ONE QUESTION, IF YOU DON'T MIND...
WOW.
YOU'RE STRONG.
DO I KNOW YOU FROM SOME-WHERE? I HAVE THE STRANGEST FEELING I'VE MET YOU BEFORE.
SHHRRRIP
YOU SEEM TO KNOW ME TOO, COME TO THINK OF IT.
HA-HAH! GOOD QUESTION, MASTER TIM. NOTED. ANSWER FORTHCOMING A.S.A.P.
NAMELY, ONCE YOU'RE OUT OF DANGER.
SHOULD HAVE UPWARDS OF FIVE MINUTES BEFORE THE RIVER REALLY COMES SLASHING THROUGH HERE.
Oh, WE HAVE TIME, THEN.
ENOUGH, MASTER TIM.
JUST ENOUGH, I'D SAY.

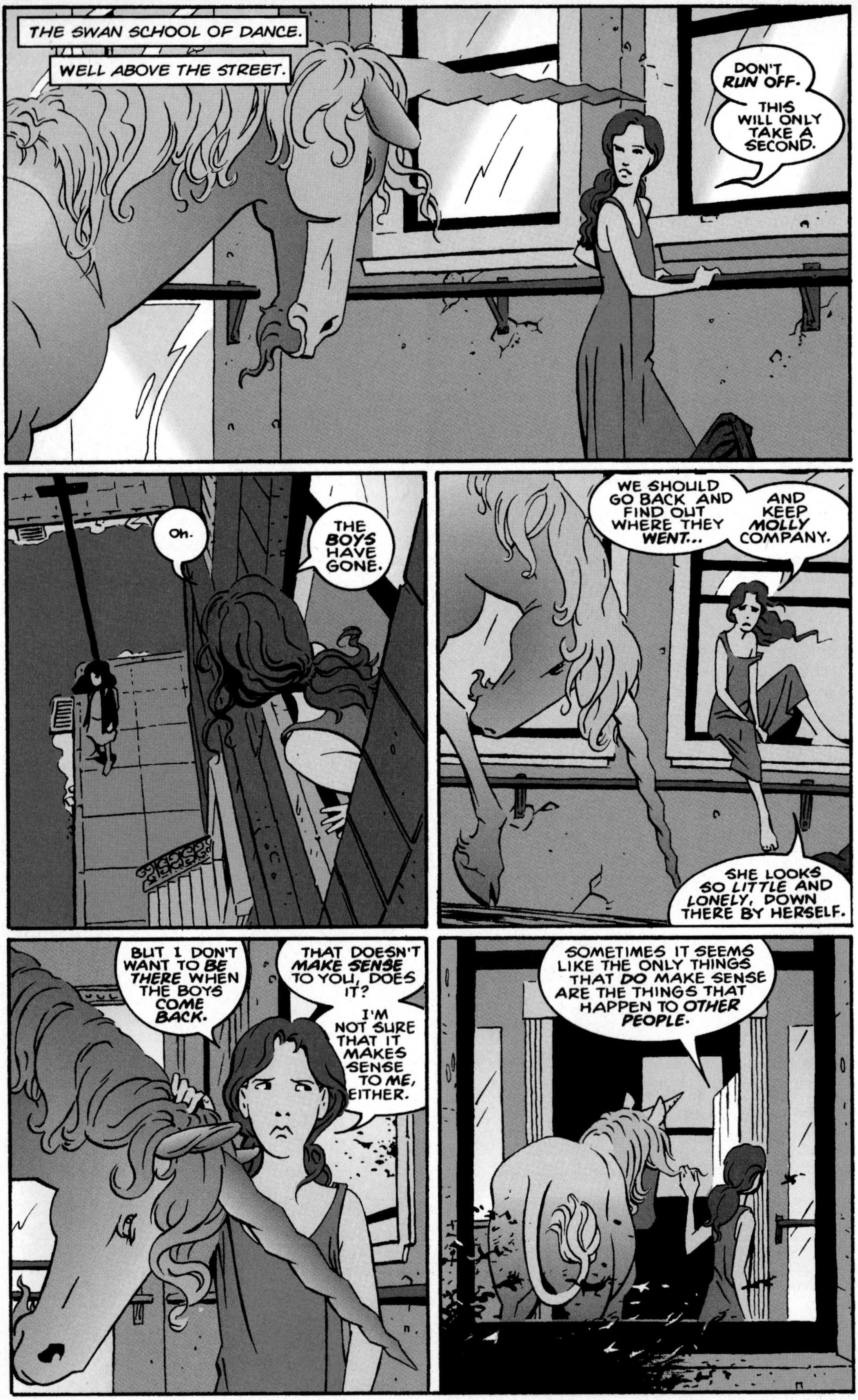
THE SWAN SCHOOL OF DANCE.
WELL ABOVE THE STREET.
DON'T RUN OFF. THIS WILL ONLY TAKE A SECOND.
Oh.
THE BOYS HAVE GONE.
WE SHOULD GO BACK AND FIND OUT WHERE THEY WENT...
AND KEEP MOLLY COMPANY.
SHE LOOKS SO LITTLE AND LONELY, DOWN THERE BY HERSELF.
BUT I DON'T WANT TO BE THERE WHEN THE BOYS COME BACK.
THAT DOESN'T MAKE SENSE TO YOU, DOES IT?
I'M NOT SURE THAT IT MAKES SENSE TO ME, EITHER.
SOMETIMES IT SEEMS LIKE THE ONLY THINGS THAT DO MAKE SENSE ARE THE THINGS THAT HAPPEN TO OTHER PEOPLE.

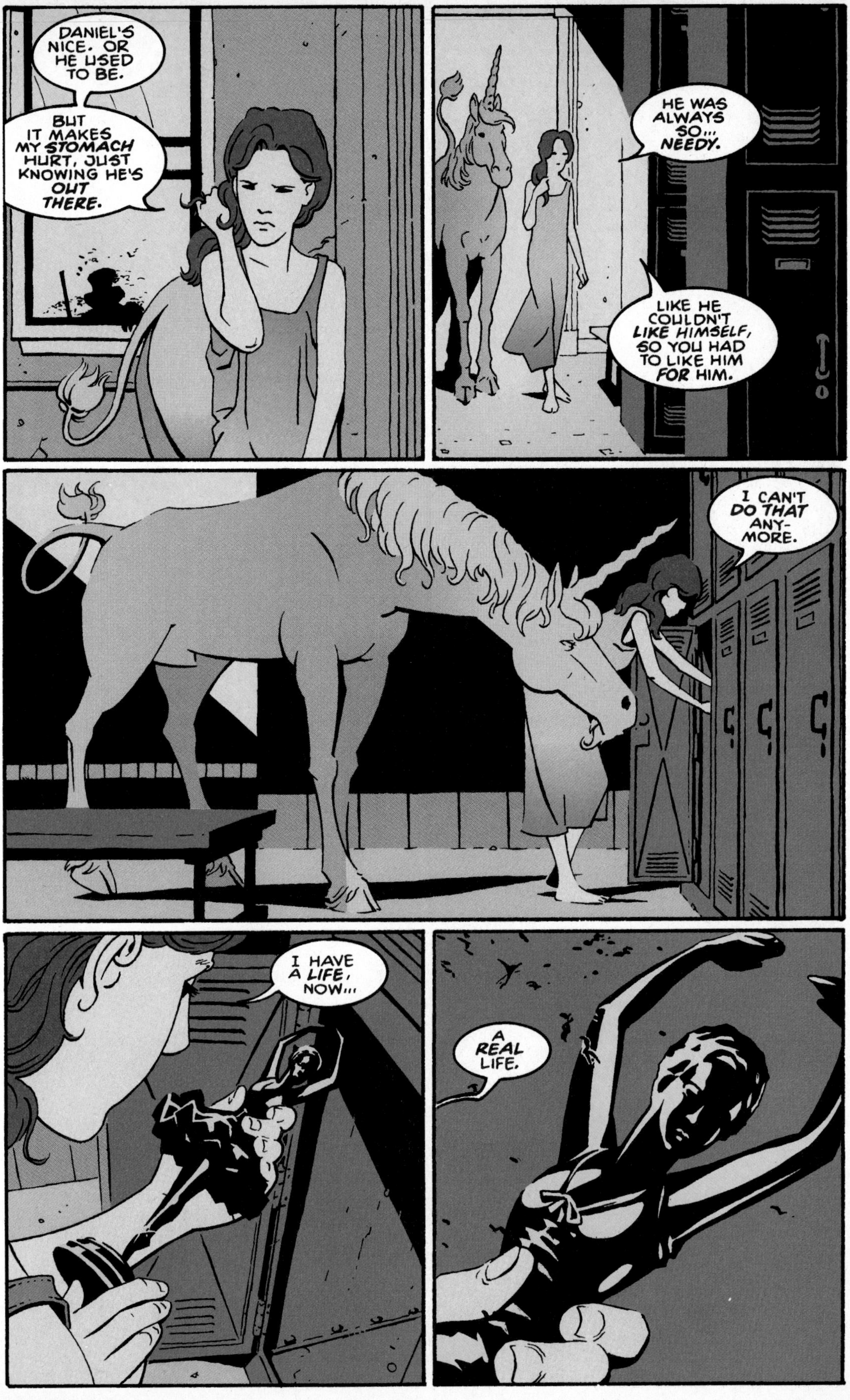
DANIEL'S NICE. OR HE USED TO BE.
BUT IT MAKES MY STOMACH HURT, JUST KNOWING HE'S OUT THERE.
HE WAS ALWAYS SO... NEEDY.
LIKE HE COULDN'T LIKE HIMSELF, SO YOU HAD TO LIKE HIM FOR HIM.
I CAN'T DO THAT ANY-MORE.
I HAVE A LIFE, NOW...
A REAL LIFE.

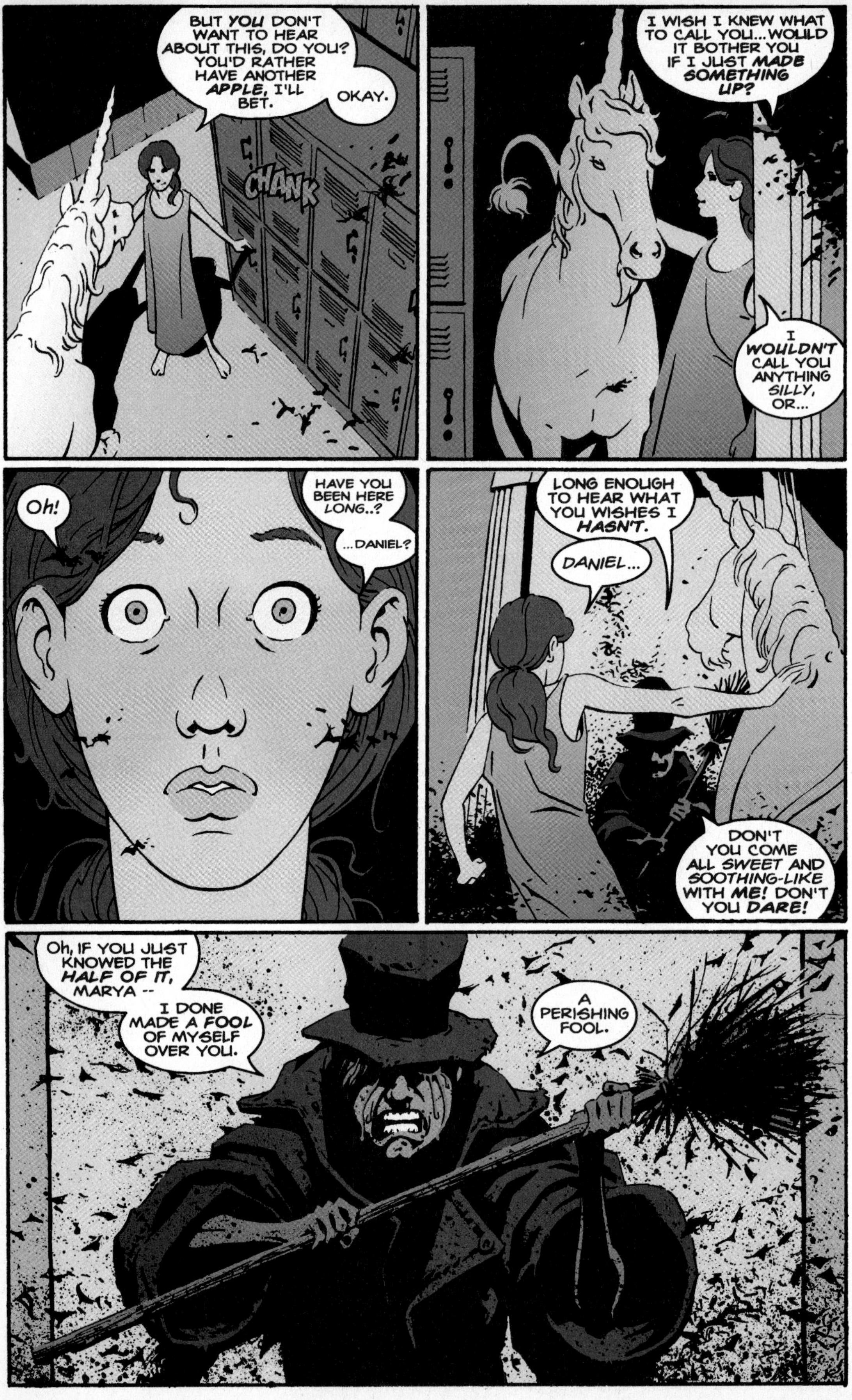
BUT YOU DON'T WANT TO HEAR ABOUT THIS, DO YOU? YOU'D RATHER HAVE ANOTHER APPLE, I'LL BET.
OKAY.
CHANK
I WISH I KNEW WHAT TO CALL YOU... WOULD IT BOTHER YOU IF I JUST MADE SOMETHING UP?
I WOULDN'T CALL YOU ANYTHING SILLY, OR...
Oh!
HAVE YOU BEEN HERE LONG..?
...DANIEL?
LONG ENOUGH TO HEAR WHAT YOU WISHES I HASN'T.
DANIEL...
DON'T YOU COME ALL SWEET AND SOOTHING-LIKE WITH ME! DON'T YOU DARE!
Oh, IF YOU JUST KNOWED THE HALF OF IT, MARYA --
I DONE MADE A FOOL OF MYSELF OVER YOU.
A PERISHING FOOL.

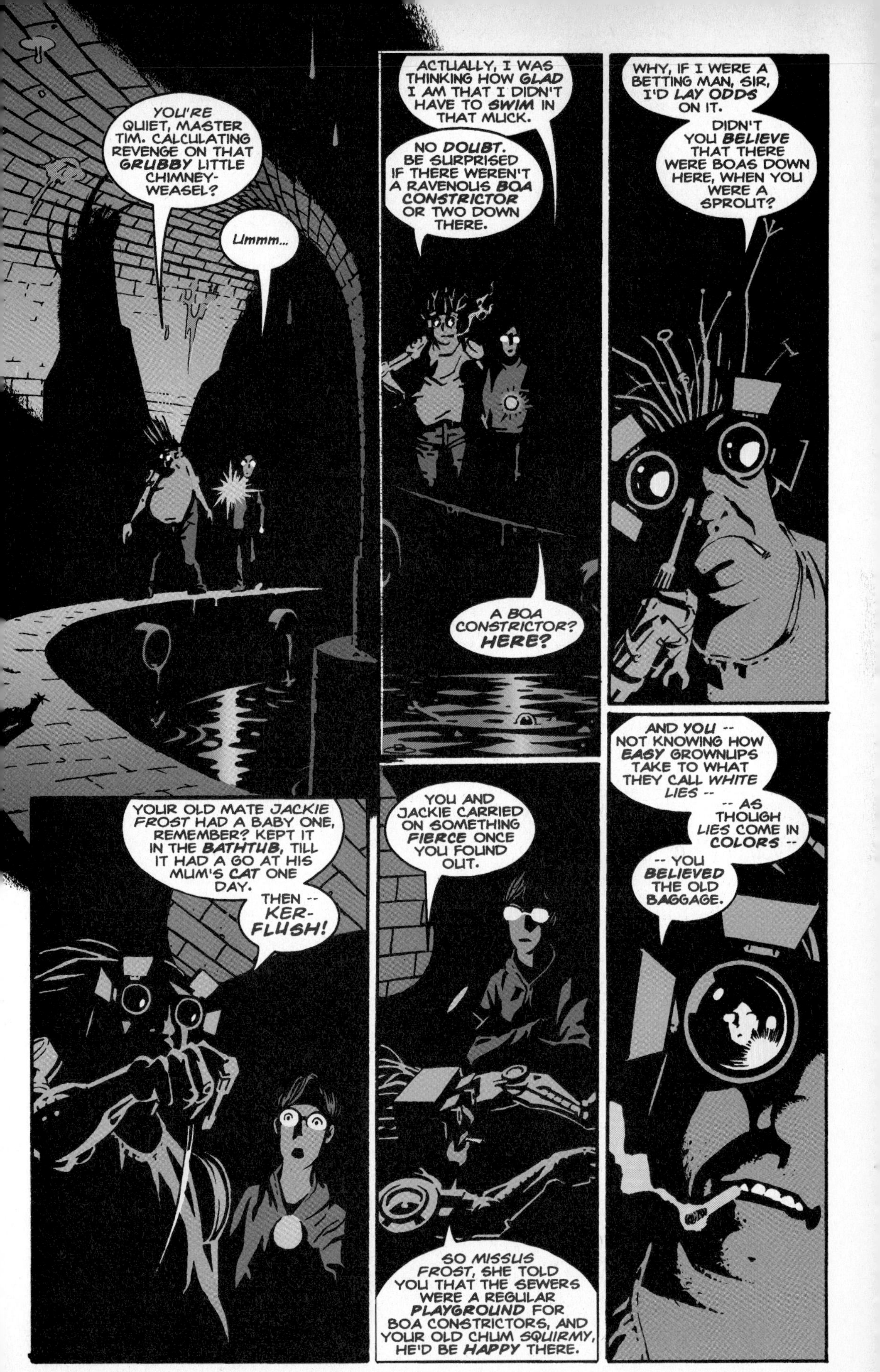
YOU'RE QUIET, MASTER TIM. CALCULATING REVENGE ON THAT GRUBBY LITTLE CHIMNEY-WEASEL?
Ummm...
ACTUALLY, I WAS THINKING HOW GLAD I AM THAT I DIDN'T HAVE TO SWIM IN THAT MUCK.
NO DOUBT. BE SURPRISED IF THERE WEREN'T A RAVENOUS BOA CONSTRICTOR OR TWO DOWN THERE.
A BOA CONSTRICTOR? HERE?
WHY, IF I WERE A BETTING MAN, SIR, I'D LAY ODDS ON IT.
DIDN'T YOU BELIEVE THAT THERE WERE BOAS DOWN HERE, WHEN YOU WERE A SPROUT?
YOUR OLD MATE JACKIE FROST HAD A BABY ONE, REMEMBER? KEPT IT IN THE BATHTUB, TILL IT HAD A GO AT HIS MUM'S CAT ONE DAY.
THEN -- KER-FLUSH!
YOU AND JACKIE CARRIED ON SOMETHING FIERCE ONCE YOU FOUND OUT.
SO MISSUS FROST, SHE TOLD YOU THAT THE SEWERS WERE A REGULAR PLAYGROUND FOR BOA CONSTRICTORS, AND YOUR OLD CHUM SQUIRMY, HE'D BE HAPPY THERE.
AND YOU -- NOT KNOWING HOW EASY GROWNUPS TAKE TO WHAT THEY CALL WHITE LIES --
-- AS THOUGH LIES COME IN COLORS --
-- YOU BELIEVED THE OLD BAGGAGE.

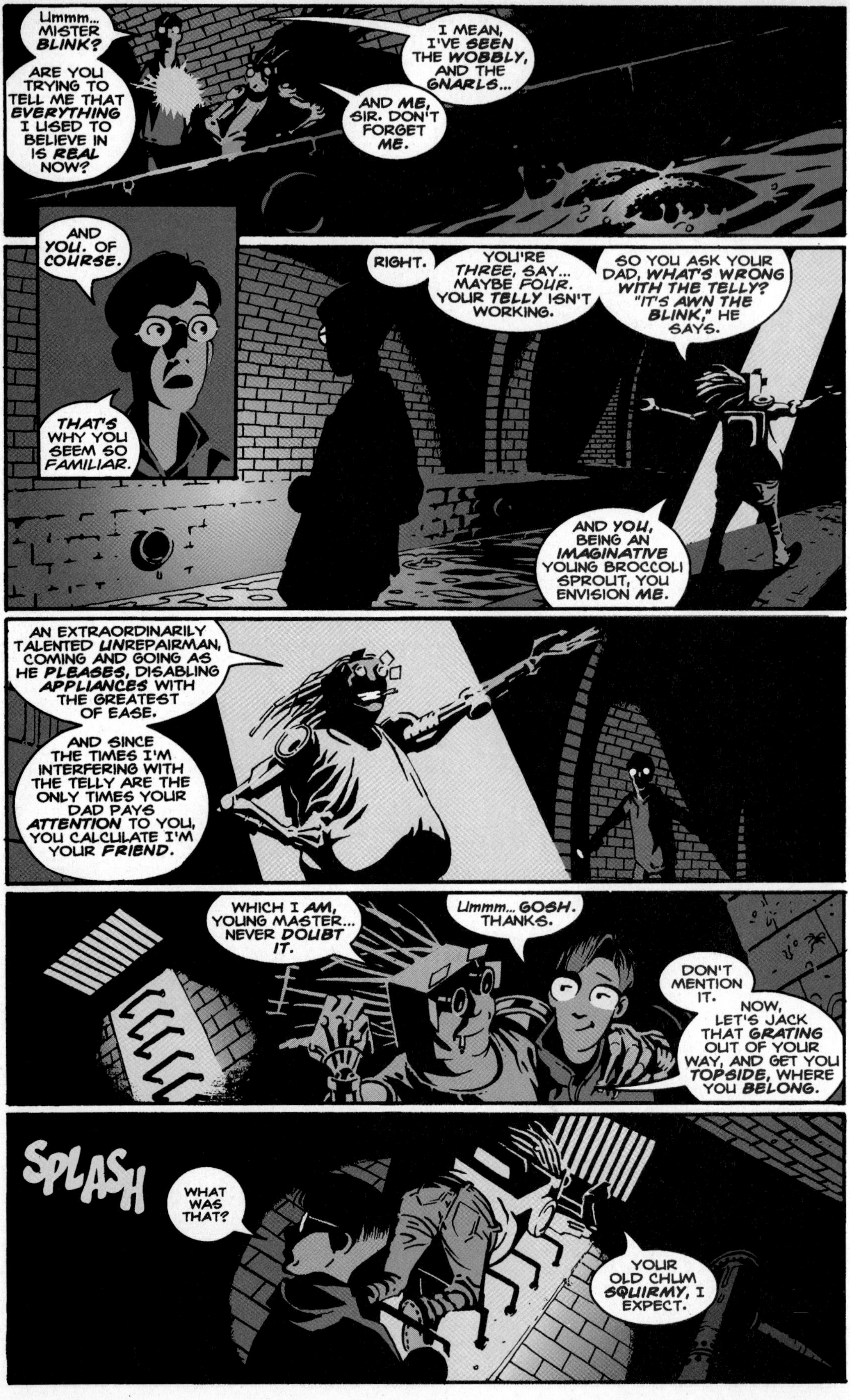
Ummm... MISTER BLINK?
ARE YOU TRYING TO TELL ME THAT EVERYTHING I USED TO BELIEVE IN IS REAL NOW?
I MEAN, I'VE SEEN THE WOBBLY, AND THE GNARLS...
AND ME, SIR. DON'T FORGET ME.
AND YOU. OF COURSE.
THAT'S WHY YOU SEEM SO FAMILIAR.
RIGHT.
YOU'RE THREE, SAY... MAYBE FOUR. YOUR TELLY ISN'T WORKING.
SO YOU ASK YOUR DAD, WHAT'S WRONG WITH THE TELLY? "IT'S AWN THE BLINK," HE SAYS.
AND YOU, BEING AN IMAGINATIVE YOUNG BROCCOLI SPROUT, YOU ENVISION ME.
AN EXTRAORDINARILY TALENTED UNREPAIRMAN, COMING AND GOING AS HE PLEASES, DISABLING APPLIANCES WITH THE GREATEST OF EASE.
AND SINCE THE TIMES I'M INTERFERING WITH THE TELLY ARE THE ONLY TIMES YOUR DAD PAYS ATTENTION TO YOU, YOU CALCULATE I'M YOUR FRIEND.
WHICH I AM, YOUNG MASTER... NEVER DOUBT IT.
Ummm... GOSH. THANKS.
DON'T MENTION IT.
NOW, LET'S JACK THAT GRATING OUT OF YOUR WAY, AND GET YOU TOPSIDE, WHERE YOU BELONG.
SPLASH
WHAT WAS THAT?
YOUR OLD CHUM SQUIRMY, I EXPECT.

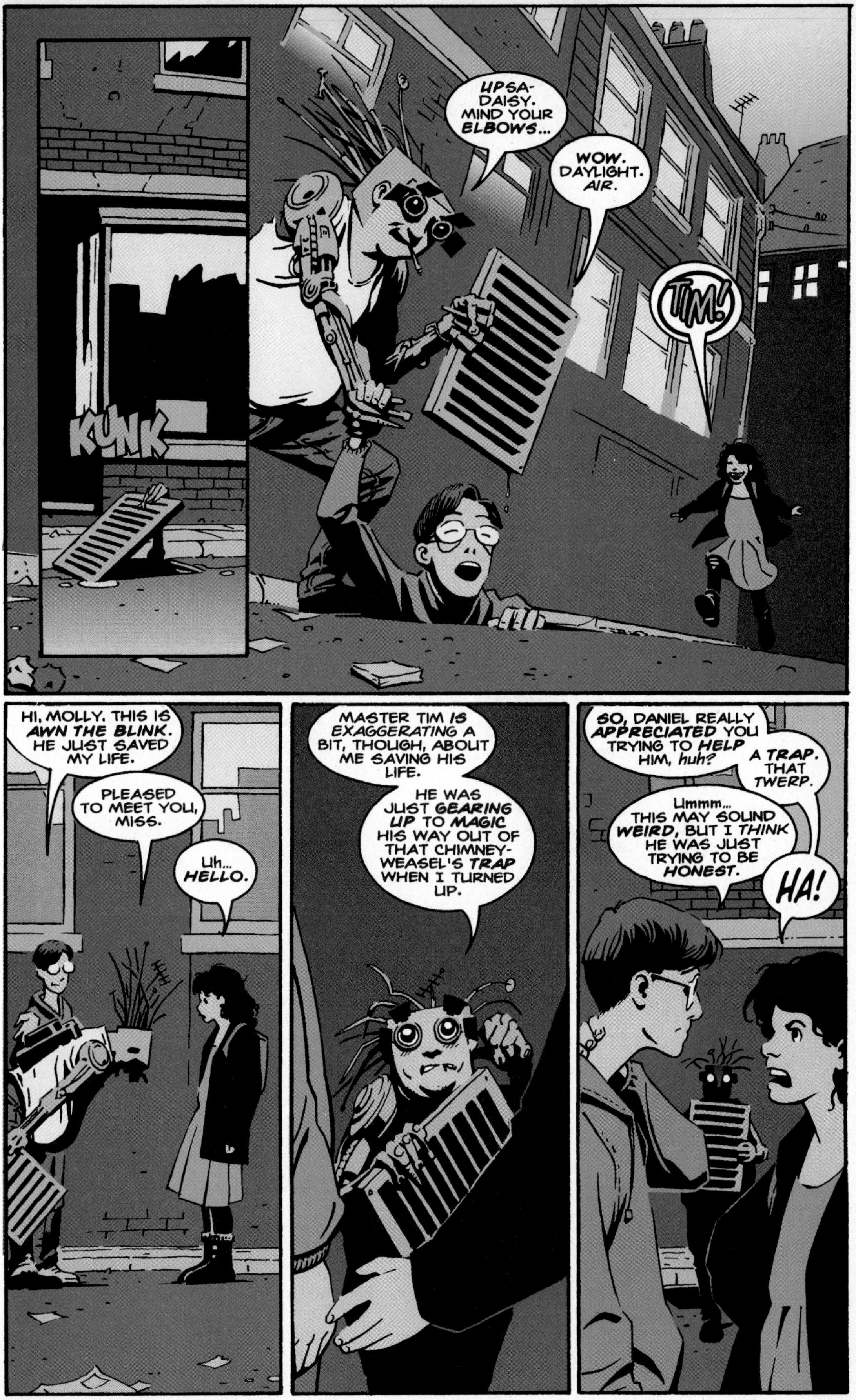
KUNK
UPSA-DAISY. MIND YOUR ELBOWS...
WOW. DAYLIGHT. AIR.
TIM!
HI, MOLLY. THIS IS AWN THE BLINK. HE JUST SAVED MY LIFE.
PLEASED TO MEET YOU, MISS.
Uh... HELLO.
MASTER TIM IS EXAGGERATING A BIT, THOUGH, ABOUT ME SAVING HIS LIFE.
HE WAS JUST GEARING UP TO MAGIC HIS WAY OUT OF THAT CHIMNEY-WEASEL'S TRAP WHEN I TURNED UP.
SO, DANIEL REALLY APPRECIATED YOU TRYING TO HELP HIM, huh?
A TRAP. THAT TWERP.
Ummm... THIS MAY SOUND WEIRD, BUT I THINK HE WAS JUST TRYING TO BE HONEST.
HA!

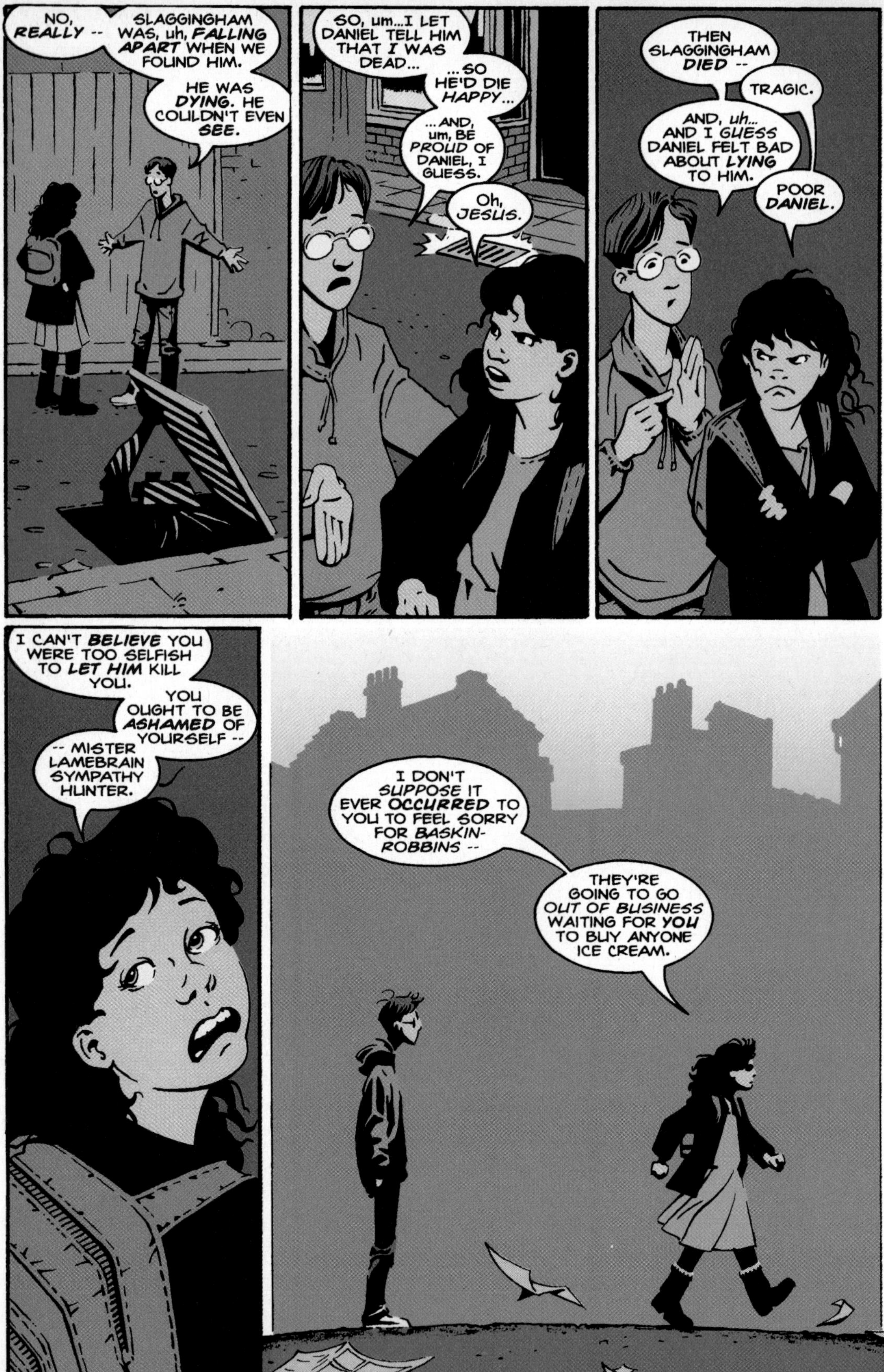

NO, REALLY --
SLAGGINGHAM WAS, uh, FALLING APART WHEN WE FOUND HIM.
HE WAS DYING. HE COULDN'T EVEN SEE.
SO, um...I LET DANIEL TELL HIM THAT I WAS DEAD...
...SO HE'D DIE HAPPY...
...AND, um, BE PROUD OF DANIEL, I GUESS.
Oh, JESUS.
THEN SLAGGINGHAM DIED --
TRAGIC.
AND, uh... AND I GUESS DANIEL FELT BAD ABOUT LYING TO HIM.
POOR DANIEL.
I CAN'T BELIEVE YOU WERE TOO SELFISH TO LET HIM KILL YOU.
YOU OUGHT TO BE ASHAMED OF YOURSELF --
-- MISTER LAMEBRAIN SYMPATHY HUNTER.
I DON'T SUPPOSE IT EVER OCCURRED TO YOU TO FEEL SORRY FOR BASKIN-ROBBINS --
THEY'RE GOING TO GO OUT OF BUSINESS WAITING FOR YOU TO BUY ANYONE ICE CREAM.

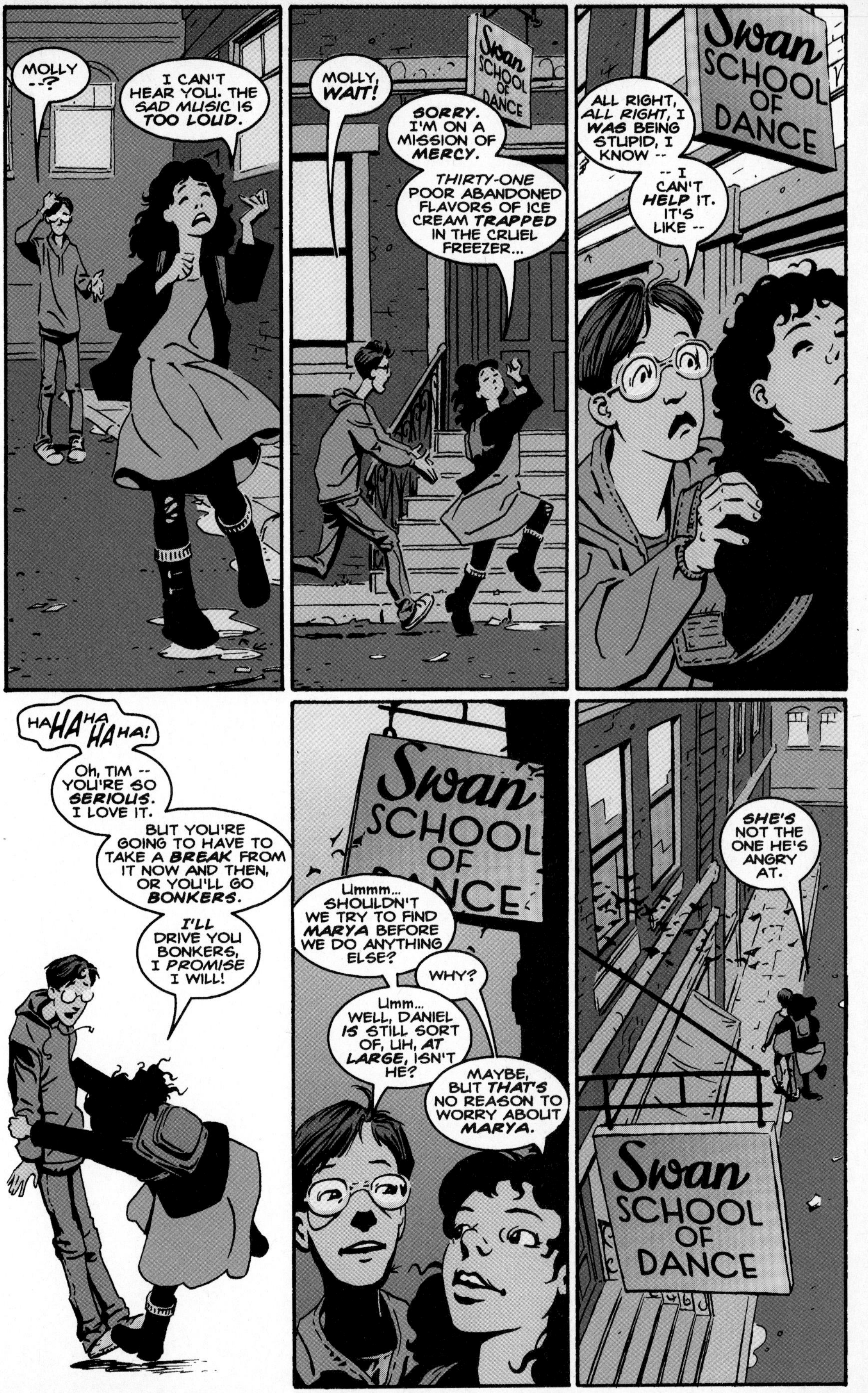
MOLLY --?
I CAN'T HEAR YOU. THE SAD MUSIC IS TOO LOUD.
Swan SCHOOL OF DANCE
MOLLY, WAIT!
SORRY. I'M ON A MISSION OF MERCY.
THIRTY-ONE POOR ABANDONED FLAVORS OF ICE CREAM TRAPPED IN THE CRUEL FREEZER...
Swan SCHOOL OF DANCE
ALL RIGHT, ALL RIGHT, I WAS BEING STUPID, I KNOW --
-- I CAN'T HELP IT. IT'S LIKE --
HAHAHA HAHA!
Oh, TIM -- YOU'RE SO SERIOUS. I LOVE IT.
BUT YOU'RE GOING TO HAVE TO TAKE A BREAK FROM IT NOW AND THEN, OR YOU'LL GO BONKERS.
I'LL DRIVE YOU BONKERS, I PROMISE I WILL!
Swan SCHOOL OF DANCE
Ummm... SHOULDN'T WE TRY TO FIND MARYA BEFORE WE DO ANYTHING ELSE?
WHY?
Umm... WELL, DANIEL IS STILL SORT OF, UH, AT LARGE, ISN'T HE?
MAYBE, BUT THAT'S NO REASON TO WORRY ABOUT MARYA.
SHE'S NOT THE ONE HE'S ANGRY AT.
Swan SCHOOL OF DANCE

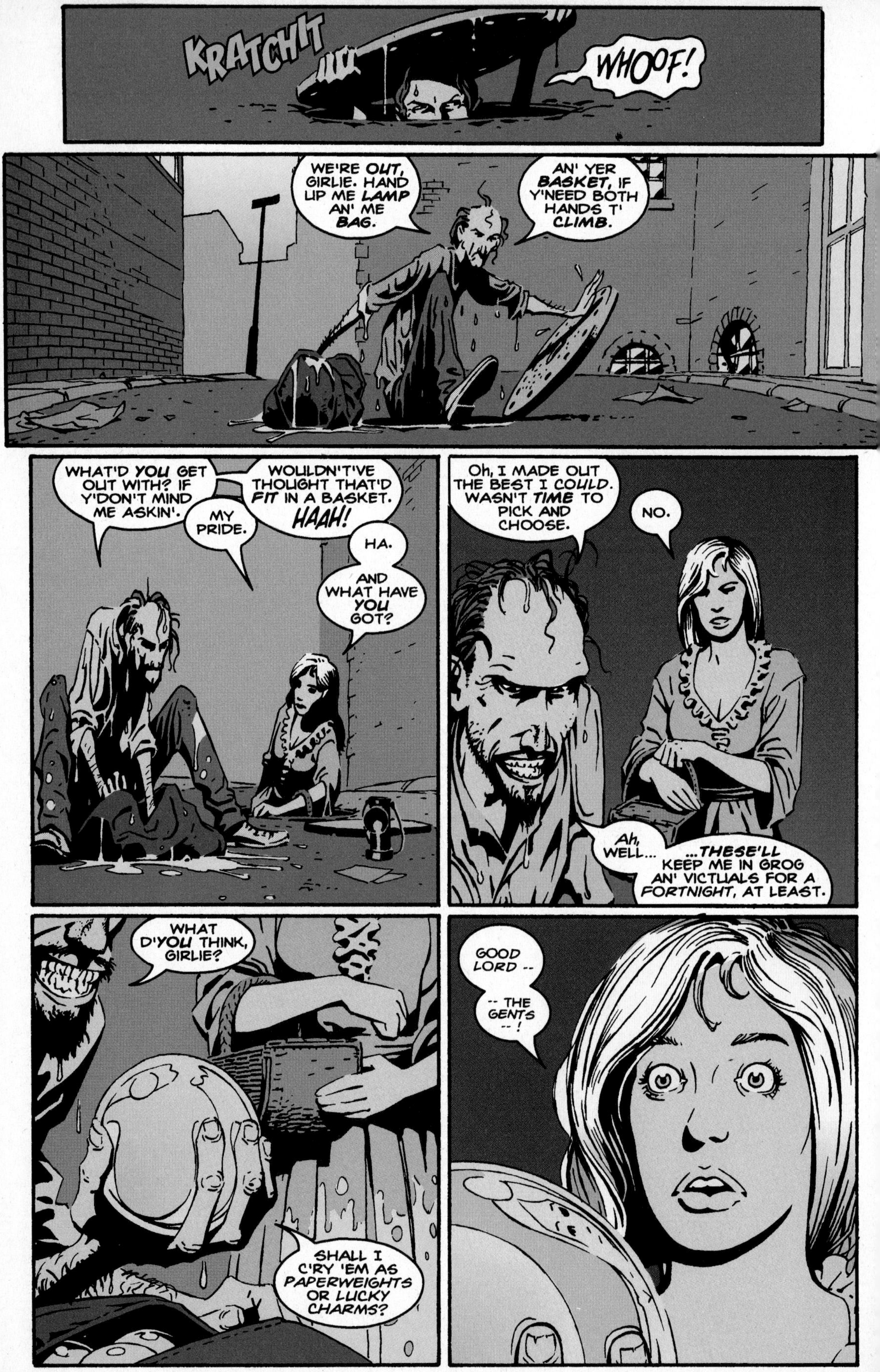

KRATCHIT
WHOOF!
WE'RE OUT, GIRLIE. HAND UP ME LAMP AN' ME BAG.
AN' YER BASKET, IF Y'NEED BOTH HANDS T' CLIMB.
WHAT'D YOU GET OUT WITH? IF Y'DON'T MIND ME ASKIN'.
MY PRIDE.
WOULDN'T'VE THOUGHT THAT'D FIT IN A BASKET. HAAH!
HA.
AND WHAT HAVE YOU GOT?
Oh, I MADE OUT THE BEST I COULD. WASN'T TIME TO PICK AND CHOOSE.
NO.
Ah, WELL...
...THESE'LL KEEP ME IN GROG AN' VICTUALS FOR A FORTNIGHT, AT LEAST.
WHAT D'YOU THINK, GIRLIE?
SHALL I C'RY 'EM AS PAPERWEIGHTS OR LUCKY CHARMS?
GOOD LORD --
-- THE GENTS -- !

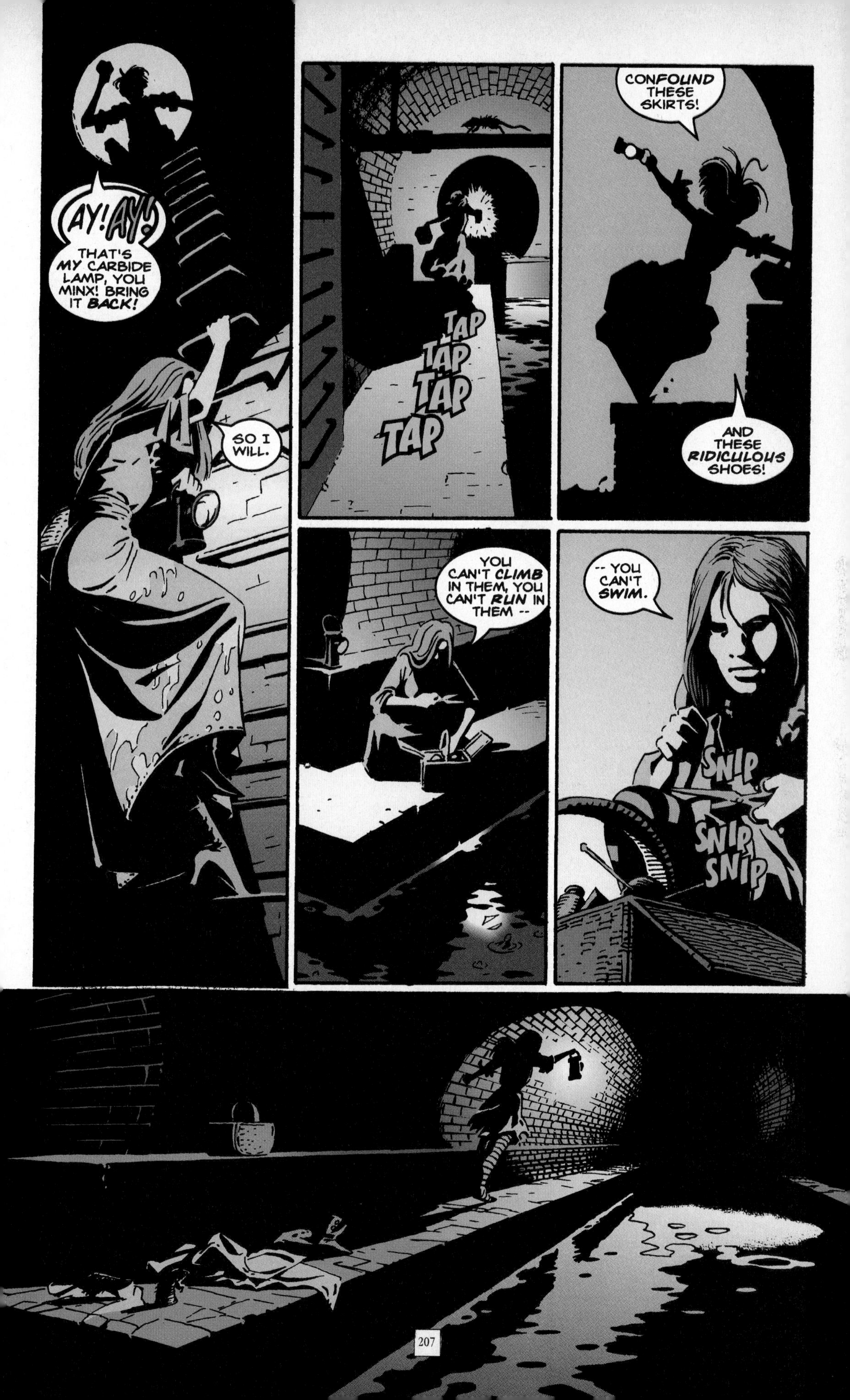
AY! AY!
THAT'S MY CARBIDE LAMP, YOU MINX! BRING IT BACK!
SO I WILL.
TAP TAP TAP TAP
CONFOUND THESE SKIRTS!
AND THESE RIDICULOUS SHOES!
YOU CAN'T CLIMB IN THEM, YOU CAN'T RUN IN THEM --
-- YOU CAN'T SWIM.
SNIP SNIP SNIP

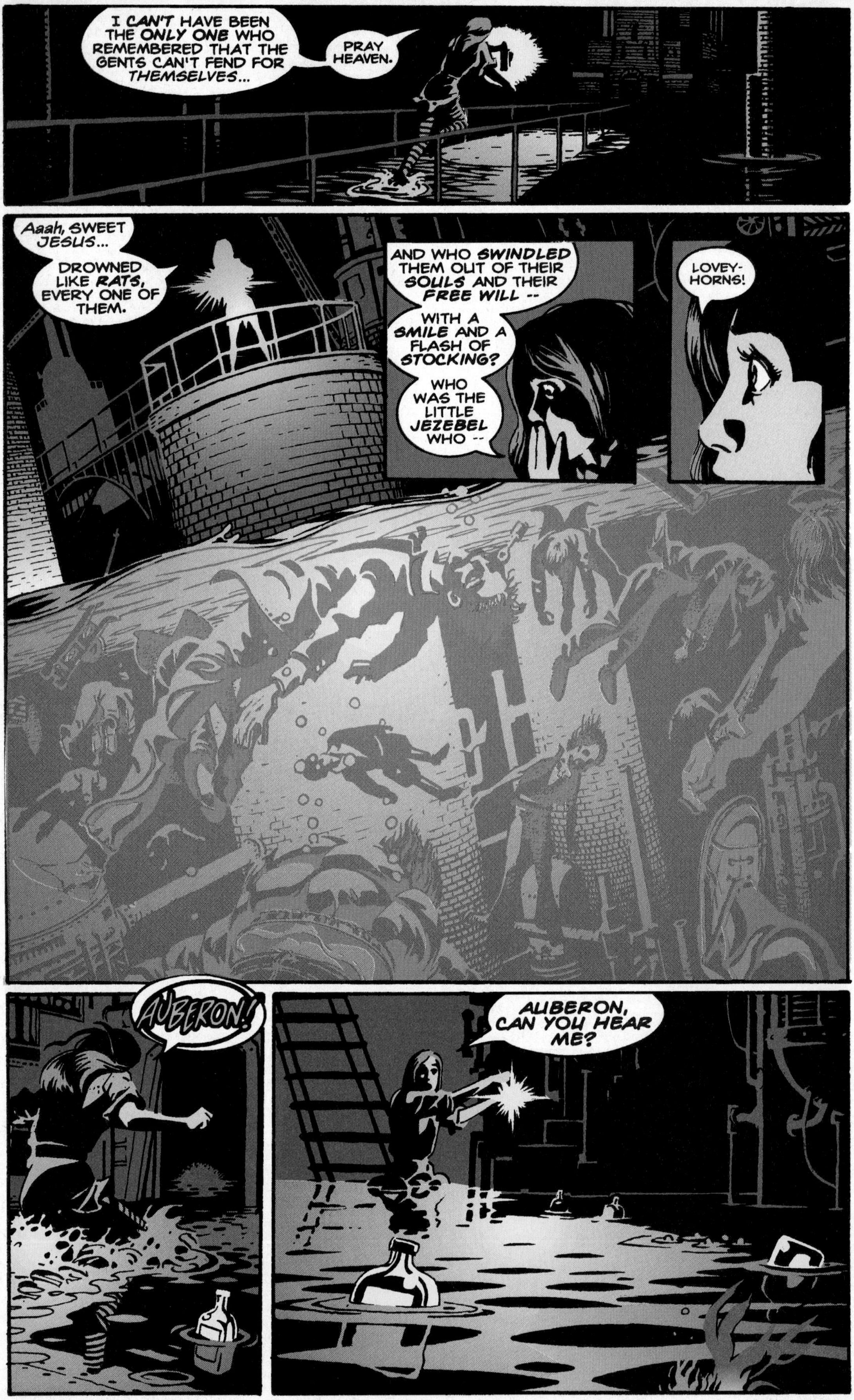
I CAN'T HAVE BEEN THE ONLY ONE WHO REMEMBERED THAT THE GENTS CAN'T FEND FOR THEMSELVES...
PRAY HEAVEN.
Aaah, SWEET JESUS...
DROWNED LIKE RATS, EVERY ONE OF THEM.
AND WHO SWINDLED THEM OUT OF THEIR SOULS AND THEIR FREE WILL --
WITH A SMILE AND A FLASH OF STOCKING?
WHO WAS THE LITTLE JEZEBEL WHO --
LOVEY-HORNS!
AUBERON!
AUBERON, CAN YOU HEAR ME?

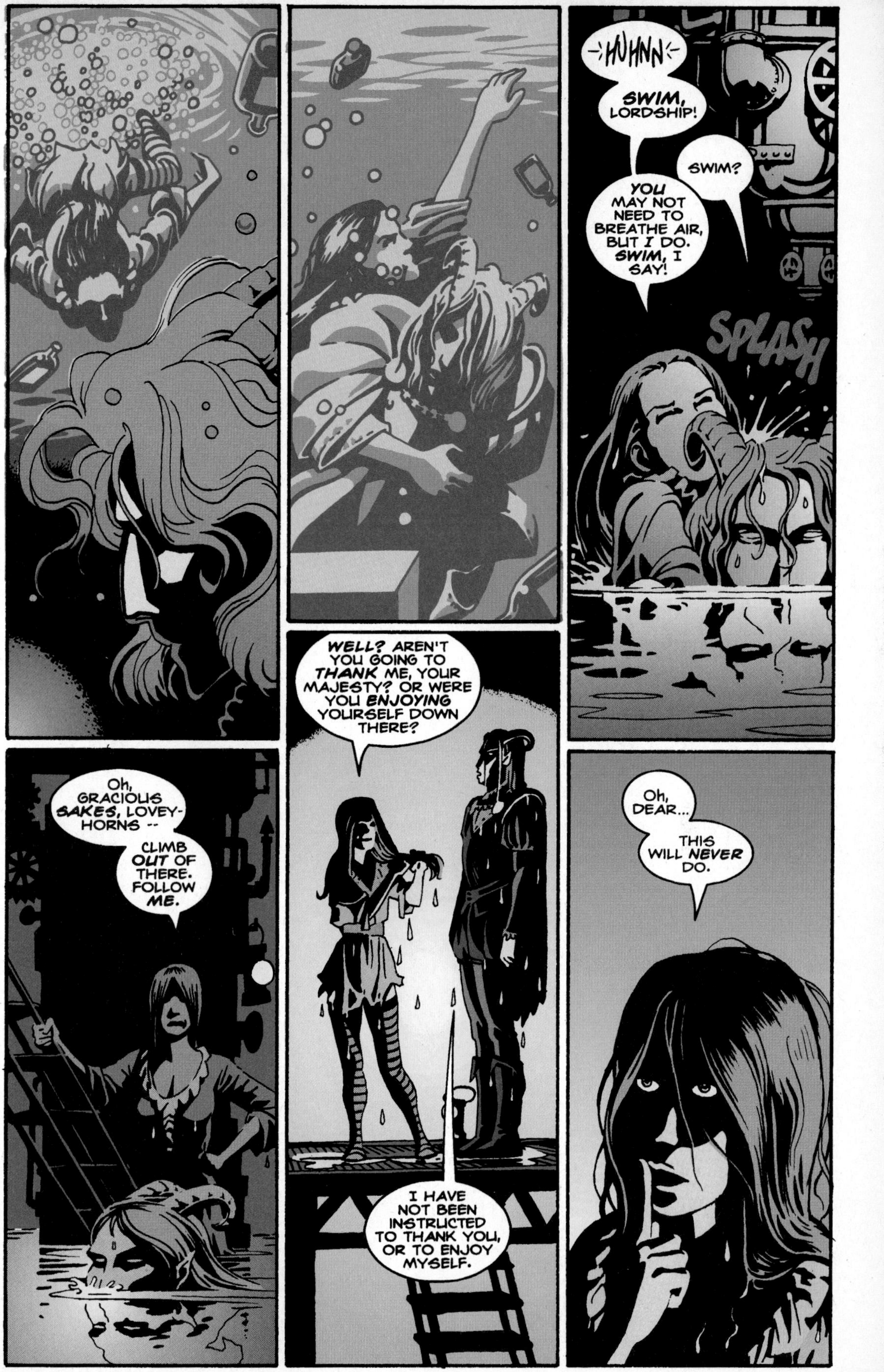
HUHNN
SWIM, LORDSHIP!
SWIM?
YOU MAY NOT NEED TO BREATHE AIR, BUT I DO. SWIM, I SAY!
SPLASH
WELL? AREN'T YOU GOING TO THANK ME, YOUR MAJESTY? OR WERE YOU ENJOYING YOURSELF DOWN THERE?
Oh, GRACIOUS SAKES, LOVEY-HORNS --
CLIMB OUT OF THERE. FOLLOW ME.
I HAVE NOT BEEN INSTRUCTED TO THANK YOU, OR TO ENJOY MYSELF.
Oh, DEAR...
THIS WILL NEVER DO.

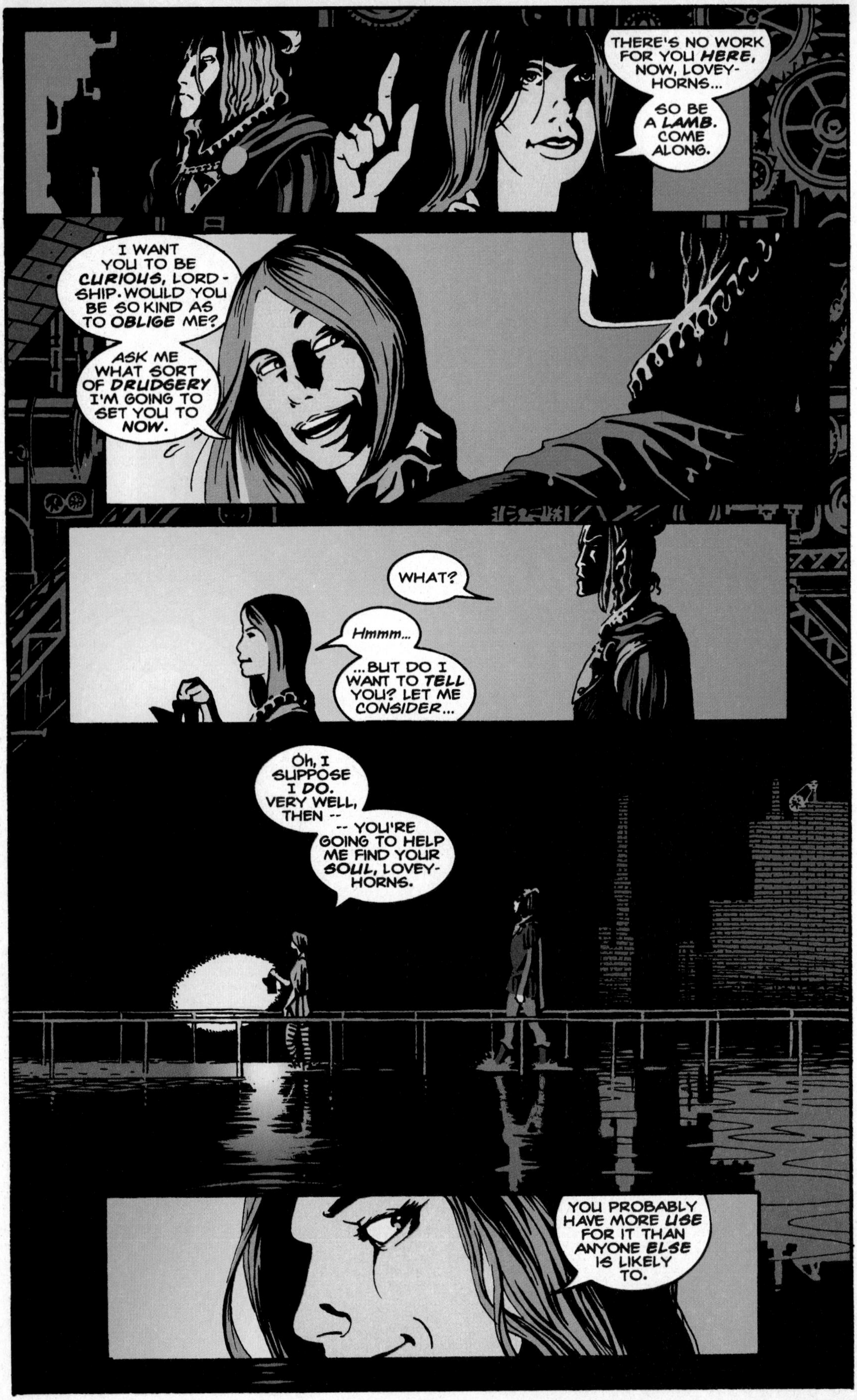
THERE'S NO WORK FOR YOU HERE, NOW, LOVEY-HORNS...
SO BE A LAMB. COME ALONG.
I WANT YOU TO BE CURIOUS, LORDSHIP. WOULD YOU BE SO KIND AS TO OBLIGE ME?
ASK ME WHAT SORT OF DRUDGERY I'M GOING TO SET YOU TO NOW.
WHAT?
Hmmm...
...BUT DO I WANT TO TELL YOU? LET ME CONSIDER...
Oh, I SUPPOSE I DO. VERY WELL, THEN --
-- YOU'RE GOING TO HELP ME FIND YOUR SOUL, LOVEY-HORNS.
YOU PROBABLY HAVE MORE USE FOR IT THAN ANYONE ELSE IS LIKELY TO.

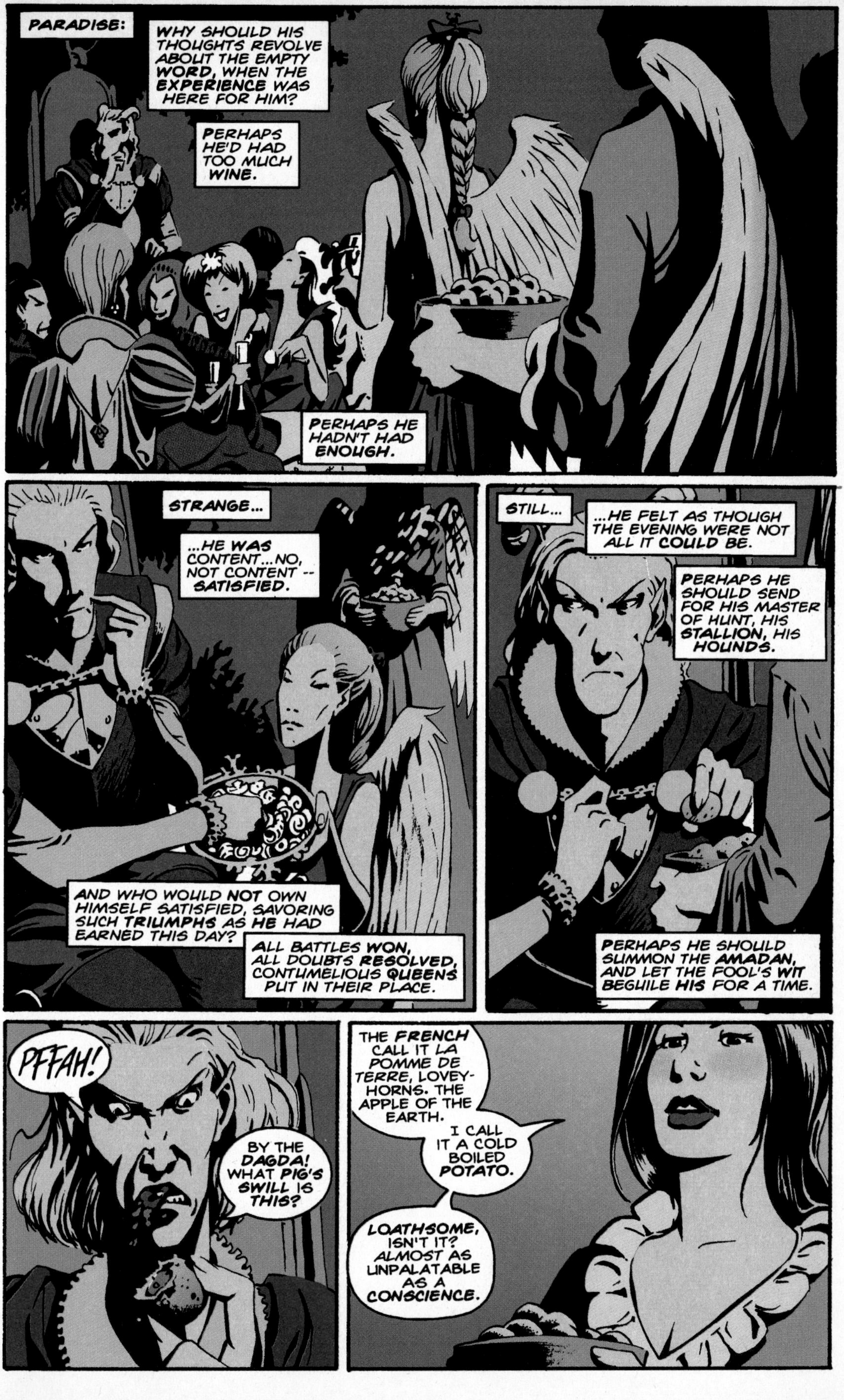
PARADISE:
WHY SHOULD HIS THOUGHTS REVOLVE ABOUT THE EMPTY WORD, WHEN THE EXPERIENCE WAS HERE FOR HIM?
PERHAPS HE'D HAD TOO MUCH WINE.
PERHAPS HE HADN'T HAD ENOUGH.
STRANGE...
...HE WAS CONTENT...NO, NOT CONTENT -- SATISFIED.
AND WHO WOULD NOT OWN HIMSELF SATISFIED, SAVORING SUCH TRIUMPHS AS HE HAD EARNED THIS DAY?
ALL BATTLES WON, ALL DOUBTS RESOLVED, CONTUMELIOUS QUEENS PUT IN THEIR PLACE.
STILL...
...HE FELT AS THOUGH THE EVENING WERE NOT ALL IT COULD BE.
PERHAPS HE SHOULD SEND FOR HIS MASTER OF HUNT, HIS STALLION, HIS HOUNDS.
PERHAPS HE SHOULD SUMMON THE AMADAN, AND LET THE FOOL'S WIT BEGUILE HIS FOR A TIME.
PFFAH!
BY THE DAGDA! WHAT PIG'S SWILL IS THIS?
THE FRENCH CALL IT LA POMME DE TERRE, LOVEY-HORNS. THE APPLE OF THE EARTH.
I CALL IT A COLD BOILED POTATO.
LOATHSOME, ISN'T IT? ALMOST AS UNPALATABLE AS A CONSCIENCE.

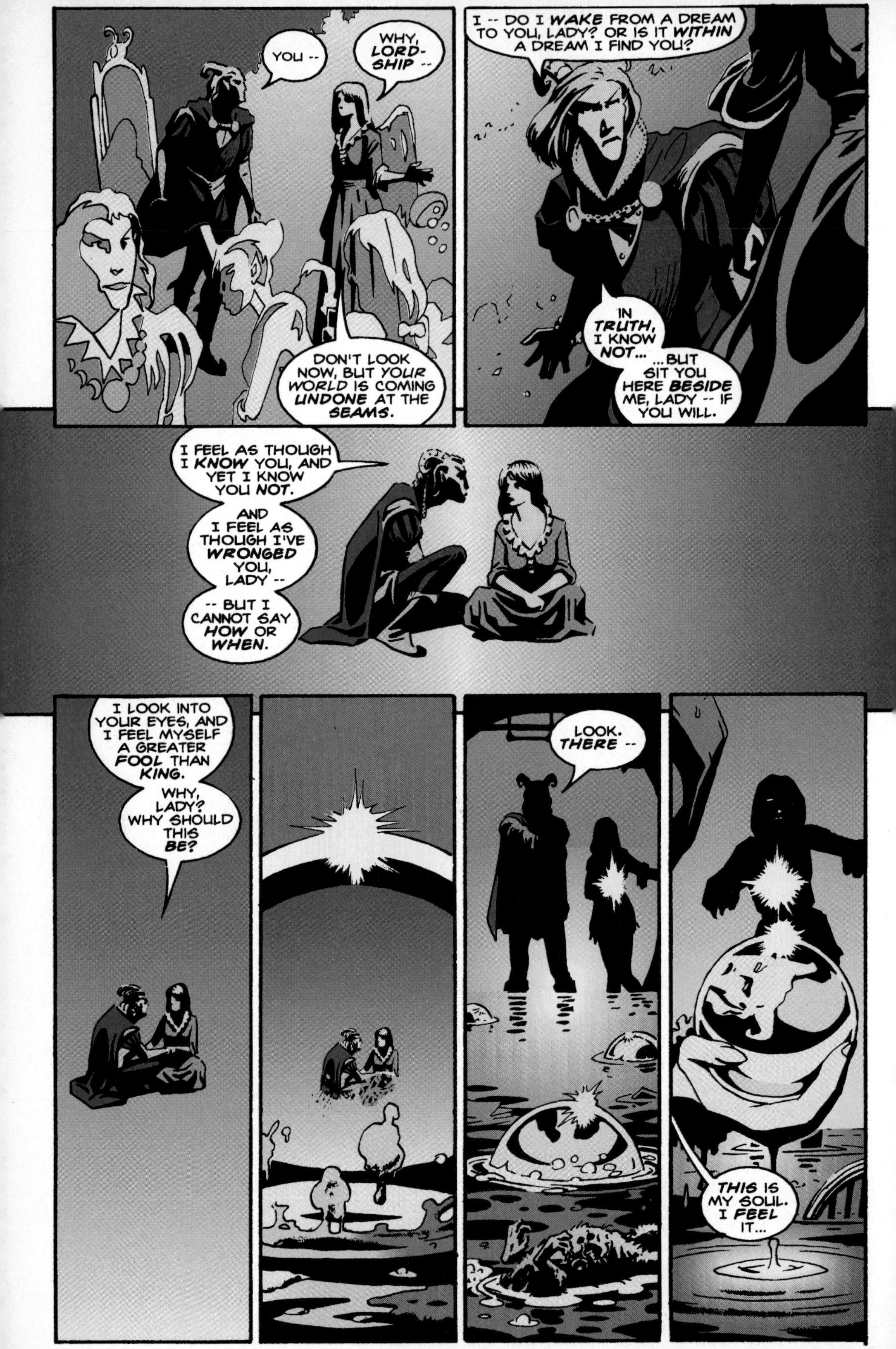
YOU --
WHY, LORDSHIP --
DON'T LOOK NOW, BUT YOUR WORLD IS COMING UNDONE AT THE SEAMS.
I -- DO I WAKE FROM A DREAM TO YOU, LADY? OR IS IT WITHIN A DREAM I FIND YOU?
IN TRUTH, I KNOW NOT...
...BUT SIT YOU HERE BESIDE ME, LADY -- IF YOU WILL.
I FEEL AS THOUGH I KNOW YOU, AND YET I KNOW YOU NOT.
AND I FEEL AS THOUGH I'VE WRONGED YOU, LADY --
-- BUT I CANNOT SAY HOW OR WHEN.
I LOOK INTO YOUR EYES, AND I FEEL MYSELF A GREATER FOOL THAN KING.
WHY, LADY? WHY SHOULD THIS BE?
LOOK. THERE --
THIS IS MY SOUL. I FEEL IT...

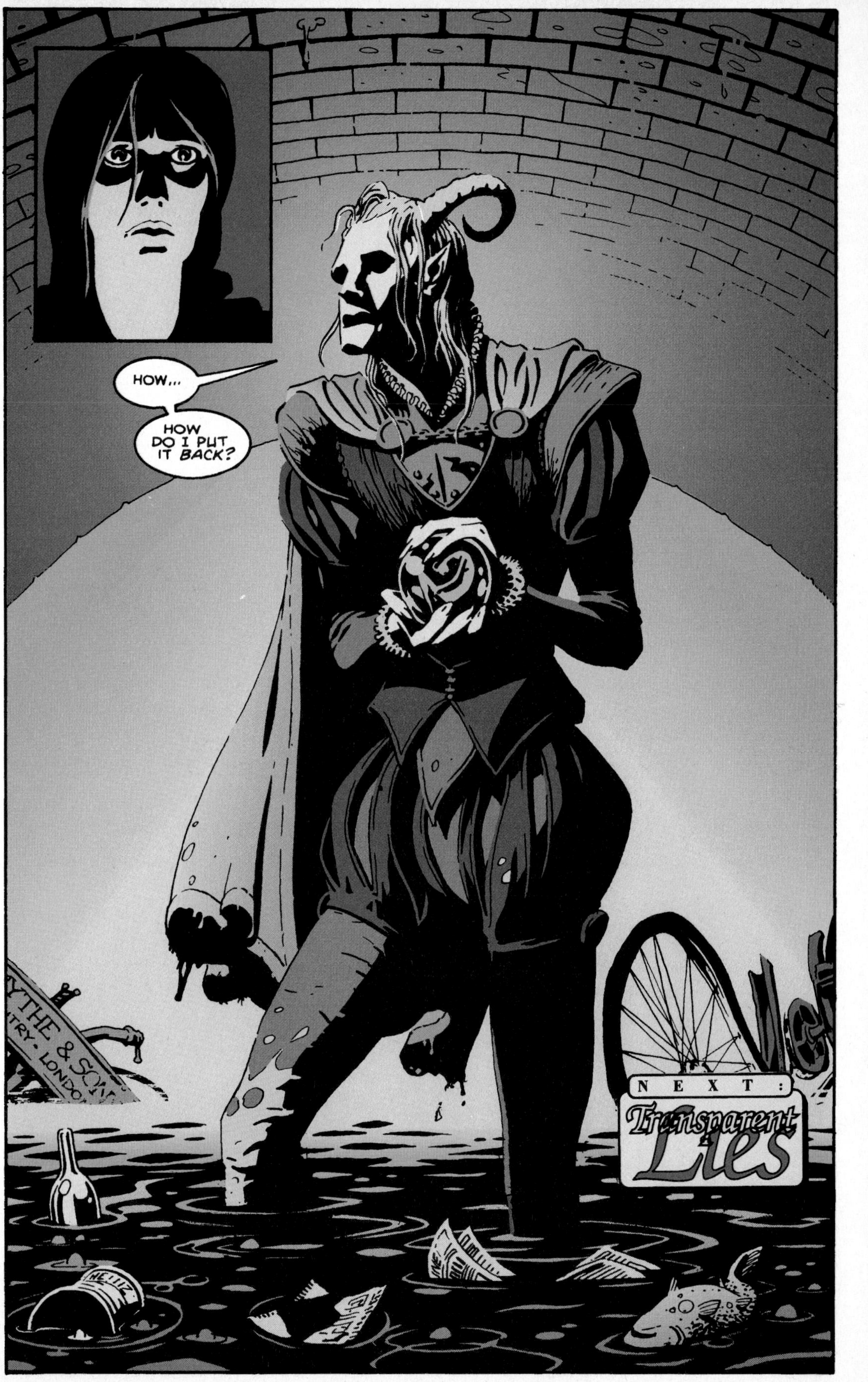
HOW...
HOW DO I PUT IT BACK?
NEXT:
Transparent Lies

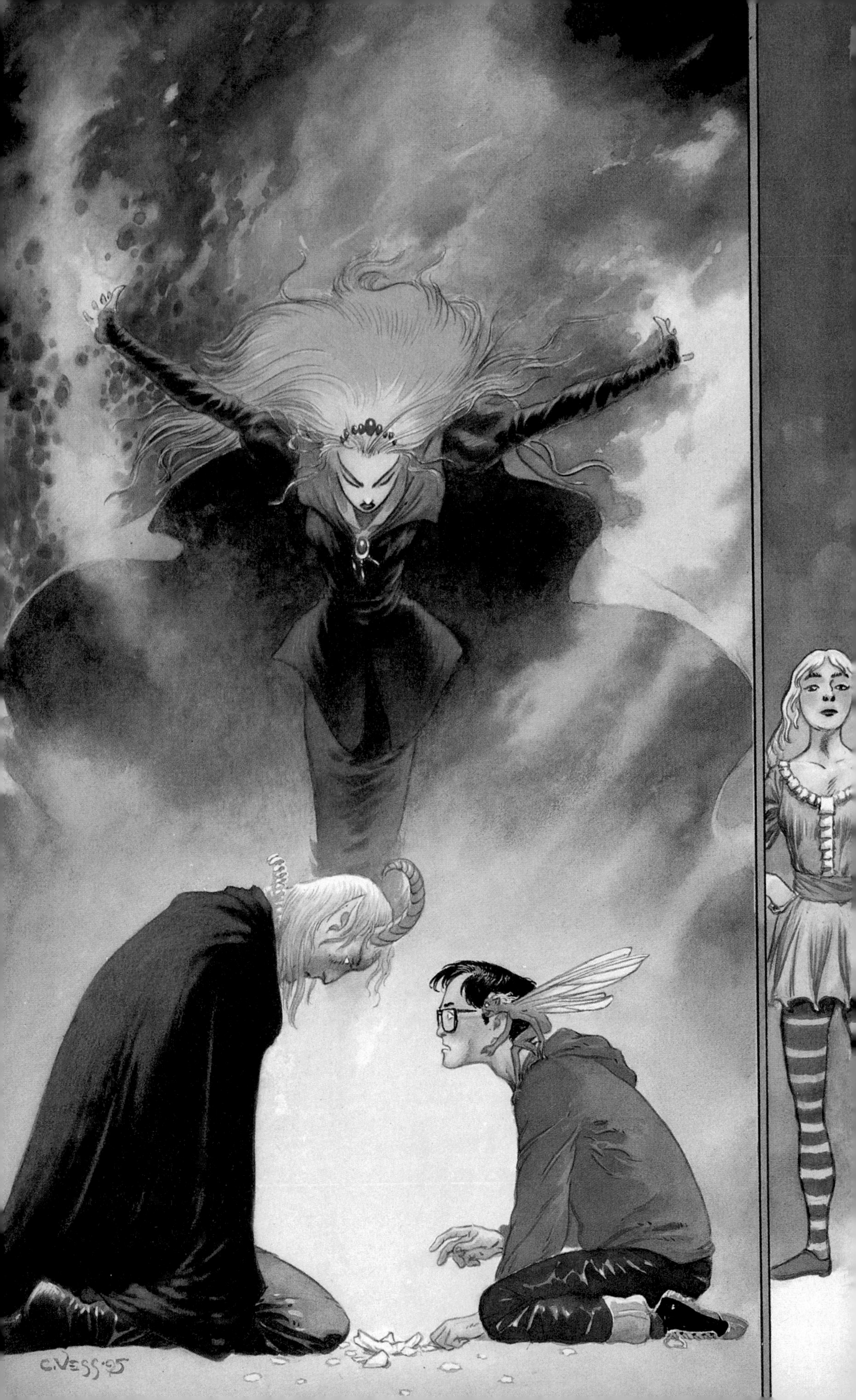
C.VESS·95

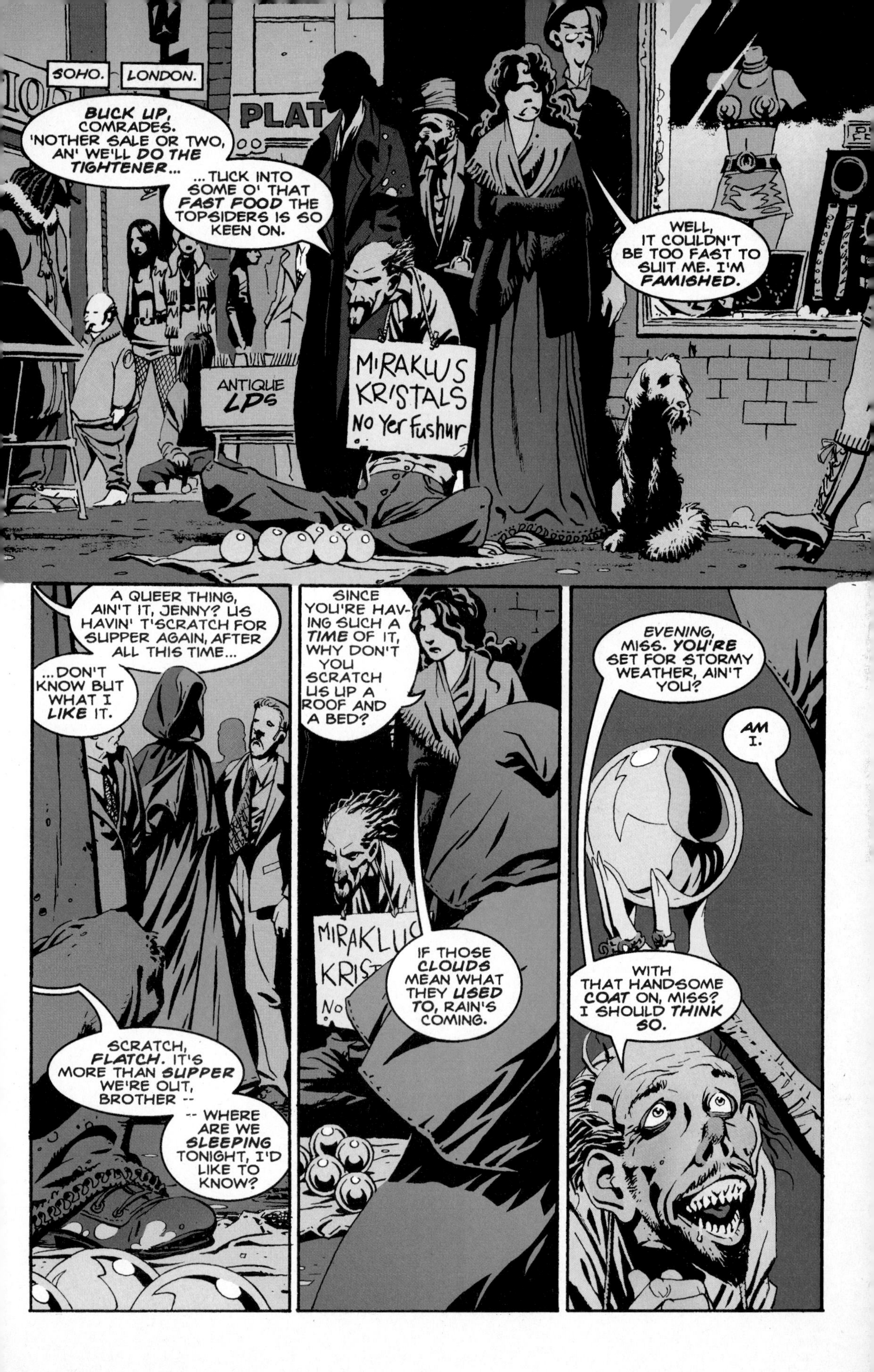

SOHO. LONDON.
BUCK UP, COMRADES. 'NOTHER SALE OR TWO, AN' WE'LL DO THE TIGHTENER...
...TUCK INTO SOME O' THAT FAST FOOD THE TOPSIDERS IS SO KEEN ON.
WELL, IT COULDN'T BE TOO FAST TO SUIT ME. I'M FAMISHED.
PLAT
ANTIQUE LPs
MIRAKLUS KRISTALS No Yer Fushur
A QUEER THING, AIN'T IT, JENNY? US HAVIN' T'SCRATCH FOR SUPPER AGAIN, AFTER ALL THIS TIME...
...DON'T KNOW BUT WHAT I LIKE IT.
SCRATCH, FLATCH. IT'S MORE THAN SUPPER WE'RE OUT, BROTHER --
-- WHERE ARE WE SLEEPING TONIGHT, I'D LIKE TO KNOW?
SINCE YOU'RE HAVING SUCH A TIME OF IT, WHY DON'T YOU SCRATCH US UP A ROOF AND A BED?
IF THOSE CLOUDS MEAN WHAT THEY USED TO, RAIN'S COMING.
EVENING, MISS. YOU'RE SET FOR STORMY WEATHER, AIN'T YOU?
AM I.
WITH THAT HANDSOME COAT ON, MISS? I SHOULD THINK SO.

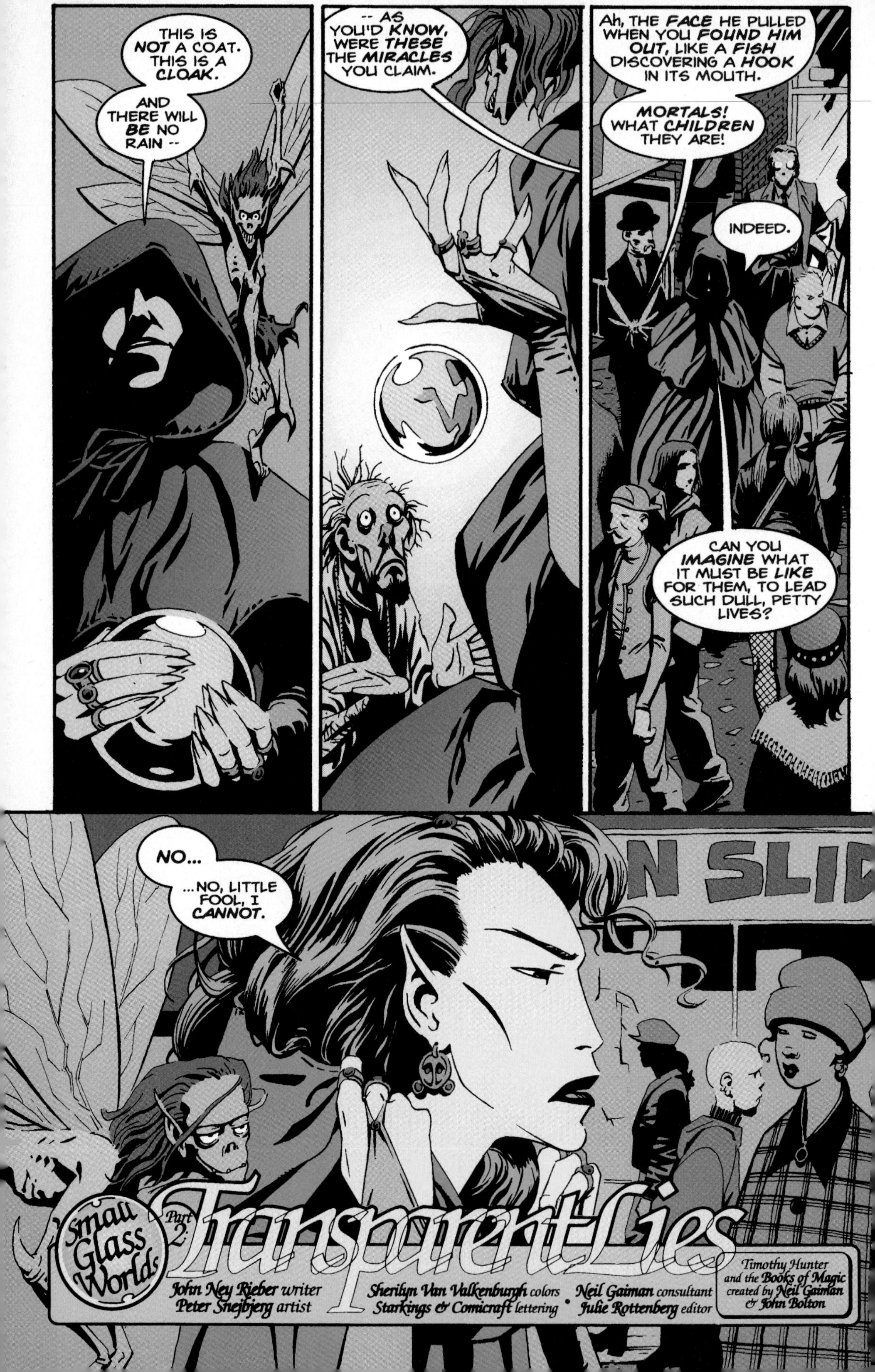
THIS IS NOT A COAT. THIS IS A CLOAK.
AND THERE WILL BE NO RAIN --
-- AS YOU'D KNOW, WERE THESE THE MIRACLES YOU CLAIM.
Ah, THE FACE HE PULLED WHEN YOU FOUND HIM OUT, LIKE A FISH DISCOVERING A HOOK IN ITS MOUTH.
MORTALS! WHAT CHILDREN THEY ARE!
INDEED.
CAN YOU IMAGINE WHAT IT MUST BE LIKE FOR THEM, TO LEAD SUCH DULL, PETTY LIVES?
NO...
...NO, LITTLE FOOL, I CANNOT.
N SLID
Small Glass Worlds
Part 2: Transparent Lies
John Ney Rieber writer
Peter Snejbjerg artist
Sherilyn Van Valkenburgh colors
Starkings & Comicraft lettering
Neil Gaiman consultant
Julie Rottenberg editor
Timothy Hunter and the Books of Magic created by Neil Gaiman & John Bolton

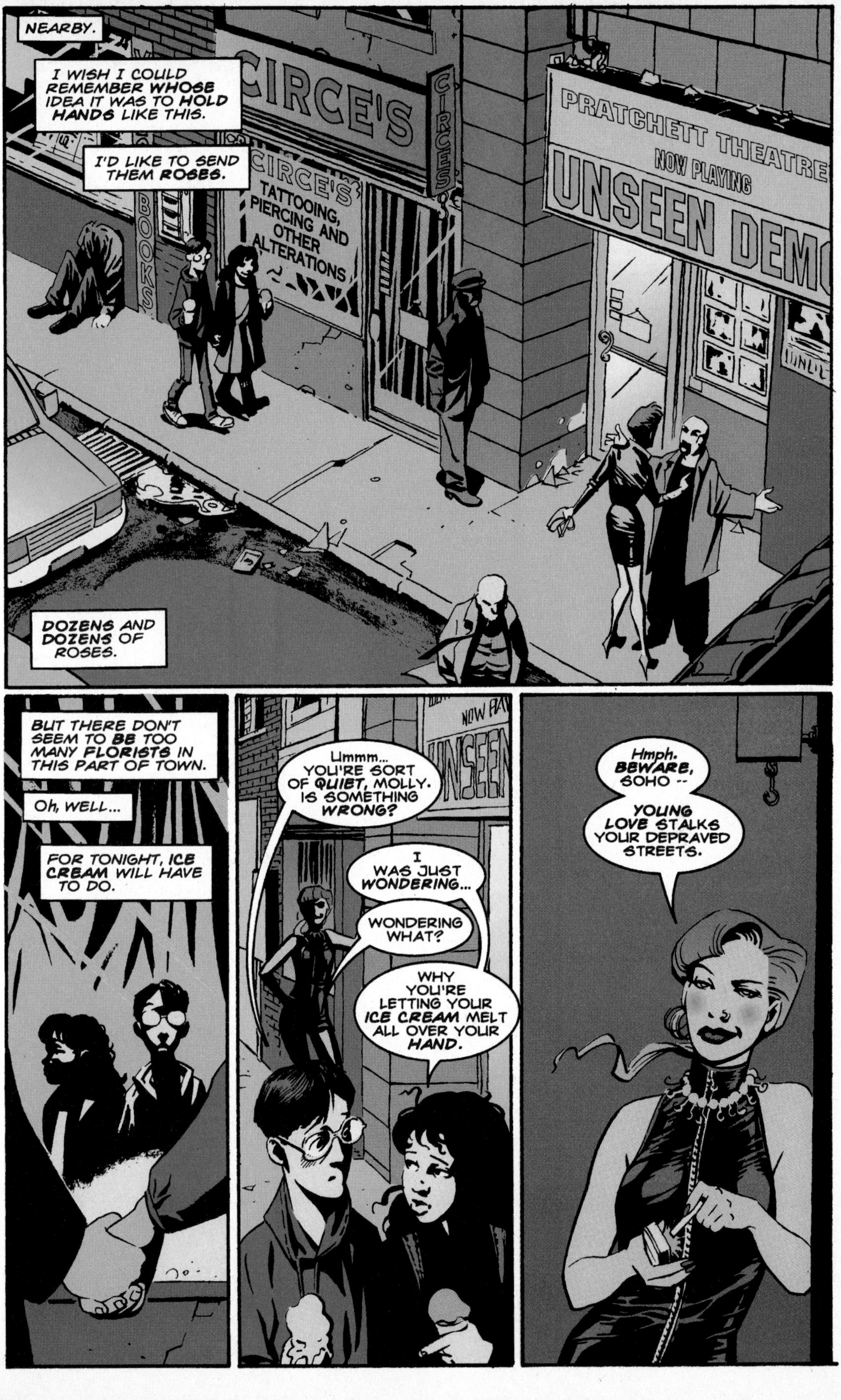

NEARBY.
I WISH I COULD REMEMBER WHOSE IDEA IT WAS TO HOLD HANDS LIKE THIS.
CIRCE'S
CIRCE'S
I'D LIKE TO SEND THEM ROSES.
CIRCE'S TATTOOING, PIERCING AND OTHER ALTERATIONS
BOOKS
PRATCHETT THEATRE NOW PLAYING UNSEEN DEM
DOZENS AND DOZENS OF ROSES.
BUT THERE DON'T SEEM TO BE TOO MANY FLORISTS IN THIS PART OF TOWN.
Oh, WELL...
FOR TONIGHT, ICE CREAM WILL HAVE TO DO.
NOW PLA
UNSEEN
Ummm... YOU'RE SORT OF QUIET, MOLLY. IS SOMETHING WRONG?
I WAS JUST WONDERING...
WONDERING WHAT?
WHY YOU'RE LETTING YOUR ICE CREAM MELT ALL OVER YOUR HAND.
Hmph. BEWARE, SOHO --
YOUNG LOVE STALKS YOUR DEPRAVED STREETS.

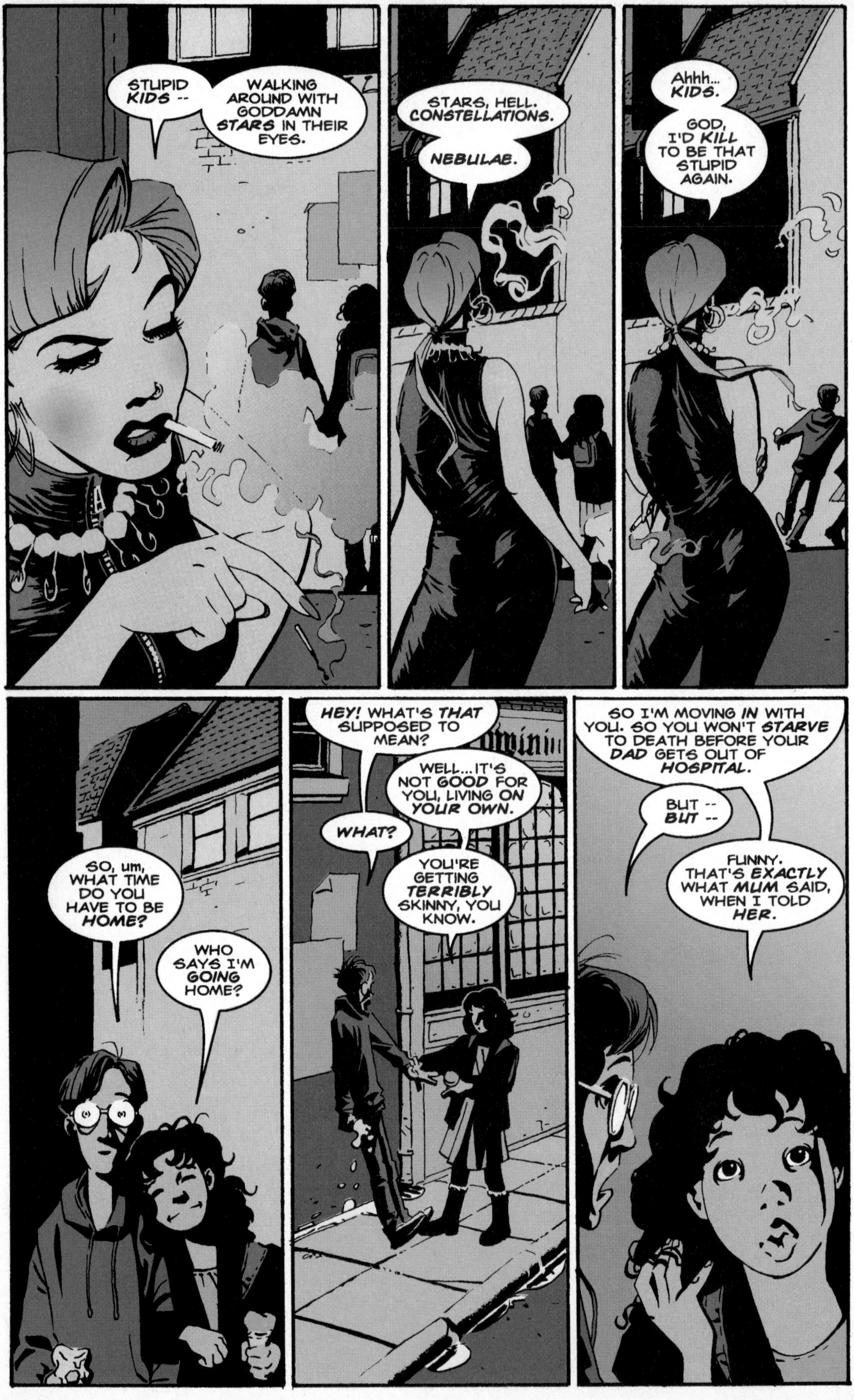
STUPID KIDS --
WALKING AROUND WITH GODDAMN STARS IN THEIR EYES.
STARS, HELL. CONSTELLATIONS.
NEBULAE.
Ahhh... KIDS.
GOD, I'D KILL TO BE THAT STUPID AGAIN.
SO, um, WHAT TIME DO YOU HAVE TO BE HOME?
WHO SAYS I'M GOING HOME?
HEY! WHAT'S THAT SUPPOSED TO MEAN?
WHAT?
WELL...IT'S NOT GOOD FOR YOU, LIVING ON YOUR OWN.
YOU'RE GETTING TERRIBLY SKINNY, YOU KNOW.
SO I'M MOVING IN WITH YOU. SO YOU WON'T STARVE TO DEATH BEFORE YOUR DAD GETS OUT OF HOSPITAL.
BUT -- BUT --
FUNNY. THAT'S EXACTLY WHAT MUM SAID, WHEN I TOLD HER.

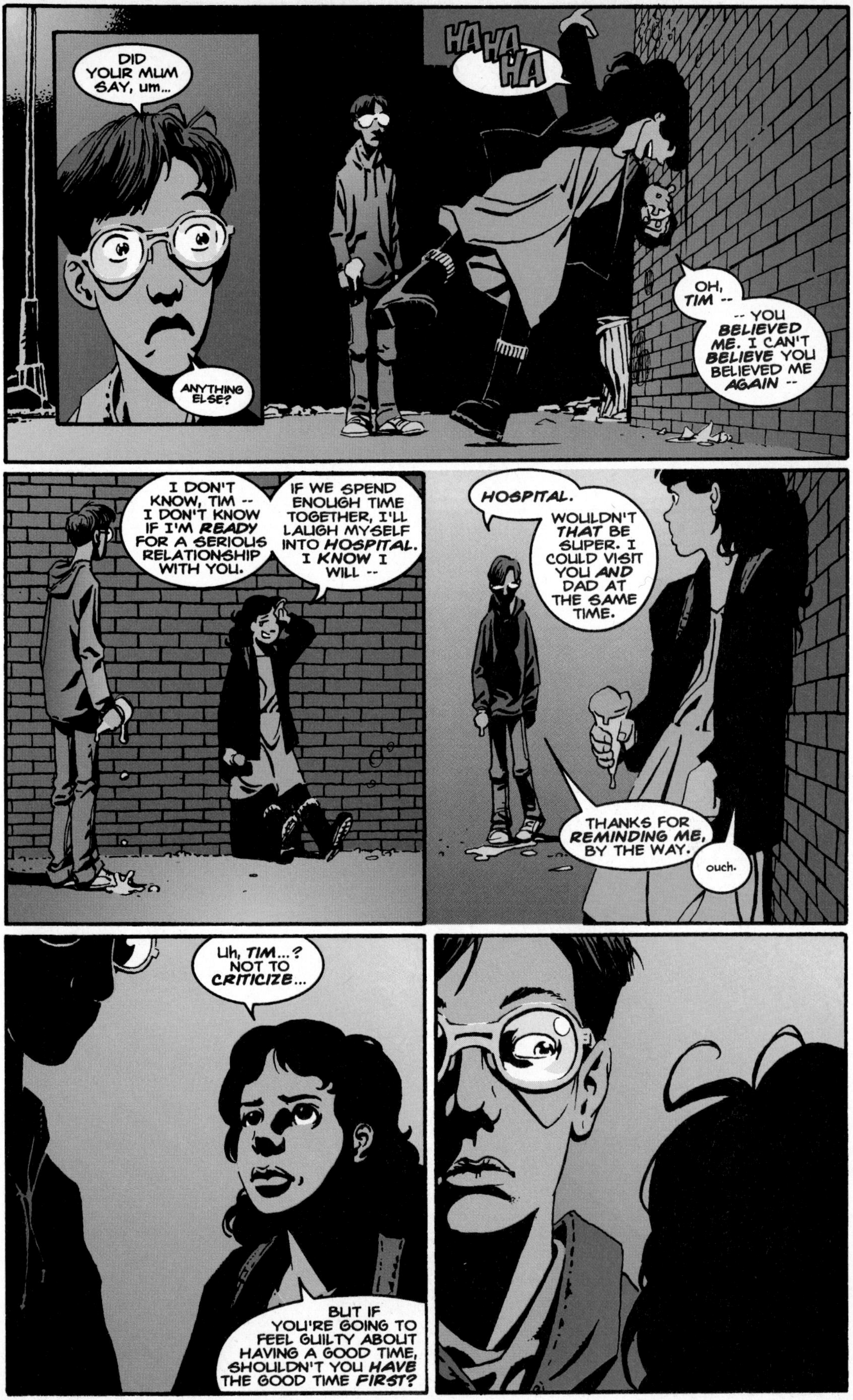
DID YOUR MUM SAY, um...
ANYTHING ELSE?
HAHAHA
OH, TIM --
-- YOU BELIEVED ME. I CAN'T BELIEVE YOU BELIEVED ME AGAIN --
I DON'T KNOW, TIM -- I DON'T KNOW IF I'M READY FOR A SERIOUS RELATIONSHIP WITH YOU.
IF WE SPEND ENOUGH TIME TOGETHER, I'LL LAUGH MYSELF INTO HOSPITAL. I KNOW I WILL --
HOSPITAL.
WOULDN'T THAT BE SUPER. I COULD VISIT YOU AND DAD AT THE SAME TIME.
THANKS FOR REMINDING ME, BY THE WAY.
ouch.
Uh, TIM...? NOT TO CRITICIZE...
BUT IF YOU'RE GOING TO FEEL GUILTY ABOUT HAVING A GOOD TIME, SHOULDN'T YOU HAVE THE GOOD TIME FIRST?

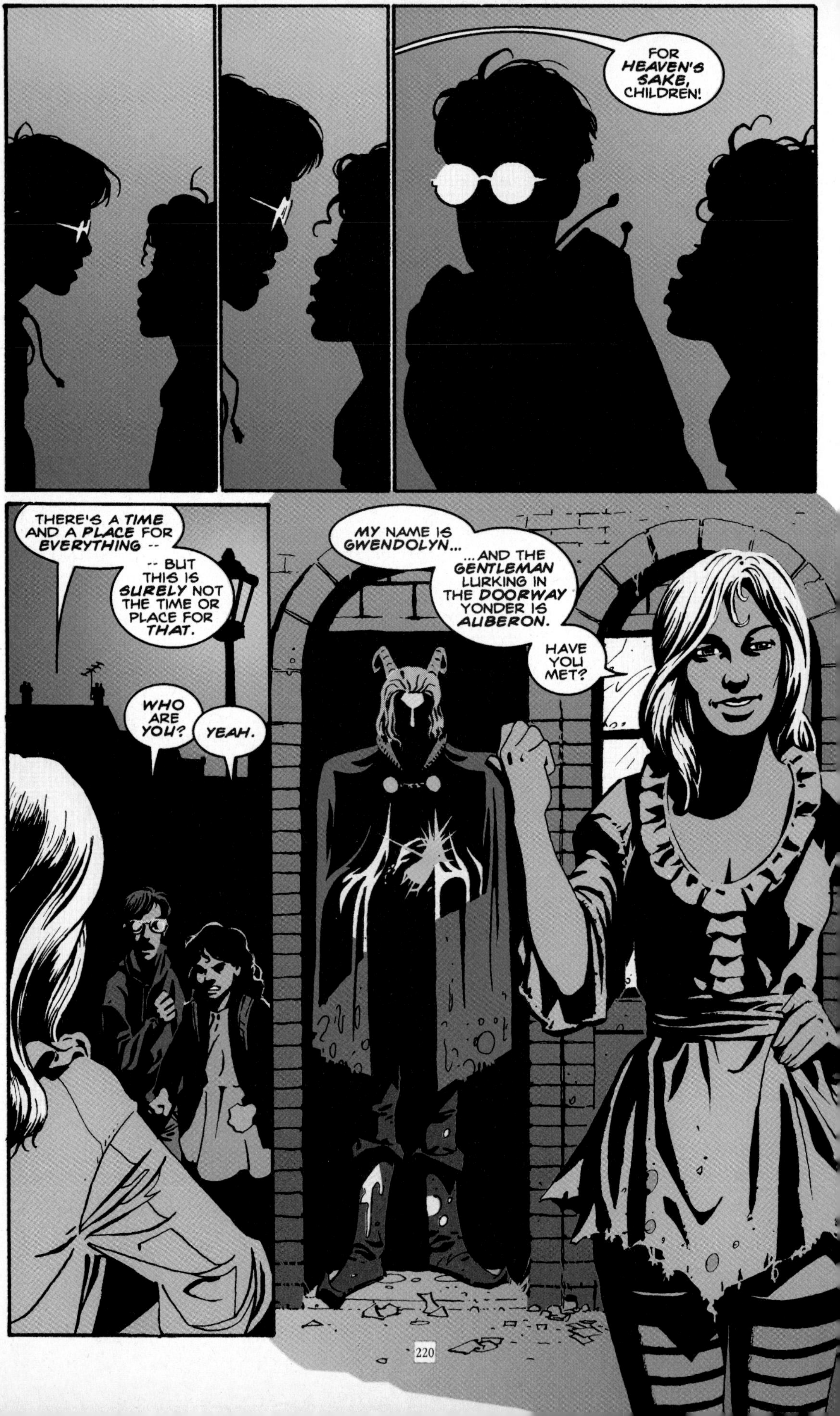
FOR HEAVEN'S SAKE, CHILDREN!
THERE'S A TIME AND A PLACE FOR EVERYTHING --
-- BUT THIS IS SURELY NOT THE TIME OR PLACE FOR THAT.
WHO ARE YOU?
YEAH.
MY NAME IS GWENDOLYN...
...AND THE GENTLEMAN LURKING IN THE DOORWAY YONDER IS AUBERON.
HAVE YOU MET?

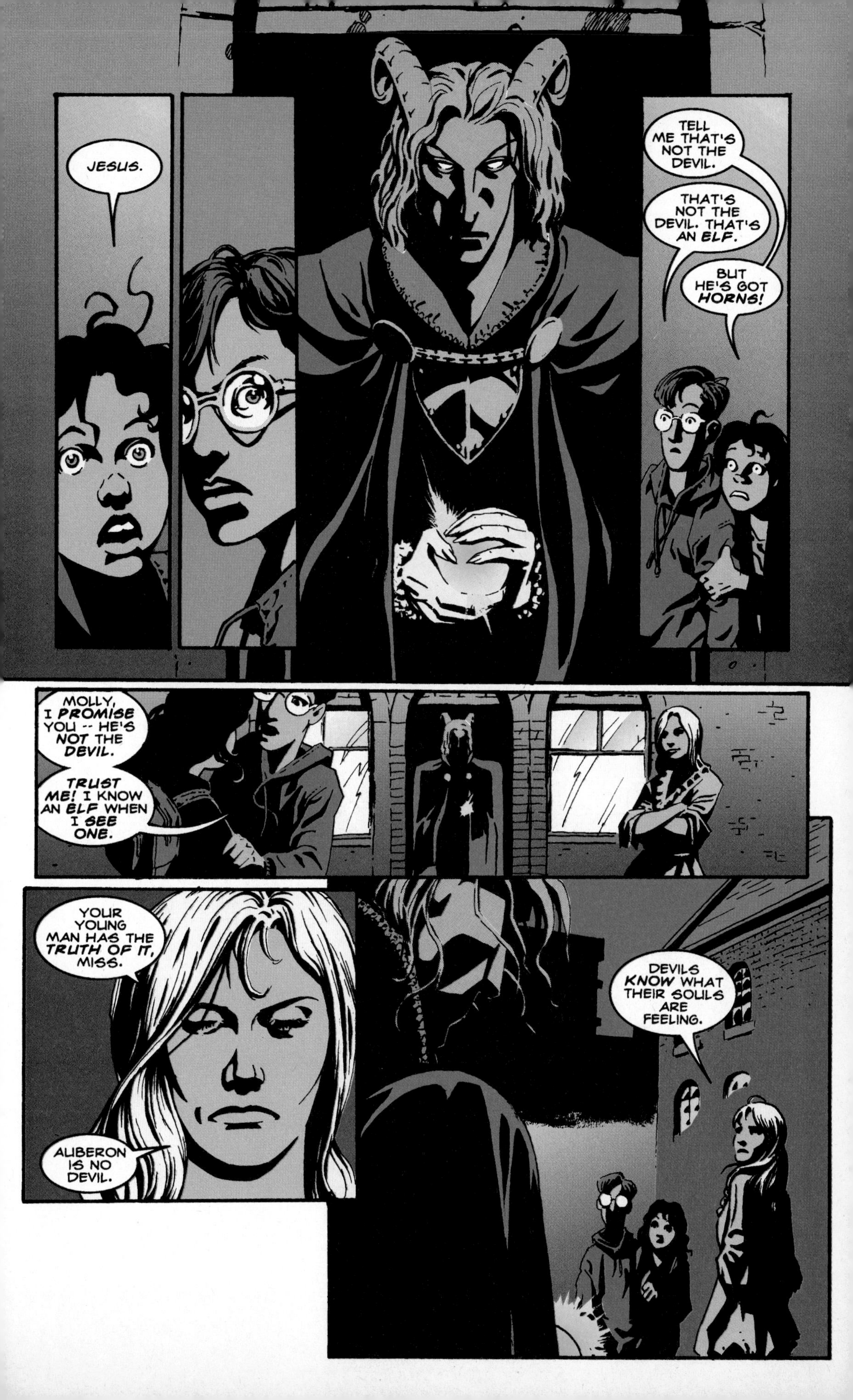
JESUS.
TELL ME THAT'S NOT THE DEVIL.
THAT'S NOT THE DEVIL. THAT'S AN *ELF*.
BUT HE'S GOT *HORNS!*
MOLLY, I *PROMISE* YOU -- HE'S *NOT* THE *DEVIL.*
TRUST ME! I KNOW AN *ELF* WHEN I *SEE* *ONE*.
YOUR YOUNG MAN HAS THE *TRUTH OF IT*, MISS.
ALIBERON IS NO DEVIL.
DEVILS *KNOW* WHAT THEIR SOULS ARE FEELING.

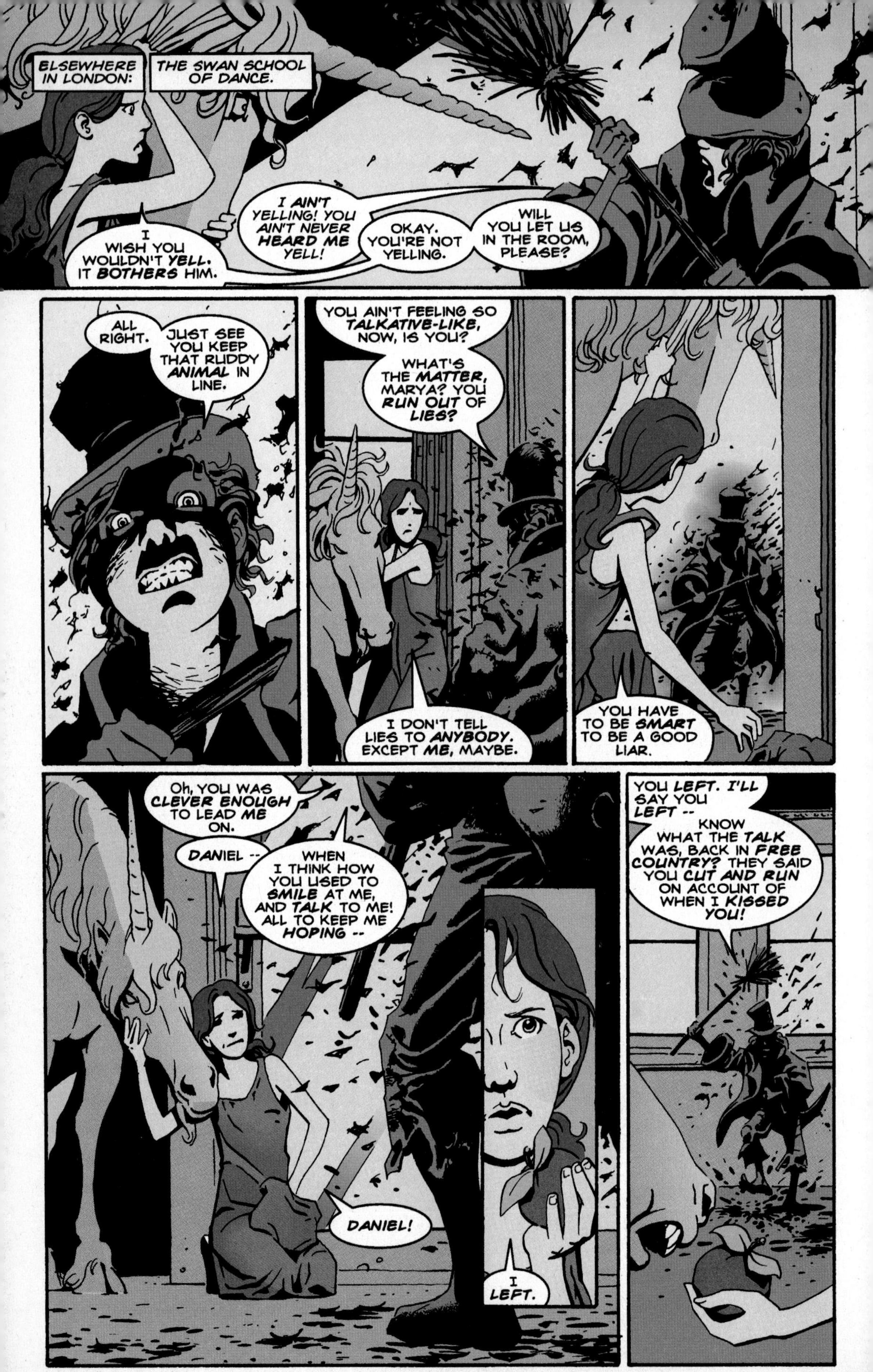
ELSEWHERE IN LONDON:
THE SWAN SCHOOL OF DANCE.
I WISH YOU WOULDN'T YELL. IT BOTHERS HIM.
I AIN'T YELLING! YOU AIN'T NEVER HEARD ME YELL!
OKAY. YOU'RE NOT YELLING.
WILL YOU LET US IN THE ROOM, PLEASE?
ALL RIGHT.
JUST SEE YOU KEEP THAT RUDDY ANIMAL IN LINE.
YOU AIN'T FEELING SO TALKATIVE-LIKE, NOW, IS YOU?
WHAT'S THE MATTER, MARYA? YOU RUN OUT OF LIES?
I DON'T TELL LIES TO ANYBODY. EXCEPT ME, MAYBE.
YOU HAVE TO BE SMART TO BE A GOOD LIAR.
Oh, YOU WAS CLEVER ENOUGH TO LEAD ME ON.
DANIEL --
WHEN I THINK HOW YOU USED TO SMILE AT ME, AND TALK TO ME! ALL TO KEEP ME HOPING --
DANIEL!
I LEFT.
YOU LEFT. I'LL SAY YOU LEFT --
KNOW WHAT THE TALK WAS, BACK IN FREE COUNTRY? THEY SAID YOU CUT AND RUN ON ACCOUNT OF WHEN I KISSED YOU!

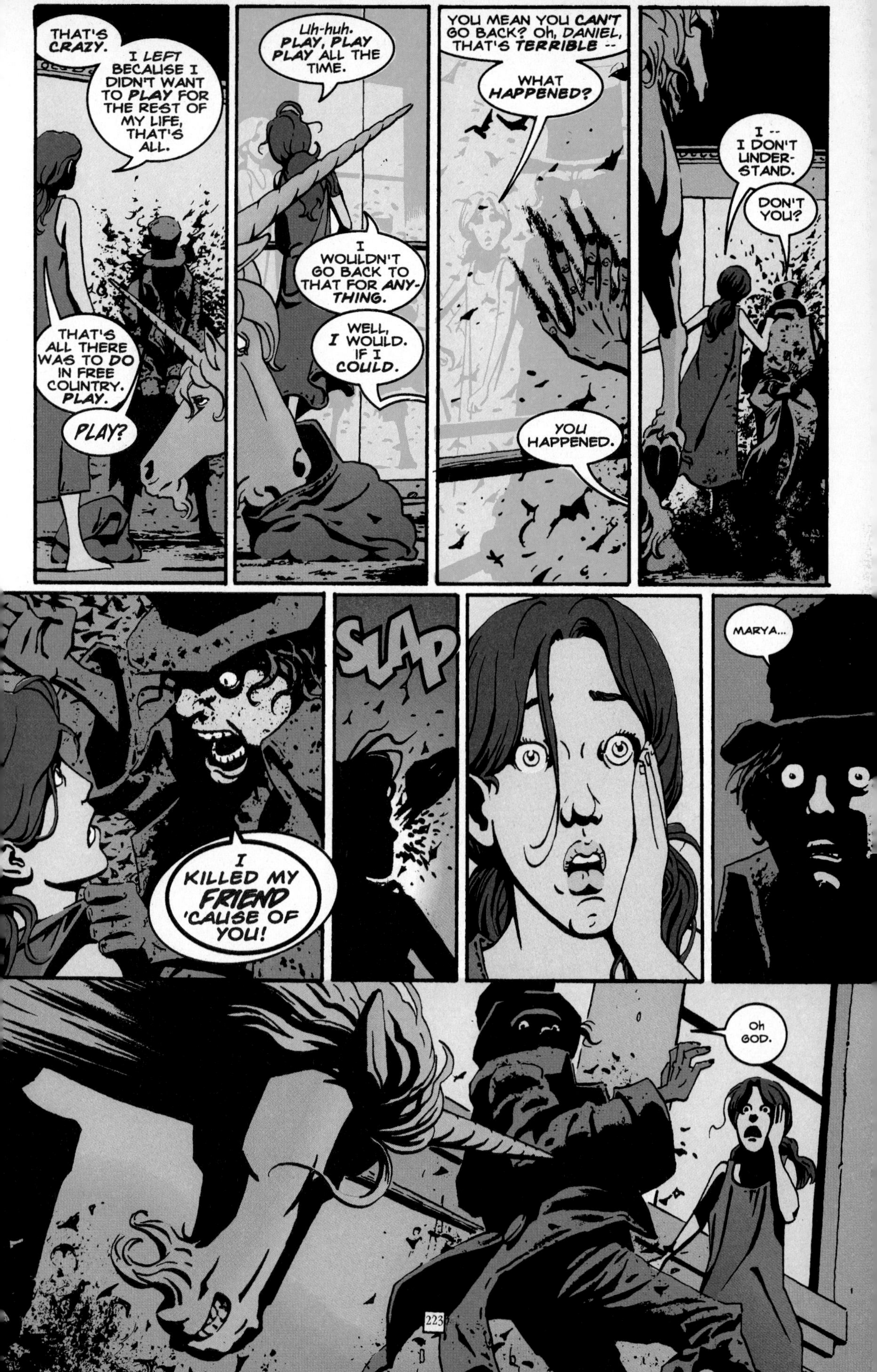
THAT'S CRAZY.
I LEFT BECAUSE I DIDN'T WANT TO PLAY FOR THE REST OF MY LIFE, THAT'S ALL.
THAT'S ALL THERE WAS TO DO IN FREE COUNTRY. PLAY.
PLAY?
Uh-huh. PLAY, PLAY PLAY ALL THE TIME.
I WOULDN'T GO BACK TO THAT FOR ANY-THING.
WELL, I WOULD. IF I COULD.
YOU MEAN YOU CAN'T GO BACK? Oh, DANIEL, THAT'S TERRIBLE --
WHAT HAPPENED?
YOU HAPPENED.
I -- I DON'T UNDER-STAND.
DON'T YOU?
I KILLED MY FRIEND 'CAUSE OF YOU!
SLAP
MARYA...
Oh GOD.

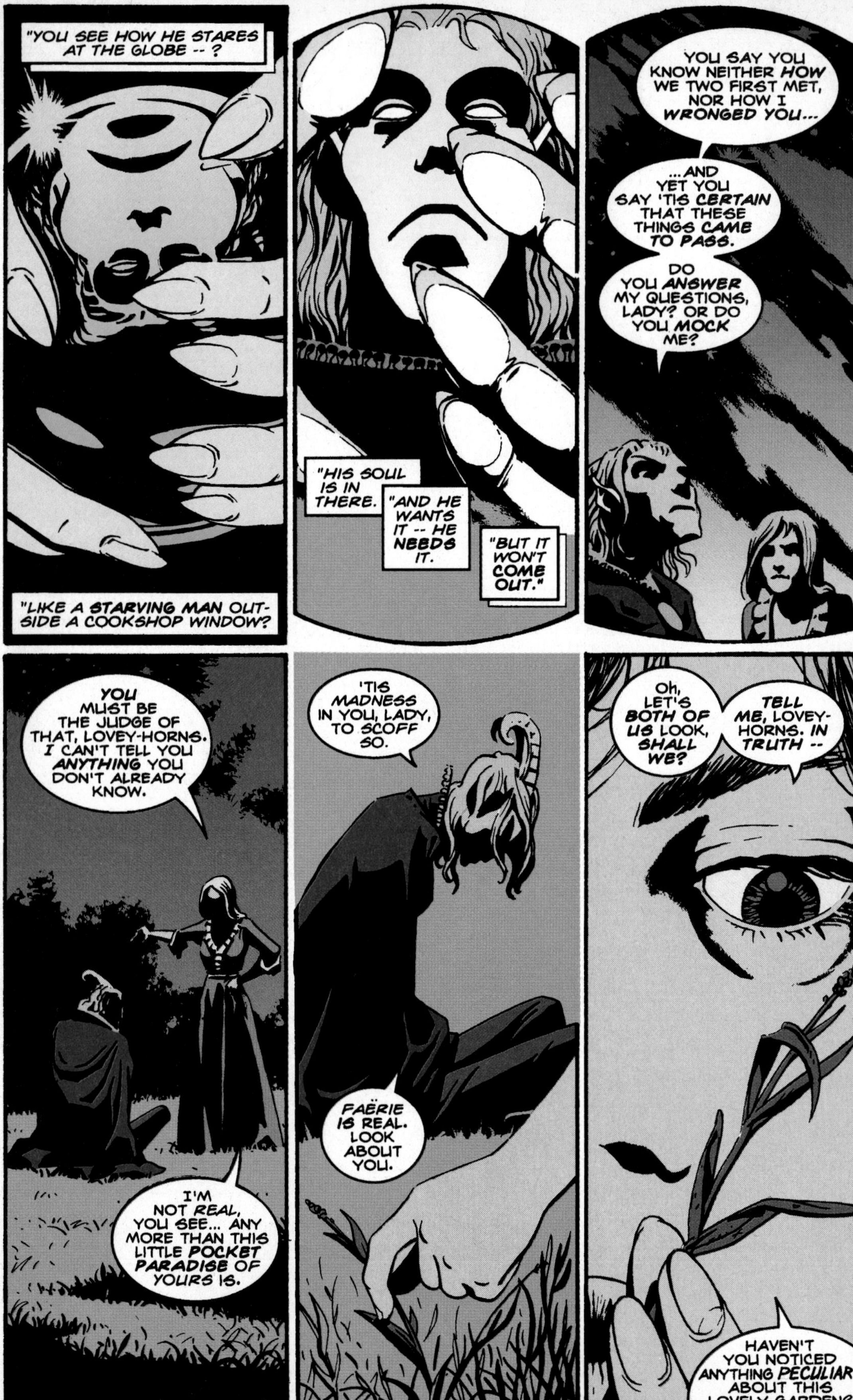
"YOU SEE HOW HE STARES AT THE GLOBE -- ?
"LIKE A STARVING MAN OUTSIDE A COOKSHOP WINDOW?
"HIS SOUL IS IN THERE.
"AND HE WANTS IT -- HE NEEDS IT.
"BUT IT WON'T COME OUT."
YOU SAY YOU KNOW NEITHER HOW WE TWO FIRST MET, NOR HOW I WRONGED YOU...
...AND YET YOU SAY 'TIS CERTAIN THAT THESE THINGS CAME TO PASS.
DO YOU ANSWER MY QUESTIONS, LADY? OR DO YOU MOCK ME?
YOU MUST BE THE JUDGE OF THAT, LOVEY-HORNS. I CAN'T TELL YOU ANYTHING YOU DON'T ALREADY KNOW.
I'M NOT REAL, YOU SEE... ANY MORE THAN THIS LITTLE POCKET PARADISE OF YOURS IS.
'TIS MADNESS IN YOU, LADY, TO SCOFF SO.
FAËRIE IS REAL. LOOK ABOUT YOU.
Oh, LET'S BOTH OF US LOOK, SHALL WE?
TELL ME, LOVEY-HORNS. IN TRUTH --
HAVEN'T YOU NOTICED ANYTHING PECULIAR ABOUT THIS LOVELY GARDEN?

FAËRIE **IS** ONE OF THOSE OTHER-SIDE-OF-THE-FENCE PLACES, ISN'T IT?

WHERE THE **GRASS** IS ALWAYS **GREENER,** AS THE MORTAL SAYING GOES?

WELL...

ONCE UPON A TIME, DEAR, YOU **LIVED** IN THAT SUMMER-LAND...

...AND YOU WERE **CONTENT** -- **SATISFIED** WITH THE **GRAZING** THERE, IF YOU **FOLLOW** ME --

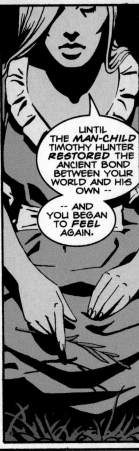

UNTIL THE **MAN-CHILD** TIMOTHY HUNTER **RESTORED** THE ANCIENT BOND BETWEEN YOUR WORLD AND HIS **OWN** --

-- AND YOU BEGAN TO **FEEL** AGAIN.

POOR LOVEY-HORNS.

YOU'D **FORGOTTEN** WHAT IT WAS **LIKE** TO HAVE FEELINGS, HADN'T YOU?

TO **WANT,** TO BE **HURT...** AND **FRIGHTENED.** TO **DOUBT** YOURSELF.

IT'S NO **WONDER** YOU **CLING** TO THIS FANTASY-LAND SO DESPERATELY...

NO DOUBT **TITANIA** WOULD **DO** THE **SAME...** IF SHE WERE GIVEN THE **OPPORTUNITY.**

YOU MAY BE THOUSANDS OF YEARS OLD, LOVEY-HORNS, BUT YOU'RE **CHILDREN,** BOTH OF YOU --

LOVE ISN'T **WISHING.** LOVE IS **WORK.**

AND NEITHER OF YOU KNOWS THE FIRST **THING** ABOUT WORK.

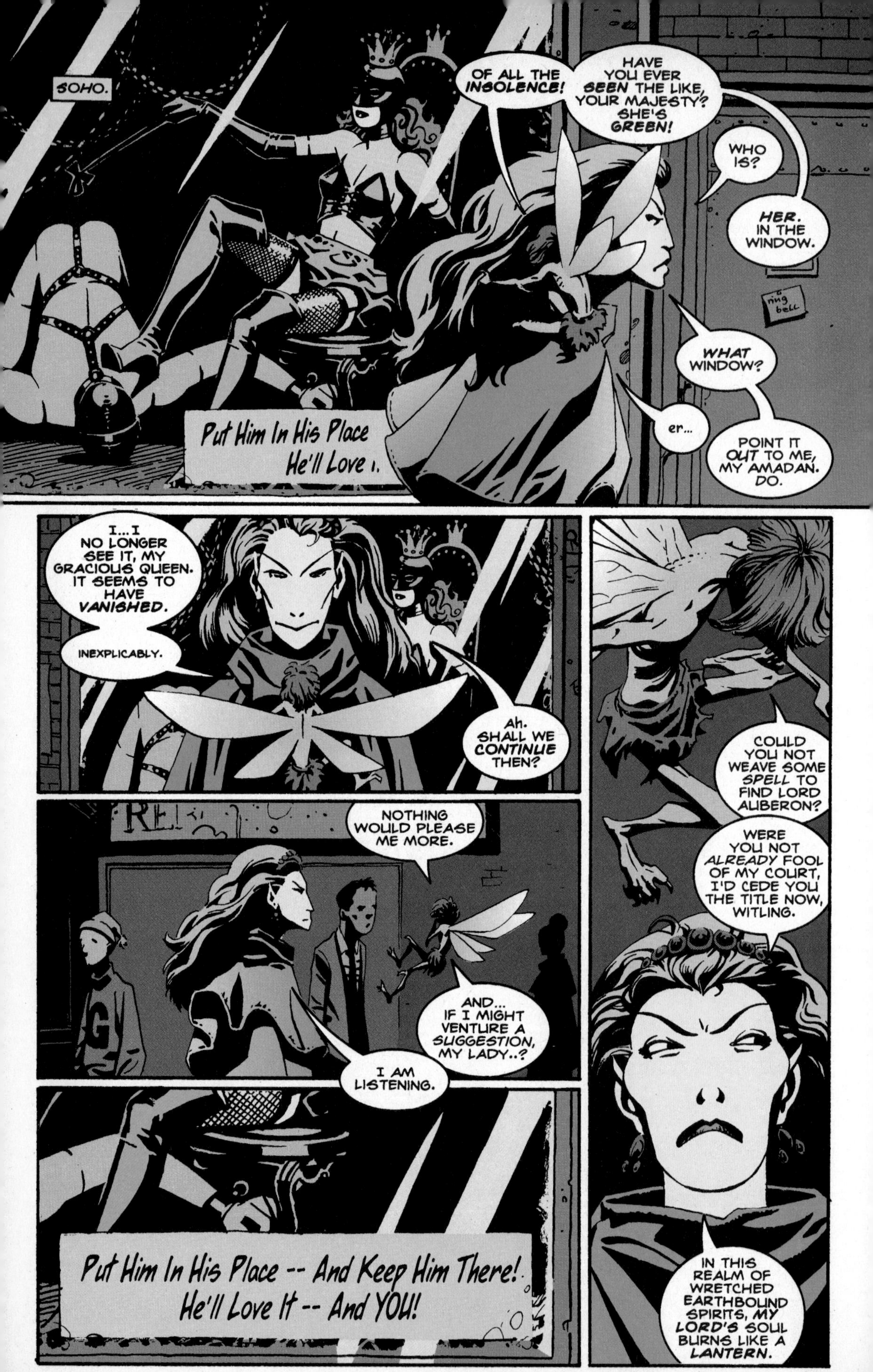
SOHO.
OF ALL THE INSOLENCE!
HAVE YOU EVER SEEN THE LIKE, YOUR MAJESTY? SHE'S GREEN!
WHO IS?
HER. IN THE WINDOW.
WHAT WINDOW?
er...
POINT IT OUT TO ME, MY AMADAN. DO.
Put Him In His Place
He'll Love i.
I... I NO LONGER SEE IT, MY GRACIOUS QUEEN. IT SEEMS TO HAVE VANISHED.
INEXPLICABLY.
Ah. SHALL WE CONTINUE THEN?
NOTHING WOULD PLEASE ME MORE.
AND... IF I MIGHT VENTURE A SUGGESTION, MY LADY..?
I AM LISTENING.
Put Him In His Place -- And Keep Him There!
He'll Love It -- And YOU!
COULD YOU NOT WEAVE SOME SPELL TO FIND LORD AUBERON?
WERE YOU NOT ALREADY FOOL OF MY COURT, I'D CEDE YOU THE TITLE NOW, WITLING.
IN THIS REALM OF WRETCHED EARTHBOUND SPIRITS, MY LORD'S SOUL BURNS LIKE A LANTERN.

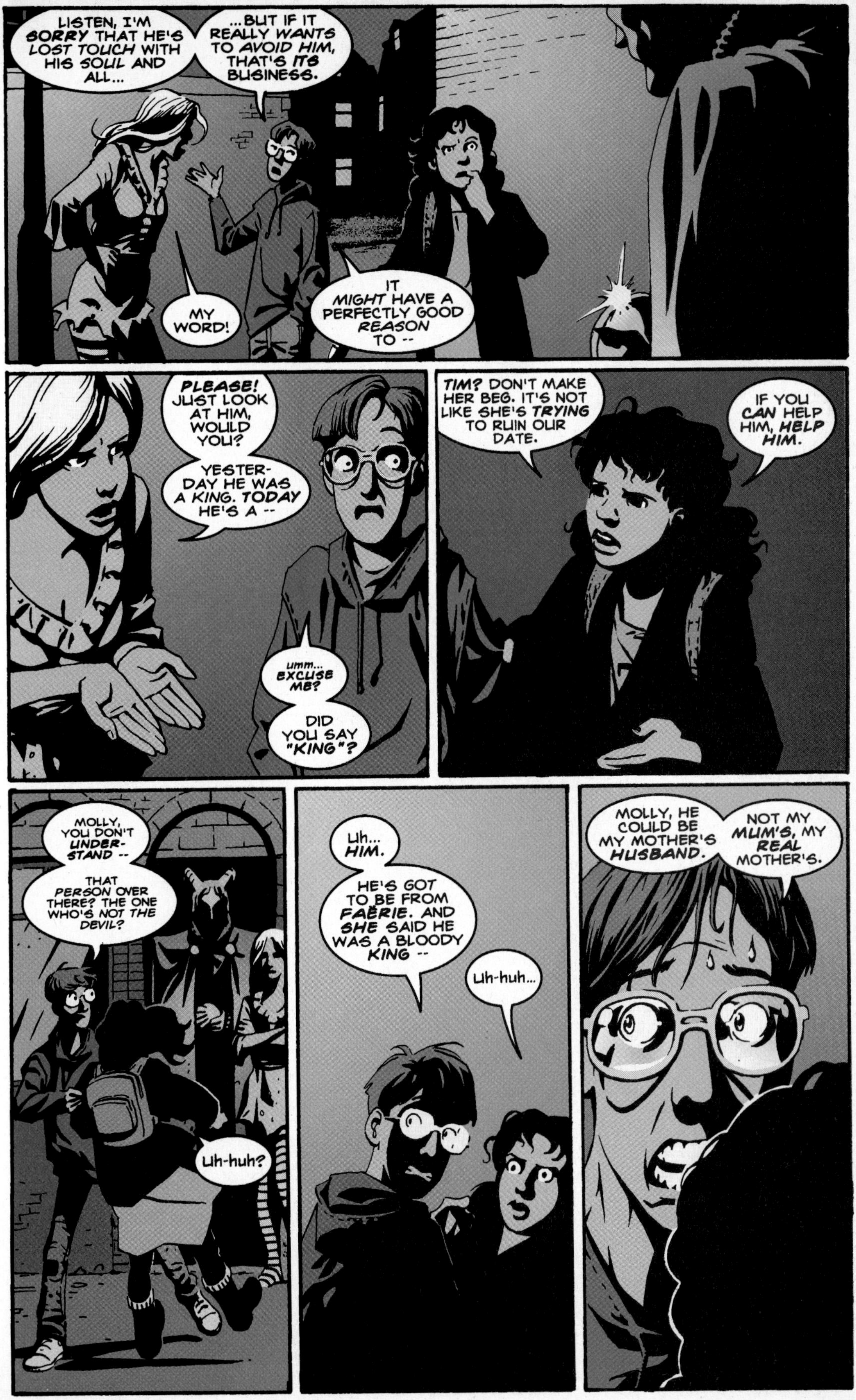
LISTEN, I'M SORRY THAT HE'S LOST TOUCH WITH HIS SOUL AND ALL...
...BUT IF IT REALLY WANTS TO AVOID HIM, THAT'S ITS BUSINESS.
MY WORD!
IT MIGHT HAVE A PERFECTLY GOOD REASON TO --
PLEASE! JUST LOOK AT HIM, WOULD YOU?
YESTER-DAY HE WAS A KING. TODAY HE'S A --
umm... EXCUSE ME?
DID YOU SAY "KING"?
TIM? DON'T MAKE HER BEG. IT'S NOT LIKE SHE'S TRYING TO RUIN OUR DATE.
IF YOU CAN HELP HIM, HELP HIM.
MOLLY, YOU DON'T UNDER-STAND --
THAT PERSON OVER THERE? THE ONE WHO'S NOT THE DEVIL?
Uh-huh?
Uh... HIM.
HE'S GOT TO BE FROM FAERIE. AND SHE SAID HE WAS A BLOODY KING --
Uh-huh...
MOLLY, HE COULD BE MY MOTHER'S HUSBAND.
NOT MY MUM'S, MY REAL MOTHER'S.

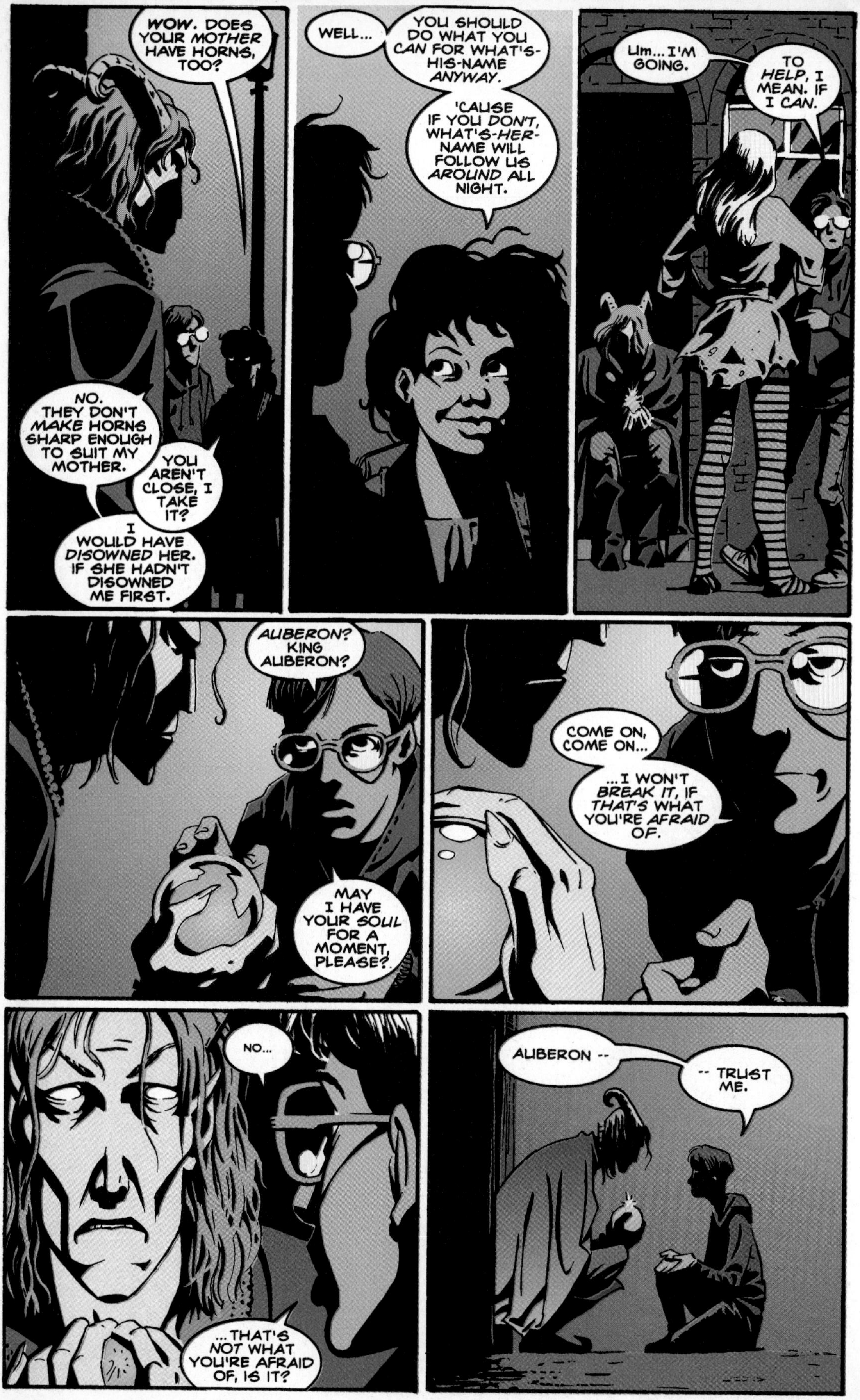
WOW. DOES YOUR MOTHER HAVE HORNS, TOO?
NO. THEY DON'T MAKE HORNS SHARP ENOUGH TO SUIT MY MOTHER.
YOU AREN'T CLOSE, I TAKE IT?
I WOULD HAVE DISOWNED HER. IF SHE HADN'T DISOWNED ME FIRST.
WELL...
YOU SHOULD DO WHAT YOU CAN FOR WHAT'S-HIS-NAME ANYWAY.
'CAUSE IF YOU DON'T, WHAT'S-HER-NAME WILL FOLLOW US AROUND ALL NIGHT.
UM... I'M GOING.
TO HELP, I MEAN. IF I CAN.
AUBERON? KING AUBERON?
MAY I HAVE YOUR SOUL FOR A MOMENT, PLEASE?
COME ON, COME ON...
...I WON'T BREAK IT, IF THAT'S WHAT YOU'RE AFRAID OF.
NO...
...THAT'S NOT WHAT YOU'RE AFRAID OF, IS IT?
AUBERON --
-- TRUST ME.

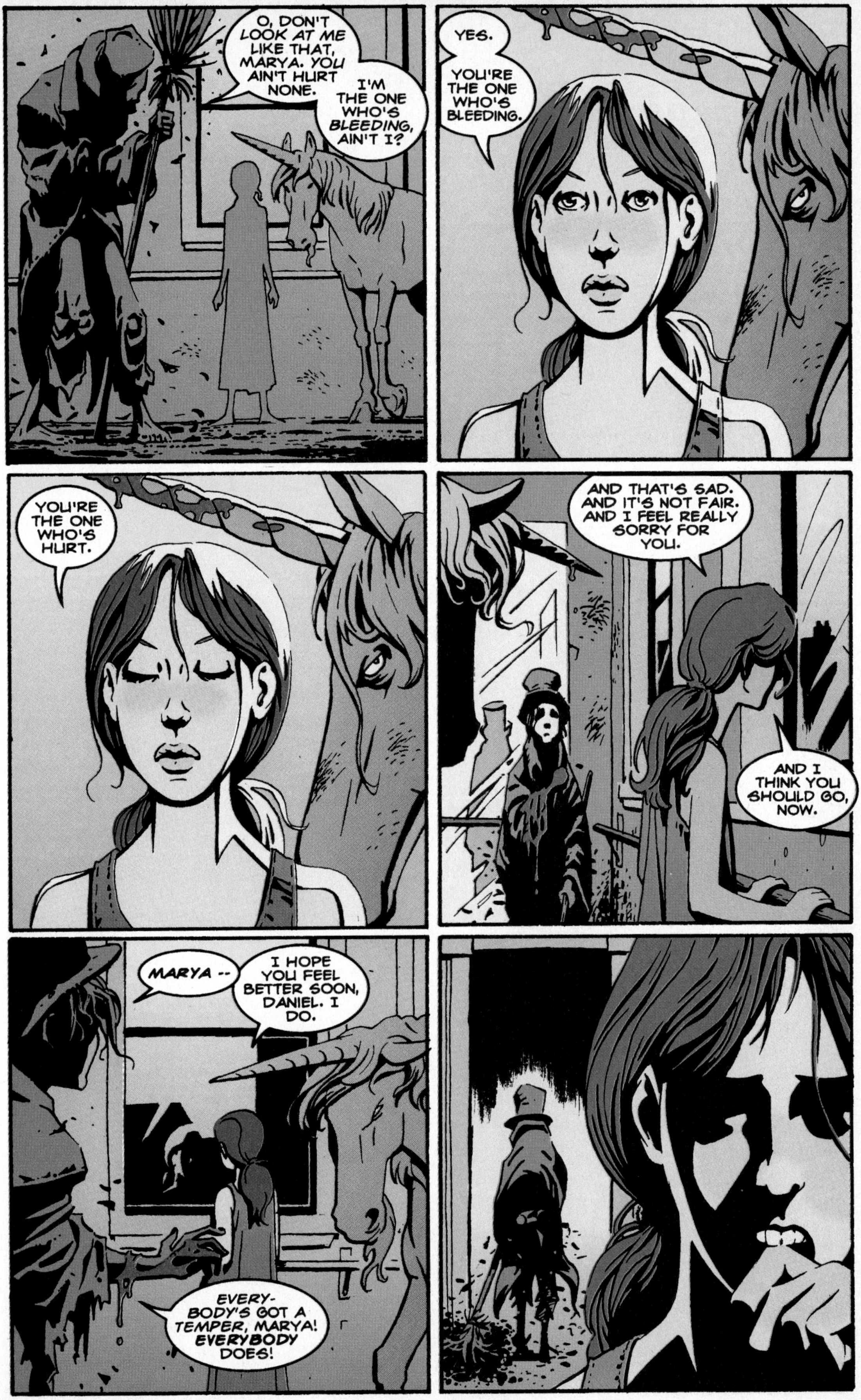
O, DON'T LOOK AT ME LIKE THAT, MARYA. YOU AIN'T HURT NONE.
I'M THE ONE WHO'S BLEEDING, AIN'T I?
YES.
YOU'RE THE ONE WHO'S BLEEDING.
YOU'RE THE ONE WHO'S HURT.
AND THAT'S SAD. AND IT'S NOT FAIR. AND I FEEL REALLY SORRY FOR YOU.
AND I THINK YOU SHOULD GO, NOW.
MARYA --
I HOPE YOU FEEL BETTER SOON, DANIEL. I DO.
EVERY-BODY'S GOT A TEMPER, MARYA! EVERYBODY DOES!

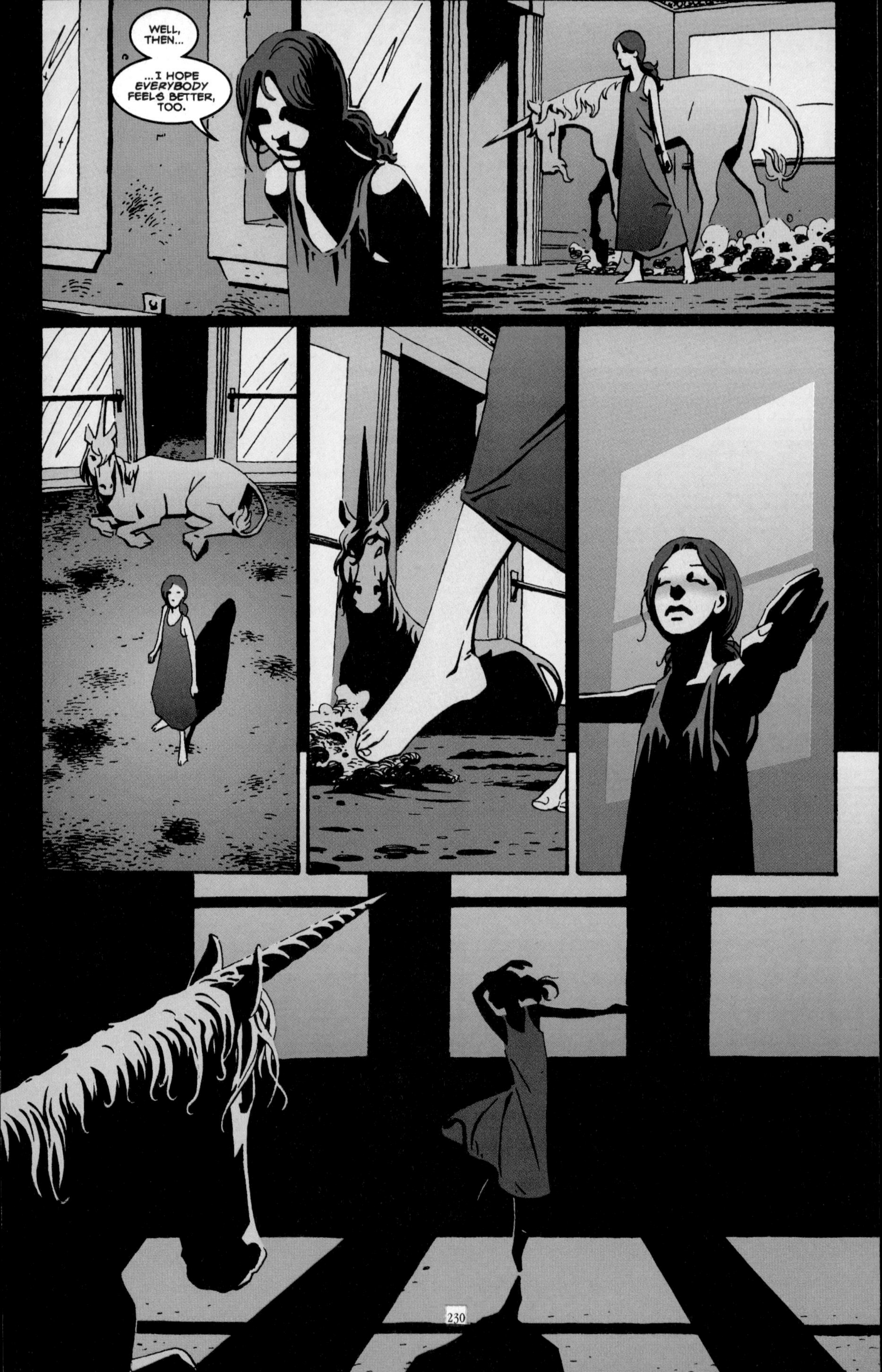

WELL, THEN...
...I HOPE EVERYBODY FEELS BETTER, TOO.

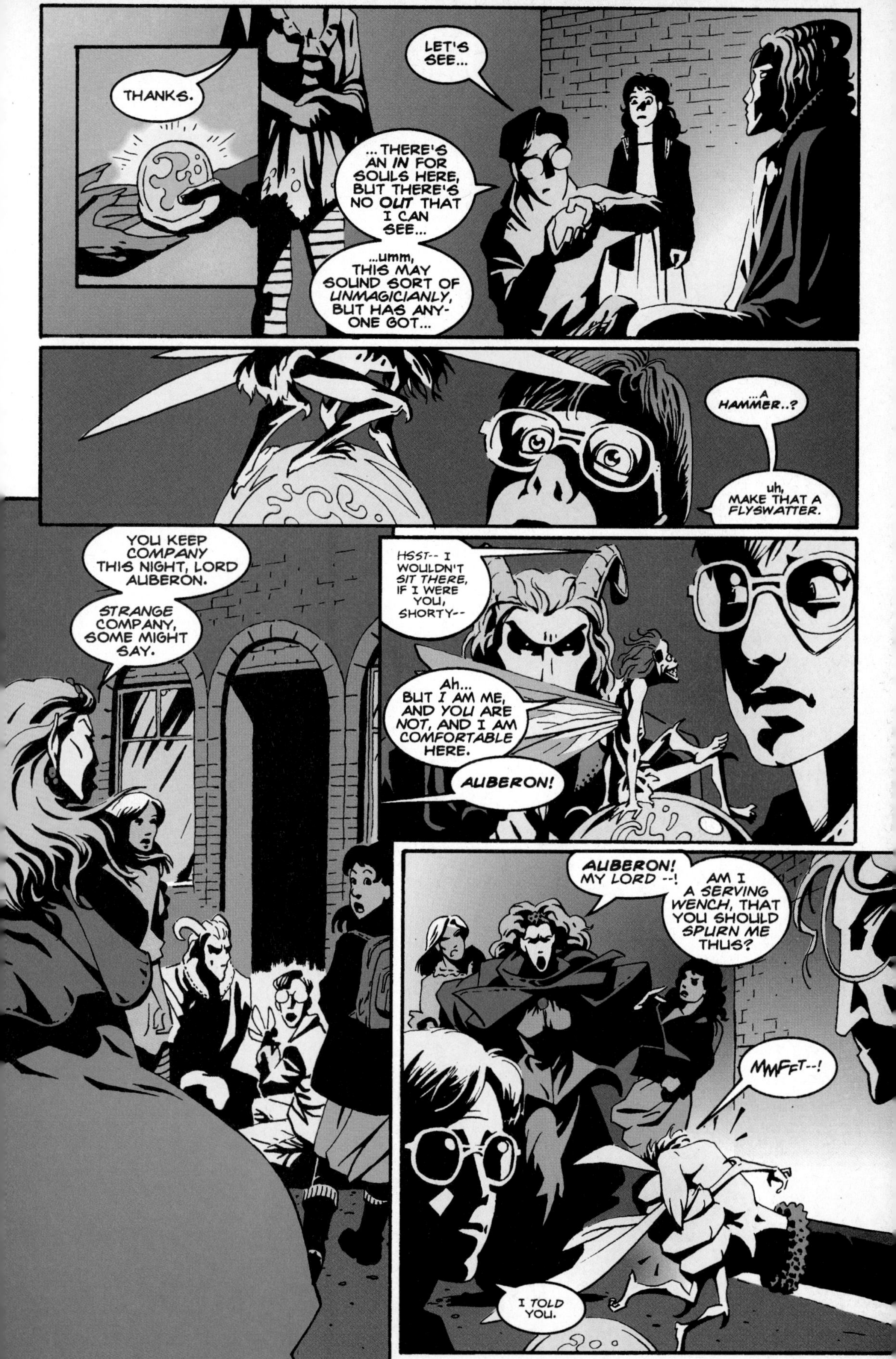
THANKS.
LET'S SEE...
...THERE'S AN IN FOR SOULS HERE, BUT THERE'S NO OUT THAT I CAN SEE...
...umm, THIS MAY SOUND SORT OF UNMAGICIANLY, BUT HAS ANY-ONE GOT...
...A HAMMER..?
uh, MAKE THAT A FLYSWATTER.
YOU KEEP COMPANY THIS NIGHT, LORD AUBERON.
STRANGE COMPANY, SOME MIGHT SAY.
HSST-- I WOULDN'T SIT THERE, IF I WERE YOU, SHORTY--
Ah... BUT I AM ME, AND YOU ARE NOT, AND I AM COMFORTABLE HERE.
AUBERON!
AUBERON! MY LORD --!
AM I A SERVING WENCH, THAT YOU SHOULD SPURN ME THUS?
MMFFT--!
I TOLD YOU.

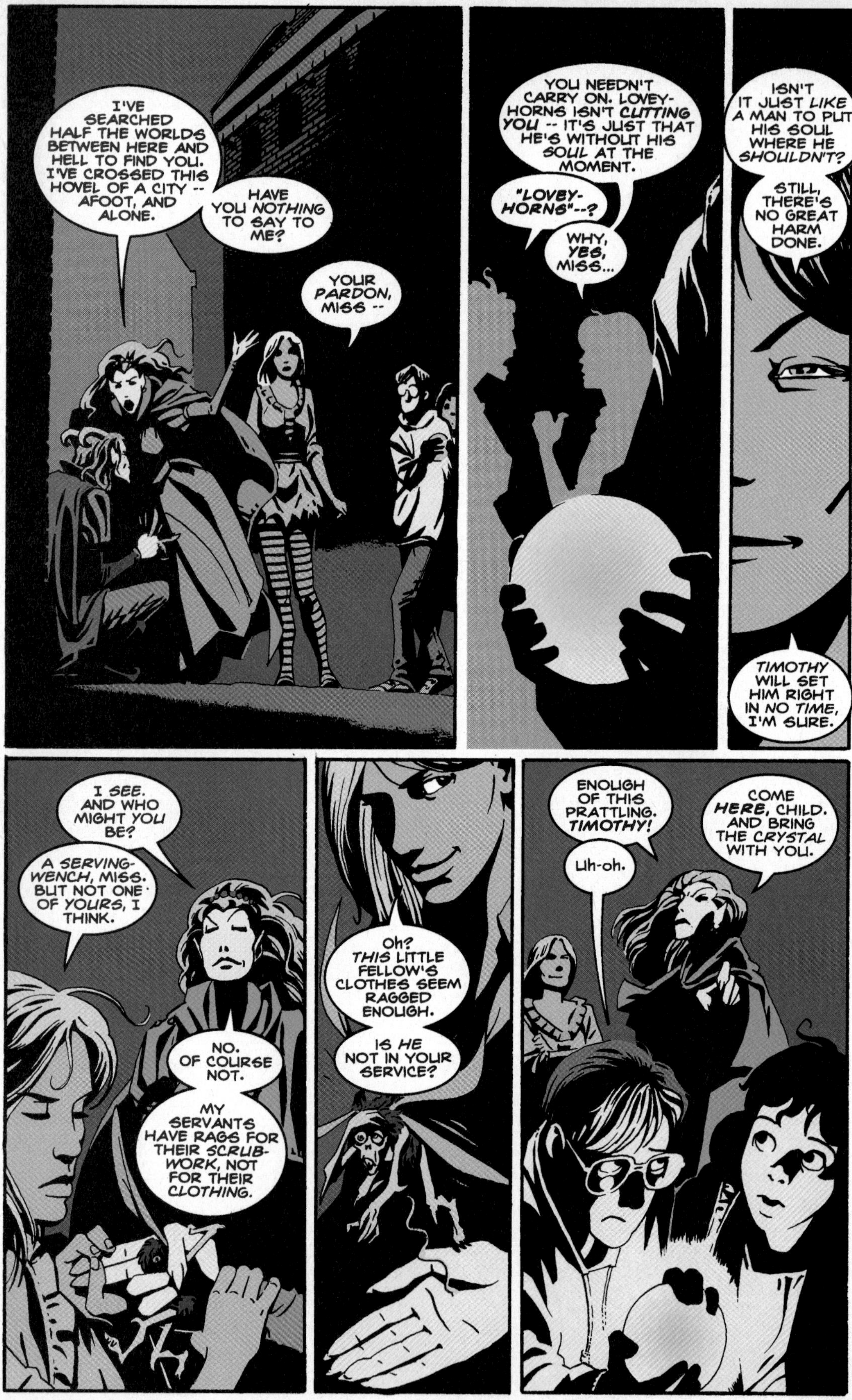
I'VE SEARCHED HALF THE WORLDS BETWEEN HERE AND HELL TO FIND YOU. I'VE CROSSED THIS HOVEL OF A CITY -- AFOOT, AND ALONE.
HAVE YOU NOTHING TO SAY TO ME?
YOUR PARDON, MISS --
YOU NEEDN'T CARRY ON. LOVEY-HORNS ISN'T CUTTING YOU -- IT'S JUST THAT HE'S WITHOUT HIS SOUL AT THE MOMENT.
"LOVEY-HORNS"--?
WHY, YES, MISS...
ISN'T IT JUST LIKE A MAN TO PUT HIS SOUL WHERE HE SHOULDN'T?
STILL, THERE'S NO GREAT HARM DONE.
TIMOTHY WILL SET HIM RIGHT IN NO TIME, I'M SURE.
I SEE. AND WHO MIGHT YOU BE?
A SERVING-WENCH, MISS. BUT NOT ONE OF YOURS, I THINK.
NO. OF COURSE NOT.
MY SERVANTS HAVE RAGS FOR THEIR SCRUB-WORK, NOT FOR THEIR CLOTHING.
OH? THIS LITTLE FELLOW'S CLOTHES SEEM RAGGED ENOUGH.
IS HE NOT IN YOUR SERVICE?
ENOUGH OF THIS PRATTLING. TIMOTHY!
UH-OH.
COME HERE, CHILD. AND BRING THE CRYSTAL WITH YOU.

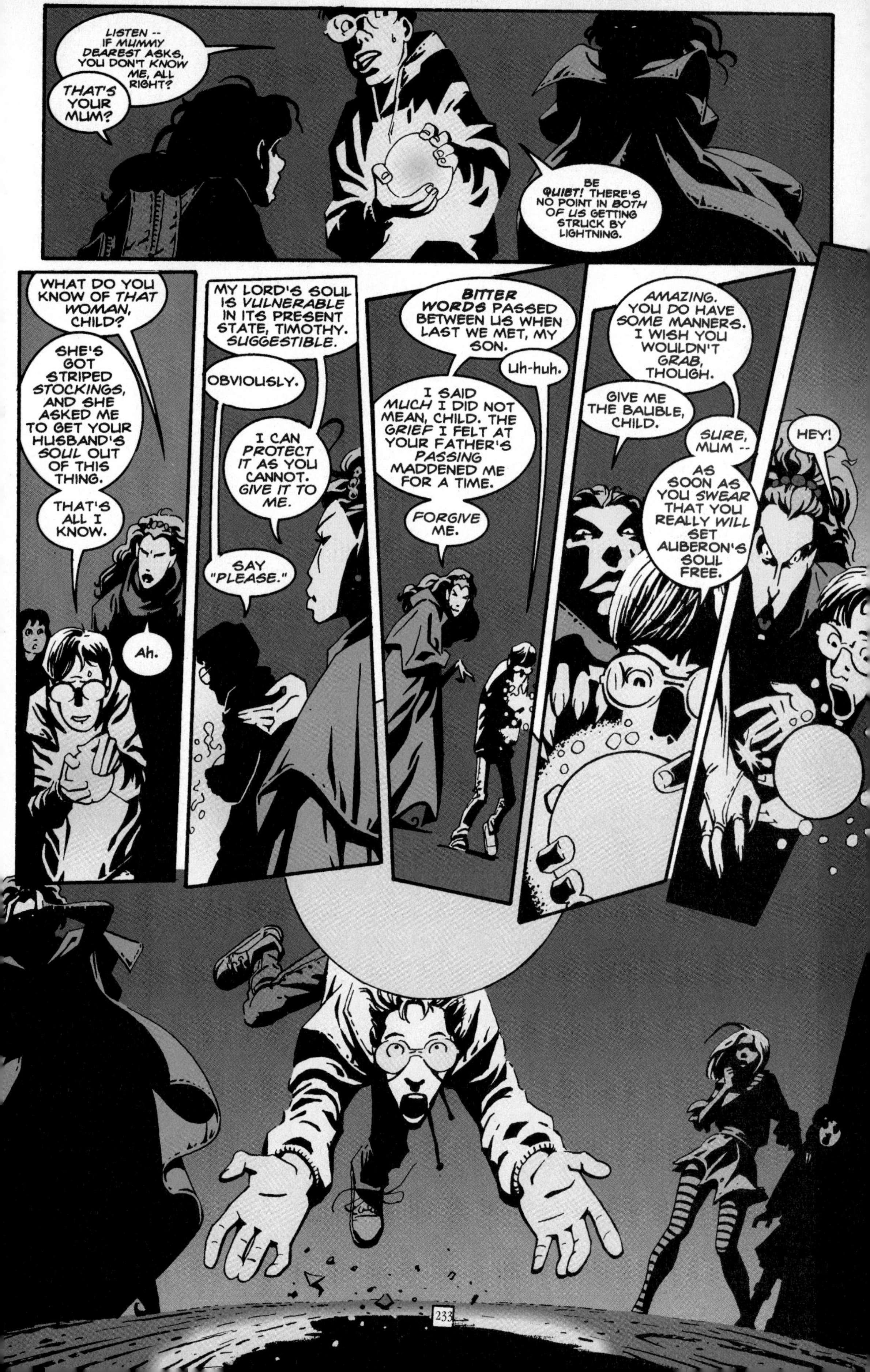

LISTEN -- IF MUMMY DEAREST ASKS, YOU DON'T KNOW ME, ALL RIGHT?
THAT'S YOUR MUM?
BE QUIET! THERE'S NO POINT IN BOTH OF US GETTING STRUCK BY LIGHTNING.
WHAT DO YOU KNOW OF THAT WOMAN, CHILD?
SHE'S GOT STRIPED STOCKINGS, AND SHE ASKED ME TO GET YOUR HUSBAND'S SOUL OUT OF THIS THING.
THAT'S ALL I KNOW.
Ah.
MY LORD'S SOUL IS VULNERABLE IN ITS PRESENT STATE, TIMOTHY. SUGGESTIBLE.
OBVIOUSLY.
I CAN PROTECT IT AS YOU CANNOT. GIVE IT TO ME.
SAY "PLEASE."
BITTER WORDS PASSED BETWEEN US WHEN LAST WE MET, MY SON.
Uh-huh.
I SAID MUCH I DID NOT MEAN, CHILD. THE GRIEF I FELT AT YOUR FATHER'S PASSING MADDENED ME FOR A TIME.
FORGIVE ME.
AMAZING. YOU DO HAVE SOME MANNERS. I WISH YOU WOULDN'T GRAB, THOUGH.
GIVE ME THE BAUBLE, CHILD.
SURE, MUM --
AS SOON AS YOU SWEAR THAT YOU REALLY WILL SET AUBERON'S SOUL FREE.
HEY!

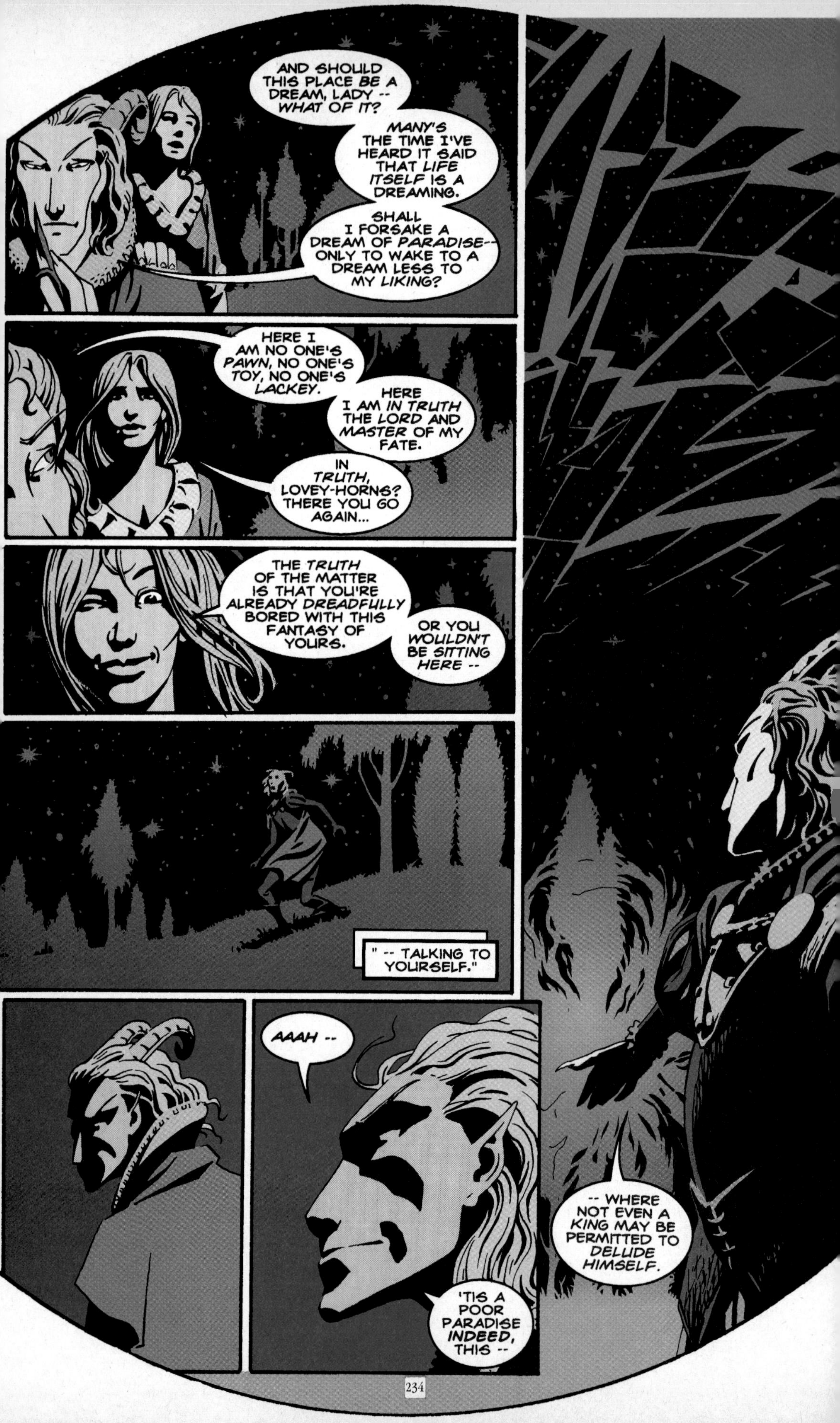

AND SHOULD THIS PLACE BE A DREAM, LADY -- WHAT OF IT?
MANY'S THE TIME I'VE HEARD IT SAID THAT LIFE ITSELF IS A DREAMING.
SHALL I FORSAKE A DREAM OF PARADISE-- ONLY TO WAKE TO A DREAM LESS TO MY LIKING?
HERE I AM NO ONE'S PAWN, NO ONE'S TOY, NO ONE'S LACKEY.
HERE I AM IN TRUTH THE LORD AND MASTER OF MY FATE.
IN TRUTH, LOVEY-HORNS? THERE YOU GO AGAIN...
THE TRUTH OF THE MATTER IS THAT YOU'RE ALREADY DREADFULLY BORED WITH THIS FANTASY OF YOURS.
OR YOU WOULDN'T BE SITTING HERE --
" -- TALKING TO YOURSELF."
AAAH --
'TIS A POOR PARADISE INDEED, THIS --
-- WHERE NOT EVEN A KING MAY BE PERMITTED TO DELUDE HIMSELF.

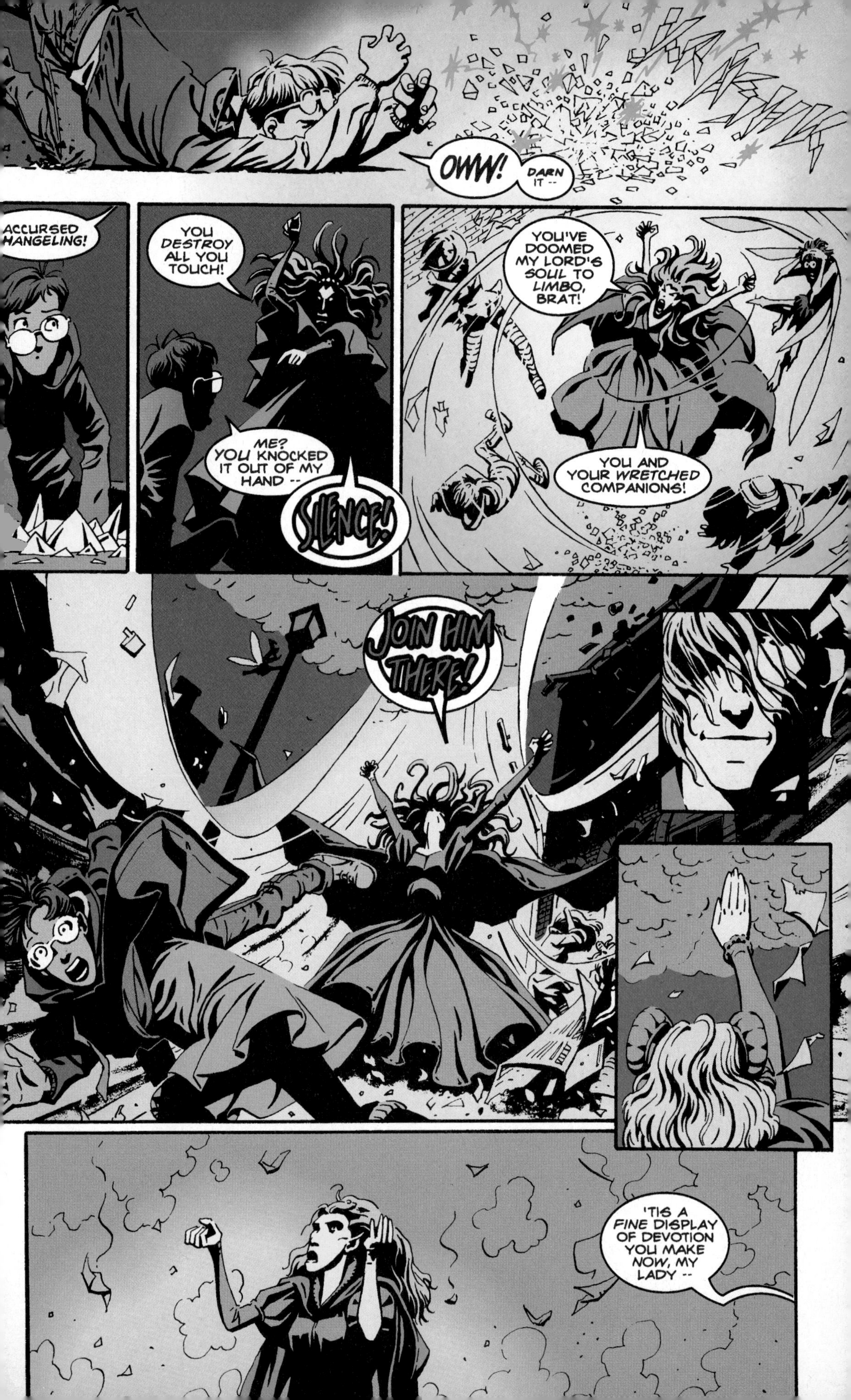
OWW!
DARN IT --
ACCURSED CHANGELING!
YOU DESTROY ALL YOU TOUCH!
ME? YOU KNOCKED IT OUT OF MY HAND --
SILENCE!
YOU'VE DOOMED MY LORD'S SOUL TO LIMBO, BRAT!
YOU AND YOUR WRETCHED COMPANIONS!
JOIN HIM THERE!
'TIS A FINE DISPLAY OF DEVOTION YOU MAKE NOW, MY LADY --

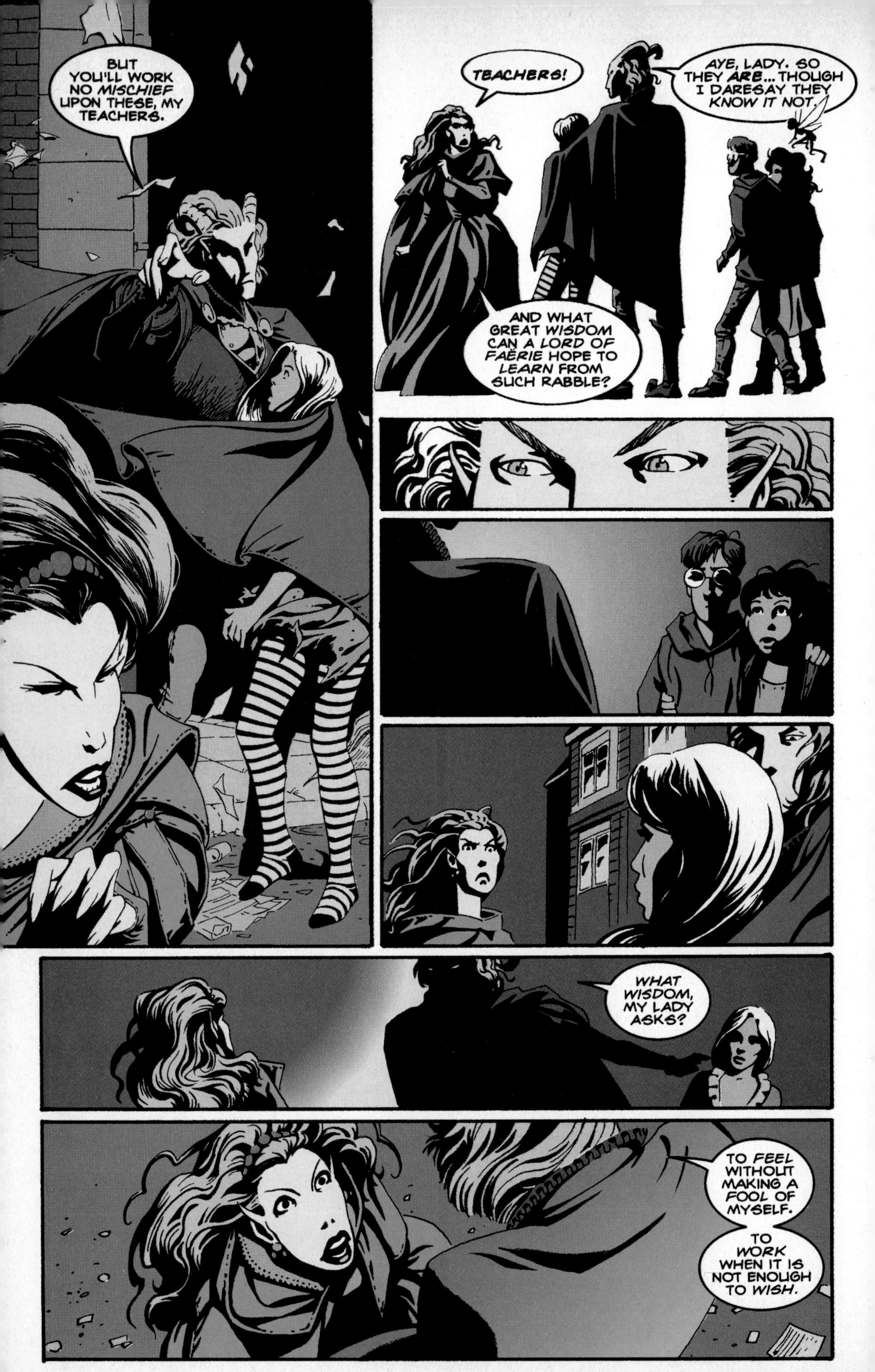
BUT YOU'LL WORK NO MISCHIEF UPON THESE, MY TEACHERS.
TEACHERS!
AYE, LADY. SO THEY ARE... THOUGH I DARESAY THEY KNOW IT NOT.
AND WHAT GREAT WISDOM CAN A LORD OF FAËRIE HOPE TO LEARN FROM SUCH RABBLE?
WHAT WISDOM, MY LADY ASKS?
TO FEEL WITHOUT MAKING A FOOL OF MYSELF.
TO WORK WHEN IT IS NOT ENOUGH TO WISH.

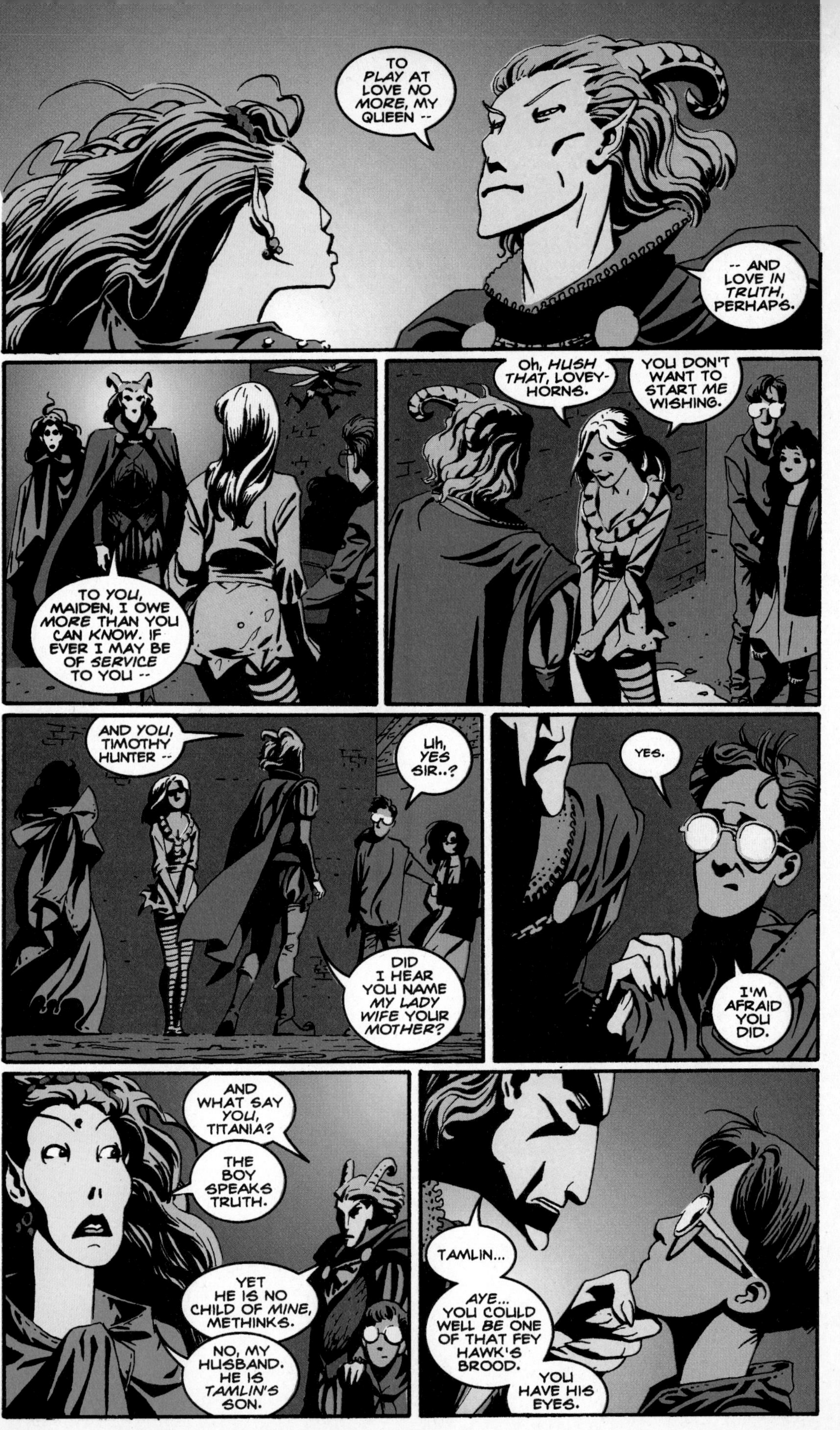
TO PLAY AT LOVE NO MORE, MY QUEEN --
-- AND LOVE IN TRUTH, PERHAPS.
TO YOU, MAIDEN, I OWE MORE THAN YOU CAN KNOW. IF EVER I MAY BE OF SERVICE TO YOU --
Oh, HUSH THAT, LOVEY-HORNS.
YOU DON'T WANT TO START ME WISHING.
AND YOU, TIMOTHY HUNTER --
Uh, YES SIR..?
DID I HEAR YOU NAME MY LADY WIFE YOUR MOTHER?
YES.
I'M AFRAID YOU DID.
AND WHAT SAY YOU, TITANIA?
THE BOY SPEAKS TRUTH.
YET HE IS NO CHILD OF MINE, METHINKS.
NO, MY HUSBAND. HE IS TAMLIN'S SON.
TAMLIN...
AYE... YOU COULD WELL BE ONE OF THAT FEY HAWK'S BROOD.
YOU HAVE HIS EYES.

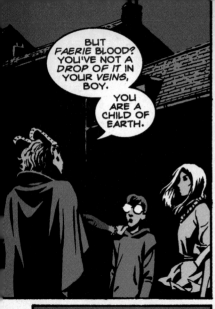

BUT *FAERIE BLOOD?* YOU'VE NOT A *DROP* OF IT IN YOUR VEINS, BOY.

YOU ARE A CHILD OF EARTH.

INDEED, I'D SCARCELY *CREDIT* THAT MY LADY COULD BELIEVE YOU HER CHILD...

...DID I NOT KNOW *FULL WELL* HOW *CUNNINGLY* THE HEART PERSUADES THE MIND TO FOLLY.

um... EXCUSE ME?

ARE YOU TRYING TO TELL ME THAT *SHE* ISN'T REALLY MY MOTHER?

YES.

umm...

GOSH.

TAKE US *HOME,* AUBERON...

...IT TEARS MY *HEART* TO SEE THE POOR CHILD GRIEVE SO.

AS YOU WILL, MY LADY.

AWAY, THEN... AND TO WORK.

TIM! TIM, ARE YOU ALL RIGHT?

YEAH... I'M ALL RIGHT. OF COURSE, I'M ALL RIGHT.

I'M AN ORPHAN...

...AGAIN.

The End

Many Thanks

The writer of this stuff would like to thank (trot out your magnifying glass):

MY KOALA OF KOALAS, NICOLE•JASMINE, QUEEN OF THE ROOS•MY GUARDIAN ANGELS, KENT AND SHERRI•BLAIR, FOR GETTING ME THROUGH THE BIRTHDAY FROM HELL•KAREN, WHO BELIEVED THAT I COULD WRITE TIM-STORIES IN SPITE OF MY LAME PROPOSALS• NEIL, FOR TEACHING ME TO PUT OBLIQUITY IN ITS PLACE•STUART, FOR NOT HANGING UP ON ME EARLY ON, WHEN I MOANED A LOT•JULIE, UPON WHOM THE SUN TRULY DOES RISE AND SET• PATTY, WHO HAS ANGELWINGS AND AIN'T AFRAID TO USE 'EM•RICHARD AND CREW, FOR LETTERING AS MAGICAL AS ANY WRITER COULD WISH FOR•CHARLES, FOR THE FINE MELLOW SINGLE-MALT COVERS, AND FOR LETTING ME SIT BEHIND HIS TABLE•DAN, WITHIN WHOSE CRUSTY BINDING THE NICEST POSSIBLE PAGES CAN BE FOUND•DAVE, FOR INVALUABLE PYROTECHNIC ADVICE AND ODD CAMARADERIE •MICHAEL OF THE CLOTTED PLUMES AND SARAH OF THE UNWRAPPED KITE•GRAHAM AND ELIZABETH, WHO LET ME LIVE IN THEIR WOODS WHEN I NEEDED TO•ANN AND BRUNSON, FOR WINE AND PUSH-HANDS IN THE YARD•SUNSHINE, FOR THE VERY BEST UNPUNCTUATED STORIES •IAN, FOR ASKING ABOUT MY GHOST, AND WRITING ABOUT OTHERS •MARK HADEN FRAZER, FOR SHARING THE UNTRIVIAL STUFF•WENDY CASTRO, WHO LIVES IN BLISS BUT KICKS ASS ANYWAY•GRAEME MCMILLAN, FOR WORRYING ABOUT THE WHY OF THINGS•DANA EVANS, FOR LAUGHING AT HOLLYWOOD• MIGUEL, FOR THE FIRE LESSON FIRE•MEKINDA LI, FOR ONE PARTICULAR UNFORGETTABLE SMILE, AND FOR IMAGINING GUMMI BARBATOSES•JENN BAZILIUS, FOR REMINDING ME THAT A GOOD SWIM CAN FIX JUST ABOUT ANYTHING •HENRIK, FOR THE INTERVIEW, AND FOR BLUSHING WHEN THE ACTRESS-MODELS WINKED•ED, FOR SHARING THE ALTERNATIVE, WELL-MIXED•DAVE LOMAX, FOR SNEAKING FANTASY INTO THE CURRICULUM, AND INVITING ME INTO IT, TOO•DOUG GIFFEN, WHO MAY GIVE ME PITCHING LESSONS SOMEDAY •HAL PHILLIPS, FOR DARING THE SCHOOL OF HARD KNOCKS•BAD ROAD ADAM, THE ENIGMATIC C, ELAYNE, AND ALL THE REST OF THE FOLKS AT REC.ARTS.COMICS.DC.VERTIGO FOR THE :)S AND >>S AND WHATNOT•PAUL JENKINS, FOR BEING THE GOOD FOX• GARTH ENNIS AND STEVE DILLON, FOR THE BLARNEY STONE, AND THE HELICOPTER RIDE I FADED OUT OF•JIM MCLAUGHLIN, FOR LIKING THE BOOKS AND SAYING SO•AND LAST BUT NOT LEAST OF ALL, YOU.

Gary Amaro would like to thank:
JUSTIN BERTHELSEN, MICHELLE BRYANT, RENATA HENLEY, GWENDOLYN KANIES, AND PAUL SCHNEIDER.

Peter Gross would like to thank:
KAREN PLATT, BARBARA SCHULZ, AND CHRISTI ATKINSON, FOR INKING ASSISTANCE...AND CHRISTI AGAIN, FOR ALL THE OTHER THINGS IN LIFE.

Peter Snejbjerg would like to thank:
LAILA, MY WIFE, AND GONZO THE WONDER DOG — BEST DOG-IN-LAW A GUY EVER HAD.

LOOK FOR THESE OTHER VERTIGO BOOKS:

All VERTIGO backlist books are suggested for mature readers

GRAPHIC NOVELS

DHAMPIRE: STILLBORN
Nancy A. Collins/Paul Lee

MR. PUNCH
Neil Gaiman/Dave McKean

THE MYSTERY PLAY
Grant Morrison/Jon J Muth

TELL ME, DARK
Karl Wagner/Kent Williams

VERTIGO VÉRITÉ: SEVEN MILES A SECOND
David Wojnarowicz/James Romberger

COLLECTIONS

ANIMAL MAN
Grant Morrison/Chas Truog/Tom Grummett/Doug Hazlewood

BLACK ORCHID
Neil Gaiman/Dave McKean

THE BOOKS OF MAGIC
Neil Gaiman/John Bolton/Scott Hampton/
Charles Vess/Paul Johnson

THE BOOKS OF MAGIC: BINDINGS
John Ney Rieber/Gary Amaro/Peter Gross

THE BOOKS OF MAGIC: SUMMONINGS
John Ney Rieber/Peter Gross/
Peter Snejbjerg/Gary Amaro/Dick Giordano

THE BOOKS OF MAGIC: RECKONINGS
John Ney Rieber/Peter Snejbjerg/Peter Gross/John Ridgway

DEATH: THE HIGH COST OF LIVING
Neil Gaiman/Chris Bachalo/Mark Buckingham

DEATH: THE TIME OF YOUR LIFE
Neil Gaiman/Chris Bachalo/
Mark Buckingham/Mark Pennington

DOOM PATROL:

CRAWLING FROM THE WRECKAGE
Grant Morrison/Richard Case/various

ENIGMA
Peter Milligan/Duncan Fegredo

HELLBLAZER: DANGEROUS HABITS
Garth Ennis/William Simpson/various

HELLBLAZER: FEAR AND LOATHING
Garth Ennis/Steve Dillon

HOUSE OF SECRETS: FOUNDATION
Steven T. Seagle/Teddy Kristiansen

THE INVISIBLES:

SAY YOU WANT A REVOLUTION
Grant Morrison/Steve Yeowell/Jill Thompson/Dennis Cramer

JONAH HEX: TWO-GUN MOJO
Joe R. Lansdale/Tim Truman/Sam Glanzman

PREACHER: GONE TO TEXAS
Garth Ennis/Steve Dillon

PREACHER: UNTIL THE END OF THE WORLD
Garth Ennis/Steve Dillon

SAGA OF THE SWAMP THING
Alan Moore/Steve Bissette/John Totleben

SANDMAN MYSTERY THEATRE:

THE TARANTULA
Matt Wagner/Guy Davis

THE SYSTEM
Peter Kuper

V FOR VENDETTA
Alan Moore/David Lloyd

VAMPS
Elaine Lee/William Simpson

WITCHCRAFT
James Robinson/Peter Snejbjerg/Michael Zulli/
Steve Yeowell/Teddy Kristiansen

THE SANDMAN LIBRARY

THE SANDMAN: PRELUDES & NOCTURNES
Neil Gaiman/Sam Kieth/Mike Dringenberg/Malcolm Jones III

THE SANDMAN: THE DOLL'S HOUSE
Neil Gaiman/Mike Dringenberg/Malcolm Jones III/
Chris Bachalo/Michael Zulli/Steve Parkhouse

THE SANDMAN: DREAM COUNTRY
Neil Gaiman/Kelley Jones/Charles Vess/
Colleen Doran/Malcolm Jones III

THE SANDMAN: SEASON OF MISTS
Neil Gaiman/Kelley Jones/
Mike Dringenberg/Malcolm Jones III/various

THE SANDMAN: A GAME OF YOU
Neil Gaiman/Shawn McManus/various

THE SANDMAN: BRIEF LIVES
Neil Gaiman/Jill Thompson/Vince Locke

THE SANDMAN:

FABLES AND REFLECTIONS
Neil Gaiman/various artists

THE SANDMAN: WORLDS' END
Neil Gaiman/various artists

THE SANDMAN: THE KINDLY ONES
Neil Gaiman/Marc Hempel/Richard Case/various

THE SANDMAN: THE WAKE
Neil Gaiman/Michael Zulli/Jon J Muth/Charles Vess

OTHER COLLECTIONS
OF INTEREST

CAMELOT 3000
Mike W. Barr/Brian Bolland

RONIN
Frank Miller

WATCHMEN
Alan Moore/Dave Gibbons

For the nearest comics shop carrying collected editions and monthly titles from DC Comics, call 1-888-COMIC BOOK.

970430